THE SOCIAL PSYCHOLOGY
OF GOOD AND EVIL

The Social Psychology of Good and Evil

SECOND EDITION

Edited by
ARTHUR G. MILLER

THE GUILFORD PRESS
New York   London

Copyright © 2016 The Guilford Press
A Division of Guilford Publications, Inc.
370 Seventh Avenue, Suite 1200, New York, NY 10001
www.guilford.com

All rights reserved

No part of this book may be reproduced, translated, stored in
a retrieval system, or transmitted, in any form or by any means,
electronic, mechanical, photocopying, microfilming, recording,
or otherwise, without written permission from the publisher.

Printed in the United States of America

This book is printed on acid-free paper.

Last digit is print number: 9 8 7 6 5 4 3 2 1

Library of Congress Cataloging-in-Publication Data

Names: Miller, Arthur G., 1940– editor.
Title: The social psychology of good and evil / edited by Arthur G. Miller.
Description: Second edition. | New York : The Guilford Press, 2016. | Revised
  edition of The social psychology of good and evil, 2004. | Includes
  bibliographical references and index.
Identifiers: LCCN 2016005602| ISBN 9781462525393 (paperback) | ISBN
  9781462525409 (hardcover)
Subjects: LCSH: Aggressiveness. | Violence. | Helping behavior. | Good and
  evil. | Social psychology—Research. | BISAC: PSYCHOLOGY / Social
  Psychology. | SOCIAL SCIENCE / Sociology / General.
Classification: LCC HM1116 .S63 2016 | DDC 302.072—dc23
LC record available at *http://lccn.loc.gov/2016005602*

About the Editor

Arthur G. Miller, PhD, is Professor Emeritus of Psychology at Miami University. Dr. Miller's research and publications have focused on stereotyping and stigma, biases in attribution and social judgment, and people's reactions to diverse explanations of evil and violence. He is the author of *The Obedience Experiments: A Case Study of Controversy in Social Science* (1986) and edited a special issue of *Personality and Social Psychology Review*: "Harming Other People: Perspectives on Evil and Violence" (Volume 3, Number, 3, 1999). More recently, Dr. Miller was an invited commentator on Jerry M. Burger's modification of Stanley Milgram's obedience paradigm, featured in a special issue of *American Psychologist* (Volume 64, Number 1, 2009), and on Diana Baumrind's reprise of her highly influential ethical critique of Milgram's studies in *Theoretical and Applied Ethics* (Volume 2, Number 2, 2013). He coedited, with Alex Haslam and Steve Reicher, a special issue of the *Journal of Social Issues*: "Milgram at 50: Exploring the Enduring Relevance of Psychology's Most Famous Studies" (Volume 70, Number 3, 2014).

Contributors

Nadia Y. Ahmad, PhD, St. Louis, Missouri

Johnie J. Allen, BA, Department of Psychology, Iowa State University, Ames, Iowa

Craig A. Anderson, PhD, Department of Psychology, Iowa State University, Ames, Iowa

Dan Ariely, PhD, The Center for Advanced Hindsight, Duke University, Durham, North Carolina

John A. Bargh, PhD, Department of Psychology, Yale University, New Haven, Connecticut

C. Daniel Batson, PhD, Department of Psychology (Emeritus), University of Kansas, Lawrence, Kansas

Roy F. Baumeister, PhD, Department of Psychology, Florida State University, Tallahassee, Florida

Madeleine Blackman, BA, Department of Psychology, Georgetown University, Washington, DC

Dan V. Blalock, MA, Department of Psychology, George Mason University, Fairfax, Virginia

Nyla R. Branscombe, PhD, Department of Psychology, University of Kansas, Lawrence, Kansas

Arthur P. Brief, PhD, Department of Management, University of Utah, Salt Lake City, Utah

David M. Buss, PhD, Department of Psychology, University of Texas at Austin, Austin, Texas

Maggie Campbell-Obaid, PhD, Department of Psychology and Philosophy, Framingham State University, Framingham, Massachusetts

Amy Canevello, PhD, Department of Psychology, University of North Carolina at Charlotte, Charlotte, North Carolina

Jennifer Crocker, PhD, Department of Psychology, The Ohio State University, Columbus, Ohio

John F. Dovidio, PhD, Department of Psychology, Yale University, New Haven, Connecticut

Daniel J. Dufour, MA, Department of Government, Georgetown University, Washington, DC

David Dunning, PhD, Department of Psychology, University of Michigan, Ann Arbor, Michigan

Joshua D. Duntley, PhD, Department of Criminal Justice, Stockton University, Galloway, New Jersey

Patrick C. Dwyer, PhD, Department of Psychology and Neuroscience, University of North Carolina at Chapel Hill, Chapel Hill, North Carolina

Sarah Fasano, MA, Department of Government, Georgetown University, Washington, DC

Susan T. Fiske, PhD, Department of Psychology and Woodrow Wilson School of Public Affairs, Princeton University, Princeton, New Jersey

Johanna B. Folk, MA, Department of Psychology, George Mason University, Fairfax, Virginia

Zeno E. Franco, PhD, Department of Family and Community Medicine, Medical College of Wisconsin, Milwaukee, Wisconsin

Samuel L. Gaertner, PhD, Department of Psychological and Brain Sciences, University of Delaware, Newark, Delaware

Sarah J. Gervais, PhD, Department of Psychology, University of Nebraska–Lincoln, Lincoln, Nebraska

Francesca Gino, PhD, Harvard Business School, Harvard University, Cambridge, Massachusetts

Christopher L. Groves, MS, Department of Psychology, Iowa State University, Ames, Iowa

Nick Haslam, PhD, School of Psychological Sciences, University of Melbourne, Parkville, Australia

Victoria Heckenlaible, MA, Department of Politics and Public Policy, The American University of Kurdistan, Duhok, Kurdistan Region of Iraq

Mark Levine, PhD, Department of Psychology, University of Exeter, Exeter, United Kingdom

Steve Loughnan, PhD, Department of Psychology, The University of Edinburgh, Edinburgh, United Kingdom

Arthur G. Miller, PhD, Department of Psychology (Emeritus), Miami University, Oxford, Ohio

Contributors

Fathali M. Moghaddam, PhD, Department of Psychology, Georgetown University, Washington, DC

Andrew E. Monroe, PhD, Department of Psychology, Appalachian State University, Boone, North Carolina

Allen M. Omoto, PhD, Department of Psychology, Claremont Graduate University, Claremont, California

Adam R. Pearson, PhD, Department of Psychology, Pomona College, Claremont, California

Sara Prot, PhD, School of Psychology and Behavioral Sciences, Coventry University, Coventry, United Kingdom

Muniba Saleem, PhD, Department of Communication Studies and Institute of Social Research, University of Michigan, Ann Arbor, Michigan

Kristin Smith-Crowe, PhD, Department of Organizational Behavior, Questrom School of Business, Boston University, Boston, Massachusetts

Mark Snyder, PhD, Department of Psychology, University of Minnesota, Minneapolis, Minnesota

E. L. Stocks, PhD, Department of Psychology, University of Texas at Tyler, Tyler, Texas

Jeffrey Stuewig, PhD, Department of Psychology, George Mason University, Fairfax, Virginia

June P. Tangney, PhD, Department of Psychology, George Mason University, Fairfax, Virginia

Kathleen D. Vohs, PhD, Carlson School of Management, University of Minnesota, Minneapolis, Minnesota

Johanna Ray Vollhardt, PhD, Frances L. Hiatt School of Psychology, Clark University, Worcester, Massachusetts

Ruth H. Warner, PhD, Department of Psychology, Saint Louis University, St. Louis, Missouri

Neil Wilson, PhD, College of Health and Wellbeing, University of Central Lancashire, Lancashire, United Kingdom

Michael J. A. Wohl, PhD, Department of Psychology, Carleton University, Ottawa, Ontario, Canada

Philip G. Zimbardo, PhD, Department of Psychology (Emeritus), Stanford University, Stanford, California

Preface

The major purpose of this book is to provide a contemporary view of social-psychological research on both the virtuous and cruel, often harmful features of human behavior. Following the precedent of the first edition, this volume presents the research of many of the world's leading theorists and researchers on topics that are currently receiving very active empirical inquiry. Although the basic structure of the first edition has been retained, this second edition presents a significantly new look, including chapters on new topics—free will, the role of conscious and unconscious processes, responses to historical victimization, bystander intervention, media violence, false moral superiority, dehumanization, terrorism, and heroism—and a number of new chapter authors. Good and evil in the relatively intimate dynamics of dyadic relationships as well as larger social organizations and bureaucracies are discussed. The explanatory value of considering group processes in contrast to focusing largely on the individual is an important consideration, and this edition includes a major section on this perspective. Each chapter may be read as a relatively comprehensive "state of the science" in its domain of interest, as well as an informative guide for readers wishing to pursue more intensive study.

The social-psychological perspective is relatively inclusive, and one will encounter different emphases across chapters. The power of specific situations or contexts to influence ordinary, seemingly good persons to commit good or evil deeds is clearly one major focus of the book. There are, however, social psychologists who take exception to what they regard as an exaggerated, even unwarranted focus on the situation, and instead emphasize the demonstrable fact of individual differences in response to specific circumstances. In some instances, there is considerable tension or controversy within the discipline regarding this person–situation dynamic, one rationale being the criticism that a situational explanatory approach entails not only at least partially condoning harmful acts, but also a diminished sense of individual honor or merit in doing helpful deeds. Of course, social situations don't create themselves, and people often select their own situations; thus one might contend that the person, in solitary or group contexts, inevitably is the ultimate source of behavioral outcomes. Nevertheless, the power of the situation continues to be a formidable thesis in social psychology, with many arguing that the causal role of situations is particularly unappreciated by many people who prefer instead personality or dispositional accounts.

The wealth of empirical evidence displayed in this volume is a deserved source of pride for social psychologists and lends veracity to many of its claims. Nevertheless, explanations of human behavior seem to have an inherently provocative or unnerving aspect. Science, in general, has always been characterized by skepticism and controversy, and social psychology is certainly no exception. It has been said that most people are "intuitive scientists," who are continually interested in explaining and judging the behavior of others. Encountering scientific accounts of behavior may potentially conflict strongly with one's common-sense understanding, engendering considerable resistance. Chapter 10, on Milgram's obedience experiments, is just one example of this kind of explanatory controversy and resistance.

Significant gains in theoretical understanding depend on constructive criticism and challenges to accepted ways of studying behavior. Readers of this book are encouraged to adopt a similarly questioning perspective. It will be apparent in this volume that any simple characterization of the causation of behavior will frequently be disputed or qualified. Throughout, the book presents participants in research settings who have committed either harmful, immoral acts or extraordinarily helpful deeds. It should be of interest to readers to consider how the various explanations provided for these behaviors strike them in terms of their moral implications. Punishing harm-doers or rewarding kindness often depends quite specifically on how those actions are explained. The convincingness of the social-psychological perspective may depend, to a significant degree, on the moral implications of their explanations. Whether or not this should be the case is yet another important question to be considered.

Acknowledgments

A number of individuals have played a vital role in the development of this second edition. First, of course, I wish to thank my colleagues who contributed chapters. Their interest, expertise, commitment to the project, and responsiveness to my comments and questions were crucial in bringing this new edition to fruition. The Department of Psychology at Miami University has, once again, been a very collegial and supportive context for my work. Untold numbers of undergraduate and graduate students, as well as personal colleagues, have contributed, over a period of almost five decades, to my lasting interest and enthusiasm for social psychology.

Seymour Weingarten, Editor in Chief at the The Guilford Press, was responsible for the genesis of this second edition, and Carolyn Graham, Editorial Administrator, and Anna Nelson, Senior Production Editor, have been a source of continuous support and helpful judgment. Finally, I would like to dedicate this book to my wife, Sandy, and my late parents, Mollie and Irving Miller.

Contents

1. Introduction and Overview 1
  Arthur G. Miller

PART I. CONCEPTUAL PERSPECTIVES ON GOOD AND EVIL

2. The Evolution of Good and Evil 17
  Joshua D. Duntley and David M. Buss

3. Free Will Evolved for Morality and Culture 41
  Andrew E. Monroe, Kathleen D. Vohs, and Roy F. Baumeister

4. Categories, Intent, and Harm 52
  Susan T. Fiske

5. "The Devil Made Me Do It": The Deification of Consciousness and the Demonization of the Unconscious 69
  John A. Bargh

PART II. HARMING OTHERS: CONTEXTS, CAUSES, AND IMPLICATIONS

6. Racism among the Well Intentioned: Bias without Awareness 95
  John F. Dovidio, Samuel L. Gaertner, and Adam R. Pearson

7. Understanding Media Violence Effects   119
*Sara Prot, Craig A. Anderson, Muniba Saleem,
Christopher L. Groves, and Johnie J. Allen*

8. How Dehumanization Promotes Harm   140
Nick Haslam and Steve Loughnan

9. The Social Psychology of Genocide and Mass Atrocities   159
Johanna Ray Vollhardt and Maggie Campbell-Obaid

10. Why Are the Milgram Experiments Still So Extraordinarily Famous—and Controversial?   185
Arthur G. Miller

11. A Social Interaction Approach to Objectification: Implications for the Social–Psychological Study of Sexual Violence   224
Sarah J. Gervais

PART III. THE SELF-CONCEPT IN RELATION TO GOOD AND EVIL ACTS

12. False Moral Superiority   249
David Dunning

13. Making Relationship Partners Good: A Model of the Interpersonal Consequences of Compassionate Goals   270
Jennifer Crocker and Amy Canevello

14. Evil Persons or Evil Deeds?: What We've Learned about Incarcerated Offenders   298
June P. Tangney, Dan V. Blalock, Johanna B. Folk, and Jeffrey Stuewig

15. Dishonesty Explained: What Leads Moral People to Act Immorally   322
Francesca Gino and Dan Ariely

PART IV. GROUP PERSPECTIVES ON GOOD AND EVIL

16. Bystanders and Emergencies: Why Understanding Group Processes Is Key to Promoting Prosocial Behavior   345
Mark Levine and Neil Wilson

17.	Remembering Historical Victimization: Potential for Intergroup Conflict Escalation and Conflict Reduction *Nyla R. Branscombe, Michael J. A. Wohl, and Ruth H. Warner*	367
18.	Organizations Matter *Arthur P. Brief and Kristin Smith-Crowe*	390
19.	Globalization and Terrorism: The Primacy of Collective Processes *Fathali M. Moghaddam, Victoria Heckenlaible, Madeleine Blackman, Sarah Fasano, and Daniel J. Dufour*	415

PART V. THE POSSIBILITIES FOR KINDNESS

20.	Benefits and Liabilities of Empathy-Induced Altruism: A Contemporary Review *C. Daniel Batson, Nadia Y. Ahmad, and E. L. Stocks*	443
21.	Volunteerism: Multiple Perspectives on Benefits and Costs *Mark Snyder, Allen M. Omoto, and Patrick C. Dwyer*	467
22.	The Psychology of Heroism: Extraordinary Champions of Humanity in an Unforgiving World *Zeno E. Franco and Philip G. Zimbardo*	494
	Index	525

CHAPTER 1

Introduction and Overview

Arthur G. Miller

"The evil that men [sic] do lives after them. The good is often interred with their bones." Judge George O'Toole spoke these lines from Shakespeare's *Julius Caesar* to Dzhokhar Tsarnaev after sentencing him to death for the Boston Marathon bombing. Tsarnaev had, surprisingly, just apologized to victims and their relatives in attendance. The judge continued: "So it will be for Dzhokhar Tsarnaev," telling him that no one will remember that his teachers were fond of him, that his friends found him fun to be with, or that he showed compassion to disabled people. "What will be remembered is that you murdered and maimed innocent people and that you did it willfully and intentionally," O'Toole said.

The wrenching vignette above (reported in Valencia, 2015) seems an appropriate prelude for a book about the social psychology of good and evil. Many would see evil clearly in the actions of the young man, even with his otherwise very good attributes. There are those who would also describe the imposition of the death penalty as a form of evil. Many states and numerous countries have banned it. A recent report from the Pew Research Center (2015), however, indicated that 63% of respondents still viewed capital punishment as morally acceptable, 31% negatively, and 6% undecided. In yet another instance of mass murder, the relatives of nine victims killed in a church in Charleston, South Carolina, were seen to forgive the killer in a highly emotional scene (Corasaniti, Perez-Pena, & Alvarez, 2015). Forgiveness would certainly seem to qualify as one of the very best behaviors, often shown on the part of people who have been seriously harmed. Yet there were those in the Charleston case who explicitly rejected a forgiving attitude.

From a social-psychological perspective, good and evil are complex concepts. They seem to reside within individuals, in their very "natures" or their motives, but also in their actions and in the judgments and interpretations of those who observe their deeds. Research indicates that people in fact have different beliefs about both good and evil and that these beliefs are strongly related to other views of the world. For example, greater beliefs in pure evil predict more positive attitudes toward the death penalty, whereas greater beliefs in pure good correlate with a variety of prosocial attitudes and policies, such as criminal rehabilitation and nonmilitaristic foreign relations (e.g., Campbell & Vollhardt, 2014; Webster & Saucier, 2013).

There are critics within social psychology who suggest that the discipline has been dominated by a focus on the negative, on the evil side, so to speak. For example, Krueger and Funder (2004) were critical of what they regard as an "imbalance" in social psychology:

> Mainstream social psychology focuses on how people characteristically violate norms of action through social misbehaviors such as conformity with false majority judgments, destructive obedience, and failures to help those in need. Likewise, they are seen to violate norms of reasoning through cognitive errors such as misuse of social information, self-enhancement, and an over-readiness to attribute dispositional characteristics. The causes of this negative research emphasis include the apparent informativeness of norm violation, the status of good behavior and judgment as unconfirmable null hypotheses, and the allure of counter-intuitive findings. (p. 317)

Krueger and Funder recommend a substantial revision in this "negativity" bias that would achieve significant benefits: "A more balanced social psychology would yield not only a more positive view of human nature, but also an improved understanding of the bases of good behavior and accurate judgment, coherent explanations of occasional lapses, and theoretically grounded suggestions for improvement" (p. 317). This book is designed to address some of their concerns. Many of its chapters are indeed framed in the negative mode, but within them are numerous examples of good behavior—for example, people who do not lie or cheat (Chapter 15), dehumanize (Chapter 8), or display racism (Chapter 6). There are also harmful behaviors to be seen in the positively framed chapters—for example, those who do not help (Chapter 20), do not volunteer (Chapter 21), and do not act heroically when the opportunity presents itself (Chapter 22). There is a strong reality to the thesis that people react differently to the same situation. Studying these differences in conjunction with the power of situations is extremely important in terms of any complete understanding of good or evil.

Krueger and Funder's (2004) conclusion that "A more balanced social psychology would yield . . . a more positive view of human nature" may be somewhat biased in its own right. That is, whether or not social psychology, as an academic discipline, should in fact promote a positive view of human nature is debatable. One could argue that there is no one correct or better view than another. Yet, as noted earlier, beliefs about good and evil do in fact relate empirically to other attitudes and behaviors. So, in that context, beliefs about human nature do matter, however awkward or impossible it may be to validate their inherent truthfulness. In this book, both sides of the good–evil coin are examined in considerable depth. If there is a slant toward the negative, that may indeed be something worth thinking about. There may be understandable reasons for this reaction and it would be useful to know more about this apparent asymmetry or bias (e.g., Baumeister, Bratlavsky, Finkenauer, & Vohs, 2001). Readers of this book can make up their own minds about these matters.

The essential purpose of this book is to provide the reader with highly informed portraits of the diverse phenomena that fall under the generic concepts of *good* and *evil*. Its 21 chapters each provide a window through which readers may become familiar with a significant domain of contemporary social-psychological thinking, research, and application. The chapters are written by social psychologists who have had a highly influential role in contributing to our scientific understanding of their respective areas. The social-psychological perspective is valuably inclusive. Across chapters, one will encounter many emphases—the compelling if controversial insights of an evolutionary perspective; the powerful causal role of diverse situations and contexts; the role of technology and globalization on newer forms of threat and harm; the importance of individual differences in personality, motives, and the moral emotions of shame and guilt; and a strong focus on various forms of biased perception and cognitive processes largely below the individual's threshold of awareness. Also featured is a focus on the self and the mechanisms by which it protects itself, serving in certain conditions to rationalize or justify behaviors that, in principle, go against the person's ideals or values. Group and organizational contexts, as well as dyadic relationships, all of which have their own unique dynamics, are also emphasized. Finally, although the table of contents contains categories seemingly distinct from one another in terms of their focus on good or evil, in actuality, many of the chapters, as noted, are concerned with both kinds of behavior. Individuals can differ considerably in their response to the identical (physical) situation (e.g., Funder, 2009). It is also true, however, given the logic of the experimental method, that the same individuals, were they randomly assigned to different conditions, could behave very cruelly in one and with great kindness in another. Finally, spirited controversy, no stranger to social psychology, will occasionally be encountered in this book or in the minds of readers. Intellectual combat can, at least under certain conditions, be stimulating and productive in its own right.

CHAPTER OVERVIEWS

Part I. Conceptual Perspectives on Good and Evil

Duntley and Buss (Chapter 2) address the concepts of good and evil from an evolutionary perspective. They approach these concepts as inevitable products of human adaptation to their social environment. Harm-inflicting behaviors are viewed as "universal components of human nature," independent of social psychology's emphasis on the situation, socialization, media, and culture. Adaptations to bestow good (benefits) on others are perhaps more obvious in terms of promoting survival. The perception of intentionality also seems relatively hard-wired, as if the distinction between intended and accidental harm is a valuable capacity for successful adaptation. In this context, there are some parallel concerns between this chapter and those of Chapters 3 and 5. Duntley and Buss argue intensely for the unique theoretical contributions of the evolutionary perspective, for example its claim that individual humans have the capacity for both good and evil. However, would not situationists in the Milgram–Zimbardo tradition (e.g., Ross, Lepper, & Ward, 2010) make the same claim? An indispensable feature of this chapter is the authors' discussion of considerable experimental evidence to support their conceptual ideas. They are, of course, highly aware of critics of their theoretical position, and in this context, the persuasive value of empirical evidence cannot be overstated.

Monroe, Vohs, and Baumeister (Chapter 3) discuss issues of free will and determinism. These are powerful concepts, and, as with good and evil, they have preoccupied philosophers and theologians (and perhaps lawyers) for centuries. There has always been fascination with the seeming contradiction of people believing they are free but yet faced with scientific evidence that they are not nearly as free as they presume. If, then, people do not have free will, how can they be held responsible for their actions? (See Chapter 10.) This question bears on the authors' discussion of the evolution of the idea of free will. Similar to beliefs about good and evil, people have different beliefs about free will and determinism. The accuracy or existential reality of these beliefs is, as noted by the authors, an entirely separate matter. Most people believe in free will, but their beliefs are malleable. Changes in these beliefs have a variety of significant behavioral and judgmental effects, as documented in the research reported in this chapter. Issues of free will and determinism are of particular interest to social psychology, given its strong emphasis on concepts that appear to minimize a person's freedom of choice—for example, the powerful causal influences of situations and cognitive processes inaccessible to consciousness (see Chapters 5 and 6).

Fiske (Chapter 4) focuses upon one of social psychology's strongest research domains, that of social categorization. She is interested in our natural inclination to perceive others in terms of biased preconceptions about their group membership. Categorical thinking about others appears to be inevitable, at times useful, but often extremely harmful. Of major interest in this chapter are Fiske's conclusions and recommendations regarding the individual's intentionality, control, and moral responsibility for engaging in biased thinking. She defines the concept of "right thinking people," that is, people with "the right values . . . the right organizational incentives . . . the right motivation" (p. 65). This provocative approach can be seen as engaging in its own categorical distinction, that is, the good "right thinking" people versus the "other kind." There is a concerted effort in Fiske's chapter to deal with the problems involved in exonerating perpetrators for behaviors allegedly beyond their control (see Chapters 5, 6, and 10 for related concerns).

Bargh (Chapter 5) describes the fascinating history behind the reputations of two of psychology's most famous constructs, consciousness and the unconscious. He explains both the causes and consequences of the clearly positive, "good" associations that have traditionally been bestowed upon conscious thought and the very negative, "evil" connotations of the unconscious. Bargh hardly settles for this simplistic formulation. Given the voluminous research documenting the pervasive roles of both conscious (aware, intentional) behavior and implicit unconscious (unaware) processes in social behavior, there is an obvious need for a careful synthesis, which Bargh provides. He advocates that skepticism itself not be biased in favor of one kind of thought over another. His recommendations for dealing with the difficulties raised by unconscious causation relate in interesting ways to Fiske's discussion in Chapter 4.

Part II. Harming Others: Contexts, Causes, and Implications

Dovidio, Gaertner, and Pearson (Chapter 6) discuss racism, clearly the most prominent social issue facing this country at the time of this writing. The authors provide a contemporary review of the accumulating evidence that racism typically takes a relatively subtle expression, that it is perpetrated largely by "well-intentioned and ostensibly nonprejudiced white Americans" (p. 96). This refrain, of good people doing bad things, is one that resonates throughout much of this book—reminiscent of Fiske's "right-thinking" persons. The reader is encouraged to think critically of this seemingly uncontroversial thesis. Are these individuals truly good people, and does this label subtly provide some mild form of exoneration or condoning of their harmful thoughts and actions? Does their lack of awareness provide a justification or an excuse? (See Chapter 10.) Dovidio and colleagues provide specific recommendations for solving the problems they cite. Can the interruption of unconscious, biased processes by making people insightful as to their operation be successful? Police training is now in fact adopting these techniques (Fridell & Lim, 2016; Gove, 2011).

Prot, Anderson, Saleem, Groves, and Allen (Chapter 7) address the problem of media violence effects. Media projected on a screen have long been regarded by social scientists as a source of stimuli that in principle can affect vast numbers of people. As technology has advanced, the various devices displaying media and games have increased, with the age of viewers (and players) becoming increasingly younger. The mass appeal and financial gain of producing media violence are thus part of the obvious reality here. Prot, Anderson, and colleagues assert, however, that there are in fact harmful effects, specifically in the form of increasing aggressive behaviors and also in reducing prosocial behaviors. Controversy rules here, as some observers either overattribute major tragedies (e.g., school shootings) to the single cause of a perpetrator's exposure to violent media or completely deny any effects whatsoever. The authors deal with the complexities of these issues, including both person and situational factors, as these affect different psychological processes, including brain activity. The general aggression model (GAM) is used to organize the complex processes involved in these effects. The positive effects of prosocial media are one of several promising new directions.

Haslam and Loughnan (Chapter 8) discuss how dehumanization promotes harm. Their focus is not on defining the concept too precisely (there are several workable definitions in use) but rather on the mechanisms by which dehumanization causes harmful consequences. There is a strong empirical base to support the significant correlation between (degree of) dehumanization and a variety of negative attitudes and judgments—for example, less empathy for dehumanized victims in war contexts. (See also Chapter 11 for a related discussion in the context of sexual violence.) Not unexpectedly, there are a number of different pathways from dehumanization to harm. The authors note the importance of timing, as dehumanization can occur prior to an act of harm doing or after, taking different functions depending on its proximal connection to behavior. Dehumanization can also occur in hindsight, in one's memory. Dehumanization has traditionally been viewed as a type of perception having functional value for the self. However, Haslam and Loughnan also define a variety of nonmotivated forms of the dehumanization–harm linkage, including the absence of obvious moral components of this process. Interestingly, dehumanization can be applied with similar functional value to perpetrators as well as victims.

Vollhardt and Campbell-Obaid (Chapter 9) examine the social psychology of genocide and mass atrocities. They note that it is with respect to genocide and atrocities that the word "evil" is used virtually to minimal objection, but vagueness persists. Are we speaking of evil persons, or evil deeds, or both? "Evil" can give the illusion of being explanatory of the most harmful actions imaginable when in fact it is little more than a descriptive label. The authors' analytical strategy is to view social-psychological constructs contributing to genocide as consisting largely of ordinary basic processes—for example, social identity, leadership, conformity, group norms—that can explain the behaviors of perpetrators, victims, and bystanders. This approach represents a proven strength of social psychology, but can these concepts be sufficiently convincing, given the truly extreme behaviors at issue in this chapter? The authors recognize the complex, at times blurred, roles that individual members of both perpetrator and victim groups play, as bystanders, rescuers, collaborators, or resistance fighters. Vollhardt and Campbell-Obaid present an informative analysis of the political functions of the term *evil*, for example as a rhetorical device to justify using violence or war when there may be uncertainty in the larger population. Research is cited that shows the effects of individual differences in beliefs about evil and correlations with recommended punishment strategies or increased arms for self-protection. Their closing message is "we need to move beyond the essentialist idea that people or groups involved in genocide are good or evil" (p. 178). This assertion will likely attract vigorous opposition. It will seem too situational, and thus too exonerating (see Chapters 4 and 10).

Miller (Chapter 10) examines the current status of the Milgram obedience experiments. After documenting their extraordinary visibility in recent textbook coverage and many other published works, some 50-plus years after their initial appearance, he discusses reasons for their enduring fame. Recent obedience experiments, now under more strict ethical review, are described, documenting, with a variety of methodologies, the basic resilience of the obedience effect, as well as resistance or defiance under specified situations. The chapter then shifts to the continuing controversy. One of the major elements here is the strongly situationist tradition that has long occupied the major theoretical account of these studies. This tradition highlights the "ordinary"/"good" characterization of the obedient participants, as well as a degree of exoneration that is inevitably implied by an emphasis on situational causation. This exoneration is, however, with rare but very important exceptions, vehemently denied by scholars, adding to the controversial nature of the discussion (see Chapter 4). Situationism is in sharp contrast to the development of a new model, that of social identification, what is described by Haslam and Reicher (2012) as "engaged followership." The authors have conducted several empirical studies in strong support of this model. Their views on the considerable freedom and strong culpability characterizing Milgram's obedient participants are in sharp contrast to those of the seemingly more lenient situationist perspective. The strong polarization of these conceptualizations is seen as a major basis for the continuing controversy of these studies.

Gervais (Chapter 11), citing numerous statistics and definitions of sexual assault in many contexts, asserts that in all of these harmful acts, "women are treated as things that can be used and abused by others rather than as fellow human beings" (p. 226). Resonating with Chapter 8, by Haslam and

Loughnan, Gervais likens objectification as a form of dehumanization that is a precursor to violence. The chapter is built around the authors' social interaction model of objectification. The general approach is to examine sequences or stages of (largely) dyadic interaction that, over time, result in a sexual objectification, even to a violent episode. That sexually objectifying behaviors can in certain instances be regarded positively is acknowledged, but the focus is on existing relationships turning out badly. The subtleties within dyadic interactions are given prominence as contrasted with more familiar images of a powerful person exerting blatant sexist domination. A variety of classic concepts—personality, cognition, situational factors (e.g., alcohol), affect, motivation, nonverbal as well as verbal and physical forms of aggression—characterizing both the perpetrator and victim are involved in a broad-ranging series of analytical studies. Gervais suggests that understanding dyadic interaction using this microanalytic strategy offers the best prospect for ultimately preventing this form of violence.

Part III. The Self-Concept in Relation to Good and Evil Acts

Dunning (Chapter 12) opens with a discussion of hubris, those qualities of unwarranted high self-regard and arrogance that are widely denounced in religion and other aspects of culture. Do people see their moral character accurately or suffer from false self-pride? Dunning indicates that people indeed generally fall prey to hubris. They regard themselves as better than their peers on a host of moral and ethical dimensions, and they forecast better actions on their own part than on the part of others. His chapter, replete with relevant experimental findings, is based largely on analyzing precisely why these beliefs are in error. Dunning distinguished two major errors that could give rise to false moral superiority—first, perceiving the self largely correctly but others too harshly; or, second, the reverse, that is, being right about others but too flattering about ourselves. His focus on the legal domain and the importance of intentionality and beliefs in free will in the context of crime and punishment are of particular interest, relating to similar issues considered in Chapters 3 and 10. Dunning suggests, paradoxically, that there may be benefits to society (more lawful behavior) if people indeed misjudge what social psychology preaches, that is, that their behavior is strongly constrained by outside forces. The chapter closes with an intriguing recommendation based on the surprising finding that people are generally more accurate in their predictions about others than about themselves.

Crocker and Canevello (Chapter 13) examine the complexities and difficulties of achieving relationships with partners who are both good persons and particularly good for us. They reject the widely held assumption that "there is just the right person out there for us" but emphasize the interpersonal dynamics that serve to create desirable outcomes once (just about) anyone is a potential partner. Thus their challenging and provocative thesis is that "good relationship partners are made, not found" (p. 271). For these authors, a critical question for the prospective relationship builder is: "What are your intentions?" A key distinction rests on whether, in a relationship context, persons essentially (1) are motivated to manage the impressions others have of them or (2) intend to be constructive and supportive and not regard or treat others badly. Being sure to project one's good qualities to the other at the beginning of a relationship is crucial. A central construct in this chapter is that of compassionate goals. Most people are presumed to value compassion from others, and the authors build a strong case why people should indeed provide it. Doing so is in the provider's best interest as much as in the interest of the recipient. The reader will ponder a number of issues here, including the degree to which certain seemingly necessary ingredients are present from the start, that is, characteristics of the specific individuals, or whether they evolve largely in the process of relationship development. Developing a truly good relationship is not without potential risks or costs, adding to the high emotional stakes that are typically invested in close friendships and other valued associations.

Tangney, Blalock, Folk, and Stuewig (Chapter 14) provide an opportunity for readers to think strongly about prisons, places widely regarded as among the very worst situations in this country. Acknowledging social psychology's emphasis on causal powers of the situation, the authors pose the alternative question: Are there evil *people* in the world? Among incarcerated offenders, there is a sizable minority of psychopaths, a form of mental illness that they regard as deserving of the designation "evil." Who, then, are the vast number of other persons in prison? The authors acknowledge their bad deeds, but not their evil natures. The chapter is focused on the presence of shame and guilt in prisoners. Experiences of shame and guilt have clear costs to the ordinary individual, but some crucial benefits as well, particularly in the case of guilt. It is what individuals do in response to these emotions that is vital to understand. Adding the concepts of criminogenic cognitions and capacity for self-control, the authors transition from findings observed in the psychology laboratories of universities to the contexts of jails and prisons. They analyze the concept of rehabilitation—its positive (postrelease success) and negative (recidivism) outcomes—from the perspective of their conceptually oriented research. Their interweaving of social psychology and criminology is both novel and extraordinarily important for society.

Gino and Ariely (Chapter 15) examine the paradox that although we clearly value truth and sincerity extremely highly, we often behave deceitfully. How can these two realities coexist? They open their chapter in the quagmire of the great accounting and investment firm scandals in the early stages of the 21st century. Corporate corruption thus joins the lengthy list of well-known perpetrators of deceit—in the worlds of adultery, plagiarism, "Deflategate" at the Super Bowl, performance-enhancing drugs in professional sports, shoplifting, illegal gambling, and so forth. Based on research, the occurrence of a variety of lies among ordinary citizens is a documented truism. Many consequences of interpersonal deceit can be tragic. Is there solace in their pointing out that dishonesty is more often committed on a small scale by many individuals than on a large scale by only a few? Gino and Ariely are interested in how individuals respond differently depending upon the number of opportunities they face to behave dishonestly. They draw upon the extensive research documenting our general need to maintain a positive self-image, even a sense of moral superiority to others (Chapter 12). How will our deceitful actions be integrated into this flattering self-portrait? Once again, the power of situations emerges, causing people to behave (and justify that behavior) in ways they would not anticipate. Are they to be exonerated? The authors suggest that "at least in its more liberal form, . . . morality is *malleable* and *dynamic*" (p. 336). They have the evidence to back this up, but assuredly critics will appear with a quite different point of view on this kind of "flexibility."

Part IV. Group Perspectives on Good and Evil

Levine and Wilson (Chapter 16) approach one of social psychology's "classic" studies with a new perspective. The famous Kitty Genovese case and the research it inspired were originally framed in terms of the destructive effect of the presence of apparently nonengaged others on individual judgment and action. The authors initiate their discussion with some new insights into the concept of group behavior and group processes, shedding light on what they regard as an outmoded, unjustifiably negative reputation regarding the influence of groups on the individual. Groups can clearly facilitate prosocial behavior and resistance to evil. Levine and Wilson thus argue for the essential neutrality of group influence. Their innovative approach includes an integration of social identity theory with group influence. Then, depending upon the valence of the particular group's influence, a person's identification with that group may result in very positive or very negative outcomes. A detailed critique of the Latané and Darley studies is then presented, showing the traditional effects in some emergency instances but very different effects of group presence in other circumstances. In an interesting closing, Levine and Wilson interpret the focus on the Kitty Genovese incident as not only an episode of the apparent inaction of witnesses but also a case study in sexual assault (see Chapter 11).

Branscombe, Wohl, and Warner (Chapter 17) remind us that a person's victimization hardly ends with the crime but may last for decades, even generations. There can be both good and bad outcomes of the act of remembering victimization. Forgiveness, such as recently bestowed upon the murderer of nine members of a church in Charleston, South Carolina, by the victims' immediate relatives, is case in point, reflecting (presumably) a good side of victimization. Alternatively, revenge is another understandable motive that has destructive potential of its own. Branscombe and her colleagues discuss the psychological processes and mechanisms that lead to the diverse reactions to the memory of group victimization. Their core construct is the meaning that is derived from historical victimization and the manner in which it drives diverse responses. Intuitively, it is remarkable to discover meanings other than the most negative imaginable, but successful coping may require the development of more sustaining interpretations. Alternatively, perpetrators or bystanders—those who are seen as having been able to help but did not do so—may, in the minds of victims, be dehumanized, with predictably negative results (Chapters 11 and 12). Apologies or expressed remorse from perpetrators or their descendants are also complicated responses, in principle extremely meaningful but also likely to evoke skeptical or even angry reactions because of the diverse motives that they may reflect.

Brief and Smith-Crowe (Chapter 18) open with a series of vignettes describing specific examples of good and evil in organizational settings. Having shown that both desirable and destructive actions occurs in organizations, the authors then discuss various explanations for these diverse outcomes. An important presumption is that organizations are not "reducible to individuals or even small groups" (p. 393). Their chapter documents the value, indeed the necessity, of a genuine organizational psychology perspective informed by social psychology—not a simple generalization of the predominantly individual focus of social psychology to organizational settings. They offer recommendations for the kind of research settings—for example, field experiments—that would be of great value for understanding organizational manifestations of good and evil. Focusing on obedience and conformity but applicable to far more behaviors, Hamilton and Sanders (1995) noted: "Perhaps the most commonplace acts of destructive obedience and conformity occur when people go to work and try to do their jobs" (p. 81). This observation clearly resonates with the essential thesis of this chapter.

Moghaddam, Heckenlaible, Blackman, Fasano, and Dufour (Chapter 19) discuss the internal dynamics and processes underlying the devastating outcomes of terrorist attacks. The centerpiece of their chapter is the staircase model, documenting a sequence of stages, each with a relatively distinct set of relevant psychological processes, that, over time, may (or may not) result in an actual terrorist event. Using the Boston Marathon bombing as a case study of their conceptual approach, they illustrate the complex organizational details involved in terrorism. Although their model is essentially situational, one sees different types and roles of individuals within the terrorist group, for, as in many other types of mass violence, there are instigators and leaders, as well as subordinates and followers. The perpetrators of terrorism are not all necessarily ordinary or good individuals.

The authors note a key role played by "extremists," a frequently relatively small number of persons who nevertheless are instrumental in many large-scale terrorist actions. The concept of globalization is featured throughout this chapter, as are the extraordinarily important roles played by developments of modern technology and social media. "Connectivity" is a central concept in their analysis, one that is applicable to the successful functioning both of terrorists and of those agencies designed to detect and destroy them. The authors conclude with some practical implications of their model for the solution of the terrorism threat—a task that, in terms of events in the contemporary world, will be very difficult but perhaps not as impossible as many think.

Part V. The Possibilities for Kindness

Batson, Ahmad, and Stocks (Chapter 20) discuss the empathy–altruism hypothesis, the idea that empathic emotion evokes the motivation to help another in need. Three decades of experimental research, largely very supportive, have been devoted to many features of this hypothesis. The chapter opens with some important definitions and caveats, for example, their *not* presuming that potential benefactors somehow "catch" or experience in personal terms the emotional states of the victim. Their conceptual strategy is to contrast altruistic with egoistic motivation. The interest is in the ultimate goal. Helping another can be one goal; benefitting oneself can be another; and helping another can be instrumental in reaching the latter objective. People are often disposed to treating their selves with a very high, even biased, regard (Chapter 12); thus teasing apart altruistic and egoistic motivations presents a variety of conceptual and methodological challenges. The authors and their colleagues have been extremely creative in devising experimental techniques to accomplish this difficult task. Similar to Bargh's contention (Chapter 5) that the conscious aspect of our mental lives has always been associated with the "good" in contrast to the "bad" unconscious, the authors note that altruism also has had image difficulties, that is, often perceived either as always good—one can hardly think of a more glowing attribute to bestow upon another person—or essentially weak, depending upon emotional connections that are not vital or long lasting, in contrast perhaps to other forms or rationales for helping others, for example, successful volunteerism (see Chapter 21). The authors denounce both of these generalizations, and provide a clear and highly nuanced view of empathy-induced altruism. Unexpected liabilities can occur in its pursuit. Thus our intuitions about altruism do not necessarily correspond well with the findings of the extensive research discussed in this chapter.

Snyder, Omoto, and Dwyer (Chapter 21) deal with volunteerism, a particularly intriguing form of good behavior. It takes place, at least initially, among strangers but often has a uniquely sustained aspect in that certain individuals may volunteer in the same or different settings for years. Its value to society is arguably unrivaled in terms of the vast numbers of both providers and recipients of their help. The verb *to volunteer* literally implies a high degree of choice, and, similar to altruism, volunteering might appear superficially to be a relatively self-less act. As usual, things are more complicated. There are diverse motives underlying this form of helping behavior, and some recipients can even vary in their degree of gratitude for receiving it. The chapter opens with useful distinctions among various types of helping or prosocial behavior. Many types are clearly needed and given. Visit any hospital, and one is likely to see a number of volunteers, helping patients with a wheelchair to enter the building or offering books and magazines to patients. These are small acts of great kindness. The authors discuss the many individuals who engage in volunteering, the settings in which it takes place, and the benefits and liabilities associated with it. Why do people volunteer? Motives matter, and several individuals engaged in the identical act of volunteering can be doing so for very different reasons. Knowing the underlying reasons for volunteering can illuminate its beneficial as well as costly outcomes. There are so many benefits of volunteering—for its recipients as well as providers—that it would indeed seem to represent "the good sides of human nature" (p. 486). Nonetheless, there are also costs associated with volunteerism. By recognizing and dealing with these liabilities, society can in fact strengthen the already admired and valued prosocial side.

Franco and Zimbardo (Chapter 22) discuss the psychology of heroism, a topic that would seem to represent the best, indeed the most unquestionably good, aspect of human beings. Our worshipful attitude has not translated into research, however, as Franco and Zimbardo open their chapter by noting the relatively sparse interest in the topic on the part of psychology. They identify a number of reasons for this lack of overdue attention. Among these are problems of definition. Heroism may "suffer" from seeming to be well understood (and prized) in a colloquial sense. For example, their initial emphasis on "everyday heroism" may clash with our intuition that heroic acts are rare. Once embedded into a more scientific framework, however, the conceptual nature of heroism becomes far more interesting, complex, and subject to controversy. The authors introduce an evolutionary dimension to illustrate just one among many relevant features of heroism. The authors discuss a variety of internal processes and motivations underlying heroism and approach the topic from both a prosocial and a more negative perspective. They also consider heroism from a more external point of view, in which an important issue concerns the perception of heroism—that is, that heroism can be viewed not as a specific action or person but as an ultimately positive judgment bestowed by others who have their own motivations and needs. The authors suggest that heroes can be powerful forces for improving the lives of others—that heroes "represent the ideal in human nature to which each of us can aspire" (p. 516). A description of the Heroic Imagination Project (HIP) closes the chapter.

REFERENCES

Baumeister, R. F., Bratlavsky, E., Finkenauer, C., & Vohs, K. D. (2001). Bad is stronger than good. *Review of General Psychology, 5*, 323–370.

Campbell, M., & Vollhardt, J. R. (2014). Fighting the good fight: The relationship between belief in evil and support for violent policies. *Personality and Social Psychology Bulletin, 40*(1), 16–33.

Corasaniti, N., Perez-Pena, R., & Alvarez, L. (2015, June 19). Charleston massacre suspect held as city grieves: Races unite for nine killed by gunman. *The New York Times*, pp. A1, A16.

Fridell, L., & Lim, H. (2016). Assessing the racial aspects of police force using the implicit- and counter-bias perspectives. *Journal of Criminal Justice, 44*, 36–48.

Funder, D. C. (2009). Persons, behaviors, and situations: An agenda for personality psychology in the postwar era. *Journal of Research in Personality, 43*, 120–126.

Gove, T. G. (2011). Implicit bias and law enforcement. *The Police Chief: The Professional Voice of Law Enforcement, 78*(10), 44–56.

Hamilton, V. L., & Sanders, J. (1995). Crimes of obedience and conformity in the workplace: Surveys of Americans, Russians, and Japanese. *Journal of Social Issues, 51*(3), 67–88.

Haslam, S. A., & Reicher, S. D. (2012). Contesting the "nature" of conformity: What Milgram and Zimbardo's studies really show. *PLoS Biology, 10*(11), e1001426.

Krueger, J. I., & Funder, D. C. (2004). Towards a balanced social psychology: Causes, consequences, and cures for the problem-seeking approach to social behavior and cognition. *Behavioral and Brain Sciences, 27*, 313–376.

Pew Research Center. (2015, April 16). U.S. politics and policy: Less support for death penalty, especially among democrats. Retrieved from *www.people-press.org/2015/04/16/less-support-for-death-penalty-especially-among-democrats*.

Ross, L., Lepper, M., & Ward, A. (2010). History of social psychology: Insights, challenges, and contributions to theory and application. In S. T. Fiske, D. T. Gilbert, & G. Lindzey (Eds.), *Handbook of social psychology* (5th ed., Vol. 2, pp. 3–50). New York: Wiley.

Valencia, M. J. (2015, June 24). Judge excoriates Tsarnaev before imposing death sentence. *Boston Globe*. Retrieved from *www.bostonglobe.com/metro/2015/06/24/judge-excoriates-tsarnaev-before-imposing-death-sentence/s4IVL9PTCeznIqEYcTuJMN/story*.

Webster, R. J., & Saucier, D. A. (2013). Angels and demons are among us: Assessing individual differences in belief in pure evil and belief in pure good. *Personality and Social Psychology Bulletin, 39*(11), 1455–1470.

PART I

CONCEPTUAL PERSPECTIVES ON GOOD AND EVIL

CHAPTER 2

The Evolution of Good and Evil

Joshua D. Duntley and David M. Buss

On the evening of July 24, 2002, in the thriving city of Houston, Texas, Clara Harris got into her Mercedes Benz and killed her husband, David Harris, in the parking lot of a hotel. Using her car as the device of murder, she ran into him once. Her anger still not allayed, she circled the lot and ran over him again. Witnesses differ on precisely how many times she backed up and crushed her husband with the 4,000-pound vehicle. One said five times, another four, and a third witness indicated only twice. Videotape from the hotel security cameras revealed that the correct number was three. Some think that Clara Harris is evil and deserves to rot in jail for the remainder of her life. But some view the homicide as justifiable, or at least understandable.

The circumstance that elicited the homicide was that David Harris was having an affair with Gail Bridges, his former office coworker. Clara Harris discovered this through a private detective she hired when her suspicions were initially aroused. The morning of his death, David Harris swore to Clara that he would end the affair. Later that night, Clara, along with her stepdaughter, Lindsey, began to search for David Harris. When they finally tracked him down at a hotel, according to Lindsey, "She said she could kill him and get away with it for what she's been through." Indeed, Clara had gone to great efforts to win her husband back after she discovered his affair. She made herself "real pretty so Dad would want her and not Gail," Lindsey said. During the week before the murder, Clara Harris spent time at a tanning salon, a beauty shop, and a gym. She also consulted a plastic surgeon, inquiring about breast implants.

It might also have annoyed Clara that the hotel was precisely the one where Clara and David had gotten married a decade earlier—on Valentine's Day. When she saw her husband emerge from the hotel elevator with his mistress, the two hand in hand, Clara Harris went "ballistic." She ripped the blouse off her rival's body and wrestled her to the ground. Although she clearly intended to do more damage, her husband separated the two women, and Clara was firmly escorted out of the hotel by the clerk on duty. As she left the lobby, David shouted, "It's over! It's over! It's over!"

It was then that Clara Harris became strangely calm, according to her stepdaughter, who accompanied her out of the hotel. Clara silently got into her Mercedes, and her tears stopped flowing. Clara was cool and composed as she suddenly stomped on the accelerator and rammed the car into her husband. She then ran over her husband again and again. Her stepdaughter tried to exit the vehicle but had to wait until Clara stopped the car and the damage had finally come to an end. "You killed my dad," Lindsey said, when the car finally stopped. In light of the circumstances, many in Texas do not judge Clara's horrific deed as evil. Some think that David Harris got exactly what he deserved.

Can good and evil be evaluated from an evolutionary perspective? In this chapter, we consider several related issues: Have humans evolved adaptations to commit deeds that most would consider "evil"? Have humans evolved defenses against the perpetration of evil on them? And do the apparently universal cognitive categories of "good" and "evil" have special functional uses, aiding humans in solving critical adaptive problems?

EVIL AS THE INFLICTION OF FITNESS COSTS

Evil has no direct analogue in the formal theoretical structure of evolutionary theory. Evolution by natural selection operates by the simple process of differential gene reproduction as a consequence of differences in heritable design. Heritable variants that lead to greater reproduction compared with competing variants present in the population at the time become represented in greater numbers in the next generation. Iterated over generations, the process of selection leads to the evolution of adaptations that exist solely because they contributed, either directly or indirectly, to the reproductive success of their bearers. Thus the process of natural selection is value-free. Whatever qualities lead to increased replicative success are those that evolve.

The evolutionary process of selection produces many products, and humans have little hesitation in labeling some of those products "good" and others "evil." At a first approximation, those we label as "evil" are behaviors or behavioral dispositions that result in a massive imposition of fitness costs on another individual or group. Terrorist organizations inclined to kill innocent women, children, or other victims for differences in religious beliefs would be prime examples. Indeed, as we will argue later in the chapter, humans have evolved a specialized psychological categorization system for making these judgments.

Consider fitness costs. The imposition of costs on another individual can vary in magnitude from trivial to catastrophic. At the low end, someone bumping into you in the hall or stepping on your toe might be considered annoying, but probably not evil, unless these acts were repeated to the point of torture. At the high end are events such as robbing, maiming, rape, torture, and murder, with combinations of these usually viewed as embodying evil more fully than any considered alone. Intentional premeditated murder occupies the extreme end of the continuum, but within that broad class, some murders are considered to be more evil than others—murder with malice, murder without provocation, murder of young defenseless children, murder of adolescent girls, serial murder, mass murder, and genocide. Some homicides, on the other hand, are considered excusable, justifiable, or even altruistic—killing in self-defense, killing to protect a family member from harm, or killing to prevent a helpless stranger from being raped. Of course, as Baumeister (1997) points out, the judgment of the perpetrators and victims will surely differ in how evil these deeds are evaluated to be—a point that will be taken up later. The key point here is that the acts we consider evil invariably involve the imposition of massive costs on victims, even though not all massive costs are considered to be evil.

By what metric do we judge acts to be costly? One contention of this chapter is that the deeds we view as evil occupy the extreme end of a continuum of reproductively relevant costs—that is, those that impose a massive fitness cost on the victim will be viewed to be the most evil. Humans, of course, do not think in these terms. We do not think to ourselves: "Gee, the damage done to Sally inflicts a large cost on her fitness, which impairs her relative gene replication . . . hence, it's evil." Rather, we propose that humans have evolved evaluative psychological mechanisms that function to gauge the magnitude of fitness costs inflicted on themselves, their allies, their children, and their extended families—roughly, degree of evil. We also have evolved evaluative mechanisms to assess the magnitude of fitness benefits that others bestow on us and our allies—roughly, degree of good. According to our evolutionary theory of good and evil, the degrees of evil and of good judged by a person is partially a function of their degree of genetic relatedness to the person upon whom costs are inflicted or benefits are bestowed. Costs inflicted or benefits bestowed upon closer relatives would be more evil or good, respectively, than the same amounts of costs or benefits on more distant genetic relatives. Degree of evil or good is also a function of "strategic confluence," that is, the degree to which other individuals are allied with us in achieving some goal (Buss, 1996). Thus extreme fitness costs inflicted on a close friend would be judged to be more evil than comparable costs inflicted on a stranger or on an enemy. Indeed, massive fitness costs inflicted on an enemy are often judged to be "good." In sum, the degree of strategic confluence, including individuals who are either genetic kin or non-kin allies, is predicted to mediate the degree to which an intentionally inflicted fitness cost is judged to be evil.

In order for these evaluative mechanisms to have evolved, however, there must have been evolutionarily recurrent deeds that humans performed that correspond to these psychological categorizations. Thus, before exploring the evolution of human judgments of good and evil, and the functions of the psychological mechanisms that produce them, we must first explore why people inflict extreme levels of egregious harm on other people.

HUMAN PSYCHOLOGY AS THE END PRODUCT OF A COMPETITIVE EVOLUTIONARY PROCESS

From an evolutionary perspective, modern humans are the end products of a long line of successful reproducers. Indeed, all humans are evolutionary success stories. Each one of us owes our existence to an unbroken chain of ancestors, each of whom did what was necessary to survive and reproduce. If any one of our ancestors or their ancestors had failed at these tasks—being felled before reproductive age, failing to find a mate, failing to best competitors in attracting a mate, or failing to keep their own offspring alive so that they could mate—we would not be here to ponder the momentous issues of good and evil. As end products of this vast chain of events operating over deep evolutionary time, modern humans carry with them the adaptations that led to their ancestors' success and the genes that contribute to the reliable development of these adaptations. These adaptations are the source of our universal human nature.

Aside from genetically identical twins, the fitness interests of all individuals are to some degree unique and diverge from each other. Stated differently, humans are to some extent reproductive competitors with other humans to become ancestors. Competition need not be direct and need not involve overt contests. Indeed, competitors need never meet for competition to ensue. Scramble competition, for example, involves striving for the acquisition of limited or better resources in the external environment. Intrasexual competitors can compete with each other in individual courtship displays to attract a particular mate. Parents can compete with other parents merely by investing in their children's success. Although some of these forms of individual competition, such as investing in children, do not correspond to human intuitions about competition, they do embody competition at the formal level of natural selection as much as two stags locking horns in direct combat or two humans clawing each other psychologically to get ahead in the status hierarchy.

Because all modern humans are the descendants of ancestors who succeeded countless times in direct and indirect competition, modern humans carry with them the competitive adaptations that led to their ancestors' success and pass on the genes that contribute to the development of these adaptations to their children. Some of these adaptations function to inflict costs on other humans.

WHY HUMANS INFLICT HARM ON OTHER HUMANS

At an abstract level, there are two fundamental strategies for besting a competitor in a fitness contest. One strategy involves the acquisition of benefits that aid fitness—scrambling for superior access to resources, displaying more alluring attractant signals to a mate, bestowing on children resources that aid their reproductive success, or aiding one's kin in a manner than increases inclusive fitness (Hamilton, 1964). The other strategy involves inflicting costs on competitors—impairing their access to resources, interfering with their mate attractant signals, or harming a competitor's kin.

In the world of nonhuman animals, both strategies are seen in great abundance. Baby birds compete for their parents' food resources by "begging" with beaks wide open, but they also sometimes push a sibling out of the nest, committing siblicide. Male scorpionflies compete for females by securing insects to feed them as part of the nuptial gift, but they also jostle competing males away from the female, inflicting physical costs on their rivals. Among humans, intrasexual strategies of mate competition involve both sending attraction signals (Buss, 1988) and verbally derogating rivals (Buss & Dedden, 1990; Schmitt & Buss, 1996). Although damaging a rival's reputation may not be considered "evil" in the grand scheme of things, from the victim's perspective, the lost social status and consequent failure in mate competition may approach being viewed as evil. For genes, upon which natural selection primarily operates and for which replication is the ultimate "goal," the struggle to obtain an opportunity to mate is akin to a life-and-death situation. Indeed, status losses sometimes drive people to kill those they perceive as having harmed them, and the emotion of vengeance may have evolved as a defense designed to stanch the costs or to deter others from inflicting similar costs in the future.

In summary, we can expect selection to have favored the evolution of some adaptations that function to inflict costs on intrasexual rivals specifically and conspecific competitors generally. These costs will vary from small to large in the currency of fitness damage to the recipient. As the fitness costs grow in magnitude, we become more and more inclined to label the actions as evil. According to our theory of the evolution of evil, humans have adaptations to inflict these costs—adaptations to steal a rival's resources, adaptations to damage a rival's reputation, adaptations to physically injure rivals, and adaptations to steal their mates. Humans also are likely to have evolved adaptations to kill (Duntley & Buss, 2011).

KILLING AS PROTOTYPICALLY EVIL

Probably no other class of human action is judged to be more evil than premeditated murder. And there may be no other class of actions that inflicts a greater fitness cost on the victim. Although no formal theory is needed to tell us that it's bad to be dead, killing is worse for a victim's fitness than is currently recognized by any existing psychological theory except homicide adaptation theory (Buss & Duntley, 1998; Duntley, 2015; Duntley & Buss, 2011). First, by being killed, the victim forfeits all future reproduction. He loses sexual access to his current partner and all future mating opportunities he may have acquired if he remained alive. By being dead, he is no longer around to invest in his children. Thus his children's survival and reproduction become imperiled as a result of his untimely death. It is known that the death of a parent can impair the survival of children, in some cultures by as much as 10% (Hill & Hurtado, 1996). If the children live and his mate remarries, his children become stepchildren—the single largest risk factor for physical abuse and child homicide (Daly & Wilson, 1988). Furthermore, his extended kin—his brothers and sisters, aunts and uncles, nephews and nieces, grandparents and grandchildren—all become more vulnerable as a consequence of his death through the loss of his protection and the perception of his family as exploitable. And if all of these fitness costs are not bad enough, his rivals benefit by his death. His mate becomes a potential sexual partner for his rivals. His resources become available for the taking. And his rivals' children now have a competitive edge over his own children. His death, in short, can become his rivals' gain. A death produced by homicide differs from those resulting from disease, accidents, or animal attacks. Rather than waiting for circumstances outside their control to produce a death, human killers can, with some precision, select the timing and circumstances of another's death in ways that help to maximize benefits and minimize costs to themselves. In summary, killing may inflict more momentous fitness costs on a victim than any other single act—prototypical evil from the perspective of the victim and the victim's friends and kin.

Reversing the perspective from victim to perpetrator yields interesting insights. Consider as a thought experiment that your assignment, should you choose to accept it, is to outreproduce your rival. You can do this by various means—besting him in the quest for high-quality food, developing more hygienic practices to better combat parasites and diseases, cultivating strategies that succeed in better attracting desirable mates, or investing more heavily or more skillfully in your children. But one remarkably effective strategy remains by which you could accomplish your mission in dramatic fashion—killing your rival.

Killing a rival can offer a bounty of benefits, in principle, from the perspective of the inclusive fitness of the killer. By killing a rival, you may gain access to the rival's resources, as the rival is not around to protect them—resources such as land, food, tools, weapons, or shelter. Because rivals are often in competition for the same pool of potential mates, killing a rival can eliminate mating competition. The rival's existing mate(s) become potential new mates for the killer. The killer's current and future children may have less competition in the next generation, enhancing their fitness. A victim's losses, in short, can become the killer's gains.

This brief description of the potential benefits of killing a rival, of course, ignores the costs of killing, and, indeed, killing can be a dangerous and costly strategy to carry out. Killers risk getting injured or killed while attempting to carry out a murder. Even if "successful," the kin of the victim may extract revenge in the future. In some cultures, killers can suffer retribution from the larger group. And killing may harm the reputation of the perpetrator, hindering future access to social resources, including mates. The key point is *not* that killing is always or even often beneficial to the fitness of the killer. Rather, *killing historically has been potentially beneficial in the currency of reproductive fitness under some delimited circumstances*—when the risks are low, when costs are unlikely to be incurred, when the potential yield is large in magnitude, or when killing is the least costly strategy available amidst an array of costly options. It is precisely these benefits to the killer, combined with the costs to victims, that would create strong evolutionary selection pressures that favor tactics to avoid being killed as soon as homicide enters a population as a strategy. Killing will immediately favor coevolved defenses, resulting in an antagonistic coevolutionary arms race between homicide and defenses against being killed.

DEFENDING AGAINST EVIL: ANTAGONISTIC COEVOLUTION

There can be little doubt that, from the victim's perspective, killers or would-be killers can be considered to be evil. But before we consider the possible evolution of a universal cognitive category of "evil," it is critical to consider the evolutionary events that would be set into motion once killing entered the human strategic repertoire. Because of the dramatic fitness costs of being killed, selection would act strongly to create defenses against killing—what we have called "anti-homicide mechanisms" (Duntley, 2015; Duntley & Buss, 1998).

The intensity of selection is generally a function of two critical factors—the fitness consequences and the frequency of the fitness-relevant events over evolutionary time. There is no doubt that being killed inflicts enormous fitness damage on victims, fulfilling the first criterion. Given the magnitude of damage, the frequency of killing need not be high for selection to act consistently and strongly in fashioning anti-homicide defenses. The lifetime odds of being killed in modern America are roughly 1 in 200; they are 1 in 26 for certain groups, such as inner-city males (Ghiglieri, 1999). Among more traditional societies, such as the Ghibusi tribe of Africa or the Yanomamo of Venezuela, as many as 30% of all males die at the hands of their fellow humans (Chagnon, 1988; Ghiglieri, 1999). Even among the so-called "peaceful" !Kung San of Botswana, murder rates are higher than in Los Angeles or Detroit. Bioarcheological evidence, which reveals arrowheads lodged in rib cages and skull-crushing blows to skeletal heads, points to a long human history of conspecific killing (Buss & Duntley, 1998, 2015; Duntley & Buss, 2011).

Although it is impossible to determine with precision the exact frequency of homicide over the long course of human evolutionary history, available evidence suggests that it was likely far from uncommon. And given the large fitness impact of being killed, even small rates of killing, such as a rate of one-half of 1%, as seen in modern America, would easily have met the required criteria for selection to have operated to fashion anti-homicide defenses.

Indeed, humans likely have evolved many different types of anti-homicide defenses (Duntley, 2015; Duntley & Buss, 1998). Stranger anxiety, for example, is an excellent candidate for an evolved anti-homicide strategy. It emerges predictably at 7–8 months of life, is specific to male strangers (who historically have been more dangerous to infants), and appears to be universal across cultures (Heerwagen & Orians, 2002; Marks, 1987; Marks & Nesse, 1994). Other potential anti-homicide defenses include ethnocentrism, fleeing mechanisms, mind-reading abilities specialized for detecting homicidal intent, and many others (Duntley, 2015; Duntley & Buss, 1998).

Because humans risk being killed in many different circumstances, a single anti-homicide adaptation would have been insufficient to combat all of the dangers. Being killed in infancy is different from being killed by an intrasexual rival in a status dispute as an adult. Being killed in a status dispute is different from being killed by a jealous mate who has suddenly discovered a sexual infidelity. Being killed by an enraged mate is different from being killed in tribal warfare. Given the many, varied, and evolutionarily recurrent circumstances in which the lives of humans have been endangered, selection will have forged a complex armament of defensive, anti-homicide devices.

Once anti-homicide defenses begin to evolve, however, killing becomes a more costly strategy to pursue. First, the success of the strategy becomes lower as a consequence of anti-homicide defenses; hence it results in fewer fitness benefits to the killer. Second, attempting to kill can be downright costly to the killer. Killers risk injury from intended victims. And they risk death, since "killing to prevent being killed," or killing in self-defense, is undoubtedly one of the anti-homicide defenses. Indeed, sometimes entire coalitions of individuals join forces to kill a killer. The upshot is that pursuing a homicidal strategy becomes less evolutionarily profitable.

Anti-homicide defenses, by making killing less profitable, set in motion another evolutionary process—the coevolution of new or refined killer adaptations designed to circumvent the anti-homicide defenses. Selection will favor design features in killers that choose circumstances in which the costs of killing will not be incurred—when the intended victim is particularly vulnerable or weak, when the intended victim lacks kin or coalitional support, when the victim is caught alone or by surprise. Selection will favor deceptive strategies that include concealing homicidal intent from the victim in order to circumvent the activation of the victim's anti-homicide defenses.

As these more refined killer adaptations begin to evolve, selection will then favor the further evolution of increasingly sophisticated defenses. The consequence is a perpetual antagonistic coevolutionary arms race, as depicted in Figure 2.1.

From the victim's perspective, of course, being the target of a homicide renders the would-be killer evil. From the killer's perspective, however, eliminating a victim may represent a "good," and the victim's anti-homicide strategies would thereby be viewed as evil.

THE FUNCTIONS OF COGNITIVE-EVALUATIVE MECHANISMS OF "GOOD" AND "EVIL"

It is not implausible that selection has fashioned privileged and universal cognitive categories of "evil" and "good" reserved precisely for monumental fitness-impairing motivations and fitness-bestowing motivations, respectively. The categorization of specific others as "evil" serves an important function—it targets a key threat to an individual's fitness, serves to encode an array of relevant fitness-damaging events in memory for subsequent strategic retrieval, and motivates action designed to circumvent the fitness threat (see Buss, 1989, for a more general argument about emotions as adaptations designed to deal with strategic interference).

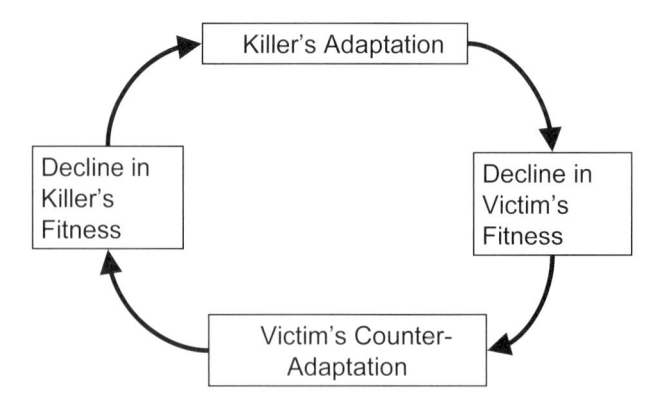

FIGURE 2.1. The coevolution of adaptations to kill and defenses to prevent being killed. Killing, when it occurred in predictable situations over evolutionary history, would create selection pressures that favor strategies to avoid being killed. These coevolved defenses against becoming a victim of homicide would create new selection pressure on mechanisms that lead people to kill, refining the strategies of killers or adding to them. Refined and new killer strategies, in turn, would select for refined and new defenses, resulting in an antagonistic coevolutionary arms race between homicide and defenses against being killed.

Consider the case of stepdaughter who is consistently beaten and sexually abused by a stepfather—events known to occur with nontrivial frequencies (Daly & Wilson, 1998). The stepdaughter's categorization of her stepfather as evil serves an important function. It tags fitness-damaging events for storage. It causes emotional arousal in response to fitness-damaging events, such as sexual abuse. And it motivates action designed to escape the fitness-damaging events. The fact that stepdaughters leave home 2 years earlier than daughters residing with both genetic parents may reflect this motivated action. Evaluative categories such as "evil" historically would have facilitated avoidance of cost inflicting individuals.

But the evolved category of evil is likely to be even more complex than this. Over our evolutionary history there would have been many recurrently costly entities in the environment. It is likely that the category of evil only applies to some of those entities, and then to different degrees. We propose that an entity is more likely to be perceived as evil when it (1) engages in behaviors that inflict asymmetrically high levels of cost on a person relative to the benefits it receives, and (2) appears to desire to inflict harm.

An entity that inflicts great costs for small gains is more likely to be put into the special category of evil than when there is no asymmetry between costs inflicted and benefits received. Other factors equal, a person who kills for $10 million is viewed as less evil than a person who kills for $10. And a person who kills someone in self-defense in order to avoid being killed herself may not be viewed as evil at all. We propose that psychological mechanisms evolved to recognize other individuals who inflict great costs for relatively little gain. Categorization of such individuals as evil would serve an important adaptive function—helping to avoid becoming a victim of heavy costs.

The *intent* to do harm is an integral part of the definition of evil (Weiner & Simpson, 1989). It is not enough that some entity is costly to one's fitness. That thing must desire, or be perceived to desire, to inflict those costs. Over our evolutionary history, some things would have been more recurrently associated with cost-inflicting events than others. Based on recurrent evolutionary experiences with cost-inflicting entities, the perception of desire to inflict costs likely evolved to be greater for some entities than others. It makes evolutionary sense that those entities that recurrently exhibited a closer causal relationship between their behavior and the infliction of costs would be perceived as more desirous of inflicting those costs and hence more evil. Snakes, for example, should be considered to be more evil than flowers (Mineka, 1992). And other humans (Buss & Duntley, 2015; Duntley & Buss, 2011) are considered the most evil entities of all. Among animals, humans are second only to mosquitoes in the number of people they kill each year (Gates, 2014). Of the 5.8 million deaths from injuries that occur globally each year, about 1 in 7 result from homicide or warfare (World Health Organization, 2008). Among 15- to 29-year-olds, who experience among the highest levels of competition for reproductively relevant resources (Buss, 2003), homicide is the fourth leading cause of death, after traffic injuries, HIV/AIDS, and tuberculosis (World Health Organization, 2008). Warfare is the ninth leading cause of death for this group. Across all ages, almost twice as many men as women die from injuries and violence. Of all causes of death, homicide is the only one with a directly and recurrently identifiable causal agent—another human. Over evolutionary time, this trend would have contributed to the evolution of a perception of other humans as potentially evil. But the recurrent association of other humans with cost-inflicting behaviors, such as homicide, was not the only factor that must have contributed to the evolution of our perceptions of evil. Uncertainty about the intentions of others also would have played an important role.

Uncertainty

There is a degree of uncertainty associated with all of our interactions with other humans. *What* does the other person hope to gain from this interaction? *How much* do they have to gain or lose as a result of this interaction? Over the history of our species, our ancestors would have had better knowledge of important factors associated with the likely costs and benefits of an interaction among the people with whom they interacted more frequently.

And they would have chosen specifically to engage in interactions that were likely to yield the highest benefits at the lowest costs. Prior experience with an individual would have been among the most accurate ways of determining whether the intentions of another individual were good or evil. In the absence of prior experience, how would our ancestors have determined the intentions of others?

Error management theory (Haselton & Buss, 2000) proposes that humans evolved strategic cognitive biases that lead them to avoid high costs and not overlook significant benefits when making decisions under conditions of uncertainty. Men but not women, for example, have been shown to overperceive the sexual interest of members of the opposite sex who are friendly to them (Haselton, 2002), thus decreasing the likelihood of overlooking a situation in which a significant boost to fitness may be achieved.

A lifelong apprehensiveness or anxiety about the intentions of strangers, particularly men who are unknown, may be a cognitive bias that evolved to protect us from individuals who may want to inflict costs on us for their own gain. The ancestral costs of assuming that an unknown male had beneficent intentions when he intended to inflict harm would have been great, providing selection pressure for the evolution of cognitive biases to assume that unknown individuals, particularly men who are more likely to inflict costs, had hostile intentions. In tribal societies, it is most often the case that an approaching unknown adult male intends to inflict costs (Chagnon, 1974; Kelly, 2000; Roscoe, 2002, 2007; Wrangham & Glowacki, 2012).

Some researchers have argued that our psychology of stereotyping may be adaptive by being an energy-saving device (Macrae, Milne, & Bodenhausen, 1994; Moya & Boyd, 2015). We propose that stereotyping may be adaptive in making judgments under conditions of uncertainty. In the absence of other sources of information, a stereotype of another individual, however inaccurate it may actually be, would be better than no information at all in making decisions about how to interact with the person. That is, even if the validity of a cue that led to the stereotype is small in predicting the actual infliction of costs, selection will favor the evolution of stereotyping, despite the possibility that such a cognitive process would lead to a large number of errors of inference. The fact that most stereotypes are negative suggests that they are patterned in our psychology by evolved mechanisms designed to avoid some of the potentially heavy costs of interacting with unknown individuals.

PRINCIPLED PERSPECTIVE SHIFTS IN EVIL BASED ON FITNESS CONFLICTS

It should be clear from the preceding discussion that categorizations of good and evil can hinge heavily on the perspective of the victim versus the perpetrator—a point that has been made by others (e.g., Baumeister, 1997). An evolutionary account, however, renders this intuitively obvious point a great deal more precise. In order to understand why, it is necessary to highlight the different levels of evolutionary analysis and the precise ways in which perspectives on evil may predictably shift.

Consider a woman who is pregnant. She is young and has many potential reproductive years ahead of her. However, she is unmarried, lacks extended kin in close proximity, and lives in a nutritionally impoverished environment. In these and other circumstances, women often "spontaneously" abort the growing fetus. From the fetus's perspective, however, this is its one and only shot at life, which sets the stage for mother–fetus conflict (Haig, 1993). What is in the best fitness interests of the fetus (being born) differs fundamentally from what is in the best fitness interests of the incipient mother (aborting the fetus). A large body of evidence points to the coevolution of adaptations in both mother and fetus to deal with this conflict. The perpetual arms race produces adaptations that may damage the mother (e.g., by producing hypertension). The key point is that what we often view as a harmonious relationship of self-evident unity of interests—mother and growing child—is actually fraught with evolutionary conflict. In this example, of course, neither the growing fetus nor the mother typically categorize the other as evil. But it makes evident that conflicts can permeate all relationships, from the moment of conception on.

Although selection is generally regarded as operating in the strongest manner at the genic level, it can play out at many levels of analysis. What's good for a particular gene in the currency of fitness may be bad for the other genes in an individual's genome—the phenomenon of intragenomic conflict (e.g., Cosmides & Tooby, 1981). What's good for the genes of an individual can be bad for the genes of other individuals—conspecific conflict. What's good for one intrasexual competitor (e.g., ascending in status) might be bad for another (e.g., being supplanted in the status hierarchy). What's good for one woman, such as mating with a highly desirable man, inevitably entails inflicting costs on intrasexual competitors who lose out and fail to obtain him as a mate. What's good for a man (e.g., obtaining sexual access to a woman through deception) might be bad for a woman (e.g., suffering reputation or other damage as a consequence of being deceived). What's good for one kinship group might be bad for another. What's good for one coalition of individuals might be bad for another. And what's good for one species (e.g., surviving through predation) might be bad for another species (e.g., those preyed upon).

In sum, evolutionary psychology provides theoretical precision to the intuitively grasped perspective differences of victims and perpetrators of horrendous deeds by yielding a precise analysis of the specific forms that conflict takes.

THE EXPLOITATION OF EVIL

Once psychological mechanisms have evolved to place other individuals into the cognitive category of "evil," these mechanisms can be exploited by others for their own purposes. People often do this in order to forge alliances designed to inflict costs on competing individuals or groups. Just as President George W. Bush used the label *Axis of Evil* in an effort to forge alliances with other groups, Osama bin Laden labeled America as *evil* in order to forge Arab alliances with other groups and to motivate and justify the infliction of massive fitness costs on Americans.

Stated differently, once the cognitive category of *evil* exists, it can be exploited by individuals or groups to justify the perpetration of massive fitness costs on their enemies. Exploitation through labeling others as *evil* operates in several ways: (1) to motivate others to join in, amplifying the fitness damage inflicted on enemies; (2) by lowering the overall costs of inflicting such damage because the larger coalition renders success more likely and defeat less likely; and (3) to justify to nonparticipants the validity of inflicting costs, thus decreasing the odds that nonparticipants will ally with the victims.

Most scholars of suicide terrorists, such as those of 9/11 who flew airplanes into the World Trade Center towers, contend that these individuals (mostly men) are most likely manipulated or exploited by others to perform these suicidal actions (e.g., Orbell & Tomonori, 2011; Thomson, 2007). Specifically, they are recruited mostly from pools of men with poor mating prospects. They are manipulated by kinship psychology (e.g., using labels such as *brothers* for peers who are not real kin). They are promised money and reputational enhancement for their real genetic relatives as a consequence of their "heroic" suicide to kill perceived enemies. They are led to believe that they will gain mating access to many virgin women after death. And they experience intense peer pressure from their "brothers" to commit the suicidal deeds.

These manipulations of male evolved psychology are apparently needed to overcome the natural human tendency to preserve one's own life and not to kill oneself for the sake of the group (Gallup & Weedon, 2013; Liddle, Bush, & Shackelford, 2011; Pinker, 2015; Qirko, 2013; Thomson & Aukofer, 2011). Suicide terrorism, in short, appears to be a byproduct of adaptations that are exploited and manipulated by religious leaders, peers, and sometimes kin.

The universal category of evil can be exploited in another way. Some individuals actively cultivate a reputation as "evil" to exploit, and to avoid being exploited by, others. In the Iraqi regime of Saddam Hussein, dissenters were often killed, decreasing the likelihood of challenges to Hussein's power. All may be regarded as attempting to exploit the evolved psychological mechanisms of others in order to achieve particular ends.

Dawkins (2001) notes that religion can be used as a vehicle to promote evil: "My point is not that religion itself is the motivation for wars, murders, and terrorist attacks, but that religion is the principal label, and the most dangerous one, by which 'they' as opposed to 'we' can be identified at all" (p. 1). Whether one subscribes to a particular belief system or not, religion is a pervasive feature of human experience. Some have argued that it appears as though our minds were prepared for religion by evolution (Boyer, 2001). This may be the case, but is more likely to have occurred in a different sequence—the ideas that make up the most popular religions exist in the form that they do because they appeal to different psychological adaptations, adaptations that evolved to solve particular ancestral problems. One problem religion helps to solve is the identification of social allies and social enemies (Dawkins, 2001). Another is establishing and maintaining group solidarity. When there is competition between groups for some tangible resource that is combined with powerfully reinforced religious beliefs that there is no end to life, psychological adaptations that embrace religious belief systems may contribute to misguided, cost-inflicting acts toward other groups who are identified by religious doctrine as evil, without fear of death or punishment in an afterlife. Such a situation from a third party's perspective, ironically, produces what appears to be evil actions against an evil group.

THE EVOLUTION OF GOOD

Although this chapter focuses primarily on the evolution of evil, a few words can be said about the evolution of good. At one level of analysis, many of the arguments made for the evolution of evil can simply be reversed for the evolution of good. That is, people evaluate "good" when fitness benefits are delivered or received. The magnitude of the fitness benefits is predicted to be highly correlated with judgments of good—an altruistic gift of a house or car would be judged to be more "good" than an altruistic gift of a candy bar. As in the evolution of evil, perspective matters greatly in evaluating good. "Good" are people who deliver fitness-relevant benefits to oneself, one's children, other genetic relatives, friends, and coalitional allies. "Evil" are people who deliver fitness benefits to one's enemies.

Just as humans have evolved adaptations to inflict costs on other humans, we have also evolved adaptations to bestow benefits. Evolutionary psychologists have explored three classes of benefit-bestowing mechanisms: (1) altruism delivered to genetic relatives (e.g., Burnstein, Crandall, & Kitayama, 1994); (2) reciprocal altruism formed among friends or allies (e.g., Bleske & Buss, 2001); and (3) benefit-delivering mechanisms that do not involve kin altruism or reciprocal altruism and in which the giver does not incur a cost to deliver a benefit (e.g., Tooby & Cosmides, 1996).

Parents sometimes sacrifice their own lives so that their children may live, an example of kin altruism. Friends bestow resources on each other, an example of reciprocal altruism. And if I give you a ride to school when I'm already heading there anyway, I deliver a benefit to you without incurring a cost to myself. Evolution by selection has undoubtedly fashioned many benefit-bestowing adaptations in humans.

But at another level, the things we tend to single out as especially deserving of the label *good* involve bestowing benefits at a great cost to oneself, *without any apparent return benefit to oneself*. Thus the soldier who throws himself on a grenade to save his buddies; Mother Teresa, who devoted her life to helping others; the bystander who risks his life to save a stranger from drowning—these are all categorized as good and noble deeds. Indeed, it is precisely when there appear to be *no* return benefits to self, kin, or friends that we are especially prone to label a deed as admirable. The parent who donates $100,000 to his or her child's college education is not deemed as good as the same donation to a stranger's child who cannot afford the tuition. When there is obvious benefit to self, kin, or allies from a beneficent deed, we tend to "discount" the amount of good we attribute to the person giving it because it is natural to invest more heavily in close kin (Hamilton, 1964) and allies (Cosmides & Tooby, 2015; Tooby & Cosmides, 1996; Trivers, 1974) than to invest in distant relations or strangers whose success or cooperation would not benefit an individual's inclusive fitness. In this way, an evolutionary analysis of "good" is not strictly the mirror image of the evolutionary analysis of evil. Whether committed against strangers or close kin, evil deeds tend to be viewed as equally evil.

People undoubtedly exploit and manipulate perceptions of "good," just as they exploit and manipulate perceptions of "evil." Thus we expect that people will sometimes put "spin" on their delivery of benefits to others, presenting them as more altruistic and less self-serving than they may be. Conversely, others may attempt to publicly discount apparent acts of good by pointing to some hidden benefit the giver is receiving. And, indeed, many acts of apparent self-sacrifice turn out to have hidden benefits to the bestower, complicating the analysis even further. Soldiers wounded in war fighting for "freedom" or "their country" often receive large boosts in prestige and social reputation through medals of valor. Women find these highly "altruistic" men to be especially attractive, and so the wounded soldier benefits in mating currency. Even the acts of suicide bombers are regarded by their group as highly "good," which leads bombers' families to benefit from their "martyr" status in the form of resources and favorable treatment from the group.

In sum, an evolutionary analysis of "good" can be expected to shed much light on how people deliver benefits to others and manipulate the perceptions of others around the delivery of those benefits. Although these brief comments cannot do this complex topic justice, they suggest a few lines along which inquiry might proceed.

A COMPARISON OF EVOLUTIONARY WITH OTHER THEORETICAL PERSPECTIVES OF EVIL

The use of violence against another person or group, particularly if it is perceived as unjustified, is undoubtedly the category of actions most likely to be viewed as evil (Anderson & Carnagey, 2004; Baumeister & Vohs, 2004). Violence is typically viewed as "not an effective way to get what one wants" (Baumeister & Vohs, 2004). In response to the question "Why is there evil?" Baumeister argues that evil stems fundamentally from a failure of self-control, an inability to stifle aggressive impulses. Our theory of the evolution of evil suggests that these formulations of evil are fundamentally wrong.

First, let's consider the contention that violence is not an effective way to get what one wants (Baumeister & Vohs, 2004). Citing the possibility that violent or aggressive strategies can result in prison sentences or other costs is beside the point from an evolutionary perspective. The key issue is whether selection has favored the contingent use of violence in some circumstances—whether the benefits of violence outweighed the costs, *on average*, relative to other strategic solutions over the sample space of relevant instances. Most social scientists, innocent of the logic of the evolutionary process, have intuitions that are wide off the mark when it comes to evaluating whether a particular strategy is "beneficial" or not. Selection, for example, can favor a strategy such as homicide, even if that strategy sometimes results in the strategist getting killed or imprisoned. The logic of this seemingly counterintuitive argument becomes clear when one realizes that selection operates *not* on whether a particular strategy is effective *in every instance* but rather on whether the benefits of the strategy outweigh the costs on average across the entire sample space of instances in which it is deployed (relative to competing designs present in the population at the time). Thus selection can produce adaptations that result in many instances of failure—bullies who sometimes get beaten up, thieves who sometimes get caught, cheaters who sometimes get ostracized, and killers who sometimes get killed. If the net fitness benefits outweighed the net fitness costs of these adaptations for evil, relative to competing designs, then selection will favor their evolution, eventually making them fundamental components of human nature.

Second, let's consider the argument that evil stems from an inability to control one's impulses (Baumeister & Vohs, 2004; Monroe, Vohs, & Baumeister, Chapter 3, this volume). Our theory of the evolution of evil suggests an alternative explanation—that humans have evolved adaptations that are "designed" to solve some adaptive problems in certain circumstances with behavior that appears "impulsive." Effective strategies sometimes require immediate action, where ponderous time delays and real-time extended reflection result in failure. Stated differently, we propose that "impulsivity" is actually a design feature of certain adaptations that promotes their tactical effectiveness. The fact that they appear to external observers (or social scientists) to be products of the lack of judicious reflection may speak to the profound inability of human intuitions to grasp the logic of evolved design, or to our moral judgments that classify certain strategies as good or bad. Speedy, immediate, real-time responses can be the product of adaptive design rather than "mechanism failure."

PRACTICAL IMPLICATIONS: FLEXIBILITY, TRACTABILITY, RESPONSIBILITY, AND MORALITY

Evolutionary psychology is a scientific discipline devoted to the understanding of the human mind and behavior, guided by a variety of evolutionarily-based theories, hypotheses, and predictions. As a scientific discipline, it is concerned with description, explanation, and understanding, *not* with prescription, recommendation, or policymaking. Nonetheless, because evolutionary psychology is so often mischaracterized and misunderstood, it is worthwhile dispelling what we anticipate might be some common misconceptions based on our analysis.

At a broad level of analysis, evolutionary psychology envisions the human mind as consisting of a large collection of complex and interrelated mechanisms whose activation (or nonactivation) is highly contingent on specific forms of environmental and endogenous input. Just as callus-producing adaptations are activated only upon the receipt of environmental friction to the skin, psychological adaptations are activated only upon the receipt of certain forms of input. Male sexual jealousy, for example, is not an invariant "biological instinct" that wells up regardless of circumstances. Instead, jealousy is activated only by highly circumscribed input, such as the perception of cues to a mate's infidelity, the threat of mate poachers, or the opening of a discrepancy in the relative "mate values" of romantic partners (Buss, 2000). Similarly, all of the actions judged to be "good" or "evil" are hypothesized to be a product of the output of the activation of evolved psychological mechanisms by specific forms of environmental, social, or endogenous input.

Human flexibility comes from our large number of psychological mechanisms, their complexity, their interrelatedness, and their dependence on activation from various forms of input. Humans are not lumbering robots insensitive to context. Rather, adaptations exist precisely to deal with varying forms of context or, in the language of evolutionary psychology, the different adaptive problems and contingencies an individual confronts over time. In short, an evolutionary analysis does not, and should not, lead to the erroneous view that human behavior is inevitable or intractable. Indeed, the greater the knowledge we have about our evolved psychological mechanisms and the contexts that trigger their activation, the greater will be our power to effect change in the domains in which change is deemed desirable.

This point becomes especially important because some people mistakenly view an evolutionary analysis as dooming us to inevitable courses of action and a pessimistic fate: "If evil has its foundation in evolved psychological mechanisms," this concern sometimes gets expressed, "then we can't hold people responsible for their actions; we are doomed to a pessimistic view of human nature; we can't judge their actions to be morally wrong."

This concern reflects several related misunderstandings. First, people can be held responsible for their actions, and holding people responsible is one of the critical forms of environmental input that can be used to deter people from committing deeds we consider to be "evil." Nothing in an evolutionary analysis implies that people cannot be held responsible for their actions. Second, standards of morality themselves have a foundation in evolved psychological mechanisms—for example, evolved moral emotions such as *disgust, moralistic anger,* and *contempt* (Haidt, 2001; see Buss, 2015, for a review). Expressed moral emotions become part of the social input that can deter the expression of certain actions people judge to be evil or wrong. Third, an evolutionary psychological analysis does not condone any deeds—a confusion of what "is" with that "ought to be," or the naturalistic fallacy, as it is commonly known. Many things exist "in nature" that we do not condone and in fact try to eradicate—certain diseases and infant mortality, for example. In the same way, we may wish to eradicate the activation of certain evolved psychological mechanisms, such as those involved in motivating homicide and genocide.

Finally, it's important to avoid what has been called the "antinaturalistic," "romantic," or "moralistic" fallacy—the belief that good or desirable behavior is found in the true nature of humans, which leads people to confuse what they want to be true with what is actually true about the nature of behavior. Many people cherish a view of human nature that is fundamentally kind and good, with acts of evil attributed to the ills of modern society, capitalism, or partriarchy. In the words of one anthropologist, "We have never quite outgrown the idea that somewhere, there are people living in perfect harmony with nature and one another, and that we might do the same were it not for the corrupting influences of Western culture" (Konner, 1991). We may want human nature to be fundamentally good and free of evil, but that utopian view should not lead us to commit the romantic fallacy and confuse what ought to be with what really is.

According to our evolutionary analysis, human nature includes adaptations to bestow benefits and adaptations to inflict costs on others, sometimes massive costs such as killing. We have the capacity for good and evil. Only through deeper knowledge of our evolved psychology can we acquire the tools to deter the expression of the more pernicious components of human nature.

CONCLUSIONS

Our theoretical framework for the evolution of evil contains several key premises that make it unique among theories of evil. First, humans have evolved adaptations designed to harm other individuals in ways small and large. In addition to whatever adaptations humans have evolved to deliver benefits to particular others (and these are many in number—see Buss, 2015, for a recent summary), humans have also evolved adaptations to lie, cheat, steal, maim, and murder. The harm-inflicting adaptations are fundamental and universal components of human nature and cannot be attributed to the particulars of media, parents, teachers, capitalism, or culture. Whether these harm-inflicting adaptations are expressed in manifest behavior is highly contingent on the particulars of the social and physical environment—contingencies that are themselves essential components of the design of the adaptations.

Second, those harm-inflicting phenomena that are especially costly in fitness currencies, when inflicted intentionally, are those that humans tend to label as *evil*. Certain types of killing are prototypical examples of evil—killings that are intentional and unprovoked and that inflict massive fitness costs on the victim.

Third, because humans have been victims of harm-producing adaptations in others, they have evolved defenses to prevent incurring these costs. Stranger anxiety, specific kinds of fears, stereotyping, xenophobia, cheater detection, ostracism, and other anti-homicide mechanisms are but a few examples of these evolved defenses. We propose that many coevolutionary arms races have been set into motion, as illustrated in Figure 2.1—adaptations to inflict harm evolve to become more sophisticated and context-contingent to counter adaptations designed to defend against harm. Many of these coevolutionary arms races are perpetual, with no stable equilibrium.

Fourth, humans have evolved special cognitive mechanisms designed to categorize some phenomena as "good" and other phenomena as "evil." These cognitive mechanisms function to identify specific humans who intend, or are likely, to inflict massive costs on the individual. Intentionality is central. An entity that accidentally delivers massive harm is not considered "evil," nor is one that unintentionally delivers benefits considered "good."

Fifth, evolutionary psychology provides a principled, theoretical framework for adding precision to the intuition that "evil" depends critically on perspective. Precise perspective shifts are predicted to occur according to who is delivering the costs and who is the unfortunate victim of the costs. We predict that degree of genetic relatedness between the perpetrator and victim, for example, will strongly affect judgments of good and evil—predictions not rendered by any other theory of good and evil.

All organisms that perceive can be deceived (Dawkins & Krebs, 1978). The psychological machinery of an organism potentially can be exploited for purposes that are contrary to the organism's fitness interests. Just as fishermen can use lures to exploit the sense organs of fish, psychopaths can exploit the cooperative mechanisms of their victims. Once a psychology of evil evolved, it became possible for other humans to exploit it in the service of their own ends. Invoking "evil" in other individuals or groups is often a psychological manipulation designed to enlist coalitional support for inflicting massive costs on the individual or group so labeled.

The theoretical framework for understanding "good" and "evil" proposed in this chapter contains many premises and predictions that are highly testable—predictions not generated by any other theory. Although we would stop short of labeling competing theories of good and evil as being "evil," none appears to afford the conceptual precision offered by this evolutionary framework. Understanding *why* people inflict massive costs on others requires understanding of the underlying psychological mechanisms involved in the perpetration of these acts. Evolutionary psychology generally, and the coevolutionary arms races proposed here specifically, provide the most cogent conceptual framework for understanding why these psychological mechanisms evolved, why humans have evolved defenses against them, and why the potential for good and evil resides within all of us today.

REFERENCES

Anderson, C. A., & Carnagey, N. L. (2004). Violent evil and the general aggression model. In A. G. Miller (Ed.), *The social psychology of good and evil* (pp. 168–192). New York: Guilford Press.

Baumeister, R. F. (1997). *Evil: Inside human violence and cruelty.* New York: Freeman.

Baumeister, R. F., & Vohs, K. D. (2004). Four roots of evil. In A. G. Miller (Ed.), *The social psychology of good and evil* (pp. 85–101). New York: Guilford Press.

Bleske, A. L., & Buss, D. M. (2001). Opposite sex friendship: Sex differences and similarities in initiation, selection, and dissolution. *Personality and Social Psychology Bulletin, 27,* 1310–1323.

Boyer, P. (2001). *Religion explained.* New York: Basic Books.

Burnstein, E., Crandall, C., & Kitayama, S. (1994). Some neo-Darwinian decision rules for altruism: Weighing cures for inclusive fitness as a function of the biological importance of the decision. *Journal of Personality and Social Psychology, 67,* 773–789.

Buss, D. M. (1988). The evolution of human intrasexual competition: Tactics of mate attraction. *Journal of Personality and Social Psychology, 54,* 616–628.

Buss, D. M. (1989). Conflict between the sexes: Strategic interference and the evocation of anger and upset. *Journal of Personality and Social Psychology, 56,* 735–747.

Buss, D. M. (1996). Social adaptation and five major factors of personality. In J. S. Wiggins (Ed.), *The five-factor model of personality: Theoretical perspectives* (pp. 180–207). New York: Guilford Press.

Buss, D. M. (2000). *The dangerous passion.* New York: Free Press.

Buss, D. M. (2003). *The evolution of desire: Strategies of human mating* (rev. ed.). New York: Free Press.

Buss, D. M. (2015). *Evolutionary psychology: The new science of the mind* (5th ed.). Boston: Allyn & Bacon.

Buss, D. M., & Dedden, L. A. (1990). Derogation of competitors. *Journal of Social and Personal Relationships, 7,* 395–422.

Buss, D. M., & Duntley, J. D. (1998, July 10). *Evolved homicide modules.* Paper presented at the annual meeting of the Human Behavior and Evolution Society, Davis, CA.

Buss, D. M., & Duntley, J. D. (2015). *Adaptations for murder: The evolution of homicide.* Manuscript in preparation.

Chagnon, N. (1988). Life histories, blood revenge, and warfare in a tribal population. *Science, 239,* 985–992.

Cosmides, L., & Tooby, J. (1981). Cytoplasmic inheritance and intragenomic conflict. *Journal of Theoretical Biology, 89,* 83–129.

Cosmides, L., & Tooby, J. (2015). Neurocognitive adaptations designed for social exchange. In D. M. Buss (Ed.), *The handbook of evolutionary psychology* (2nd ed.). Hoboken, NJ: Wiley.

Daly, M., & Wilson, M. (1988). *Homicide.* Hawthorne, NY: Aldine.

Daly, M., & Wilson, M. (1998). *The truth about Cinderella: A Darwinian view of parental love.* London: Weidenfeld & Nicolson.

Dawkins, R. (2001). Time to stand up. Written for the Freedom from Religion Foundation, Madison, WI. Retrieved February 10, 2015, from *https://ffrf.org/news/timely-topics/item/14035-time-to-stand-up.*

Dawkins, R., & Krebs, J. R. (1978). Animal signals: Information or manipulation. In J. R. Krebs & N. B. Davies (Eds.), *Behavioural ecology: An evolutionary approach* (pp. 282–309). Oxford, UK: Blackwell.

Duntley, J. D. (2015). Adaptations to dangers from humans. In D. Buss (Ed.), *Handbook of evolutionary psychology* (2nd ed., pp. 264–286). Hoboken, NJ: Wiley.

Duntley, J. D., & Buss, D. M. (1998, July). *Evolved anti-homicide modules.* Paper presented to the annual meeting of the Human Behavior and Evolution Society, Davis, CA.

Duntley, J. D., & Buss, D. M. (2011). Homicide adaptations. *Aggression and Violent Behavior, 16,* 399–410.

Gallup, G. G., Jr., & Weedon, S. L. (2013). Suicide bombers: Does an evolutionary perspective make a difference? *Evolutionary Psychology: An International Journal of Evolutionary Approaches to Psychology and Behavior, 11*(4), 791.

Gates, B. (2014). The deadliest animal in the world. Retrieved September 18, 2014, from *www.gatesnotes.com/Health/Most-Lethal-Animal-Mosquito-Week*.

Ghiglieri, M. P. (1999). *The dark side of man*. Reading, MA: Perseus Books.

Haidt, J. (2001). The emotional dog and its rational tail: A social intuitionist approach to moral judgment. *Psychological Review, 108*, 814–834.

Haig, D. (1993). Genetic conflicts in human pregnancy. *Quarterly Review of Biology, 68*, 495–532.

Hamilton, W. D. (1964). The genetical evolution of social behavior: I and II. *Journal of Theoretical Biology, 7*, 1–52.

Haselton, M. G. (2002). The sexual overperception bias: Evidence of a systematic bias in men from a survey of naturally occurring events. *Journal of Research in Personality, 37*, 34–47.

Haselton, M. G., & Buss, D. M. (2000). Error management theory: A new perspective on biases in cross-sex mind reading. *Journal of Personality and Social Psychology, 78*, 81–91.

Heerwagen, J. H., & Orians, G. H. (2002). The ecological world of children. In P. H. Kahn, Jr. & S. R. Kellert (Eds.), *Children and nature: Psychological, sociocultural, and evolutionary investigations* (pp. 29–64). Cambridge, MA: MIT Press.

Hill, K. R., & Hurtado, M. (1996). *Aché life history*. Piscataway, NJ: Transaction.

Kelly, R. C. (2000). *Warless societies and the origin of war*. Ann Arbor: University of Michigan Press.

Konner, M. (1991). *Why the reckless survive*. New York: Viking.

Liddle, J. R., Bush, L. S., & Shackelford, T. K. (2011). An introduction to evolutionary psychology and its application to suicide terrorism. *Behavioral Sciences of Terrorism and Political Aggression, 3*(3), 176–197.

Macrae, C. N., Milne, A. B., & Bodenhausen, G. V. (1994). Stereotypes as energy-saving devices: A peek inside the cognitive toolbox. *Journal of Personality and Social Psychology, 66*(1), 37–47.

Marks, I. M. (1987). *Fears, phobias, and rituals: Panic, anxiety, and their disorders*. New York: Oxford University Press.

Marks, I. M., & Nesse, R. M. (1994). Fear and fitness: An evolutionary analysis of anxiety disorders. *Ethology and Sociobiology, 15*, 247–261.

Mineka, S. (1992). Evolutionary memories, emotional processing, and the emotional disorders. *Psychology of Learning and Motivation, 28*, 161–206.

Moya, C., & Boyd, R. (2015). Different selection pressures give rise to distinct ethnic phenomena. *Human Nature, 26*(1), 1–27. Available at *http://link.springer.com/article/10.1007/s12110-015-9224-9#*.

Orbell, J., & Tomonori, M. (2011). An evolutionary account of suicide attacks: The Kamikaze case. *Political Psychology, 32*, 297–392.

Pinker, S. (2015). The false allure of group selection. In D. M. Buss (Ed.), *The handbook of evolutionary psychology* (2nd ed.). Hoboken, NJ: Wiley.

Qirko, H. N. (2013). Induced altruism in religious, military, and terrorist organizations. *Cross-Cultural Research, 47*(2), 131–161.

Roscoe, P. (2002). The hunters and gatherers of New Guinea. *Current Anthropology, 43*, 153–162.

Roscoe, P. (2007). Intelligence, coalitional killing, and the antecedents of war. *American Anthropologist, 109*, 485–495.

Schmitt, D. P., & Buss, D. M. (1996). Strategic self-promotion and competitor derogation: Sex and context effects on perceived effectiveness of mate attraction tactics. *Journal of Personality and Social Psychology, 70*, 1185–1204.

Thomson, J. A. (2007). We few, we happy few, we band of brothers (and occasional sister): The dynamics of suicide terrorism. Retrieved February 10, 2015, from *www.jandersonthomson.com/wp-content/uploads/2010/05/Suicide_Terrorism.doc*.

Thomson, J. A., & Aukofer, C. (2011). *Why we believe in God(s)*. Charlottesville, VA: Pitchstone.

Tooby, J., & Cosmides, L. (1996). Friendship and the banker's paradox: Other pathways to the evolution of adaptations for altruism. *Proceedings of the British Academy, 88*, 119–143.

Trivers, R. L. (1974). The evolution of reciprocal altruism. *Quarterly Review of Biology, 46*, 35–57.

Weiner, E. S., & Simpson, J. A. (Eds.). (1989). *Oxford English dictionary*. New York: Oxford University Press.

World Health Organization. (2008). *World Health Statistics 2008*. Geneva, Switzerland: Author.

Wrangham, R. W., & Glowacki, L. (2012). Intergroup aggression in chimpanzees and war in nomadic hunter-gatherers. *Human Nature, 23*, 5–29.

CHAPTER 3

Free Will Evolved for Morality and Culture

Andrew E. Monroe, Kathleen D. Vohs, and Roy F. Baumeister

Belief in free will is widespread. It emerges early in life and persists through old age (Kushnir, 2012). It exists across cultures (Sarkissian et al., 2010). It remains strong even when people have their own freedom restricted (Laurene, Rakos, Tisak, Robichaud, & Horvath, 2011). People's subjective everyday experience overwhelmingly confers the impression that they have free will. People perceive that there are multiple possible futures, and people feel that they are free to choose among options (easily imagining choosing other than one did) or to refrain from choosing at all (Baumeister & Monroe, 2014; Monroe & Malle, 2014).

The notion of free will is commonly invoked in multiple contexts that are relevant to culture, including morality, theology, and the law. Yet, for such an important concept, wide-ranging confusion and disagreement remain about its nature. Does free will exist? Do people have it? If so, what are the necessary conditions to demonstrate that one has free will?

We argue that the emergence and functioning of free will must be placed in the context of a broad understanding of human nature. Our view is that free will can be understood as an advanced form of action control that evolved to enable people to function and thrive in cultural groups. Baumeister (2005) argues that human beings were produced by natural selection for culture. Culture can be defined as organized groups of people that share information, develop a system of interdependent roles, cooperate to complete shared goals, and create and maintain codes of behavioral norms and morality.

If free will was a human adaptation for culture, then it would have to produce benefits to survival and reproduction (Baumeister, 2005; Dennett, 1984). In this chapter we argue that people's belief in free will increases cultural fitness by promoting virtuous behavior, including honesty, helping, restraining aggression, initiative, expressing gratitude, and upholding community standards by advocating punishment for rule breakers.

Additionally, we suggest that there must be a psychological reality behind people's belief in free will, namely people's capacity for self-regulation and rational choice. We argue that free will as the capacity to exert control over one's actions provides benefits to culture. Self-regulation promotes cooperation, the ability to inhibit one's impulses, and persistence in pursuing long-term goals, all of which are important for promoting individual and group welfare.

WHAT IS FREE WILL?

If one were to ask a man on the street whether he has free will, the man would almost undoubtedly respond "yes." But what exactly is that person asserting when he claims to have free will? Understanding the role of people's belief in free will in promoting moral behavior and culture requires knowing how ordinary people conceptualize free will.

Until recently there was a dearth of empirical work on what constitutes people's ordinary concept of free will. In the place of empirical investigation, some scholars have characterized people's concept of free will in metaphysical or scientifically untenable terms (see Bargh, 2008; Bargh & Earp, 2009; Cashmore, 2010; Montague, 2008). One extreme view of people's belief in free will characterizes it as being committed to substance dualism, which entails (among other things) the concept of a soul as an "uncaused cause" for free will. Bargh and Earp (2009) claimed that people's concept of free will is tantamount to substance dualism, "laden with the concept of a soul, a non-physical, unfettered, internal source of choice-making" (p. 13).

Not all views on free will invoke such scientifically intractable assumptions. A recent multidisciplinary consortium defined free will as the capacity for free action (Haggard, Mele, O'Connor, & Vohs, 2010), which was in turn defined as intentional action based on rational deliberation by an agent not coerced to make a particular choice. Supporting this view, Monroe and Malle (2010, 2014) tested people's concept of free will by inviting them to report "what you think it means to have free will." The findings diverged strikingly from the common claims that characterize the folk concept of free will as deeply metaphysical.

Rather than invoking substance dualism (e.g., Cashmore, 2010; Montague, 2008) or exemption from causality (e.g., Bargh, 2008; Bargh & Earp, 2009), participants offered a psychological definition of free will. Free will entailed the capacity for choice, as well as acting consistently with one's desires and being (reasonably) free of constraints (e.g., coercion, peer pressure, social status; Monroe & Malle, 2010).

In a separate study, Monroe and Malle (2014) took a novel approach to understanding people's criteria for free will when they asked community participants to imagine engineering an agent (e.g., a new biological life form or a robot) and to specify the types of abilities and capacities it would need in order to possess free will. The capacity for choice was again the dominant category (81% of participants cited it as necessary for free will). Second was the capacity for autonomy (35% cited autonomy as needed for free will), which people defined as being able to resist constraints ("It would have to be able to choose to not be persuaded by an external factor"). These findings point to a concept of free will as *responsible autonomy* (Baumeister & Monroe, 2014). In order to have free will, agents must be rational choosers—hence responsible—and act independently of other causes (e.g., coercion).

Stillman, Baumeister, and Mele (2011) took a complementary approach to testing how people understand free will. Instead of asking people to define the concept, Stillman and colleagues asked people to provide examples of everyday outcomes that either epitomized free will or unfree behaviors. Students were either asked to describe an action "that you consider to have been of your own free will" (p. 387) or to describe an action that was a result of free will. Consistent with the view that belief in free will is associated with cultural functioning, people described free-will actions as producing positive outcomes (for the self or one's social group), attaining goals, and delaying self-interest. By contrast, unfree actions were behaviors detrimental to one's social group and oneself. Stillman et al.'s (2011) findings further showed that people regard free action not as the result of external factors or coercion but indeed as resisting such external influences and pressures.

These data provide a clear picture of free will as responsible autonomy. Actors with free will must be able to respond to demands of the environment while also attaining a degree of independence from it, including presumably the ability to resist environmental influences. In addition to being autonomous, free will implies that people are responsible for their actions. Responsibility entails understanding the social implications of one's actions: knowing relevant rules, moral principles, laws, or social norms and adjusting one's behavior accordingly—or accepting the consequences for failing to do so.

These studies fit well with the view of free will as having evolved to enable people to function in culture. Free will contributes to cultural living insofar as it helps people pursue their goals (Dennett, 1984), and it fosters delaying gratification and sacrificing immediate gain for the sake of greater long-term gain.

Folk concepts categorize phenomena and organize relationships among categories (Malle, 2006). People's folk concept of free will, in particular, informs how people perceive and interact with the social world. That multiple studies using diverse methods and samples converge on a unified concept of free will opens the door to examining how beliefs about free will may operate to influence behavior. As detailed next, belief in free will appears to play an important role in structuring how people perceive and respond to aspects of the social and moral world (see Baumeister, Masicampo, & DeWall, 2009; Vohs & Schooler, 2008).

CONSEQUENCES OF THE BELIEF IN FREE WILL

Most people believe in free will to some degree, a belief that invokes responsible autonomy. People's beliefs, however, are malleable, so it is possible to study the consequences of differences in the strength of free-will belief. If the belief in free will arises from the requirements of cultural social systems—specifically, the need to regulate one's own behavior, as well as the behavior of others (e.g., punishing misdeeds)—then threatening that belief should fundamentally alter people's behavioral tendencies in both domains.

In line with this view, Vohs and Schooler (2008) reasoned that if people were induced to disbelieve in free will, they would not feel responsible for their actions and therefore would be likelier than others to perform selfish, immoral actions. Vohs and Schooler (2008) reported the first studies to manipulate beliefs about free will. They then measured whether students would cheat and take money that was being offered as a reward for good performance. Sure enough, inducing disbelief in free will led to more cheating and taking more money. Thus believing that free will is an illusion causes people to behave in ways that are personally beneficial and harmful to the broader culture.

Later studies of free-will beliefs built on Vohs and Schooler's (2008) methods for manipulating and measuring free-will beliefs. One common method for manipulating free-will beliefs involves randomly assigning participants to read a passage that either denies that free will exists (e.g., "although we appear to have free will, in fact, our choices have already been predetermined for us and we cannot change that") or a passage that describes neutral, irrelevant material (e.g., on consciousness) (Nahmias, Shepard, & Reuter, 2014). Another common method randomly assigns participants to read a series of statements that either deny the reality of free will (e.g., "Science has demonstrated that free will is an illusion") or express scientific facts irrelevant to free will (e.g., "Oceans cover 71% of the Earth's surface").

Some experiments added a third condition: Researchers presented short passages or statements that highlighted the existence and importance of free will. However, experimental manipulations designed to increase belief in free will have not generally caused much change in behavior. Typically, reducing people's belief in free will results in behavioral changes, whereas bolstering belief in free will leaves behavior similar to baseline. A likely explanation for the differential success of the manipulations is that most people already believe in free will to some degree (see Sarkissian et al., 2010). Thus manipulations that attempt to affirm free will—a belief already firmly entrenched by people's subjective experience of choosing and willing—do little to change behavior, unlike disputing the existence of free will, which departs from their normal view.

The similarity between bolstering free-will beliefs and neutral conditions suggests that people, in general, believe in free will and that they are good, responsible, and morally responsible, autonomous, self-controlled people. It is only after threatening people's belief in free will that responsible autonomy breaks down and people begin to engage in many behaviors that are detrimental to social systems: cheating, stealing, aggressing, neglecting to help, and so forth.

DISBELIEF IN FREE WILL HARMS RESPONSIBLE AUTONOMY

Subsequent studies using these methods extended the impact of free-will beliefs to phenomena relevant to our definition of responsible autonomy. In one such project, Baumeister and colleagues (2009) examined the effects of disbelieving in free will on helping and harming. Using a modified Velten procdure to manipulate free-will belief, they showed that participants who were induced to disbelieve in free will were less willing to provide help to a fellow student compared with controls. Similarly, people with dispositionally low belief in free will were less helpful than people with chronically high belief in free will. Low belief in free will led to volunteering less time to help another student who had suffered personal and family misfortunes (Baumeister et al., 2009).

Not only did threatening people's belief in free will reduce helping, but it also increased people's willingness to harm. In an additional experiment, the researchers manipulated participants' free-will beliefs and subsequently asked them to prepare food samples for a partner (who would have to eat everything participants prepared for him). Participants learned that the partner hated hot sauce. Nevertheless, participants who were induced to disbelieve in free will forced their partners to consume more of the hated hot sauce compared with control participants (Baumeister et al., 2009). Thus, similar to the findings of Vohs and Schooler (2008), disbelieving in free will reduces people's feeling of responsibility for their actions, causing them to refrain from performing morally laudable deeds and increasing immoral actions.

Threatening people's belief in free will influences their sense of responsibility; it also reduces autonomy. One study by Alquist, Ainsworth, and Baumeister (2013) showed that disbelief in free will heightened mindless conformity. People who disbelieve in free will were more prone than believers to copy the opinions of others and to produce suggestions that parroted examples they were given rather than thinking for themselves in a creative, open-minded way (Alquist et al., 2013). Similarly, people who have had their belief in free will experimentally reduced showed less inclination to learn from past mistakes, from guilt, and from other negative emotions (Stillman & Baumeister, 2010).

Conversely, believing in free will is positively associated with counterfactual thinking. A series of experiments linked higher belief in free will to generating more counterfactual thoughts about past personal misdeeds, such as having hurt someone, as well as about hypothetical (imagined) misdeeds (Alquist, Ainsworth, Baumeister, Daly, & Stillman, 2015). Counterfactual thinking is an important mechanism for responsible autonomy, as it promotes learning from and improving one's behavior (e.g., Epstude & Roese, 2008). Insofar as belief in free will increases tendencies to engage in such thoughts about one's misdeeds, it can help people become better individuals and better members of society.

BELIEF IN FREE WILL SUPPORTS CULTURAL FUNCTIONING

Whereas disbelieving in free will is associated with various behavioral tendencies that are harmful to cultural function, recent work has demonstrated positive associations between people's belief in free will and beneficial behavior. For example, belief in free will is linked to manifestations of personal agency. People who believed in free will scored higher on self-efficacy and mindfulness (Crescioni, Baumeister, Ainsworth, Ent, & Lambert, 2015). This finding fits a growing body of work suggesting that high belief in free will goes with an agentic approach to life, as in taking action and initiative to pursue goals and get things done (e.g., Alquist et al., 2013; Baumeister et al., 2009; Stillman et al., 2010). Along those lines, stronger belief in free will is associated with initiative and high work performance. Stillman and colleagues (2010) found that workers who expressed higher belief in free will were rated more favorably by their supervisors on overall work performance. They were also rated as working harder on the assigned tasks and duties, having a positive impact on fellow employees, and consistency in work attendance (Stillman et al., 2010). Thus believing in free will contributes to culture by strengthening people's sense of agency, which in turn causes people to work harder and persist in goal pursuit.

Other research has demonstrated that people who believe in free will are more likely than disbelievers to engage in socially beneficial behaviors, at least when effort is required. This pattern persists even when the agents themselves do not directly benefit from such behavior. Stillman and Baumeister (2010) found that increasing belief in free will (relative to decreasing it) caused students to volunteer their time to work in a campus recycling program, especially after they had been made to feel guilty for the ostensibly large amount of pollution and ensuing wildlife deaths caused by fellow students. Vohs and Baumeister (2015) found similar effects: Students who had had their free-will beliefs bolstered were more likely to recycle than those whose belief in free will had been weakened. In their study, students were given a can of soda to drink during the free-will-belief manipulation. The key dependent variable was what the students did with the empty can once they were finished with it. They had the option of leaving it in the lab, throwing it in the trash, or taking it to a recycling bin that was on another floor (which required extra effort). Students in the pro-free-will condition were more likely than students in the anti-free-will condition to walk to the other floor and recycle. Because recycling took more effort than the alternatives, this finding fits both patterns we have linked to believing in free will: greater prosocial action and greater agency.

Last, higher belief in free will is not only associated with personal agency, but it is also associated with perceptions of agency in others, which is key for punishing others' misdeeds (Shariff et al., 2014) and for feelings of gratitude. MacKenzie, Vohs, and Baumeister (2014) showed that high belief in free will, as compared with low belief, caused people to feel more gratitude toward a favor done for them in the context of the experiment. Central to people's feelings of gratitude was a perception that one's benefactor could have done otherwise, thereby making the favor more valuable. Conversely, disbelief in free will reduced both gratitude and the perception that one's benefactor was motivated by a sincere intention to provide help (MacKenzie et al., 2014).

These findings about the effects of beliefs in free will are highly consistent with the view that free will evolved to facilitate functioning within culture. Culture can confer immense advantages for survival and reproduction. In order for those to happen, members of the community must obey the rules of the systems, and the community must be able to enforce the rules when they are broken. The former requirement demands that people voluntarily alter their behavior to conform to the requirements of the system. The latter requirement—that of enforcing the rules—legitimatizes meting out punishment when people break society's rules (see Clark et al., 2014). Miscreants with free will can be punished for wrongdoing because (1) it is necessary for the greater good, and (2) they could have chosen to refrain from violating a social or legal rule. The aforementioned studies highlight the importance of free will for cultural living. Without a belief in free will, rule breaking abounds and rule enforcement languishes.

THE REALITY OF FREE WILL: SELF-REGULATION

People believe that free will entails choosing between options, inhibiting desires, and pursuing goals (Baumeister & Monroe, 2014; Monroe & Malle, 2010, 2014; Stillman et al., 2011). If these are the components that make up people's concept of free will, then self-regulation is the psychological reality at the heart of that concept. The folk term *willpower* is an intuitive expression of the idea that people can regulate their thoughts, emotions, or actions by exerting energy (or will; Baumeister, Bratslavsky, Muraven, & Tice, 1998; Baumeister, Heatherton, & Tice, 1994; Muraven, Tice, & Baumeister, 1998).

Similar to believing in free will, *exerting* one's will (i.e., engaging in self-regulation) serves to inhibit behavior that is harmful to culture—for example, by stopping oneself from acting aggressively, from eating or drinking too much, from smoking, or from using drugs (Baumeister & Heatherton, 1996; Baumeister et al., 1994). Abundant evidence has indicated that both short-term and long-term benefits (but especially the latter) accrue to people with strong willpower: They do better at work and school, are more popular, have better relationships, are better adjusted, have better mental and physical health, and live longer than other people with less self-control (Mischel, Shoda, & Peake, 1988; Moffitt et al., 2011; Shoda, Mischel, & Peake, 1990; Tangney, Baumeister, & Boone, 2004).

By contrast, when a person's will has been depleted (i.e., either due to experimental manipulations or individual differences), many socially adaptive behaviors deteriorate. Depleted willpower causes people to be more likely to yield to urges that one would (and perhaps should) otherwise restrain, such as impulses to eat unhealthy food (Vohs & Heatherton, 2000), to aggress against others (DeWall, Baumeister, Stillman, & Gailliot, 2007; Stucke & Baumeister, 2006), to impulsively purchase unwanted items (Vohs & Faber, 2007), to consume alcohol prior to a driving test (Muraven, Collins, & Neinhaus, 2002), to engage in inappropriate sexual activities (Gailliot & Baumeister, 2007), or to violate social norms (Gailliot, Gitter, Baker, & Baumeister, 2012).

People's belief in free will and their ability to engage in self-regulation contribute to a broad range of behaviors that are conducive to cultural functioning. As already stated, we conceptualize free will as *responsible autonomy*. This formula is consistent with how ordinary people typically understand free will: as making choices, acting on one's own, controlling one's behavior to conform to social rules, and pursuing delayed rewards over time. Hence the evolution of free will can be understood as the development of the capacity to act autonomously and responsibly within the emerging context of human culture.

Additionally, the frame of responsible autonomy for free will fits the body of research showing that believing (rather than disbelieving) in the reality of free will promotes a broad range of behaviors that are beneficial to society, including honest action, helping others, restraining aggressive impulses, thinking for oneself, feeling and expressing gratitude, upholding standards by advocating punishment for rule breakers, and learning from one's mistakes.

Finally, the extensive evidence on the limited-resource model of volition and self-regulation indicates its helpfulness for cultural animals. Self-control, intelligent thought, and rational choice are all vital for cultural beings. Free will evolved to facilitate participation in social systems, insofar as autonomy and responsibility are largely requirements of such systems. It seems highly likely that humans evolved a new, more advanced way of controlling their actions so as to be able to participate in their new forms of social life (i.e., culture). Humans tend to think of this new form of action control as free will. Thanks to multiple, competing conceptions of free will, the term has become controversial and divisive. But the idea that humans are able to act in responsibly autonomous ways that go beyond what is seen in other species should be less so.

REFERENCES

Alquist, J. L., Ainsworth, S. E., & Baumeister, R. F. (2013). Determined to conform: Disbelief in free will increases conformity. *Journal of Experimental Social Psychology*, 49, 80–86.

Alquist, J. L., Ainsworth, S. E., Baumeister, R. F., Daly, M., & Stillman, T. F. (2015). The making of might-have-beens: Effects of free will belief on counterfactual thinking. *Personality and Social Psychology Bulletin*, 41, 268–283.

Bargh, J. A. (2008). Free will is unnatural. In J. Baer, J. C. Kaufman, & R. F. Baumeister (Eds.), *Are we free?: Psychology and free will* (pp. 128–154). New York: Oxford University Press.

Bargh, J. A., & Earp, B. D. (2009). The will is caused, not "free." *Dialogue: Newsletter of the Society for Personality and Social Psychology*, 24, 13–15.

Baumeister, R. F. (2005). *The cultural animal: Human nature, meaning, and social life*. New York: Oxford University Press.

Baumeister, R. F., Bratslavsky, E., Muraven, M., & Tice, D. M. (1998). Ego depletion: Is the active self a limited resource? *Journal of Personality and Social Psychology*, 74, 1252–1265.

Baumeister, R. F., & Heatherton, T. F. (1996). Self-regulation failure: An overview. *Psychological Inquiry*, 7, 1–15.

Baumeister, R. F., Heatherton, T. F., & Tice, D. M. (1994). *Losing control: How and why people fail at self-regulation*. San Diego, CA: Academic Press.

Baumeister, R. F., Masicampo, E. J., & DeWall, C. N. (2009). Prosocial benefits of feeling free: Disbelief in free will increases aggression and reduces helpfulness. *Personality and Social Psychology Bulletin*, 35, 260–268.

Baumeister, R. F., & Monroe, A. E. (2014). Recent research on free will:

Conceptualizations, beliefs, and processes. In J. M. Olson & M. P. Zanna (Eds.), *Advances in experimental social psychology* (Vol. 50, pp. 1–52). Waltham, MA: Academic Press.

Cashmore, A. R. (2010). The Lucretian swerve: The biological basis of human behavior and the criminal justice system. *Proceedings of the National Academy of Sciences of the USA, 107,* 4499–4504.

Clark, C. J., Luguri, J. B., Ditto, P. H., Knobe, J., Shariff, A. F., & Baumeister, R. F. (2014). Free to punish: A motivated account of free will belief. *Journal of Personality and Social Psychology, 106,* 501–513.

Crescioni, A. W., Baumeister, R. F., Ainsworth, S. E., Ent, M., & Lambert, N. M. (2015). Subjective correlates and consequences of belief in free will. *Philosophical Psychology,* (ahead of print), 1–23.

Dennett, D. C. (1984). *Elbow room: The varieties of free will worth wanting.* Cambridge, MA: MIT Press.

DeWall, C. N., Baumeister, R. F., Stillman, T. F., & Gailliot, M. T. (2007). Violence restrained: Effects of self-regulation and its depletion on aggression. *Journal of Experimental Social Psychology, 43,* 62–76.

Epstude, K., & Roese, N. J. (2008). The functional theory of counterfactual thinking. *Personality and Social Psychology Review, 12,* 168–192.

Gailliot, M. T., & Baumeister, R. F. (2007). Self-regulation and sexual restraint: Dispositionally and temporarily poor self-regulatory abilities contribute to failures at restraining sexual behavior. *Personality and Social Psychology Bulletin, 33,* 173–186.

Gailliot, M. T., Gitter, S. A., Baker, M. D., & Baumeister, R. F. (2012). Breaking the rules: Low trait or state self-control increases social norm violations. *Psychology, 3,* 1074–1083.

Haggard, P., Mele, A., O'Connor, T., & Vohs, K. D. (2010). Lexicon of key terms. Retrieved from *www.freewillandscience.com/FW_Lexicon.doc.*

Kushnir, T. (2012). Developing a concept of choice. *Advances in Child Development and Behavior, 43,* 193–218.

Laurene, K. R., Rakos, R. F., Tisak, M. S., Robichaud, A. L., & Horvath, M. (2011). Perception of free will: The perspective of incarcerated adolescent and adult offenders. *Review of Philosophy and Psychology, 2,* 723–740.

MacKenzie, M. J., Vohs, K. D., & Baumeister, R. F. (2014). You didn't have to do that: Belief in free will promotes gratitude. *Personality and Social Psychology Bulletin, 40,* 1423–1434.

Malle, B. F. (2006). Of windmills and strawmen: Folk assumptions of mind and action. In S. Pockett, W. P. Banks, & S. Gallagher (Eds.), *Does consciousness cause behavior?: An investigation of the nature of volition* (pp. 207–231). Cambridge, MA: MIT Press.

Mischel, W., Shoda, Y., & Peake, P. K. (1988). The nature of adolescent competencies predicted by preschool delay of gratification. *Journal of Personality and Social Psychology, 54,* 687–696.

Moffitt, T. E., Arseneault, L., Belsky, D., Dickson, N., Hancox, R. J., Harrington, H., et al. (2011). A gradient of childhood self-control predicts health, wealth, and public safety. *Proceedings of the National Academy of Sciences of the USA, 108,* 2693–2698.

Monroe, A. E., & Malle, B. F. (2010). From uncaused will to conscious choice: The need to study, not speculate about people's folk concept of free will. *Review of Philosophy and Psychology*, *1*, 211–224.

Monroe, A. E., & Malle, B. F. (2014). Free will without metaphysics. In A. R. Mele (Ed.), *Surrounding free will* (pp. 25–48). New York: Oxford University Press.

Montague, R. P. (2008). Free will. *Current Biology*, *18*, R584–R585.

Muraven, M., Collins, L. R., & Neinhaus, K. (2002). Self-control and alcohol restraint: An initial application of the self-control strength model. *Psychology of Addictive Behaviors*, *16*, 113–120.

Muraven, M., Tice, D. M., & Baumeister, R. F. (1998). Self-control as a limited resource: Regulatory depletion patterns. *Journal of Personality and Social Psychology*, *74*, 774–789.

Nahmias, E., Shepard, J., & Reuter, S. (2014). It's OK if "my brain made me do it": People's intuitions about free will and neuroscientific prediction. *Cognition*, *133*, 502–516.

Sarkissian, H., Chatterjee, A., De Brigard, F., Knobe, J., Nichols, S., & Sirker, S. (2010). Is belief in free will a cultural universal? *Mind and Language*, *25*, 346–358.

Shariff, A. F., Greene, J. D., Karremans, J. C., Luguri, J. B., Clark, C. J., Schooler, J. W., et al. (2014). Free will and punishment: A mechanistic view of human nature reduces retribution. *Psychological Science*, *25*, 1563–1570.

Shoda, Y., Mischel, W., & Peake, P. K. (1990). Predicting adolescent cognitive and self-regulatory competencies from preschool delay of gratification: Identifying diagnostic conditions. *Developmental Psychology*, *26*, 978–986.

Stillman, T. F., & Baumeister, R. F. (2010). Guilty, free, and wise: Determinism and psychopathy diminish learning from negative emotions. *Journal of Experimental Social Psychology*, *46*, 951–960.

Stillman, T. F., Baumeister, R. F., & Mele, A. R. (2011). Free will in everyday life: Autobiographical accounts of free and unfree actions. *Philosophical Psychology*, *24*, 381–394.

Stillman, T. F., Baumeister, R. F., Vohs, K. D., Lambert, N. M., Fincham, F. D., & Brewer, L. E. (2010). Personal philosophy and personnel achievement: Belief in free will predicts better job performance. *Social Psychological and Personality Science*, *1*, 43–50.

Stucke, T. S., & Baumeister, R. F. (2006). Ego depletion and aggressive behavior: Is the inhibition of aggression a limited resource? *European Journal of Social Psychology*, *36*, 1–13.

Tangney, J. P., Baumeister, R. F., & Boone, A. L. (2004). High self-control predicts good adjustment, less pathology, better grades, and interpersonal success. *Journal of Personality*, *72*, 271–324.

Vohs, K. D., & Baumeister, R. F. (2015). *Free will beliefs influence recycling behavior*. Unpublished data, University of Minnesota.

Vohs, K. D., & Faber, R. J. (2007). Spent resources: Self-regulatory resource availability affects impulse buying. *Journal of Consumer Research*, *33*, 537–547.

Vohs, K. D., & Heatherton, T. F. (2000). Self-regulatory failure: A resource-depletion approach. *Psychological Science*, *11*, 249–254.

Vohs, K. D., & Schooler, J. W. (2008). The value of believing in free will: Encouraging a belief in determinism increases cheating. *Psychological Science*, *19*, 49–54.

CHAPTER 4

Categories, Intent, and Harm

Susan T. Fiske

When I teach the psychology of racism—a course I have now taught perhaps a dozen times at two different universities—a predictable low point occurs every semester. About halfway through the course, after we have covered the latest research on the social-cognitive origins of bias, everyone in the course becomes profoundly discouraged and even depressed. If they could, they would give up and go home. But this is a university course, so they continue, partly to avoid the W on their transcript, partly out of curiosity to see how much worse it can get, and partly because I urge them to stay tuned because the news eventually gets better. What is so unpleasant about discovering the psychology of bias? It's not the focus on a few really bad apples, the ones who make the national news for unspeakable outgroup murders. It's not the 10% of the population that harbors really extreme, bigoted views, consistent with the views of people who go on to commit hate crimes. We all know about them, by reading and watching the daily news. But what is the news from academia, and how does it depress my students?

THE LATEST NEWS FROM BIAS RESEARCH

By some counts, 80% of the populations of Western democracies harbor benign intentions about intergroup relations but display subtle forms of bias. Subtle forms of bias are automatic, unconscious, and unintentional; cool, indirect, and ambiguous; and often ambivalent. The implication of these subtle forms of bias is that people—observers and actors alike—cannot so easily detect, name, and control them. They escape notice, even the notice of those enacting the biases. Does that lack of intent remove responsibility from the individual? But we are getting ahead of ourselves. First, the news.

Automatic, Unconscious, and Unintentional Bias

By far the biggest news in research on bias at the turn of the 21st century is how far underground it can be (Dovidio & Gaertner, 2010). Automaticity shows up in stereotypes, prejudice, and associated behavior. Sparked by evidence showing that rapid categorization instantly combines top-down (labels) and bottom-up (perceptual) features (Freeman & Ambady, 2011), by findings that category labels can immediately prime stereotypes and discriminatory responses (Jonas & Sassenberg, 2006), and by studies suggesting that even relatively unprejudiced people have automatic stereotypic associations, scores of studies now support the essentially automatic side of biases (Macrae & Bodenhausen, 2000). For example, lexical decision tasks show that even subliminally presented outgroup category labels (e.g., *black*) can activate stereotypically associated terms. That is, when people have to decide rapidly whether a series of letter strings (*apple, prebam, white, carnup, athlete*) are words or nonwords, they respond more rapidly to stereotypic words (*athlete*) when initially primed with a category label (*black*), even below awareness. In a more affective vein, outgroup category exemplars (such as outgroup faces or stereotypically ethnic names) easily activate negative evaluative terms.

Recent work on brain imaging relatedly shows amygdala activation indicating what may be prejudices against unfamiliar outgroup faces based on perceived threat (Chekroud, Everett, Bridge, & Hewstone, 2014; see Derks, Scheepers, & Ellemers, 2013, for a review). The apparent automaticity of such biases at once corroborates Gordon Allport's (1954) provocative early insights about the inevitability of categorization and shocks well-intentioned people used to thinking of prejudice as conscious and controllable. Many people like to think they are color-blind, but this belief is not only misguided, it is often counterproductive because it facilitates and justifies white racial resentment, disguises racial bias, and undermines minorities' trust (Apfelbaum, Norton, & Sommers, 2012).

Cool, Indirect, and Ambiguous Bias

The biases of the moderate, well-intentioned majority not only live underground; they also wear camouflage. It turns out that people's biases reflect ingroup comfort at least as much as outgroup discomfort, so derogation is less an issue than is simple neglect. For example, people cooperate more with ingroup than outgroup members (Balliet, Wu, & De Dreu, 2014). Similarly, bias often consists in refusing positive emotions to outgroups (Seger, Smith, Kinias, & Mackie, 2009). Moderates rarely express open hostility toward outgroups, but omitting negativity can create innuendos that allow stereotypes to stagnate (Bergsieker, Leslie, Constantine, & Fiske, 2012). People's responses often represent cool neglect or scorn (Fiske, 2010). People more rapidly assign positive attributes to the ingroup than the outgroup (negative attributes often show a weaker or even no difference; Dovidio & Gaertner, 2010). People withhold rewards from the outgroup relative to the ingroup, reflecting ingroup favoritism. They do not punish or derogate the outgroup but simply fail to share positive outcomes. The damage thus is relative and indirect (Yzerbyt & Demoulin, 2010).

Biases are indirect in other ways, having to do with norms for appropriate responses. If the situational norms do allow biases, they flourish, appearing most often when people have unprejudiced excuses (Dovidio & Gaertner, 2010). If some people exercise neglect, then norms ensure that everyone does, for example, in discretionary contact or helping. If the outgroup member behaves poorly, providing a norm-based excuse for prejudice, the resulting exclusion is more swift and sure than for a comparable ingroup member. Biases also appear in shared political policy preferences that become a group norm. Although one might cite principled reasons (excuses) for one's opinion, one might also just happen to have a whole series of policy preferences that all disadvantage the outgroup relative to the ingroup (Sears & Henry, 2005). Excuses for bias fulfill the social norm requiring rational, fair judgments, but controlled comparisons reveal greater bias toward outgroup than toward comparable ingroup members.

People also make attributions that discourage sympathy by blaming the outgroup for their own unfortunate outcomes: The outgroup should try harder, but at the same time they should not push themselves where they are not wanted (a Catch-22). For example, modern prejudice scales include items reflecting both perceived laziness and perceived intrusiveness (Pettigrew, 1998; Sears & Henry, 2005).

The blame goes further than perceived lack of effort. Whereas the ingroup might be excused for its failures (due to extenuating circumstances), the outgroup brought it on themselves (due to their unfortunate dispositions). People often attribute the outgroup's perceived failings to their essence: some innate, inherent, enduring attribute, perhaps biological, that makes up the core of the category's distinctiveness (Yzerbyt & Demoulin, 2010).

In trying to make sense of outgroup category members, people exaggerate cultural differences (e.g., in ability, language, religious beliefs, sexual practices). The mere fact of categorizing into "us" and "them," ingroup and outgroup, tends to exaggerate intercategory differences and diminish intracategory difference. "They are all alike and different from us, besides" (Rubin & Badea, 2012). In all these ways, moderates' bias is cool, indirect, and ambiguous.

Ambivalent and Mixed Bias

Besides being underground and camouflaged, people's biases are often complex. For example, ambivalent racism entails, for moderate whites, a mix of sympathy (pro-black) and anti-black sentiment, which can tip over to a predominantly positive or negative response, depending on circumstances. In this view, blacks are both deviant (for allegedly not trying hard enough) and disadvantaged (given discrimination; Katz & Hass, 1988; more generally, Webster & Saucier, 2013). As another example, ambivalent sexism demonstrates two correlated dimensions that differentiate hostile sexism (directed primarily toward nontraditional women) and subjectively benevolent sexism (directed primarily toward traditional women; Connor, Glick, & Fiske, in press). In both cases, ambivalence indicates mixed forms of prejudice more subtle than unmitigated hostility.

Mixed forms of bias turn out to be the rule, rather than the exception. We find that, although various outgroups all are classified as "them," the outgroups fall into different clusters (see Figure 4.1; Fiske, Cuddy, Glick, & Xu, 2002; Kervyn, Fiske, & Yzerbyt, 2015). Some elicit relatively less

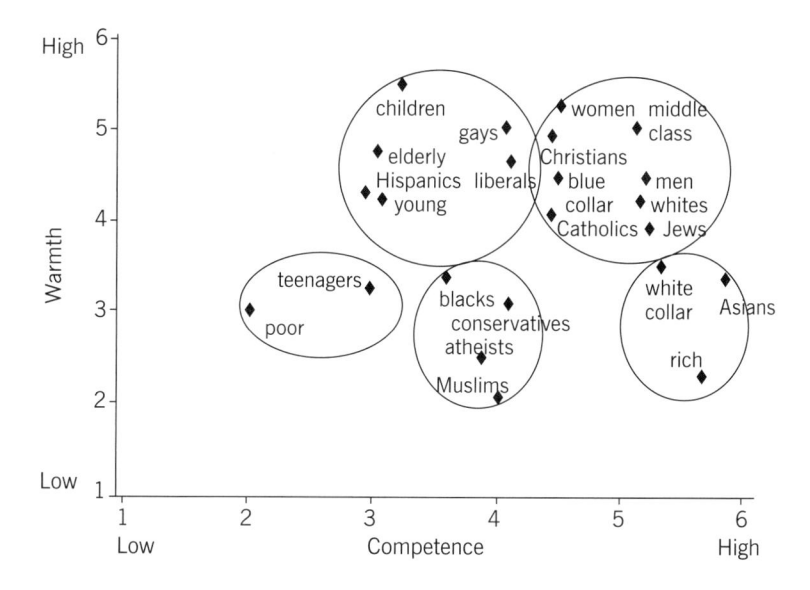

FIGURE 4.1. Clusters of American outgroups, along dimensions of perceived warmth and competence, predicted by the stereotype content model. Data from Kervyn, Fiske, and Yzerbyt (2015). Copyright Susan T. Fiske.

respect, and some elicit relatively less liking. That is, not only is the bias of well-intentioned moderates of the cool variety (withholding the positive, rather than assigning the negative), but it is not even uniformly lacking in positive views. Specifically, some outgroups (e.g., Asians, white-collar professionals, rich people) are envied and respected for their perceived competence and high status, but they are resented and disliked as lacking in warmth because they compete with the ingroup. Other outgroups (e.g., older people, gay people, children) are pitied and disrespected for their perceived incompetence and low status, but they are helped and seen as being warm because they do not threaten the ingroup. Only a few outgroups (primarily poor people of any race, but also teenagers) receive contempt, both dislike and disrespect, because they are seen as simultaneously low status and exploiting the ingroup.

The implication of the ambivalent and mixed forms of bias is system justification. The subordinated, pitied groups have an incentive to cooperate with the unequal system because they receive care, in return for not challenging the hierarchy. (Elderly people, for example, rarely protest the system that treats them as more broadly incompetent than the facts support.) And for the dominant group, the subordinated group maintains their own relative advantage in status. (Middle-aged people can feel benevolent and superior while patronizing their supposedly decrepit inferiors.) On the other hand, the envied, competitive groups (e.g., Asian people) have an incentive to support the system because they are perceived to be succeeding in it, even if they are socially excluded by the culturally dominant group (e.g., white people). And for the dominant group, respecting the envied group acknowledges the ground rules for competition (which favor them also), but disliking justifies their social exclusion.

Moderate Biases Predict Exclusion

Subtle forms of bias predict personal interactions that reek of discomfort and anxiety (e.g., Derks et al., 2013; Jones, Dovidio, & Vietze, 2014). Nonverbal indicators (distance, posture, tone of voice) and self-reports all reveal interactions that are anything but smooth, mostly due to inexperience with the outgroup.

Moreover, people treat each other in ways that tend to confirm their biased expectations, leading both parties to maintain their distance (Shelton & Richeson, 2014). The self-fulfilling prophecy, expectancy effects, and behavioral confirmation all name related phenomena, whereby biased perceivers bring about the very behavior they anticipate, which is usually negative. All these interpersonal processes result in subsequent avoidance whenever people have any choice about the company they keep. Discretionary contact is minimized (Pettigrew & Tropp, 2006).

Furthermore, exclusion and avoidance extend to decisions about employment, housing, education, and justice that tend to favor the ingroup and disadvantage the outgroup (Massey, 2008). Ample evidence indicates that relatively automatic, cool, indirect, ambiguous, and ambivalent biases permit allocation of resources to maintain ingroup advantage.

How Do Moderate Biases Originate?

Subtle prejudice comes from people's internal conflict between ideals and biases, both acquired from the culture at large. People experience constant exposure to examples of bias in the media. At the same time, their direct, personal experience with outgroup members may be limited. Given substantial de facto residential and occupational segregation, people lack experience in constructive intergroup interactions. The general media, then, supply their main sources of information about outgroups (e.g., Weisbuch, Pauker, & Ambady, 2009), so people easily develop unconscious associations and feelings that reinforce bias.

Nevertheless, the ideals of Western cultures tend to encourage tolerance of most outgroups. Complying with antiprejudice ideals requires a conscious endorsement of egalitarian norms against prejudice. Moderates also generally share personal values against prejudice.

The upshot is a conflict between relatively implicit, unconscious biases and explicit, conscious ideals to be unprejudiced. The conflict between one's biases and one's ideals tends to make the biases go into camouflage underground. The result is prejudice that is, as just reviewed, subtle (more than overt), modern (more than old-fashioned), and aversive to the people who hold it (occurring despite their best intentions).

Summary: The Dilemma

We have seen that people categorize each other automatically and unintentionally on the basis of race, gender, age, and other group memberships legally protected under civil rights statutes. Further, stereotypes, prejudice, and discrimination tend to follow such categorization. Does a glimmer of hope suggest that, if properly motivated, people can move beyond their initial categorical reactions, responding to other people as unique individuals? In other words, where does this analysis leave us in the quest to understand the moral implications of the newly discovered subtle biases?

THE NIGHTMARE ON OUR STREET: RESPONSIBILITY FOR BIASES

Until recently, these analyses would suggest that people are not responsible for their initial category-based reactions but only for what they do afterward. That is, if people can't help launching their impression formation processes along a trajectory guided by outgroup categories, then how can they possibly prevent themselves from responding in a biased manner? Precisely this issue was raised early on by E. E. Jones et al. (1984, p. 300): "Contemporary cognitive approaches to stereotyping . . . project a rather weary fatalism . . . [about] ingrained human proclivities." Hamilton (1979, p. 80) called the same problem "a rather depressing dilemma." This kind of concern was described by Bargh (1999, p. 363) as paranoia about the "cognitive monster":

> If it were indeed the case . . . that stereotyping occurs without an individual's awareness or intention, then the implications for society . . . were tremendously depressing. Most ominously, how could anyone be held responsible, legally or otherwise, for discriminatory or prejudicial behavior when psychological science had shown such effects to occur unintentionally? The legal profession has a term for such a dilemma: "the parade of horribles."

Legal Attributions of Responsibility

The responsibility dilemma is made explicit in legal settings. For most legal purposes, discrimination is defined as intentional. To show discrimination, the plaintiff must demonstrate that the perpetrator meant for the legally protected group member(s) to be disadvantaged on account of gender, race, age, disability, religion, and the like. Arguing that the alleged perpetrator was recklessly discriminating or accidently discriminating will not show discrimination. Unlawful discrimination has no category equivalent to involuntary manslaughter in the legal arena of murder.

The two legal standards for establishing discrimination both rely on intent. Disparate *treatment* must discriminate against one group precisely because of race, gender, age, and so forth. (Saying that one refuses to hire certain people because they are black would be the baldest example of disparate treatment discrimination.) One might consider this direct discrimination.

In contrast, disparate *impact* discrimination is indirect, operating by way of a practice that is on its face neutral but has differential impact on a protected category. (Requiring all firefighters to be over 200 pounds would differentially impact women.) The plaintiffs complain in such a case that the supposedly neutral practice is actually a pretext for excluding their category of people. If the defendants cannot demonstrate that the practice is in fact a business necessity (e.g., testing for upper body strength in a firefighter), the inference is made that it was indeed a pretext and that the defendant intended to discriminate.

The point here is that both types of discrimination assume intent. If one could show that all people universally operate on the basis of protected categories and that they do so without intent or control, that is, automatically, then perhaps one could argue that discrimination is an inevitable and blameless fact of social life.

This scenario gave me pause, more than once, when I served as an expert witness in discrimination cases. As I was educating the fact finder (judge or jury) about the automaticity of ingroup–outgroup categorization and subsequent bias, I waited for the opposing attorney to demand how anyone could possibly be held responsible for unintentional discrimination, according to the cognitive-social account.

Indeed, ordinary people see unintentional harms as less harmful than intentional ones (Ames & Fiske, 2013, 2015). Across a series of exactly equivalent harms (e.g., water shortage, medications switched), an intentional harm was estimated literally to cost more than the identical harm caused by nature or by human accident. Intentional harms motivate people to blame, condemn, and punish, which in turn predicts their exaggerating the harm's actual cost.

To return to the social-cognitive dilemma about (un)intentional discrimination: Because of the importance of intent in estimating harm, several answers to the question eventually arose. One psychological answer developed, the lawyers proposed another, and the research community eventually generated a third.

Psychological Analysis of Intent

One response to this dilemma is to examine closely the meaning of intent, according to lay, psychological, and legal definitions (Fiske, 1989). They do agree somewhat on three criteria for inferring intent, applicable to the situation of perceiver bias. First, observers must agree that the perceiver had a *choice* between two modes of response. For example, most people would agree that one can hardly avoid flinching from touching an unexpectedly hot surface, even though one might choose, in an emergency, to grab a burning object in order to extinguish it. In social life, the equivalent perspective would argue that although people may feel uncomfortable around unfamiliar outgroup members, it's not a burning surface; they do have a choice about how they respond.

Corroborating this lay analysis, various psychological models argue for two modes of social cognition, one a more automatic form of response and the other a more deliberate, thoughtful form of response (Sherman, Gawronski, & Trope, 2014). In impression formation specifically, people's impression formation processes arguably form a continuum, from relatively automatic category-based processes to relatively thoughtful individuated processes (Fiske, Lin, & Neuberg, 1999; Fiske & Neuberg, 1990). People have alternative modes available, so they have a choice.

The law makes a similar distinction between, for example, murder in self-defense (automatic) and premeditated murder (deliberate). Individuals are responsible for the latter but not for the former. Partly, this hinges on the idea that people have a choice in the latter case but not in the former one.

But the inference of intent in premeditated murder brings us to the second lay, psychological, and legal criterion for intent. People are more clearly acting with intention when they make the *hard choice*. The person who refuses to commit a murder, despite extreme provocation and strong impulse (e.g., in the moment of discovering one's spouse in flagrante delicto), is more obviously making a choice than the person who follows what is seen as a natural homicidal impulse. The person who grabs the burning object to extinguish it is attributed more intent than the person who flinches. In impression formation, the person who individuates another person by gathering additional information is acting with intent. The person who automatically categorizes another person and acts accordingly is less clearly acting with intent. Impulse is less often viewed as operating with intent; controlling the impulse is more clearly intentional.[1]

The third criterion for inferring intent is *attention*. People are responsible for premeditated murder precisely because it involves deliberate thought and attention. People are seen as deliberately controlling their individuation process because it requires attention and motivation. People have to gather information, consider it, synthesize it, and weigh it in the final impression; all that requires attention.

In summary, a psychological analysis of intent provides a basis in lay, legal, and social-cognitive terms for inferring an individual's intent. Intent is most clear when the individual has a choice, makes the hard choice, and pays attention.

But what about meeting subsets of these criteria? What if a person has a choice and apparently makes the hard choice but without thinking about it? A person who rushes into a burning building to save a child is widely acclaimed a hero—clearly having had a choice and having made the hard choice—though often the person reports doing it without thinking. Nevertheless, we laud the person as responsible. What about a person who has a choice and makes the easy choice, although by thinking about it? An individual who follows an impulse to murder an unfaithful spouse but does so after an interval of planning is held more responsible than someone who does so in the passion of the moment. Similarly, what about an individual who has an impulse to exclude an outgroup member (but has a choice), thinks about it and justifies the exclusion (gives it attention), and acts accordingly (makes the easy choice)? That person would seem responsible for intentional action. What about the hardest case: An individual has an impulse to exclude the outgroup member (we know the person has a choice to follow or resist the impulse) but doesn't bother to think (no attention) and acts accordingly (makes the easy choice)?

Less prejudiced people are more likely to recognize that even relatively automatic responses are in some sense intentional (Cooley, Payne, & Phillips, 2014). Perhaps we should have a category of involuntary but unlawful discrimination, slightly less egregious than premeditated discrimination. Drawing on the legal distinctions among types of murder, we could go from involuntary discrimination (like manslaughter, acting on impulse that greater control might have prevented) or negligent discrimination (like accidental homicide, acting in a thoughtless manner that attention might have prevented), up the levels to deliberate bigotry (like premeditated murder). The legal world has yet to adopt this theory, but it has devised another answer to the dilemma of individual responsibility in a world of relatively automatic bias.

Legal Analysis of Intent

Because people are motivated by social situations, organizations may be viewed as responsible for the actions of their individual members. The Supreme Court held, in a case I know because of my role as an expert witness at the lower court level, that an organization acts as a body that cannot hold its employees to gender stereotypes (*Price Waterhouse vs. Hopkins*, 1989): "We are beyond the day when an employer could evaluate employees by assuming or insisting that they matched the stereotype associated with their group" (p. 1790).

In a similar way, in another case in which I was an expert witness (*Robinson vs. Jacksonville Shipyards*, 1989), a Florida appeals court held that an organization knows—or should know—that its male employees are likely to act on sexually explicit materials (pinup calendars in the workplace) in ways that sexually harass the female employees:

> Corporate defendant liability may be proved under one of two theories. Direct liability is incurred when an agent of the corporate employer is responsible for the behavior that comprises the hostile work environment, and the agent's actions were taken within the scope of the agency. . . . Indirect liability attaches where the hostile environment is created by one who is not the plaintiff's employer, such as a coworker, or by an agent of the employer who is acting outside the scope of the agency, and the plaintiff can establish that the employer knew or should have known of the harassment and failed to take prompt, effective remedial action. (Par. 25)

Besides the attribution of intent to an organization, legal analyses complement psychological analyses in another manner. The *Price Waterhouse* decision is known in legal circles not for its relevance to organizational responsibility but for its relevance to the problem of mixed-motive discrimination. Suppose a decision is admittedly tainted by protected-class membership (i.e., it took gender into account), but, regardless, other factors would have denied the benefit (hiring, promotion) anyway. In a recent mixed-motive decision, the Supreme Court ruled that the burden of proof shifts to the defendant (employer). In other words, when the decision is tainted by a protected category (outgroup) membership, the decision maker is responsible for showing that prejudice was not the cause of the decision.

What's more, the Court recently ruled that indirect evidence (i.e., circumstantial evidence) of discriminatory animus is sufficient in a mixed-motive case in which protected-class membership is just one motivating factor in the decision (*Desert Palace, Inc. v. Costa,* 2003). This means that an outgroup member does not necessarily need overt evidence of discriminatory intent but could use more subtle indicators, such as those described earlier as indicating modern forms of bias. In this case, Desert Palace employed the plaintiff as its only female warehouse worker. The company treated her less favorably than comparable men but also failed to protect her from a supervisor who stalked her. Notice that all these actions are failures to act, consistent with subtle forms of discrimination in which people withhold benefits from outgroup members and neglect them while benefiting the ingroup.

These legal analyses, then, address the intent issue in two ways that complement psychological analyses. First, they accept the concept of organizational responsibility, which would be outside the purview of a psychological analysis (both because of attributing intent to a group and because of allocating moral responsibility). Second, the legal analyses complement psychological perspectives on intent by analyzing mixed-motive settings, in which both the category and individual attributes are in play. The results suggest suspicious motives whenever a group makes a decision tainted by category membership.

Recent Research on Intent

Earlier in this section I listed three possible answers to the automaticity dilemma: the initial psychological analysis of intent, some legal analyses of responsibility, and the recent research on automaticity and control. This third response to the question of automaticity—which so dismays well-intentioned people—comes from the same researchers whose work provoked the dilemma in the first place.

All is not lost for the well intentioned. Recent evidence suggests that people's initial gut-level responses may be influenced by their frame of mind, that is, by their motivation. People do not inevitably activate and use their ingroup–outgroup categories. It depends on how overloaded and motivated they are, and it depends on their values and goals, as well as the nature of the information they confront.

In other words, category activation apparently is not *unconditionally* automatic. Although people can instantly identify another person's category membership (especially gender, race, and age), they may not always activate the associated stereotypic content, for example, under intense distraction (e.g., multitasking). People's long-term attitudes also can moderate access to biased associations: Lower levels of chronic prejudice can attenuate activation of stereotypes. And temporary processing goals matter as well: Category activation can depend on various short-term motivations, including relevance for self-enhancement and accurate understanding.

Promising as they are, these findings remain controversial. For example, they may depend on the nature of the stimuli: Ease of category activation probably differs depending on whether perceivers encounter verbal labels (easy, because they supply the category name), photographs (harder, because the label must be inferred), or a real person (hardest, because the label must be inferred during live interaction). Some researchers believe that social categories inevitably activate associated biases, whereas others believe the activation depends entirely on short-term situational goals and long-term individual differences (Devine, 2001).

Whether bias is conditionally or unconditionally automatic, either way people's long- and short-term motives do matter (Fiske, 1998). If category activation is unconditionally automatic, less prejudiced perceivers still can override their automatic associations with subsequent controlled processes. If category activation is conditionally automatic, then people may be able to inhibit the biased associations in the first place.

What's more, even if people do *activate* biases associated with a category, they may not *apply* (or use) those biases. For example, once the category is activated, other information may be consistent or inconsistent with it, and perceivers have to decide what to do about the conflicting information. Inconsistency resolution and subsequent individuation of the other person require resources, which are allocated according to the perceiver's motivation and capacity. Overriding category activation to avoid using the category depends on metacognitive decisions (thinking about one's thinking patterns) and higher-level executive functions (i.e., deliberate control), not just on sheer brute attentional capacity. Other qualifications to the use of activated categories go beyond the perceiver's motivation and capacity: For example, category use depends on the nature of the stimuli (category abstractions are more likely to encourage assimilation, whereas exemplars encourage contrast) and on the perceiver's or the culture's theory about whether people's dispositions are fixed entities or flexible states (Morris, Chiu, & Liu, 2015). Also, people inhabit multiple categories simultaneously, and multiple factors determine which category is most active: the current task (Kang & Bodenhausen, 2015) and the intergroup situation (Crisp & Hewstone, 2007).

Inhibition of category activation and of its application both turn out to challenge even the most determined moderate. Direct suppression sometimes causes only a rebound of the forbidden biases. Depending on cognitive capacity, practice, age, and motivation, people can suppress or inhibit many effects of social categories.

Indeed, even amygdala activation to cross-race faces vanishes when people adopt individuating goals (Would this person like broccoli?) or nonsocial goals (Is there a dot on this photograph?) (Wheeler & Fiske, 2005).

The take-home message to lay people is: Bias is more automatic than you think, but less automatic than we psychologists thought.

WHERE DOES THIS LEAVE THE RESPONSIBILITY FOR GOOD AND EVIL IN INTERGROUP PERCEPTIONS?

Categories Can Help or Harm

An underlying assumption of this chapter has been that categories are harmful and all but inevitable. To be sure, categories can be pragmatic in many respects: They are convenient for the perceiver because they import knowledge from the general case to the specific individual. The categorized target may embrace that identity, which then creates mutual understandings. Recognizing the other's category may indicate how society treats this person and so indicate frequent experiences. The category-based knowledge may even carry a grain of truth.

For example, medical diagnosis and treatment may depend on age, weight, or gender, presumably based on population probabilities. Medical research regularly includes such factors. One would not want one's doctor to ignore them. At the same time, one would not want one's doctor to jump to conclusions based entirely on one's demographic categories. Presumably, tests are ordered; evidence is gathered. If the data do not support the category-based hunches, one wants the doctor to go with the individualized evidence.

In daily encounters, too, although other people notice one's categories, one may not even prefer that the associated information act as a hunch. The hunch anchors the encounter, so many intergroup encounters require sweeping away stereotypic assumptions: Asians don't speak English well, women are too nice, black people are athletic, older people are confused.... How many times does one have to prove oneself otherwise?

Not only do categories serve as an initial anchor, but they also fence targets within their group boundaries in an ongoing way. The fence limits how far one can deviate from the stereotyped norm. Mechanisms such as stereotype threat, self-fulfilling prophecy, and societal norms all limit the behavior of categorized targets.

Tied to the anchor and confined inside the fence, targets blur into a seemingly homogeneous group that are all the same. Interchangeable category members have no individuality. Even if the category stereotype were accurate on average (assuming objective benchmarks), the average takes no account of variability around that mean. In all these ways, categories shortchange the individual by blurring distinctions.

Finally, categories usually demean the outgroup—someone else's group. As the stereotype content model indicates, most outgroups are not respected, viewed as having inferior abilities. And many outgroups are not liked, excluded for seeming less trustworthy than the ingroup. Categories create anchors, fences, blur, and subordination. Although they can be useful, they are also harmful.

Implications of Psychological Criteria for Intent

This chapter's analyses create a new set of criteria for attributing intent (and therefore responsibility) for biased responses. The recent research findings, in particular, take responsibility and situational pressures one step further back in the psychological processes of biased impression formation. Assume that right-thinking people want to avoid biases against people from other groups. People with the right values (e.g., egalitarianism), the right organizational incentives (e.g., cross-category teamwork), and the right motivation (e.g., motivation to avoid prejudice) can in fact get beyond (sometimes even prevent) their automatic use of category-driven impression formation and decision making. People demonstrably have a choice and can choose the hard choice if they pay sufficient attention.

This conclusion suggests legal and ethical implications for the unbiased treatment of others. Organizations can know that people's initial impulse is to categorize others and to favor the ingroup. Organizations can structure their incentives so that people from different categories learn to work well together. Individuals can be accountable for their treatment of others. Interdependent teams can learn to work together. In each case, overriding the default response is key, and knowing that it is indeed the default can help individuals and organizations to take responsibility for treatment of underrepresented groups—for good or ill.

NOTE

1. This is not to say that the automatic impulse is always negative and the deliberate response is always positive. For example, selfless behavior might be an automatic response, whereas selfish behavior might require calculating self-interest.

REFERENCES

Allport, G. (1954). *The nature of prejudice*. Reading, MA: Addison-Wesley.
Ames, D. L., & Fiske, S. T. (2013). Intentional harms are worse, even when they're not. *Psychological Science, 24*(9), 1755–1762.
Ames, D. L., & Fiske, S. T. (2015). Perceived intent motivates people to magnify

observed harm. *Proceedings of the National Academy of Sciences of the USA, 112*(12), 3599–3605.

Apfelbaum, E. P., Norton, M. I., & Sommers, S. R. (2012). Racial color blindness: Emergence, practice, and implications. *Current Directions in Psychological Science, 21,* 205–209.

Balliet, D., Wu, J., & De Dreu, C. K. W. (2014). Ingroup favoritism in cooperation: A meta-analysis. *Psychological Bulletin, 140*(6), 1556–1581.

Bargh, J. A. (1999). The cognitive monster: The case against the controllability of automatic stereotype effects. In S. Chaiken & Y. Trope (Eds.), *Dual-process theories in social psychology* (pp. 361–382). New York: Guilford Press.

Bergsieker, H. B., Leslie, L. M., Constantine, V. S., & Fiske, S. T. (2012). Stereotyping by omission: Eliminate the negative, accentuate the positive. *Journal of Personality and Social Psychology, 102*(6), 1214–1238.

Chekroud, A. M., Everett, J. A. C., Bridge, H., & Hewstone, M. (2014). A review of neuroimaging studies of race-related prejudice: Does amygdala response reflect threat? *Frontiers in Human Neuroscience, 8,* Article ID 179.

Connor, R. A., Glick, P., & Fiske, S. T. (in press). Ambivalent sexism in the 21st century. In C. Sibley & F. Barlow (Eds.), *Cambridge handbook of the psychology of prejudice.* New York: Cambridge University Press.

Cooley, E., Payne, B. K., & Phillips, K. J. (2014). Implicit bias and the illusion of conscious ill will. *Social Psychological and Personality Science, 5*(4), 500–507.

Crisp, R. J., & Hewstone, M. (2007). Multiple social categorization. In M. P. Zanna (Ed.), *Advances in experimental and social psychology* (Vol. 39, pp. 163–254). New York: Academic Press.

Derks, B., Scheepers, D., & Ellemers, N. (Eds.). (2013). *Neuroscience of prejudice and intergroup relations.* New York: Psychology Press.

Desert Palace, Inc. v. Costa, S. Ct. 679 (2003).

Devine, P. G. (2001). Implicit prejudice and stereotyping: How automatic are they? Introduction to the special section. *Journal of Personality and Social Psychology, 81,* 757–759.

Dovidio, J. F., & Gaertner, S. L. (2010). Intergroup bias. In S. T. Fiske, D. T. Gilbert, & G. Lindzey (Eds.), *Handbook of social psychology* (5th ed., Vol. 2, pp. 1084–1121). Hoboken, NJ: Wiley.

Fiske, S. T. (1989). Examining the role of intent: Toward understanding its role in stereotyping and prejudice. In J. S. Uleman & J. A. Bargh (Eds.), *Unintended thought* (pp. 253–283). New York: Guilford Press.

Fiske, S. T. (1998). Stereotyping, prejudice, and discrimination. In D. T. Gilbert, S. T. Fiske, & G. Lindzey (Eds.), *Handbook of social psychology* (4th ed., Vol. 2, pp. 357–411). New York: McGraw Hill.

Fiske, S. T. (2010). Envy up, scorn down: How comparison divides us. *American Psychologist, 65*(8), 698–706.

Fiske, S. T., Cuddy, A. J., Glick, P., & Xu, J. (2002). A model of (often mixed) stereotype content: Competence and warmth respectively follow from perceived status and competition. *Journal of Personality and Social Psychology, 82,* 878–902.

Fiske, S. T., Lin, M. H., & Neuberg, S. L. (1999). The continuum model: Ten years later. In S. Chaiken & Y. Trope (Eds.), *Dual-process theories in social psychology* (pp. 231–254). New York: Guilford Press.

Fiske, S. T., & Neuberg, S. L. (1990). A continuum of impression formation, from category-based to individuating processes: Influences of information and motivation on attention and interpretation. In M. P. Zanna (Ed.), *Advances in experimental social psychology* (Vol. 23, pp. 1–74). New York: Academic Press.

Freeman, J. B., & Ambady, N. (2011). A dynamic interactive theory of person construal. *Psychological Review, 118*, 247–279.

Hamilton, D. L. (1979). A cognitive-attributional analysis of stereotyping. In L. Berkowitz (Ed.), *Advances in experimental social psychology* (Vol. 12, pp. 53–84). New York: Academic Press.

Jonas, K. J., & Sassenberg, K. (2006). Knowing how to react: Automatic response priming from social categories. *Journal of Personality and Social Psychology, 90*(5), 709–721.

Jones, E. E., Farina, A., Hastorf, A. H., Markus, H., Miller, D. T., & Scott, R. A. (1984). *Social stigma: The psychology of marked relationships*. New York: Freeman.

Jones, J. M., Dovidio, J. F., & Vietze, D. L. (2014). *The psychology of diversity: Beyond prejudice and racism*. Malden, MA: Wiley-Blackwell.

Kang, S. K., & Bodenhausen, G. V. (2015). Multiple identities in social perception and interaction: Challenges and opportunities. *Annual Review of Psychology, 66*, 7.1–7.28.

Katz, I., & Hass, R. G. (1988). Racial ambivalence and American value conflict: Correlational and priming studies of dual cognitive structures. *Journal of Personality and Social Psychology, 55*(6), 893–905.

Kervyn, N., Fiske, S. T., & Yzerbyt, Y. (2015). Foretelling the primary dimension of social cognition: Symbolic and realistic threats together predict warmth in the stereotype content model. *Social Psychology, 46*, 36–45.

Macrae, C. N., & Bodenhausen, G. V. (2000). Thinking categorically about others. *Annual Review of Psychology, 51*, 93–120.

Massey, D. S. (2008). *Categorically unequal: The American stratification system*. New York: Russell Sage.

Morris, M. W., Chiu, C.-Y., & Liu, Z. (2015). Polycultural psychology. *Annual Review of Psychology, 66*, 631–659.

Pettigrew, T. F. (1998). Reactions toward the new minorities of Western Europe. *Annual Review of Sociology, 24*, 77–103.

Pettigrew, T. F., & Tropp, L. R. (2006). A meta-analytic test of intergroup contact theory. *Journal of Personality and Social Psychology, 90*(5), 751–783.

Price Waterhouse v. Hopkins, 109 S. Ct. 1775 (1989).

Robinson v. Jacksonville Shipyards, Inc. (M.D. Fla. 1989; Case No. 86-927).

Rubin, M., & Badea, C. (2012). They're all the same! . . . But for several different reasons: A review of the multicausal nature of perceived group variability. *Current Directions in Psychological Science, 21*(6), 367–372.

Sears, D. O., & Henry, P. J. (2005). Over thirty years later: A contemporary look at symbolic racism. In M. P. Zanna (Ed.), *Advances in experimental social psychology* (Vol. 37, pp. 95–150). San Diego, CA: Elsevier Academic Press.

Seger, C. R., Smith, E. R., Kinias, Z., & Mackie, D. M. (2009). Knowing how they feel: Perceiving emotions felt by outgroups. *Journal of Experimental Social Psychology, 45*(1), 80–89.

Shelton, J. N., & Richeson, J. A. (2015). Interacting across racial lines. In M. Mikulincer, P. R. Shaver, J. F. Dovidio, & J. A. Simpson (Eds.), *APA handbook of personality and social psychology: Vol. 2. Group processes* (pp. 395–422). Washington, DC: American Psychological Association.

Sherman, J. W., Gawronski, B., & Trope, Y. (Eds.). (2014). *Dual-process theories of the social mind*. New York: Guilford Press.

Webster, R. J., & Saucier, D. A. (2013). Angels and demons are among us: Assessing individual differences in belief in pure evil and belief in pure good. *Personality and Social Psychology Bulletin, 39*(11), 1455–1470.

Weisbuch, M., Pauker, K., & Ambady, N. (2009). The subtle transmission of race bias via televised nonverbal behavior. *Science, 326*(5960), 1711–1714.

Wheeler, M. E., & Fiske, S. T. (2005). Controlling racial prejudice and stereotyping: Social cognitive goals affect amygdala and stereotype activation. *Psychological Science, 16*, 56–63.

Yzerbyt, V., & Demoulin, S. (2010). Intergroup relations. In S. T. Fiske, D. T. Gilbert, & G. Lindzey (Eds.), *Handbook of social psychology* (5th ed., Vol. 2, pp. 1024–1083). Hoboken, NJ: Wiley.

CHAPTER 5

"The Devil Made Me Do It"
The Deification of Consciousness and the Demonization of the Unconscious

John A. Bargh

Other chapters in this book on the social psychology of good and evil address important questions such as: What are the psychological processes that lead to positive, selfless, prosocial, and constructive behavior on the one hand or to negative, selfish, antisocial, and destructive behavior on the other? Such questions concern how the state of a person's mind and his or her current context or situation influences his or her actions upon the outside world. In this chapter, however, the causal direction is reversed. The focus is instead on how the outside world of human beings—with its religious, medical, cultural, philosophical, and scientific traditions, its millennia-old ideologies and historical forces—has placed a value on types of psychological processes. It is on how these historical forces, even today, slant the field of psychological science, through basically a background frame or mind set of implicit assumptions, to consider types of psychological processes themselves as being either good or evil (or at least problematic and producing negative outcomes).

There exists a long historical tendency to consider one type of mental process to be the "good" one—our conscious and intentional, deliberate thought and behavior processes—and another type as the "bad" and even "evil" one—our automatic, impulsive, unintentional, and unconscious thought and behavioral processes. These valuations are part of a historical tradition dating back at least 2,000 years to early Christianity (as in "the spirit is willing but the flesh is weak") in the writings of Saints Paul and Augustine, a legacy that continued into the Renaissance with Descartes's explicit equating of the conscious mind with the God-like soul and the automatic or reflexive mind with base animal instincts; then to Freud's literal demonization of the unconscious as a separate destructive mind inside each of us, the source of self-destructive and maladaptive thoughts, emotions, and motivations; and to the psychological science (especially the subdomains of self-regulation, judgment, and decision making) of today.

To give a flavor of how this good-versus-evil characterization continues to play out today, here are a few examples. In their comprehensive review of self-regulation theory and research, Mischel, Cantor, and Feldman (1996) summarize the relation between conscious, intentional processes and automatic, unconscious ones as follows:

> The encoding of the features of particular situations is often highly automatized (Bargh & Gollwitzer, 1994), making conscious control unnecessary and, even if desirable, difficult. These automatic construals may be *problematic* when they are linked with *maladaptive reflexive patterns* of affect and behavior, such as *uncontrolled impulsiveness*, that jeopardize the person's own long-term goals. For example, *aggressive adolescents* may readily encode ambiguous events . . . as personal violations to which they respond instantly with aggression. . . . *Physically abusive men* are prone to respond to perceived rejection with *uncontrollable anger and physical violence* . . . [and then there are] the automatic construals of *rejection-sensitive, abusive individuals or of depressed individuals*. . . . (p. 335; emphasis added)

This passage is not taken out of context. It is the *only* mention of automatic or unconscious mental processes appearing in the chapter; it is exclusively (and vividly) negative; and no positive effects are ever mentioned, even though the one paper cited here (Bargh & Gollwitzer, 1994) concerned the automatic operation of positive achievement motivations. Nor is this an isolated example; mainstream self-regulation theorists have repeatedly dismissed the idea of unconsciously operating motivational and behavioral processes as "warmed-over behaviorism" (Ainslie, 2014; Mischel, 1997; see later discussion) or argued that effective self-regulation is exclusively conscious and intentional in nature (Bandura, 1986).

As a second example from a quite different research domain, the popular dual-process "System 1 and System 2" model (Kahneman, 2011) assigns very similar negative-versus-positive roles to automatic (unconscious) and deliberate (conscious) thought, respectively. In the opening paragraph (abstract) of Morewedge and Kahneman's (2010) presentation of the two systems, System 1 is described as fast, associative, and not controlled, whereas System 2 is slower and under executive control. This is followed by the summary: "System 1 makes the errors, System 2 corrects them" (p. 435). In its historical context, this simple statement can be seen as a continuation of the Freudian idea that the unconscious is the source of errors and suffering that can only be corrected by bringing the unconscious material into the light of consciousness (Higgins & Bargh, 1992).

Our tendency to equate our conscious mind with goodness and our unconscious or "animal" mind with badness is driven by a very deep historical, religious, and cultural current, one that can be traced back at least 2,000 years. It is such a part of our fundamental Western ideology that it operates quite implicitly, as part of our unexperienced but important background, as water is to a fish or greed to a banker (no joke: see Cohn, Fehr, & Maréchal, 2015). This is an important point because my goal here is to call attention to this tendency and thus, hopefully, decrease it. Cultural ideologies can be remarkably long-lasting and persistent, carrying over from one generation to the next, operating implicitly on our judgments and behavior even centuries after their original reason and context have ceased to exist (Uhlmann, Poehlman, & Bargh, 2008, 2009).

THREE POWERFUL INFLUENCES

The deification of consciousness and the corresponding demonization of unconscious or automatic processes are overdetermined; many powerful forces contribute to our favoritism toward one over the other—historical, religious, cultural, motivational, and ideological.

The Unconscious as Historical Scapegoat

"The spirit is willing but the flesh is weak." Aggressive or self-indulgent, destructive animal impulses have long been said to come from the physical, animal body and could be prevented or corrected only by application of the spirit, or conscious mind, riding in like a white knight to the rescue. According to Hannah Arendt's (1978) historical analysis of the concept of free will, this idea can be traced back at least 2,000 years, to St. Paul (letters to the Corinthians and to the Romans). It is repeated 1,600 years later by Descartes (1641/1931) in his division of the mind into metaphysical and physical aspects. It is repeated again in Freud's assignment of destructive and self-defeating impulses and motivations to the primary process of the unconscious, which can be overcome and cured only by bringing them into the light of consciousness. And it is repeated today in canonical models of (exclusively conscious) self-regulation abilities and of judgment and decision making.

Saint Paul and Saint Augustine

Hannah Arendt, in the first chapter of her *The Life of the Mind* (1978), distinguishes between political and psychological conceptions of free will. The ancient Greek philosophers were concerned with the political concept only, with the ability to choose between courses of action without external coercion. The political concept of free will assumes that otherwise the person is free to choose—that is, that there are no *internal* determinants of the choice other than consciously aware and intentional choice processes. Thus the political concept of free will (freedom from external coercion or causation) assumes the existence of psychological free will (freedom from internal, nonconscious causation); thus, according to Arendt, the issue of purely psychological free will never arose for the ancient Greek philosophers.

It did become an issue for the early Christian theologians many centuries later. The issue of *psychological* free will developed into a real problem for the early Christian church, given its twin axioms that God was all good and also all powerful. As evil was recognized to exist in the world—people did bad things such as theft, murder, and rape, and there were also evil natural catastrophes such as floods and volcanic eruptions (see Neiman, 2002)—how then could evil exist if God were all powerful (and all good)? The influential Manichean heresy during the early years of the Christian church solved this problem by asserting that good and evil were separate forces and thus that God was all good but not all powerful.

Augustine, in fact, was originally a Manichean whose influential theological writings solved the problem through the argument that while God was indeed both all good and all powerful, He had to permit the existence of evil in order for there to be a fair and just basis for the Final Judgment on each of our souls. That is, humans must be given the ability to freely choose and do evil, so that they and they alone would be responsible for it and be fairly judged on their actions after death. Our free will was thus another way in which, as early Christian theology held, humans were created in God's image; just as God was the original, uncaused cause and source of the universe and creation, so too were we the original (uncaused) source of our actions. Arendt concludes that hence the concept of free will was originally a religious concept. With the rise and political domination of the Christian church over Europe and then Western civilization for the next 1,500 years, the doctrine of human free will as an original uncaused cause of our actions became legal, ideological, and cultural dogma as well (see Arendt, 1978; Neiman, 2002).

And a thousand years later, with Descartes, it became philosophical doctrine as well.

Descartes and the Renaissance

Following Christianity's theological position that humans were created in God's image, Descartes (1641/1931) equated the conscious mind with the metaphysical soul, for which he gave a physical location, the pineal gland. This was the key transition from the supernatural, metaphysical soul to its physical, natural instantiation as the conscious mind. Descartes took the supernatural soul and located it in our physical body. But at the same time he made a sharp division of the conscious mind from the rest of the (animal) body, thus preserving the supernatural aspect of the soul (as embodied in the conscious mind) as separate and distinct. Conscious, aware thought was distinguished from animal, automatic mental processes (which Descartes explicitly acknowledged). This was a turning point in the philosophy of mind, the first dual-process model: a good, causal conscious mind (soul) that must control the individual's base animal impulses and reflexes.

Descartes's division of the mind into the conscious and the physical identified the conscious mind (or, today, "System 2") with the soul, and it was our God-like component. He acknowledged a "System 1" component to the mind as well; the automatic, fast, emotional workings of the mind were identified not with our soul but with the physical world, the one we shared with animals. Our conscious mind was our *superpower*—in comparison to the other animals, it made us God-like and superior. Descartes's division of the conscious mind from the animal unconscious was more than a mind–body dualism; it also incorporated the division between heaven and earth themselves: Unique among terrestrial animals, humans had a foot in both worlds.

"The Devil Made Me Do It"

Despite Augustine's arguments against the Manichean heresy, the belief in separate good and evil forces in the universe persisted in common thought. As God was all good, and we were God's children, evil was generally attributed to external supernatural forces and not to human nature. For example, shortly after John Wilkes Booth's assassination of President Lincoln, a lithograph appeared in newspapers—and was endorsed by an Act of Congress—depicting the devil tempting Booth to perform the evil act (see Figure 5.1). In the illustration, the devil isn't forcing Booth to do anything, but is rather persuading him; thus the devil is depicted here as the source of the evil thoughts and decisions that Booth himself ultimately makes (of his own free will). In this way, the cause of the assassination is portrayed as an evil force acting upon Booth's normal thoughts and choices, changing them into something not human (i.e., evil). (The cultural legacy of this belief is still with us. The popular 20th-century American comedian Flip Wilson (1970) became famous for his "the devil made me do it" routine:

his character Geraldine's standard excuse for anything wild and crazy she impulsively did, such as buy an expensive dress she couldn't afford.)

In the Middle Ages, disturbed or counternormative (strange) behavior was attributed to demonic possession. Because the abnormal behavior could not be considered to be from our good, God-like human nature itself, it must be caused by supernatural evil forces, an evil demon who had possessed the individual and caused the abnormal behavior. The prevalence of this attribution of odd, abnormal, or psychotic behavior to supernatural forces was commonplace as recently as 1890, still prevalent in Western culture—including among medical doctors (see Crabtree, 1993)—about the time that Freud began his research and treatment of clinical patients.

However, in the late 19th century, recourse to supernatural forces was increasingly becoming anathema to the emerging medical scientific understanding and treatment of mental disorders, which acknowledged only physical, not metaphysical, causes. Freud took these external, supernatural demons and moved them into the patient's physical body itself—as a "second mind" replete with self-destructive and maladaptive impulses and motivations. Just as Descartes put the good soul in a physical location in the human body, 250 years later Freud put the evil demons inside the human body. *Descartes put the supernatural good soul in our conscious mind, and Freud put the supernatural evil demon in our unconscious mind.* Thus did Freud quite literally demonize the unconscious workings of the human mind.

Freud and the Demonization of the Unconscious

Freud himself credited the discovery of the unconscious mind to Anton Mesmer and the early hypnotists (see Brill, 1938). According to Adam Crabtree's (1993) detailed and comprehensive account, Mesmer did not consider himself a hypnotist and was in fact not in favor of psychological interpretations of his "animal magnetism" treatment of physical ailments, problems that the medical science of the time could not cure. He took on these lost causes and tried to alleviate the patients' suffering and symptoms through what we recognize today as a very Eastern notion of bodily energy fields (*ka*), which he believed could be effectively manipulated through his treatment techniques. Mesmer did not believe he was treating mental illnesses, but rather was treating physical illnesses through manipulations of these presumed physical energy fields.

Still, these manipulations, involving hand waving and movements around the patient's body, did have some success—not great or highly reliable success, but still better than the mainstream medical treatments of the time, which had given up on these cases entirely. And as it turned out, over many decades of refinement and some research on these techniques—some of which were adjudicated by Benjamin Franklin, among others—the

FIGURE 5.1. Satan tempting John Wilkes Booth to the murder of President Abraham Lincoln (1865 lithograph by John L. Magee). From Library of Congress Prints and Photographs Division.

successes, such as they were, were not to be due to manipulations of any actual energy fields but instead to their psychological effects on the patients. Mesmer himself did not know (and did not live to find out) that these were, largely, mental illnesses he was treating, and he personally strongly resisted the conclusions that his techniques worked on the patients' psychology instead of their physical body processes. Nonetheless, his and his followers' techniques became the forerunner of the hypnotic therapies of the middle

1800s, which for the first time revealed physical illnesses that had an exclusively psychological or emotional cause and that could be somewhat effectively treated by hypnosis and the other emerging psychotherapeutic techniques (see Crabtree, 1993).

Freud arrived rather late in this transitional period, in which hysterically and psychopathologically caused physical symptoms were eventually, over a span of 125 years, discovered to have psychological origins and to be treated through hypnosis and other emerging psychotherapies (such as the eventual "talking cure"). Thus Freud was not the historical *origin* of the psychotherapeutic treatment of these illnesses but actually the culmination of over a century of slow development of the psychotherapeutic idea, traced in detail in Crabtree's (1993) account. As a good medical doctor at the dawn of the 20th century, Freud eschewed the location of these illnesses in supernatural forces such as demonic possession. Moved, as were so many others at that time, by the *Zeitgeist* of Darwin and the goal of providing natural, scientific explanations for phenomena (such as the creation of life) that had long been explained through recourse to religious or supernatural causal forces, Freud instead located these psychopathologies in the workings of the patient's physical body itself.

But if the causes of maladaptive and odd behavior were no longer supernatural evil demons possessing the God-like body and soul of the human victim and now, instead, resided within the patient's physical body, they still could not be attributed to the person's God-like conscious mind. And so Freud took the external demons of possession and placed them in physical form within the patient's body, as a "second mind" that existed separately and in secret from the conscious mind. This was, historically and literally, *the demonization of the unconscious.* Thus the human unconscious—unintended influences of which the person was not aware—became the new, and medical, scientific home for the demons of the Middle Ages, the modern "I didn't mean to" scapegoat for bad behavior and negative outcomes.

In *Psychopathology of Everyday Life* (1901/1914), Freud discusses a wide variety of mundane errors, a collection of slips of the tongue, forgetfulness, and other mistakes taken from real life, many starring Freud himself. Each of these numerous examples is explained through recourse to some kind of unconscious process (i.e., something else going on in the person's life: a problem, strong desire, or reminder of a past traumatic event); in one, for example, Freud leaves his favorite cigar store without paying for the cigars, which he describes as "a most harmless omission" caused by his focus that day on budgetary matters (p. 97).

It is unfortunate that Freud did not limit his "second mind" account to the cases of mental illness and psychopathology he treated. Instead, he generalized from these pathological individuals to the view that *all* of us had this error-prone "second mind" inside us, operating in secret from the conscious mind. Tellingly, Freud's contemporary, Pierre Janet, who saw the same types of patients and dealt with the same psychopathologies, disagreed with Freud on this point; Janet believed instead that the maladaptive and self-destructive "second mind" was an abnormal and relatively rare condition (Crabtree, 1993) and not a characteristic of normal human functioning. But as we know, it was Freud's position that prevailed in psychiatry and so greatly influenced popular culture.

Still Fighting the Cognitive Revolution

Freud's model of the "secret second mind" also influenced modern-day cognitive science, which persists in defining unconscious processes as those which operate entirely outside of conscious awareness—including awareness of the triggering external stimulus event itself. By operationalizing unconscious processes in this manner—which is not the way they have been defined historically by Darwin, Freud, Dawkins, and others—the domain of unconscious influences is dramatically restricted to that which the human mind can do with subliminal stimuli. Intentionally or not, this delimitation of the role of unconscious influences in the higher mental processes to include only those that can occur with subliminal stimulus presentation is in the service of championing the causal role of conscious processes. By the "subliminal" definition of the unconscious, all of the mental processes that operate—even unintentionally—when the person is aware of the stimulus itself are considered conscious processes. Because these are by far most mental processes, the subliminal definition of unconscious processes effectively defines the unconscious out of existence. We return to this definitional issue later, but we first consider its roots, not only in Freud's "second mind" but also in the heat of the battles of the cognitive revolution against behaviorism.

The cognitive revolution (Chomsky, 1959; Neisser, 1967) marked a return to the study of conscious thought, memory, and the higher mental processes. It was a rejection of the behaviorist approach, which sought to explain even the higher mental processes of human language and social behavior as stimulus–response (S–R) chains. Skinner (1957) pushed the S–R principle as far as he could, in an attempt to account for the higher mental processes in humans such as language and social interaction behavior, and failed utterly (Chomsky, 1959; Koestler, 1967). This failure more than anything else opened the door to cognitive psychology, which was founded on the completely opposite set of basic assumptions. Now, everything except for primitive sensory and perceptual processes (such as figural synthesis and pattern recognition) was assumed at the outset of cognitive psychology to be under conscious and intentional "executive control." Thus in the remarkably short span of 10 years between the 1957 publication of Skinner's *Verbal Behavior* and the 1967 publication of Ulric Neisser's *Cognitive Psychology,* the field of psychology (especially in North

America) underwent a seismic paradigm shift, from the presumption of complete external stimulus control over the higher mental processes to the presumption of a complete *absence* of any external stimulus control. (In an irony of psychology's history, Neisser wrote *Cognitive Psychology* while at Harvard, in a small basement office in William James Hall, under the very nose of Skinner. They often found themselves on the elevator together, but according to Neisser [personal communication, 2003], never spoke.)

Thus the founding axiom and ideology of the cognitive paradigm in psychology was that conscious, intentional mental processes were the exclusive cause of the higher mental processes such as judgment and social behavior. It was directly opposed to the behaviorist assumption that external environmental events were the exclusive cause. But today, 50 years later, the cognitive revolution is still being fought by some. They view with suspicion any model that posits a positive role for unconscious processes in judgment or self-regulatory behavior and explicitly label it a "return to behaviorism" or "warmed-over behaviorism" and wonder aloud why we ever fought the cognitive revolution in the first place (Mischel 1997; Ainslie, 2014; see also Bandura, 1986). Though pains have been taken to point out how the modern research on the unconscious operation of internal cognitive and motivational processes is actually antithetical to behaviorism, because in the modern models the external stimulus by itself determines nothing and internal cognitive and motivational processes are always the proximal causes (see Bargh & Ferguson, 2000; Wood & Ruenger, 2016), there nonetheless remains today an almost visceral rejection by influential psychological scientists of an unconscious role in the higher mental processes.

If unconscious processes are viewed as a return to behaviorism, then one tactical way to continue to fight the cognitive revolution against it would be to "define away" unconscious processes, as cognitive psychology has done for many years now, by operationally defining them as "what the mind can do with subliminal stimuli." In 1992, a special issue of the *American Psychologist* with articles by an expert panel of cognitive psychologists reached the overall conclusion that the unconscious was rather dumb (Loftus & Klinger, 1992). Why? Because it could not do very much complex processing with such low intensity or briefly presented (i.e., subliminal) stimuli. (As Tim Wilson pointed out at the time [personal communication, 1992], the unconscious processes were still smarter than the conscious processes, which didn't even know a stimulus had been presented at all!)

The contemporary cognitive psychology definition of unconscious processes in terms of lack of awareness even of the causal stimulus events themselves is not the one that was used by scientists and scholars prior to the cognitive revolution, nor is it used this way in common language. The historical definition of an unconscious process did not focus on the awareness (of the stimulus itself) dimension but on its *unintentional* nature. Unconsciously produced behaviors, as through posthypnotic suggestion, are those the person does not intend and the cause of which the person is not aware of. This is how the early hypnotists used the term (see Brill, 1938; Crabtree, 1993), how Darwin (1859) used it in *Origin of Species* (referring to how the farmers and herders of his time unconsciously used the principle of natural selection in their trades), how Freud consistently used it (Brill, 1938), and how Dawkins (1976, 1986) and evolutionary biologists use it today (see Bargh & Morsella, 2008).

When one considers the evolution of the human mind, which operated unconsciously for eons in an adaptive and functional manner prior to the late development of consciousness (Deacon, 1997), defining unconscious processes as those that operate on subliminally presented stimuli makes little sense. Unconscious causation of often quite sophisticated and adaptive behavioral tendencies is by far the rule in the animal kingdom (Dawkins, 1976). Contemporary evolutionary psychology has extended this principle to human beings, demonstrating and delineating the innate tendencies, motivations, and needs that humans are born with or which develop quite quickly after birth through epigenetic mechanisms responsive to the individual's early environment (e.g., Bargh & Huang, 2014; Kenrick & Griskevicius, 2013; Neuberg & Schaller, 2014)—all of which evolved to operate on normal, not (weak, brief, low intensity) subliminal strength stimuli. To draw the conclusion, based on studies of subliminal stimulus presentation, that the unconscious was rather dumb is like taking a dolphin out of the water, testing its abilities on dry land, and concluding dolphins are not very smart after all.

As might be expected, defining unconscious processes in terms of subliminal information processing has led to the conclusion by some in the fields of cognitive psychology and judgment and decision making that only conscious mental processes can produce the higher mental processes. Methodological criticisms of studies that conclude a role for unconscious influences in the higher mental processes hold them to a different standard than those for conscious processes: An unconscious process must satisfy *all* of the "four horsemen" defining features, but a conscious process need satisfy only one (as pointed out by Dijksterhuis & Aarts, 2010; Hassin, 2013). This leads to an overestimation of the causal role of conscious processes and an underestimation of the role of unconscious influences.

Ironically, defining away one type of process in favor of the other is to make the same type of mistake—but in the opposite direction—that the behaviorists made a century ago. Back then, the hard-nosed experimental psychologists of the time concluded that *conscious* processes were not causal, because there were (at that time) no reliable methods, in their opinion, to measure them (Watson, 1913). The behaviorists derided the study of consciousness and conscious processes as unscientific. And as Arthur Koestler argued so eloquently in *The Ghost in the Machine* (1967), this dogmatic and rigid position of experimental psychology against conscious causation of the higher mental processes then proceeded to dominate American psychology for the next 50 years and prevented advances in psychological science at the same time that the other sciences were making huge strides in discoveries and advancement of knowledge. We would do well to avoid making this same mistake again.

It's What We *Want* to Believe

Finally, the tendency to demonize our automatic and unconscious mental processes goes hand in glove with our basic self-serving motivation to believe that our own conscious and intentional decisions and behaviors are good. Anything selfish or hurtful to others can be attributed to these "not-conscious" influences instead, and this permits us to maintain our belief in the basic goodness of conscious mental processes. After all, consciousness is our very own superpower among the animals of the earth, and we cherish it, we want to think of ourselves as more than "just" an animal. This powerful desire to possess superpowers is easily seen in our tastes and preferences in escapist entertainment—the most common plotlines and characters in the most popular television shows and movies (*Superman, Avengers*, etc.) are about people with special abilities and superpowers. We yearn and long to have such superpowers so much that we are hardly likely to give up valuing and thinking very positively about the one we actually *do* have over other animals—our conscious mental processes.

This general motivated-cognition human tendency—to attribute good outcomes to conscious intentional processes and to place blame for any bad outcomes elsewhere—was noted very early in attribution research, in the self-serving tendency to make dispositional causal attributions (take credit) for successes and positive outcomes but situational attributions (place blame elsewhere) for failures and negative outcomes (Bradley, 1978).

These self-serving attributions, or rationalizations, are the product of conscious processes in service of the goal of reaching a positive, self-serving conclusion regarding the behavior and its outcome. As we will see, these conscious rationalizations can facilitate continued negative and even evil behavior by justifying it in some abstract, positive way, as in "the ends justify the means." In fact, some have recently argued that the evolved purpose of consciousness itself was to be able to argue, to act as one's own defense attorney, in order to maintain good standing in one's social group (Mercier & Sperber, 2010). In order to remain in good standing in the group, and avoid its retribution when one produces bad or unwanted outcomes, it was important to be able to effectively deny personal responsibility and to produce a plausible, positively intentioned version of one's actions.

Just how facile the conscious mind is at generating this ongoing positive narrative of one's actions was shown 30 years ago by the pioneering neuroscientist Michael Gazzaniga. He argued in *The Social Brain* (1985) that impulses to action arise unconsciously in the right brain hemisphere and are "interpreted" in an ongoing narrative fashion by the left hemisphere. This conscious interpretation of what one is doing and why is thus not a direct readout of the actual reasons but an after-the-fact inference or interpretation of what they must be (see also Wegner & Wheatley, 1999), and it functions to build a plausible (and positive) story. Gazzaniga recounts some of his early research involving posthypnotic suggestion; for example, telling his patients while they are in the hypnotic trance that at the count of 3, he will snap his fingers and they will get down on the floor on all fours, or that they will get up and leave the room: 3, 2, 1, *snap*! and they are on the floor or out the door. But immediately the patient is explaining this bizarre behavior in some plausible positive manner: "I think I lost an earring down here" or "I need to get a drink of water." It was striking how quickly the patient generated a good reason for what was actually a strange or rude thing to do—walking around on the floor on hands and knees in front of your doctor or abruptly leaving the room while he is sitting there talking to you. These plausible and self-servingly positive spins of our actions—often inaccurate as to the actual reasons for them—are then incorporated into the ongoing narrative account of our lives (for empirical demonstrations of this effect, see Bar-Anan, Wilson, & Hassin, 2010). And so each of us continuously builds our life story, one populated almost exclusively by positive versions of our conscious intentions and actions.

UNCONSCIOUS PROCESSES ARE USUALLY GOOD, CONSCIOUS PROCESSES ARE OFTEN BAD (SOMETIMES VERY BAD)

In case there was any doubt, here are some counterexamples to the overdetermined tendency to value conscious processes as "good" and devalue unconscious ones as "bad." These are offered merely as reminders that conscious and unconscious cognitive processes do not in reality sort themselves neatly into "good" and "bad" boxes, respectively; it is not intended to be an exhaustive list.

Good (Beneficial) Unconscious Processes

Natural selection has shaped human beings (and other social animals) to be able to get along with others in social groups, to cooperate with and to help each other, to instinctively respond to the needs of infants and young children, to contagiously "catch" and thus empathize with the emotions of whomever we are with (Sober & Wilson, 1998). What a bleak and misleading view of human nature it is to consistently portray our evolved and unconsciously operating impulses as mostly negative and selfish, as well as frequently self-destructive. It is certainly true that in extreme pathological cases such as addictions, or for those in dire need of an anger management class, these impulses can be self-destructive and a danger to others as well. But the generalization of those cases to a general model of how the mind works—that self-regulation consists of the conscious control through willpower of exclusively negative automatic impulses, or that automatic processes make the errors and conscious processes correct those errors—is to make the same mistake that Freud made when he generalized from his mentally ill patients to normal human functioning.

To relentlessly paint a picture in which our automatic impulses are negative or harmful (to ourselves or to others) misses the point that we would not be able to function at all without them. Over a half century ago, Miller, Galanter, and Pribram (1960) called our attention to the fact that without fast and automatically operating muscular coordination processes, we would not even be able to get out of bed in the morning. The hard-won skills of coordinating our numerous muscle movements, gained through often painful experience over the years of infancy and early childhood, become automated through skill acquisition processes so that eventually they require little if any conscious attention. Any complex skill—walking, driving, reading—has considerable unconscious components in order to free limited conscious processing capacity that would otherwise be overwhelmed. Just remember when you started to learn how to read or to drive a car—you probably don't remember how many months it took you to learn to stand up, and then many more months to be able to walk—and how effortless those experiences are now. As adults we take these hardwon skills for granted, but just because the details of their operation are no longer part of our conscious awareness does not mean all that greatly beneficial and absolutely essential work is not taking place behind the scenes.

Now let's take habits, described by some exclusively in terms of "evil" impulses to overeat or overdrink, to assume the worst about others, to react to insults with violence, and so on. We do need effortful, conscious self-regulation skills to overcome them. But research has more recently shown that the best and most reliable method of self-regulation turns out to be the development of *positive* habits that are triggered automatically and unconsciously by external situational cues. The extensive research program of Wendy Wood and colleagues (see Wood & Ruenger, 2016) has shown that the best way to actually perform desired behaviors—healthy, prosocial habits to exercise, to eat right, to take time out for one's kids, to get one's work or studying done first before relaxing and doing something more enjoyable, and so on—is to develop them as habits and then to rely on regular situational cues to activate the desired behavior.

For example, one study showed that nearly 90% of effective self-regulators in the domain of exercise, those who did exercise on a regular basis, relied on a dependable location or time cue to trigger the desired behavior (see Wood & Ruenger, 2016). What the environmental cue most helpfully does is to activate the goal-directed behavior it has become habitually associated with, even when the conscious mind is—as it often is—occupied elsewhere. So when you arrive home from work still mentally rehashing the day at the office, so that you are distracted from the conscious intention of exercising, you still find yourself upstairs in your bedroom changing out of your "work clothes" (as you always do) and putting on your T-shirt, shorts, and running shoes. Or routinely stopping by your children's bedrooms to say goodnight or check on them before retiring yourself. Wood and Ruenger (2016) summarized the benefits of habitual self-regulation as follows:

> The research we reviewed highlights a number of advantages to acting habitually. For example, habit knowledge is protected from short-term whims and occasional happenings, given that habits form through incremental experience and do not shift readily with changes in people's goals and plans. Also, by outsourcing action control to environmental cues, people have a ready response when distraction, time pressure, lowered willpower, and stress reduce the capacity to deliberate about action and tailor responses to current environments. Furthermore, habit systems are smart in the sense that they enable people to efficiently capitalize on environmental regularities. (p. 307)

The point is that habits—automatic impulses to act in a goal-directed manner that do not rely on conscious intentions to produce the actions—can be good as well as bad. It is not that fast automatic processes are bad and slow deliberate ones are good; what is really the determinant of whether a person behaves in a good or evil way are the goals and motives activated by those impulses. Having power over other people can automatically trigger selfishness and exploitation of those others in some people but greater concern and caring about them in other people, depending on one's chronic interpersonal goals (Chen, Lee-Chai, & Bargh, 2001). The goal to exercise or to take time out for one's family can be just as habitual as the goal to drink or eat or take drugs. It is not habit per se that is bad (or good), but the person's goals or desires that have become habitual.

Well, you might say, these nice habits are all well and good, but how does one overcome the bad ones and develop the good ones in the first place? If the bad ones are already there, then they will rule the person's behavior and be difficult to overcome. Yes, they will be, especially if one relies only on the vagaries and unreliability of conscious means to overcome them. Once again, it turns out, the most effective way to do difficult intentional things, those that you really want to do but are having trouble getting done, is by using automatic, unconscious means of enacting those desired behaviors.

Gollwitzer and colleagues' (Gollwitzer, 1999; Brandstatter, Lengfelder, & Gollwitzer, 2001) extensive work on *implementation intentions* is the short-term version of the same principle—reliable behavior control through environmental cuing—that underlies the effective habitual self-regulation processes reviewed by Wood and Ruenger (2016). Relying on slow and unreliable conscious choice processes to get the difficult behavior accomplished often fails because the person forgets to carry out the intention when the golden opportunity arises or because of consciously generated excuses or rationalizations as to why the hard thing doesn't need to be done right now ("I'll do it tomorrow"; "one more donut won't matter"). Implementation intentions, on the other hand, specify in advance the place, time, and method of how one will enact the desired behavior in concrete terms, so that when the specified future event occurs, the situation unconsciously cues the intended action.

In one early implementation intention study (Gollwitzer, 1999), some male college students reported having the goal, while home on Christmas vacation, to tell their fathers they loved them; this was something they were having trouble doing despite really wanting to. Those who made a concrete implementation intention on how to do this—"when I get into the car at the train station when he picks me up, I will tell him I love him"—were markedly more likely to successively carry out their intention than others who also wanted to do this but did not first form an implementation intention.

The principle of delegating control of difficult but desired intentions to the environment (instead of conscious choice at that time) has significant health benefits as well; Sheeran and Orbell (1999) found that, over a 6-month period, elderly patients were much more likely to remember to take their several important medications if they had formed implementation intentions about them than if they had not. Other studies showed marked increases produced by implementation intentions in getting screened for various forms of cancer, something we often avoid consciously thinking about and doing. And implementation intentions are especially helpful for people who have difficulty in conscious, willpower-based self-regulation, such as recovering drug addicts and schizophrenics (Brandstatter et al., 2001). Thus the delegation of a desired but difficult behavior to a reliable future situation would seem the best way to break an existing bad habit ("I'll have a piece of fruit for dessert after dinner tonight; I'll go get some out of the fridge right after I put my dinner plate in the sink") and get a good new habit started.

There are other evolved and "fast-automatic" positive behavior triggers beyond the self-regulation domain. For example, unconsciously produced imitation and mimicry tendencies produce greater bonding and liking of one's interaction partner and also greater empathy toward him or her (e.g., Chartrand & Bargh, 1999; Chartrand & Lakin, 2013). In mundane, normal, 24/7 mental functioning, our innate impulses to act and behave are often quite positive; they cause us to smile at the baby, to run into the ocean to save someone from drowning, to cooperate instead of compete as our first option (e.g., Peysakhovich, Nowak, & Rand, 2014). For people with communal goals who characteristically put others' interests before their own, prosocial and selfless acts are the natural and spontaneous reactions to having authority or power over those others' outcomes (Chen et al., 2001). Again, these are just some examples; the larger point is that human beings evolved to be on good terms with each other, to cooperate and coordinate with them, as well as to effectively pursue our important needs and goals. Our evolved unconscious machinery, which is along with our habits the main source of automatic impulses to action, was never in the business of producing maladaptive outcomes (which would never have been selected for). It is mainly geared toward producing prosocial and personally beneficial (via goal pursuit) ends.

Evil (Producing) Conscious Processes

At this writing came the news of the Charleston, South Carolina, church massacre. A young white man came into the church during a Bible study session and sat there for over an hour before walking up to and shooting each of his nine black victims, who had on his arrival invited him to come up and join their study group. His was not an impulsive or automatic violent outburst but a coldly premeditated mass murder. It is a sad and sobering reminder that many acts of pure evil are consciously intended, planned, and then deliberately carried out. Evil acts are hardly the exclusive domain of impulsive, unconscious influences.

In psychological science, conscious intentional processes are equated with executive processes that exert a top-down influence on responses to the world. This is the opposite causal direction to that championed by behaviorism, in which causation came exclusively from external environmental stimuli. Our executive processes give us the ability to overcome the influence of those stimuli, as in Mischel's (2014) famous marshmallow studies, transforming the meaning of those stimuli in order to better serve one's current goal (such as to delay gratification). Effective regulation of our emotional states as well often relies on internal cognitive transformation of the external reality into something less threatening or demoralizing (Gross, 1998), as when one engages in downward social comparison ("at least I'm not as bad off as poor Joe") or repeats to oneself "It's only a movie, it's only a movie" while watching a horror film.

The Charleston example illustrates that although executive processes carry out one's important goals, not all goals are good ones, and some are especially evil. Some might be good for the individual but bad for others and society in general. The top-down transformations of external reality by executive processes show that it is not external reality—the causal stimuli of behaviorism—that drives these evil behaviors but the conscious and deliberate process that changes it. Thus these evil deeds are not due to unconscious impulses driven by external situations or stimuli (i.e., automatic processes, or System 1) but the internal conscious and deliberate transformations of that world in the service of the individual's goals and needs. Each of us, unfortunately, is quite adept at *rationalizing* our selfish deeds that harm or cost others, spinning their meaning to be not so bad after all or even as benefiting the others who are harmed ("We destroyed the village in order to save it"). These rationalizations are in the service of maintaining the positive illusion that we are good people and merit the esteem of others (Taylor, 1989).

These rationalizations or transformations of external reality that maintain our high opinion of ourselves are very conscious, very deliberate, and often very creative cognitive processes, and they have contributed significantly to some of the greatest evils in human history. In Roy Baumeister's (1996) analysis of the sources and causes of evil, the most powerful source he identified was clear threats to the unjustified but very high self-esteem of individuals and nations. For the sake of brevity, let's take Adolf Hitler as an example, as there is little debate that he was one of the most evil individuals and played a large role in some of the most savage and unspeakable evil behavior in recent human history. Hitler was the prime mover and shaker of many of the worst atrocities of the Second World War, and his aggressive territorial expansion policy was the proximal cause of the war itself. But in his youth he was out of work and homeless, a complete failure at becoming the great artist (or architect) he so strongly believed himself to be (e.g., Kershaw, 1998). Today, we much better understand the motivational reasons and processes through which Hitler identified himself so strongly with the German nation and greater, pan-German *Volk,* his absolute identification with the larger culture of which he was a part, in his apparent deep need to overcome and compensate for his own personal failures and lack of control over his own important outcomes (Kay, Gaucher, Napier, Callan, & Laurin, 2008). He so strongly identified himself with the historic, culturally and militarily renowned German nation that he became, in his own mind and in the image he relentlessly portrayed to its citizens, the human embodiment of Germany itself—he *was* Germany and Germany was him (Kershaw, 1998).

This transformation was certainly the product of conscious and deliberate executive processes. But more than that and far more destructive were the rationalizations of failure, the distortions and transformations of actual reality, that laid the blame elsewhere for first his artistic and then the nation's own failure, the defeat and surrender of the German army (in which he served for 4 years) at the end of the First World War. In his mind, the cause was not any shortcomings of the armed forces on the foreign front lines but a "stab in the back" by Jews and socialist politicians back home. This defeat was so shocking and taken so personally by Hitler that he became hysterically blind for several weeks following the surrender in November 1918. He had tied his ego and identity to that of Germany and could not accept that the German army could have been defeated on the field.

The evils that Hitler propagated in the service of this twisted and distorted version of reality—with powers no longer limited to himself as a single individual but now as the dictator of a powerful totalitarian government and armed forces—were some of the greatest in human history. And on smaller scales they continue to occur today. The early accounts of the Charleston shooter paint a similar picture of an individual strongly identifying with a larger social group to which he belongs (whites) and hatred toward a less powerful social group, viewed as the enemy of his group and as deserving of retribution for imagined wrongs they had committed against his group. It is all too eerily reminiscent of Hitler's blaming of the Jews and Bolsheviks for his own and the German army's past failures. And the Charleston shooter carried out his evil in a systematic and quite deliberate fashion, as did Hitler. The main point, that evil is often the product of conscious, intentional, deliberate thought and deed, should not require any further elaboration here. The ability to consciously transform the realities of the world is a double-edged sword; when used to further the pursuit of one individual's or one group's goals at the cost of others' goals and even lives, it can facilitate evildoing to an extent no unconscious or impulsive acts can.

CONCLUSIONS

Extreme positions may be convenient, they may simplify our world, but they are usually wrong and get in the way of increased understanding. Regarding human higher mental processes and behavior, the Freudian theory of the causal primacy of the secret-second-mind unconscious, the behaviorist position of exclusive external stimulus causation, and the cognitive science position of exclusive conscious causation are all equally wrong. The higher mental processes in human beings are guided and influenced by both conscious and unconscious mental processes, one causing the other in dynamic and reciprocal fashion (Baumeister & Bargh, 2014).

Moreover, despite thousands of years of tradition to the contrary, neither type of process is inherently good or bad on its own merits. Both are to a large extent evolved adaptations to the mind, and so both tend more than not to afford us adaptive advantages. Conscious mental processes in particular have given us a tremendous advantage over all other animals, and, through their facilitation of our ability to communicate and cooperate with others, they are mainly responsible for the incredible achievements of human civilization. But they are limited, and much necessary good work is also done by unconscious processes in the background (Baumeister & Masicampo, 2010; Nordgren, Bos, & Dijksterhuis, 2011).

It is encouraging, however, that recent reviews and theoretical treatments of the relative scope and abilities of conscious (aware, intentional) and unconscious (the operation and influence of which the person is not aware) mental processes no longer view them as oppositional, one against the other; instead, each is treated as adaptive and helpful in the human navigation of the modern world (e.g., Baumeister & Bargh, 2014; Baumeister &

Masicampo, 2010; Dijksterhuis & Aarts, 2010). For example, implementation intentions are a combination of a consciously intended behavior and its delegation to a future event with high reliability of occurrence. Good habits, the most effective method of self-regulation, are a combination of conscious intention and willpower, with control over that desired behavior transferred over time to reliable environmental cues. Thus the most reliable path to good outcomes in our most important life domains is the combination of conscious and unconscious means to those ends.

As many have argued recently, progress in our understanding of the relative roles played by conscious (intentional, awareness of cause) and unconscious (unintentional, no awareness of cause) processes in the human higher mental processes will be made when we finally push beyond the traditional "one versus the other" conceptions (Bargh, 1994; Inzlicht, Barthalow, & Hirsh, 2015; Keren & Schul, 2009; Suhler & Churchland, 2009), which appeal to us for their convenience but are oversimplified and misleading. Even more importantly, we need to become explicitly aware of our implicit biases regarding their relative value and utility in life, values handed down to us over the centuries by historical and ideological forces and which thus may be operating implicitly inside of us. As Hassin (2013) noted, tremendous advances are often made in the sciences when dominant background assumptions are finally put to the test. A good way to start on this path would be to become just as skeptical and evidence-demanding regarding claims of conscious causation of higher mental processes as many are today regarding their possible unconscious causation. As all-too-fallible human beings in search of underlying scientific truths, we should be on our guard against the deep currents and traditions that lead us to cheer for one horse against the other.

REFERENCES

Ainslie, G. (2014). Selfish goals must compete for the common currency of reward. *Behavioral and Brain Sciences, 37,* 135–136.

Arendt, H. (1978). *The life of the mind.* New York: Harcourt.

Bandura, A. (1986). *Social foundations of thought and action: A social cognitive theory.* Englewood Cliffs, NJ: Prentice Hall.

Bar-Anan, Y., Wilson, T. D., & Hassin, R. R. (2010). Inaccurate self-knowledge formation as a result of automatic behavior. *Journal of Experimental Social Psychology, 46,* 884–894.

Bargh, J. A. (1994). The Four Horsemen of automaticity: Awareness, efficiency, intention, and control in social cognition. In R. S. Wyer, Jr. & T. K. Srull (Eds.), *Handbook of social cognition* (2nd ed., pp. 1–40). Hillsdale, NJ: Erlbaum.

Bargh, J. A., & Ferguson, M. J. (2000). Beyond behaviorism: The automaticity of higher mental processes. *Psychological Bulletin, 126,* 925–945.

Bargh, J. A., & Gollwitzer, P. M. (1994). Environmental control over goal-directed action. *Nebraska Symposium on Motivation, 41*, 71–124.

Bargh, J. A., & Huang, J. Y. (2014). The evolutionary unconscious: From selfish genes to selfish goals. In J. Forgas & E. Harmon-Jones (Eds.), *Motivation and its regulation: The Sydney Symposium on Social Cognition* (pp. 35–54). Philadelphia: Taylor & Francis.

Bargh, J. A., & Morsella, E. (2008). The unconscious mind. *Perspectives on Psychological Science, 3*, 73–79.

Baumeister, R. F. (1996). *Evil: Inside human violence and cruelty.* New York: Freeman.

Baumeister, R. F., & Bargh, J. A. (2014). Conscious and unconscious: Toward an integrative understanding of human life and action. In J. Sherman (Ed.), *Dual-process theories of the social mind* (pp. 35–49). New York: Guilford Press.

Baumeister, R. F., & Masicampo, E. J. (2010). Conscious thought is for facilitating social and cultural interactions: How mental simulations serve the animal–culture interface. *Psychological Review, 117*, 945–971.

Bradley, G. W. (1978). Self-serving biases in the attribution process: A reexamination of the fact or fiction question. *Journal of Personality and Social Psychology, 36*, 56–71.

Brandstatter, V., Lengfelder, A., & Gollwitzer, P. M. (2001). Implementation intentions and efficient action initiation. *Journal of Personality and Social Psychology, 81*, 946–960.

Brill, A. A. (1938). Introduction. In A. A. Brill (Ed. & Trans.), *The basic writings of Sigmund Freud* (pp. 1–32). New York: Modern Library.

Chartrand, T. L., & Bargh, J. A. (1999). The chameleon effect: The perception–behavior link and social interaction. *Journal of Personality and Social Psychology, 76*, 893–910.

Chartrand. T. L., & Lakin, J. (2013). Antecedents and consequences of human behavioral mimicry. *Annual Review of Psychology, 64*, 285–308.

Chen, S., Lee-Chai, A. Y., & Bargh, J. A. (2001). Relationship orientation as a moderator of the effects of social power. *Journal of Personality and Social Psychology, 80*, 173–187.

Chomsky, N. (1959). A review of B. F. Skinner's *Verbal Behavior. Language, 35*, 26–58.

Cohn, A., Fehr, E., & Maréchal, M. A. (2015). Business culture and dishonesty in the banking industry. *Nature, 516*, 86–89.

Crabtree, A. (1993). *From Mesmer to Freud: Magnetic sleep and the roots of psychological healing.* New Haven, CT: Yale University Press.

Darwin, C. (1859). *The origin of species.* London: Collier.

Dawkins, R. (1976). *The selfish gene.* New York: Oxford University Press.

Dawkins, R. (1986). *The blind watchmaker.* New York: Freeman.

Deacon, T. W. (1997). *The symbolic species: The co-evolution of language and the brain.* New York: Norton.

Descartes, R. (1931). *The philosophical works of Descartes* (E. S. Haldane & G. R. T. Ross, Trans.). New York: Cambridge University Press. (Original work published 1641)

Dijksterhuis, A., & Aarts, H. (2010). Goals, attention and (un)consciousness. *Annual Review of Psychology, 61*, 467–490.

Freud, S. (1914). *Psychopathology of everyday life* (A. A. Brill, Trans.). London: T. Fisher Unwin. (Original work published 1901)

Gazzaniga, M. (1985). *The social brain*. New York: Free Press.

Gollwitzer, P. M. (1999). Implementation intentions: Strong effects of simple plans. *American Psychologist, 54*, 493–503.

Gross, J. J. (1998). The emerging field of emotion regulation: An integrative review. *Review of General Psychology, 2*, 271–299.

Hassin, R. R. (2013). Yes it can: On the functional abilities of the human unconscious. *Perspectives on Psychological Science, 8*, 195–207.

Higgins, E. T., & Bargh, J. A. (1992). Unconscious sources of subjectivity and suffering: Is consciousness the solution? In A. Tesser & L. Martin (Eds.), *The construction of social judgments* (pp. 67–110). Hillsdale, NJ: Erlbaum.

Inzlicht, M., Barthalow, B. D., & Hirsh, J. B. (2015). Emotional foundations of cognitive control. *Trends in Cognitive Science, 19*(3), 126–132.

Kahneman, D. (2011). *Thinking, fast and slow*. New York: Farrar, Straus & Giroux.

Kay, A. C., Gaucher, D., Napier, J. L., Callan, M. J., & Laurin, K. (2008). God and the government: Testing a compensatory control mechanism for the support of external systems. *Journal of Personality and Social Psychology, 95*, 18–35.

Kenrick, D. T., & Griskevicius, V. (2013). *The rational animal*. New York: Basic Books.

Keren, G., & Schul, Y. (2009). Two is not always better than one: A critical evaluation of two-system theories. *Perspectives on Psychological Science, 4*, 533–550.

Kershaw, I. (1998). *Hitler: Vol. 1. 1889–1936: Hubris*. New York: Norton.

Koestler, A. (1967). *The ghost in the machine*. London: Hutchinson

Loftus, E. F., & Klinger, M. R. (1992). Is the unconscious smart or dumb? *American Psychologist, 47*, 761–765.

Mercier, H., & Sperber, D. (2010). Why do humans reason?: Arguments for an argumentative theory. *Behavioral and Brain Sciences, 34*, 57–111.

Miller, G. A., Galanter, E., & Pribram, K. H. (1960). *Plans and the structure of behavior*. New York: Holt.

Mischel, W. (1997). Was the cognitive revolution just a detour on the road to behaviorism? On the need to reconcile situational control and personal control. In R. S. Wyer, Jr. (Ed.), *Advances in social cognition* (Vol. 10, pp. 181–186). Mahwah, NJ: Erlbaum.

Mischel, W. (2014). *The marshmallow test*. New York: Little, Brown.

Mischel, W., Cantor, N., & Feldman, S. (1996). Goal-directed self-regulation. In E. T. Higgins & A. W. Kruglanski (Eds.), *Social psychology: Handbook of basic principles* (pp. 329–360). New York: Guilford Press.

Morewedge, C. K., & Kahneman, D. (2010). Associative processes in intuitive judgment. *Trends in Cognitive Sciences, 14*, 435–440.

Neiman, S. (2002). *Evil in modern thought*. Princeton, NJ: Princeton University Press.

Neisser, U. (1967). *Cognitive psychology*. Englewood Cliffs, NJ: Prentice-Hall.

Neuberg, S. L., & Schaller, M. (2014) Evolutionary social cognition. In E. Borgida & J. Bargh (Eds.), *APA handbook of personality and social psychology* (Vol. 1, pp. 3–45). Washington, DC: American Psychological Association.

Nordgren, L. F., Bos, M. W., & Dijksterhuis, A. (2011). The best of both worlds:

Integrating conscious and unconscious thought best solves complex decisions. *Journal of Experimental Social Psychology, 47,* 509–511.

Peysakhovich, A., Nowak, M. A., & Rand, D. G. (2014). Humans display a "cooperative phenotype" that is domain general and temporally stable. *Nature Communications, 5.* Available at *www.nature.com/ncomms/2014/140916/ncomms5939/full/ncomms5939.html.*

Sheeran, P., & Orbell, S. (1999). Implementation intentions and repeated behaviors: Augmenting the predictive validity of the theory of planned behavior. *European Journal of Social Psychology, 29,* 349–370.

Skinner, B. F. (1957). *Verbal behavior.* Acton, MA: Copley.

Sober, E., & Wilson, D. S. (1998). *Unto others: The evolution and psychology of unselfish behavior.* Cambridge, MA: Harvard University Press.

Suhler, C. L., & Churchland, P. S. (2009). Control: Conscious and otherwise. *Trends in Cognitive Sciences, 13,* 341–347.

Taylor, S. E. (1989). *Positive illusions.* New York: Basic Books.

Uhlmann, E. L., Poehlman, T. A., & Bargh, J. A. (2008). Implicit theism. In R. Sorrentino & S. Yamaguchi (Eds.), *Handbook of motivation and cognition within and across cultures* (pp. 71–94). San Diego, CA: Academic Press.

Uhlmann, E. L., Poehlman, T. A., & Bargh, J. A. (2009). American moral exceptionalism. In J. Jost, A. Kay, & H. Thorisdottir (Eds.), *Social and psychological bases of ideology and system justification* (pp. 27–52). New York: Oxford University Press.

Watson, J. B. (1913). Psychology as the behaviorist views it. *Psychological Review, 20,* 158–177.

Wegner, D. M., & Wheatley, T. (1999). Apparent mental causation: Sources of the experience of will. *American Psychologist, 54,* 480–492.

Wilson, F. (1970). *The devil made me buy this dress* [LP]. Hollywood, CA: Little David Records.

Wood, W., & Ruenger, D. (2016). Psychology of habit. *Annual Review of Psychology, 67,* 280–314.

PART II

HARMING OTHERS
Contexts, Causes, and Implications

CHAPTER 6

Racism among the Well Intentioned
Bias without Awareness

John F. Dovidio, Samuel L. Gaertner,
and Adam R. Pearson

Blatant expressions of bias continue to have a significant negative impact on the well-being of black Americans, but overt prejudice has substantially declined in the United States. Public opinion polls have revealed significant decreases in expressions of prejudice by white Americans toward minority groups, and toward blacks in particular (Bobo, 2001). Indeed, many have argued that Barack Obama's election as President of the United States is evidence that racism is "a thing of the past" and that America is currently a "postracial" society. However, race still matters in the United States. Significant racial and ethnic disparities persist in health (National Center for Health Statistics, 2012), in income and wealth (Shapiro, Meschede, & Osoro, 2013), and in opportunities for social advancement (Reeves, 2013), generally at a magnitude comparable to that at the time Obama first assumed office.

In his influential book *Racism without Racists*, Bonilla-Silva (2003) argued that new forms of racism may be less overt but just as insidious as old-fashioned racism. Whereas Bonilla-Silva (see also Bonilla-Silva & Dietrich, 2011) emphasizes institutional and cultural manifestations of color-blind racism, biases within individuals form the foundation for the perpetuation of societal disparities. In this chapter, we examine how aversive racism, a form of individual-level prejudice characterizing the thoughts, feelings, and behaviors of the majority of well-intentioned and ostensibly nonprejudiced white Americans, contribute to the perpetuation of unfair racial disparities in the United States (Dovidio & Gaertner, 2004; Gaertner & Dovidio, 1986). Although we focus on race relations within the United States, we note that similar processes have been observed among members of advantaged and disadvantaged groups in other nations, such as Canada (Son Hing, Chung-Yan, Hamilton, & Zanna, 2008), Portugal (De Franca & Monteiro, 2013), and the Netherlands (Kleinpenning & Hagendoorn, 1993), in which overt forms of prejudice are similarly recognized as inappropriate. We illustrate how good and well-intentioned people can contribute systematically to maintaining and reinforcing disadvantage in society.

We begin by describing the psychological underpinnings of aversive racism and then demonstrating its consequences for whites' treatment of blacks, the quality and nature of interracial interactions, and race relations more generally. We then consider how social policies that promote color-blindness can perpetuate subtle biases and discrimination by obscuring the role of race in these outcomes. Specifically, we explain how emphasizing color-blindness and commonalities between members of different groups that seemingly help promote positive intergroup relations can reinforce biases and hierarchical relations between blacks and whites. After that, we discuss the potential ways that aversive racism and color-blindness can operate in complementary and mutually reinforcing ways to perpetuate bias without awareness. We conclude by reviewing promising strategies and interventions, at the individual and societal level, to combat nonconscious forms of bias.

CONTEMPORARY RACIAL ATTITUDES AND AVERSIVE RACISM

Research from the 1920s through the 1950s typically portrayed prejudice as a psychopathology (Dovidio & Gaertner, 2004). For example, the classic work on the authoritarian personality (Adorno, Frenkel-Brunswik, Levinson, & Sanford, 1950) described negative socialization experiences (e.g., involving excessively strict parental influence) that produced a general tendency to be biased against low-status groups in ways that could erupt into aggression and large-scale violence. Other researchers discussed how low levels of self-esteem promote prejudice and how threats to one's well-being arouse negative actions toward negatively valued groups, even when such groups do not contribute to the threat (i.e., scapegoating).

However, stimulated by developments in the area of social cognition, by the mid-1960s and early 1970s much more attention was devoted to examining how *normal*, often adaptive, cognitive (e.g., social categorization), motivational (e.g., needs for status), and sociocultural (e.g., social transmission of beliefs) processes can contribute to the development of whites' biases toward blacks (see Dovidio & Gaertner, 2004). Because racial distinctions between whites and blacks have played a central role in U.S. history, social categorization by race within the United States is largely automatic: The actual or imagined presence of a black person is often enough to automatically activate racial categories without conscious effort or control (Dovidio & Gaertner, 2004). Social categorization spontaneously activates more positive feelings and beliefs about ingroup members ("us") than outgroup members ("them"; see Gaertner & Dovidio, 2012, for a review). Moreover, thinking of groups in this way spontaneously arouses motivations (e.g., for competition: us vs. them) to demonstrate or establish the superiority of one's group over others (Tajfel & Turner, 1979). In addition, intergroup processes such as system-justifying ideologies, as well as perceived competition over material resources, can also form a basis for negative racial attitudes (see Sidanius & Pratto, 1999).

At the same time, principles of egalitarianism and "justice for all"—core American values—are stronger today than ever before. As Bobo (2001) concluded in his review of U.S. racial attitudes, "The single clearest trend in studies of racial attitudes has involved a steady and sweeping movement toward general endorsement of the principles of racial equality and integration" (p. 269). This tension between a deep commitment to egalitarianism and often nonconscious negative feelings and beliefs that are byproducts of sociocultural influences (such as negative media portrayals of blacks) and social categorization processes (which promote intergroup competition and attempts to establish the superiority of one's group) is at the core of aversive racism.

In 1970, Kovel first distinguished between dominative and aversive racism. Dominative racism is said to reflect the traditional, blatant form. According to Kovel (1970), the dominative racist is the "type who acts out bigoted beliefs—he represents the open flame of racial hatred" (p. 54). Aversive racists, in contrast, sympathize with victims of past injustice, support principles of racial equality, and genuinely regard themselves as nonprejudiced, but at the same time possess conflicting, often nonconscious, negative feelings and beliefs about blacks that are rooted in basic psychological processes. The negative feelings that aversive racists have toward blacks typically do not reflect open antipathy but rather consist of more avoidant reactions of discomfort, anxiety, or fear. That is, they find blacks "aversive," while at the same time find any suggestion that they might be prejudiced "aversive" as well.

Other frameworks for understanding contemporary racial bias, such as *modern racism* (McConahay, 1986), and *symbolic racism* (Sears, Henry, & Kosterman, 2000), also hypothesize a fundamental conflict between the denial of personal prejudice and underlying unconscious negative feelings and beliefs. However, whereas modern and symbolic racism characterize the attitudes of political conservatives, aversive racism characterizes the biases of those who are politically liberal and openly endorse egalitarian views but whose unconscious negative feelings and beliefs are expressed in subtle, indirect, and often rationalizable ways (Dovidio & Gaertner, 2004; Nail, Harton, & Decker, 2003).

Aversive racists are characterized as having egalitarian conscious, or explicit, attitudes but negative unconscious, or implicit, racial attitudes (Dovidio & Gaertner, 2004). Methodological techniques for assessing implicit attitudes have become increasingly useful for differentiating aversive racists (those who endorse egalitarian values but harbor implicit racial biases) from individuals who are truly nonprejudiced (those who endorse egalitarian ideals but do not harbor negative implicit biases; see Son Hing, Chung-Yan, Grunfeld, Robichaud, & Zanna, 2005). Implicit attitudes are typically assessed using response latency procedures (the Implicit Association Test, or IAT; Greenwald, Poehlman, Uhlmann, & Banaji, 2009), memory tasks, physiological measures (e.g., heart rate and galvanic skin response), and indirect self-report measures (e.g., biases in behavioral and trait attributions). Whereas a majority of whites in the United States appear nonprejudiced on self-report (explicit) measures of prejudice, a similar percentage of whites typically show evidence of racial biases on implicit measures that are largely dissociated from their explicit views (Greenwald et al., 2009). For example, although most whites now explicitly disavow negative stereotypes of blacks, most white Americans implicitly and automatically activate stereotypes of whites as intelligent, successful, and educated, and of blacks as aggressive, impulsive, and lazy in response to the mere image or presence of a member of that racial group (Blair, 2001). Thus a substantial proportion of whites in the United States can be characterized as exhibiting reactions toward blacks consistent with aversive racism.

Although people may not be fully aware of their implicit prejudice and stereotypes, these biases can have profound effects on behavior. For instance, because of generally cultural associations of blacks with crime and violence, whites tend to misperceive harmless objects (e.g., a wallet or comb) as a weapon (e.g., a gun). As a consequence, in simulations in which they have to make decisions in the role of a police officer to shoot or not shoot a suspect, they are more likely to erroneously shoot a black than a white suspect holding a harmless object. Moreover, this effect is more pronounced among individuals higher in implicit bias (Payne, 2006). Because extensive training in this context can reduce the impact of race in erroneous decisions to shoot, police officers tend to display less of this bias than do college students or community members (although they still show some evidence of bias; Correll et al., 2007; Plant & Peruche, 2005), unless their duties (e.g., as special unit officers who routinely deal with minority gang members) tend to reinforce associations between blacks and violence

(Sim, Correll, & Sadler, 2013). Thus bias, even if unconscious, can have profound social consequences.

CONSEQUENCES OF AVERSIVE RACISM

In contrast to more traditional forms of racism, which are blatant and expressed openly and directly, aversive racism operates in more subtle and indirect ways. Specifically, whereas blatant racists exhibit a direct and overt pattern of discrimination, aversive racists' actions appear more variable and inconsistent: Sometimes they discriminate (manifesting their negative feelings), and sometimes they do not (reflecting their egalitarian beliefs). Nevertheless, their behavior is predictable.

Because aversive racists consciously recognize and endorse egalitarian values and truly aspire to be nonprejudiced, they will *not* act inappropriately in situations with strong social norms when discrimination would be obvious to others and to themselves. Specifically, when they are presented with a situation in which the normative response is clear (e.g., right and wrong are clearly defined), aversive racists will not discriminate against blacks. In these contexts, aversive racists will be especially motivated to avoid feelings, beliefs, and behaviors that could be associated with racist intent. However, the nonconscious feelings and beliefs that aversive racists also possess will produce discrimination in situations in which normative structure is weak, when the guidelines for appropriate behavior are unclear, when the basis for social judgment is vague, or when one's actions can be justified or rationalized on the basis of some factor other than race. Under these circumstances, aversive racists may engage in behaviors that ultimately harm blacks but in ways that allow whites to maintain a nonprejudiced self-image and insulate them from recognizing that their behavior is not color-blind.

Support for the aversive racism framework has been obtained across a broad range of experimental paradigms and participant populations, including emergency and nonemergency helping behavior inside and outside of the laboratory, selection decisions in employment and college admission, interpersonal judgments, and policy and legal decisions (see Dovidio & Gaertner, 2004; Knight, Guiliano, & Sanchez-Ross, 2001; Sommers & Ellsworth, 2000). For example, Dovidio and Gaertner (2000) examined white college students' support for hiring black and white applicants for a selective campus position within the same college in the years 1989 and 1999. When the candidates' credentials clearly qualified or disqualified them for the position, there was no discrimination against the black candidate (i.e., the highly qualified black candidate was just as likely to be hired as the highly qualified white candidate). However, when candidates' qualifications for the position were less obvious and the appropriate decision was more ambiguous (moderate qualifications), white participants recommended a black candidate significantly less often than a white candidate with exactly the same credentials. Whereas overt expressions of prejudice (measured by items on a self-report scale) declined over this 10-year period, the pattern of subtle discrimination in selection decisions remained essentially unchanged.

Additional research offers further insight into processes that underlie these effects. When ambiguous or mixed credentials are involved, people systematically weigh credentials differently based on their unconscious biases. For example, when providing input to college admission decisions for candidates with mixed credentials (e.g., strong high school grades but modest standardized scores, or vice versa), white college students emphasized the credential that white candidates were stronger in, relative to black candidates, as being the more valid predictor of success in college. This differential weighting of the credentials, in turn, justified students' stronger recommendations of white than black candidates for admission (Hodson, Dovidio, & Gaertner, 2002; see also Brief, Dietz, Cohen, Pugh, and Vaslow, 2000, for employment bias against blacks; Rooth, 2007, for hiring biases against Muslims).

In general, explicit attitudes, which are consciously endorsed, shape deliberative, well-considered responses in which the costs and benefits of various courses of action are weighed. By contrast, implicit attitudes, which are automatically activated, often without awareness, typically influence spontaneous actions or behaviors that people are not aware of as expressions of bias (e.g., decisions that can be justified on the basis of some factor other than race, or less controllable responses, such as averting one's gaze or appearing unduly anxious in the presence of a black person).

Consistent with this distinction and paralleling the findings of subtle bias against blacks in the United States, a study by Son Hing et al. (2008) with a Canadian sample found that when assessing candidates with more moderate qualifications, evaluators recommended white candidates more strongly for a position than Asian candidates with identical credentials. However, when evaluating candidates with exceptionally strong qualifications, no such selection bias emerged. Moreover, the researchers found that implicit bias against Asians (as measured by an IAT), but not explicit prejudice, predicted weaker support for hiring Asian candidates who had moderate qualifications. However, when the Asian candidate had distinctively strong qualifications, neither implicit nor explicit prejudice predicted the hiring decision. Divergent effects of implicit and explicit racial attitudes can also fuel divergent perspectives and experiences of blacks and whites in interracial interactions. For example, Dovidio, Kawakami, and Gaertner (2002) demonstrated that whereas whites' explicit (self-reported) racial attitudes predicted their relatively controllable verbal expressions in their interactions with blacks, whites' implicit attitudes, which were generally negative, predicted their nonverbal behaviors (e.g., looking less directly at their black interaction partners). Moreover, black interaction partners weighed the nonverbal behavior more heavily than the verbal behavior in their impressions of the white partner and the interaction. Thus whites and blacks had divergent perspectives in their interactions, and blacks' awareness of conflicting positive verbal behavior (e.g., politeness) and negative nonverbal behavior (averted gaze; cues of discomfort, such as higher rates of blinking) undermined how trustworthy they saw the white interaction partner. In general, blacks are sensitive to a range of nonverbal behaviors as cues of whites' racial bias. These cues include standing or sitting at a greater than normal distance, less direct posture, speaking quickly with disfluencies (e.g., "um"), less direct and sustained looking, and tense rather than relaxed posture and gestures.

The dynamics associated with implicit biases can ultimately have a substantial impact on the health and well-being of blacks. White physicians generally see themselves as nonprejudiced and color-blind (Epstein, 2005; Sabin, Rivara, & Greenwald, 2008), but they also harbor negative implicit racial biases toward blacks (Sabin, Nosek, Greenwald, & Rivara, 2009; Sabin et al., 2008). Physicians' implicit biases predict medical recommendations, including lower quality of coronary care for black patients (Green et al., 2007) and less willingness to prescribe narcotics to ease the pain of black patients (Sabin & Greenwald, 2012), in ways independent of explicit racial bias. Moreover, consistent with research on the influence of implicit racial bias in social interactions (Dovidio et al., 2002), doctors higher in implicit bias speak faster to and have shorter visits with black patients (Cooper et al., 2012), and they display less warmth in their medical interactions (Penner et al., 2010). Overall, physicians higher in implicit bias are less patient-centered in their care of black patients (Blair et al., 2013; Cooper et al., 2012).

Black patients' responses to these interactions directly relate to doctors' implicit biases. Following their interactions, black patients have less respect for, confidence in, and trust in the advice of medical professionals higher in implicit bias (Cooper et al., 2012). This distrust predicts lower levels of adherence to the doctor's prescriptions and recommendations, which ultimately adversely affects health. Thus, even among highly educated individuals in helping professions, who are deeply committed to the welfare of patients and espouse nonprejudiced views, implicit biases produce systematic disparities in health care and, ultimately, contribute to racial disparities in health.

COLOR-BLIND INCLUSIVENESS

The challenge of combating unconscious biases is that people are often not aware that they possess these biases, and, when they consciously monitor their behavior, their actions reinforce their egalitarian self-image. How, then, can the effects of unconscious biases be addressed? One technique has targeted a core process at the psychological root of the problem: social categorization. The process of categorizing people into groups automatically activates stereotypes and biases toward members of those groups and increases affinity to members of one's ingroup. The principle behind the common ingroup identity model (Gaertner & Dovidio, 2012) is that inducing people to recategorize ingroup and outgroup members within a common group (a one-group representation based, for example, on common school, organization, or national identity) can redirect the motivational and cognitive processes that produce ingroup favoritism to include former outgroup members. The common ingroup identity model for improving intergroup attitudes has received considerable empirical support internationally (see Gaertner & Dovidio, 2012).

An important variant of a common ingroup identity that may be viewed as less threatening and more inclusive by members of disadvantaged groups is the development of a common identity that also includes aspects of a subgroup identity. Indeed, individuals may activate two (or more) of their multiple social identities simultaneously (Roccas & Brewer, 2002) or sequentially (Abrams & Hogg, 2010)—a dual identity. For example, people can conceive of two groups (e.g., science and art majors) as distinct units within the context of a superordinate social entity (e.g., university students).

Although both forms of recategorization, substituting separate group identities with a common ingroup identity or creating dual identities, can produce more positive intergroup attitudes (see Gaertner & Dovidio, 2012, for a review), we illustrate how there can be a "darker side" of intergroup harmony achieved solely by emphasizing a common identity. Creating a sense of common identity can deflect attention away from group-based disparities, reducing the likelihood that members of high-status groups perceive social injustice, and can promote a feeling of harmony and optimism that undermines collective action by members of low-status groups. Moreover, recategorization in the form of a single common ingroup identity (vs. a dual identity), relating directly to the concept of color-blind racism (Bonilla-Silva, 2003), may be a strategy employed by members of a majority group to reinforce the status quo that benefits their group.

In the next two sections, we examine (1) differences in preferences of members of high-status and low-status groups for different representations (one group or dual identity) and associated cultural ideologies (color-blind or multicultural), and (2) how a one-group representation can improve attitudes but undermine action to achieve social equality.

Group Status and Preferences for Common Identity versus Dual Identity

In his classic acculturation framework, Berry (1997; see also Sam & Berry, 2010) presents four forms of cultural relations in pluralistic societies that represent the intersection of "yes–no" responses to two relevant questions: (1) Are cultural identity and customs of value to be retained? and (2) are positive relations with the larger society of value, and to be sought? These combinations reflect four adaptation strategies for intergroup relations: (1) *integration*, in which cultural identities are retained and positive relations with the larger society are sought; (2) *separatism*, in which cultural identities are retained but positive relations with the larger society are not sought; (3) *assimilation*, in which cultural identities are abandoned and positive relations with the larger society are desired; and (4) *marginalization*, in which cultural identities are abandoned and are not replaced by positive identification with the larger society.

Although this framework has been applied primarily to the ways in which immigrants acclimate to a new society, it can be adapted to apply to intergroup relations between high-status and low-status groups generally. Substituting the separate strengths of the subgroup and subordinate group identities for the answers to Berry's (1997) two questions, the combinations map onto the four main representations considered in the common ingroup identity model: (1) *dual identity* (subgroup and superordinate group identities are high, representing a form of integration); (2) *separate groups* (subgroup identity is high and superordinate identity is low, reflecting separatism); (3) *one group* (subgroup identity is low and superordinate group identity is high, similar to assimilation); and (4) *separate individuals* (subgroup and superordinate group identities are low, as with marginalization).

Two of the ideologies that have received the most attention in the study of intergroup relations are assimilation, which involves a form of common identity, and integration in terms of multiculturalism, which reflects a dual identity. Whereas assimilation requires minority-group members to conform to dominant values and ideals, often requiring the abandonment of racial or ethnic group values, multicultural integration, by contrast, strives to be inclusive by recognizing, and even celebrating, group differences and the unique contributions of different groups to society.

Research in the area of immigration suggests that members of the host society (the high-status group) and immigrant groups (low-status groups) often have different preferences for assimilation and multicultural integration. For example, Verkuyten (2006) summarized the results of eight studies of adolescents and young adults in Europe, consistently finding that minority group members supported multiculturalism (integration) more than did majority group members (see also Verkuyten & Martinovic, 2012). These preferences also apply to the preferences of whites and racial and ethnic minorities. In the United States, whites prefer assimilation, whereas racial and ethnic minorities favor multiculturalism (Ryan, Hunt, Weible, Peterson, & Casas, 2007).

In intergroup interactions, members of high-status and low-status groups are often motivated to shape discourse in ways that emphasize their preferred representation. Across two studies, one with laboratory groups varying in control over a valued resource (credits for experimental participation) and the other with ethnic groups varying in status in Israel (Ashkenazim, high status; Mizrahim, low status), Saguy, Dovidio, and Pratto (2008) found that whereas members of high-status groups preferred discourse that focused virtually exclusively on commonality rather than on group differences, members of low-status groups showed equivalently strong preferences for talking about commonality *and* difference (the two critical elements of a dual identity). Moreover, low-status group members' greater desire to discuss points of difference, relative to that of high-status group members, occurred because they had a greater motivation for a change in the power structure.

These different preferences for members of high- and low-status groups appear to be strategic perspectives that promote the interests of one's group. Hehman et al. (2012) studied the preferences of whites and blacks at two public universities in the United States, one a state college in which whites represent the majority (85%) of the student body and one a historically black college in which blacks are the majority (76%). This contextual status significantly affected identity preferences. White students showed a much stronger preference for multiculturalism when they were in the institutional minority than in the majority; black students exhibited stronger endorsement of assimilation when they were the majority than when they were the minority.

In summary, members of high-status groups, who are motivated to maintain the status quo, show a preference for focusing on commonalities to the exclusion of differences and greater support for assimilation over multiculturalism. Members of low-status groups, who desire to alter the status quo to improve their group's position, exhibit both a desire to discuss commonalities between groups and to talk about differences and show greater endorsement of multiculturalism compared with assimilation.

Thus far we have discussed the different preferences of members of high-status (or majority) and low-status (or minority) groups for different group representations and ideologies, as well as the conditions and goals that moderate these preferences. Next, we examine the possibility that factors that promote common identity (e.g., positive intergroup contact), assimilation, or color-blindness may undermine the motivation of both high- and low-status group members to engage in collective action to address inequality.

The Irony of Harmony

As we noted earlier, the subtle nature of contemporary bias typically limits recognition of unfair treatment. Subtle bias is more difficult to detect and respond to than blatant bias, even for low-status group members (Ellemers & Barreto, 2009), and high-status group members are less attuned to cues of subtle discrimination than are members of low-status groups (Salvatore & Shelton, 2007). Thus focusing only on commonalities between groups may decrease the likelihood that high-status group members will recognize and respond to injustice, and particularly subtle biases, against minority-group members (see Saguy & Chernyak-Hai, 2012).

We (Banfield & Dovidio, 2013) examined this issue in a study in which white participants in the United States were exposed to a manipulation that emphasized (1) common-group (American) identity of blacks and whites, (2) separate racial-group memberships, or (3) a control condition that did not emphasize identities. Participants then read a hiring scenario that involved either subtle or blatant discrimination, in which a black candidate was not offered a job (Salvatore & Shelton, 2007). The outcomes of interest were perceptions of discrimination and expressions of willingness to protest on behalf of the applicant who was denied the job.

Because emphasizing only common ingroup identity can distract people from attending to race-based differences, when the bias witnessed was subtle, white participants for whom common identity was emphasized perceived lower levels of racial bias than those for whom separate identities were emphasized and those in a control condition, and these perceptions mediated less willingness to protest a negative outcome for a black person who was disadvantaged. That is, thinking primarily about Americans as just one group makes it easier to overlook, perceptually and behaviorally, race-based bias that is not obvious or overt. By contrast, when discrimination was blatant, emphasizing a common identity produced greater perceptions of bias and moderately more willingness to engage in collective action.

In another set of studies, we investigated the effects of commonality frames on the perceptions and responses of members of low-status disadvantaged groups. In a laboratory study (Saguy, Tausch, Dovidio, & Pratto, 2009, Study 1), power was manipulated between two randomly assigned groups by giving the high-status group the position of assigning extra course credits to the two groups (see Saguy et al., 2008). Before the members of the high-status group allocated the credits, members of both the high-status and low-status groups interacted, with instructions that prompted them to focus on either intergroup commonalities or differences.

As expected, commonality-focused interaction produced more positive intergroup attitudes for high-status and low-status group members than did difference-focused contact. In addition, for both groups, attention to inequality between groups was lower in the commonality-focused condition. Moreover, members of the low-status group expected the high-status group to be fairer in allocating the resources and to distribute the credits in a more equitable fashion following commonality-focused, rather than differences-focused, interaction. These effects were mediated by more positive intergroup attitudes and decreased attention to inequity during the interaction.

However, when the low-status group members' expectations were compared with the high-status group's actual allocation, there was a significant discrepancy. As the members of the low-status groups anticipated, high-status groups were substantially biased against the low-status groups in the allocation of credits after differences-focused contact; but, unexpectedly from the perspective of low-status group members, high-status groups were just as biased in allocating the credits after commonality-focused interaction. The more positive intergroup attitudes of high-status group members in the commonality-focused versus differences-focused condition did not translate into more material support to achieve equality, and the high-status group's allocation fell significantly below what low-status groups anticipated. These findings, therefore, indicate that focusing on what different groups have in common effectively improves the attitudes of members of high-status groups toward low-status groups and promotes feelings of intergroup harmony, which is a primary goal for members of high-status groups in interaction with members of low-status groups (Bergsieker, Shelton, & Richeson, 2010). However, perhaps because their main goal to achieve harmony has been satisfied, the improved attitudes of members of high-status groups do not necessarily translate into fairer treatment. Harmony has been established without requiring them to give up their privilege or resources. This relaxed motivation to provide the low-status group with the resources they need to achieve true equality reflects the darker side of harmony achieved through common identity.

Another study investigated these processes in a naturalistic intergroup context. A study of Arabs in Israel (Saguy et al., 2009, Study 2) examined correlations among friendships with Jews (a type of positive contact that is particularly likely to involve a focus on commonalities), attitudes toward Jews, awareness of inequality, and perceptions of Jews as fair. It further measured Arabs' support for social change toward equality. Saguy and colleagues hypothesized that, because more positive connections with Jews would produce less attention to illegitimate aspects in the inequality between Arabs and Jews in Israel, more positive intergroup contact would relate to *weaker* support for social action for change among Arabs.

Consistent with the results of the laboratory experiment, more positive contact with Jews was associated with more positive attitudes toward Jews and with reduced awareness of inequality between Jews and Arabs. In addition, improved attitudes were associated with increased perceptions of Jews as fair. Moreover, and consistent with our theorizing, both perceptions of Jews as fair and reduced awareness of inequality were associated with reduced support for social change, including less willingness to engage personally in political activities to improve the social and economic opportunities for their group. Thus, through its effects on the way low-status group members viewed social inequality and members of the other group, positive contact was associated with a *decrease* in support for social change.

In summary, the subtlety of contemporary bias makes it particularly likely that unfair disadvantage will be overlooked or dismissed when there is a focus on common identity (or, relatedly, assimilation or color-blindness). Focusing on only a common identity distracts attention away from group-based disparities (see also Neville, Awad, Brooks, Flores, & Bluemel, 2013), and when disparities are detected by members of low-status groups, feelings of common identity can reduce motivation to take action because of greater trust in the system (e.g., Kay et al., 2009). Nevertheless, when members of high-status groups recognize that the disadvantage of low-status groups is unfair, they can be genuinely motivated to restore equity (Saguy et al., 2008, Study 2).

COLOR-BLINDNESS, SUBTLE BIAS, AND THE PERPETUATION OF DISADVANTAGE

Our focus, thus far, has been on processes that perpetuate racial bias among whites in its contemporary form, in terms of whites' assessments, decisions, and interactions. This bias is typically exhibited in subtle ways, often cloaked by a commitment to color-blindness at a personal and societal level. These individual- and institutional-level processes can operate in reciprocal and mutually reinforcing ways. At the individual level, to maintain an egalitarian self-image, aversive racists are motivated to emphasize factors other than race to justify negative intergroup actions (e.g., discrimination). At a societal level, whites endorse a color-blind perspective in social and institutional policies (e.g., organizational practices; Plaut, Thomas, & Goren, 2009); denying racial differences insulates whites from perceiving their actions as racially motivated.

In general, because they are typically sincerely committed to behaving in a moral and fair manner, whites are usually motivated to avoid seeing themselves as biased. However, efforts to be unbiased can sometimes produce "rebound effects," causing biases to become activated even more. Because suppressing unwanted thoughts is cognitively taxing, implicit biases, which are automatically and effortlessly activated, may exert a particularly strong effect (the rebound effect) when people are cognitively fatigued or relax their efforts to control their biases. Indeed, Uhlmann and Cohen (2005) found that participants who were more confident in the objectivity of their judgments were also more likely to discriminate against equally qualified female candidates for a stereotypically male job (chief of police), inflating criteria that favored male over female candidates. Normally, this form of bias occurs without conscious awareness; indeed, making people aware of their subtle bias usually distresses them and motivates compensatory efforts to address the immediate injustice. However, the subtle nature of this bias—emphasizing criteria that justifies, for oneself and to others, that the decision is appropriate and fair—reduces the likelihood that the selection process was systematically discriminatory.

Moreover, the act of affirming a nonprejudiced self-image can, ironically, further increase the likelihood that even ostensibly nonprejudiced individuals will discriminate. Monin and Miller (2001) found that, when given the opportunity to disagree with a prejudicial statement (and thus affirm a nonprejudiced self-image), individuals were *more* likely to discriminate against women or a racial minority group when making a subsequent hiring decision. The authors reasoned that the opportunity to reinforce one's egalitarian image (even when done privately) gave participants a "license" to act in a discriminatory manner (see also Effron, Cameron, & Monin, 2009). As Monin and Miller explain, this license allows people to engage in subtle discrimination because demonstrating their egalitarianism in one context subsequently allows them to dismiss personal bias as an explanation for their current or future behavior.

At an institutional level, a dominant color-blind ideology exerts a cultural influence that can affect the thoughts and actions of minority-group, as well as majority-group, members in ways that perpetuate disadvantage. Bonilla-Silva and Dietrich (2011) observed that "the ideology of color-blindness is increasingly affecting even those who are at or near the bottom of the economic and social hierarchies in the United States: blacks and Latinos" (p. 195). A social psychological approach offers a complementary perspective to Bonilla-Silva's (2003) structural approach (see also Bonilla-Silva & Dietrich, 2011), which emphasizes the role of policies and cultural standards independent of the intentions or actions of a given individual, by identifying psychological mechanisms and propensities that may underlie the enactment of individual actions that enforce and transmit these cultural frames. Specifically, social psychological research has revealed a tendency to perceive prevailing hierarchies and disparities as what "should" be (Kay et al., 2009), as well as a general motivation to preserve the status quo, even at a high cost to one's group (see system justification theory; Jost, Banaji, & Nosek, 2004; Jost, Federico, & Napier, 2013).

These psychological processes can help to explain why members of disadvantaged groups may endorse color-blind racism. In one study (Kay et al., 2009, Study 3), female Canadian participants read a brief description of the responsibilities of Canadian members of Parliament, accompanied by a graph showing that only 20% of the members of Parliament were women. As hypothesized, women who were led to believe that they were more highly dependent on the government were more likely to defend the status quo. These women were less likely than those who believed that they were low in dependency to endorse statements that there should be more women in politics and in Parliament. From their perspective, having women account for only 20% of the members of Parliament was fair and acceptable. Women were highly motivated to preserve the status quo, even at a high cost to themselves and fellow group members. In a subsequent study (Kay et al., 2009, Study 4), women who felt more dependent on the current social system, and thus more motivated to justify the system, actively derogated a woman whose ambitions in business threatened the status quo of gender relations. These processes may help members of disadvantaged groups cope with their situation, at least in the short term, by preserving a sense of justice, while shaping their behavior in the longer term in ways that reinforce the low social status of their group.

ADDRESSING BIASES AMONG THE WELL-INTENTIONED

Thus far, we have considered how biases that operate at both the individual and societal levels (e.g., color blindness) can contribute to group-based inequities and disadvantage. In this section we explain how subtle biases can be addressed effectively by strategic interventions. Indeed, because aversive racists are well intentioned and because color blindness may often be motivated by egalitarian intentions, illuminating the cognitive and motivational processes that contribute to subtle biases is a critical step in combating their effects.

Prejudice-reduction techniques have traditionally been concerned with changing conscious attitudes (overt racism); however, because of its subtlety and complexity, conventional interventions and practices for eliminating racial bias are often ineffective for combating aversive racism. Nevertheless, to the extent that implicit attitudes and stereotypes are learned through socialization (Karpinski & Hilton, 2001), they can also be unlearned or inhibited by well-learned countervailing influences (Lai, Hoffman, & Nosek, 2013; Lai et al., 2014).

Individual-Level Interventions

As described earlier, aversive racism is characterized by conscious (explicit) egalitarian attitudes and negative unconscious (implicit) attitudes and beliefs. To the extent that aversive racists are made aware of their nonconscious biases, it may thus be possible to recruit their conscious egalitarian values to help control or compensate for the potential effects of implicit bias. Son Hing, Li, and Zanna (2002) tested this possibility by examining responses of people identified as aversive racists (low in explicit prejudice but high in implicit prejudice) to self-awareness of their own hypocrisy. In a study conducted in Canada with Asians as the target minority group, participants were assigned to either a hypocrisy condition, in which they reflected on situations in which they had reacted negatively or unfairly toward an Asian person, or to a control condition in which they were not asked to write about such situations. The researchers predicted that making people aware of violations of their egalitarian principles would arouse more guilt among aversive racists (who harbor negative feelings toward Asians) than among people who were nonprejudiced (low in both explicit and implicit prejudice) and thus produce compensatory behavior among aversive racists but not among nonprejudiced participants when recommending funding for Asian student groups.

The results supported the predictions. Aversive racists in the hypocrisy condition experienced uniquely high levels of guilt and displayed the most generous funding recommendations for the Asian Students' Association. The funding recommendations of truly low-prejudice participants, however, were not affected by the hypocrisy manipulation. Son Hing et al. (2002) concluded that making people aware of their biases is particularly effective at reducing bias among people who explicitly endorse egalitarian principles while also possessing implicit biases—aversive racists.

Similarly, work by Monteith and colleagues (see Monteith, Arthur, & Flynn, 2010, for a review) also reveals that when people low in explicit prejudice recognize discrepancies between their behavior toward minorities (i.e., what they *would* do) and their personal standards (i.e., what they *should* do), they feel guilt and compunction, which motivates them to respond without prejudice in the future. With practice, these individuals learn to reduce prejudicial responses and to respond in ways that are consistent with their nonprejudiced personal standards. Over time, this process of self-regulation can produce sustained changes in even automatic negative responses. For example, extended practice can create *implicit* motivations to control prejudice, which can inhibit the activation of spontaneous racial biases (Park, Glaser, & Knowles, 2008). Moreover, Moskowitz and colleagues (see Moskowitz & Ignarri, 2009, for a review) found that interventions that enhance motivations to be egalitarian (e.g., having participants describe a personal incident in which they failed to be egalitarian toward African Americans) can not only attenuate but actively *inhibit* nonconscious stereotyping.

Research on nonconscious goal pursuit suggests additional ways to address implicit bias. For example, work by Aarts, Gollwitzer, and Hassin (2004) on goal contagion reveals that goals such as motivations not to be prejudiced can become automatically activated simply in the presence of egalitarian-minded others, suggesting the importance for controlling automatic biases of observing others' egalitarian behavior and egalitarian social norms more generally. Other research reveals that some goals that may not seem directly relevant to egalitarianism but that can interfere with the processes contributing to bias may be effective in combating implicit bias. Sassenberg and Moskowitz (2005), for example, showed that priming creativity (a goal that conflicts with the energy-saving and simplifying features of stereotyping) also reduced stereotype activation, suggesting that any goal that is incompatible with stereotyping (in this case, the goal to form atypical associations) may contribute to successful bias control. Thus, the fact that implicit biases may be activated automatically, and often without awareness, among people who believe that they are egalitarian does not mean that implicit bias is inevitable or immutable. However, simply becoming aware of one's implicit bias is not enough; assuming responsibility for addressing this bias is a necessary step. Understanding the psychological dynamics of aversive racism can thus help guide effective interventions for combating subtle bias.

Cultural Frame Interventions

Successfully addressing group-based disparities also requires being conscious of subgroup identities. As we illustrated earlier, emphasizing only the common ingroup identity of Americans in a way that distracts attention from socially relevant racial identities, such as black Americans or white Americans, reduces sensitivity to race-based bias and efforts to address this bias (Banfield & Dovidio, 2013). By contrast, acknowledging both common (American) and racial subgroup (black, white American) identities facilitates recognition of group-based disparities and differences but in a context of interdependence and positive connection. Specifically, a common, inclusive identity helps people view differences between groups as complementary resources that can benefit all. In addition, when both common and subgroup identities are simultaneously salient, unfair treatment of one subgroup is seen as a threat to the integrity of the larger group, motivating both dominant and nondominant group members to restore justice (Tyler & Blader, 2003).

From the perspective of members of high-status groups, recognition of a subgroup identity (as in multiculturalism) conveys greater respect for their group than focusing only on a common identity and thus satisfies a basic need of low-status group members in intergroup relations (Bergsieker et al., 2010; Shnabel, Nadler, Canetti-Nisim, & Ullrich, 2008). These feelings of respect, along with the sense of belonging and inclusion conveyed by common ingroup identity, can both improve intergroup attitudes and empower members of low-status groups. For example, in a study of racial/ethnic minority-group members in the United States, Glasford and Dovidio (2011) found that emphasizing multicultural values within a shared American identity (a dual identity), compared with assimilation within a common American identity, generally elicited more positive attitudes. The condition emphasizing dual identity, relative to common identity, also produced greater willingness to engage in contact while maintaining a strong motivation for social change toward equality. Relative to a common identity, a dual identity elicited stronger feelings of shared values and optimism about future relations, which mediated greater interest in contact and willingness to engage in action to achieve equality.

As discussed earlier, one of the challenges for intergroup relations is that members of high-status and low-status groups typically prefer different representations and ideologies: Members of high-status groups typically prefer a single common identity, color-blindness, and assimilation; members of low-status groups generally prefer a dual identity, multiculturalism, and integration. This discordance in preferred identity representation preferences and acculturation ideologies between members of the host society and immigrant groups, in itself, can produce negative intergroup outcomes. According to the interactive acculturation model (Bourhis, Montreuil, Barrette, & Montaruli, 2009), immigrants' adjustment is better and intergroup relations less strained when acculturation ideologies of members of the host society and of immigrants converge (see also Plaut et al., 2009; Pfafferott & Brown, 2006).

Although greater convergence may generally improve attitudes, we propose that whether the convergence in preference is for common or dual identity can further influence the basic motivations experienced in intergroup relations. When there is a mutual focus on dual identity or multiculturalism, group differences are acknowledged and potentially valued. By contrast, a mutual focus on assimilation, or color-blindness, may produce positive attitudes but may lead to complacency with respect to the status quo because people fail to attend to disparity (Saguy et al., 2009). Consistent with this idea, Vorauer, Gagnon, and Sasaki (2009), who prompted both members of their intergroup dyads to adopt a corresponding ideology, found that a mutual focus on multiculturalism produced greater positive, other-directed behavior in the intergroup interactions than a mutual focus on color-blindness. Thus, whereas common identity when solely emphasized may create a superficial and potentially unstable form of harmony, a truly inclusive form of recategorization—a dual identity that recognizes and values different subgroup identities as an integrated element of a common ingroup identity—can promote positive attitudes and facilitate positive action for equality among high-status, as well as low-status group members.

CONCLUSION

Both aversive racism and color-blindness can represent well-intentioned intergroup orientations, but they may play important, complementary roles in perpetuating racial hierarchy and disparities, often without conscious awareness. In practice, understanding the nature of subtle bias at the individual level and the automatic processes that underlie it can help illuminate how well-meaning interventions can create a veneer of tolerance while reinforcing structures that perpetuate injustice in the United States. The influence of aversive racism is pervasive, and it persists because it remains largely unrecognized and thus unaddressed. In mind, aversive racists truly believe that they are nonprejudiced, but in action they discriminate in subtle but consequential ways. Without sufficient recognition of the subtle nature of contemporary biases and without the appropriate tools for combating these particular biases, significant progress toward a truly just society will be difficult to achieve.

Nevertheless, aversive racism can be combated with approaches and strategies that are uniquely targeted at unconscious racial prejudice. For example, because aversive racists are motivated to be nonprejudiced, making them aware of their unconscious biases (in a nonthreatening way) can arouse powerful motivations for change. Increasing sensitivity to the discrepancy between their genuine commitment to egalitarian principles and the nature of their biased actions produces self-regulatory responses that can help aversive racists control their bias in the short run and, with practice and effort over time, reduce their unconscious biases in the long run.

Color-blindness may have broad appeal in principle because it seems to represent, at least superficially, the core American value of equal treatment and is consistent with an acculturation tradition emphasizing assimilation. At an individual level, emphasizing color-blindness through commonality may represent a step toward reducing intergroup tensions and thus appear to be a well-intentioned effort. However, adopting this perspective permits the perpetuation of systems reinforcing existing racial dominance that appear to be fair on the surface but that are actually unjust. Thus, although color-blindness may have immediate benefits for alleviating intergroup tensions and promoting harmony, it has a darker side that can reduce recognition of unfair group-based treatment or outcomes and, consequently, inhibit action to ameliorate injustice.

Addressing racial inequalities at both the societal and individual levels requires being race conscious, not color-blind, to recognize racial disparities and to understand their basis in unfair treatment. Good intentions by themselves are not sufficient to guarantee fairness. Bias commonly occurs without awareness, despite conscious well-meaning intentions. Nevertheless, good intentions, if we are "wise" to underlying psychological processes that impede them, can also be realized to form a more socially responsible, just, and fair society.

ACKNOWLEDGMENT

Preparation of this chapter was supported, in part, by Grant Nos. RO1HL 0856331-0182 and 1R01DA029888-01 from the National Institutes of Health to John F. Dovidio.

REFERENCES

Aarts, H., Gollwitzer, P. M., & Hassin, R. (2004). Goal contagion: Perceiving is for pursuing. *Journal of Personality and Social Psychology, 87,* 23–37.

Abrams, D., & Hogg, M. E. (2010). Social identity and self-categorization. In J. F. Dovidio, M. Hewstone, P. Glick, & V. M. Esses (Eds.), *Sage handbook of prejudice, stereotyping, and discrimination* (pp. 179–194). London: Sage.

Adorno, T. W., Frenkel-Brunswik, E., Levinson, D. J., & Sanford, R. N. (1950). *The authoritarian personality.* New York: Harper.

Banfield, J. C., & Dovidio, J. F. (2013). Whites' perceptions of discrimination against blacks: The influence of common identity. *Journal of Experimental Social Psychology, 49,* 833–841.

Bergsieker, H. B., Shelton, J. N., & Richeson, J. A. (2010). To be liked versus respected: Divergent goals in interracial interaction. *Journal of Personality and Social Psychology, 99,* 248–264.

Berry, J. W. (1997). Immigration, acculturation, and adaptation. *Applied Psychology: An International Review, 46,* 5–34.

Blair, I. V. (2001). Implicit stereotypes and prejudice. In G. B. Moskowitz (Ed.), *Cognitive social psychology: The Princeton symposium on the legacy and future of social cognition* (pp. 359–374). Mahwah, NJ: Erlbaum.

Blair, I. V., Steiner, J. F., Fairclough, D. L., Hanratty, R., Price, D. W., Hirsh, H. K., et al. (2013). Clinicians' implicit ethnic/racial bias and perceptions of care among black and Latino patients. *Annals of Family Medicine, 11,* 43–52.

Bobo, L. (2001). Racial attitudes and relations at the close of the twentieth century. In N. J. Smelser, W. J. Wilson, & F. Mitchell (Eds.), *Racial trends and their consequences* (Vol. 1, pp. 264–301). Washington, DC: National Academy Press.

Bonilla-Silva, E. (2003). *Racism without racists.* Lanham, MD: Rowman & Littlefield.

Bonilla-Silva, E., & Dietrich, D. (2011). The sweet enchantment of color-blind racism in Obamerica. *Annals of the American Academy of Political and Social Science, 634,* 190–206.

Bourhis, R. Y., Montreuil, A., Barrette, G., & Montaruli, E. (2009). Acculturation and immigrant/host community relations in multicultural settings. In S. Demoulin, J. P. Leyens, & J. F. Dovidio (Eds.), *Intergroup misunderstanding: Impact of divergent social realities* (pp. 39–61). New York: Psychology Press.

Brief, A. P., Dietz, J., Cohen, R. R., Pugh, S. D., & Vaslow, J. B. (2000). Just doing business: Modern racism and obedience to authority as explanations for employment discrimination. *Organizational Behavior and Human Decision Processes, 81,* 72–97.

Cooper, L. A., Roter, D. L., Carson, K. A., Beach, M. C., Sabin, J. A., Greenwald, A. G., et al. (2012). The associations of clinicians' implicit attitudes about race with medical visit communication and patient ratings of interpersonal care. *American Journal of Public Health, 102,* 979–987.

Correll, J., Park, B., Judd, C. M., Wittenbrink, B., Sadler, M. S., & Keesee, T. (2007). Across the thin blue line: Police officers and racial bias in the decision to shoot. *Journal of Personality and Social Psychology, 92,* 1006–1023.

De Franca, D. X., & Monteiro, M. B. (2013). Social norms and the expression of

prejudice: The development of aversive racism in children. *European Journal of Social Psychology, 43,* 263–271.
Dovidio, J. F., & Gaertner, S. L. (2000). Aversive racism and selection decisions: 1989 and 1999. *Psychological Science, 11,* 319–323.
Dovidio, J. F., & Gaertner, S. L. (2004). Aversive racism. In M. P. Zanna (Ed.), *Advances in experimental social psychology* (Vol. 36, pp. 1–51). San Diego, CA: Academic Press.
Dovidio, J. F., Kawakami, K., & Gaertner, S. L. (2002). Implicit and explicit prejudice and interracial interaction. *Journal of Personality and Social Psychology, 82,* 62–68.
Effron, D. A., Cameron, J. S., & Monin, B. (2009). Endorsing Obama licenses favoring whites. *Journal of Experimental Social Psychology, 45,* 590–593.
Ellemers, N., & Barreto, M. (2009). Collective action in modern times: How modern expressions of prejudice prevent collective action. *Journal of Social Issues, 65,* 749–768.
Epstein, R. A. (2005). Disparities and discrimination in health care coverage: A critique of the Institute of Medicine study. *Perspectives in Biology and Medicine, 48*(1, Suppl.), S26–S41.
Gaertner, S. L., & Dovidio, J. F. (1986). The aversive form of racism. In J. F. Dovidio & S. L. Gaertner (Eds.), *Prejudice, discrimination, and racism* (pp. 61–89). Orlando, FL: Academic Press.
Gaertner, S. L., & Dovidio, J. F. (2012). Reducing intergroup bias: The common ingroup identity model. In P. A. M. Van Lange, A. W. Kruglanski, & E. T. Higgins (Eds.), *Handbook of theories of social psychology* (Vol. 2, pp. 439–457). Thousand Oaks, CA: Sage.
Glasford, D. E., & Dovidio, J. F. (2011). *E pluribus unum*: Dual identity and minority group members' motivation to engage in contact, as well as social change. *Journal of Experimental Social Psychology, 47,* 1021–1024.
Green, A. R., Carney, D. R., Pallin, D. J., Ngo, L. H., Raymond, K. L., Iezzoni, L. I., et al. (2007). The presence of implicit bias in physicians and its predictions of thrombolysis decisions for black and white patients. *Journal of General Internal Medicine, 22,* 1231–1238.
Greenwald, A. G., Poehlman, T. A., Uhlmann, E. L., & Banaji, M. R. (2009). Understanding and using the Implicit Association Test: III. Meta-analysis of predictive validity. *Journal of Personality and Social Psychology, 97,* 17–41.
Hehman, E., Gaertner, S. L., Dovidio, J. F., Mania, E. W., Guerra, R., Wilson, D. C., et al. (2012). Group status drives majority and minority integration preferences. *Psychological Science, 23,* 46–52.
Hodson, G., Dovidio, J. F., & Gaertner, S. L. (2002). Processes in racial discrimination: Differential weighting of conflicting information. *Personality and Social Psychology Bulletin, 28,* 460–471.
Jost, J. T., Banaji, M., & Nosek, B. A. (2004). A decade of system justification theory: Accumulated evidence of conscious and unconscious bolstering of the status quo. *Political Psychology, 25,* 881–919.
Jost, J. T., Federico, C. M., & Napier, J. L. (2013). Political ideologies and their social psychological functions. In M. Freeden, L. M. Sargent, & M. Stears (Eds.), *Oxford handbook of political ideologies* (pp. 232–250). New York: Oxford University Press.

Karpinski, A., & Hilton, J. L. (2001). Attitudes and the Implicit Association Test. *Journal of Personality and Social Psychology, 81,* 774–788.

Kay, A. C., Gaucher, D., Peach, J. M., Laurin, K., Friesen, J., Zanna, M. P., et al. (2009). Inequality, discrimination, and the power of the status quo: Direct evidence for a motivation to see the way things are as the way they should be. *Journal of Personality and Social Psychology, 97,* 421–434.

Kleinpenning, G., & Hagendoorn, L. (1993). Forms of racism and the cumulative dimension. *Social Psychology Quarterly, 56,* 21–36.

Knight, J. L., Guiliano, T. A., & Sanchez-Ross, M. G. (2001). Famous or infamous?: The influence of celebrity status and race on perceptions of responsibility for rape. *Basic and Applied Social Psychology, 23,* 183–190.

Kovel, J. (1970). *White racism: A psychohistory.* New York: Pantheon.

Lai, C. K., Hoffman, K. M., & Nosek, B. A. (2013). Reducing implicit bias. *Social and Personality Compass, 7,* 315–330.

Lai, C. K., Marini, M., Lehr, S. A., Cerruti, C., Shin, J.-E. L., Joy-Gaba, J. A., et al. (2014, March 24). Reducing implicit racial preferences: I. A comparative investigation of 17 interventions. *Journal of Experimental Psychology: General, 143*(4), 1765–1785.

McConahay, J. B. (1986). Modern racism, ambivalence, and the Modern Racism Scale. In J. F. Dovidio & S. L. Gaertner (Eds.), *Prejudice, discrimination, and racism* (pp. 99–125). Orlando, FL: Academic Press.

Monin, B., & Miller, D. T. (2001). Moral credentials and the expression of prejudice. *Journal of Personality and Social Psychology, 81,* 33–43.

Monteith, M. J., Arthur, S. A., & Flynn, S. M. (2010). Self-regulation and bias. In J. F. Dovidio, M. Hewstone, P. Glick, & V. M. Esses (Eds.), *Sage handbook of prejudice, stereotyping, and discrimination* (pp. 493–507). London: Sage.

Moskowitz, G. B., & Ignarri, C. (2009). Implicit volition and stereotype control. *European Review of Social Psychology, 20,* 97–145.

Nail, P. R., Harton, H. C., & Decker, B. P. (2003). Political orientation and modern versus aversive racism: Tests of Dovidio and Gaertner's (1998) integrated model. *Journal of Personality and Social Psychology, 84,* 754–770.

National Center for Health Statistics. (2012). *Health, United States, 2012: With special feature on emergency care.* Hyattsville, MD: U.S. Government Printing Office.

Neville, H. A., Awad, G. H., Brooks, J. E., Flores, M. P., & Bluemel, J. (2013). Color-blind racial ideology: Theory, training, and measurement implications in psychology. *American Psychologist, 68,* 455–466.

Park, S. H., Glaser, J., & Knowles, E. D. (2008). Implicit motivation to control prejudice moderates the effect of cognitive depletion on unintended discrimination. *Social Cognition, 26,* 401–419.

Payne, B. K. (2006). Weapon bias: Split-second decisions and unintended stereotyping. *Current Directions in Psychological Science, 15,* 287–291.

Penner, L. A., Dovidio, J. F., West, T. W., Gaertner, S. L., Albrecht, T. L., Dailey, R. K., et al. (2010). Aversive racism and medical interactions with black patients: A field study. *Journal of Experimental Social Psychology, 46,* 436–440.

Pfafferott, I., & Brown, R. (2006). Acculturation preferences of majority and minority adolescents in Germany in the context of society and family. *International Journal of Intercultural Relations, 30,* 703–717.

Plant, E. A., & Peruche, B. M. (2005). The consequences of race for police officers' responses to criminal suspects. *Psychological Science, 16*, 180–183.

Plaut, V. C., Thomas, K. M., & Goren, M. J. (2009). Is multiculturalism or color blindness better for minorities? *Psychological Science, 20*, 444–446.

Reeves, R. V. (2013). The other American dream: Social mobility, race and opportunity. Brookings Institute Social Mobility Memos. Retrieved from *www.brookings.edu/blogs/social-mobility-memos/posts/2013/08/28-social-mobility-race-opportunity-reeves*.

Roccas, S., & Brewer, M. (2002). Social identity complexity. *Personality and Social Psychology Review, 6*, 88–106.

Rooth, D. (2007). Automatic associations and discrimination in hiring: Real world evidence. *Labour Economics, 17*, 523–534.

Ryan, C. S., Hunt, J. S., Weible, J. A., Peterson, C. R., & Casas, J. F. (2007). Multicultural and colorblind ideology, stereotypes, and ethnocentrism among black and white Americans. *Group Processes and Intergroup Relations, 10*, 617–637.

Sabin, J. A., & Greenwald, A. G. (2012). The influence of implicit bias on treatment recommendations for 4 common pediatric conditions: Pain, urinary tract infection, attention deficit hyperactivity disorder, and asthma. *American Journal of Public Health, 102*, 988–995.

Sabin, J. A., Nosek, B. A., Greenwald, A. G., & Rivara, F. P. (2009). Physicians' implicit and explicit attitudes about race by MD race, ethnicity, and gender. *Journal of Healthcare for the Poor and Underserved, 20*, 896–913.

Sabin, J. A., Rivara, F. P., & Greenwald, A. G. (2008). Physician implicit attitudes and stereotypes about race and quality of medical care. *Medical Care, 46*, 678–685.

Saguy, T., & Chernyak-Hai, L. (2012). Intergroup contact can undermine disadvantaged group members' attributions to discrimination. *Journal of Experimental Social Psychology, 48*, 714–720.

Saguy, T., Dovidio, J. F., & Pratto, F. (2008). Beyond contact: Intergroup contact in the context of power relations. *Personality and Social Psychology Bulletin, 34*, 432–445.

Saguy, T., Tausch, N., Dovidio, J. F., & Pratto, F. (2009). The irony of harmony: Intergroup contact can produce false expectations for equality. *Psychological Science, 29*, 114–121.

Salvatore, J., & Shelton, J. N. (2007). Cognitive costs of exposure to racial prejudice. *Psychological Science, 18*, 810–815.

Sam, D. L., & Berry, J. W. (2010). Acculturation: When individuals of different cultural backgrounds meet. *Perspectives on Psychological Science, 5*, 472–481.

Sassenberg, K., & Moskowitz, G. B. (2005). Do not stereotype, think different!: Overcoming automatic stereotype activation by mindset priming. *Journal of Experimental Social Psychology, 41*, 506–514.

Sears, D. O., Henry, P. J., & Kosterman, R. (2000). Egalitarian values and the origins of contemporary American racism. In D. O. Sears, J. Sidanius, & L. Bobo (Eds.), *Racialized politics: The debate about racism in America* (pp. 75–117). Chicago: University of Chicago Press.

Shapiro, T., Meschede, T., & Osoro, S. (2013, February). The roots of the widening racial wealth gap: Explaining the black–white economic divide. Institute on Assets and Social Policy: Research and Policy Brief. Retrieved from *http://iasp.brandeis.edu/pdfs/Author/shapiro-thomas-m/racialwealthgapbrief.pdf.*

Shnabel, N., Nadler, A., Canetti-Nisim, D., & Ullrich, J. (2008). The role of acceptance and empowerment from the perspective of the needs-based model. *Social Issues and Policy Review, 2*, 159–186.

Sidanius, J., & Pratto, F. (1999). *Social dominance: An intergroup theory of social hierarchy and oppression.* New York: Cambridge University Press.

Sim, J. J., Correll, J., & Sadler, M. S. (2013). Understanding police and expert performance: When training attenuates (vs. exacerbates) stereotypic bias to shoot. *Personality and Social Psychology Bulletin, 39*, 291–304.

Sommers, S. R., & Ellsworth, P. C. (2000). Race in the courtroom: Perceptions of guilt and dispositional attributions. *Personality and Social Psychology Bulletin, 26*, 1367–1379.

Son Hing, L. S., Chung-Yan, G., Grunfeld, R., Robichaud, L., & Zanna, M. P. (2005). Exploring the discrepancy between implicit and explicit prejudice: A test of aversive racism theory. In J. P. Forgas, K. Williams, & S. Latham (Eds.), *The Sydney symposium of social psychology: Vol. 5. Social motivation: Conscious and unconscious processes* (pp. 274–293). New York: Psychology Press.

Son Hing, L. S., Chung-Yan, G. A., Hamilton, L. K., & Zanna, M. P. (2008). A two-dimensional model that employs explicit and implicit attitudes to characterize prejudice. *Journal of Personality and Social Psychology, 94*, 771–987.

Son Hing, L. S., Li, W., & Zanna, M. P. (2002). Inducing hypocrisy to reduce prejudicial responses among aversive racists. *Journal of Experimental Social Psychology, 38*, 71–78.

Tajfel, H., & Turner, J. C. (1979). An integrative theory of intergroup conflict. In W. G. Austin & S. Worchel (Eds.), *The social psychology of intergroup relations* (pp. 33–48). Monterey, CA: Brooks/Cole.

Tyler, T. R., & Blader, S. L. (2003). The group engagement model: Procedural justice, social identity, and cooperative behavior. *Personality and Social Psychology Review, 7*, 349–361.

Uhlmann, E. L., & Cohen, G. L. (2005). Constructed criteria: Redefining merit to justify discrimination. *Psychological Science, 16*, 474–480.

Verkuyten, M. (2006). Multicultural recognition and ethnic minority rights: A social identity perspective. *European Review of Social Psychology, 17*, 148–184.

Verkuyten, M., & Martinovic, B. (2012). Immigrants' national identification: Meanings, determinants, and consequences. *Social Issues and Policy Review, 6*, 82–112.

Vorauer, J. D., Gagnon, A., & Sasaki, S. J. (2009). Salient intergroup ideology and intergroup interaction. *Psychological Science, 20*, 838–845.

CHAPTER 7

Understanding Media Violence Effects

Sara Prot, Craig A. Anderson, Muniba Saleem,
Christopher L. Groves, and Johnie J. Allen

More than six decades of research demonstrate significant effects of violent media use on affect, cognition, and behavior. Media violence effects on aggression have received the most attention and are now well understood. There is a clear consensus among researchers that media violence is linked to aggressive behavior and that this relationship is causal (Bushman, Gollwitzer, & Cruz, 2014; Taylor & Huesmann, 2014). Short-term and long-term effects of violent media use on aggressive behavior have been demonstrated by scores of empirical studies using strong methodology and over a dozen meta-analytic reviews (e.g., Anderson et al., 2010; Bushman & Huesmann, 2006; Greitemeyer & Mügge, 2014). A smaller but growing number of studies also demonstrates detrimental effects of media violence on prosocial behavior (Anderson et al., 2010; Greitemeyer & Mügge, 2014). Overall, the research literature suggests that media violence effects are not large but accumulate over time to produce significant changes in behavior that can significantly influence both individuals and society.

Unfortunately, these research findings are often misinterpreted and misunderstood by members of the general public, policymakers, and even some researchers (Gentile, 2014). Media violence effects have been a topic of public debate for decades and are frequently labeled as controversial.

Extreme claims are often made. In the wake of violent acts such as the Aurora, Colorado, theater massacre, violent media tend to be vilified and singled out as "the" cause of the tragedy. On the other hand, critics of media violence research deny the existence of any effects of media violence on behavior (Ferguson & Kilburn, 2010). Both of these types of extreme claims are unwarranted and unsupported by research evidence but persist in the public discourse (Gentile, 2014; Taylor & Huesmann, 2014).

The goal of this chapter is to provide a review of current theory and research findings concerning media violence effects on good (prosocial behavior) and evil (aggression, violence, stereotyping, and intergroup conflict). Several theoretical perspectives are discussed that can be used to understand media violence effects (the general aggression model, the general learning model, and the risk and resilience approach). Next, an overview of research findings is given concerning short-term and long-term effects of violent media use on aggressive and prosocial outcomes. Finally, several key mechanisms are discussed that underlie these effects (aggressive cognitions, affect, desensitization and empathy, attention deficits, and executive control). It is our hope that this review will help increase understanding of how media violence contributes to complex social behaviors and dispel persisting myths and misunderstandings that fuel the media violence debate.

THEORETICAL FRAMEWORKS

The General Aggression Model and the General Learning Model

Much of the recent research examining media violence effects on aggression has been guided by the general aggression model (GAM; Anderson & Carnagey, 2014; DeWall, Anderson, & Bushman, 2011); earlier research is easily accommodated by it. This is hardly surprising, because the GAM was created in part to integrate decades of prior research on all forms of aggression into a common framework and language. More precisely, the GAM integrates several domain-specific theories of aggression and outlines the personal and situational factors and the psychological processes that influence an individual's aggressive behavior in both short-term and long-term contexts.

According to the GAM, all proximate variables (i.e., person and situation variables that are operative in the present social encounter) increase aggression in the short term by influencing at least one (often more than one) of three key types of internal state variables: aggressive thoughts, hostile affect, and physiological arousal. Of course, recent exposure to violent media is one such situational variable.

These changes in one's present internal state influence judgment and decision making in the current social encounter. For instance, if a person is provoked after watching a violent movie, the risk of an aggressive response is increased because of primed aggressive thoughts, affect, and physiological arousal. Figure 7.1 displays these episodic, short-term, proximate processes of the GAM.

In the long term, habitual media violence use leads to stable changes in cognition, affect, and behavior through well-established learning processes. Regular media violence consumption involves repeated rehearsal and use of aggressive knowledge structures. Over time, this can lead to the development of pro-violence attitudes, hostile attribution biases, and desensitization to violence. Together, these factors contribute to increases in aggressive behavior over time (Anderson & Carnagey, 2014; DeWall et al., 2011). Long-term developmental and personality processes in the GAM are shown in Figure 7.2. The short-term and long-term processes proposed by the GAM have been empirically supported by findings from a broad set of studies examining media violence effects (Anderson et al., 2003; Anderson et al., 2010; Greitemeyer & Mügge, 2014), as well as many other aggression domains such as domestic violence (e.g., Warburton & Anderson, 2015), personality disorders involving violence (e.g., Hosie, Gilbert, Simpson, & Daffern, 2014), male on female aggression (e.g., Anderson & Anderson, 2008), and violence in prisons (e.g., DeLisi et al., 2010). Recent research also demonstrates how the GAM can be applied to understanding the effects of violent stereotype portrayals in the media on increased stereotyping, prejudice, and aggression toward outgroup members (Saleem & Anderson, 2013; Yang et al., 2014).

The general learning model (GLM; Buckley & Anderson, 2006; Gentile, Groves, & Gentile, 2014) extends the GAM and broadens the model to

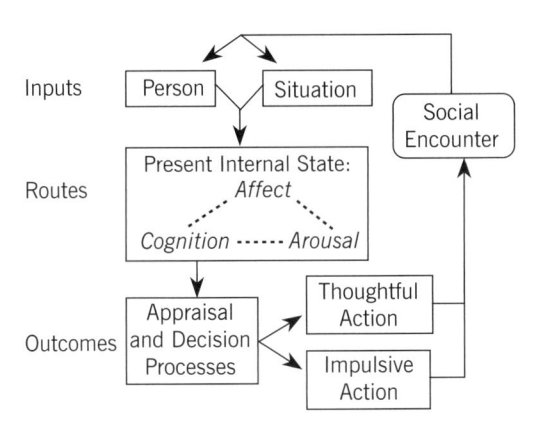

FIGURE 7.1. The GAM: Episodic processes. From Anderson and Bushman (2002). Copyright 2002 by Annual Reviews. Reprinted by permission.

```
                    ┌─────────────────────────────┐
                    │ Repeated violent game playing:│
                    │ Learning, rehearsal, &        │
                    │ reinforcement of aggression-  │
                    │ related knowledge structures  │
                    └─────────────────────────────┘
```

Diagram: Repeated violent game playing (Learning, rehearsal, & reinforcement of aggression-related knowledge structures) branches into five categories: Aggressive beliefs & attitudes; Aggressive perceptual schemas; Aggressive expectation schemas; Aggressive behavior scripts; Aggression desensitization. These feed into "Increase in aggressive personality," which along with Personological variables (e.g., Aggressive personality) and Situational variables (e.g., Social situations, New peer group) leads to: General Aggression Model, as in Episodic Figure.

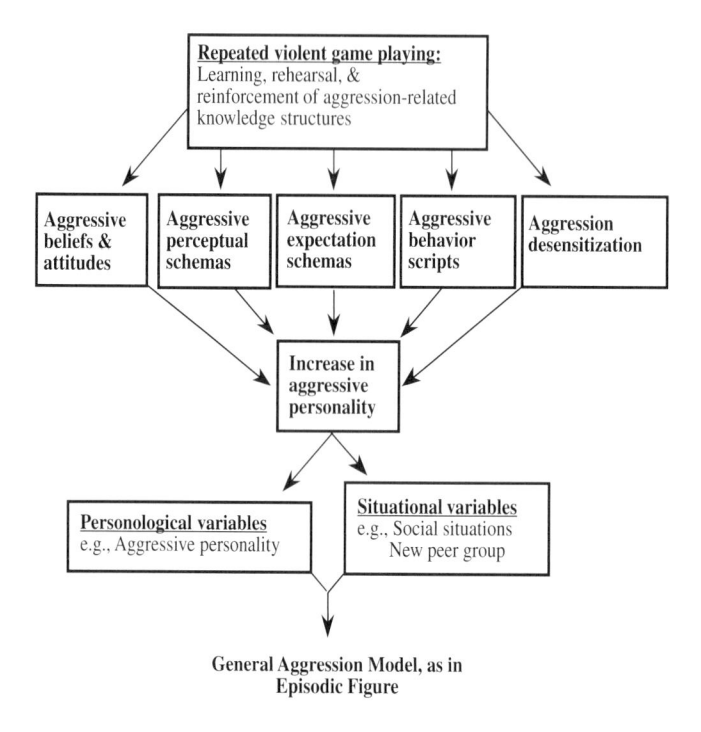

FIGURE 7.2. The GAM: Long-term developmental/personality processes in relation to five categories of aggression-related variables. From Anderson and Bushman (2002). Copyright 2002 by Annual Reviews. Reprinted by permission.

examine different kinds of social behaviors. For instance, the same learning processes through which media violence increases aggressive attitudes and behavior also lead to reductions in prosocial behavior (Anderson et al., 2010; Greitemeyer & Mügge, 2014). Short-term mechanisms proposed by the GLM are similar to those in the GAM—that situational and personality factors influence one's internal state, which, in turn, affects judgment, decision making, and behavior. In the long term, different experiences affect social behaviors through effects on perceptual and cognitive constructs (such as normative beliefs and behavioral scripts), cognitive-emotional constructs (such as attitudes and stereotypes), and emotional constructs (such as affective traits). Figure 7.3 illustrates some of the key variables highlighted by the GLM.

The Risk Factor Approach

In the public debate on media violence effects, research findings are often misunderstood. Media violence effects are most frequently discussed in

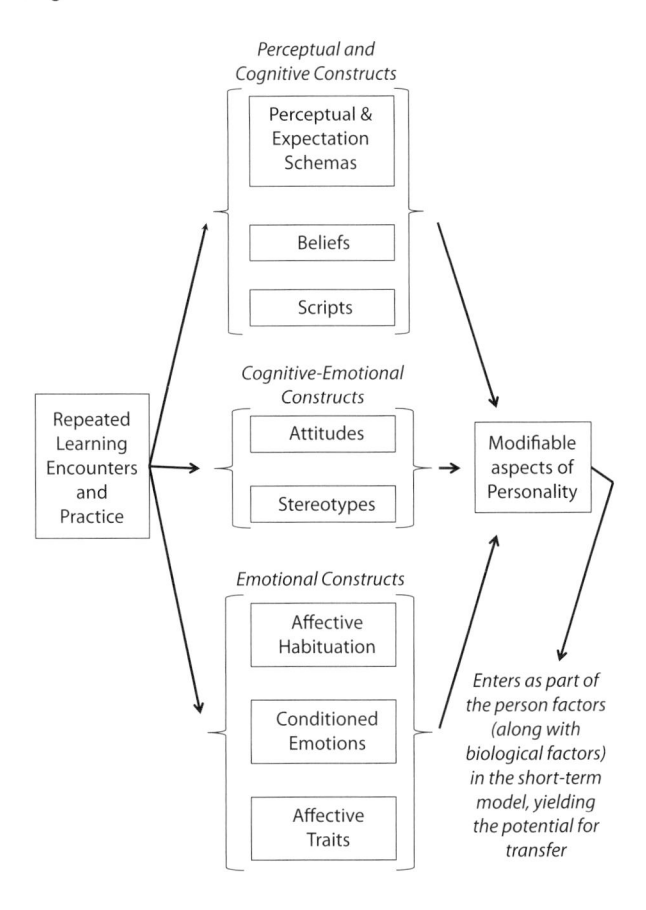

FIGURE 7.3. Long-term processes in the GLM. From Gentile, Groves, and Gentile (2014). Copyright 2014 by Oxford University Press. Reprinted by permission.

response to rare but shocking acts of violence, such as the Columbine high school shooting and the Aurora theater massacre. When such events occur, violent video games, television shows, and movies are often vilified and labeled as "the" cause of the violent act (Gentile, 2014). Other overly simplistic "primary" causes invoked by politicians, pundits, and news media to explain such events include mental illness, easy availability of guns, not enough guns, lax parenting, overly strict parenting, and drugs.

In reality, aggression is a complex behavior that is caused and moderated by a large number of interacting risk factors (Anderson, Gentile, & Buckley, 2007). No respectable researcher would claim that media violence is "the" cause of aggression and violence; it is one of many contributing causal risk factors. Because of this, media violence effects can best be understood within a risk and resilience framework. Within this framework, behavior is viewed as a product of protective factors (which foster healthy development) and risk factors (which disrupt healthy development and increase the risk of maladaptation). Examples of other risk factors that contribute to aggression include genetic predispositions, aggressive personality traits, abusive parenting, and living in a violent neighborhood. Examples of protective factors that reduce the risk of aggression include parental involvement, having prosocial peers, and prosocial media use. Effects of different risk and protective factors accumulate; the likelihood of problematic functioning is increased by every risk factor present (Masten, 2001). No single risk factor is sufficient to elicit a violent act. However, each can increase the risk of violence, especially for individuals who already have multiple risk factors and few protective factors present (Anderson et al., 2007).

Several researchers have advocated for a conceptual shift in the media violence domain toward a risk and resilience perspective (Anderson et al., 2007; Gentile & Bushman, 2012; Gentile, 2014; Prot & Gentile, 2014). Such a conceptual shift may help clarify the role media violence plays in the context of other risk and protective factors of aggression and help resolve current debates about violent media effects. Most studies examining media violence effects on aggression show small to moderate effect sizes, leading some critics to dismiss these effects as unimportant (e.g., Ferguson & Kilburn, 2010). On the other hand, research within the risk and resilience framework reveals that media violence acts the same as any other risk factor for aggression (such as low parental involvement and prior physical victimization), deserving neither special attention nor dismissal (Anderson et al., 2007; Gentile & Bushman, 2012).

MEDIA VIOLENCE EFFECTS

Violent Media Effects on Aggression

Violent media are any media that portray characters intentionally attempting to harm others. Such violent depictions are common in movies, video games, music videos, television shows, and even cartoons (Anderson et al., 2003). More than 60 years of research demonstrates clear evidence that media violence influences aggressive behavior in both short-term and long-term contexts. Laboratory and field experiments show that short-term exposure to violent media content causes an increase in physically and verbally aggressive behavior immediately afterward (Anderson et al., 2003; Anderson et al., 2010). For example, in a study by Engelhardt, Bartholow, and Saults (2011), participants were randomly assigned to play a violent or nonviolent video game. Participants who played a violent game subsequently delivered more intense aversive noise blasts to a supposed partner, demonstrating increased physical aggression. Similar short-term effects have been observed across different forms of media, including violent television shows, movies, video games, and music lyrics (Anderson et al., 2003).

Cross-sectional and longitudinal studies provide converging evidence of long-term media violence effects on aggression. Cross-sectional studies consistently show associations between violent media consumption and aggressive behavior, and many rule out a host of alternative explanations. For example, in one study (Anderson et al., 2007, Study 2), high school students reported their screen media habits, beliefs, and attitudes about aggression and various types of aggressive and violent behaviors which they had engaged in during the past year. The self-reported amount of exposure to violent video games was significantly associated with mild physical aggression (e.g., fights, hitting others) and violent behavior (e.g., assault, robbery). These violent video game effects on behavior remained significant after statistically controlling for sex, total time on screen media, normative beliefs about aggression, trait anger and hostility, and attitudes toward violence.

Large-sample longitudinal studies demonstrate links between frequent exposure to violent media in childhood and aggression later in life. For example, Huesmann, Moise, Podolski, and Eron (2003) found that viewing televised violence at ages 6–10 predicted adult aggressive behavior measured 15 years later when statistically controlling for aggressiveness in childhood, socioeconomic status, intellectual ability, demographic characteristics, and parenting factors.

Finally, the existence of media violence effects on aggression is supported by a series of meta-analyses (e.g., Anderson et al., 2010; Greitemeyer & Mügge, 2014; Paik & Comstock, 1994). Meta-analytic reviews show significant effects of violence in television shows, movies, and video games on aggressive behavior that are consistent across experimental, cross-sectional, and longitudinal studies. Such findings also generalize across cultures, including Western individualistic, Eastern European, and East Asian collectivistic countries. There is some evidence that media violence effects may be stronger in Western countries than in East Asian countries, suggesting that collectivism perhaps acts as a protective factor that mitigates media violence effects (Anderson et al., 2010). However, there is currently insufficient empirical evidence in the media violence literature to clearly support this hypothesis. Instead, most studies demonstrate significant effects of violent media on aggression that are similar across different cultures (Anderson et al., 2010; Greitemeyer & Mügge, 2014). Several researchers have also suggested that sex may act as a moderator of media violence effects given that men tend to demonstrate higher levels of aggression and higher levels of media violence use than women (e.g. Anderson et al., 2007). However, meta-analytic reviews show that effects of media violence on aggressive behavior are of equal magnitudes for men and women (Anderson et al., 2010). These findings suggest that, in spite of mean differences in levels of aggression and media violence use, effects of media violence on aggression are the same for men and women.

Violent Media Effects on Violent Outcomes

Although the influence of violent media on low-level, everyday forms of aggression is well established, less empirical attention has been paid to media effects on more extreme, violent forms of aggressive behavior. Experimental research regarding violent behavior is much more difficult to conduct because it is unethical to provide opportunities for research participants to engage in violent behavior. An additional problem, inherent in longitudinal and correlational studies, results from the relative rarity of violent behaviors exhibited by the general population. This makes the effects of any given risk factor for violence more difficult to statistically detect unless one uses large sample sizes.

There have, however, been several investigations of this topic. For example, as noted earlier, the cross-sectional study by Anderson et al. (2007, Study 2) found significant associations between violent video game use and violent behavior after partialing out a host of individual difference and personality variables. Similarly, DeLisi, Vaughn, Gentile, Anderson, and Shook (2013) found that institutionalized juvenile delinquents who played more violent video games also exhibited relatively more delinquent and more violent behaviors as measured by thefts of drugs or vehicles, carrying a weapon, and attacking another person. Perhaps most fascinating in the DeLisi study was the finding of significant video game violence effects on serious violent behavior even after controlling for psychopathic traits (such as callousness, unemotionality, remorselessness, and impulsiveness), demonstrating that the relationship between video game violence and violent behavior is not a spurious relationship due to psychopathic personality traits.

A number of longitudinal studies also have examined media violence effects on violent behavior. As mentioned previously, the longitudinal study by Huesmann et al. (2003) showed that children who had viewed more television violence at ages 6–10 were more likely to have been convicted of a crime 15 years later. In a study by Gentile and Bushman (2012), several risk factors for aggression (e.g., violent media use, hostile attribution biases) were found to cumulatively increase the probability of being involved in a physical fight at a later time point. Delinquent and violent behavior has also been specifically linked to habitual exposure to violent video games, as shown by studies of German fifth to ninth graders (Hoph, Huber, & Weib, 2008), and American sixth to eighth graders (Graber, Nichols, Lynne, Brooks-Gunn, & Botvin, 2006). One longitudinal study found a significant media violence effect on teen dating violence, violence directed at a current or former romantic partner that may range from less severe acts such as slapping to more severe acts such as punching and shoving (Friedlander, Connolly, Pepler, & Craig, 2013). Another found that exposure to violent X-rated (pornographic) material predicted later sexually aggressive behavior (including both in-person sexual assault and technology-based sexual harassment, such as sending a sexual text message to a person who did not want to receive it; Ybarra, Mitchell, Hamburger, Diener-West, & Leaf, 2011). Interestingly, exposure to nonviolent X-rated material did not increase sexual aggression, which demonstrates that it is violent media content and not sexual media content that contributes to the risk of sexual aggression.

A number of additional cross-sectional and longitudinal studies have been published in the six decades since research on screen violence began, studies that have included violent behavior as outcome variables. Most such studies have found reliable media violence effects. However, as one should expect in any research literature, a few studies have failed to observe a significant influence of violent media on violent outcomes. This is not unusual in any domain of research and may be attributed to a variety of factors, including chance. Other factors that often (but not always) characterize studies that fail to find significant effects include inappropriately small sample sizes (i.e., insufficient power), poor measures of media violence (e.g., measuring only total time on screen media but not time on violent media), inappropriate outcome measures (e.g., using a trait measure in a short-term experimental study), and inappropriate data analyses (e.g., statistically controlling for trait aggression in a cross-sectional study; see Groves, Prot, & Anderson, 2016). Indeed, the most recent comprehensive meta-analysis of violent video game effects found that studies with poorer methodological characteristics (such as using inappropriate outcome measures or failing to manipulate media violence exposure effectively) tended to yield weaker video game effects on aggressive behavior (Anderson et al., 2010). These methodological limitations can make it more difficult to detect media violence effects. Nonetheless, when all relevant studies are included in such meta-analyses, the overall result is overwhelming evidence that violent media exposure is a significant risk factor for aggressive behavior and for variables known to lead to aggressive behavior, such as aggressive cognition (e.g., pro-violence attitudes) and aggressive affect (e.g., anger and hostility).

Effects of Presentation of Racial/Ethnic Groups within Violent Contexts

The fact that media stereotypes can influence cognitions, affect, and behaviors toward the targeted group members is well established (e.g., Mastro & Tukachinsky, 2013). Beyond general negative attitudes, studies reveal that presenting a racial/ethnic group within violent media contexts can influence aggressive cognitions, affect, and behaviors toward the targeted group (Dixon, 2008; Saleem & Anderson, 2013; Saleem, Prot, Anderson, & Lemieux, 2015; Yang et al., 2014). For example, cross-sectional evidence reveals that exposure to overrepresentation of blacks as criminals on local news programs is positively associated with perceptions of blacks as violent and with increased culpability judgments of hypothetical black criminal suspects (Dixon, 2008).

Brief experimental studies that measure short-term media violence effects after a single instance of media violence exposure show similar effects, and of course they establish causal direction. For example, in two studies, Saleem and Anderson (2013) randomly assigned non-Arab/non-Muslim participants to play one of five video games: a violent game in which the targets were Arab terrorists; a violent game in which the targets were Russian terrorists; a violent game without terrorists or Arabs; a nonviolent game with Arabs; or a nonviolent game without Arabs. After playing the assigned game, implicit and explicit measures of anti-Arab attitudes and affect were taken. Results revealed that playing the Arabs-as-terrorists violent game yielded significant increases in anti-Arab attitudes and emotions (Saleem & Anderson, 2013). Figure 7.4 presents these results. One of the experiments also asked participants to draw "typical" Arab and European males and females, after completing all other measures. Not surprisingly, the drawings of Arabs were more likely to include some type of

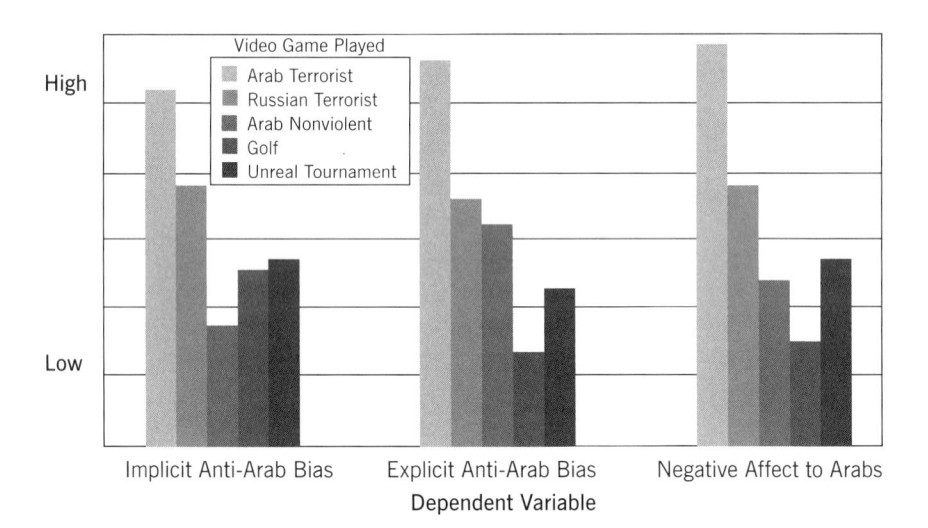

FIGURE 7.4. Standardized mean differences for three dependent variables resulting from playing one of five randomly assigned video games. From Saleem and Anderson (2013). Copyright 2013 by the American Psychological Association. Reprinted by permission.

weapon if they were drawn by someone who had just played the Arabs-as-terrorists game. Figure 7.5 displays sample drawings from that experiment.

In another experimental study, white participants who played a video game as a black avatar within a violent context were more likely (relative to those in a nonviolent game context) to express negative attitudes toward blacks (Yang et al., 2014). Importantly, playing the game within a violent or nonviolent context as a white avatar did not significantly influence negative attitudes toward blacks. Additionally, white participants who played a violent video game as a black, relative to white, avatar were more likely to hold implicit attitudes that blacks are violent and, subsequently, behaved more aggressively in a standard lab aggression task (giving hot sauce to a supposed partner known to dislike spicy food).

Beyond these cognitive and affective effects, evidence from cross-sectional and experimental studies suggest that exposure to news portraying Muslims as terrorists influences support for aggressive public policies against Muslim immigrants and Muslim Americans (Saleem et al., 2015). In sum, the presentation of racial/ethnic minorities within violent contexts in media influences aggressive perceptions, affect, and behaviors toward members of that group.

Violent Media Effects on Prosocial Behavior

A small but highly consistent research literature suggests that violent media also decrease prosocial behavior both in the short term and in the long

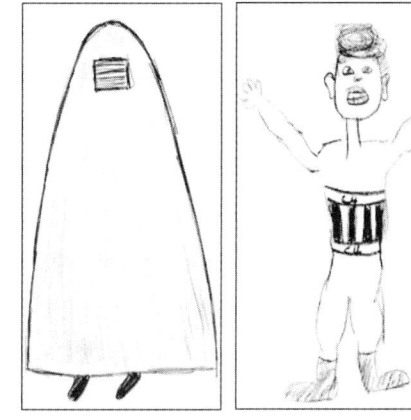

FIGURE 7.5. Sample human figure drawings of the "typical" Arab and European male and female. From Saleem and Anderson (2013). Copyright 2013 by the American Psychological Association. Reprinted by permission.

term. Laboratory experiments demonstrate immediate negative effects of violent media use on helping. For instance, Saleem, Anderson, and Gentile (2012) randomly assigned children to play a violent, neutral, or prosocial video game for 30 minutes. Playing a violent game prompted children to show less helpful and more hurtful behavior in a subsequent puzzle assignment task.

Cross-sectional and longitudinal research suggests that short-term effects accumulate over time to produce lasting changes in prosocial behavior. A cross-sectional study by Gentile et al. (2009) demonstrated a significant negative relationship between violent video game playing habits and prosocial behavior among Singaporean children even when statistically controlling for sex, age, total screen time, and prosocial video game play. Longitudinal studies demonstrate similar findings and show that violent media use predicts lower prosocial behavior over time (Anderson et al., 2007; Prot et al., 2014). Lastly, the existence of significant detrimental effects of media violence on prosocial behavior is supported by several meta-analytic reviews (Anderson et al., 2010; Greitemeyer & Mügge, 2014).

Detrimental effects of violent media on prosociality may have widespread consequences that affect both individuals and our society. Recent correlational research by Anderson (2014) demonstrates that violent gaming predicts more negative attitudes toward civic engagement and less civic engagement behavior among youth. Not surprisingly, prosocial gaming had opposite effects on both attitudes and civic engagement behavior. These effects remained significant even after controlling for sex, age, parent education, parent involvement, and parent civic engagement.

MECHANISMS OF MEDIA VIOLENCE EFFECTS ON AGGRESSION AND PROSOCIAL BEHAVIOR

Aggressive Cognitions

As the GAM outlines, the relationship between media violence exposure and aggressive behavior (or violence) is at least partially mediated by cognitive factors (Anderson et al., 2010). Exposure to violent media can lead to both short-term increases in aggressive cognitions (via priming) and long-term changes in personality (via altered knowledge structures).

Many experimental studies have shown that exposure to violent media causes short-term increases in the accessibility of aggressive cognitions. For example, Bushman (1998) found that after viewing a violent video (as compared with viewing a nonviolent video), participants were quicker at identifying aggressive words in a word/nonword lexical decision task. Similarly, Anderson et al. (2004) found that playing violent video games increased the accessibility of aggressive cognitions as measured by a word completion task. Participants who played a violent (as compared with a nonviolent) video game created a higher percentage of aggressive words when asked to fill in words with missing letters. A similar experiment by Uhlmann and Swanson (2004) showed that playing a violent video game can temporarily increase aggressive self-associations as measured by an IAT.

Cross-sectional and longitudinal studies have also shown that repeated exposure to violent media can have long-term cognitive consequences. These consequences may take the form of aggressive beliefs and attitudes, aggressive perceptual schemata, aggressive expectation schemata, or aggressive behavioral scripts (Anderson et al., 2010). For example, Gentile and Gentile (2008) conducted a longitudinal study and found that third- to fifth-grade students who played multiple violent video games developed more hostile attribution biases over the course of a school year (i.e., they changed to perceive ambiguous situations more aggressively). Another longitudinal study by Möller and Krahé (2009) found that in a sample of German adolescents, exposure to violent video games influenced physical aggression 30 months later, an effect that was mediated by an increased acceptance of aggression as normative behavior and by an increase in hostile attribution bias. Basically, repeated exposure to violent screen media leads to systematic increases in the person's readiness to perceive threats to oneself, accessibility of aggressive solutions to problems, and beliefs that support and justify using such aggressive solutions.

Aggressive Affect

Affect serves as another mediating variable between media violence exposure and aggressive behavior (or violence). Exposure to violent media can lead to short-term increases in aggressive affect (i.e., anger and hostility). For example, Anderson, Carnagey, and Eubanks (2003) conducted several experiments showing that college students felt more hostile after hearing a violent song as compared with those who heard a similar but nonviolent song. Another experiment conducted by Barlett and Rodeheffer (2009) found that playing a realistic violent video game (Conflict Desert Storm) increased hostility even more than playing an unrealistic violent video game (Star Wars Battlefront 2).

The long-term affective consequences of violent media exposure have not been studied as extensively, but meta-analytic data (Anderson et al., 2010) suggest that the long-term effects are not as powerful as the short-term effects (at least for video games). The average effect sizes for longitudinal and cross-sectional studies were only $r = .075$ and $r = .101$, respectively, as compared with an average effect size of $r = .294$ for experimental studies. A more recent meta-analysis (Greitemeyer & Mügge, 2014) found an overall effect size (including experimental, cross-sectional, and longitudinal data) of $r = .17$ for the relationship between violent video games and aggressive affect.

Desensitization

Violent media use also contributes to desensitizing consumers, a process that engenders a reduced physiological and emotional response to viewing images of actual violence and suffering. Initial responses to media violence among children and adults involve physiological arousal, fear, and anxiety. However, prolonged exposure to violent media leads to reductions in physiological and emotional responsiveness to violence. For example, Carnagey, Anderson, and Bushman (2007) found that violent game play for 20 minutes caused reductions in physiological arousal when viewing scenes of actual violent acts. In other work, violent game play led to reduced activity in a part of the brain normally associated with aversive motivations (Bartholow, Bushman, & Sestir, 2006). Whereas desensitization plays a role in the production of aggressive behavior (e.g., Engelhardt, Bartholow, Kerr, & Bushman, 2011), these findings also suggest it contributes to violent media effects on lack of helping behavior.

In a telling set of experiments conducted by Bushman and Anderson (2009), participants played either a violent or nonviolent video game and subsequently overheard a physical fight occurring outside of the lab. Those who had played the violent game were less likely to rate the fight as severe, were even less likely to report having heard the fight in the first place, and took longer to go to the aid of the injured party. In a second study, a female confederate feigned difficulty with retrieving her crutches outside of a movie theater. Moviegoers who were headed into a movie responded in pretty much the same way regardless of whether they were headed to a violent or a nonviolent movie. After the movie, though, those who had just watched a violent film took longer to help the struggling confederate than those who had just watched a nonviolent film. These findings are supported by a large-scale meta-analysis in which violent video game play was significantly related to reduced helping behavior in experimental, correlational, and longitudinal studies (Anderson et al., 2010).

A number of studies of brain function also support the hypothesis that repeated exposure to violent media can lead to desensitization and to subsequent increases in aggressive behavior and/or decreases in helping behavior. For example, Gentile, Swing, Anderson, Rinker, and Thomas (in press) compared brain function (with functional magnetic resonance imaging [fMRI]) of gamers who habitually play violent games versus gamers who habitually play nonviolent games, while both groups were playing a violent video game. Nonviolent gamers displayed an increase in recruitment of emotional response regions when playing the violent game; violent gamers demonstrated an active suppression of these same regions. Bartholow et al. (2006) used event-related potential brain data and aggressive behavioral data in the same lab study and found that violent game players showed desensitization in brain function and that this desensitization effect was associated with higher aggressive behavior in a later laboratory task.

Attention Deficits and Cognitive Control

Several recent studies suggest an additional mechanism through which habitual violent media use may increase aggressive behavior—disinhibition of aggression due to attention deficits and reduced executive control. The fast pace and rapid changes of focus that occur in many violent television shows, movies, and video games prompt consumers to direct attention broadly. Researchers have hypothesized that using such exciting and fast-paced media could make it more difficult to control attention and to inhibit responses to distracting stimuli (Bartholow & Hummer, 2014; Gentile, Swing, Lim, & Khoo, 2012).

Research evidence from a diverse set of studies examining both behavior and neural functioning provides support for this hypothesis. Short-term experimental studies demonstrate immediate effects of media use on executive function. For example, Hummer and colleagues (2010) randomly assigned participants to play a violent or nonviolent game for 30 minutes. Subsequently, participants completed a measure of cognitive control (the go/no-go task) while undergoing fMRI. Violent video game play led to reduced prefrontal cortex activity while withholding a motor response in the go/no-go task, indicating poorer behavioral control. These results are consistent with findings from correlational studies that demonstrate associations between habitual media violence use and poorer executive functioning (Bailey, West, & Anderson, 2010; Hummer, Kronenberger, Wang, Anderson, & Mathews, 2014). For instance, Bailey and colleagues (2010) found a negative relationship between video gaming experience and proactive cognitive control, a form of self-regulation that involves sustained maintenance of goal-relevant information within the prefrontal cortex and enables an optimal response to cognitively demanding events.

A related line of research indicates that both television use and video game use are related to attention deficits and impulsivity (Swing, Gentile, Anderson, & Walsh, 2010). A recent longitudinal study found a bidirectional relationship of video game use with attention problems and impulsiveness over a period of 2 years. Individuals who were initially more impulsive or had more attention problems spent more time playing video games, which, in turn, increased subsequent attention problems and impulsiveness (Gentile et al., 2012). A recent cross-sectional study (Swing & Anderson, 2014) specifically tested the associations among media exposure variables, attention and impulsivity problems, aggression-related cognitions and affect, and two types of aggressive behavior. The data best fit the a priori theoretical model in which: (1) violent media exposure is positively linked to higher levels of both impulsive and premeditated aggressive behavior; (2) this link was mediated through the violent media effects on attention and impulsivity problems, aggressive cognition, and aggressive affect; (3) overall screen media exposure was linked to aggressive behavior through its effect on attention and impulsivity problems; and (4) the link between attention and impulsivity problems and aggressive behavior was much stronger for impulsive aggressive behavior than for premeditated aggression. Figure 7.6 displays these results.

Of course, being of a cross-sectional design, this study doesn't provide strong causal evidence of the entire hypothesized sequence from high exposure to fast-paced screen media to attention and impulsivity problems to impulsive aggression. However, as noted earlier, longitudinal and experimental studies have established causal links between screen media and attention/impulsivity problems and between violent media and aggression. Thus, although more research is needed, the overall pattern of findings supports a causal interpretation.

It is important to note that playing fast-paced (and often violent) video games has also been found to lead to improvements in visuospatial functioning (Bavelier, Green, Schrater, & Pouget, 2012). Unfortunately, these visuospatial benefits seem to come at a cost: They may be accompanied by reduced executive control, attention deficits, and increased impulsivity. Further research is needed in this area to explore whether these negative media effects on cognitive functioning truly lead to disinhibition of aggressive behavior.

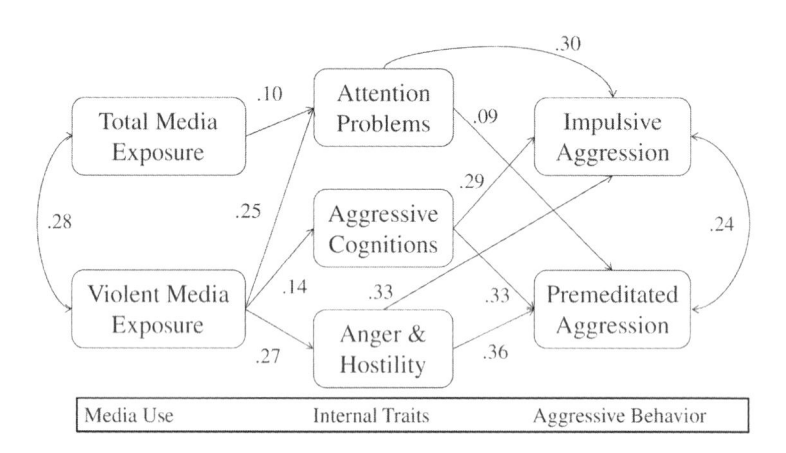

FIGURE 7.6. Effects of screen media on aggressive behavior, through the three theoretically hypothesized mediation variables of attention and impulsivity problems, aggressive cognitions, and aggressive affect. Standardized path coefficients are reported. All paths shown are statistically significant. Overall model-fit indicators: chi-square: 5.06, degrees of freedom = 8, $p < .75$, goodness-of-fit index: 1.00, adjusted goodness-of-fit index: .99, comparative fit index: 1.00, Akaike information criterion: 61.06, root mean square error of approximation: .000 (90% confidence interval: 0.000, 0.042). Adapted from Swing and Anderson (2014). Copyright 2014 by Wiley Periodicals, Inc. Adapted by permission.

CONCLUSION

It cannot be denied that media violence is appealing and exciting to viewers—a common favorite form of entertainment. Unfortunately, many consumers believe that violent media can also provide catharsis and help people become less aggressive by giving them an opportunity to blow off steam (Gentile, 2014). In contrast, empirical research clearly shows that media violence use does not reduce aggression—it increases it. Dozens of methodologically rigorous empirical studies, as well as numerous comprehensive meta-analyses, demonstrate significant short-term and long-term effects of violent media use on aggression. Both in short-term and long-term contexts, violent media alter cognitions and affect, produce desensitization, and can even lead to reductions in attention and executive control. Together, these processes contribute to increased aggressive behavior. When media violence portrayals focus on racial and ethnic minorities, they also increase stereotyping and prejudice toward these groups. Media violence also reduces prosocial behavior by desensitizing viewers and reducing empathy toward victims of violence. These findings leave little doubt that media violence effects are important and can contribute to evil (aggression, violence, prejudice) while also reducing good (empathy, prosocial behavior).

Finally, although the majority of research in the media effects literature has focused on detrimental effects of violent media, an emerging research literature suggests that prosocial media that portray helpful behaviors among characters can have equally strong positive effects, reducing antisocial outcomes and increasing prosocial outcomes. It is our hope that future research efforts and public discourse will eschew the question of *whether* media effects matter and will instead focus on finding ways to apply our current knowledge of media effects to increase prosocial outcomes and decrease antisocial outcomes.

REFERENCES

Anderson, C. A. (2014). *Violent, nonviolent, and prosocial gaming effects on teens' civic engagement* (Oxford Handbooks Online). New York: Oxford University Press.

Anderson, C. A., & Anderson, K. B. (2008). Men who target women: Specificity of target, generality of aggressive behavior. *Aggressive Behavior, 34*, 605–622.

Anderson, C. A., Berkowitz, L., Donnerstein, E., Huesmann, L. R., Johnson, J., Linz, D., et al. (2003). The influence of media violence on youth. *Psychological Science in the Public Interest, 4*, 81–110.

Anderson, C. A., & Bushman, B. J. (2002). Human aggression. *Annual Review of Psychology, 53*, 27–51.

Anderson, C. A., & Carnagey, N. L. (2014). The role of theory in the study of media violence: The general aggression model. In D. A. Gentile (Ed.) *Media violence and children* (2nd ed., pp. 103–133). Westport, CT: Praeger.

Anderson, C. A., Carnagey, N. L., & Eubanks, J. (2003). Exposure to violent media: The effects of songs with violent lyrics on aggressive thoughts and feelings. *Journal of Personality and Social Psychology, 84*(5), 960–971.

Anderson, C. A., Carnagey, N. L., Flanagan, M., Benjamin, A. J., Eubanks, J., & Valentine, J. C. (2004). Violent video games: Specific effects of violent content on aggressive thoughts and behavior. *Advances in Experimental Social Psychology, 36,* 200–251.

Anderson, C. A., Gentile, D. A., & Buckley, K. E. (2007). *Violent video game effects on children and adolescents: Theory, research, and public policy.* Oxford, UK: Oxford University Press.

Anderson, C. A., Shibuya, A., Ihori, N., Swing, E. L., Bushman, B. J., Sakamoto, A., et al. (2010). Violent video game effects on aggression, empathy, and prosocial behavior in Eastern and Western countries. *Psychological Bulletin, 136,* 151–173.

Bailey, K., West, R., & Anderson, C. A. (2010). A negative association between video game experience and proactive cognitive control. *Psychophysiology, 47,* 34–42.

Barlett, C. P., & Rodeheffer, C. (2009). Effects of realism on extended violent and nonviolent video game play on aggressive thoughts, feelings, and physiological arousal. *Aggressive Behavior, 35*(3), 213–224.

Bartholow, B. D., Bushman, B. J., & Sestir, M. A. (2006). Chronic violent video game exposure and desensitization: Behavioral and event-related brain potential data. *Journal of Experimental Social Psychology, 42,* 532–539.

Bartholow, B. D., & Hummer, T. A. (2014). Cognitive neuroscience approaches to the study of media violence effects. In D. Gentile (Ed.), *Media violence and children: A complete guide for parents and professionals* (2nd ed., pp. 329–354). Westport, CT: Praeger.

Bavelier, D., Green, C. S., Schrater, P., & Pouget, A. (2012). Brain plasticity through the life span: Learning to learn and action video games. *Annual Reviews of Neuroscience, 35,* 391–416.

Buckley, K. E., & Anderson, C. A. (2006). A theoretical model of the effects and consequences of playing video games. In P. Vorderer & J. Bryant (Eds.), *Playing video games: Motives, responses, and consequences* (pp. 363–378). Mahwah, NJ: Erlbaum.

Bushman, B. J. (1998). Priming effects of media violence on the accessibility of aggressive constructs in memory. *Personality and Social Psychology Bulletin, 24*(5), 537–545.

Bushman, B. J., & Anderson, C. A. (2009). Comfortably numb: Desensitizing effects of violent media on helping others. *Psychological Science, 20,* 273–277.

Bushman, B. J., Gollwitzer, M., & Cruz, C. (2014, October 6). There is broad consensus: Media researchers agree that violent media increase aggression in children, and pediatricians and parents concur. *Psychology of Popular Media Culture, 4*(3), 200–214.

Bushman, B. J., & Huesmann, L. R. (2006). Short-term and long-term effects of violent media on aggression in children and adults. *Archives of Pediatric and Adolescent Medicine, 160,* 348–352.

Carnagey, N. L., Anderson. C. A., & Bushman, B. J. (2007). The effect of video game violence on physiological desensitization to real-life violence. *Journal of Experimental Social Psychology, 43*, 489–496.

DeLisi, M., Drury, A. J., Kosloski, A. E., Caudill, J. W., Conis, P. J., Anderson, C. A., et al. (2010). The cycle of violence behind bars: Traumatization and institutional misconduct among juvenile delinquents in confinement. *Youth Violence and Juvenile Justice, 8*, 107–121.

DeLisi, M., Vaughn, M. G., Gentile, D. A., Anderson, C. A., & Shook, J. (2013). Violent video games, delinquency, and youth violence: New evidence. *Youth Violence and Juvenile Justice, 11*, 132–142.

DeWall, C. N., Anderson, C. A., & Bushman, B. J. (2011). The general aggression model: Theoretical extensions to violence. *Psychology of Violence, 1*, 245–258.

Dixon, T. L. (2008). Crime news and racialized beliefs: Understanding the relationship between local news viewing and perceptions of African Americans and crime. *Journal of Communication, 58*(1), 106–125.

Engelhardt, C. R., Bartholow, B. D., Kerr, G. T., & Bushman, B. J. (2011). This is your brain on violent video games: Neural desensitization to violence predicts increased aggression following violent video game exposure. *Journal of Experimental Social Psychology, 47*, 1033–1036.

Engelhardt, C. E., Bartholow, B. D., & Saults, J. S. (2011). Violent and nonviolent video games differentially affect physical aggression for individuals high versus low in dispositional anger. *Aggressive Behavior, 37*, 539–546.

Ferguson, C. J., & Kilburn, J. (2010). Much ado about nothing: The misestimation and overinterpretation of violent video game effects in Eastern and Western nations: Comment on Anderson et al. (2010). *Psychological Bulletin, 136*, 174–178.

Friedlander, L. J., Connolly, J. A., Pepler, D. J., & Craig, W. M. (2013). Extensiveness and persistence of aggressive media exposure as longitudinal risk factors for teen dating violence. *Psychology of Violence, 3*, 310–322.

Gentile, D. A. (2014). Why don't media violence effects look the same on everyone?: Developmental approaches to understanding media effects. In D. Gentile (Ed.), *Media violence and children: A complete guide for parents and professionals* (2nd ed., pp. 45–69). Westport, CT: Praeger.

Gentile, D. A., Anderson, C. A., Yukawa. S., Ihori, N., Saleem, M., Ming, L. K., et al. (2009). The effects of prosocial video games on prosocial behaviors: International evidence from correlational, experimental, and longitudinal studies. *Personality and Social Psychology Bulletin, 35*, 752–763.

Gentile, D. A., & Bushman, B. J. (2012). Reassessing media violence effects using a risk and resilience approach to understanding aggression. *Psychology of Popular Media Culture, 1*(3), 138–151.

Gentile, D. A., & Gentile, J. R. (2008). Violent video games as exemplary teachers: A conceptual analysis. *Journal of Youth and Adolescence, 37*(2), 127–141.

Gentile, D. A., Groves, C., & Gentile, J. R. (2014). The general learning model: Unveiling the learning potential of video games. In F. C. Blumberg (Ed.), *Learning by playing: Video gaming in education* (pp. 121–142). New York: Oxford University Press.

Gentile, D. A., Swing, E. L., Anderson, C. A., Rinker, D., & Thomas, K. M. (in press). Differential neural recruitment during violent video game play in violent and nonviolent game players. *Psychology of Popular Media Culture.*

Gentile, D. A., Swing, E. L., Lim, C. G., & Khoo, A. (2012). Video game playing, attention problems, and impulsiveness: Evidence of bidirectional causality. *Psychology of Popular Media Culture, 1*(1), 62–70.

Graber, J. A., Nichols, T., Lynne, S. D., Brooks-Gunn, J., & Botvin, G. J. (2006). A longitudinal examination of family, friend, and media influences on competent versus problem behaviors among urban minority youth. *Applied Developmental Science, 10,* 75–85.

Greitemeyer, T., & Mügge, D. O. (2014). Video games do affect social outcomes: A meta-analytic review of the effects of violent and prosocial video game play. *Personality and Social Psychology Bulletin, 40,* 578–589.

Groves, C. L., Prot, S., & Anderson, C. A. (2016). Violent media effects: Theory and evidence. In H. S. Friedman (Ed.) *Encyclopedia of mental health* (2nd ed., Vol. 4, pp. 362–369). Waltham, MA: Academic Press.

Hoph, W. H., Huber, G. L., & Weib, R. H. (2008). Media violence and youth violence: A 2-year longitudinal study. *Journal of Media Psychology, 20,* 79–96.

Hosie, J., Gilbert, F., Simpson, K., & Daffern, M. (2014). An examination of the relationship between personality and aggression using the general aggression and five-factor models. *Aggressive Behavior, 40*(2), 189–196.

Huesmann, L. R., Moise, J., Podolski, C. P., & Eron, L. D. (2003). Longitudinal relations between childhood exposure to media violence and adult aggression and violence: 1977–1992. *Developmental Psychology, 39*(2), 201–221.

Hummer, T. A., Kronenberger, W. G., Wang, Y., Anderson, C. A., & Mathews, V. P. (2014). Association of television violence exposure with executive functioning and white matter volume in young adult males. *Brain and Cognition, 88,* 26–34.

Hummer, T. A., Wang, Y., Kronenberger, W. G., Mosier, K. M., Kalnin, A. J., Dunn, D. W., et al. (2010). Short-term violent video game play by adolescents alters prefrontal activity during cognitive inhibition. *Media Psychology, 13,* 136–154.

Masten, A. S. (2001). Ordinary magic: Resilience processes in development. *American Psychologist, 56,* 227–238.

Mastro, D., & Tukachinsky, R. (2013). The influence of media exposure on the formation, activation, and application of racial/ethnic stereotypes. In A. N. Valdivia (Ed.), *The International encyclopedia of media sudies* (pp. 295–315). Boston: Blackwell.

Möller, I., & Krahé, B. (2009). Exposure to violent video games and aggression in German adolescents: A longitudinal analysis. *Aggressive Behavior, 35*(1), 75–89.

Paik, H., & Comstock, G. (1994). The effects of television violence on antisocial behavior: A meta-analysis. *Communication Research, 21,* 516–546.

Prot, S., & Gentile, D. A. (2014). Applying risk and resilience models to predicting the effects of media violence on development. *Advances in Child Development and Behavior, 46,* 215–244.

Prot, S., Gentile, D. G., Anderson, C. A., Suzuki, K., Swing, E., Lim, K. M., et al. (2014). Long-term relations between prosocial media use, empathy and prosocial behavior. *Psychological Science, 25,* 358–368.

Saleem, M., & Anderson, C. A. (2013). Arabs as terrorists: Effects of stereotypes within violent contexts on attitudes, perceptions, and affect. *Psychology of Violence, 3*(1), 84.

Saleem, M., Anderson, C. A., & Gentile, D. A. (2012). Effects of prosocial, neutral, and violent video games on children's helpful and hurtful behaviors. *Aggressive Behavior, 38*, 281–287.

Saleem, M., Prot, S., Anderson, C. A., & Lemieux, A. (2015). *Effects of terrorism news on American/Muslim intergroup relations.* Manuscript submitted for publication.

Swing, E. L., & Anderson, C. A. (2014). The role of attention problems and impulsiveness in media violence effects on aggression. *Aggressive Behavior, 40*, 197–203.

Swing, E. L., Gentile, D. A., Anderson, C. A., & Walsh, D. A. (2010). Television and video game exposure and the development of attention problems. *Pediatrics, 126*, 214–221.

Taylor, L., & Huesmann, L. R. (2014). Answering the attacks on the media violence consensus. In D. Gentile (Ed.), *Media violence and children: A complete guide for parents and professionals* (2nd ed., pp. 355–380). Westport, CT: Praeger.

Uhlmann, E., & Swanson, J. (2004). Exposure to violent video games increases automatic aggressiveness. *Journal of Adolescence, 27*(1), 41–52.

Warburton, W. A., & Anderson, C. A. (2015). Social psychology of aggression. In J. Wright & J. Berry (Eds.), *International encyclopedia of social and behavioral sciences* (2nd ed., Vol. 1, pp. 373–380). Oxford, UK: Elsevier.

Yang, G. S., Gibson, B., Lueke, A. K., Huesmann, L. R., & Bushman, B. J. (2014). Effects of avatar race in violent video games on racial attitudes and aggression. *Social Psychological and Personality Science, 5*(6), 698–704.

Ybarra, M. L., Mitchell, K. J., Hamburger, M., Diener-West, M., & Leaf, P. J. (2011). X-rated material and perpetration of sexually aggressive behavior among children and adolescents: Is there a link? *Aggressive Behavior, 37*, 1–18.

CHAPTER 8

How Dehumanization Promotes Harm

Nick Haslam and Steve Loughnan

The psychology of dehumanization has experienced a renaissance in the past decade. Pioneering theoretical studies in the 1970s and 1980s established the concept as a legitimate topic for psychological study, too important and too complex to be left only to historians, philosophers, and culture theorists; but it was only in the new millennium that social psychologists made it their own. Dehumanization might hold the key, they hoped, to understanding the evil that people do to one another and the good they fail to do. Seeing others as less than human surely makes it easier to harm them, and humanizing them surely makes it harder.

There have been several attempts to collect and review this recent surge of psychological research and theory (Bain, Vaes, & Leyens, 2014; Gervais, 2013; Haslam & Loughnan, 2014). However, the question of *how* dehumanization enables harm—the question that ultimately drives that scholarship—has been largely overlooked. The literature teaches us that dehumanization keeps bad company, that it is linked to an assortment of undesirable acts, emotions, and attitudes. However, if we wish to learn how dehumanization produces these harmful consequences, past research gives no simple answer.

In this chapter we argue that there is no simple answer. Instead, the psychological literature shows that dehumanization can promote harm in diverse ways. Clarifying these pathways from dehumanization to harm should pay theoretical, empirical, and perhaps even practical dividends. After laying out the evidence that dehumanization is indeed linked to many forms of vice, violence, and villainy, we then try to map these pathways into a useful taxonomy. In doing so, we propose that dehumanization promotes harm in ways that depend crucially on the temporal dimension. Simply put, dehumanization can prepare the ground for future harm, facilitate present harm, and justify and perpetuate past harm.

LINKS BETWEEN DEHUMANIZATION AND HARM

Social psychologists have shown that dehumanization is associated with a remarkable variety of harmful correlates and consequences. Although they have defined dehumanization in different ways—such as perceptions of people as feral beasts or as mindless objects—and assessed varieties of dehumanization that range from the blatant to the subtle and unconscious, we put these differences to one side. We focus instead on the many ways in which dehumanization has been linked to harmful acts and ideas.

The first theoretical discussions of dehumanization within psychology emphasized its role in war, ethnopolitical conflict, and genocide (Kelman, 1976; Staub, 1989). The more recent empirical literature confirms that dehumanizing the enemy has real implications in these contexts. Jackson and Gaertner (2010) showed that perceiving enemies as less than human was associated with stronger support for continued U.S. military presence in Iraq among American participants. Maoz and McCauley (2008) found that Israelis who dehumanized Palestinians to a greater extent were more likely to support harsh policies such as forced population transfers. In the same context, Leidner, Castano, and Ginges (2013) demonstrated that the more Palestinian and Jewish Israeli participants dehumanized one another, the more they supported retributive rather than restorative forms of justice, and the more they favored violent responses over peace deals. Greater dehumanization has also been linked to lesser empathy for victims in the context of the Bosnian war by Čehajić, Brown, and Gonzalez (2009). Finally, Viki, Osgood, and Phillips (2013) found that British Christians who dehumanized Muslims were more likely to support the torture of Muslim prisoners of war. Seeing enemies as less than human is clearly associated with treating them in inhumane ways.

Dehumanizing perceptions are not restricted to external enemies of the state but also target citizens who violate its laws and social norms. Several studies have established that dehumanization, particularly the likening of people to animals, plays a role in the punishment of criminals and social deviants. Bastian, Denson, and Haslam (2013) and Zhang, Chan, Teng, and Zhang (2015) both showed that greater dehumanization of criminals was associated with preference for harsher sentencing of offenders. In part, these punishments appear to reflect a belief that criminals are animal-like, and this in turn fosters the belief that they are likely to reoffend (Vasquez, Loughnan, Gootjes-Dreesbach, & Weger, 2014). In a study of attitudes toward sex offenders in particular, Viki, Fullerton, Raggett, Tait, and Wiltshire (2012) showed that greater dehumanization—as measured by associating offenders with animal rather than human terms—was associated not only with support for longer sentences and more violent punishments, such as castration, but also with a preference for the complete social exclusion of offenders and a lack of support for rehabilitation.

Dehumanization has also been implicated in the treatment of ethnic and racial minorities and displaced people. For example, indigenous groups are ill served by the dehumanizing perceptions of the majority. Castano and Giner-Sorolla (2006) showed that U.S. citizens reminded of massacres of Native Americans tended to see them as less capable of experiencing uniquely human emotions. Similar findings were obtained by Čehajić et al. (2009) in the Chilean context, in which nonindigenous people who were reminded of suffering inflicted by their group on indigenous Mapuche tended to see them as less fully human and consequently felt less empathy for their plight. Goff, Eberhardt, Williams, and Jackson (2008) have documented how white Americans dehumanize black Americans by implicitly associating them with apes and have shown that this perception has dire consequences. For example, these dehumanizing perceptions were associated with judging the beating of a black suspect to be justified, and the presence of dehumanizing language in media reports of capital crimes committed by black suspects was associated with these suspects being put to death. Less stark but still concerning are Canadian findings that dehumanizing perceptions of immigrants and refugees are associated with more negative and exclusionary attitudes toward these groups (Esses, Veenvliet, Hodson, & Mihic, 2008; Hodson & Costello, 2007) and Chinese findings that seeing a low-income group as less than human was associated with greater support for a policy of forced migration (Zhang et al., 2015).

The link between dehumanization and harm can also be found in the context of gender. Viki and Abrams (2003) found that men holding harmful attitudes such as hostile sexist beliefs tended to deny women complex emotions (e.g., nostalgia, remorse, love). Men who hold these harmful beliefs not only deny women the complex emotionality necessary to be fully human but also fail to see them as human beings, indicated by an underactivation of brain regions associated with viewing other humans (Cikara, Eberhardt, & Fiske, 2011). This denial of mental states may in turn be linked to a general reduction in perceived moral standing. Women who are objectified are deemed less worthy of moral concern (Loughnan et al., 2010), and people see them as having suffered less when they are the victims of crime (Loughnan, Pina, Vasquez, & Puvia, 2013). Most tellingly, Rudman and Mescher (2012) assessed the speed with which men were able to associate words related to women (e.g., *woman, girl*) with words related to animals (e.g., *animals, nature, instinct*) and words related to objects (e.g., *object, device, tool*). They found that men who rapidly associated women with animal and object words also had a greater propensity for sexual aggression and harassment.

This short review of the evidence linking dehumanizing perceptions to various forms of harm does not exhaust the contexts in which these links have been established. For example, Obermann (2011) examined the ways in which playground bullies view other children. She found that the more bullies agreed with statements such as "some people deserve to be treated like animals," the more they reported bullying other children, and the more other children reported being bullied by them. Looking at a different type of play, Bastian, Jetten, and Radke (2012) and Greitemeyer and McLatchie (2011) found that players of violent video games were apt to dehumanize their cyber-warrior opponents and to behave more aggressively toward others outside these games. People who dehumanize the mentally ill are especially prone to reject them socially (Martinez, Piff, Mendoza-Denton, & Hinshaw, 2011). Those who denied human traits to a person with a physical ailment were especially prone to endorse a more painful treatment, albeit one with better long-term outcome (Lammers & Stapel, 2011). Finally, a body of personality research demonstrates that tendencies to dehumanize others correlate with an assortment of traits—psychopathy, narcissism, social dominance orientation—that have well-established associations with aggressive and nonempathic behavior (e.g., Gray, Jenkins, Heberlein, & Wegner, 2011; Hodson & Costello, 2007).

In sum, then, social psychology's "new look" at dehumanization over the past decade or so has revealed a multiplicity of links between dehumanization and harm. Seeing others as less than human is associated with hostile and rejecting acts and attitudes toward enemies and offenders, toward indigenous people and immigrants, toward the mentally ill, and toward groups defined by race, gender, and class. These links have been demonstrated in many countries on five continents, among adults and children. Dehumanization is ubiquitous, and its harmful implications are legion.

HOW DEHUMANIZATION PROMOTES HARM

The evidence linking dehumanization and harm is strong and varied, but the mechanisms that account for these links are uncertain. Several early theorists proposed accounts of these mechanisms, but rarely have their proposals been tested. For example, Kelman (1976) argued that when dehumanization occurs in the context of mass violence, it weakens the perpetrator's normal restraints on violent behavior. In essence, dehumanization disinhibits violence when conflict already exists. Bandura (1999) gave a more specific account of this process of disinhibition, suggesting that dehumanization disengages the perpetrator's moral self-sanctions: the internal restraints of guilt and related moral emotions that normally apply the brakes to aggressive conduct. Opotow (1990) presented an alternative account of why moral restraints are disengaged, focusing on the process of "moral exclusion," placing someone "outside the boundary in which moral values, rules, and considerations of fairness apply" (p. 1). Bar-Tal (1989) proposed yet another explanation, arguing that attaching a subhuman or demonic label to a hated outgroup enables violence by supplying a legitimate justification of the ingroup's aggression.

These alternative accounts of the dehumanization–aggression relationship have some shared elements and some subtle differences. They address situations in which there is an existing conflict and an ongoing potential for aggression, and they focus on processes taking place in the heat of that conflict. The implied context is war (Kelman, 1976), intense ethnic conflict (Bar-Tal, 1989), or a present temptation to commit a violent act (Bandura, 1999). They also tend to emphasize how dehumanization involves a moral conflict, whether an internal struggle between conscience and aggressive impulses (Bandura, 1999), a contraction of the moral circle to exclude a potential victim (Opotow, 1990), or an external release of moral restraints on violence (Kelman, 1976). However, these accounts part company in other ways. Opotow's idea of moral exclusion offers an account of dehumanization's effects that draws heavily on cognitive processes, one that depends on drawing a conceptual boundary around the moral domain, whereas the explanations presented by Kelman (1976), Bandura (1999), and Bar-Tal (1989) involve more emotional processes. Opotow, Kelman, and Bandura's accounts seem to show how dehumanization might *enable* violence, making it more likely to happen, whereas Bar-Tal's seems to show how dehumanization might also *justify* it, providing an explicit reason for the rightness and necessity of that violence. Relatedly, the moral exclusion, weakened restraint, and disengaged self-sanctions accounts all explain the processes that *precede* or *accompany* acts of violence, Bar-Tal's justification-based account could also explain processes that *follow* those acts. If dehumanization can legitimate aggression, portraying one's enemies as animals or devils, then it might be able to do so post hoc.

This last point raises an important possibility. If there are indeed several mechanisms or pathways linking dehumanization to harmful behavior, these might be organized along a temporal dimension. Dehumanizing perceptions of others might come before harmful acts, making them more likely to happen in future. Dehumanization processes might accompany harmful acts in the present, enabling them in the heat of the moment. Finally, dehumanization might occur after some harm has taken place, occurring as a response that might make the original harm more likely to persist or to be repeated. In the pages that follow, we elaborate on this schema, identifying 10 distinct ways in which dehumanization can promote harm, which are summarized in Table 8.1. Our goal in doing so is to organize existing empirical work on dehumanization in a way that guides future research and theory.

DEHUMANIZATION AND FUTURE HARM

One way in which dehumanizing perceptions might promote harm is by preparing the psychological ground for it. Dehumanization might precede acts of violence, aggression, or social exclusion, making these outcomes more likely to occur in the future. We propose three distinct ways in which this might happen. First, *dehumanizing group stereotypes* may exist that predispose people to act harmfully toward group members. These stereotypes may lie dormant, in a sense, but exert a destructive influence on behavior when activated by conflict situations. Second, particular *ideologies* might predispose people to dehumanize outgroups and promote harmful behavior. Third and finally, people might morally exclude a victim prior to behaving aggressively toward the person in an effort to diminish anticipatory guilt—what might be called *preparatory moral disengagement*.

Some stereotypes portray groups as lacking humanity, being closer to animals or objects than the rest of "us." These enduring representations may not be harmful in themselves, but they leave these groups vulnerable to dehumanizing perceptions and treatment, especially when conflict arises. Some of these stereotypes may not have explicitly dehumanizing content, as in those identified by Harris and Fiske's (2006) model of dehumanization. These authors propose that groups stereotyped as low in both warmth and competence—such as drug addicts, the homeless, and prostitutes—are particularly liable to be dehumanized. Indeed, social neuroscience research (Harris & Fiske, 2006) has found that these social groups fail to elicit activation of brain regions typically associated with viewing humans (e.g., medial prefrontal cortex). At a neural level, it seems that they are not processed as fully human. Other stereotypes have blatantly dehumanizing content. For example, Tileagă (2007) demonstrated that Roma—often known by the exonym "gypsies"—are stereotyped as animal-like, and Saminaden, Loughnan, and Haslam (2010) similarly demonstrated that indigenous people are implicitly associated with animals. The best example of a dehumanizing group stereotype is supplied by Goff and colleagues' (Goff et al., 2008; Goff, Jackson, Di Leone, Culotta, & DiTomasso, 2014) work on the black-ape metaphor, a tendency for white Americans to unknowingly associate blacks with apes. Goff's powerful research shows that this lasting stereotype has dire consequences when it is activated, whether in response to priming within the lab or to violations of

TABLE 8.1. Processes by Which Dehumanization Can Promote Harm

Perspective	Process	Definition
Future: Dehumanization prepares harm.	Dehumanizing stereotypes	Representations of groups that make them vulnerable to dehumanizing perceptions
	Dehumanizing ideologies	General belief systems that promote dehumanizing perceptions of groups
	Preparatory moral disengagement	Dehumanizing others in advance of harmful acts motivated by desire to disinhibit those acts
Present: Dehumanization enables harm.	Strong emotion	Dehumanizing others under the influence of disgust or contempt
	Threat	Dehumanizing others under the influence of fear and threat
	Disconnection	Dehumanizing others when feeling socially disconnected from them
	Self-dehumanization	Dehumanizing the self in the context of ongoing aggression
Past: Dehumanization justifies and prolongs harm.	Post hoc rationalization	Dehumanizing others following harms committed against them, motivated by desire to minimize their suffering and ingroup responsibility
	Reconciliation blocking	Dehumanizing others as a process that obstructs compassion, forgiveness, helping, and reparation
	Reciprocal dehumanization	Dehumanizing of perpetrators by victims, including as a response to feeling dehumanized by them

social norms outside it. His research implicates this stereotype in endorsement by white participants of violent conduct toward black criminal suspects and death sentences carried out disproportionately on black defendants in capital cases.

Group stereotypes are not the only preexisting belief systems that may promote harm via dehumanizing perceptions. An assortment of organized ideas that might be referred to as dehumanizing ideologies may play the same role. For example, Maoz and McCauley (2008) showed that Jewish

Israelis who held a hawkish political ideology in relation to the Arab–Israeli conflict were more supportive of harsh and coercive treatment of Palestinians, and this support was partially mediated by dehumanizing perceptions of that group. Similarly, there is extensive evidence that people who hold a very hierarchical view of social relations (i.e., high "social dominance orientation" [SDO]) and those who hold a similarly hierarchical view of the supremacy of humans over other animals (Costello & Hodson, 2010) are especially likely to dehumanize outgroups. For example, people high in SDO are more likely to dehumanize refugees (Esses et al., 2008) and wartime enemies (Jackson & Gaertner, 2010). Importantly, this dehumanization went beyond how people viewed the groups and influenced how they believed the group should be treated. Specifically, people's support for restrictive refugee policies was higher if they dehumanized refugees (Esses et al., 2008), and their support for continued military intervention in Iraq was higher if they dehumanized America's enemies (Jackson & Gaertner, 2010). In short, ideologies such as hawkishness and SDO, rather like the delegitimating beliefs identified by Bar-Tal (1989), increase the likelihood that some people will be seen as less than human, with harmful consequences.

A third way in which dehumanization may set the scene for future harm, rather than facilitating it in the present or sanitizing it once it has transpired, involves what Bandura (1999) referred to as "moral disengagement." This concept refers to aggressors' withdrawal of moral concern for their victims, which allows them to commit acts of violence without being restrained by guilt or empathy. Moral disengagement is often conceptualized as a complex process of which dehumanization is just one facet, alongside such processes as euphemistic labeling of one's actions and displacement of responsibility for their consequences. However, it can equally be conceptualized as a process through which dehumanization enables harm. A person considering a future act of aggression may dehumanize his or her intended victims as a way to reduce their moral standing and remove moral inhibitions against harming them. This use of dehumanization as a motivated strategy for disinhibiting future violence is supported by early research of Bandura, Underwood, and Fromson (1975), as well as by later research by Bandura, Barbaranelli, Caprara, and Pastorelli (1996), which showed that people who endorse sentiments such as "Some people deserve to be treated like animals" were particularly likely to behave violently toward others.

DEHUMANIZATION AND PRESENT HARM

Dehumanizing stereotypes and ideologies and moral disengagement strategies may prepare the ground for future harm doing by picturing some people as mindless, bestial, and morally unworthy. These perceptions predispose people to act against others at a later time, or to tolerate such acts committed on their behalf by their governments or militaries. However, dehumanization may also play a more immediate role in enabling harm in the present. Seeing someone as less than human in the heat of the moment may make it easier to harm the person then and there. We argue that this sort of present-focused enabling involves several distinct processes, which we refer to as *strong emotion*, *threat*, *disconnection*, and *self-dehumanization*.

There is now considerable research evidence that dehumanization increases under conditions of strong emotion. In particular, people are more likely to dehumanize others when they experience the emotion of disgust and the closely associated emotion of contempt. Harris and Fiske (2006) showed that participants who viewed an image of a homeless person or drug addict failed to activate the regions of the brain that serve social cognition and mentalizing, instead showing strong activation in the insula, the neural seat of disgust. Buckels and Trapnell (2013) demonstrated further that experimentally induced disgust facilitated the dehumanization of arbitrary outgroups, and Esses and colleagues (2008) established that contempt is associated with dehumanizing perceptions of refugees. This evidence suggests that when intense aversion-based emotions are activated, they diminish the perception of outgroup humanity, and this may in turn make harmful acts against outgroup members easier to commit or support. Strong emotions of disgust and contempt, therefore, represent one factor that helps to account for the link between dehumanization and harm doing in the present.

Disgust and contempt are strong, anger-tinged aversions whose targets are seen as impure, tainted, or revolting; for example, drug addicts, homeless people, and prostitutes (Harris & Fiske, 2006). A different kind of aversion, based on fear rather than anger and hatred, involves the perception of threat. Several researchers have shown that perceptions of threat also promote dehumanizing perceptions of the threatening person or group. Maoz and McCauley (2008), for example, demonstrated that Israeli participants who perceived Palestinians as more threatening were more likely to dehumanize them by seeing them as disgusting and contemptuous, and this dehumanizing perception was in turn associated with support for coercive policies such as population transfers, curfews, use of rubber bullets to break up demonstrations, and administrative detention. In another study, Viki et al. (2013) showed that British participants who saw Muslims as more threatening showed a greater proclivity to torture Muslim prisoners of war, but only to the extent that they also dehumanized Muslims. The threat posed by the dehumanized individual need not represent a threat to one's personal safety. Vasquez et al. (2014) showed that perceived threat of reoffending linked dehumanization to increased sentencing for a hypothetical criminal. Thus perceived threat intensified the link between dehumanization and harm.

These two present-focused mechanisms linking dehumanization to harm—based on disgust and threat—both implicate emotions. They are ways in which strong affective states can promote dehumanization and its effects on aggression. However, dehumanizing perceptions can also enable harm through cooler mechanisms that involve attenuated rather than emotionally intensified connections between dehumanizer and dehumanized. There is some evidence that dehumanization can increase when people feel disconnected from others. In particular, Waytz and Epley (2012) showed that when people's needs for social connection are temporarily satisfied, they are more likely to dehumanize distant others. For example, participants who completed a study in the company of a friend were more likely to endorse harsh treatment of terrorist detainees than those who completed the same study in the company of a stranger. This idea that dehumanization can reflect feelings of disconnection rather than hatred, disgust, or fear is consistent with Haslam's (2006) account of the "mechanistic" form of dehumanization and with evidence that people who feel chronically disconnected (e.g., people high in autistic and psychopathic traits) tend to have more difficulty imagining the minds and mental experiences of others (Gray et al., 2011).

A final mechanism through which dehumanization may promote harm in the present differs from the others by focusing on the perception of the self rather than others. Bastian and colleagues (Bastian et al., 2012; Bastian, Jetten, et al., 2013) have argued that in some circumstances people may see themselves as less than human, and this "self-dehumanization" may have destructive consequences. In a study of video gaming (Bastian et al., 2012), for example, people who played a more violent game (Mortal Kombat) perceived themselves as well as their opponents as less human compared with playing a less violent game. Bastian et al. (2012) did not show that this self-dehumanization facilitated aggression within the context of the game, and later work in the context of social exclusion (Bastian, Jetten, et al., 2013) indicated that self-dehumanization may have prosocial consequences. In their study, Bastian, Jetten, and colleagues (2013) showed that when people feel that their actions have undermined their humanity, they are more likely to volunteer to help others. Although some findings may point to prosocial, reparatory process in dehumanization, most people who come to see themselves as lacking normal human traits of empathy and civility may not feel normal inhibitions on harming their fellow humans.

DEHUMANIZATION AND PAST HARM

We have seen how dehumanization can prepare the ground for future harm and how it can enable present harm, but it may also make the outcomes of past harms seem worse than they might have otherwise been. After a damaging interpersonal or intergroup event has taken place, dehumanizing perceptions may perpetuate or even escalate its harmful consequences and stand in the way of reconciliation. Once again, several different ways in which dehumanization can have these destructive effects can be distinguished. We label these as *post hoc rationalization*, *reconciliation blocking*, and *reciprocal dehumanization*.

Post hoc rationalization occurs when, confronted with evidence that a person or his or her group has harmed others in the past, he or she sees these victims as lesser humans. This denial of humanity can be motivated by the desire to minimize the harm that was perpetrated, perhaps by denying the affected people the capacity to suffer or by the desire to disown responsibility for that harm, or perhaps by viewing them as violent savages. The best demonstration of this mechanism was provided by Castano and Giner-Sorolla (2006), who presented British and American participants with descriptions of atrocities committed many years earlier by their respective nations against Australian Aborigines and Native Americans. Participants who received such descriptions judged the respective groups less capable of experiencing uniquely human emotions (e.g., love, remorse, nostalgia) than participants who read descriptions that did not mention atrocities. By implication, victim groups were dehumanized—perceived as wild and bestial—in an effort to restore the perpetrator group's sense of themselves as moral people. Similar findings were obtained by Čehajić et al. (2009), who found that nonindigenous Chileans who were informed that their group was collectively responsible for the suffering and subjugation of the indigenous Mapuche were less likely to attribute uniquely human emotions to the Mapuche compared with participants informed that a few nonindigenous Chileans were individually responsible. Čehajić et al. (2009) obtained parallel findings in the aftermath of the Bosnian war, when Serbian participants reminded of ingroup responsibility for atrocities committed against Bosnian Muslims were less likely to attribute distinctively human emotions to this victim group.

Rationalizing away harms committed by one's ingroup may be an effective way to reduce collective guilt when faced with reminders of ingroup responsibility. It allows people to see the outgroup as incapable of suffering, morally undeserving, or even as necessitating the harsh treatment they received. This form of past-focused dehumanization can therefore allow perpetrator groups to restore a sense of moral worth in the face of a troubled history. However, although this maneuver may help perpetrator groups to live with themselves, it is unlikely to help them live with victim groups. For this to happen there must generally be some kind of reconciliation, and perceiving historically victimized groups as unfeeling savages is unlikely to advance this goal.

Reconciliation is a powerful way to promote intergroup harmony, and one which has a profoundly psychological dimension (Staub, 2006; Staub,

Pearlman, Gubin, & Hagengimana, 2005). Dehumanizing perceptions of outgroups can be one important obstruction to intergroup reconciliation following conflict. Studies have established that in situations of intergroup conflict, dehumanization is associated with a lack of compassion, forgiveness, and efforts to make amends for past mistakes. An additional aspect of Čehajić and colleagues' (2009) studies in Chile and Bosnia was that the tendency to deny uniquely human emotions to victim groups was associated with reduced empathy for them, such as admissions of feeling touched by their loss and suffering. Zebel, Zimmermann, Viki, and Doosje (2008) went beyond feelings of empathy to investigate the consequences of dehumanization on support for reparations to victim groups. In two studies they demonstrated that Dutch participants who perceived Bosnian Muslims as relatively animal-like were less likely to believe that the Dutch government should provide reparations to victims of the Srebrenica massacre in 1995, which Dutch United Nations peacekeepers failed to prevent. Similarly, in a study set in Northern Ireland, Tam and colleagues (2007) found that Catholic and Protestant participants who attributed fewer uniquely human emotions to the other group were less forgiving, showing a lesser willingness to seek reconciliation and a greater reluctance to let go of historical grievances against the other community. Together these studies reveal that dehumanization can retard the process of repairing harms past, and therefore make them more likely to fester and recur.

A final dynamic that links dehumanization to past harms is the tendency for victims to dehumanize perpetrators, a possibility that is the mirror image of the retrospective dehumanization of victims by perpetrators and that is likely to have similarly negative effects. When people have been harmed, they may respond by perceiving the perpetrator as inhuman. Research on this possibility is limited, but Bastian and Haslam (2010) found that individuals who had been socially excluded tended to perceive the person who ostracized them as lacking humanity. Furthermore, those who had been excluded not only saw the excluder as less human but also believed that the excluder saw them in a dehumanizing way as well. There is some evidence for reciprocal dehumanization at an intergroup level. In an early study, Leyens and colleagues (2000) found that Mainland Spanish and Canary Island Spanish participants both viewed the other as relatively lacking in uniquely human emotions. They named this effect "infrahumanization" to capture both the dehumanizing and the everyday nature of this derogation. Since this original finding, multiple studies have demonstrated that people will infrahumanize others at an intergroup level, effects that can occur outside of conscious awareness (Paladino et al., 2002) and alter behavior in ways that undermine intergroup helping (Cuddy, Rock, & Norton, 2007; Vaes, Paladino, & Leyens, 2002). These findings imply that vicious cycles of reciprocal dehumanization can be set in motion, both parties denying humanity to the other in a mutually reinforcing spiral.

BROADER SENSES OF HARM

Much like the original formulations of dehumanization, we have focused our temporal analysis on examining the links between dehumanization and harm manifested as aggression or violence. However, harm is not limited to violence and aggression. Rather, harm can take a range of forms, including undermining the self and neglecting or failing to offer appropriate help to others. In briefly turning to these broader senses of harm, we can see that dehumanization again has a role to play.

We have already outlined how people can self-dehumanize, seeing themselves as less than fully human (Bastian & Haslam, 2010). Research examining objectification—a related construct to dehumanization, occurring when people are perceived as sexual objects or instrumental tools—has revealed a cascade of intrapersonal harms that result. We now know that experiencing objectification from another person causes reductions in intellectual performance (Gay & Castano, 2010) and a narrowing of social engagement (Saguy, Quinn, Dovidio, & Pratto, 2010), effectively damaging the victim's ability to behave competently and socially. More recently, experienced objectification has been found to foster a view of the self as immoral or dirty (Chen, Teng, & Zhang, 2013). Finally, these effects extend outside of the self, with women who experience this form of dehumanization subsequently less willing to work with others (Teng, Chen, Poon, & Zhang, 2015). In short, experiencing dehumanization—in the form of being seen as an object—can have harmful implications for how people see themselves.

We have already touched on the idea that dehumanization is linked to social withdrawal (Waytz & Epley, 2012) and ostracism (Bastian & Haslam, 2010). It may also promote a failure to help others: acts of harmful omission rather than commission. In a recent study, Andrighetto, Baldissarri, Lattanzio, Loughnan, and Volpato (2014) examined the willingness of Italian participants to offer help to Japanese and Haitians following the aftermath of devastating natural disasters. They found that the more Italians dehumanized Haitians and Japanese, the less willing they were to offer assistance to these groups. Thus, in addition to undermining reconciliation following harm performed by one's group, dehumanization additionally stifles helping behavior when unintentional harm has befallen others.

BENEFITS OF DEHUMANIZATION?

There should be no doubt or debate that dehumanization—seeing other people as less than fully human—is generally a harmful perception that is best avoided. However, research has started to explore the marginal cases in which dehumanization may work to enhance or benefit people, even if that only occurs within a narrow scope. When dehumanization is beneficial, it seems to convey its benefits by letting people make good, if inhumane, decisions.

Situations that present people with hard choices, requiring them to inflict short-lived pain or suffering on others for a greater good, appear to benefit from some degree of dehumanization. In an important paper, Lammers and Stapel (2011) manipulated people to feel high or low in power and then asked them to make a series of tough decisions. These tough decisions involved acting in a way that created harm and pain, but in the pursuit of a clear and real greater good. For instance, in Study 2, participants had the choice to force a group of people to move for the group's benefit, and in Study 3 they had the choice to administer a painful but highly effective treatment to a hypothetical patient. They found in both cases that powerful people tended to dehumanize the group and the patient, and that the more they dehumanized, the easier it became to take the painful but ultimately more beneficial route. Just as dehumanization can help mute our moral concern for others and enable intergroup and interpersonal harm, so too it might mute our spontaneous aversion to inflict harm on others and enable us to ultimately help them.

This last finding, that dehumanization can help us make tough decisions about others' health, was expanded by Haque and Waytz (2012) in a review of medical dehumanization. They argued that dehumanization can be functional within a medical setting. One function may be to protect health care workers from the emotional toll of working with stressful and sometimes ultimately futile cases. In a study of health care workers who cared for terminally ill patients, Vaes and Muratore (2013) found that dehumanization helped health care workers to avoid feelings of disillusionment, futility, and exhaustion. In short, by dehumanizing their patients, they were able to reduce the emotional toll of working in this highly stressful medical setting. In this way, dehumanization can help protect us from the emotional toll of unpleasant, stressful, and necessary tasks.

This short review has done little more than raised the possibility that dehumanization is not solely linked to harm. In a narrow sense, it appears to allow us to overcome an immediate aversive environment and to make better choices (Lammers & Stapel, 2011) with a lighter heart (Vaes & Muratore, 2013). It seems to us that these small benefits are a very thin silver lining to a vast, dark cloud. Future research would have to uncover many more benefits before we can seriously consider the upside of dehumanization.

CONCLUSIONS

We have proposed 10 different mechanisms through which dehumanization may be associated with harm and harm doing. In distinguishing these processes, we have tried to show that the pathways from dehumanizing perceptions to harm are diverse and complex. Although some theorists have emphasized single explanations, we suggest that the truth is more complex.

For example, it is common for writers to assert that dehumanization promotes violence by providing a justification for it. In our view, this account is lacking in two respects. First, it fails to specify whether the justification comes before the violent act so as to enable it, or whether it comes after the act to rationalize or whitewash it. Both of these forms of dehumanizing justification—preparatory and post hoc—exist, but they are importantly different. One serves to free us of moral prohibitions (Bandura et al., 1975), whereas the other serves to free us from moral obligations (Castano & Giner-Sorolla, 2006). Second, the justification account implies that all dehumanization is a motivated process, driven by a desire to minimize the suffering it causes the victim and the responsibility of the perpetrator or to maximize the perceived rightness and necessity of the harmful act. However, our list of processes linking dehumanization and harm includes many mechanisms that are not motivated. Stereotypes that represent groups as animals need not be a motivated process, and neither is the exacerbation of dehumanizing perceptions by disgust or tendency for people to see themselves as less human after they have been objectified.

Similarly, many writers emphasize the moral dimension of dehumanization, implying that dehumanization fosters harm via moral exclusion or disengagement. However, our list of processes includes some that are not primarily matters of moral cognition or immoral motives. The tendency for threat and social disconnection to promote dehumanizing perceptions, for example, implies that dehumanization processes are not always best viewed through a moral psychology lens. Similarly, the tendency to see oneself as less than human—whether a response to ostracism or objectification—does not appear to have a clear moral dimension. Moral disengagement and exclusion may include processes of dehumanization, and thus increase harm. However, dehumanization can be harmful without a moral component.

Our set of processes linking dehumanization to harm is almost certainly incomplete and provisional. There may well be additional mechanisms besides those that we have identified, and some of the distinctions we have made among the latter may be questionable. In particular, in any ongoing conflict it may be impossible to separate out future, present, and past. The repercussions of earlier intergroup incidents form the psychological contexts of current perceptions and future actions. We believe that this temporal framework has some conceptual value nonetheless. This framework makes it clear that dehumanization may work differently in leading up to harmful acts, during those acts, and in their aftermath.

For example, someone who engages in an act of violence may have held stereotyped views of the victim's group that made him or her seem less worthy of protection, may have been aware of dehumanizing labels that justified aggression, and may have deliberately morally disengaged from the victim in anticipation of the act. At the time of the act, the perpetrator's dehumanizing perception of the victim may have been exacerbated by disgust or fear and the violent act further enabled by a self-dehumanizing perception that he or she, as a perpetrator, was a mere instrument of a greater cause. Afterward, the perpetrator may further dehumanize the victim in order to rationalize the violent act, in the process making empathy and reconciliation less likely. Meanwhile, the victim may come to see the perpetrator as an unfeeling monster or an uncivilized beast, to see him- or herself as less human, and struggle to find others willing to help him or her. At every step of the way, dehumanizing perceptions may contribute to harmful and destructive outcomes.

REFERENCES

Andrighetto, L., Baldissarri, C., Lattanzio, S., Loughnan, S., & Volpato, C. (2014). Humanitarian aid?: Two forms of dehumanization and willingness to help after natural disasters. *British Journal of Social Psychology, 53*, 573–584.

Bain, P., Vaes, J., & Leyens, J. P. (Eds.). (2014). *Humanness and dehumanization*. London: Psychology Press.

Bandura, A. (1999). Moral disengagement in the perpetration of inhumanities. *Personality and Social Psychology Review, 3*, 193–209.

Bandura, A., Barbaranelli, C., Caprara, G. V., & Pastorelli, C. (1996). Mechanisms of moral disengagement in the exercise of moral agency. *Journal of Personality and Social Psychology, 71*, 364–374.

Bandura, A., Underwood, B., & Fromson, M. E. (1975). Disinhibition of aggression through diffusion of responsibility and dehumanization of victims. *Journal of Research in Personality, 9*, 253–269.

Bar-Tal, D. (1989). Delegitimization: The extreme case of stereotyping. In D. Bar-Tal, C. F. Grauman, A. Kruglanski, & W. Stroebe (Eds.), *Stereotyping and prejudice: Changing conceptions* (pp. 169–182). New York: Springer.

Bastian, B., Denson, T., & Haslam, N. (2013). The roles of dehumanization and moral outrage in retributive justice. *PLoS ONE, 8*(4), e61842.

Bastian, B., & Haslam, N. (2010). Excluded from humanity: Ostracism and dehumanization. *Journal of Experimental Social Psychology, 46*, 107–113.

Bastian, B., Jetten, J., Chen, H., Radke, H. R. M., Harding, J. F., & Fasoli, F. (2013). Losing our humanity: The self-dehumanizing consequences of social ostracism. *Personality and Social Psychology Bulletin, 39*(2), 156–169.

Bastian, B., Jetten, J., & Radke, H. (2012). Cyber-dehumanization: Violent video game playing diminishes our humanity. *Journal of Experimental Social Psychology, 48*, 486–491.

Buckels, E. E., & Trapnell, P. D. (2013). Disgust facilitates outgroup dehumanization. *Group Processes and Intergroup Relations, 16*(6), 771–780.

Castano, E., & Giner-Sorolla, R. (2006). Not quite human: Infrahumanization in response to collective responsibility for intergroup killing. *Journal of Personality and Social Psychology, 90*, 804–818.

Čehajić, S., Brown, R., & Gonzalez, R. (2009). What do I care?: Perceived ingroup responsibility and dehumanization as predictors of empathy felt for the victim group. *Group Processes and Intergroup Relations, 12*, 715–729.

Chen, Z., Teng, F., & Zhang, H. (2013). Sinful flesh: Sexual objectification threatens women's moral self. *Journal of Experimental Social Psychology, 49*, 1042–1048.

Cikara, M., Eberhardt, J. L., & Fiske, S. (2011). From agents to objects: Sexist attitudes and neural responses to sexualized targets. *Journal of Cognitive Neuroscience, 3*, 540–551.

Costello, K., & Hodson, G. (2010). Exploring the roots of dehumanization: The role of animal–human similarity in promoting immigrant humanization. *Group Processes and Intergroup Relations, 13*, 3–22.

Cuddy, A., Rock, M., & Norton, M. (2007). Aid in the aftermath of Hurricane Katrina: Inferences of secondary emotions and intergroup helping. *Group Processes and Intergroup Relations, 10*, 107–118.

Esses, V. M., Veenvliet, S., Hodson, G., & Mihic, L. (2008). Justice, morality, and the dehumanization of refugees. *Social Justice Research, 21*, 4–25.

Gay, R. K., & Castano, E. (2010). My body or my mind: The impact of state and trait objectification on women's cognitive resources. *European Journal of Social Psychology, 40*(5), 695–703.

Gervais. S. J. (Ed.). (2013). *Objectification and (de)humanization: The 60th Nebraska Symposium on Motivation*. New York: Springer.

Goff, P. A., Eberhardt, J. L., Williams, M. J., & Jackson, M. C. (2008). Not yet human: Implicit knowledge, historical dehumanization, and contemporary consequences. *Journal of Personality and Social Psychology, 94*, 292–306.

Goff, P. A., Jackson, M. C., Di Leone, B. A. L., Culotta, C. M., & DiTomasso, N. A. (2014). The essence of innocence: Consequences of dehumanizing black children. *Journal of Personality and Social Psychology, 106*, 526–545.

Gray, K., Jenkins, A. C., Heberlein, A. S., & Wegner, D. M. (2011). Distortions of mind perception in psychopathology. *Proceedings of the National Academy of Sciences, 108*, 477–479.

Greitemeyer, T., & McLatchie, N. (2011). Denying humanness to others: A newly discovered mechanism by which violent video games increase aggressive behavior. *Psychological Science, 22*, 659–665.

Haque, O., & Waytz, A. (2012). Dehumanization in medicine: Causes, solutions, and functions. *Perspectives in Psychological Science, 7*, 176–186.

Harris, L. T., & Fiske, S. (2006). Dehumanizing the lowest of the low: Neuroimaging responses to extreme out-groups. *Psychological Science, 17*, 847–853.

Haslam, N. (2006). Dehumanization: An integrative review. *Personality and Social Psychology Review, 10*, 252–264.

Haslam, N., & Loughnan, S. (2014). Dehumanization and infrahumanization. *Annual Review of Psychology, 65*, 399–423.

Hodson, G., & Costello, K. (2007). Interpersonal disgust, ideological orientations, and dehumanization as predictors of intergroup attitudes. *Psychological Science, 18*, 691–698.

Jackson, L. E., & Gaertner, L. (2010). Mechanisms of moral disengagement and their differential use by right-wing authoritarianism and social dominance orientation in support of war. *Aggressive Behavior, 36*, 238–250.

Kelman, H. C. (1976). Violence without restraint: Reflections on the dehumanization of victims and victimizers. In G. M. Kren & L. H. Rappoport (Eds.), *Varieties of psychohistory* (pp. 282–314). New York: Springer.

Lammers, J., & Stapel, D. A. (2011). Power increases dehumanization. *Group Processes and Intergroup Relations, 14*, 113–126.

Leidner, B., Castano, E., & Ginges, J. (2013). Dehumanization, retributive and restorative justice, and aggressive versus diplomatic intergroup conflict resolution strategies. *Personality and Social Psychology Bulletin, 39*, 181–192.

Leyens, J.-P., Paladino, P., Rodriguez-Torres, R., Vaes, J., Demoulin, S., Rodriguez-Perez, A., et al. (2000). The emotional side of prejudice: The attribution of secondary emotions to ingroups and outgroups. *Personality and Social Psychology Review, 4*, 186–197.

Loughnan, S., Haslam, N., Murnane, T., Vaes, J., Reynolds, C., & Suitner, C. (2010). Objectification leads to depersonalization: The denial of mind and moral concern to objectified others. *European Journal of Social Psychology, 40*, 709–717.

Loughnan, S., Pina, A., Vasquez, E., & Puvia, E. (2013). The impact of objectification on perceptions of rape victim blame and suffering. *Psychology of Women Quarterly, 37*, 455–461.

Maoz, I., & McCauley, C. (2008). Threat, dehumanization, and support for retaliatory aggressive policies in asymmetric conflict. *Journal of Conflict Resolution, 52*, 93–116.

Martinez, A. G., Piff, P. K., Mendoza-Denton, R., & Hinshaw, S. P. (2011). The power of a label: Mental illness diagnoses, ascribed humanity, and social rejection. *Journal of Social and Clinical Psychology, 30*, 1–23.

Obermann, M. (2011). Moral disengagement in self-reported and peer-nominated bullying. *Aggressive Behavior, 37*, 133–144.

Opotow, S. (1990). Moral exclusion and injustice: An introduction. *Journal of Social Issues, 46*, 173–182.

Paladino, M., Leyens, J.-P., Rodriguez-Torres, R., Rodriguez-Perez, A., Gaunt, R., & Demoulin, S. (2002). Differential association of uniquely and non-uniquely human emotions to the ingroup and the outgroup. *Group Processes and Intergroup Relations, 5*, 105–117.

Rudman, L. A., & Mescher, K. (2012). Of animals and objects: Men's implicit dehumanization of women and likelihood of sexual aggression. *Personality and Social Psychology Bulletin, 38*, 734–746.

Saguy, T., Quinn, D. M., Dovidio, J. F., & Pratto, F. (2010). Interacting like a body: Objectification can lead women to narrow their presence in social interactions. *Psychological Science, 21*, 178–182.

Saminaden, A., Loughnan, S., & Haslam, N. (2010). Afterimages of savages: Implicit associations between "primitives," animals and children. *British Journal of Social Psychology, 49*, 91–105.

Staub, E. (1989). *The roots of evil: The origins of genocide and other group violence*. New York: Cambridge University Press.

Staub, E. (2006). Reconciliation after genocide, mass killing, or intractable conflict:

Understanding the roots of violence, psychological recovery, and steps toward a general theory. *Political Psychology, 27,* 867–894.

Staub, E., Pearlman, L., Gubin, A., & Hagengimana, A. (2005). Healing, reconciliation, forgiving and the prevention of violence after genocide or mass killing: An intervention and its experimental evaluation in Rwanda. *Journal of Clinical and Social Psychology, 24,* 297–334.

Tam, T., Hewstone, M., Cairns, E., Tausch, N., Maio, G., & Kenworthy, J. (2007). The impact of intergroup emotions on forgiveness in Northern Ireland. *Group Processes and Intergroup Relations, 10,* 119–136.

Teng, F., Chen, Z., Poon, K. T., & Zhang, D. (2015). Sexual objectification pushes women away: The role of decreased likability. *European Journal of Social Psychology, 45,* 77–87.

Tileagă, C. (2007). Ideologies of moral exclusion: A critical discursive reframing of depersonalization, delegitimization and dehumanization. *British Journal of Social Psychology, 46,* 717–737.

Vaes, J., & Muratore, M. (2013). Defensive dehumanization in medical practice: A cross-sectional study from a health care worker's perspective. *British Journal of Social Psychology, 52,* 180–190.

Vaes, J., Paladino, M., & Leyens, J.-P. (2002). The lost email: Pro-social reactions induced by uniquely human emotions. *British Journal of Social Psychology, 41,* 521–534.

Vasquez, E. A., Loughnan, S., Gootjes-Dreesbach, E. L., & Weger, U. (2014). The animal in you: Animalistic descriptions of a violent crime bias sentencing decisions. *Aggressive Behavior, 40,* 337–344.

Viki, G. T., & Abrams, D. (2003). Infra-humanization: Ambivalent sexism and the attribution of primary and secondary emotions to women. *Journal of Experimental Social Psychology, 39,* 492–499.

Viki, G. T., Fullerton, I., Raggett, H., Tait, F., & Wiltshire, S. (2012). The role of dehumanization in attitudes toward the social exclusion and rehabilitation of sex offenders. *Journal of Applied Social Psychology, 42,* 2349–2367.

Viki, G. T., Osgood, D., & Phillips, S. (2013). Dehumanization and self-reported proclivity to torture prisoners of war. *Journal of Experimental Social Psychology, 49,* 325–328.

Waytz, A., & Epley, N. (2012). Social connection enables dehumanization. *Journal of Experimental Social Psychology, 48,* 70–76.

Zebel, S., Zimmermann, A., Viki, G. T., & Doosje, B. (2008). Dehumanization and guilt as distinct but related predictors of support for reparation policies. *Political Psychology, 29,* 193–219.

Zhang, H., Chan, D. K., Teng, F., & Zhang, D. (2015). The role of interpersonal security and preference for harsh actions against others: The role of dehumanization. *Journal of Experimental Social Psychology, 56,* 165–171.

CHAPTER 9

The Social Psychology of Genocide and Mass Atrocities

Johanna Ray Vollhardt and Maggie Campbell-Obaid

Attempts at understanding the psychological principles that drive human behavior in genocide and mass atrocities often invoke discussions about the concepts of good and evil. Genocide and mass atrocities are commonly described as a particular evil, among the cruelest behaviors human beings engage in. Social psychologists aiming to understand this phenomenon often use the term *evil* in their titles of books and articles on this topic and refer to genocide and mass atrocities to discuss the "evil side of human nature" more broadly (e.g., *The Roots of Evil: The Origins of Genocide and Other Group Violence*, Staub, 1989; *Evil: Inside Human Violence and Cruelty*, Baumeister, 1997; *Becoming Evil: How Ordinary People Commit Genocide and Mass Killing*, Waller, 2007; and *The Lucifer Effect: Understanding How Good People Turn Evil*, Zimbardo, 2008). As Furey (2012) notes in his review of Mikulincer and Shaver's (2012) *The Social Psychology of Morality: Exploring the Causes of Good and Evil*, "psychologists who study morality are increasingly comfortable using the term *evil*" (p. 2).

Indeed, the concept of genocide in particular often brings to mind what are seen as prototypes of pure evil, such as Hitler, Stalin, or Pol Pot, who were responsible for the deaths of millions of innocent (i.e., "good") people. In this way, lay perceptions of genocide and mass atrocities may often involve an understanding of the events as a "triumph of evil" (Public Broadcasting System, n.d.), by which an active force of pure evil among the perpetrators prevails over the pure good elements of society, including the seemingly passive victim group. However, historical and social psychological scholarship illustrates that the full picture of genocide and mass atrocities is often more complicated. For example, beyond the actions of the perpetrator group, the tacit support or silence of bystanders allows mass atrocities to occur (Staub, 1989). Starting with Hannah Arendt's (1963) groundbreaking work on the Eichmann trials, described in her book *Eichmann in Jerusalem: A Report on the Banality of Evil*, and continuing with Milgram's (1974) famous studies on obedience, social scientists have increasingly focused on mundane psychological processes such as obedience and conformity (Browning, 1992; Miller, 2014 and Chapter 10, this volume) or the need for restoring control in the face of difficult life circumstances (Frey & Rez, 2002; Staub, 1989) to explain why and how human beings engage in or support extreme violence. Further, despite the characterization of the perpetrator group as "pure evil," in every genocide there are examples of heroic rescuers in this group (Bilewicz & Jaworska, 2013). Additionally, there is increasing recognition of resistance groups in the Holocaust and other cases of genocide and mass atrocities (Haslam & Reicher, 2012; Middleton-Kaplan, 2014; Tec, 2013). This resistance under such extreme circumstances, which is often viewed as heroic and even as a moral imperative, also involves moral dilemmas and violence that were not always an obvious or easy decision for those involved (Glass, 2004). Moreover, in any genocide, some members of the victim group collaborate with the perpetrator group to ensure their survival or the survival of some at the expense of others' demises (e.g., Frankl, 1959/1984; Trunk, 1996).

Thus the distinction between victims, bystanders, and perpetrators during genocide and mass killing (Hilberg, 1993) is not always so clear-cut, and the lines between these social roles are, in many cases, blurred (see Bilewicz & Vollhardt, 2012). Accordingly, the clear distinction between "good" and "evil" is also not always a given. Although we do not argue against the fact that genocide and mass atrocities are among the worst events imaginable and involve evil actions, we believe it is important to take into account the moral complexity of these situations and also to consider the possible effects it may have when perpetrators and victim groups are morally typecast into roles of those who are (or experience) good versus evil (Gray & Wegner, 2009). We therefore preface this chapter with a brief review of the use of the terms *good* and *evil* in discourse about genocide and mass killing. This includes several examples from political rhetoric, as well as recent social psychological research suggesting that this very process of labeling people and groups as good and evil in itself contributes to support for mass atrocities and killing.

SOCIAL-PSYCHOLOGICAL CONSEQUENCES OF USING THE TERM *EVIL*

Some social psychologists and other scholars note that there are potential pitfalls in conceptualizing genocide and mass atrocities through the lens of a "good versus evil" mind set. Waller (2001) contends that human beings want to understand genocide as a product of "purely evil people" (p. 14) in order to distance ourselves from the possibility of committing such evil actions, but that neither the purely evil nor purely good exist in reality. Baumeister (1997) argues similarly that the "myth of pure evil" is "always a false image that is imposed or projected on the opponent" (p. 62) in order to keep our distance from the possibility of evil. This helps us to view good and evil as oppositional forces, with ourselves on the side of the good, and can legitimize violence to address the evil—which biblical scholar Wink (1992) refers to as "redemptive violence." During warfare, an exaggerated view of the enemy's evilness—communicated through propaganda depicting the enemy as monstrous or as allied with the devil (Herf, 2006; Keen, 1986)—is a major catalyst for violence and spiraling hostilities (White, 2004). Abundant anecdotal evidence of the use of this "good versus evil" rhetoric to garner support for the use of violence can be found in the United States' political discourse of the so-called War on Terror, from both liberal and conservative politicians. For example, in his farewell address to the nation, former President George W. Bush (2009) recognized his repeated use of this framing and stood by it, saying, "America must maintain our moral clarity. I've often spoken to you about good and evil, and this has made some uncomfortable. But good and evil are present in this world, and between the two there can be no compromise." Similar divisions and support for violence were evident in President Barack Obama's (2009) Nobel Peace Prize acceptance speech: "Evil does exist in the world. A nonviolent movement could not have halted Hitler's armies. Negotiations cannot convince al Qaeda's leaders to lay down their arms." The label *evil* has continued to be used in recent years in discussions related to the use of force and militarism against enemy groups, most recently applied to the group known as either the Islamic State of Iraq and Syria (ISIS) or the Islamic State of Iraq and the Levant (ISIL). Finally, the use of the term *evil* for former perpetrators of violence may even affect the political course in the aftermath of violence. Specifically, this can reduce the chances of reconciliation because "it is hard to reconcile with infinite evil; it is perhaps easier to reconcile with bad that is not entirely evil" (Gibson, 2006, p. 101).

Recent social-psychological research has begun to empirically examine the effects of perceiving others as evil. For example, the findings show that criminal offenders are demonized more when they are described according to a prototype of evil—such as displaying a lack of remorse for their actions or having a history of antisocial behavior (Ellard, Miller, Baumle,

& Olson, 2002; van Prooijen & van de Veer, 2010). Similarly, labeling a sex offender as evil was associated with more hatred toward the offender and more punitive responses (Burris & Rempel, 2011). In the intergroup realm, we found that the belief that some people are "just evil" predicted stronger support for a number of violent intergroup positions, including the death penalty for Muslim perpetrators of shootings in the United States, the continued possession of nuclear weapons by the United States, and the use of enhanced interrogation techniques at Guantanamo Bay (Campbell & Vollhardt, 2014). Further, believing that some people are just evil was associated with less support for nonviolent strategies to intergroup conflict, such as the creation of a U.S. Department of Peace, forgiving suspected terrorists, and U.S. reparations to the people of Fallujah in Iraq who have been severely harmed as a result of the U.S. sieges. In almost all cases, the underlying process driving these effects was that people who believe in evil and support violence against perceived enemies also tend to endorse redemptive violence, that is, the belief that violence is the best way of dealing with evil in the world. Importantly, these effects were found above and beyond the influence of demographic variables, political ideology, closed-mindedness, implicit theories of morality as fixed (as opposed to malleable), belief in a dangerous world, right-wing authoritarianism, and religious fundamentalism (Campbell & Vollhardt, 2014). Webster and Saucier (2013) similarly found that believing in pure evil predicted stronger levels of support for military action against Iran given provocation, preemptive military action by the United States, and the use of torture techniques by the United States. These effects were again found above and beyond other influential factors, such as empathic concern and social dominance orientation.

Taken together, the work on this topic suggests that some caution is needed when applying the labels of *good* and *evil* to groups of people, particularly in situations of mass atrocities, as such rhetoric may serve to legitimize ongoing violence and render any other diplomatic actions less feasible options. Additionally, as argued by Dawes (2014) in the context of the conflict with ISIS, calling a group evil may undermine the attempt to understand the terror group's recruitment strategies and tactics, thus making it more difficult to overcome this problem. That said, the use of the term *evil* may help draw attention to genocide and mass atrocities and galvanize bystanders to action. Perhaps it is possible to label the *acts* of genocide and mass atrocities as evil without applying this terminology to the actors involved, thus creating the space for constructive dialogue regarding diplomatic actions and the difficult process of reconciliation following such violence. However, it is also important to keep in mind that many people reject such explanations that are focused on situational rather than individual factors contributing to violence, because such explanations are often viewed as condoning the perpetrators (see Miller, Chapter 10, this volume).

ORGANIZATION OF THE REMAINDER OF THIS CHAPTER

In the remainder of this chapter, we discuss some of the social-psychological influences that shape behavior among perpetrator, victim, and bystander groups during genocide and mass atrocities. Within each of these social roles, we explore both the processes that contribute to negative, destructive (what could be considered "evil") behaviors in genocide and mass atrocities and the processes that contribute to positive, prosocial (what could be considered "good") phenomena in this context. This discussion of both processes within each of the social roles provides further support for the notion that the distinctions between perpetrators, bystanders, and victims are sometimes blurred (Bilewicz & Vollhardt, 2012) and, likewise, that portrayals of perpetrators as "purely evil" and bystanders and victims as "purely good" are often not accurate (Campbell & Vollhardt, 2014).

Definitions of genocide and mass atrocities are difficult and often contested and have resulted in many cases of such violence not being acknowledged. We base our definitions on Straus (2011), who defined *genocide* as "a form of extensive, group-selective violence whose purpose is the destruction of that group in a territory under the control of a perpetrator" (p. 4). "Group-selective" means that people are targeted because of their membership in certain groups, which are not limited to race, ethnicity, religion, or nationality but can also include class, political ideology, or other social categories (Straus, 2011). *Mass atrocities* is a broader term and includes not only genocide but also other attacks against civilians that are not always group-selective, such as crimes against humanity and war crimes (Straus, 2011). A lot of the available social-psychological research on genocide has focused on the Holocaust, and our chapter reflects that. However, whenever possible we integrate available research on other contexts in which mass atrocities occurred, such as in Darfur and Rwanda or the Armenian genocide. We also refer the interested reader to several extensive books reviewing research and scholarship on this topic from a social-psychological perspective, such as by Baumeister (1997), Newman and Erber (2002), Staub (1989, 2011), and Waller (2007). Although it is beyond the scope of this chapter to summarize these works here, we select a few examples of social-psychological research and theorizing in each of the categories described above (destructive and constructive processes among perpetrators, bystanders, and victims)—without attempting to be in any way complete, but aiming to portray the complex social-psychological and moral dynamics involved in mass atrocities and genocide. Notably, there is a different degree of work on each of these intersections, and some make more (moral, intuitive, as well as empirical) sense than others. Finally, it is important to note that social-psychological research on the *aftermath* of genocide is growing (Vollhardt & Bilewicz, 2013) and has become more common than research on genocide and mass atrocities themselves. There are several reasons for this: The aftermath of mass atrocities is easier to study than situations of ongoing violence; there is generally increased attention in global society toward addressing historical trauma and human rights violations (Barkan, 2000; Fassin & Rechtman, 2009); and the aftermath of violence has important implications for reconciliation and the prevention of future genocide and mass atrocities (Staub, 2013). Although a discussion of these dynamics is beyond the scope of this chapter, we refer to another chapter in this volume that addresses some of the social-psychological processes involved in the aftermath of genocide (Branscombe, Wohl, & Warner, Chapter 17, this volume).

PERPETRATORS

Although several important strands of psychological research in the decades following the Second World War were stimulated by the urgent need to understand Nazi Germany and the Holocaust (e.g., research on the "authoritarian personality" or F [Fascism] scale: Adorno, Frankel-Brunswick, Levinson, & Sanford, 1950; Milgram's obedience experiments: Miller, 2014 and Chapter 10, this volume), more comprehensive psychological models of genocide and mass atrocities have been developed only more recently. The perhaps most well-known model was proposed by Staub (1989). Because this model is also the most comprehensive, we use Staub's framework to organize other findings that relate to and build on his model of the "continuum of destruction." In regard to the empirical evidence for this model and related theories and constructs, it is important to note that due to the nature of genocide and mass atrocities, the controlled empirical studies that are commonly favored in social psychology are difficult if not impossible in this context. Therefore, the available empirical evidence for these models and theories is triangulated from historical scholarship, archival analysis (e.g., of diaries, letters, official documents, and propaganda), and anecdotal evidence, as well as findings from less severe contexts of intergroup conflict and artificially created contexts in the lab in times of relative peace.

Basic Societal and Psychological Processes

The basic model of the perpetration of genocide and mass atrocities that Staub (1989) proposes takes societal conditions as a starting point. Specifically, Staub proposes that "difficult life conditions," such as a sudden economic crisis or conditions of war, frustrate basic human needs for security, control, a positive social identity, and meaning. When these frustrated needs are then satisfied in destructive ways, it can initiate a continuum of destruction whereby genocide and mass atrocities gradually develop and unfold (as opposed to suddenly erupting). Two central examples of how frustrated human needs are satisfied in destructive ways include scapegoating and following destructive ideologies: People often scapegoat minority groups who are blamed for societal problems and whose marginalization and ultimate removal from society is seen as a solution to the problems society faces. Similarly, destructive ideologies are promulgated that glorify the ingroup while derogating other groups in society. This basic model Staub presents is very much in the social-psychological tradition of examining both individual-level and situational factors and how they interact with each other (see also Newman, 2002).

Situational- and Societal-Level Factors

Staub (1989) notes that genocide is particularly likely under conditions of group conflict and war, in part because these conditions create difficult life circumstances that frustrate basic human needs. In addition, preexisting violent conflict normalizes violence and provides political opportunities for authorities to take extreme measures to deal with the challenges (Harff, 2003). This is empirically supported by political scientist Barbara Harff's (2003) comparative analysis of 126 cases of internal wars and regime collapses between 1955 and 1997, 35 of which led to genocide or politicide. Harff identified six factors that differentiated these cases from those that did not lead to genocide or politicide with 74% accuracy. In all but one of the studied cases, genocide occurred either during or in the aftermath of political upheaval (defined as "an abrupt change in the political community" and including "defeat in wars, revolutions, anticolonial rebellions, separatist wars, coups, and regime transitions"; Harff, 2003, p. 62).

Other political- and societal-level risk factors for genocide that Harff identified include previous genocides; an ethnic minority group being in power; low trade openness, which means low international economic interdependence and control; and an autocratic (as opposed to a democratic or semidemocratic) state form. The latter corresponds to Staub's (1989) analysis, which focuses on "monolithic" (as opposed to pluralistic) societies that follow one particular set of values and goals—rather than allowing for the expression of diverse opinions—as one of the societal-level conditions that facilitate genocide and mass atrocities. Finally, Harff's empirical analysis also shows that the presence of exclusionary ideologies among the ruling elites is one of the predictors of genocide. An ideology is defined as exclusionary when it "identifies some overriding purpose or principle that justifies efforts to restrict, persecute, or eliminate certain categories of people" (Harff, 2003, p. 63). For example, Jews in Nazi Germany were targeted based on ideas about alleged racial purity and building an "Aryan" nation of ethnic Germans; the Khmer Rouge ideology that culminated in the

Cambodian genocide was based on the idea of eliminating all social classes except for the peasant class; and the "Hutu Power" ideology that resulted in the Rwandan genocide called for the exclusion of Tutsis from political power and public institutions. These ideologies correspond to what Staub refers to as "moral exclusion" (see also Opotow, 2011) and are part of the "destructive ideologies" he identifies as part of any genocide and mass atrocities. Because these ideologies occur on a broader, collective level and require political leadership in order to spread, we place them within the category of societal-level factors that contribute to genocide. However, obviously people within a given society agree with these ideologies to different degrees, and ideologies therefore also belong in the category of individual differences that predict varying levels of support for violent conflict (see also Cohrs, 2012). The same is true for the roles of obedience and respect for authority, which many social scientists present as one of the key factors in explaining how genocide and mass atrocities unfold (Adorno et al., 1950; Milgram, 1974; Miller, 2014 and Chapter 10, this volume; Prunier, 1995; Staub, 1989; Suedfeld & Schaller, 2002): Obedience and authoritarianism can refer to both individual-difference variables and to characteristics that are widespread in a given society (as frequently discussed in regard to Rwanda: e.g., Prunier, 1995; and prewar Germany: e.g., Staub, 1989).

Ideology and Intergroup Attitudes

Social-psychological research helps us understand the elements and psychological functions of the "destructive ideologies" (Staub, 1989) that are at the core of any genocide or mass atrocities. As noted above, one characteristic of ideologies that are part of genocide is that they are based on restricting the rights of and persecuting members of certain groups. However, this does not happen automatically once group distinctions are made; and social categorization of people into "us" versus "them" is only a necessary and not a sufficient condition for genocidal ideologies. This mere distinction between ingroup and outgroup members (Tajfel & Turner, 1979) does not by itself explain why people become violent against other groups. It predicts favoring the ingroup but not aggression against the outgroup; or, as Marilynn Brewer (1999) put it, ingroup love is not the same as outgroup hate. Therefore, the specific content of the identity as well as ideology is important, and the following additional elements are needed in order to turn into a destructive ideology that contributes to genocide and mass atrocities.

First, destructive ideologies entail that the outgroup is defined as a problem and an obstacle to a better society (Baumeister, 1997, 2002; Staub, 1989). In other words, a group is selected as a scapegoat, and the problems of society are blamed on the presence and influence of this group (Glick, 2002; Staub, 1989). Sociologist Zygmunt Bauman (1991) compares this to social engineering, in which the elements (including groups and people) that disrupt or stand in the way of a societal ideal are identified, and their elimination is portrayed as the only way to achieve the ideal. Thus destructive ideologies leading to genocide and mass atrocities are not based simply on the moral exclusion of outgroups, whereby moral standards regarding the treatment of other human beings are not applied to the targeted outgroup (Opotow, 2011). Rather, destructive ideologies also include the idea that this exclusion and elimination of the targeted outgroup serves a higher purpose, namely to achieve a better society. These characteristics of destructive ideologies suggest that they serve a psychological function, as Staub (1989) points out: Because these ideologies clearly identify a problem as well as a solution, they satisfy certain human needs that are frustrated in the face of difficult life conditions, such as the need for control over one's life and the need for meaning and understanding (see also Frey & Rez, 2002). Here it is also important to distinguish between those who instigate and those who perpetrate the violence by physically carrying it out (see Mandel, 2002): It is presumably the instigators of genocide who are responsible for crafting and promoting destructive ideologies that "serve a catalytic role in the development of collective violence" (Mandel, 2002, p. 262) that is carried out by perpetrators who respond to the destructive ideologies.

But which groups are targeted by these destructive ideologies that eventually can lead to genocide and mass atrocities? Glick's work on an ideological model of scapegoating (2002) extends Staub's initial ideas, proposing theoretically driven predictions of which groups will be selected as scapegoats that are blamed for society's problems. Specifically, and based on the general stereotype content model (Fiske, Cuddy, Glick, & Xu, 2002), Glick argues that those groups that are stereotyped as powerful and competent, as well as cold (giving rise to so-called "envious prejudice"), are chosen as scapegoats. For example, Jews were stereotyped by Nazis (and others) as rich and as influencing political and economic affairs through global conspiracies (see also Herf, 2006). Similar stereotypes (in regard to wealth and status) of Armenians and Tutsis existed before and throughout the Armenian genocide and the Rwandan genocide as well. Although this may at first appear counterintuitive based on what we know about the derogation of victim groups during genocide, it makes sense that groups stereotyped as high in status and influence (and not low in status and competence) are selected as scapegoats, because only groups with these perceived characteristics would actually create a serious threat (Glick, 2002; see also Bilewicz & Vollhardt, 2012). Additionally, Glick (2002), as well as Staub (1989), argue that groups selected as scapegoats have often already been historically derogated and blamed such that there is a cultural narrative that leaders and other ideologists can easily tap into and activate.

In addition to these particular views of the targeted outgroup, Staub (1989) argues that destructive ideologies also entail a certain view of the ingroup: namely, a belief in the ingroup's superiority (cultural and otherwise) that is accompanied by a sense of vulnerability, for example, due to the contrast between the past glory of the ingroup and its later decline. This sense of fragility in regard to the collective identity and self-esteem of the group corresponds to the notion of "threatened egotism," which Baumeister (1997, 2002) identifies as one of the sources of genocide and mass atrocities. A related line of research similarly suggests that collective narcissism—which describes an idealized view of the ingroup's greatness that is, however, unstable and sensitive to threats to the ingroup's image—predicts intergroup hostility and aggression (Golec de Zavala, Cichocka, Eidelson, & Jayawickreme, 2009). Likewise, empirical tests of an important distinction between attachment to versus glorification of the ingroup (Roccas, Sagiv, Schwartz, Halevy, & Eidelson, 2008) reveal that only ingroup glorification, not mere attachment to the ingroup, predicts support for intergroup violence (Leidner, Castano, Zaiser, & Giner-Sorolla, 2010). These theories and findings once again demonstrate that it is not the distinction between ingroups and outgroups per se that is responsible for intergroup violence, but rather the specific ways in which these social categories and group identities are construed and the ideologies that are attached to them (see also Livingstone & Haslam, 2008).

Psychological Processes Facilitating Destruction

Staub (1989) and several other scholars suggest additional psychological processes that facilitate the gradual progression of violence and enable human beings and societies to participate in mass atrocities and genocide. One group of processes concerns psychological changes among individual perpetrators and the perpetrator group as a whole (see also Bilewicz & Vollhardt, 2012). As the moral exclusion of victim groups, as well as violence against them, progresses, new norms are established, and this violence is normalized in society. Additionally, people can become habituated to violence and desensitized after an initial period of shock and physical discomfort (e.g., Carnagey, Anderson, & Bushman, 2007). Psychiatrist Robert Jay Lifton (1986), who analyzed accounts of Nazi doctors, Hiroshima bombers, and others who carried out or witnessed mass atrocities, refers to this as "psychic numbing."

Another group of relevant psychological processes involve how the targeted group is treated and labeled. In addition to the moral exclusion and delegitimization of the victim group (see also Bar-Tal & Hammack, 2012) that goes along with the deprivation of civil rights, victim groups are also dehumanized. Dehumanization (see Haslam, 2006; Haslam & Loughnan, Chapter 8, this volume) can take many different forms, but during genocide and mass atrocities animalistic dehumanization is often observed in which the victim group is compared to animals—for example,

Nazis likened Jews to lice or rats; in the Rwandan genocide, Tutsi were referred to as cockroaches; and in the genocide in Darfur, documented epithets included several animal comparisons, such as with dogs, donkeys, or monkeys (Hagan & Rymond-Richmond, 2008). Dehumanization is among the mechanisms of moral disengagement outlined by Bandura (1999), who argued—along with several other social scientists (e.g., Opotow, 2001)—that portraying victim groups as less than human facilitates mistreatment and killing because most people have less moral concern about doing this to animals than to other human beings. Notably, this process does not appear to be at odds with the selection of otherwise high-status victim groups, as described in the scapegoating model by Glick (2002). The two distinct depictions of the same victim group can happen concurrently or can transition from high-status to low-status dehumanized depictions as the genocide progresses (Bilewicz & Vollhardt, 2012). Similarly, euphemistic labeling is another mechanism of moral disengagement, whereby people avoid direct terms such as *killing* and instead use terms that do not carry any moral implications, thereby allowing people to evade thinking or talking about the nature of their actions (Bandura, 1999). For example, Nazis invented a number of euphemisms, such as *Sonderbehandlung* ("special treatment") to refer to executions and *Endlösung* ("final solution") to refer to the goal of killing all Jews in Europe (Klemperer, 2006). Likewise, in the Rwandan genocide, Hutus were summoned to participate in the killings that were referred to as part of *umuganda* (community service or communal work), which traditionally in Rwandan society has involved tasks that benefit the community (Des Forges, 1999).

Finally, Baumeister (1997, 2002) points to two additional motives that are not centrally addressed in Staub's model, namely sadism and instrumentalism. Getting sadistic pleasure from harming other people can be a motive during genocide and mass atrocities, but Baumeister notes that this is presumably a rather minor factor and limited to a few individual cases (see also Waller, 2007, Chapter 3). Instrumental gain, on the other hand, is a more common motive for participating in genocide. Looting and appropriation of the victim group's possessions is part of every genocide. For example, political scientist Scott Straus (2006) found in his interviews with prisoners in Rwanda who were incarcerated for their participation in the genocide that many had joined in because of the opportunities to loot—which, in the face of the difficult life conditions that are often the context of genocide, could be particularly tempting (see also Dean, 2008; Gross, 2012; Üngör & Polatel, 2013, for analyses of the role of economic gains in other genocides).

In sum, with some exceptions (e.g., the "psychopathology hypothesis"; see Waller, 2007, Chapter 3), psychological theories of why people perpetrate genocide and mass atrocities have tended to focus on ordinary processes. Additionally, while many of these theories highlight individual processes, it is obvious that societal-level, macrolevel factors trigger and interact with these processes. In other words, it is only in the presence of specific societal conditions and political structures that ordinary psychological processes such as obedience and conformity or the need for security and control transform into such destructive dynamics as in genocide and mass atrocities. For example, in times of relative peace and in the presence of prosocial norms, conformity and obedience can contribute to prosocial behavior and cooperation (e.g., Tomasello, 2014). Moreover, even in times of conflict and genocide, conformity with prosocial role models and authorities can result in rescuing behavior rather than participation in the violence (see Oliner & Oliner, 1988; Rochat & Modigliani, 1995). Therefore, the role of constructive versus destructive leaders and ideologies is crucial in determining how situations evolve that carry the risk factors for violence (see Haslam & Reicher, 2012; Staub, 2011). For example, many people have speculated about how post-apartheid South Africa may have developed had Nelson Mandela not been the leader of the country.

Prosocial Processes among Perpetrators

As noted by sociologist Bradley Campbell (2010), most studies on genocide focus on either perpetrator or rescuer behavior but rarely address the fact that even perpetrators sometimes help members of the victim group while also continuing to participate in killing others. Thereby (as we have noted above), these behaviors are often treated as if they belonged to mutually exclusive categories of people, rather than focusing on the act itself. In result, many interesting cases of seemingly "contradictory behavior" (Campbell, 2010) during genocide are overlooked and excluded by researchers. This creates a gap in our knowledge and understanding of human behavior during mass killing and genocide. As Campbell (2010) notes, this oversight may be motivationally driven: "Contradictory behavior by individuals during genocides may seem shocking and incomprehensible. . . . It may even be morally shocking, since it challenges common notions of good and evil" (p. 310).

However, historical examples of perpetrators who occasionally also helped members of the victim group can be drawn from many different cases of genocide and mass atrocities (Campbell, 2010). For example, in the Rwandan genocide some Hutu perpetrators also saved individual Tutsi victims, usually family members or other people they knew (Mamdani, 2001; Waldorf, 2009). Because personal connections seemed to be present in many of these instances of helping behavior, Campbell (2010) proposed that interpersonal closeness and interdependence between members of different groups can explain these seemingly contradictory behaviors—a prediction that would be supported by social-psychological research on the contact hypothesis and the role of individuation or personalization (i.e., being able to see the individual and not just the group membership through personal interactions) in explaining positive effects of intergroup contact (Miller, 2002). However, historical research on any genocide is also replete with examples of neighbors killing or turning in neighbors and sometimes even family members (e.g., des Forges, 1999; Hilberg, 1993), and therefore this explanation is not sufficient. Moreover, other historical examples show that in some cases perpetrators refused to kill or evaded orders to kill, even if those targeted were strangers (Browning, 1992). Therefore, much more research is needed in order to illuminate the individual and situational conditions under which perpetrators differentiate between victims and come to experience inhibitions and moral qualms even when they have already been engaged in the act of killing. This kind of research would also acknowledge individual differences between perpetrators, as well as within perpetrators, showing that perpetrators are not "evil" all the time and that there are situational variations and conditions under which perpetrators may be compelled to engage in "good" actions.

BYSTANDERS

An important contribution of Staub's (1989) analysis of genocide and mass atrocities is his emphasis on the role of bystanders in allowing the violence to unfold. Staub argues that the passivity of bystanders and complicity in the face of evil acts encourages perpetrators and provides a sense of normalcy and acceptance of these acts. Moreover, passivity of bystanders contributes to a sense of pluralistic ignorance, whereby many people may disagree with what is happening but think they are alone in their views because nobody else is voicing dissent (and many others in the collective may be thinking the same; see Newman, 2002).

It is important to distinguish between internal and external bystanders (Staub, 1989, 2011). Internal bystanders are those who are members of the society at the time of mass atrocities but are not targeted or actively participating as perpetrators, and external bystanders are those who are not present in the given society but are in a position to know about the mass atrocities (Staub, 2011). Psychological research on both categories of bystanders is scarce.

External Bystanders

Several recent studies have used the context of the genocide in Darfur to study reactions of external bystanders to genocides happening in other countries. Two sets of studies focused on factors that reduce external bystanders' willingness to support interventions and aid to victims of genocide. One of these factors is the tendency to blame victims for their fate. A series of studies conducted among British students demonstrated that people were more likely to donate money to aid victims of the 2004 tsunami in Asia than to aid victims of the genocide in Darfur, because victims of the genocide were blamed more for their plight than were victims of the natural disaster (Zagefka, Noor, Brown, de Moura, & Hopthrow, 2011). Another series of studies demonstrated a "collapse of compassion" in the face of the enormous suffering caused by genocide (Cameron & Payne, 2011; see also Slovic, 2007). In the context of reports on the genocide in Darfur, these studies show that people become increasingly numb to human suffering and exhibit less empathy and prosocial behavior as the number of victims increases (Cameron & Payne, 2011). This happens because people regulate their emotions in order to protect themselves from increased distress that would occur when being confronted with greater human suffering. Interestingly, other instrumental, self-protective motives may be involved as well: In one experiment, participants who were told that they would be asked to donate money to aid the victims of the genocide in Darfur exhibited the "collapse of compassion" to a greater degree (Cameron & Payne, 2011).

Factors that promote prosocial attitudes and behaviors of external bystanders toward genocide in a foreign country include the ingroup's historical experience of genocide in other contexts and the perception of similarity between the ingroup's historical victimization and a present-day genocide or other case of collective victimization (Vollhardt, 2015). For example, the Jewish community in the United States was a major actor in the "Save Darfur" campaign, driven by the perceived moral duty to prevent other groups from suffering the same fate as Jews during the Holocaust (Vollhardt, 2012). An experiment among Jewish American students demonstrated that participants were most likely to sign a petition urging their senators to act against the genocide in Darfur when they had been reminded of the fact that the Holocaust had targeted both Jewish and non-Jewish victims and when this was done in such a way that the ingroup's particular fate was acknowledged (Vollhardt, 2013). Similarly, Warner, Wohl, and Branscombe (2014) demonstrated that Jewish participants who were asked to reflect on the lessons of the Holocaust for Jews reported that they felt morally obliged to help victims of the genocide in Darfur (but not victims who were perceived as adversaries in a conflict; i.e., Palestinians), which was mediated by perceived similarity with the other victim group and the desire to find benefits in the ingroup's suffering (see also Branscombe et al., Chapter 17, this volume). These empirical findings mirror what Klar, Schori-Eyal, and Klar (2013) have identified as one of the four lessons or "voices" of the Holocaust that developed in Jewish-Israeli society: "to never be a passive bystander."

Internal Bystanders

Social-psychological studies on internal bystanders during genocide and mass atrocities are even more scarce because of the difficulties of conducting this research, and they all rely on either archival analyses of historical documents or on retrospective self-reports in interviews and surveys. The most extensive psychological study on people who became what Staub (1989) refers to as "active bystanders" by rescuing Jews during the Holocaust was conducted by Oliner and Oliner (1988), who interviewed hundreds of rescuers and compared them with nonrescuers. This study revealed several situational factors that contributed to people's decisions to put their lives at risk to help members of the victim group. For example, a seemingly trivial but crucial factor was that rescuers had often been approached and asked to help (see also Varese & Yaish, 2000). This was more likely among those who had previous contact or extended contact with Jews, that is, among people who either had Jewish friends or colleagues or whose friends or family did. This was also found in a study on rescuers during the Armenian genocide, which revealed that they often had had previous contact with the person they rescued (Hovannisian, 1992).

Additionally, both Oliner and Oliner's (1988) study and archival analyses of the arguments that were used to save Bulgarian Jews during the Holocaust (Reicher, Cassidy, Wolpert, Hopkins, & Levine, 2006) suggests that group norms and communication about the ingroup's identity and values are crucial in explaining how internal bystanders become active and decide to help the victim group. More than half of the sample interviewed by Oliner and Oliner (1988) reported that they were motivated by perceived group norms, such that influential ingroup members (relatives, priests, other authorities) had conveyed the idea or had modeled through their own behavior that rescuing Jews was in line with their ingroup's norms and values. Similarly, Reicher et al.'s (2006) analysis of the arguments that were used to persuade Bulgarian citizens of the importance of saving Bulgarian Jews from being deported and killed revealed that helping fellow citizens who were threatened was framed as a normative act for the ingroup, that is, as being in line with Bulgarian identity and shared values.

Finally, several individual differences were identified as important factors in explaining who decided to help the victims and why. Above all, this involved inclusive attitudes that entailed perceiving the targeted victim group as part of a shared, superordinate identity (Reicher et al., 2006). Motivations to engage in rescuing behavior also included a sense of responsibility for and connection with members of other groups, which Oliner and Oliner (1988) refer to as "extensivity." Similarly, Suedfeld and de Best (2008) found in a content-analytic study of memoirs and interviews that universal values (including social justice and equality; see the conceptualization and measure developed by Schwartz, 1992) were higher among rescuers during the Holocaust (as compared to resistance fighters).

Blurred Lines between "Good" and "Evil" Behaviors among Bystanders

The question of whether bystanders act in "good" or "evil" ways is also not so clear-cut, and many complexities are apparent in the available studies of this role during genocide. Even seemingly "good" rescuers may engage in this behavior for reasons that are not always altruistic in nature (Oliner & Oliner, 1988). For example, many rescuers had instrumental motives and strategic reasons to help the victim group: Reicher et al.'s (2006) analysis suggests that leaders also appealed to ingroup interests in order to motivate Bulgarians to support the rescue of Jews, and almost half of the cases reported in Hovannisian's (1992) study of rescuers in the Armenian genocide had helped because they received money or were paid with labor. Similar motives were often reported in Oliner and Oliner's (1988) interviews as well. It is important, though, to take into account that these payments in form of money or labor did not always mean that the rescuers had a financial gain and enriched themselves. Because food was scarce in times of war, it was often simply a necessary condition in order to be able to provide for the additional people who were being hidden in people's houses or farms (Oliner & Oliner, 1988). However, some rescuers also took advantage of the situation by extorting money from people they offered to rescue. In Nazi-occupied Poland, people who blackmailed Jews who were in hiding were referred to as *szmalcovniks* (Ringelblum, 1976). Additionally, some rescuers during genocide eventually betrayed those they had previously helped, and others rescued some while turning in or even killing others (Campbell, 2010). Therefore, the lines between good and evil were often blurred among bystanders as well, and some bystanders slipped into the role of perpetrators at times.

VICTIMS

Most of the available psychological research on the perspective of the victim group in mass atrocities has, understandably, focused on how people manage to cope with and survive such extreme circumstances (e.g., Barel, Van IJzendoorn, Sagi-Schwartz, & Bakermans-Kranenburg, 2010; Frankl, 1959/1984). Much less is known about resistance, that is, how members of the victim group engage in acts that are "motivated by the intention to thwart, limit, or end the exercise of power of the oppressor group over the oppressed" (Tec, 2013, p. 4). This is perhaps due to the still fairly common characterization of members of the victim group as going passively "like lambs to the slaughter." Indeed, this view was often held even by members of the victim group itself—for example, the Israeli attorney general who prosecuted Adolf Eichmann described in his memoirs a letter he received stating: "I could not honor all my relatives about whom I had heard from my father. I loathed them for letting themselves be slaughtered" (Hausner, 1966, p. 43, as cited in Haslam & Reicher, 2012).

However, despite early views of the victim group as passive, resistance in its various forms was omnipresent during the Holocaust, on both individual and collective levels (Haslam & Reicher, 2012; Middleton-Kaplan, 2014; Tec, 2013). Even in circumstances of extreme oppression, such as in the ghettos and extermination camps, uprisings and rebellions occurred. Further, individual resistance in many forms, such as shirking work, hiding, maintaining one's religious practices, and so forth, was also widespread (see Tec, 2013, for a discussion of various types of psychological and physical resistance). In the past two decades, there has been a small but growing body of social science research on what constitutes resistance and under what circumstances resistance is most likely to occur (e.g., Haslam & Reicher, 2012; Hollander & Einwohner, 2004; Einwohner, 2014; Tec, 2013). This work has primarily examined the context of the Holocaust. In the following we briefly summarize the available findings on the social-psychological factors and processes that contributed to collective resistance during the Holocaust. Collective resistance is defined as organized, unarmed, and (sometimes) armed resistance activities in coordination with others, such as in the ghetto underground, partisan groups, or camp and ghetto uprisings, as well as "collective humanitarian activities on behalf of others" (Tec, 2013, p. 13), such as escape networks or providing food, shelter, and education for other group members.

Perceptions of the Chance of Survival

Interestingly, though attempts at survival during a situation of genocide could in and of itself be viewed as a form of resistance, survival does not seem to have been the ultimate goal of many people involved in resistance activities (Haslam & Reicher, 2012; Tec, 2013). Indeed, a feeling of inevitability about one's death at the hands of the Nazis appears to have made resistance more likely, which is one reason why the Nazi regime tried to hide its intentions (Einwohner, 2009; Tiedens, 1997). This may go against the intuitive notion that some degree of hope or optimism is necessary for resistance. However, psychological and sociological analyses comparing the Warsaw ghetto—where an armed uprising took place—to other ghettos in which there was no sustained, collective resistance (e.g., Łódź) suggest that the opposite was the case: Resistance was often triggered by the knowledge of one's sure impending death, whereas the illusion of survival inhibited resistance activities (Einwohner, 2009; Tiedens, 1997).

Tiedens (1997) points to a number of factors that led the Jews in Łódź to be more optimistic about their chances of survival than the Jews in Warsaw: The Warsaw ghetto seemed temporary, and therefore the imminent danger of deportation or liquidation of the ghetto was more apparent; it was also less isolated from life outside the ghetto (e.g., many ghetto residents worked throughout the city), thus leading the Jews living in the Warsaw ghetto to obtain more information about the mass murder of Jews in other parts of the country. In contrast, the Łódź ghetto was more geographically isolated and insular in its functioning. It also appeared more permanent, for example, having its own currency and postal system. This encouraged the belief that Jews could live in the ghetto long term and work in a manner that was economically advantageous to the Nazi regime, thus ensuring their survival.

Similarly, Einwohner (2009) argues that when Jews in the ghetto both had access to information about the genocidal intentions of the Nazis and believed that information, collective resistance was more likely to occur. Those who believed survival in the ghetto was possible would likely not put themselves in danger by joining an uprising, but those who knew that the Nazis intended to kill all Jews wanted to at least die with dignity (Einwohner, 2003, 2009) while fighting. Einwohner's (2009) analysis suggests that barriers to acknowledging the genocidal intent of the Nazis and thus engaging in resistance included both "structural ignorance" (lack of access to information) and "cultured ignorance" (being unable to believe this extreme scenario of mass killings could be true). The latter corresponds to a "positivity bias" (see Bilewicz & Vollhardt, 2012, p. 295), namely the tendency toward optimism and the denial of negative information, which may be a reason for the passivity sometimes seen in victim groups.

Social Identity and Leadership

As is the case with bystanders and perpetrators, some research suggests that social identity processes also play a role in shaping behaviors during genocide among victim groups, including resistance activities. Haslam and Reicher's (2012) analysis of the famous uprising at the Nazi extermination camp of Sobibor suggests that the Nazis intuitively drew on social identity processes to demobilize the prisoners and thwart resistance. Specifically, they prevented a cohesive group identity from forming among the prisoners through policies that enforced separation among various oppressed groups and promoted the idea of individual mobility (as opposed to collective action to improve the group's situation; Tajfel & Turner, 1979) by awarding privileges to a selected few. These demobilization processes were counteracted in the case of Sobibor when roughly 80 Jewish soldiers from the Red Army arrived as new prisoners, a group that had formed a cohesive identity with norms for fighting and a clearly organized structure that facilitated collective resistance and ultimately led to an uprising in the camp. Haslam and Reicher (2012) stress, in addition to the preexisting shared identity of these Red Army soldiers, the importance of the emergent group identity in the camp that encouraged resistance and that was formed over time through a "common experience of subordination" (p. 168) and a perceived lack of opportunity to individually improve one's status.

In addition, both Einwohner (2007) and Haslam and Reicher (2012) stress the importance of leadership in explaining resistance, and it has been suggested that obedience to authority can in fact play a role in resistance among victim groups as well (Einwohner, 2014), just as it plays a role in explaining behaviors among bystanders and perpetrator groups.

The "Dark Side" of Resistance

Similar to the bystander and perpetrator roles, the victim category in genocide and mass atrocities is also heterogeneous and has complexities. For example, despite the heroic nature of resistance in such extreme circumstances, it can also involve violence and other behaviors, such as stealing food from civilians, that resisters themselves sometimes felt morally conflicted about (see Glass, 2004; Tec, 1993). It seems possible that some resisters may have undergone a moral transformation, parallel to what is often discussed for perpetrators (e.g., Staub, 1989), which allowed people under these extreme circumstances to commit what they would consider to be antisocial actions under other circumstances in the service of the greater cause of resistance to Nazi oppression (see also Monroe, 2008). As noted by Bilewicz and Vollhardt (2012), there were also non-Jewish resistance groups who killed Jews during the Holocaust, and some Jewish resistance groups killed Polish civilians in response to murders of hidden Jews by Nazis and the Polish Home Army (see also Perelman, 2003). Tec (1993) describes how some resisters in the partisan movement felt personally gratified through violent action against the Nazis, the German army, or other enemy groups.

Victor Frankl (1959/1984), a psychiatrist who survived Auschwitz and Dachau, later wrote a book about his experiences from the perspective of a survivor as well as a clinician analyzing the behavior of other prisoners. He described similar themes of moral complexity in the actions of members of the victim group:

> On the average, only those prisoners could keep alive who, after years of trekking from camp to camp, had lost all scruples in their fight for existence; they were prepared to use every means, honest and otherwise, even brutal force, theft, and betrayal of their friends, in order to save themselves. We who have come back, by the aid of many lucky chances or miracles—whatever one may choose to call them—we know: the best of us did not return. (pp. 5–6)

This quote is not included to suggest that all survivors of the Holocaust survived by immoral means, or that certain means of survival were not understandable and justifiable under the circumstances. Rather, we believe this additionally exemplifies the difficulty of uniformly and homogeneously labeling any group in a situation of mass atrocities as solely good or solely evil—even the victim group, which may be the most controversial claim because of the tendency to morally typecast victims as incapable of committing evil acts (Gray & Wegner, 2009). However, there are many accounts of members of the victim group collaborating to some extent with the perpetrators—for example, serving as accomplices in the camps by becoming guards in exchange for privileges (e.g., Hilberg, 1993). Additionally, although heavy blame has been placed on Jewish leaders in the ghettos (the so-called *Judenrat*) who were forced to help orchestrate oppression and deportation, these leaders did not always know that they were sending fellow Jews to their deaths, and the dilemmas they faced were created by the Nazis (Tiedens, 1997; Trunk, 1996). This further highlights the problem with using mutually exclusive labels of *good* or *evil* even in the extreme case of genocide and mass atrocities.

CONCLUSION

In sum, the social-psychological processes and factors that contribute to genocide and mass atrocities are often basic, ordinary processes that are relevant to other, peaceful contexts as well and that play a role (albeit in different manifestations) in shaping behaviors among victim, perpetrator, and bystander groups alike. For example, social identity processes, leadership, conformity, and group norms are relevant to all three categories. Therefore, it is the specific ideological content of group norms and identities as well as the interaction with particular situational and societal factors (including scarcity of resources and the conditions of war) that explain human behavior in times of genocide and mass atrocities, rather than a set of unique psychological processes and individual differences.

Moreover, our review demonstrates that within each of the social roles during genocide (bystander, victim, and perpetrator roles) there is fluidity and variation within the category, as well as between categories, such that individuals within each of these roles can act in good or evil ways. In order to gain a more complete understanding of the psychology of genocide and mass killing, we need to move beyond the essentialist idea that people or groups involved in genocide are good or evil. Instead, we should focus on the nature of the actions and the complexity of the social roles involved, as well as the potential for fluidity and transformations among people in these roles.

REFERENCES

Adorno, T., Frenkel-Brunswick, E., Levinson, D., & Sanford, N. (1950). *The authoritarian personality*. New York: Harper.

Arendt, H. (1963). *Eichmann in Jerusalem: A report on the banality of evil*. New York: Viking Press.

Bandura, A. (1999). Moral disengagement in the perpetration of inhumanities. *Personality and Social Psychology Review, 3*, 193–209.

Barel, E., Van IJzendoorn, M. H., Sagi-Schwartz, A., & Bakermans-Kranenburg, M. J. (2010). Surviving the Holocaust: A meta-analysis of the long-term sequelae of a genocide. *Psychological Bulletin, 136*, 677–698.

Barkan, E. (2000). *The guilt of nations: Restitution and negotiating historical injustices*. Baltimore, MD: John Hopkins University Press.

Bar-Tal, D., & Hammack, P. (2012). Conflict, delegitimization, and violence. In L. R. Tropp (Ed.), *Oxford handbook of intergroup conflict* (pp. 29–52). New York: Oxford University Press.

Bauman, Z. (1991). *Modernity and the Holocaust*. Ithaca, NY: Cornell University Press.

Baumeister, R. (1997). *Evil: Inside human violence and cruelty*. New York: Freeman/Holt.

Baumeister, R. (2002). The Holocaust and the four roots of evil. In L. Newman & R. Erber (Eds.), *Understanding genocide: The social psychology of the Holocaust* (pp. 241–258). New York: Oxford University Press.

Bilewicz, M., & Jaworska, M. (2013). Reconciliation through the righteous: The narratives of heroic helpers as a fulfillment of emotional needs in Polish–Jewish intergroup contact. *Journal of Social Issues, 69*, 162–179.

Bilewicz, M., & Vollhardt, J. R. (2012). Social psychological processes underlying genocide and mass killing. In A. Golec de Zavala & A. Cichocka (Eds.), *Social psychology of social problems: The intergroup context* (pp. 280–307). New York: Palgrave Macmillan.

Brewer, M. B. (1999). The psychology of prejudice: Ingroup love and outgroup hate? *Journal of Social Issues, 55*, 429–444.

Browning, C. (1992). *Ordinary men: Reserve police battalion 101 and the final solution in Poland*. New York: Harper Collins.

Burris, C. T., & Rempel, J. K. (2011). "Just look at him": Punitive responses cued by "evil" symbols. *Basic and Applied Social Psychology, 33*, 69–80.

Bush, G. W. (2009, January 15). Farewell address to the nation [Speech]. Retrieved from *www.americanrhetoric.com/speeches/gwbushfarewelladdress.htm*.

Cameron, C., & Payne, B. (2011). Escaping affect: How motivated emotion regulation creates insensitivity to mass suffering. *Journal of Personality and Social Psychology, 100*, 1–15.

Campbell, B. (2010). Contradictory behavior during genocides. *Sociological Forum, 25*, 296–314.

Campbell, M., & Vollhardt, J. R. (2014). Fighting the good fight: The relationship between belief in evil and support for violent policies. *Personality and Social Psychology Bulletin, 40*, 16–33.

Carnagey, N. L., Anderson, C. A., & Bushman, B. J. (2007). The effect of video game violence on physiological desensitization to real-life violence. *Journal of Experimental Social Psychology, 43,* 489–496.

Cohrs, J. C. (2012). Ideological bases of violent conflict. In L. R. Tropp (Ed.), *Oxford handbook of intergroup conflict* (pp. 53–71). New York: Oxford University Press.

Dawes, J. (2014, August 22). Should we call ISIS "evil"? *CNN Opinion.* Retrieved from *www.cnn.com/2014/08/22/opinion/dawes-isis-evil.*

Dean, M. (2008). *Robbing the Jews: The confiscation of Jewish property in the Holocaust, 1933–1945.* New York: Cambridge University Press.

Des Forges, A. L. (1999). *"Leave none to tell the story": Genocide in Rwanda.* New York: Human Rights Watch.

Einwohner, R. L. (2003). Opportunity, honor, and action in the Warsaw ghetto uprising of 1943. *American Journal of Sociology, 109,* 650–675.

Einwohner, R. L. (2007). Leadership, authority, and collective action: Jewish resistance in the ghettos of Warsaw and Vilna. *American Behavioral Scientist, 50,* 1306–1326.

Einwohner, R. L. (2009). The need to know: Cultured ignorance and Jewish resistance in the ghettos of Warsaw, Vilna, and Łódź. *Sociological Quarterly, 50,* 407–430.

Einwohner, R. L. (2014). Authorities and uncertainties: Applying lessons from the study of Jewish resistance during the Holocaust to the Milgram legacy. *Journal of Social Issues, 70,* 531–543.

Ellard, J. H., Miller, C. D., Baumle, T. L., & Olson, J. M. (2002). Just world processes in demonizing. In M. Ross & D. T. Miller (Eds.), *The justice motive in everyday life* (pp. 350–362). New York: Cambridge University Press.

Fassin, D., & Rechtman, R. (2009). *The empire of trauma: An inquiry into the condition of victimhood.* Princeton, NJ: Princeton University Press.

Fiske, S. T., Cuddy, A. J., Glick, P., & Xu, J. (2002). A model of (often mixed) stereotype content: Competence and warmth respectively follow from perceived status and competition. *Journal of Personality and Social Psychology, 82,* 878–902.

Frankl, V. (1984). *Man's search for meaning.* New York: Pocket Books/Simon & Shuster. (Original work published 1959)

Frey, D., & Rez, H. (2002). Population and predators: Preconditions for the Holocaust from a control-theoretical perspective. In L. S. Newman & R. Erber (Eds.), *Understanding genocide: The social psychology of the Holocaust* (pp. 188–221). New York: Oxford University Press.

Furey, R. (2012, February 8). The good, the bad, and the bystanders [Review of the book *The social psychology of morality: Exploring the causes of good and evil*]. *PsycCRITIQUES, 57.* Retrieved from *http://psqtest.typepad.com/blogPostPDFs/201200851_psq_57- 6_theGoodTheBadAndTheBystanders.pdf.*

Gibson, J. L. (2006). Overcoming apartheid: Can truth reconcile a divided nation? *Annals of the American Academy of Political and Social Science, 603,* 82–111.

Glass, J. M. (2004). *Jewish resistance during the Holocaust: Moral uses of violence and will.* New York: Palgrave Macmillan.

Glick, P. (2002). Sacrificial lambs dressed in wolves' clothing: Envious prejudice, ideology, and the scapegoating of Jews. In L. Newman & R. Erber (Eds.), *Understanding genocide: The social psychology of the Holocaust* (pp. 113–142). New York: Oxford University Press.

Golec de Zavala, A., Cichocka, A., Eidelson, R., & Jayawickreme, N. (2009). Collective narcissism and its social consequences. *Journal of Personality and Social Psychology*, 97, 1074–1096.

Gray, K., & Wegner, D. M. (2009). Moral typecasting: Divergent perceptions of moral agents and moral patients. *Journal of Personality and Social Psychology*, 96, 505–520.

Gross, J. T. (2012). *Golden harvest: Events at the periphery of the Holocaust*. New York: Oxford University Press.

Hagan, J., & Rymond-Richmond, W. (2008). The collective dynamics of racial dehumanization and genocidal victimization in Darfur. *American Sociological Review*, 73, 875–902.

Harff, B. (2003). No lessons learned from the Holocaust?: Assessing risks of genocide and political mass murder since 1955. *American Political Science Review*, 1, 57–73.

Haslam, N. (2006). Dehumanization: An integrative review. *Personality and Social Psychology Review*, 10, 252–264.

Haslam, S. A., & Reicher, S. D. (2012). When prisoners take over the prison: A social psychology of resistance. *Personality and Social Psychology Review*, 16, 154–179.

Herf, J. (2006). *The Jewish enemy: Nazi propaganda during World War II and the Holocaust*. Cambridge, MA: Harvard University Press.

Hilberg, R. (1993). *Perpetrators, victims, bystanders: The Jewish catastrophe 1933–1945*. New York: Harper Perennial.

Hollander, J. A., & Einwohner, R. L. (2004). Conceptualizing resistance. *Sociological Forum*, 19, 533–554.

Hovannisian, R. G. (1992). The question of altruism during the Armenian Genocide. In P. M. Oliner, S. P. Oliner, L. Baron, L. A. Blum, D. L. Krebs, & M. Smolenska (Eds.), *Embracing the other: Philosophical, psychological, and historical perspectives on altruism* (pp. 282–305). New York: New York University Press.

Keen, S. (1986). *Faces of the enemy: Reflections of the hostile imagination*. San Francisco: Harper & Row.

Klar, Y., Schori-Eyal, N., & Klar, Y. (2013). The "never again" state of Israel: The emergence of the Holocaust as a core feature of Israeli identity and its four incongruent voices. *Journal of Social Issues*, 69, 125–143.

Klemperer, V. (2006). *The language of the Third Reich*. London: Continuum.

Leidner, B., Castano, E., Zaiser, E., & Giner-Sorolla, R. (2010). Ingroup glorification, moral disengagement, and justice in the context of collective violence. *Personality and Social Psychology Bulletin*, 36, 1115–1129.

Lifton, R. J. (1986). *The Nazi doctors: Medical killing and the psychology of genocide*. New York: Basic Books.

Livingstone, A., & Haslam, S. A. (2008). The importance of social identity content in a setting of chronic social conflict: Understanding intergroup relations in Northern Ireland. *British Journal of Social Psychology*, 47, 1–21.

Mamdani, M. (2001). *When victims become killers: Colonialism, nativism, and the genocide in Rwanda.* Princeton, NJ: Princeton University Press.

Mandel, D. (2002). Instigators of genocide: Examining Hitler from a social psychological perspective. In L. S. Newman & R. Erber (Eds.), *Understanding genocide: The social psychology of the Holocaust* (pp. 259–284). New York: Oxford University Press.

Middleton-Kaplan, R. (2014). The myth of Jewish passivity. In P. Henry (Ed.), *Jewish resistance against the Nazis* (pp. 3–26). Washington, DC: Catholic University of America Press.

Mikulincer, M., & Shaver, P. M. (Eds.). (2012). *The social psychology of morality: Exploring the causes of good and evil.* Washington, DC: American Psychological Association.

Milgram, S. (1974). *Obedience to authority: An experimental view.* New York: Harper & Row.

Miller, A. G. (2014). The explanatory value of Milgram's obedience experiments: A contemporary appraisal. *Journal of Social Issues, 70,* 558–573.

Miller, N. (2002). Personalization and the promise of contact theory. *Journal of Social Issues, 58,* 387–410.

Monroe, K. R. (2008). Cracking the code of genocide: The moral psychology of rescuers, bystanders, and Nazis during the Holocaust. *Political Psychology, 29,* 699–736.

Newman, L. S. (2002). What is a "social-psychological" account of perpetrator behavior?: The person versus the situation in Goldhagen's *Hitler's Willing Executioners.* In L. S. Newman & R. Erber (Eds.), *Understanding genocide: The social psychology of the Holocaust* (pp. 43–67). New York: Oxford University Press.

Newman, L. S., & Erber, R. (Eds.). (2002). *Understanding genocide: The social psychology of the Holocaust.* New York: Oxford University Press.

Obama, B. (2009, December). *A just and lasting peace.* Talk presented at the Nobel Peace Prize Ceremony, Oslo, Norway. Retrieved from *www.nobelprize.org/nobel_prizes/peace/laureates/2009/obama-lecture_en.html.*

Oliner, S. P., & Oliner, P. M. (1988). *The altruistic personality: Rescuers of Jews in Nazi Europe.* New York: Collier Macmillan.

Opotow, S. (2001). Reconciliation in times of impunity: Challenges for social justice. *Social Justice Research, 14,* 149–170.

Opotow, S. (2011). How this was possible: Interpreting the Holocaust. *Journal of Social Issues, 67,* 205–224.

Perelman, M. (2003, August 8). Poles open probe into Jewish role in killings. *The Forward.* Retrieved from *www.forward.com/articles/7832.*

Prunier, G. (1995). *The Rwanda crisis: History of a genocide.* New York: Columbia University Press.

Public Broadcasting System. (n.d.). The triumph of evil: How the West ignored warnings of the 1994 Rwanda genocide and turned its back on the victims [Online documentary]. Retrieved from *www.pbs.org/wgbh/pages/frontline/shows/evil.*

Reicher, S., Cassidy, C., Wolpert, I., Hopkins, N., & Levine, M. (2006). Saving Bulgaria's Jews: An analysis of social identity and the mobilisation of social solidarity. *European Journal of Social Psychology, 36,* 49–72.

Ringelblum, E. (1976). *Polish–Jewish relations during the Second World War.* New York: Fertig.

Roccas, S., Sagiv, L., Schwartz, S., Halevy, N., & Eidelson, R. (2008). Toward a unifying model of identification with groups: Integrating theoretical perspectives. *Personality and Social Psychology Review, 12,* 280–306.

Rochat, F., & Modigliani, A. (1995). The ordinary quality of resistance: From Milgram's laboratory to the village of Le Chambon. *Journal of Social Issues, 51,* 195–210.

Schwartz, S. (1992). Universals in the content and structure of values: Theoretical advances and empirical tests in 20 countries. In M. Zanna (Ed.), *Advances in experimental social psychology* (Vol. 25, pp. 1–65). San Diego, CA: Academic Press.

Slovic, P. (2007). "If I look at the mass I will never act": Psychic numbing and genocide. *Judgment and Decision Making, 2,* 79–95.

Staub, E. (1989). *The roots of evil: The origins of genocide and other group violence.* New York: Cambridge University Press.

Staub, E. (2011). *Overcoming evil: Genocide, violent conflict, and terrorism.* New York: Oxford University Press.

Staub, E. (2013). A world without genocide: Prevention, reconciliation, and the creation of peaceful societies. *Journal of Social Issues, 69,* 180–199.

Straus, S. (2006). *The order of genocide: Race, power, and war in Rwanda.* Ithaca, NY: Cornell University Press.

Straus, S. (2011). Identifying genocide and related forms of mass atrocity (Working paper, United States Holocaust Memorial Museum). Retrieved from *www.ushmm.org/m/pdfs/20111219-identifying-genocide-and-mass-atrocity-strauss.pdf.*

Suedfeld, P., & de Best, S. (2008). Value hierarchies of Holocaust rescuers and resistance fighters. *Genocide Studies and Prevention, 3,* 31–42.

Suedfeld, P., & Schaller, M. (2002). Authoritarianism and the Holocaust: Some cognitive and affective implications. In L. Newman & R. Erber (Eds.), *Understanding genocide: The social psychology of the Holocaust* (pp. 68–90). New York: Oxford University Press.

Tajfel, H., & Turner, J. (1979). An integrative theory of intergroup conflict. In W. Austin & S. Worchel (Eds.), *The social psychology of intergroup relations* (pp. 33–48). Monterey, CA: Brooks-Cole.

Tec, N. (1993). *Defiance: The Bielski partisans.* New York: Oxford University Press.

Tec, N. (2013). *Resistance: Jews and Christians who defied the Nazi terror.* New York: Oxford University Press.

Tiedens, L. Z. (1997). Optimism and revolt of the oppressed: A comparison of two Polish Jewish ghettos of World War II. *Political Psychology, 18,* 45–69.

Tomasello, M. (2014). The ultra-social animal. *European Journal of Social Psychology, 44,* 187–194.

Trunk, I. (1996). *Judenrat: The Jewish councils in Eastern Europe under Nazi occupation.* Lincoln: University of Nebraska Press.

Üngör, U. U., & Polatel, M. (2013). *Confiscation and destruction: The Young Turk seizure of Armenian property.* London: Bloomsbury Academic.

van Prooijen, J. W., & van de Veer, E. (2010). Perceiving pure evil: The influence of cognitive load and prototypical evilness on demonizing. *Social Justice Research, 23*, 259–271.

Varese, F., & Yaish, M. (2000). The importance of being asked: The rescue of Jews in Nazi Europe. *Rationality and Society, 12*, 307–334.

Vollhardt, J. R. (2012). Interpreting rights and duties after mass violence. *Culture and Psychology, 18*, 133–145.

Vollhardt, J. R. (2013). "Crime against humanity" or "crime against Jews"?: Acknowledgment in construals of the Holocaust and its importance for intergroup relations. *Journal of Social Issues, 69*, 144–161.

Vollhardt, J. R. (2015). Inclusive victim consciousness in advocacy, social movements, and intergroup relations: Promises and pitfalls. *Social Issues and Policy Review, 9*, 89–120.

Vollhardt, J. R., & Bilewicz, M. (2013). After the genocide: Psychological perspectives on victim, bystander, and perpetrator groups. *Journal of Social Issues, 69*, 1–15.

Waldorf, L. (2009). Revisiting Hotel Rwanda: Genocide ideology, reconciliation, and rescuers. *Journal of Genocide Research, 11*, 101–125.

Waller, J. (2001). Perpetrators of genocide: An explanatory model of extraordinary human evil. *Journal of Hate Studies, 1*, 5–22.

Waller, J. (2007). *Becoming evil: How ordinary people commit genocide and mass killing* (2nd ed.). New York: Oxford University Press.

Warner, R. H., Wohl, M. J. A., & Branscombe, N. R. (2014). When do victim group members feel a moral obligation to help suffering others? *European Journal of Social Psychology, 44*, 231–241.

Webster, R. J., & Saucier, D. A. (2013). Angels and demons are among us: Assessing individual differences in belief in pure evil and belief in pure good. *Personality and Social Psychology Bulletin, 39*, 1455–1470.

White, R. K. (2004). Misperception and war. *Peace and Conflict: Journal of Peace Psychology, 10*, 399–409.

Wink, W. (1992). *Engaging the powers: Discernment and resistance in a world of domination*. Minneapolis, MN: Augsburg Fortress.

Zagefka, H., Noor, M., Brown, R., de Moura, G. R., & Hopthrow, T. (2011). Donating to disaster victims: Responses to natural and humanly caused events. *European Journal of Social Psychology, 41*, 353–363.

Zimbardo, P. (2008). *The Lucifer effect: Understanding how good people turn evil*. New York: Random House.

CHAPTER 10

Why Are the Milgram Obedience Experiments Still So Extraordinarily Famous—and Controversial?

Arthur G. Miller

Social psychology textbook and journal authors, in introducing the subject of obedience, invariably describe the Milgram experiments as famous and controversial (emphasis added in all):

> "Understanding when and why people obeyed authority, even if doing so harmed others, became Milgram's main concern, and his findings became perhaps *the best known and controversial* in social psychology" (Smith, Mackie, & Claypool, 2015, p. 371).
>
> "Milgram did not realize it at the time . . . but they were about to make history in *one of the most famous psychology experiments ever conducted*" (Kassin, Fein, & Markus, 2014, p. 279).
>
> "For half a century, the findings from Stanley Milgram's obedience studies have been among *the most intriguing and widely discussed data ever to come out of a psychology lab*" (Burger, 2014, p. 489).
>
> "Just over 50 years ago, in July, 1961, Stanley Milgram embarked on what were to become *the most famous studies in social psychology, if not the discipline of psychology as a whole*" (Reicher, Haslam, & Smith, 2012, p. 315).

Historically, the Milgram experiments are often tied to another group of "classic studies" in social psychology, by Sherif, Asch, Darley and Latané, Rosenhan, and Zimbardo (Smith & Haslam, 2012; Tavris, 2014). All of them, conducted within approximately a decade of one another, were conceptualized in strongly situationist terms, a conceptual orientation that Ross, Lepper, and Ward (2010) have described as "a major feature of our field, and with that perspective, the implicit suggestion that stable personality traits or dispositions matter less than lay observers assume, or at least that they can be outweighed by particular features or manipulations of the immediate situation at hand" (p. 5). As will be seen, however, this conceptualization has not been to everyone's liking, both within and outside of social psychology.

The enduring fame and controversiality of the Milgram obedience experiments are intriguing phenomena. This longevity is particularly remarkable given their long-acknowledged shortcomings—that is, as being unethical, as subject to demand characteristics preventing the perception of real harm occurring, as lacking a convincing theoretical explanation, and as producing little follow-up research. Burger's study (2009) was the first significant behavioral experiment on harmful obedience in over 20 years. One might have reasonably expected a gradual decline of preoccupation with the obedience experiments, their being regarded more for historical interest and as lacking contemporary relevance. This did not occur. The prestige of the obedience experiments understandably has long been important for the image of social psychology itself (e.g., Benjamin & Simpson, 2009; Ross, Lepper, & Ward, 2010), but the "fame" (or "infamy") label can present difficulties in studying them objectively. Griggs and Whitehead (2015), in a content analysis of the most recent social psychology texts, have argued that the strongest criticisms of the Milgram experiments (e.g., Nicholson, 2011; Perry, 2013, as well as earlier criticisms) have had difficulty in receiving a fair hearing, if any at all. This bias reflects the power of what they term the standard "Milgram-friendly" view of the experiments as well as textbook authors' reluctance to disrupt the classic stature and widely viewed importance of the experiments by including criticisms "that would muddle the story line . . . , resulting in student confusion and disengagement" (p. 319). The authors make a similar argument with respect to Zimbardo's prison study (Griggs & Whitehead, 2014). Thus the Milgram experiments unquestionably *are* widely regarded as famous. Whether they *should* be so regarded is a different issue. A goal of this chapter is to put readers in an informed position to answer or to seek information and reconsider this question for themselves.

Three significant developments occurring within the past decade are discussed. First, several new experimental studies on harmful obedience have been published. Second, there have been renewed efforts to develop convincing theoretical explanations for Milgram's findings. Third, there have been revisions in the generalization of these studies to the Holocaust. There have also appeared new research and criticisms based on documents in the Milgram archives at Yale University. This chapter also discusses a number of core issues not specific to the obedience experiments per se but that play a central role in the manner in which these studies have been embraced by many social scientists and yet rejected by others. These include the ideological tensions between situationist and other perspectives, the question of whether explanations exonerate perpetrators, social psychology's presumption of the good nature of most people, and the role of free will and the assignment of moral responsibility and punishment to perpetrators. These issues are considered after a discussion of the fame of these studies and a brief synopsis of Milgram's original findings and interpretation, as well as a number of more recent experiments and theoretical developments on harmful obedience.

THE FAME AND CONTROVERSY OF THE OBEDIENCE EXPERIMENTS

Their Visibility and Prominence

If one defines academic fame (or infamy) in terms of visibility and prominence, the Milgram experiments are likely unsurpassed in the social sciences. Consider the recent presence of these studies in research and scholarship: (1) in virtually every introductory and social psychology textbook, frequently with numerous pages dealing exclusively with the experiments (e.g., Kassin et al., 2014, pp. 278–288; Smith et al., 2015, pp. 370–382); (2) in books about the experiments (Blass, 2000; Lunt, 2009; Perry, 2013); (3) in a biography of Milgram (Blass, 2004); (4) in book chapters (e.g., Miller, 2004; Reicher & Haslam, 2012); (5) in a special issue of *Theoretical and Applied Ethics* (Herrera, 2013) devoted to a renewed ethical critique of the obedience experiments; (6) in a special issue of *Theory & Psychology* (Brannigan, Nicholson, & Cherry, 2015) containing highly critical evaluations of the conduct and meaning of the experiments; and (7) in an issue of the *Journal of Social Issues* marking the 50th year since Milgram's first publication of his findings (Haslam, Miller, & Reicher, 2014). Conferences and symposia on the obedience research have also been held. Millard (2014), using archival material, has written an informative, somewhat critical analysis of Milgram's film *Obedience* (1965) in contributing to the continuing fame of the studies. A new film, *Experimenter: The Stanley Milgram Story: Illusion Sets the Stage, Deception Reveals the Truth*, directed by Michael Almereyda, premiered at the New York Film Festival on October 6, 2015, and was released in U.S. theaters on October 16 (*http://www.imdb.com/title/tt3726704/*). Illustrative reviews may be found at Dargis (2015) and *http://www.ioncinema.com/reviews/experimenter-review*.

New experiments on obedience (e.g., Beauvois, Courbet, & Oberle, 2012; Burger, 2009) have been published, in addition to a theoretical model (Reicher & Haslam, 2011; Haslam, Reicher, & Birney, 2016), and numerous commentaries in social psychology and in other disciplines as well—in business ethics (e.g., Werhane, Hartman, Archer, Englehardt, & Pritchard, 2013), political science (e.g., Wolfe, 2011), history (e.g., Overy, 2014; Valentino, 2004), the law (e.g., Hanson & Yosifon, 2003; Perlman, 2007), and philosophy (e.g., Card, 2005). In March 2014, Google Scholar listed Milgram's first (1963) obedience publication as having more than 3,000 citations, and his 1974 book close to 7,000. The rate of citations is rising (e.g., Reicher, Haslam, & Miller, 2014). Websites that feature rankings of the most famous social psychologists invariably include Milgram (e.g., *www.socialpsychology.org/social-figures.htm*).

The Ethical Controversy

The ethical criticisms have unquestionably played a vital if ironic role in the fame of the obedience experiments, starting at the very beginning (Baumrind, 1964; Blass, 2004). One could have expected that a study judged as unethical would gradually have lost its credibility, resulting in its being marginalized from the usual academic venues. The opposite, in fact, seems to have occurred. The value of the research, for some, has been so imposing as to render the ethical issues to a somewhat lesser role, as they in fact had at the time Milgram conducted the experiments (e.g., Benjamin & Simpson, 2009; Elms, 2009). Others, however, have viewed the deficient ethics of the experiments (and of Milgram himself) as negating their value, past and present. The discovery of relevant documents in the Yale archives have given investigators the opportunity for new ethical criticisms. For example, Nicholson (2011) remarked: "For contemporary social psychologists, Milgram is a poor role model and the obedience research is a dark chapter, instructive not for its intellectual merit, but as a cautionary tale in scientific excess and hubris" (p. 755). Perry (2013) commented: "I have concluded that evidence from Milgram's unpublished papers and original recordings and transcripts casts doubt on Milgram's reliability as a narrator of the obedience research and of his role in safeguarding the welfare of his subjects" (p. 90). The precise target of these very *recent* ethical critiques (see also Baumrind, 2014; Herrera, 2013) is unclear. It cannot be Milgram, who died in 1984, nor the more recent obedience studies, which have received ethical approval from their departmental review boards. These current ethical criticisms may, then, be aimed at the very high regard in which Milgram's experiments are held by so many others, in academic as well as other contexts. The persistent fame of the experiments is likely to be very disturbing to current critics.

In their analysis of research ethics, Sieber and Tolich (2013) acknowledge that Milgram was studying an issue of great importance: "We defend

Milgram scientifically . . . recognizing his great importance to understanding our moral failings as humans" (p. 53). They note that Milgram (in the late 1950s/early 1960s) was operating largely in an ethical vacuum without formal guidelines for protection of participants and that Milgram did in fact use a detailed debriefing (Milgram, 1964), described as "ahead of his time" (p. 56). Although the use of deception is not, in principle, considered unethical by Sieber and Tolich, they are critical of Milgram's use of deceptions to achieve his goal of pressuring individuals to behave counter to their moral principles. Milgram's major ethical violation, by today's guidelines, was his failure to respect his participants' right to withdraw: "Informed consent is essentially about ensuring the autonomy of persons throughout the research process" (Sieber & Tolich, p. 139). Thus a difficult question faces the researcher: Can the experimental study of destructive obedience be studied ethically? The answer was, for several decades, "no." As will be seen, it now appears to be "yes."

The Obedience Experiments and the Holocaust

Milgram generalized his findings to the Holocaust in the opening paragraph of his first publication (Milgram, 1963, p. 371), an association that unquestionably would soon contribute to the fame and controversiality of the studies both for Milgram and the field of social psychology itself (e.g., Miller, 2004). The concepts of the pathological "Nazi mind" and authoritarian personality were the prevailing understanding of perpetrators when Milgram initiated the obedience project. Milgram's findings were strikingly different, that is, that *ordinary people*, under certain conditions of authorization, would be willing to inflict unexpectedly high levels of intolerable pain on a protesting victim. Social psychologists have widely (but not universally) endorsed the association. Ross et al. (2010) noted, for example, that "fully appreciating the implication of these studies . . . reduces the surprise experienced on learning that most of the low-level perpetrators of the Holocaust . . . were ordinary people who lived unexceptional lives before and after their infamous deeds rather than self-selected psychopaths and sadists" (p. 10). Similarly, Holocaust historian Richard Overy (2014) has observed that "Milgram's influence has expanded as historians look for scientific corroboration of the argument that 'normal men' can perform horrific acts without necessarily imbibing a hate-filled ideology or being driven by a visceral popular racism" (p. 520).

There have, however, always been severe critics of the "normality" view of perpetrators. Lang (2014), for example, focuses on the issue of moral responsibility:

> When Milgram invoked the Holocaust as an analogy to his obedience experiments, he inadvertently deprived the Nazi genocide of its historical meaning and relegated perpetrator behavior to a function of hierarchical

social structures. The result, which continues to exert considerable influence both inside and outside the discipline of social psychology, is an ahistorical explanation of perpetrator behavior that eviscerates any forceful conception of individual agency, reduces political action to acts of submission, and finally calls into question the very idea of personal responsibility. (p. 665)

Similarly, the political scientist Alan Wolfe (2011) has noted: "No matter how flawed Milgram's work and no matter how unsupported his conclusions, the notion that ordinary people are quite capable of inflicting terrible harm on innocent others when pressured to do so by respected people in authority has become so widely accepted that nothing is ever likely to shake it. We are, or so we are told, all part of genocide now" (p. 69). A number of social psychologists (e.g., Blass, 2004) have criticized the discipline for glossing over the gratuitous brutality of the Holocaust and, preoccupied with the obedience experiments, slighting the crucial role of the Holocaust's instigators and high-level planners. The exonerating implications of the Milgram experiments have also been extremely problematic for some Holocaust analysts (e.g., Mandel, 1998). Valentino (2004, p. 50) has also pointed out that Milgram's participants lacked any prior justification for hating their victim. In fact, from the participants' perspective, that the teacher and learner roles had been assigned randomly (Milgram, 1974, p. 18) could reasonably be interpreted as humanizing the learner. Milgram, in fact, envisioned a study combining the role of malevolent authority and victim dehumanization (1974, p. 10). This would be extremely important research, but it remains to be conducted. Most of Milgram's experimental variations yielded considerably less than 100% obedience, thus allowing a clear potential for added punishment directed at a dehumanized learner (e.g., Bandura, 1999; Haslam & Loughnan, Chapter 8, this volume).

Milgram (1974, p. 6) associated his experimental findings with Hannah Arendt's (1963) provocative description of the high-ranking Nazi official Adolf Eichmann as unexpectedly ordinary and primarily motivated to be a good Nazi bureaucrat—that is, the "banality of evil" (1974, p. 6). For decades, Eichmann's photograph has often been included in social psychology textbook coverage of the Milgram experiments (e.g., Gilovich, Keltner, & Nisbett, 2011, p. 11). Relevant to social psychology's traditional linkage between Eichmann and the Milgram experiments is the recent publication (Kershner, 2016) of a previously unknown plea written by Eichmann to the Israeli Court. Having been convicted and sentenced to death, Eichmann pointed to the condoning aspects of his situation (to which, he argues, the judges were insensitive) and that he was a subordinate following orders, not a leader issuing them:

> The judges made a fundamental mistake in their judgment of me, because they are not able to empathize with the time and situation in which I

found myself during the war years. . . . there is a need to draw a line between the leaders responsible and the people like me forced to serve as mere instruments in the hands of the leaders. I was not a responsible leader, and as such do not feel myself guilty. (in Kershner, 2016)

A few days after writing this plea, he was hanged on June 1, 1962. Many would, of course, argue that Eichmann was simply fabricating, demonstrating what Mandel (1998) has termed the "obedience alibi," and are, in this context, strongly against generalizing Milgram's findings to Eichmann's role in the Holocaust. Consistent with this argument are three biographies of Eichmann which have cast severe doubt on Arendt's apparently benign depiction of Eichmann (e.g., Cesarani, 2004; Lipstadt, 2011; Stangneth, 2014). Lipstadt (2011) noted: "In Eichmann's case her [Arendt's] analysis seems strangely out of touch with the reality of his historical record" (pp. 169–170), noting his postwar zeal about having caused the deaths of Hungarian Jews in particular, and millions of others. In reviewing a film by Claude Lanzmann, which features an interview with a formerly imprisoned rabbi who worked under Eichmann, Lane (2014) states that "Short shrift is given to Hannah Arendt and her celebrated coining . . . of 'the banality of evil.' The man was far from banal, as Murmelstein explains: 'He was a *demon*'" (p. 84). Why have social psychologists been wrong on Eichmann? Newman (2001) suggested a bias: "Social psychologists interpreted her work in a way that was consistent with their preferred conclusion" (p. 16), that is, that Eichmann was unexpectedly normal and not a sadistic monster. Newman suggests that Arendt's more complete argument may in fact have been less exonerating toward Eichmann (see Lang, 2014, for a similar conclusion). The banality of evil remains a powerful idea. However, Eichmann now appears to have been "the wrong man" for this role. Also, it is likely that *not all* of Milgram's obedient participants were banal. Different motives could have driven the obedient behavior (e.g., Reicher & Haslam, 2011).

The relevance of Milgram's findings for harm doing in complex organizational structures—the Nazi regime being a case study—has emphasized the ambiguous and, at times, intentionally hidden moral responsibility and habitual obedience at different levels of authority or subordination (e.g., Kelman & Hamilton, 1989; Russell, 2014; Werhane et al., 2013). Fermaglich (2006) noted that "Milgram's work, with its emphasis on the ordinary evils of the bureaucracy, made a significant impact on Holocaust scholars that lasts to this day" (p. 116). Leadership, of course, is also paramount in "successful" organizations. As Valentino (2004) stated: "The centerpiece of Hitler's political philosophy was the 'Fuhrer Principle,' a doctrine that demanded unquestioning obedience to a single leader" (p. 62).

Overy (2014), emphasizing the power of authority, considers as a major finding Milgram's evidence (1974, Chapter 3) that his colleagues predicted that very few volunteers would go beyond the lowest shock levels. People similarly underestimated their own obedience. Why does this occur? Epley (2015) has suggested that "you know your conscious aversion to harming another person, but you miss the difficulty you would have in saying no to a clear and reassuring authority figure in the heat of the moment after having lived much of your life following orders from authority figures. You are missing the construction that happens inside your own brain" (p. 29). Overy (2014), similarly, notes:

> In most cases, the power of ordinary people to confront or withdraw from the imperatives to comply, whether these are intellectual or institutional or social or psychological, is evidently much more limited that the black/white division between perpetration and dissent would suggest. If the power of ordinary people to say no were greater, they would perhaps say no more often. (p. 527)

In a recent, particularly thoughtful and compelling analysis of genocide and mass murder, de Swann (2015) discusses the Milgram experiments in some detail. Although harboring questions and doubts about the experiment's direct relevance to historical genocide as well as participants' actual view of the experimental set-up, he acknowledges the value of Milgram's findings, in a manner very similar to Overy (2014):

> The experiment does not warrant either the popular conclusion that in real life most people will comply with a genocidal dictatorship or its contrary, much less popular conclusion that a sizable minority would resist it in reality. It is hard to decide whether the subjects actually believed they were administering severe torture or even a death penalty to their subject or, rather, that they experienced the setup as a very serious game. Moreover, the difference between the compliers and the naysayers was never thoroughly explored by Milgram and his followers. But Milgram did establish that people are much more prone to obey a person of authority ordering them to harm someone else than just about anyone had expected before his experiments. (de Swann, 2015, p. 254)

This shattering of the illusion of personal autonomy appears to be a particularly important discovery by Milgram, particularly when one remembers that his research took place barely over a decade following the Holocaust.

Fame: The Result of an Enduring Great Idea

The physicist Freeman Dyson (2015) recently noted, in discussing the fame of Albert Einstein:

> But there are a few scientists whose lives and thought are of perennial interest, because they permanently changed our way of thinking. To the few belong Galileo and Newton and Darwin, and now Einstein. For the select few, there will be no end to the writing of books [about them]. New

books will need to be written and read, because these people had enduring ideas that throw light on new problems as the centuries go by. (p. 14)

Many admirers of Milgram's experiments would add his name to Dyson's list. For example, Benjamin and Simpson (2009):

> It is critically important to understand why this study so captivates psychologists and psychology students today as well as ordinary citizens. It has all the elements of an *experimentum crucis,* an experiment designed to answer a question of great importance. It asked a big question, an important question—how far will a person go in inflicting severe pain on a stranger when instructed to do so by an authority figure? It is not just a psychological question. It is a moral question. Indeed it is a societal question. (p. 17)

In a recent essay, Gazda (2015) describes painful distant memories of graduate school dealing with his administering punishment to laboratory rats and other animals. He is

> astonished that the daily grind of depriving, shocking, and killing these animals did not move me to leave my job. . . . My rationalization is that I was a student and younger worker in institutions of higher learning, programmed to receive the wisdom of academia. I was studying how the science that supposedly advanced our civilization was done. (p. 8)

He then adds:

> Speaking of his infamous experiments in which human subjects followed orders thinking they were giving extremely painful shocks to other humans, the Yale University psychologist Stanley Milgram said, "*Ordinary people, simply doing their jobs, and without any particular hostility on their part, can become agents in a terrible destructive process.*" I think that describes me pretty well. (p. 8, emphasis added)

Milgram himself considered it "the most fundamental lesson of our study" (1974, p. 6). Gazda's reference to Milgram in a context of animal research would likely spark more controversy. Nevertheless, his quotation would define, for many, Milgram's most enduring idea.

RESEARCH ON OBEDIENCE TO AUTHORITY

Milgram's Original Findings and Current Theoretical Explanations

Milgram's major findings were: (1) an unexpectedly high rate of obedience (65%) in the baseline experiment (1963), indications of extreme stress in many participants, and evidence that observers vastly underestimated the actual obedience when given descriptions of the basic paradigm; (2) sharply varying obedience rates in over two dozen situational variations, including a predominance of *disobedience* in many of them (1974) (for an informative comparative analysis of the obedience rates in 21 of Milgram's experimental variations, including several studies from the Yale archives not included in Milgram [1974], see Haslam, Loughnan, and Perry [2014]); and (3) considerable individual differences among participants within the experimental variations. Two chapters (1974) provided a rich, if highly impressionistic, analysis by Milgram of specific individuals' reactions to being in his study. Personality factors were intended for further research, but only one brief study was conducted (Elms & Milgram, 1966). (For informative discussions of the origins of the experiments, see Blass [2004] and Russell [2011]).

Current explanations largely echo Milgram's own situational accounts but cite important empirical support (not available to Milgram) for the relevant processes—although in research contexts not dealing with obedience per se. Burger (2014) identified four key situational factors likely to have increased obedience: (1) small increments in administering the shocks, (2) the novelty of the situation and the absence of normative information regarding appropriate behavior, (3) an opportunity to deny or diffuse responsibility, and (4) little opportunity to reflect because of the fast pace of the tasks. Miller (2014) also emphasized the factors of moral disengagement and dehumanization, for example the greater punishment inflicted with increasing physical distance from the victim (e.g., Bandura, 1999), and what Milgram (1974) termed "cognitive tuning," in which subordinates are often primarily oriented to those individuals with greater power or authority (e.g., Werhane et al., 2013). Note that these constructs or processes are all tied to specific situational arrangements or roles and do not deal with personality factors or individual differences in moral judgment or reasoning among those participating in the studies.

The explanatory status of Milgram's central concept of the agentic state (the participant's ceding personal responsibility to the authority) is at best marginal. Reicher and Haslam (2011), for example, argued that this construct cannot readily account for the extremely varied rates of obedience across his experimental variations, as, presumably, the agentic-state orientation, activated by the presence of legitimate authority, would have been operative in all of them. Beauvois et al. (2012) report positive evidence, but most recent studies do not (e.g., Burger, Girgis, & Manning, 2011). Nevertheless, some researchers and writers appear to presume the agentic state's validity. For example, Moore and Gino (2013) observed that, when debriefed, many participants in the obedience experiments commented, "'if it were up to me, I would not have administered shocks to the learner' (Milgram, 1974). Of course, their behavior *was* up to them, but the presence of a legitimate authority figure allowed them to pass off their responsibility to another" (p. 66, emphasis in original). It is not clear, however, how many of Milgram's participants voiced this particular idea (i.e., "if it were up to me . . ."), and the certainty with which Moore and Gino attribute responsibility to Milgram's participants is hardly a consensus point of view, as will be shown.

The gradual escalation of punishment has been a particularly widely cited theoretical idea, for which there is an abundant and supportive research literature. One likely underlying process involves a change in self-perception during the course of committing increasingly punitive acts. For example, this concept can explain actors in a "bug-killing" paradigm (e.g., Martens, Kosloff, & Jackson, 2010), or observers of harm doing by others. Hartson and Sherman (2012) demonstrated that the "gradual escalation of behavior can alter how individuals perceive the problematic behavior of others, reducing the severity of moral judgments and leading individuals to hold others less accountable for their actions" (p. 1287). Writing in a legal context, Perlman (2007) endorsed many of Milgram's theoretical concepts, but regarding the escalation dynamic, he pointed out that "although each step up on the shock generator was only fifteen volts, subjects did not experience each step in precisely the same way" (p. 467). Here, he refers to the sudden emergence of significant disobedience at the 150-volt stage, an observation later emphasized by Burger (2009) and Packer (2008).

The lack of theoretical precision in explaining Milgram's findings remains problematic, particularly consequential when the experiments are generalized to other settings—for example, to obedience in fraudulent corporate settings (e.g., Werhane et al., 2013) or to atrocities such as the My Lai massacre (Milgram, 1974) or the Holocaust. Applications of this kind rest on the viability of generalizing the *theoretical processes underlying Milgram's findings* to these other contexts and to the underlying causes for what happened there (e.g., Mook, 1983). In certain instances, one can indeed find persuasive generalizations of process. For example, the escalation phenomenon, central to Milgram's basic paradigm, has been cited by historians as an important dynamic of the Holocaust. Stargardt (2015) noted, in reference to the 1941 decree that all Jews (over age 5) had to wear a yellow star:

> The yellow star was the most visible nation-wide measure taken since the November 1938 pogrom (Kristallnacht) and it came into effect across the whole Reich on the same day, 19 September 1941. Its mandatory character could not be in doubt and it was immediately *recognized as an important escalation, conditioning how the burghers of Minden digested the news a few weeks later of the deportation and first mass shootings of Jews from their town.* (p. 236, emphasis added)

Without a convincing theory and a conceptual understanding of the target domains, however, many generalizations are largely guesswork, and hence fertile ground for controversies. However, there is a recent promising development of a theoretical model, with empirical support, to explain Milgram's findings (e.g., Reicher et al., 2012), which may significantly facilitate generalizations. This research is discussed later in this chapter.

Experiments on Obedience to Authority Using Variations on Milgram's Paradigm

The first major obedience study in several decades was reported by Burger (2009). He introduced key procedural changes in order to receive ethical approval from his university's institutional review board (IRB): (1) a detailed informed-consent form, specifying the participants' freedom to end their involvement at any time; (2) preexperimental screenings to rule out anyone who would experience undesired stress (or who had been familiar with the obedience research)—the experimenter himself was a clinical psychologist; and (3) the decision to terminate the experiment after the 150-volt level (a unique point in the shock sequence at which the learner, on tape, first protests loudly and demands to be released). Burger based the 150-volt maximum on Milgram's Experiment 5 (1963), which indicated that a clear majority of those who exceeded 150 volts went to the 450-volt maximum. Packer (2008) had analyzed disobedience rates in the data tables for eight of Milgram's variations (1974) and demonstrated that the highest rate of disobedience (37%) occurred at 150 volts. The underlying ethical premise here, of course, was that the experiment would be experienced as far less stressful below 150 volts. Burger also included a "modeled-refusal" condition, in which another participant (an accomplice) refused to continue past the 90-volt switch; this was analogous to Milgram's "two peers rebel" variation (1974, Experiment 17), which had shown a marked reduction in the obedience rate. Out of a much larger initial group of volunteers, 70 males and females, ranging in age and other demographics, were in the final sample.

The major finding was that 70% of participants were obedient, comparable statistically to Milgram's finding (82.5%). Men and women were similarly obedient (as had been found by Milgram). However, the modeled-refusal condition had no effect. In addition, participants who ultimately refused to continue past 150 volts had received the first prod (to continue) *significantly earlier* than those who were willing to exceed 150 volts—suggesting that it is easier to disobey if one starts the hesitation process relatively early. Burger did not mention any expressions of emotional conflict or strain during the study. These reactions were, of course, one of Milgram's major findings.

In a follow-up analysis of participants' (tape-recorded) spontaneous postexperimental reports, Burger et al. (2011) observed that very few obedient but a majority of disobedient participants expressed a sense of personal responsibility for what happened to the learner. However, these groups did not differ in the percentage attributing responsibility to *someone other than themselves*, thus *not* supporting Milgram's agentic-shift hypothesis. In a detailed analysis of the prods, they observed that obedience was highest for the quite reasonable Prod 1 ("Please continue"), but, surprisingly, no participant who reached what was viewed as a true order—Prod 4 ("you have no other choice, you *must* go on")—obeyed it. Acknowledging the confounding of the wording of the prods with their sequential position, Burger et al. (2011) suggested that if obeying orders was not in fact what Milgram was studying (as implied in refusals to obey Prod 4), then alternative interpretations of his findings should be considered. As will be shown, an alternative has indeed been advanced (Haslam, Reicher, & Birney, 2014). Another possibility, however, is that a number of Burger's participants may have remembered the explicit assurance about being free to leave given to them at the informed-consent phase, thus accounting for those receiving the last (fourth) order-like prod not obeying it. Sieber and Tolich (2013) found Burger's (2009) study ethically impressive but are critical of his continued use of the four strident prods. They recommend that "the research assistant would tell the research subject only once, 'The experiment must continue.' The second time the subject protests, his or her right to withdraw must be respected" (p. 58).

Beauvois et al. (2012) conducted an obedience study on the set of a television studio in a game show context. In three similar conditions, involving electric shock as punishment in a quiz game, they reported obedience rates ranging from 72 to 81%. Similar to Burger's modeled-refusal condition, there was no effect of a defiant model; however, a "host withdrawal" condition (analogous to Milgram's "experimenter absent" variation) lowered obedience significantly. As Milgram (but not Burger) had observed, these researchers noted nervous laughter and cheating in the form of cueing the contestant with voice tones as to the correct answer (thereby not requiring electric shocks). Similar to Burger's finding, use of the final prod was ineffective, with only one of 16 (hearing it) yielding to it.

Zeigler-Hill, Southard, Archer, and Donohoe (2013) used (apparent) blasts of white noise as punishment. An obedience rate of 94% was obtained, as only two participants disobeyed orders (on the last trial). Rochat and Blass (2014) reported an unpublished study by Milgram titled the "bring a friend condition." This was apparently his last variation, conducted at Bridgeport in 1962 and located in the Yale archives. Of 20 male volunteers, only 3 went to 450 volts, an obedience rate of 15%. Clearly, for the majority of participants, the motivation to help a friend in the learner role prevailed over any obligation to the experimenter. Perry (2013) terms this study Milgram's "secret" experiment and is critical of his not publishing it.

Different Paradigms

Bocchiaro, Zimbardo, and Van Lange (2012) introduced a new obedience paradigm to investigate whistle-blowing. The basic design involved presenting participants with an unethical request by an authority—to send a deceptive letter encouraging their (real) acquaintances to participate in a painful study that they, however, described as pleasant. Participants had three options—obedience, defiance, or whistle-blowing (reporting, anonymously, the unethical study to the university research committee). Obedience was relatively high, 76.5%, with disobedience low at 14.1% and whistle-blowing at an unexpectedly low 9.4%. To assess estimated behavior in this setting, an earlier independent sample was simply given a description of the study and asked to predict their own (and the average student's) responses. As had been shown by Milgram (and others), predicted behavior for oneself and for the average person differed sharply from actual behavior in their study and in a radically more socially desirable direction (highest for whistle-blowing, lowest for obedience). This sharp discrepancy between predicted and actually observed behavior, with Milgram's being one of the first empirical documentations, has been a reliable phenomenon for decades in social psychology, one which testifies to the informational value of social-psychological inquiry.

Bocchiaro and Zimbardo (2010) adopted a variation of Milgram's paradigm (Meeus & Raaijmakers, 1986), using "personal insults" instead of physical punishment. They set up procedures specifically to encourage disobedience (authority and participant in different rooms, participant and learner in close proximity). Disobedience prevailed, as only 30% of participants obeyed all insult instructions (to an accomplice working on a task). Participants indicated considerable amounts of tension, as well as verbal utterances of dissent, regardless of whether they were ultimately obedient or resistant. As observed by Burger et al. (2011) and Packer (2008), there was a critical decision point at the 11th of 19 trials, in which the performer's script required him to try to physically free himself from the apparatus and leave. At this point 67% of participants immediately disobeyed.

Several studies using a variety of computer-based technologies and virtual reality simulations have also investigated obedience (e.g., Cheetham, Pedroni, Antley, Slater, & Jancke, 2009; Dambrun & Vatine, 2010). The ethical gains of these role-playing studies are important, and obedience–disobedience rates are generally comparable to those of Milgram (whose findings are always included as the benchmark). Dambrun and Vatine (2010) used an immersive video environment with a French sample of participants, with a real actor filmed, recorded, and displayed on a computer screen. Using a comparable experimental condition (victim hidden), they observed an obedience rate similar to Milgram's baseline result (1963). Obedience dropped sharply in the visible condition. The inclusion of a new variable, the victim's ethnicity (North African), did not result in significantly higher obedience, though participants were less anxious and reported a lower level of distress (in comparison with a French-victim condition). Role-playing procedures have, in the past, always generated critics who doubted their realism, but the new technologies may have the potential to minimize this self-consciousness.

Individual Differences in Harmful Obedience

Berger (2009) found no significant differences between obedient and defiant participants on measures of empathic concern or desire for control. Higher empathy (but not desire for control) scores were related to lower first-prod scores. Begue et al. (2015) brought most of the participants in the Beauvois et al. (2012) study back 8 months after the experiment and administered various measures (e.g., the Big Five personality inventory). There were small but significant correlations between agreeableness and conscientiousness with highest shock intensity reached, but not with actual obedience rates. They also observed a correlation between liberal social attitudes and lower intensity of shocks delivered, reminiscent of a similar early finding on authoritarianism by Elms and Milgram (1966). Females (but not males) who scored higher on political rebelliousness administered lower shocks. Zeigler-Hill et al. (2013) report that lower neuroticism scores on the Big Five personality inventory were associated with more prods, that is, with a greater reluctance to obey the experimenter.

The results reviewed here reveal correlations that are either negative or relatively small, and the measures are typically different across studies. Meaningful causes for the dramatic evidence of individual differences in these studies thus have yet to be discovered. Another individual-difference issue pertains to the consistency of behavior. Criticizing the dominance of a situational perspective, Funder (2009) noted: "The classic studies of social psychology placed subjects into evocative situations (e.g., Milgram's obedience experiments, the Zimbardo prison study), but almost never, if ever, placed the same participants into *more than one* situation so that consistent patterns of behavior and associated traits could be detected" (p. 125; emphasis in original). Perhaps variations on some of the recent ethical obedience paradigms may be capable of this kind of needed inquiry.

Political attitudes, first suggested by Elms and Milgram (1966), may be the most promising. Research by Graham et al. (2011) has shown that liberals (vs. conservatives) give significantly lower priority to issues of authority/respect, one of five basic moral virtues in intuitive judgments, a finding consistent with less obedience shown by participants rating themselves to the political left in the Beauvois et al. (2012) study. Frimer, Gaucher, and Schaefer (2014) suggest that past research on the conservative–obedience relationship has been confounded with the assumption that the authorities are also conservative. They suggest that liberals are more obedient than conservatives when the authorities are also liberal, that is, that "obedience itself is not ideologically divisive" (p. 1205). Is Milgram's experimenter perceived as relatively politically conservative? The evidence tentatively points in this direction. Finally, at least a small number of participants in these studies may in fact enjoy the opportunity to harm the learner. Buckels, Jones, and Paulhus (2013) reported that college students scoring high on a sadistic impulse inventory were more cruel on the bug-killing task of Martens et al. (2010) and more willing to harm an innocent victim in a (deceptive) computer game.

Summary

The studies reviewed here have successfully demonstrated that predictably harmful obedience (or resistance) can be elicited from ordinary individuals (except in Burger's use of screening) *in an ethically acceptable manner.* Burger's (2009) groundbreaking study has, not surprisingly, been controversially received (Benjamin & Simpson, 2009; Blass, 2009), some viewing it as not inducing sufficiently intense moral conflict to carry the same significance as Milgram's original (e.g., Elms, 2009; Miller, 2009). Nevertheless, there is clear acknowledgment that the new ethical guidelines must be followed. Although none of the studies have produced major advances in terms of a *theoretical understanding* of their (or Milgram's) findings, ideally this will occur in future research. Moral conflict can be introduced ethically in obedience research settings without the *extreme* anguish reported by Milgram.

All of the recent studies have used Milgram's findings as a benchmark with which to compare their results. For example, Burger (2009) concluded: "I am as confident as a psychology researcher can ever be that my findings can be legitimately compared with Milgram's" (p. 10). These newer studies, however, are so procedurally different from Milgram's that comparisons of outcomes, in terms of specifying underlying causal processes, are largely uninterpretable (e.g., Miller, 2009). Perhaps it is the fame of the Milgram studies that is exerting itself in these understandable but conceptually inconclusive comparisons.

AT THE CENTER OF THE MILGRAM CONTROVERSY: THE PROBLEM OF MORAL RESPONSIBILITY

There is another source of great controversy, one that is related to generalizations from the experiments to the Holocaust and other settings. The focus here is on moral responsibility. To what degree are the obedient participants in the studies considered fully responsible for their behavior? There are very strong differences of opinion on this issue. The remainder of this chapter examines several areas of contemporary research and thought relevant to this question.

Good Persons Doing Evil

The participants in Milgram experiments have always been viewed as ordinary, presumably good persons (Milgram, 1974, p. 6). Presumptions of the ordinariness and good nature of people typically studied by social psychologists and related disciplines are explicit in the titles of many books and articles. For example (emphasis added):

> Why *ordinary people* torture enemy prisoners (Fiske, Harris, & Cuddy, 2004).
> Contemporary racial bias: When *good people* do bad things (Dovidio, Gaertner, Nier, Kawakami, & Hodson, 2004).
> The Lucifer effect: Understanding how *good people* turn evil (Zimbardo, 2007a.)
> The righteous mind: Why *good people* are divided by politics and religion (Haidt, 2012).
> Blind spots: Hidden biases of *good people* (Banaji & Greenwald, 2013).

These titles forecast to readers that their intuitions—that good people like themselves don't do these "bad things"—are going to be shattered with counterintuitive insights and challenges to commonly held, more comforting views. Certainly the terms *ordinary* and *good* seem to be reasonable descriptions of the typical research populations studied by social psychologists, for example, the common reliance on college students.

One important if unintended consequence, however, of the "ordinary or good person" focus may be a perceived condoning of the harmful actions (or thoughts) about to be explained. That good people engage in bad actions seems to soften the meaning of the harm doing. For example, research on ingroup versus outgroup biases suggests that a good person, that is, a member of one's ingroup, will be judged significantly more leniently for committing a harmful act than will a bad person (outgroup member) engaging in the identical act (e.g., Smith et al., 2015, p. 507). There is also the implication that if ordinary people engage in these undesirable behaviors, then they are more common than people think, and, in turn, somewhat less serious—similar to the "prevalence rule" in judgments of illness (e.g., Martin, Rothrock, Leventhal, & Leventhal, 2003).

Challenging the "Good/Ordinary Person" Thesis of Situationism

A number of social psychologists, not favoring strong situationism, have explicitly challenged the "good person–evil deeds" thesis. For example, if one moves to paid volunteers, as in Milgram (1963), or screened (and paid) volunteers, as in Zimbardo et al. (2007a) and Burger (2009), there is more room for questioning the ordinariness of the research sample. Carnahan and McFarland (2007) hypothesized that there was a selection bias among Zimbardo's volunteers. In Carnahan and McFarland's study, their volunteers for a prison study scored significantly higher than a control group on measures of the abuse-related dispositions of aggressiveness, authoritarianism, Machiavellianism, narcissism, and social dominance and lower on empathy and altruism. These individuals would not seem quite as ordinary or good as a random sample of college students. Among their counterarguments, Haney and Zimbardo (2009) highlighted the (pretested) normalcy of their participants and accused Carnahan and McFarland of being dispositionalists, with an erroneously liberal view of the freedom people have: "In fact, most people's choices—even about serious or consequential matters—are often highly situationally constrained" (p. 813).

In his recent very comprehensive analysis of mass murder, de Swann (2015), a sociologist, acknowledges the ordinariness of many killers, as well as the power of the immediate situation, but he argues that this view of "ordinary perpetrators" has been too influential in social science:

> But the killers did not just share the collective past of their nation; they had a biography of their own. They had particular experiences, developed their individual inclinations and opinions. The critical question is whether the killers differed from others who lived through the same times, in the same society, but who did *not* join the murderers' ranks. The search for such differences has been neglected for over half a century because of this insistence that the genocidaires were all "ordinary men." Rather than look more closely at the perpetrators, people were to search their own soul, since "you and I or anyone under the same circumstances might have done the same thing." In fact, no one knows what "anyone" might do under these circumstances. The question is at once haunting and meaningless. . . . The idea that in a certain social context, in a given situation, people will commit acts that they would not dream of otherwise is quite plausible. Some people are more likely to do so than others, and some will resist even at considerable personal risk. Others may be willing and even eager to follow orders. That depends not only on the situation of the moment but also on their prior experience and personal history, in a word, a term that with so many words has been declared out of bounds: on their personal dispositions. And in other words: on their particular personality. (pp. 263–264)

de Swann (2015) cogently surmises that had most of us of us—good and ordinary persons at the outset—been raised as children and young adults in the earlier phases of the Third Reich, "if this had been the course of our lives, then, yes, maybe then, some of us might have become genocidal killers. But then, you or I, we would have been someone else. The impact of the genocidal situation on the behavior of the perpetrators has rightly been stressed in the past half-century. There is a renewed interest in the influence of historical-cultural conditions on the formation of a genocidal mentality. What is overdue is an assessment of the importance of personal biography, or the individual dispositions that may lead to genocidal actions" (pp. 264–265).

Another issue concerns possible changes that occur in "good" or "ordinary" research participants. They may be good or ordinary *before* being assigned to certain conditions of the experiments, but less so *afterward*. Should Milgram's obedient participants be considered to be as good as those who defied the experimenter, especially when the former later justified their harmful actions toward the learner (e.g., Haslam, Reicher, Millard, & McDonald, 2015b)? Although successful debriefing represents a kind of reversal of experimentally induced changes "so that they [research participants] are restored to a state of emotional well-being" (Sieber & Tolich, 2013, p. 151), the harmful, perhaps immoral conduct in these studies has in fact occurred in the minds of the participants (and researchers) and cannot simply be deleted for ethical convenience.

A particularly interesting challenge to the good/ordinary thesis can be seen in a letter to the editor of the *APS Observer* (Donnellan, Fraley, & Krueger, 2007). The authors criticize what they regarded as that journal's endorsement (Herbert, 2007) of Zimbardo's situationist explanation of the Abu Ghraib prison scandal:

> Our concern is that Zimbardo has misrepresented scientific evidence in an attempt to offer a purely situational account of the antisocial acts perpetrated at Abu Ghraib. . . . The scientific consensus, based on existing data, is that people vary in their propensity for antisocial behavior and that environments transact with personalities. Some people are more likely to turn out to be bad apples than others, and this is particularly evident in certain situations. (p. 5)

Below this letter appear 40 signatures of well-known psychologists, most of them social psychologists with a strong interest in personality (e.g., S. Alexandra Burt, David M. Buss, Samuel D. Gosling, Robert Hogan, Deborah A. Kashy, David A. Kenny, Laura A. King, Scott O. Lilienfeld, Brent W. Roberts, William B. Swann, Jr., Jessica L. Tracy, David Watson).

One can readily imagine a virtually identical letter voicing protest against generalizing Milgram's studies to the Holocaust. In his rebuttal letter, after some denials of fact (e.g., he agrees that there *are* "bad apples"), Zimbardo (2007b) reaffirmed a cornerstone of situationism: "The central issue is not the relative predictive power of person vs. situation, rather it is the typical underestimation of situational factors and channel factors that lead to erroneous predictions and misattributions of behavior whenever such external factors are operating" (p. 6). Milgram (1979) had earlier voiced a very similar position: "It is surprising how difficult it is for people to keep situational forces in mind, as they seek a totally personalistic interpretation of obedience, divorced from the specific situational pressures acting on the individual, which . . . we know to be crucial in determining whether the person will submit or rebel" (p. 9). This underestimation-of-the-situation argument is, however, not persuasive to opponents, who interpret it as giving clear priority to situational factors *over* personality (e.g., Funder, 2009). Situationists still have to account for individual differences in behavior in the same situation. Jetten and Mols (2014) have argued, with some empirical evidence, that it was Milgram's decision to publish *first* (1963) only one of his many experiments, specifically one showing a very high rate of obedience, which was consequential in many readers' drawing an incorrect message—that is, that most people are unexpectedly, blindly obedient. Yet, for decades, millions of college students have in fact learned about many of Milgram's specific experiments (showing strong variations in obedience) in generally superb textbook coverage (e.g., Kassin et al., 2014, Fig. 7.8, p. 282; Smith et al., 2015, Figs. 10.4 and 10.5, pp. 377, 378). Still, the take-away message may well be an erroneous dispositional one for many people, informed or not (e.g., Reicher et al., 2014).

Rejecting the Accusation that "to Explain Is to Condone"

There is an interesting phenomenon related to the criticisms of situationism noted above and, in turn, relevant to the Milgram experiments. This is the widespread concern among social scientists well known for their analyses of harm doing and evil that, in the process of explaining the perpetrators' actions, they will convey an exonerating tone or implication. They are adamant in rejecting this charge. For example (emphasis added):

> "To offer a psychological explanation for the atrocities committed by perpetrators is *not to forgive, justify, or condone* their behaviors. Instead the explanation simply allows us to understand the conditions under which many of us could be transformed into killing machines" (Waller, 2007, p. xvii).
> "Throughout this book, I repeat the mantra that attempting to understand the situational and systemic contributions to any individual's behavior *does not excuse the person or absolve him or her from responsibility* in engaging in immoral, illegal, or evil deeds" (Zimbardo, 2007a, p. xi).
> "*Make no mistake: Understanding is not condoning* . . . I learned the hard way that the public assumes that the understanding excuses the doing. In a painful BBC interview, victims of torture accused us of collusion: by explaining the circumstances that could drive almost anyone to commit immoral heinous acts, we were letting them off the hook. . . . Social science is particularly vulnerable to this understanding = excusing view because we explain how situations cause behavior, even extreme behavior. Observers prefer to

blame other humans for horrible outcomes, the more horrible, the more human responsibility must be blamed" (Fiske, 2013, pp. 605–606).

"Some [historians] fear that explaining the killers' motives and actions might seem to lessen their guilt. Auschwitz survivor Primo Levi warned against trying to understand the murderers, 'because to understand is almost to justify.' Yet every murderer acted with free will and had no reason to fear punishment if he refused to commit murder. *No explanation can diminish the killers' terrible guilt*" (McMillan, 2014, p. viii).

The circumstances of the perpetrators are, of course, included in many scientific explanations of harm doing, violence, and genocide—their socialization histories, life conditions, specifics of the harming situations, their roles as members of social organizations and bureaucracies (e.g., Baumeister, 1997; Russell, 2014; Staub, 2014). In a court setting, these kinds of factors can, in principle, be used as mitigating evidence in decisions regarding a convicted defendant's sentence. Why, then, is there a resolute refusal on the part of these scholars to acknowledge that their explanations will suggest, at least to a degree, an exoneration of the perpetrators' moral responsibility?

One reason is that scholars may anticipate, correctly, that their readers' sympathies will be far greater with the victims than with their perpetrators (e.g., Baumeister, 1997). For example, Mandel (1998) commented on the Milgram–Holocaust linkage: "It is offensive to survivors (and to our memories of victims) who know all too well that there was much more behind the way they were viciously brutalized, mocked, and tormented than a mere obligation to follow orders . . . care should be taken in how explanations are communicated, especially when they have a clear potential to cause harm" (p. 91). That scientific explanations should never be constrained by the acceptability of their conclusions to certain audiences may be a worthy ideal, but clearly one not always comfortably achieved. Another reason is that, similar to laypersons, many social scientists may feel that a firm position on moral responsibility, what Tetlock, Self, and Singh (2010) have termed a "prosecutorial mindset," is simply the appropriate professional value to espouse. They may privately acknowledge that exceptions can be made, but the general rule, not to exonerate, appears much safer and perhaps more objective, befitting the scientific role.

The Other Side: Explaining Does in Fact Lead to a Degree of Exoneration

A number of social psychologists have, however, suggested that an effort to understand a perpetrator's motives does in fact lead to a more exonerating position. For example, Ross and Shestowsky (2012), stated:

If society's goal is to have a criminal justice system that is not only effective but also logically and ethically coherent, additional implications of a situationist perspective come to the fore. One such implication would surely be a more "forgiving" response to transgressors who have been subjected to unusually strong situational pressures, including pressures whose strength is unlikely to be appreciated by lay observers who have never faced those pressures. Another implication, we would argue, would be a greater willingness to mitigate punishment in cases where the situational forces that weighed on the transgressors were ones to which they did not choose to expose themselves or ones whose impact they could not have anticipated in advance. (pp. 7–8)

Baumeister (1997), in discussing the nature of evil, took a similar position: "Unfortunately, there is ample reason to fear that understanding can promote forgiving. Seeing deeds from the perpetrator's point of view does change things in many ways" (p. 386). These emphases on forgiveness and mitigation capture the essence of the controversy regarding exoneration. Contrast these expressions with Fiske's (2013) previously noted disclaimer, "Make no mistake: Understanding is not condoning."

From Ross and Shestowsky's perspective, Milgram's obedient participants should clearly be judged more leniently than might be the case were their situation to be minimized or ignored. They acknowledge that wrongdoers are often free to act otherwise (e.g., the defiant participants in obedience experiments) but insist that a just treatment of perpetrators demands a fuller, more sophisticated appreciation of the power of situational forces. In legal decisions, responsibility for harmful conduct is often partitioned among several parties, thereby in effect exonerating some perpetrators, perhaps many, from at least total responsibility (e.g., Card, 2005; Kelman & Hamilton, 1989). Were the learner to be (hypothetically) harmed in Milgram's study and to pursue legal action, the list of defendants could be quite long: the teacher, the learner himself, Milgram, his research assistants, Yale University, and the government agency funding the research (e.g., Hanson & Yosifon, 2003). Presumably we would want exoneration for a close friend, a loved one, or ourselves were these individuals the accused perpetrator (e.g., Shalvi et al., 2015). Exoneration thus appears to be dependent, to a degree at least, upon whose wrongdoing is at issue and who are standing in judgment of it.

Do Situational Explanations Have Exonerating Implications? Research Evidence

Newman and Bakina (2009) presented participants with descriptions of the results of two hypothetical studies of wrongdoing (cheating and domestic abuse). Participants were randomly assigned to one of three types of explanations for those results—dispositional, situational/contextual, and interactionism. They then made judgments regarding the similarity of the researcher's explanations to their own beliefs and other judgments from three perspectives—their own, the researcher's, and the average student's. The key finding was that *"participants assumed that researchers promoting what has been referred to as the 'most central, defining' message of social psychology—that is, those arguing for the strong situational causation of evil behavior—were less likely to believe that evildoers could be blamed or held responsible for their wrongdoing than those presenting dispositional accounts"* (p. 265; emphasis added). Participants were most favorable to the interactionist and least to the situational explanation. Blame and responsibility judgments were relatively high regardless of perspective or which explanation they read—thus a clear rejection of situationism and a reluctance of participants to exonerate perpetrators. These findings replicated those observed by Miller, Gordon, & Buddie (1999). (See Tang, Newman, & Huang, 2014, for confirming evidence.)

Why do lay persons prefer dispositional or interactionist explanations? In responding to an essay by Lilienfeld (2012a), in which he discussed various reasons underlying public skepticism about psychology, Newman, Bakina, and Tang (2012) suggested that "laypeople are suspicious of accounts of human wrongdoing that feature situational/contextual facts, and they prefer dispositional ones" (p. 805). Lilienfeld (2012b), in response, noted: "To the extent that social psychologists who communicate with the media at times underplay the potency of dispositional influences on behavior and portray situations as generating a virtually ineluctable drive toward antisocial actions, public skepticism of such proclamations may be warranted" (p. 809). (Lilienfeld signed the "not so situational" protest letter against Zimbardo.) Observers of harm doing often respond to perpetrators in terms of anger and attributions of blame and deserved punishment (e.g., Tetlock et al., 2010). From this perspective, the partial exoneration of perpetrators—a direct implication of situationism (e.g., Ross & Shestowsky, 2012)—can readily be seen as violating norms of retribution and fair justice (e.g., for interesting further discussions of these issues, see Levy [2015] and Ciurria [2013]).

Haslam and Reicher's Social-Identification Theory and Research on Obedience

An important advance in understanding of Milgram's findings has been the research of Reicher and Haslam (e.g., 2011), who have developed a social-identification model and conducted several experiments to test its validity. According to their account, the participant is a highly engaged, active decision maker, not a relatively passive respondent to contextual forces, which, in Reicher and Haslam's view, has been the prevailing depiction of situationist accounts for decades. In their model, the participant (teacher) ultimately must decide with whom to identify from the two competing voices in Milgram's paradigm—the increasingly demanding experimenter or the protesting learner. As the experiment begins, the experimenter's role is, of course, more salient, but this can change for many participants over the course of the study. Ultimate obedience or disobedience is thus "predicated upon perceptions of shared identity" (2011, p. 168). Reaching the decision as to "with whom shall I identify?" may be fraught with difficulty for many participants, accounting for the intense emotion, nervous laughter, and conflict described graphically by Milgram (1963).

Haslam and Reicher have published four studies testing their model. In the first, Reicher et al. (2012) asked a group of individuals to read a synopsis of Milgram's baseline study, then summaries of 15 of Milgram's variations (1974), rating each as to the degree to which (1) each situation would likely have motivated participants in the teacher role to identify with the experimenter as a scientist or (2) to identify with the learner as a member of the general public. The investigators then correlated the two ratings with the actual rates of obedience reported by Milgram (1974). The results strongly supported their prediction. Identification with the experimenter correlated positively with percentage of obedience, whereas identification with the learner correlated negatively. Reicher et al. (2012) concluded that rather than the blind obedience frequently ascribed to Milgram's experiments, what is more accurately revealed is "an act of engaged followership that flows from social identification with those in positions of leadership" (p. 322).

In a second study, Haslam, Reicher, and Birney (2014) hypothesized that Prod 4 was ineffective in the study by Burger et al. (2011) because the harshly worded "You have no other choice, you must go on" produced reactance, rupturing any bond that participants might have established with the experimenter. They first asked a group of individuals to read the four prods (verbatim from Milgram) in random order and to rate each of them as to whether the prod represented an order, a reference to the scientific importance to the experimenter, a request, or a justification for continuing. The results clearly indicated that Prod 4 was viewed uniquely as an order. These results enabled the investigators to ask their key question in the next study: What effect would Prod 4 (and the other prods) have on participants specifically when *not* confounded by its order of presentation (i.e., always following Prods, 1, 2, and 3)? Haslam, Reicher, & Birney (2014) devised an increasingly unpleasant task of asking participants to choose highly negative trait adjectives to describe increasingly pleasant groups (e.g., photos of the Ku Klux Klan, a family group on a walk). The results indicated that participants assigned to *Prod 2* continued much further in the trial series than those exposed to *Prod 4* and were much more likely to complete the study's postexperimental measures. The authors concluded that their findings do not support Milgram's theory (emphasizing obedience to orders) but rather "an engaged followership model . . . that participants' willingness to continue with an objectionable task is predicated upon active identification with the scientific project and those leading it" (p. 473). In their view, continuing a course of destructive action is not a slippery slope "down which perpetrators fall helplessly, but rather a mountain that has to be climbed with, and for, a purpose" (p. 484).

In a third study, on the assumption that Milgram's participants' postexperimental comments could reveal attitudes relevant to the social-identification model, Haslam, Reicher, Millard, and McDonald (2015b) examined Box 44 in the Milgram archives. A content analysis was formed on the cards in this box, each containing a respondent's qualitative comments, expanding on the questionnaire they had filled out at Milgram's request, reported in Milgram's (1964) rebuttal to Baumrind. Major themes derived in this analysis included support for Milgram's project (e.g., "felt pride at being chosen to participate," p. 71), support for the behavioral investigation (e.g., "I consider research essential to progress and think everyone should encourage and aid when possible," p. 73), and support for Yale (e.g., "My only desire is that someday I will be able to afford to go and learn more about the human race. And I hope I will be able to attend the greatest school in this country Yale of course," p. 74). Haslam and colleagues report that there were relatively few negative comments (e.g., "I have no way of knowing if the experiment was of value or whether further experiments are necessary to prove anything," p. 74; "To me, psychology remains a pseudoscience. These types of studies are little value in the study of human behavior since the variables are too many," p. 74).

The authors concluded that the vast majority of the comments relating to participants' experience are indeed positive and have to do either with the benefits of scientific inquiry or the worthiness of the institution that promotes the scientific value of research. Although the content of the cards included references to the stress and dilemmas faced *during* the experiment, there appears to have been a pronounced *lack* of stress *after* the experiment, coupled with the generally positive evaluation and engagement with the experiment. Haslam, Reicher, Millard, et al. (2015b) concluded: "A belief in the science does not remove the dilemma that participants face. It does not make them unaware that they are inflicting pain . . . but it does help them resolve the key dilemma they confront, it does help them live with themselves, and . . . makes them prepared to support more of the same in the future" (p. 76). Haslam, Reicher, Millard, et al. (2015b) regard these findings as consistent with their engaged-follower explanation but not with the agentic-state account. They point, however, to another ethical issue in suggesting that Milgram, in his debriefing, succeeded in making participants comfortable at the cost of accepting an ideology (science) with considerable potential for social destructiveness. They conclude:

> Our close investigation of what Milgram's participants had to say about their experiences in his studies points to the way in which "science" itself has the potential to be invoked as a "warrant for abuse." This in turn suggests that the horizons of scientific ethics (and the practices of ethics committees) need to extend beyond a concern to ensure that participants are content, to also reflect on what they are encouraged to be content about. Certainly, all the evidence suggests that Milgram's participants were "happy to have been of service." As scientists, we need to ask whether this is the kind of service with which we want people to be quite so happy. (pp. 79–80)

There were likely a variety of motives driving post-experimental "happiness," for example, the operation of cognitive dissonance reduction (i.e., justifying or rationalizing their immoral deeds in order to achieve a relatively stable and positive sense of self [e.g., Cooper, 2007]). Identifying with the experimenter may have been one means of reducing dissonance. Perhaps other participants simply enjoyed the experiment, seeing it as stressful but also interesting and important, as millions of others have found the experiments over the past 5 decades. In their most recent study, Haslam, Reicher, and Millard (2015a) used a technique called digital immersive realism, in which professional actors essentially played the role of participants in a version of the Milgram paradigm. A variety of features, including the size and appearance of Milgram's laboratory, were replicated. Paid actors were prepared ahead of time by a director to learn the role of someone who would participate in a social psychology experiment. The aim was to separate the actor's (real) self from the role he or she played, thereby enabling the research to be clearly ethical. The actors took part in a modified restaging of Milgram's new baseline condition and four of the experimental variations in Milgram's (1974) series of studies (e.g., two peers rebel; experimenter absent; learner proximal to participant; no learner feedback [remote]). In this technique, a major goal was to obtain behaviors that would indicate that the actors had genuinely entered the role. Hence their behaviors would need to resemble Milgram's behavioral findings, not the vastly underestimated (idealistic) estimates noted earlier.

Major findings included: 100% of the participants in the baseline condition administered shocks exceeding 150 volts, on average reaching 300 volts; only 1 of 10 participants received what the investigators regarded as the only true order, that is, Prod 4, and obeyed it; and the average shock level across the variations corresponded closely with Milgram's original findings ($r = .59$, $p < .03$). Most participants were agitated and stressed during the study but expressed, during debriefing, being pleased to have been in it. To test their social-identification model, Haslam, Reicher, and Millard (2015a) first asked participants to rate their degree of identification with the learner and the experimenter. Average ratings were similar on both measures and higher than the midpoint. Thus the moral conflict, crucially important in Milgram's original conception of the studies, seemed to be present in the participants' perceptions of the situation they were in. The primary effect seemed to be lesser punishment correlating with higher identification with the learner ($r(13) = -.59, p < .03$) and an insignificant though positive correlation between identification with the experimenter and more punishment ($r(13) = .36, p < .21$). The authors acknowledge fully the limitations of this research in terms of small sample size and relatively extraordinary time and expense involved in the use of trained actors. A useful next step would incorporate an experimental manipulation of social identification as an independent variable, as a complement to the correlational results of these studies.

Haslam, Reicher, and Millard (2015a) concluded that their study provides clear evidence to support claims that obedience is not an ineluctable proclivity but a *choice*, seen most vividly when almost all participants refuse to "obey" the fourth prod. This is not simply less obedience but active resistance, in their view: "Far from . . . showing that the landscape of tyranny is bereft of human agency, we see instead that identity-based choice is what makes tyranny possible—and also what makes tyranny vulnerable to overthrow."

Collectively, their four studies provide powerful support for Haslam and Reicher's model. A particular virtue of their theory is that it is a general conceptual approach applicable to *all* of Milgram's specific variations (not just the baseline experiment), as well as to generalizations that have been made to the Holocaust and other contexts. Social-identification theory emphasizes the role of leadership and followers who are strongly (or perhaps weakly) identified with the leader's mission. For example, in describing female Nazi guards at the Majdanek concentration camp, Evans (2015) quotes from Elissa Mailander: "She uses memoirs, filmed interviews, and postwar trial . . . records to show how the experience of almost unlimited power over the inmates brought them to identify closely with the regime, whose propaganda and pressure to deliver 'results' strengthen the women's allegiance to Nazi ideology" (p. 54). One sees elements of both the Milgram and Zimbardo studies here. This is not to minimize the role of situational pressures on relatively ordinary, lower-level perpetrators as one causal factor in the Holocaust (e.g., Browning, 1992), but clearly the emphasis here on leadership and zealous ideological followers is very different from the typical social-psychological portrait of the morally conflicted participants in the Milgram experiments.

Who Is Responsible?

The question "Who is responsible?" is central to the Milgram experiments and to the generalizations made from those studies. Milgram himself changed his views on responsibility. In an early response to Baumrind's (1964) ethical critique, he noted, "The critic feels that the experimenter made the subject shock the victim. This conception is alien to my view. . . . I started with the belief that every person who came to the laboratory was free to accept or to reject the dictates of authority" (1964, p. 97). Later, however (1974), the central construct in his model of obedience, the agentic state, portrayed the obedient person as abandoning a sense of personal responsibility: "The most far-reaching consequence of the agentic shift is that a man feels responsible *to* the authority directing him but feels no responsibility *for* the content of the actions that the authority prescribes" (pp. 145–146; emphasis in original). One complexity is whether responsibility is defined from the perpetrator's view or that of an observer. Are subordinates being sincere when claiming that their harmful actions were performed under orders? Military law requires disobedience to illegal commands, but the "duty to obey and the duty to disobey" are at times very difficult decisions (e.g., Kelman & Hamilton, 1989). Milgram seemed clear on the sincerity issue: "The disappearance of a sense of responsibility is the most far-reaching consequence of submission to authority" (1974, p. 8). Still, "following orders" can at times be used as an excuse or lie (noted earlier in connection with Eichmann's plea) to evade punishment. (For an imaginative neuroscience-based study supporting the potential sincerity of the "I was only following orders" claim, see Caspar, Christensen, Cleeremans, and Haggard, 2016).

Card (2005), in a philosophical analysis of individual responsibility in organization contexts, recognizes the power of situational forces but suspects that Milgram's obedient participants were still, to a degree, responsible: "Requiring one to abstain from cruel actions against defenseless persons is not unreasonably demanding" (p. 399). Milgram noted that in bureaucratic situations (e.g., the Holocaust), "it is psychologically easy to ignore responsibility when one is only an intermediate link in a chain of evil action but is far from the final consequences of the action" (1974, p. 11). Card, agreeing with Milgram's legalistic perspective that in complex organizations there can be a fragmentation of both action and responsibility, concluded: "both individuals and organizations bear moral responsibility for actions performed within organization contexts, and the degree of responsibility is to be determined on a case by case basis" (p. 402).

Haslam and Reicher's Position on Moral Responsibility

Of particular interest are Haslam and Reicher's strong conclusions regarding the moral responsibility of those individuals harming others under the presence of authority: "Followership of this form is not thoughtless. It is the *conscious endeavor of committed subjects*" (Reicher et al., 2012, p. 323; emphasis added); "It is time to reject the comforts of the obedience alibi. It is time, instead, to engage with the uncomfortable truth that, when people inflict harm to others, they often *do so wittingly and willingly*" (Haslam, Reicher, and Millard, 2015a; emphasis added); "To understand tyranny, we need to transcend the prevailing orthodoxy that this tyranny derives from something for which humans have a natural inclination, a 'Lucifer effect' to which they succumb *thoughtlessly and helplessly (and for which, therefore, they cannot be held accountable)*" (Haslam & Reicher, 2012a; emphasis added).

In an earlier experiment, Reicher and Haslam (2006) reported on their BBC prison study, a partial replication (televised) of Zimbardo's prison study that largely failed to reproduce his findings. However, this was not totally unexpected, as their study was designed precisely to test social identification theory, with different expected outcomes. Their discussion section, highly critical of Zimbardo's study, understandably provoked Zimbardo (2006), who in turn rebutted both their study and their criticisms of him with his own view: "These actions also make evident to me that their underlying personal objective was to highjack this media opportunity to advance their evangelical worldview that rational people with free will can rise above situational forces to live in communal harmony as long as they can sustain a social identity in accord with prosocial values and norms of their community" (p. 52). Haslam and Reicher (2006) then responded, in part, as follows: "The fact that Zimbardo's analysis of those events [Abu Ghraib] was invoked in order *to deny responsibility* for acts of appalling brutality should also serve as a warning to social psychology. For ... it points to the way that our theories are used to justify and normalize oppression, rather than to problematize it and identify ways in which it can be overcome. In short, representing abuse as 'natural' makes us apologists for the inexcusable" (p. 62, emphasis in original). It is hard not to imagine a similarly vitriolic exchange occurring between Haslam and Reicher and Milgram, were he still alive. The larger and more significant issue here is not their personal attack on Zimbardo but rather their highly critical view of the condoning aspects of situationism itself. In this context, they are speaking for many of Milgram's critics, who for decades have argued along very similar lines. *It is this extreme disparity of conceptual views on moral responsibility, as illustrated by Haslam and Reicher on the one hand and by Ross and Shestowsky (and, by extension, Zimbardo and Milgram) on the other, that constitutes the most profound and enduring controversy surrounding the Milgram experiments.*

The issue of recommended punishment becomes an immediately relevant consideration. Relatively severe punishment for obedient perpetrators would seem to follow logically from Haslam and Reicher's model: "It is striking how destructive acts were presented as constructive, particularly in Milgram's case, where scientific progress was the warrant for abuse" (Haslam & Reicher, 2012a). That is, in their view, obedient participants identified with the destructive scientific ideology of the experimenter (i.e., to inflict severe shocks for errors) and hence would warrant a harsh penalty were it in a nonlaboratory setting. Conversely, a more lenient sentence, taking into account the mitigating role of situational factors, would clearly follow from Ross and Shestowsky's analysis. There is, fortunately, a new line of research that tests these ideas.

Beliefs in Free Will, Moral Responsibility, and Punishment

Two studies have examined the effects of beliefs in free will on judgments of moral responsibility and punishment. Vohs and Schooler (2008) randomly assigned participants to read an anti-free-will essay or a control essay. Participants in the anti-free-will condition cheated more on a subsequent task. A second experiment included a pro-determinism essay condition, as well as a neutral control. Those assigned to the determinism condition cheated significantly more than in the other conditions. Mediation analysis indicated that lower beliefs in free will were the significant determinant of cheating. The authors concluded: "The fact that brief exposure to a message asserting that there is no such thing as free will can increase both passive and active cheating raises the concern that advocating a deterministic worldview could undermine moral behavior" (p. 53). Why does dismissing free will lead to wrongdoing? Vohs and Schooler suggested, in a parallel to Milgram's agentic state: "Doubting one's free will may undermine the sense of self as agent" (2008, p. 54). From this perspective, participants in the obedience studies continue to shock the learner because the experiment (e.g., the prods) effectively places them in a "low free will belief" situation, allowing them to pursue a harmful course of action with a greater sense of self-justification. This motivation would seem very different from that advocated by Haslam and Reicher, that is, the obedient participant's active, freely chosen social identification with the experimenter's scientific mission.

In a related study focusing on observers, Shariff et al. (2014) asked whether a reduced belief in free will would lead people to see wrongful behavior as less morally reprehensible, resulting in less retributive punishment. Two studies supported this hypothesis. A third study both hypothesized and observed that exposure to a neuroscience article (emphasizing a deterministic view of human behavior) would reduce the reader's belief in free will and thereby reduce retributive punishment. Perceived blame mediated the effects of conditions on punishment. Thus the neuroscience article led to exoneration, that is, less blame and, in turn, less punishment. A fourth study showed lower beliefs in free will and recommended punishment after as compared to before taking a neuroscience course. No differences occurred in a geography control course. Exposure to a strongly situationist perspective in social psychology can be likened, functionally, to the neuroscience article or course in the Shariff et al. (2014) studies. Both send relatively low-free-will messages and are thus seen as exonerating.

Thus we now have important empirical proof for the exoneration that is often attributed to situational explanations. From this perspective, instructors and researchers discussing or favoring a more purely situationist account of harm doing should address the condoning implications in a forthright manner, including their controversiality, and not simply (intentionally or not) leaving them out of the discussion. Their readers or students will almost certainly be thinking about these matters on their own, based on the research reviewed here. The analysis of Ross and Shestowsky (2012) is a particularly useful resource for this type of discussion, regardless of whether one endorses it or not. Thus informed, readers can then draw their own conclusions and have a more nuanced, clearer rationale for holding them. (One envisions some spirited discussions here.)

CONCLUSIONS

The continuing controversial status of the Milgram experiments is understandable, because deeply held values and attitudes about causality and free will, as well as moral responsibility and punishment, are driving the polarized opinions. Controversy is sometimes a strength, not a weakness. For example, the legal justice system is not viewed as flawed simply because of the continuous adversarial positions of the defense and prosecution. These biases are, in fact, desired and built into the system itself. As long as situationists claim conceptual ownership of the obedience studies, there is going to be considerable opposition. A more pronounced interactionist position would seem one viable resolution to some of the conflict discussed in this chapter (e.g., Newman & Bakina, 2009). The social-identification model of Haslam and Reicher is clearly the most promising conceptual development at the present time. Their conceptually focused research is particularly relevant because one major reason for the endless controversies concerning the Milgram experiments has been the absence of a convincing, empirically based theory. For decades, this significant gap has been filled with speculations and personal views regarding the basis of Milgram's findings and their implications. Consider Mandel's (1998) disparaging phrase, "obedience alibi," in reaction to Milgram's stating, in the Nuremberg context, that "it would be wrong to think of it [the claim of following orders] as a thin alibi concocted for the occasion. Rather, it is a fundamental mode of thinking for a great many people once they are locked into a subordinate position in a structure of authority" (1974, p. 8). As long as these constructions of what happened are simply left to resonate in thin air, the controversy will continue. A subordinate's sincerity could be legitimate or fabricated, but the only way to resolve this disagreement would be theory-driven research on underlying processes and a convincing methodology to ask, and not prematurely answer, the "is it an alibi?" question.

Jetten and Mols (2014) have noted that "a complete account of what makes people obedient also has to focus on what makes people disobedient" (p. 591). Researchers should also account for resistance (e.g., Einwohner, 2014; Gibson, 2014; Hollander, 2015). (See also Haslam & Reicher, 2012b, for an instructive analysis of prison resistance.) As noted, understanding precisely why different specific individuals in the same experimental condition decide to obey or withdraw remains a major unanswered question in the obedience story. This chapter has attempted to explore the important dimensions of the Milgram controversies. It has not attempted to resolve these controversies nor to promote a specific conceptual ideology, although elements of bias may be apparent. Inevitably, and appropriately, readers will have their own views on these intriguing matters.

A closing thought: An interesting question would be what factors draw professional social psychologists to adopt the different, often antagonistic theoretical orientations we have considered here. Information on this difficult issue could provide greater insight into the continuing controversies regarding the Milgram experiments. For example, consider their basic position on punishment. Evidence indicates that for laypersons, at least, having strong beliefs on free will or autonomy is caused by an underlying desire to blame and punish perpetrators (Clark et al., 2014). That is, if one gives priority to the idea that perpetrators should be punished, one then is motivated to adopt a specific theory on matters pertaining to free will that will justify that punishment. Carey and Paulhus (2013) have suggested that holding to a politically conservative worldview may drive both strong beliefs in free will and harshly punitive reactions to perpetrators of harm. There are doubtless a number of reasons why social psychologists select themselves into different theoretical camps. Clearly, they are not ordinarily viewed as primarily driven by thoughts of punishment (or exoneration). These motives could nevertheless be powerful, even if subtle and unwitting, influences—that is, causes rather than solely effects of their specific theorizing—thus accounting for some of the controversies and heated rhetoric noted in this chapter. It is hardly the whole story, but it remains an intriguing possibility.

REFERENCES

Arendt, H. (1963). *Eichmann in Jerusalem: A report on the banality of evil*. New York: Penguin.

Banaji, M. R., & Greenwald, A. G. (2013). *Blind spots: Hidden biases of good people*. New York: Delacorte Press.

Bandura, A. (1999). Moral disengagement in the perpetration of inhumanities. *Personality and Social Psychology Review, 3,* 193–209.

Baumeister, R. F. (1997). *Evil: Inside human violence and cruelty.* New York: Freeman.

Baumrind, D. (1964). Some thoughts on ethics of research: After reading Milgram's "Behavioral study of obedience." *American Psychologist, 19,* 421–423.

Baumrind, D. (2014). Is Milgram's deceptive research ethically acceptable? *Theoretical and Applied Ethics, 2,* 11–18.

Beauvois, J. L., Courbet, D., & Oberle, D. (2012). The prescriptive power of the television host: A transposition of Milgram's obedience paradigm to the context of a TV game show. *European Review of Applied Psychology, 62,* 111–119.

Begue, L., Beauvois, J. L., Courbet, D., Oberle, D., Lepage, J., & Duke, A. A. (2015). Personality predicts obedience in a Milgram paradigm. *Journal of Personality, 83*(3), 299–306.

Benjamin, L. T., & Simpson, J. A. (2009). The power of the situation: The impact of Milgram's obedience studies on personality and social psychology. *American Psychologist, 64,* 12–19.

Blass, T. (Ed.). (2000). *Obedience to authority: Current perspectives on the Milgram paradigm.* Mahwah, NJ: Erlbaum.

Blass, T. (2004). *The man who shocked the world: The life and legacy of Stanley Milgram.* New York: Basic Books.

Blass, T. (2009). From New Haven to Santa Clara: A historical perspective on the Milgram obedience experiments. *American Psychologist, 64,* 37–45.

Bocchiaro, P., & Zimbardo, P. G. (2010). Defying unjust authority: An exploratory study. *Current Psychology, 29,* 155–170.

Bocchiaro, P., Zimbardo, P. G., & Van Lange, P. (2012). To defy or not to defy: Unpacking disobedience and whistle-blowing as extraordinary forms of disobedience to authority. *Social Influence, 7,* 35–50.

Brannigan, A., Nicholson, I., & Cherry, F. (Eds.) (2015). Unplugging the Milgram machine. *Theory and Psychology, 25,* 551–696.

Browning, C. (1992). *Ordinary men: Reserve police battalion 101 and the final solution in Poland.* London: Harper Collins.

Buckels, E. E., Jones, D. N., & Paulhus, D. L. (2013). Behavioral confirmation of everyday sadism. *Psychological Science, 20*(10), 1–9.

Burger, J. M. (2009). Replicating Milgram: Would people still obey today? *American Psychologist, 64,* 1–11.

Burger, J. M. (2014). Situational features in Milgram's experiment that kept his participants shocking. *Journal of Social Issues, 70*(3), 489–500.

Burger, J. M., Girgis, Z. M., & Manning, C. C. (2011). In their own words: Explaining obedience to authority through an examination of participants' comments. *Social Psychological and Personality Science, 2,* 460–466.

Card, R. (2005). Individual responsibility within organizational contexts. *Journal of Business Ethics, 62,* 397–405.

Carey, J. M., & Paulhus, D. L. (2013). Worldview implications of believing in free will and/or determinism: Politics, morality, and punitiveness. *Journal of Personality, 81*(2), 130–141.

Carnahan, T., & McFarland, S. (2007). Revisiting the Stanford prison experiment:

Could participant self-selection have led to the cruelty? *Personality and Social Psychology Bulletin, 33*(5), 603–614.

Caspar, E. A., Christensen, J. F., Cleeremans, A., & Haggard, P. (2016). Coercion changes the sense of agency in the human brain. *Current Biology, 26*, 1–8.

Cesarani, D. (2004). *Becoming Eichmann: Rethinking the life, crimes, and trial of a "desk murderer."* Cambridge, MA: Da Capo Press.

Cheetham, M., Pedroni, A. F., Antley, A., Slater, M., & Jancke, L. (2009). Virtual Milgram: Empathic concern or personal distress? Evidence from functional MRI and dispositional measures. *Human Neuroscience, 3*, 29.

Ciurria, M. (2013). Situationism, moral responsibility, and blame. *Philosophia, 41*, 179–193.

Clark, C. J., Luguri, J. B., Ditto, P. H., Knobe, J., Shariff, A., & Baumeister, R. F. (2014). Free to punish: A motivated account of free will belief. *Journal of Personality and Social Psychology, 16*, 501–513.

Cooper, J. (2007). *Cognitive dissonance: 50 years of a classic theory*. New York: Sage.

Dambrun, M., & Vatine, E. (2010). Reopening the study of extreme social behaviors: Obedience to authority within an immersive video environment. *European Journal of Social Psychology, 40*, 760–773.

Dargis, M. (2015, October 15). In "Experimenter," are they following orders or instincts? [Review]. *New York Times*. Retrieved from *www.nytimes.com/2015/10/16/movies/review-in-experimenter-are-they-following-orders-or-instincts.html?ref=arts&_r=0*.

de Swaan, A. (2015). *The killing compartments: The mentality of mass murder*. New Haven, CT: Yale University Press.

Donnellan, M. B., Fraley, R. C., & Krueger, R. F. (2007). Not so situational [Letter to the editor]. *APS Observer, 20*(6), 5.

Dovidio, J. F., Gaertner, S. L., Nier, J. A., Kawakami, K., & Hodson, G. (2004). Contemporary racial bias: When good people do bad things. In A. G. Miller (Ed.), *The social psychology of good and evil* (pp. 141–167). New York: Guilford Press.

Dyson, F. (2015, May 7). Einstein as a Jew and a philosopher. *The New York Review of Books*, pp. 14–17.

Einwohner, R. L. (2014). Authorities and uncertainties: Applying lessons from the study of Jewish resistance during the Holocaust to the Milgram legacy. *Journal of Social Issues, 70*(3), 531–543.

Elms, A. C. (2009). Obedience lite. *American Psychologist, 64*, 32–36.

Elms, A. C., & Milgram, S. (1966). Personality characteristics associated with obedience and defiance toward authoritative commands. *Journal of Experimental Research in Personality, 1*, 282–289.

Epley, N. (2015). *Mindwise: Why we misunderstand what others think, believe, feel, and want*. New York: Vintage.

Evans, R. J. (2015, July 9). The anatomy of hell. *The New York Review of Books*, pp. 52–54.

Fermaglich, K. (2006). *American dreams and Nazi nightmares: Early Holocaust consciousness and liberal America, 1957–1965*. Waltham, MA: Brandeis University Press

Fiske, S. T. (2013). A millennial challenge: Extremism in uncertain times. *Journal of Social Issues, 69*(3), 605–613.

Fiske, S. T., Harris, L. T., & Cuddy, A. J. C. (2004). Why ordinary people torture enemy prisoners. *Science, 306,* 1482–1483.

Frimer, J. A., Gaucher, D., & Schaefer, N. K. (2014). Political conservatives' affinity for obedience to authority is loyal, not blind. *Personality and Social Psychology Bulletin, 40*(9), 1205–1214.

Funder, D. C. (2009). Persons, behaviors, and situations: An agenda for personality psychology in the postwar era. *Journal of Research in Personality, 43,* 120–126.

Gazda, P. (2015, April 19). I was an animal experimenter. *New York Times,* p. 8.

Gibson, S. (2014). Discourse, defiance, and rationality: "Knowledge work" in the "obedience" paradigm. *Journal of Social Issues, 70*(3), 424–438.

Gilovich, T., Keltner, D., & Nisbett, R. E. (2011). *Social psychology* (2nd ed.). New York: Norton.

Graham, J., Nosek, B. A., Haidt, J., Iyer, R., Koleva, S., & Ditto, P. H. (2011). Mapping the moral domain. *Journal of Personality and Social Psychology, 101,* 366–385.

Griggs, R. A., & Whitehead, G. I., III. (2014). Coverage of the Stanford prison experiment in introductory social psychology textbooks. *Teaching of Psychology, 41*(4), 318–324.

Griggs, R. A., & Whitehead, G. I., III. (2015). Coverage of Milgram's obedience experiments in social psychology textbooks: Where have all the criticisms gone? *Teaching of Psychology, 42*(4), 315–322.

Haidt, J. (2012). *The righteous mind: Why good people are divided by politics and religion.* New York: Pantheon.

Haney, C., & Zimbardo, P. G. (2009). Persistent dispositionalism in interactionist clothing: Fundamental attribution error in explaining prison abuse. *Personality and Social Psychology Bulletin, 35,* 807–814.

Hanson, J., & Yosifon, D. (2003). The situation: An introduction to the situational character, critical realism, power economics, and deep capture. *University of Pennsylvania Law Review. 152,* 129–346.

Hartson, K. A., & Sherman, D. K. (2012). Gradual escalation: The role of continuous commitments in perceptions of guilt. *Journal of Experimental Social Psychology, 48,* 1279–1290.

Haslam, N., Loughnan S., & Perry G. (2014). Meta-Milgram: An empirical synthesis of the obedience experiments. *PLoS ONE, 9*(4), e93927.

Haslam, S. A., Miller, A. G., & Reicher, S. D. (Eds.). (2014). Milgram at 50: Exploring the enduring relevance of psychology's most famous studies. *Journal of Social Issues, 70*(3), 393–602.

Haslam, S. A., & Reicher, S. D. (2006). Debating the psychology of tyranny: Fundamental issues of theory, perspectives, and science. *British Journal of Social Psychology, 45,* 55–63.

Haslam, S. A., & Reicher, S. D. (2012a). Contesting the "nature" of conformity: What Milgram and Zimbardo's studies really show. *PLoS Biology, 10*(11), e1001426.

Haslam, S. A., & Reicher, S. D. (2012b). When prisoners take over the prison: A social psychology of resistance. *Personality and Social Psychology Review, 16*(2), 154–179.

Haslam, S. A., Reicher, S. D., & Birney, M. E. (2014). Nothing by mere authority: Evidence that in an experimental analogue of the Milgram paradigm, participants are motivated not by orders but by appeals to science. *Journal of Social Issues, 70*(3), 473–488.

Haslam, S. A., Reicher, S. D., & Birney, M. E. (2016). Questioning authority: New perspectives on Milgram's "obedience" research and its implications for intergroup relations. *Current Opinion in Psychology, 11*, 6–9.

Haslam, S. A., Reicher, S. D., & Millard, K. (2015a). Shock treatment: Using immersive digital realism to restage and re-examine Milgram's "obedience to authority" research. *PLoS ONE, 10*(3), e109015.

Haslam, S. A., Reicher, S. D., Millard, K., & McDonald, R. (2015b). "Happy to have been of service": The Yale archive as a window into the engaged followership of participants in Milgram's "obedience" experiments. *British Journal of Social Psychology, 54*, 55–83.

Herbert, W. (2007). The banality of evil. *APS Observer, 20*(4), 11–12.

Herrera, C. (Ed.). (2013). Stanley Milgram and the ethics of social science research. *Theoretical and Applied Ethics, 2*(2), 1–145.

Hollander, M. M. (2015). The repertoire of resistance: Non-compliance with directives in Milgram's "obedience" experiments. *British Journal of Social Psychology, 54*, 425–444.

Jetten, J., & Mols, F. (2014). 50:50 hindsight: Appreciating anew the contributions of Milgram's obedience experiments. *Journal of Social Issues, 70*(3), 587–602.

Kassin, S., Fein, S., & Markus, H. R. (2014). *Social psychology* (9th ed.). Belmont, CA: Wadsworth.

Kelman, H. C., & Hamilton, V. L. (1989). *Crimes of obedience: Toward a social psychology of authority and responsibility.* New Haven, CT: Yale University Press.

Kershner, I. (2016, January 28). Letter reveals plea for mercy by Eichmann. *The New York Times*, pp. A1, A8.

Lane, A. (2014, February 10). The cost of survival: Review of "The last of the unjust." *The New Yorker*, pp. 84–85.

Lang, J. (2014). Against obedience: Hannah Arendt's overlooked challenge to social-psychological explanations of mass atrocity. *Theory & Psychology, 24*(5), 649–667.

Levy, K. (2015). Does situationism excuse? The implications of situationism for moral responsibility and criminal responsibility. *Arkansas Law Review, 68*, 775–831.

Lilienfeld, S. O. (2012a). Public skepticism of psychology: Why many people perceive the study of human behavior as unscientific. *American Psychologist, 67*, 111–129.

Lilienfeld, S. O. (2012b). Further sources of our field's embattled public reputation. *American Psychologist, 67*(9), 808–809.

Lipstadt, D. (2011). *The Eichmann trial.* New York: Shocken.

Lunt, P. (2009). *Stanley Milgram: Understanding obedience and its implications.* New York: Palgrave Macmillan.

Mandel, D. (1998). The obedience alibi: Milgram's account of the Holocaust reconsidered. *Analyse und Kritik, 20*, 74–94.

Martens, A., Kosloff, S., & Jackson, L. E. (2010). Evidence that initial obedient killing fuels subsequent volitional killing beyond effects of practice. *Social Psychology and Personality Science, 1*, 268–273.

Martin, R., Rothrock, N., Leventhal, H., & Leventhal, E. (2003). Common-sense models of illness: Implications for symptom perception and health-related behavior. In J. Sulls & K. A. Wallston (Eds.), *Social psychological foundations of health and illness* (pp. 200–225). New York: Wiley.

McMillan, D. (2014). *How could this happen: Explaining the Holocaust*. New York: Basic Books.

Meeus, W. H. J., & Raaijmakers, Q. A. W. (1986). Administrative obedience: Carrying out orders to use psychological administrative violence. *European Journal of Social Psychology, 16*(4), 311–324.

Milgram, S. (1963). Behavioral study of obedience. *Journal of Abnormal and Social Psychology, 67*, 371–378.

Milgram, S. (1964). Issues in the study of obedience: A reply to Baumrind. *American Psychologist, 19*, 848–852.

Milgram, S. (1974). *Obedience to authority: An experimental view*. New York: Harper & Row.

Milgram, S. (1979). *Obedience to authority: An experimental view* [Preface] (2nd French ed., p. 9). Paris: Calmann-Levy.

Millard, K. (2014). Revisioning obedience: Exploring the role of Milgram's skills as a filmmaker in bringing his shocking narrative to life. *Journal of Social Issues, 70*(3), 439–453.

Miller, A. G. (2004). What can the Milgram experiments tell us about the Holocaust?: Generalizing from the social psychology laboratory. In A. G. Miller (Ed.), *The social psychology of good and evil* (pp. 193–239). New York: Guilford Press.

Miller, A. G. (2009). Reflections on "Replicating Milgram" (Burger, 2009). *American Psychologist, 64*(1), 20–27.

Miller, A. G. (2014). The explanatory value of Milgram's obedience experiments: A contemporary appraisal. *Journal of Social Issues, 70*(3), 558–573.

Miller, A. G., Gordon, A. K., & Buddie, A. M. (1999). Accounting for evil and cruelty: Is to explain to condone? *Personality and Social Psychology Review, 3*, 254–268.

Mook, D. G. (1983). In defense of external invalidity. *American Psychologist, 38*, 379–387.

Moore, C., & Gino, F. (2013). Ethically adrift: How others pull our moral compass from true North, and how we can fix it. *Research in Organizational Behavior, 33*, 53–77.

Newman, L. S. (2001). *The banality of secondary sources: Why social psychologists have misinterpreted Arendt's thesis*. Unpublished manuscript, Department of Psychology, Syracuse University, NY.

Newman, L. S., & Bakina, D. A. (2009). Do people resist social-psychological perspectives on wrongdoing?: Reactions to dispositional, situational, and interactionist explanations. *Social Influence, 4*(4), 256–273.

Newman, L. S., Bakina, D. A., & Tang, Y. (2012). The role of preferred beliefs in skepticism about psychology. *American Psychologist, 67*(9), 805–806.

Nicholson, I. (2011). "Torture at Yale": Experimental subjects, laboratory torment

and the "rehabilitation" of Milgram's "Obedience to authority." *Theory & Psychology, 21*(6), 737–761.
Overy, R. (2014). "Ordinary men," extraordinary circumstances: Historians, social psychology, and the Holocaust. *Journal of Social Issues, 70*(3), 515–530.
Packer, D. J. (2008). Identifying systematic disobedience in Milgram's obedience experiments: A meta-analytic review. *Perspectives on Psychological Science, 3*, 301–304.
Perlman, A. M. (2007). Unethical obedience by subordinate attorneys: Lessons from social psychology. *Hofstra Law Review, 36*(2), 451–477.
Perry, G. (2013). *Behind the shock machine: The untold story of the notorious Milgram psychology experiments*. New York: New Press.
Reicher, S. D., & Haslam, S. A. (2006). Rethinking the psychology of tyranny: The BBC prison study. *British Journal of Social Psychology, 45*, 1–40.
Reicher, S. D., & Haslam, S. A. (2011). After shock?: Towards a social identity explanation of the Milgram "obedience" studies. *British Journal of Social Psychology, 50*, 163–169.
Reicher, S. D., & Haslam, S. A. (2012). Obedience: Revisiting Milgram's shock experiments. In J. R. Smith & S. A. Haslam (Eds.), *Social psychology: Revisiting the classic studies* (pp. 106–125). Thousand Oaks, CA: Sage.
Reicher, S. D., Haslam, S. A., & Miller, A. G. (2014). What makes a person a perpetrator?: The intellectual, moral, and methodological arguments for revisiting Milgram's research on the influence of authority. *Journal of Social Issues, 70*(3), 393–408.
Reicher, S. D., Haslam, S. A., & Smith, J. R. (2012). Working toward the experimenter: Reconceptualizing obedience within the Milgram paradigm as identification-based followership. *Perspectives on Psychological Science, 7*(4), 315–324.
Rochat, F., & Blass, T. (2014). Milgram's unpublished obedience variation and its historical relevance. *Journal of Social Issues, 70*(3), 456–472.
Ross, L., Lepper, M., & Ward, A. (2010). History of social psychology: Insights, challenges, and contributions to theory and application. In S. T. Fiske, D. T. Gilbert, & G. Lindzey (Eds.), *Handbook of social psychology* (5th ed., Vol. 2, pp. 3–50). New York: Wiley.
Ross, L., & Shestowsky, D. (2012). Two social psychologists' reflections on situationism and the criminal justice system. In J. Hanson (Ed.), *Ideology, psychology, and the law* (pp. 612–649). New York: Oxford University Press.
Russell, N. J. (2011). Milgram's obedience to authority experiments: Origins and early evolution. *British Journal of Social Psychology, 50*, 140–162.
Russell, N. J. (2014). The emergence of Milgram's bureaucratic machine. *Journal of Social Issues, 70*(3), 409–423.
Shalvi, S., Gino, F., Barkan, R., & Ayal, S. (2015). Self-serving justifications: Doing wrong and feeling moral. *Current Directions in Psychological Science, 24*(2), 125–130.
Shariff, A. F., Greene, J. D., Karremans, J. C., Luguri, J. B., Clark, C. J., Schooler, J. W., et al. (2014). Free will and punishment: A mechanistic view of human nature reduces retribution. *Psychological Science, 25*(8), 1563–1570.
Sieber, J. E., & Tolich, M. B. (2013). *Planning ethically responsible research*. Los Angeles: Sage.

Smith, E. R., Mackie, D. M., & Claypool, H. M. (2015). *Social psychology* (4th ed.). New York: Psychology Press.
Smith, J. R., & Haslam, S. A. (2012). *Social psychology: Revisiting the classic studies*. Los Angeles: Sage.
Stangneth, B. (2014). *Eichmann before Jerusalem: The unexamined life of a mass murderer*. New York: Knopf.
Stargardt, N. (2015). *The German war: A nation under arms, 1939–1945: Citizens and soldiers*. New York: Basic Books.
Staub, E. (2014). Obeying, joining, following, resisting, and other processes in the Milgram studies, and in the Holocaust and other genocides: Situations, personality, and bystanders. *Journal of Social Issues, 70*(3), 501–514.
Tang, Y., Newman, L. S., & Huang, L. (2014). How people react to social-psychological accounts of wrongdoing: The moderating effects of culture. *Journal of Cross-Cultural Psychology, 45*(5), 752–763.
Tavris, C. (2014). Teaching contentious classics. *APS Observer, 27*(8), 12–16.
Tetlock, P. E., Self, W. T., & Singh, R. (2010). The punitive paradox: When is external pressure exculpatory and when a signal just to spread blame? *Journal of Experimental Social Psychology, 46*, 388–395.
Valentino, B. A. (2004). *Final solutions: Mass killing and genocide in the 20th century*. Ithaca, NY: Cornell University Press.
Vohs, K. D., & Schooler, J. W. (2008). The value of believing in free will: Encouraging a belief in determinism increases cheating. *Psychological Science, 19*(1), 49–54.
Waller, J. (2007). *Becoming evil: How ordinary people commit genocide and mass killing* (2nd ed.). New York: Oxford University Press.
Werhane, P. H., Hartman, L. P., Archer, C., Englehardt, E. E., & Pritchard, M. S. (2013). *Obstacles to ethical decision-making: Mental models, Milgram, and the problem of obedience*. New York: Cambridge University Press.
Wolfe, A. (2011). *Political evil: What it is and how to combat it*. New York: Knopf.
Zeigler-Hill, V., Southard, A. C., Archer, L. M., & Donohoe, P. L. (2013). Neuroticism and negative affect influence the reluctance to engage in destructive obedience in the Milgram paradigm. *Journal of Social Psychology, 153*(2), 161–174.
Zimbardo, P. G. (2006). On rethinking the psychology of tyranny: The BBC prison study. *British Journal of Social Psychology, 45*, 47–53.
Zimbardo, P. G. (2007a). *The Lucifer effect: Understanding how good people turn evil*. New York: Random House.
Zimbardo, P. G. (2007b). Person × situation × system dynamics [Letter to the editor]. *APS Observer, 20*(8), 6.

CHAPTER 11

A Social Interaction Approach to Objectification
Implications for the Social-Psychological Study of Sexual Violence

Sarah J. Gervais

> Like most survivors of sexual assault, I knew the man who attacked me. We met while working at the same restaurant, we had mutual friends and we had gone out before. The night it happened, a Friday in late January, he attended my sorority's date function with me. Late in the evening, he brought me a drink, my fourth of the evening; I started to feel sick shortly thereafter. Back on a daybed in the living room of my apartment, he sexually assaulted me. I have never remembered all of the details from that night, but I do remember thinking that he was raping me and that I needed to get away. Finally I did just that, dragging myself into my bedroom. . . . I went back to class on Monday morning a different person, not only because I had been assaulted, but because I had chosen to speak to the police and deal with the consequences of that. Even surrounded by supportive friends, I felt as if there was a huge flashing arrow over my head. I felt as if everyone knew what had happened, even though in reality few people knew anything. I felt like a victim.
>
> —Jenny Wilkinson (2015)

Unfortunately, such instances of sexual violence are an all-too-common reality for women in the United States and around the world. More than one-third of men, for example, report perpetrating a sexual assault toward a woman (e.g., Abbey, McAuslan, Zawacki, Clinton, & Buck, 2004; DeGue & DiLillo, 2004). Likewise, sexual harassment is extraordinarily common, with approximately 45% of women experiencing it at work (e.g., Pina, Gannon, & Saunders, 2009). Because sexual violence often takes place behind closed bedroom and office doors, it has historically remained an unspoken issue. Yet recent films and books, such as *The Hunting Ground* (Ziering & Dick, 2015) and *Missoula: Rape and the Justice System in a College Town* (Krakauer, 2015), have documented that sexual violence on college campuses is remarkably common and is often ignored or mishandled by college administrators, as well as local law enforcement, further traumatizing victims. Because of recent legislation holding universities more accountable for dealing with this significant public health problem, sexual violence has made its way to the forefront of a national debate. People are discussing the ways it can be prevented from happening, as well as how it should be handled once it has occurred. As these conversations unfold, college administrators, law enforcement, policymakers, and the public have turned to social psychologists to better understand the causes and consequences of this particular form of evil.

The World Health Organization (2014) defines sexual violence as "any sexual act, attempt to obtain a sexual act, unwanted sexual comments or advances, or acts to traffic, or otherwise directed, against a person's sexuality using coercion, by any person regardless of their relationship to the victim, in any setting, including but not limited to home and work." Sexual violence can take many forms (e.g., ogling, catcalls, appearance commentary, verbal coercion, unwanted touching, and physical force), can occur in distinct contexts (e.g., work, home, public spaces), and can emerge in many types of relationships (e.g., between strangers, acquaintances, casual dating partners, committed relationship partners, peers, bosses and coworkers, teachers and students). It also exerts several negative short-term and long-term health consequences on victims. Sexual assault, for example, results in immediate physical pain and injuries, as well as several psychological symptoms, including shock, denial and guilt, fear, anxiety, distrust of others, and posttraumatic stress disorder (PTSD; Felitti et al., 1998). Likewise, although many people believe that sexual behaviors at work are benign and harmless, such hostile work environments cause severe headaches, shortness of breath, and exhaustion, as well as anxiety, depression, and reduced psychological well-being (Fitzgerald, Drasgow, Hulin, Gelfand, & Magley, 1997). Sexual violence in work settings comes with significant costs to the organization, including reduced job satisfaction, more work withdrawal, and increased turnover (see Cortina & Berdahl, 2008, for a review).

As the preceding review reveals, sexual violence most often unfolds in dynamic and ongoing interactions between at least two people—the perpetrator and victim.[1] Unlike stereotypes that suggest that strangers perpetrate rape toward women walking alone on sidewalks at night, rape more often occurs in the context of existing relationships (e.g., between acquaintances, casual dating partners, those in committed relationships) in private rather than public spaces (Koss, Gidycz, & Wisniewski, 1987). Likewise, an image of quid pro quo behavior—a supervisor requests sex from a subordinate in exchange for a raise—is easily evoked with regard to sexual harassment, but sexual harassment often unfolds over time, starting with subtle nonverbal behaviors and escalating into verbal and physical behaviors that create a hostile work environment (Fitzgerald, Gelfand, & Drasgow, 1995).

Although various forms of sexual violence can differ in several regards (e.g., rapists abuse physical power while sexual harassers abuse organizational power; Gutek & Morasch, 1982), it is clear that when women's bodies become locations of sexual violence—from catcalls or ogling to sexual harassment or sexual assault—women are treated as things that can be used and abused by others rather than as fellow human beings. Unfortunately, dehumanization is often a precursor to violence (Bandura, Underwood, & Fromson, 1975). When a man sexually aggresses against a woman, he is less concerned about the woman's thoughts, feelings, desires, and consent and is more concerned with his own uses for her, such as his own sexual fulfillment, feelings of dominance, or display of masculinity. When treated in this manner, the woman is objectified (Fredrickson & Roberts, 1997).

THE SOCIAL INTERACTION MODEL OF OBJECTIFICATION

Sexual violence has been conceptualized as a form of objectification in which "a woman's body is literally treated as a mere instrument or thing by her perpetrator" (Fredrickson & Roberts, 1997, p. 186). Sexual behaviors that are uninvited, unwanted, or not consented to represent forms of sexual violence. However, women sometimes enjoy being sexualized by specific people and in certain contexts (Liss, Erchull, & Ramsey, 2011). During consensual casual sex, for example, both partners may sexually objectify each other, but this scenario would not represent sexual violence because it has been consented to by both parties. Despite the overlap between these two constructs, researchers have only recently started to incorporate sexual violence into the study of objectification and objectification into the study of sexual violence (Carr & Szymanski, 2011; Davidson & Gervais, 2015; Gervais, DiLillo, et al., 2015; Gervais, DiLillo, & McChargue, 2014; Haikalis, DiLillo, & Gervais, 2015; Loughnan, Pina, Vasquez, & Puvia, 2013; Rudman & Mescher, 2012). The social interaction model of objectification (SIMO; see Figure 11.1) complements this work to determine when sexually objectifying behavior in interactions will be welcomed and consented to and when it will not.

Overview

Figure 11.1 depicts the SIMO (Gervais, Bernard, Klein, Riemer, & Haikalis, 2015), which builds on Fredrickson and Roberts's (1997) framework by incorporating Patterson's (1982) functional sequential model of social interaction and related extensions of this model (Hebl & Dovidio, 2005). These frameworks propose that there are sequential phases that dyads pass through when interacting. Specifically, as Figure 11.1 shows, personal (1A), experiential (1B), and relational–situational (1C) *antecedents* (see Figure 11.1, Column 1) influence both interactants to have certain preinteraction cognitions and affect (2A), motivations and goals (2B), and behavioral dispositions (2C). These *preinteraction mediators* (see Figure 11.1, Column 2) set the stage for actual *interaction* behaviors (see Figure 11.1, Column 3) exchanged between the two parties. Thus, preinteraction mediators can predict the expression of various forms of objectification ranging from nonverbal behaviors (3A, e.g., objectifying gazes), verbal behaviors (3B, e.g., appearance commentary, coercion) and physical behaviors (3C, e.g., unwanted touching). During and immediately following these behaviors (see Figure 11.1, Column 4, *interaction consequences*), interactants determine whether their expressed level of involvement and their partners' involvement match their expectations, contributing to subsequent cognitions and affect (4A, e.g., this person is likeable, I'm sexually attracted to this person, this person is a creep), motivations and goals (4B, e.g., I want to have sex with this person, I am concerned about my safety, this person is abusing his power), resulting in continuation or termination (4C) of the interaction.

Patterson's (1982) original model was based on nonverbal and verbal intimacy in social interactions. Because sexual behaviors can sometimes be mutual, reciprocal, consented to, or welcomed, this model is a helpful starting point for considering interactions when nonverbal, verbal, and physical sexual behaviors occur. This approach can also simultaneously incorporate both members of the dyad, allowing for an integration of both potential perpetrator and victim perspectives during an objectifying exchange. It also conceptualizes social interactions in terms of antecedents, preinteraction mediators, actual interaction processes (including behaviors and simultaneous and subsequent cognitions, affect, motivations, and goals), capturing the dynamic and complex nature of social interactions. Social interactions are often cyclical in nature, which is reflected in a feedback loop in which the interaction influences subsequent antecedents, mediators, interaction behaviors, and consequences.

Patterson's model is also useful because it can explicitly incorporate

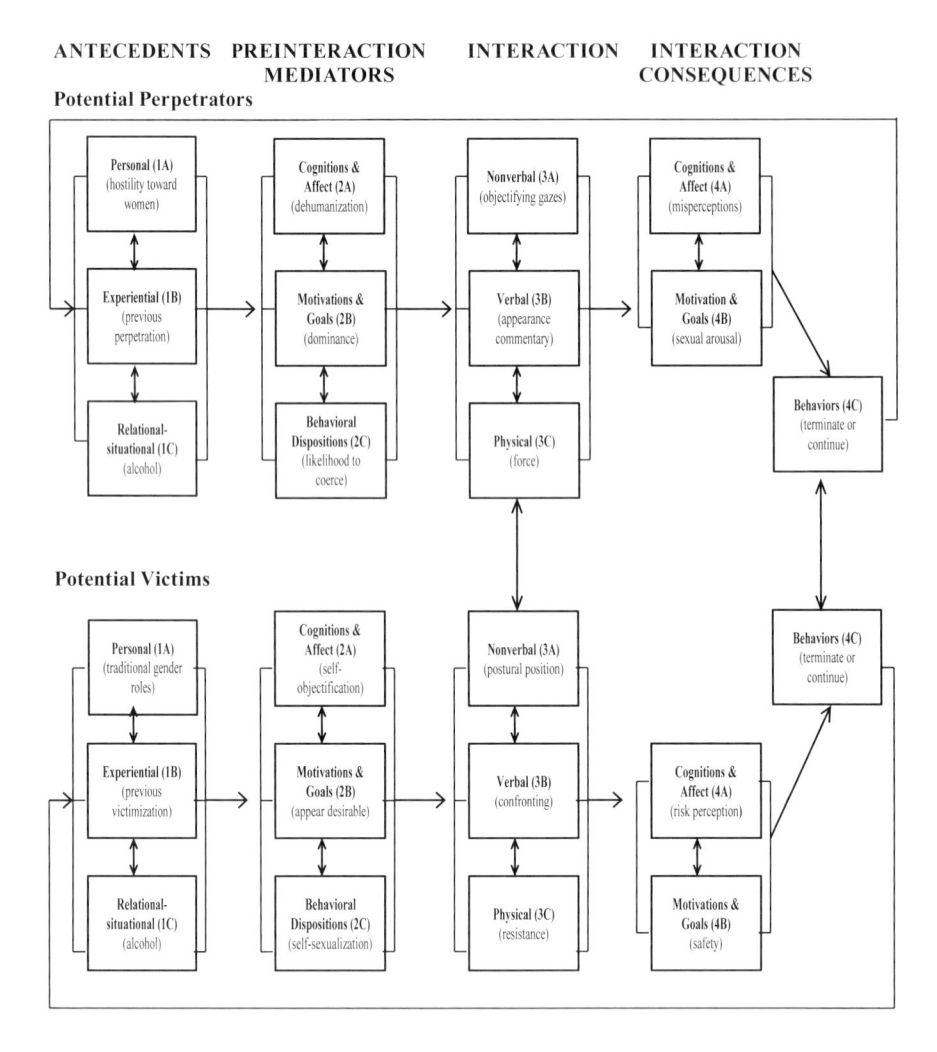

FIGURE 11.1. The SIMO applied to sexual violence.

nonverbal, objectifying behaviors (e.g., objectifying gazes) and responses, which still have negative consequences and often serve as antecedents for more extreme forms of sexual violence. In some situations of sexual assault, for example, sexual behaviors (e.g., gazes, appearance commentary) provide the foundation (in the perpetrator's mind at least) for subsequent sexual aggression (Gervais et al., 2014).

I now delineate this model more fully by considering potential perpetrators and victims of sexual violence across each of the different stage components of the social interaction. I describe the model by including both perspectives simultaneously, rather than focusing separately on the perpetrator (see top half of Figure 11.1) and the victim (see bottom half of Figure 11.1). Although most research in the area of sexual violence focuses on perpetrators *or* victims, but not both, this approach allows for exploration of the similarities and differences between the interactants, as well as explaining the dynamic nature of the interactions. As shown in Figure 11.1, the processes may be similar for potential perpetrators and potential victims (e.g., a situation in which both are drinking) or dissimilar (e.g., a situation in which one is high in power and the other is low in power). This discussion is meant to be an illustrative, rather than a comprehensive, review of research in these areas. Excellent reviews on respective forms of sexual violence (sexual assault, Abbey et al., 2004; sexual harassment, Pina et al., 2009), as well as objectification (Moradi & Huang, 2008), are already available.

Antecedents Phase

The content of social interactions often has antecedents in the differing background variables that interactants bring to a social exchange. Consistent with Patterson (1982), the SIMO specifies personal, experiential, and relational–situational factors that constitute antecedent conditions that influence potentially objectifying and sexually violent interactions.

Personal

There are a number of individual differences that predispose people to objectify and aggress against others. The confluence model (Malamuth, Linz, Heavy, Barnes, & Acker, 1995), an influential theory of sexual assault perpetration, identifies two constellations of individual differences that predict sexual assault: impersonal sex beliefs (i.e., beliefs that sex is a game to be won rather than about emotional closeness) and hostility toward women (i.e., beliefs that women cannot be trusted and corresponding anger toward women). Also focusing on negative attitudes toward women, but in the context of sexual harassment, Pryor (1987) found that men who held negative attitudes toward women and who reported higher likelihoods of rape if they could get away with it sexually harassed women. Ambivalent sexism theory (Glick & Fiske, 1996) complements these approaches with a gender-role perspective, suggesting that hostility toward women who violate the feminine gender role contributes to sexual aggression, whereas benevolence toward women who fit the feminine gender role contributes to sexual protection. Although most research focuses on people's explicit attitudes and emotions, personal factors also may be implicit. As an example, individual differences in the degree to which men implicitly associate women with objects predict their rape proclivity (Rudman & Mescher, 2012).

Personal antecedents also can influence potential victims. To be clear, perpetrators are responsible for sexual violence, and researchers have had considerable difficulty identifying personality characteristics or beliefs that reliably predict sexual victimization in women (Abbey, et al., 2004). Yet the feedback loop posited by Patterson (1982) and the SIMO suggests that initial objectifying behaviors can influence women's personal features, making them more vulnerable to subsequent sexual victimization. Consistent with this idea, Franz, DiLillo, and Gervais (2015) found that sexual objectification experiences predicted sexual victimization, but this relation was explained by self-objectification and related lack of sexual assertiveness. Women high on self-objectification (presumably from previous objectification experiences; see Figure 11.1) also hold more system-legitimizing beliefs that a woman's value is based primarily on her appearance and sex appeal (Calogero & Jost, 2011), and self-objectification is associated with false beliefs that place the blame on rape victims rather than perpetrators (Fox, Ralston, Cooper, & Jones, 2015). Thus prior objectifying experiences may trigger a sequence of events that make women more vulnerable to sexual violence.

Experiential

A second set of antecedent factors include past experiences of objectification and violence. In the context of sexual violence—which often occurs in repeated interactions (e.g., social exchanges between coworkers over the course of days, weeks, or months or a series of interactions between men and women at a party over the course of an evening)—initial interactions between potential perpetrators and victims may significantly influence subsequent interactions and whether the behaviors escalate to sexual violence. According to Patterson (1982), recent or similar experiences exert a strong influence on later interactions; if the initial interaction is pleasant (or unpleasant), interactants will experience increased (or decreased) likelihood of seeking similar interactions. If a man and a woman engage in consensual flirting, for example, this pleasant experience should result in the man and woman seeking out similar interactions. However, if one partner seeks greater sexual involvement than the other (e.g., one flirts, but the other wants to kiss), this will ultimately lead to a host of cognitions and affect, goals and motivations, and behaviors that will likely result in termination of the interaction. When sexual aggression occurs, unwanted behaviors from the perpetrator continue after the victim desires termination. Researchers have identified previous objectification and sexual abuse experiences as strong predictors of objectification and violence perpetration (DeGue & DiLillo, 2004; Malamuth et al., 1995) and victimization (Carr & Szymanski, 2011). Unfortunately, repeated perpetration often represents the norm (Lisak & Miller, 2002), and being victimized makes women vulnerable to revictimization (Messman-Moore, Walsh, & DiLillo, 2010).

Relational–Situational

Personal and experiential antecedents should be strong predictors of sexual violence, but they will likely interact with relational and situational (Patterson, 1982) factors that make the expression of objectification and related sexual aggression more likely. Sexual violence is more likely to occur in hookup situations than work situations, and, although sexual harassment is common at work, it is even more common from strangers in public places (e.g., street harassment; Fairchild & Rudman, 2008).

One important situational factor that researchers have examined is alcohol use. This focus has occurred with good reason; half of all sexual assaults involve alcohol consumption by the perpetrator, victim, or both (see Abbey, 2002 for a review). To examine the reasons for this alarming link, my colleagues and I have relied on alcohol myopia theory (Steele & Josephs, 1990), which suggests that intoxication produces disinhibited behaviors because of a two-pronged biased response to cues in the situation. First, alcohol intoxication restricts the range of cues that are perceived in a situation. When people drink, they attend to and encode fewer available internal and external cues, focusing only on the most salient cues in the situation. Second, intoxication reduces people's ability to process and extract meaning from the cues and information that they do perceive. When people are drunk, they are less able to elaborate on incoming information, relate it to existing knowledge, and thereby extract meaning from it. We have suggested that because alcohol use is associated with a myopic narrowing of the perceptual field, drinking may be associated with a tendency to sexually objectify women—focusing on women's salient sexual attributes (e.g., sex appeal, sexual functions) compared with their less salient attributes (e.g., thoughts, desires, feelings). Consistent with this idea, we have found that women's self-reported drinking, objectification, and sexual victimization are significantly related, and objectification emerges as a significant mediator of the correlation between drinking and victimization in path analysis (Haikalis et al., in press). Likewise, men's self-reported drinking, objectification perpetration, and sexual aggression are correlated, and objectification perpetration is a significant mediator of the link between alcohol consumption and sexual assault perpetration (Gervais et al., 2014).

In addition to the specific contexts and people from which objectification and aggression can occur, social psychologists have brought to bear several additional theories that predict situational antecedents to sexual violence. For example, social identity theory predicts that aggression can follow from identity threat. Consistently, when men were told that they were responding in feminine ways on a diagnostic gender test, they were more likely to send pornographic material to a female confederate (Maass, Cadinu, Guarnieri, & Grasselli, 2003). More recent but similar investigations have examined threat through a precarious-masculinity framework, showing that men are more likely to aggress against women following insults directed at their bodies (Mescher & Rudman, 2014). This presumably occurs because body insults cause masculinity threats and aggression can assuage these threats. Theories of power have also been utilized to predict objectification and aggression. When sex is primed, for example, powerful (vs. powerless) individuals are more likely to objectify women (Gruenfeld, Inesi, Magee, & Galinksy, 2008). Likewise, only men who have automatic cognitive associations linking sex and power show tendencies to sexually harass women (Bargh, Raymond, Pryor, & Strack, 1995). Finally, perceived norms are powerful predictors of sexual violence, but most norms are implicitly rather than explicitly conveyed. Social and organizational norms regarding the perceived permissiveness of sexual harassment, for example, cause sexually harassing behaviors in the workplace (Pryor, Giedd, & Williams, 1995). If people engage in sexual behaviors at work (e.g., looking and commenting on women's bodies, making sexually suggestive jokes) without reprimand from supervisors or coworkers, people may assume that these and related behaviors are acceptable and appropriate. Likewise, perceived peer norms regarding sex are strong predictors of sexual aggression (Norris, Nurius, & Dimeff, 1996).

Preinteraction Mediators Phase

Antecedent conditions directly influence preinteraction states of perpetrators and victims (see Figure 11.1, Column 2), leading interactants to adopt and reinforce cognitions and affect, motivations and goals, and behavioral dispositions in potentially objectifying and violent interactions. Although disentangling the different interaction elements can prove difficult (e.g., the directionality between cognitions and motivations remains unclear) and although they often work together to produce outcomes, I discuss them separately and make suggestions for future research.

Cognitions and Affect

The majority of past objectification perpetration research can be captured within this model component. As a result, much is known about objectifiers' social perceptions about objectified women. Overall, a substantial literature converges on the notion that objectified perceptions fundamentally influence social perception. For example, sexually objectified women are often viewed in piecemeal ways (Bernard, Gervais, Allen, Campomizzi, & Klein, 2012) and are seen as fungible and interchangeable with one another (Gervais, Vescio, & Allen, 2012) at a basic cognitive level. Likewise, sexually objectified women are regarded as less human, likened to animals (Vaes, Paladino, & Puvia, 2011), attributed less agency (Loughnan et al., 2010), and perceived as less competent and warm (Heflick & Goldenberg, 2009). Although most of this work does not focus on actual behaviors, it is suggestive regarding links between objectification and aggression; Loughnan et al. (2013), for example, found that people were more accepting and less concerned about the harm inflicted from sexual assault on a sexually objectified (compared with a humanized) woman.

Motivations and Goals

Likewise, personal, experiential, and relational–situational antecedents may set the stage for different motivations and goals, which may in turn trigger sexual aggression. Sex goals are strong predictors of both objectification and sexual violence. The confluence model (Malamuth et al., 1995) suggests that one of the primary motivations underlying sexual assault is the motivation for impersonal sex (i.e., the belief that sex is a game). Although this is often conceptualized as a chronic motivation, in order for it to manifest in a specific form of sexual violence, that goal must be activated (consciously or unconsciously) at some point preceding the objectifying exchange. Likewise, objectification researchers have found that men dehumanize sexually objectified women when sex goals are salient and they are sexually attracted to the women (Vaes et al., 2011). Importantly, most research shows that sex goals are not sufficient to prompt sexual violence. Feelings of power significantly increase the likelihood of men perpetrating sexual behaviors toward women against their will. When sex goals are primed, for example, high-power but not low-power men objectify women (Gruenfeld et al. 2008).

Potential victims are also influenced by preinteraction motivations and goals. For example, qualitative research (Nurius & Norris, 1996) suggests that during sexual interactions, women often see themselves as walking a cognitive tightrope, "balancing expectations imposed by traditional gender roles to be attractive and managing social interactions with men while avoiding sexual assault" (Norris, 2011, pp. 369). In other words, women are pressured to appear desirable and pleasing to men without becoming victims of sexual assault. Men may be unaware of the tightrope that women perceive themselves to be walking, contributing to misperceptions of sexual interest during interactions (see Figure 11.1, column 4, "Interaction Consequences").

Behavioral Tendencies

Additionally, antecedents may predispose men to behave in sexually aggressive ways. For example, men high on the Likelihood to Sexually Harass scale (Pryor, 1987), as well as men high in their likelihood to rape (Malamuth, 1981), engage in more sexually aggressive behaviors toward women, particularly in situations in which they perceive the norms as more accepting of sexual violence and in which there is less chance they will get caught (Malamuth, 1981; Pryor, 1987).

There are also correlates that make women more vulnerable to sexual victimization. For example, due to personal (e.g., traditional gender role beliefs), experiential (e.g., previous victimization), and situational–relational (e.g., peer norms) factors, some women enjoy sexualization (Liss et al., 2011) and engage in self-sexualizing behaviors (Nowatzki & Morry, 2009). However, other factors, such as self-defense training and empowerment, may serve as important protective factors. Clearly there is not a direct linear relationship between these factors and subsequent sexual victimization. There are many women who self-sexualize and yet have not been victimized by men, and even if women know resistance strategies, nothing can completely allow them to avoid experiencing sexual assault or sexual harassment. In the end, the responsibility of sexual violence falls on perpetrators. Victim characteristics (e.g., provocative dress), however, can make people (e.g., witnesses, Equal Employment Opportunity Commission officers, lawyers, jurors, judges, campus administrators, women themselves) place more blame on victims. Although it is beyond the scope of this chapter, whether sexual violence becomes legally actionable depends on a number of factors that are far from clear-cut and depend on whether the violence occurs in civil (which relies on a preponderance-of-evidence standard) or criminal (which relies on a beyond-a-reasonable-doubt standard) contexts. Regardless, the SIMO approach to sexual violence can identify potential perpetrator and/or victim factors that could be targeted through interventions to reduce the likelihood of sexual violence occurring.

Interaction Phase

According to the SIMO, preinteraction mediators directly influence the expression of nonverbal, verbal, and physical behaviors and responses in social interactions. One of the most important strengths of a social interactive model of violence and related aggression is the ability to investigate the behaviors that potential perpetrators and potential victims display toward one another in initial interactions. This is an important feature because many common forms of sexual violence occur in the context of repeated interactions. Sexual assault may follow from consensual sexual behavior, such as flirting or kissing, whereas hostile work environment sexual harassment may start with subtle, nonverbal behaviors but escalate to more verbal and physical behaviors over time. Understanding the dynamics that emerge between potential perpetrators and victims of sexual violence that ultimately escalate to sexual violence (or do not) is a critical step toward stopping sexual aggression from occurring in the first place.

Nonverbal Behaviors

Nonverbal behaviors that typically emerge during interpersonal interactions are often referred to as *immediacy behaviors* (Word, Zanna, &

Cooper, 1974). Gazing behaviors (e.g., eye contact, avoidance), bodily postures (e.g., leaning in or out, expansiveness or constriction), facial expressions (e.g., smiling, frowning), and head movements (e.g., tilting, nodding) represent common nonverbal behaviors that emerge in interpersonal interactions. Objectification tends to manifest in a very specific immediacy behavior—the objectifying gaze. Conceptualized as staring at a woman's body or sexual body parts (Fredrickson & Roberts, 1997), the objectifying gaze is thought to be the most ubiquitous form of objectification and is often referred to as "checking out" or "ogling" a woman. Although few studies have examined objectifying behaviors, a recent study using eye-tracking technology showed that people who were prompted to focus on the appearances (vs. personalities) of women gazed more at their sexual body parts and less at their faces (Gervais, Holland, & Dodd, 2013). Interestingly, there were no participant gender differences in this pattern of findings, suggesting that both men and women objectify women. Likewise, men who scored higher (vs. lower) on subtle sexism measures were more likely to exhibit dominant and sexually interested behaviors (e.g., sat closer to participants, maintained an open posture with shoulders back and knees wide apart, looked at the participant often) during interactions with classmates (Logel et al., 2009).

Although common adages such as "You can look as long as you don't touch" often condone such behaviors as normal and appropriate rather than inappropriate and aggressive, such behaviors have profound effects on women's behaviors. Generally speaking, nonverbal immediacy behaviors can exert a strong, self-fulfilling prophecy during interactions. For instance, in an initial study, Word et al. (1974) found that white interviewers sat further away and made less eye contact with black relative to white applicants during a simulated job interview. When trained white interviewers modeled the treatment that black applicants had received, white applicants performed poorly in the interview. Similar self-fulfilling prophecies likely occur in interactions with sexually objectified women, but as a result of other, inappropriate immediacy behaviors. The behaviors that result from seeing objectified women as less human (e.g., gazing at women's bodies instead of their faces, focusing on women's sex appeal rather than what they are saying) may elicit confirmatory behaviors from women themselves. Although not focused on objectification per se, a classic study revealed that when men believed they were speaking with an attractive woman (unbeknownst to the women), women acted friendlier, presumably because men were first friendly to the woman they believed to be attractive (Snyder, Tanke, & Berscheid, 1977). With regard to sexual objectification specifically, Gervais, Vescio, and Allen (2011) trained male confederates to exhibit objectifying gazes (i.e., visually scanning women's bodies and briefly staring at their chests), and objectified women performed less well on cognitive tests. Following such exchanges, women also reported that the men engaged in unwelcome, severe, and pervasive sexual conduct that would create a hostile work environment and undermine their psychological well-being (Wiener, Gervais, Allen, & Marquez, 2013; see also Woodzicka & LaFrance, 2001). These examples illustrate that even nonverbal objectifying behaviors directed toward women by men can cause predictable behaviors from women, resulting in subsequent cognitions, affect, motivations, and goals on the behalf of the perpetrator or victim (see Figure 11.1, column 4).

Verbal Behaviors

Objectified perceptions can also result in verbal behaviors, such as appearance compliments and criticisms, catcalls, sexist jokes, and coercion. There has been less research examining the objectifying and aggressive verbal behaviors directed at women by men. It may be the case that verbal objectification is less common than nonverbal objectification due to perceived norms regarding appropriate behavior during interactions or social desirability concerns. For example, Logel et al. (2009) found that subtly sexist men engaged in dominant and sexually interested nonverbal behaviors toward a female confederate, but these nonverbal behaviors did not manifest in verbal behaviors toward the woman. Likewise, research utilizing the Interpersonal Sexual Objectification Scale—Perpetration Version (Gervais et al., 2014; Gervais, Davidson, Canivez, Strack, & DiLillo, 2015) shows that men report engaging in more nonverbal than verbal objectifying behaviors. Some computer-simulated research also shows that men will engage in "verbal" behaviors—sharing sexist jokes over the Internet—and that harassment proclivity, hostile sexism, and male identity contribute to these effects (Siebler, Sabelus, & Bohner, 2008). Yet, more research is clearly needed in this area.

One verbal response that people commonly assume women will engage in as a result of objectifying behaviors is interpersonal confrontation. Although women may believe that they might actually say "My eyes are up here" in response to objectification and verbal aggression from a man, unfortunately most women fail to confront such instances of sexism because of the interpersonal costs (e.g., being seen as complainers or impolite; Swim & Hyers, 1999).

Physical Behaviors

Less research has been conducted with respect to the immediate consequences of physical behaviors composed of objectifying and aggressive behaviors that involve unwanted physical contact. Yet, in one classic study, Pryor (1987) found that when men were given an innocuous excuse for touching a woman (actually a trained female confederate)—teaching her to golf—men who had reported ahead of time that they would sexually harass women in the workplace if they could get away with it were more likely to touch the confederate in intimate and sexual ways. Likewise, using a computer paradigm, Maass et al. (2003) found that when men's social identity was threatened, they were more likely to email pornographic images to a female confederate.

One potential limitation of some of these approaches is that women have not explicitly indicated that the sexual content (e.g., film, images, jokes) is unwanted, which is a central component of sexual violence (e.g., unwelcomeness in the context of sexual harassment and lack of consent in the context of sexual assault). In one of the recent studies from my lab, my colleagues and I remedied this issue by telling male participants that they would be doing a media-preferences task with a female confederate. After a computer-mediated exchange, intoxicated (vs. sober) male participants learned that the woman did not like sexually explicit material. When intoxicated (vs. sober) men were given the opportunity to have the woman watch a sexual or neutral video, they were more likely to expose the woman to the sexually explicit video against her will (Gervais, DiLillo, et al., 2015).

Although there are obvious ethical and practical issues related to examining women's responses to men's physical objectification and aggression (see later in the chapter), a complementary approach has been used to explore women's risk for sexual victimization in the lab. Tasks such as the Risk Perception Survey (Messman-Moore & Brown, 2006) show participants written or audio vignettes depicting forced sexual intercourse by a male acquaintance at a party or a male stranger in a nonsocial setting. The vignettes include clear (sexual comments, male persistence) and ambiguous (alcohol consumption, physical isolation) risk factors for victimization. The vignettes are composed of chronological statements that become progressively riskier as the man increases his coercion. Respondents imagine themselves interacting with the man and choose whether to continue or leave the scenario after each statement. Unfortunately, women who have a history of victimization tend to indicate that they will stay in these situations, even as risk escalates.

As the preceding instances show, nonverbal, verbal, and physical forms of sexual aggression on the behalf of the perpetrator results in profound changes in the behaviors of victims. Unfortunately, such behaviors from perpetrators and victims can influence subsequent cognitions and affect, which influence motivations and goals and related behaviors that increase the propensity for sexual violence.

Interaction Consequences Phase

During and following interactions between perpetrators and victims, a host of cognitions and affect, motivations and goals, as well as behaviors can immediately emerge. In addition to the immediate and long-term consequences of sexual violence for physical and mental health, objectification theory (Fredrickson & Roberts, 1997) and related research (Moradi & Huang, 2008) suggest that objectifying experiences may trigger a cascade of negative consequences for women, making them less likely to leave the interaction and more likely to experience subsequent objectification and violence. That is, the objectifying behaviors displayed in interactions may influence how both parties assess themselves, each other, and the interaction in ways that increase the propensity for subsequent violence.

Cognitions and Affect

Although objectification research has not focused on outcomes for perpetrators per se, sexual violence research suggests that initial objectifying interactions with women can lead to misperceptions of sexual interest (Abbey et al., 2004). Cues indicating sexual interest are often ambiguous; people sometimes misperceive immediacy behaviors indicative of friendliness as flirtation. If a man and a woman meet at a party and start talking about his job, for example, a man may see the woman's interest as a sign of sexual attraction, whereas the woman may be attentive because: (1) she is attracted to him, (2) she is being friendly, (3) she is interested in pursuing the job herself, or (4) another reason altogether. Often these initial behaviors are subtle, so that the interactants can save face and avoid embarrassment if rejected. Furthermore, due to the self-fulfilling nature of social interactions, people process ambiguous information in ways that confirm their initial hypotheses; if a man has already objectified a woman during the preinteraction mediator stage, then he may seek out additional information that she is indeed attracted to him during the interaction. Women's behaviors can inadvertently confirm men's expectations through behavioral confirmation. If a man has objectified a woman and she talks less during the interaction (as a result of his objectifying gazes toward her; Saguy, Quinn, Dovidio, & Pratto, 2010), he may then believe that she has less to say and is less intelligent, not realizing the effect his original beliefs had on his and her subsequent behaviors.

Objectification theory and related research has proven useful in predicting women's cognitive and affective responses to objectifying interactions (Moradi & Huang, 2008). One cognitive outcome is that women self-objectify or adopt their partners' perspectives of their bodies. Self-objectification is associated with disruptive cognitions, such as persistent body surveillance and reduced performance on intellectual tests. It can also undermine women's assertiveness in sexual situations. For example, self-objectification is associated with decreased willingness to insist on contraceptive use with sexual partners (Impett, Schooler, & Tolman, 2006). Likewise, recent research shows that more sexual objectification experiences are correlated with more sexual victimization, but this link is explained by women engaging in more self-objectification and consequently being less sexually assertive in their interactions with men (Franz et al., 2015). Finally, experiences with sexual violence are associated with greater self-objectification and body shame (Carr & Szymanski, 2011; Davidson & Gervais, 2015).

Based on this work, researchers know that objectifying and aggressive behaviors in interactions result in adverse cognitive (e.g., self-objectification, body surveillance resulting in disrupted cognitions) and emotional (e.g., body shame) reactions from women directed at themselves. However, more research is needed to examine how women perceive men and their sexual behaviors during their initial objectifying interactions. Indeed, this will be critical toward understanding when people regard sexual behavior as unwelcome or unwanted, the key aspect of conceptualizations of sexual violence. The SIMO could prove enormously useful in this regard. Whereas some objectifying behaviors may be almost universally regarded as unwelcome (e.g., those involving physical force), others are more ambiguous, depending on the antecedents, preinteraction mediators, and behaviors posited by the SIMO. Some research suggests that when men act in dominant and sexually interested ways, women are more attracted to them (Logel et al., 2009; see also Gervais et al., 2011). Yet, other research suggests that sexual behavior in particular contexts (e.g., workplace) is largely regarded negatively (Berdahl & Aquino, 2009).

Motivations and Goals

In addition to cognitions and affect, people's motivations and goals may change as the interaction unfolds and may influence subsequent termination or continuation behaviors. Again, less research has been conducted with regard to men's motivations and goals after an objectifying scenario (relative to before). However, among self-reported misperceptions of sexual behavior, a quarter of respondents indicated that the perpetrator kept trying to engage in sexual behavior even after respondents had said they were not interested (Abbey, 1987). Thus, even when it is clear the other party does not desire sexual contact, some perpetrators may continue to pursue such interactions with victims.

Likewise, some research suggests that following interactions with an objectifying man, women report more motivation to subsequently interact with him (Gervais et al., 2011). Although it is unclear why the woman would want to continue to interact with the man (e.g., to prove that she is not a sex object; because she appreciated the objectification), this response could contribute to a vicious cycle in which women are objectified but continue to seek interactions with those who objectify them. Another response to objectification, however, is restriction of movement in an effort to avoid objectifying men due to safety concerns (Fairchild & Rudman, 2008).

Clearly the valence (e.g., complimentary vs. critical appearance remarks) and the degree of objectification (e.g., gazing vs. touching) are important moderators to consider in future research.

Behaviors

Finally, perpetrators and targets ultimately decide whether to continue or terminate the interaction. This critical decision is based on the behaviors that they display toward each other in the interaction and resulting cognitions, emotions, motivations, and goals. The continuation of an interaction is a negotiation in which both interactants contribute. However, disparities may exist; for instance, in the case of sexual assault, a potential perpetrator may misperceive friendliness for flirtation, assuming that the potential victim wants to continue even though she wants to terminate. Likewise, in the case of sexual harassment, women may "go along" with sexual jokes or sexual attention to "get along," but if the behaviors reach a certain threshold, they may wish to terminate the interaction. However, certain situational features may make this more difficult, such as power differences and perceived permissiveness norms.

A BRIEF WORD ON METHODOLOGICAL OBSTACLES

I hope that by now I have convinced you that using the SIMO or other social interactive approaches could prove useful to understanding the causes and consequences of sexual violence. Yet there are methodological and ethical challenges with such approaches. Clearly, it would be difficult, if not impossible, to ethically study both a perpetrator and a victim of sexual assault in the laboratory in the same setting. However, more research examining dyadic interactions between men and women in which more subtle forms of sexual aggression (e.g., gazes, commentary) and victim responses (e.g., silencing or confronting), as well as antecedents, mediators, and cognitions, emotions, motivations, and goals would be enormously helpful.

More focused examinations of the model (e.g., focusing primarily on victims or perpetrators) could also take the interactive approach into account, for example by measuring actual behaviors by perpetrators or examining victims' responses to aggressive behaviors. Social-psychological researchers have many methodological tools at their disposal to understand the social dynamics involved in sexual violence. As this chapter shows, researchers have used clever experimental analogues to examine when and why people engage in sexual aggression, with the use of confederates (actual and computer simulated, Gervais, DiLillo, et al., 2015; Logel et al., 2009; Maass et al., 2003; Pryor, 1987; Siebler et al., 2008). Likewise, researchers have trained confederates to engage in nonverbal and verbal aggressive behaviors and examined the impact on victims (Gervais et al., 2011; Wiener et al., 2013; Woodzicka & LaFrance, 2001). Of course, careful debriefing procedures are required in these studies to minimize potential harm.

Although laboratory approaches are useful to assess the social dynamics of sexually aggressive behaviors, these approaches are limited with regard to ethically measuring more extreme forms of sexual violence in more realistic settings. One promising, complementary approach that can allow researchers to assess a wider range of experiences as they unfold in the real world is ecological momentary assessment (EMA). EMA represents a range of methods that allow the collection of measures at specified time intervals. They follow in the tradition of daily diary studies and are believed to be superior to traditional, self-report questionnaire methods because participants complete the measures much closer in time to occurrence. Presumably this reduces reliance on memory and is more accurate. Given advances in technology (e.g., smartphones), researchers are now able to assess experiences as they unfold in real time (e.g., signal- or event-contingent reporting; see Moskowitz & Young, 2006, for a review). EMA approaches facilitate ecological validity through intensive assessments of participants in their natural environments, allowing researchers to examine a wide range of experiences for perpetrators and victims.

Finally, this chapter has focused primarily on sexual assault and sexual harassment, but other forms of sexual violence exist—trafficking, genital mutilation, and prostitution—and these other forms might be quite complex. Yet the study of these phenomena would likely further benefit from a consideration of objectification and the SIMO. Furthermore, although I have focused on potential perpetrators and victims, future research should consider the role of bystanders in preventing sexual violence (e.g., Banyard, 2008).

CONCLUDING REMARKS

Sexual violence is a significant personal and public health issue in the United States and around the world. When people engage in sexual violence, they treat women less as fellow human beings and more as sexual objects by using women's bodies for their own ends. Integrating objectification theory with the study of sexual violence, I discussed an integrated model of objectification that can predict the causes and consequences of a range of sexually aggressive behaviors by focusing on the sequential and dynamic interactions between potential perpetrators and victims. I first defined sexual violence and identified its adverse consequences. I then introduced objectification theory, discussed the value of incorporating approaches that integrate interactions between perpetrators and victims, and reviewed the social interaction model of objectification (SIMO). I then integrated classic and recent research that fit into this model. Such approaches to the study of sexual violence are fruitful opportunities for theoretical advances with strong practical implications for reducing the impact of sexual violence and preventing this form of evil from occurring in the first place.

NOTE

1. In this chapter, I focus on sexual violence directed from male perpetrators to female victims. Of course, female–male, male–male, and female–female sexual violence also exist, but sexual violence is typically directed from relatively powerful (e.g., physical, societal) male perpetrators to relatively powerless female victims. Additionally, the terms *perpetrators* and *victims* refer to *potential* perpetrators and victims, because sexual violence is hardly inevitable. Indeed, the model presented in this chapter could prove useful in identifying a range of antecedents, mediators, and behaviors that may disrupt sexual violence from occurring in interactions.

REFERENCES

Abbey, A. (1987). Misperceptions of friendly behavior as sexual interest: A survey of naturally occurring incidents. *Psychology of Women Quarterly, 11*, 173–194.

Abbey, A. (2002). Alcohol-related sexual assault: A common problem among college students. *Journal of Studies on Alcohol, 14*, 118–128.

Abbey, A., McAuslan, P., Zawacki, T., Clinton, A., & Buck, P. O. (2004). Attitudinal, experiential, and situational predictors of sexual assault perpetration. *Journal of Interpersonal Violence, 16*, 784–807.

Bandura, A., Underwood, B., & Fromson, M. E. (1975) Disinhibition of aggression through diffusion of responsibility and dehumanization of victims. *Journal of Research in Personality, 9*, 253–269.

Banyard, V. (2008). Measurement and correlates of prosocial bystander behavior: The case of interpersonal violence. *Violence and Victims, 23*, 83–97.

Bargh, J. A., Raymond, P., Pryor, J., & Strack, F. (1995). Attractiveness of the underling: An automatic power → sex association and its consequences for sexual harassment and aggression. *Journal of Personality and Social Psychology, 68*, 768–781.

Berdahl, J. L., & Aquino, K. (2009). Sexual behavior at work: Fun or folly? *Journal of Applied Psychology, 94*, 34–47.

Bernard, P., Gervais, S. J., Allen, J., Campomizzi, S., & Klein, O. (2012). Integrating sexual objectification with object versus person recognition: The sexualized body-inversion hypothesis. *Psychological Science, 23*, 469–471.

Calogero, R. M., & Jost, J. T. (2011). Self-subjugation among women: Exposure to sexist ideology, self-objectification, and the protective function of the need to avoid closure. *Journal of Personality and Social Psychology, 100*, 211–228.

Carr, E. R., & Szymanski, D. R. (2011). Sexual objectification and substance abuse in young adult women. *Counseling Psychologist, 39*, 39–66.

Cortina, L. M., & Berdahl, J. L. (2008). Sexual harassment in organizations: A decade of research in review. In J. Barling & C. L. Cooper (Eds.), *The Sage handbook of organizational behavior* (pp. 469–497). Thousand Oaks, CA: Sage.

Davidson, M. M., & Gervais, S. J. (2015). Violence against women through the lens of objectification theory. *Violence against Women, 21,* 330–354.

DeGue, S., & DiLillo, D. (2004). Understanding perpetrators of nonphysical sexual coercion: Characteristics of those who cross the line. *Violence and Victims, 19,* 673–688.

Fairchild, K., & Rudman, L. (2008). Everyday stranger harassment and women's objectification. *Social Justice Research, 21,* 338–357.

Felitti, V. J., Anda, R. F., Nordenberg, D., Williamson, D. F., Spitz, A. M., Edwards, V., et al. (1998). Relationship of childhood abuse and household dysfunction to many of the leading causes of death in adults. *American Journal of Preventive Medicine, 14,* 245–258.

Fitzgerald, L. F., Drasgow, F., Hulin, C. L., Gelfand, M. J., & Magley, V. J. (1997). Antecedents and consequences of sexual harassment in organizations: A test of an integrated model. *Journal of Applied Psychology, 82,* 578–589.

Fitzgerald, L. F., Gelfand, M. J., & Drasgow, F. (1995). Measuring sexual harassment: Theoretical and psychometric advances. *Basic and Applied Social Psychology, 17,* 425–445.

Fox, J., Ralston, R. A., Cooper, C. K., & Jones, K. A. (2015). Sexualized avatars lead to women's self-objectification and acceptance of rape myths. *Psychology of Women Quarterly, 39*(3), 349–362.

Franz, M., DiLillo, D., & Gervais, S. J. (2015). Sexual objectification and sexual assault: Do self-objectification and sexual assertiveness account for the link. *Psychology of Violence.*

Fredrickson, B. L., & Roberts, T. A. (1997). Objectification theory: Toward understanding women's lived experiences and mental health risks. *Psychology of Women Quarterly, 21,* 173–206.

Gervais, S. J., Bernard, P., Klein, O., Riemer, A., & Haikalis, M. (2015). *Objectification in interactions: The social interaction model of objectification (SIMO).* Manuscript submitted for publication.

Gervais, S. J., Davidson, M. M., Canivez, G., Strack, K., & DiLillo, D. (2015). *Toward a comprehensive objectification theory: Sexual objectification perpetration.* Manuscript submitted for publication.

Gervais, S. J., DiLillo, D., Haikalis, M., Nuss, G., Riemer, A., & Franz, M. (2015, June). *The real danger of beer goggles: Objectification as a mechanism of alcohol-related sexual violence.* Paper presented at the European Association of Social Psychology Small Groups Meeting, Rovereto, Italy.

Gervais, S. J., DiLillo, D., & McChargue, D. (2014). Understanding the link between men's alcohol use and sexual violence: The mediating role of sexual objectification. *Psychology of Violence, 4,* 156–169.

Gervais, S. J., Holland, A., & Dodd, M. (2013). My eyes are up here: The nature of the objectifying gaze toward women. *Sex Roles, 69,* 557–570.

Gervais, S. J., Vescio, T. K., & Allen, J. (2011). When what you see is what you get: The consequences of the objectifying gaze for women and men. *Psychology of Women Quarterly, 35,* 5–17.

Gervais, S. J., Vescio, T. K., & Allen, J. (2012). When are people interchangeable sexual objects?: The effect of gender and body type on sexual fungibility. *British Journal of Social Psychology, 51,* 499–513.

Glick, P., & Fiske, S. T. (1996). The Ambivalent Sexism Inventory: Differentiating hostile and benevolent sexism. *Journal of Personality and Social Psychology, 70,* 491–512.

Gruenfeld, D. H., Inesi, M. E., Magee, J. C., & Galinsky, A. D. (2008). Power and the objectification of social targets. *Journal of Personality and Social Psychology, 95,* 111–127.

Gutek, B. A., & Morasch, B. (1982). Sex-ratios, sex-role spillover, and sexual harassment of women at work. *Journal of Social Issues, 38,* 55–74.

Haikalis, M., DiLillo, D., & Gervais, S. J. (2015). Up for grabs?: Sexual objectification as a mediator between women's alcohol use and sexual victimization. *Journal of Interpersonal Violence.*

Hebl, M. R., & Dovidio, J. F. (2005). Promoting the "social" in the examination of social stigmas. *Personality and Social Psychology Review, 9,* 156–182.

Heflick, N. A., & Goldenberg, J. L. (2009). Objectifying Sarah Palin: Evidence that objectification causes women to be perceived as less competent and less fully human. *Journal of Experimental Social Psychology, 45,* 598–601.

Impett, E. A., Schooler, D., & Tolman, D. L. (2006). To be seen and not heard: Femininity ideology and adolescent girls' sexual health. *Archives of Sexual Behavior, 35,* 131–144.

Koss, M. P., Gidycz, C. A., & Wisniewski, N. (1987). The scope of rape: Incidence and prevalence of sexual aggression and victimization in a national sample of higher education students. *Journal of Consulting and Clinical Psychology, 55,* 162–170.

Krakauer, J. (2015). *Missoula: Rape and the justice system in a college town.* New York: Doubleday.

Lisak, D., & Miller, P. M. (2002). Repeat rape and multiple offending among undetected rapists. *Violence and Victims, 17,* 73–84.

Liss, M., Erchull, M., & Ramsey, L. (2011). Empowering or oppressing?: Development and exploration of the Enjoyment of Sexualization scale. *Personality and Social Psychology Bulletin, 37,* 55–68.

Logel, C., Walton, G. M., Spencer, S. J., Iserman, E. C., von Hippel, W., & Bell, A. E. (2009). Interacting with sexist men triggers social identity threat among female engineers. *Journal of Personality and Social Psychology, 96,* 1089–1103.

Loughnan, S., Haslam, N., Murnane, T., Vaes, J., Reynolds, C., & Suitner, C. (2010). Objectification leads to depersonalization: The denial of mind and moral concern to objectified others. *European Journal of Social Psychology, 40,* 709–717.

Loughnan, S., Pina, A., Vasquez, E. A., & Puvia, E. (2013). Sexual objectification increases rape victim blame and decreases perceived suffering. *Psychology of Women Quarterly, 37,* 455–461.

Maass, A., Cadinu, M., Guarnieri, G., & Grasselli, A., (2003). Sexual harassment under social identity threat: The computer harassment paradigm. *Journal of Personality and Social Psychology, 85,* 853–870.

Malamuth, N. M. (1981). Rape proclivity among males. *Journal of Social Issues, 37,* 139–157.

Malamuth, N. M., Linz, D., Heavy, C. L., Barnes, G., & Acker, M. (1995). Using the confluence model of sexual aggression to predict men's conflict with women: A 10-year follow-up study. *Journal of Personality and Social Psychology, 69,* 353–369.

Mescher, K., & Rudman, L. (2014). Men in the mirror: The role of men's body shame in sexual aggression. *Personality and Social Psychology Bulletin, 40,* 1063–1075.

Messman-Moore, T. L., & Brown, A. L. (2006). Risk perception, rape, and sexual revictimization: A prospective study of college women. *Psychology of Women Quarterly, 30,* 159–172.

Messman-Moore, T. L., Walsh, K., & DiLillo, D. (2010). Emotion dysregulation and risky sexual behavior in revictimization. *Child Abuse and Neglect, 34,* 967–976.

Moradi, B., & Huang, Y. (2008). Objectification theory and psychology of women: A decade of advances and future directions. *Psychology of Women Quarterly, 32,* 377–398.

Moskowitz, D. S., & Young, S. N. (2006). Ecological momentary assessment: What it is and why it is a method of the future in clinical psychopharmacology. *Journal of Psychiatry and Neuroscience, 31,* 13–20.

Norris, J. (2011). "Fresh" thoughts on studying sexual assault. *Psychology of Women Quarterly, 35,* 369–374.

Norris, J., Nurius, P. S., & Dimeff, L. A. (1996). Through her eyes: Factors affecting women's perception of and resistance to acquaintance sexual aggression threat. *Psychology of Women Quarterly, 20,* 123–145.

Nowatzki, J., & Morry, M. M. (2009). Women's intentions regarding, and acceptance of, self-sexualizing behavior. *Psychology of Women Quarterly, 33,* 95–107.

Nurius, P. S., & Norris, J. A. (1996). A cognitive ecological model of women's response to male sexual coercion in dating. *Journal of Psychology and Human Sexuality, 8,* 117–139.

Patterson, M. L. (1982). A sequential functional model of nonverbal exchange. *Psychological Review, 89,* 231–249.

Pina, A., Gannon, T. A., & Saunders, B. (2009). An overview of the literature on sexual harassment: Perpetrator, theory, and treatment issues. *Aggression and Violent Behavior, 14,* 126–138.

Pryor, J. B. (1987). Sexual harassment proclivities in men. *Sex Roles, 17,* 269–290.

Pryor, J. B., Giedd, J. L., & Williams, K. B. (1995). A social psychological model for predicting sexual harassment. *Journal of Social Issues, 51,* 69–84.

Rudman, L. A., & Mescher, K. (2012). Of animals and objects: Men's implicit dehumanization of women and likelihood of sexual aggression. *Personality and Social Psychology Bulletin, 38,* 734–746.

Saguy, T., Quinn, D. M., Dovidio, J. F., & Pratto, F. (2010). Interacting like a body: Objectification can lead women to narrow their presence in social interactions. *Psychological Science, 21,* 178–182.

Siebler, F., Sabelus, S., & Bohner, G. (2008). A refined computer harassment paradigm: Validation, and test of hypotheses about target characteristics. *Psychology of Women Quarterly, 32,* 22–35.

Snyder, M., Tanke, E. D., & Berscheid, E. (1977). Social perception and interpersonal behavior: On the self-fulfilling nature of social stereotypes. *Journal of Personality and Social Psychology, 35*, 656–666.

Steele, C. M., & Josephs, R. A. (1990). Alcohol myopia: Its prized and dangerous effects. *American Psychologist, 45*, 921–933.

Swim, J. K., & Hyers, L. L. (1999). Excuse me—what did you just say?!: Women's public and private responses to sexist remarks. *Journal of Experimental Social Psychology, 35*, 68–88.

Vaes, J., Paladino, M. P., & Puvia, E. (2011). Are sexualized females complete human beings?: Why males and females dehumanize sexually objectified women. *European Journal of Social Psychology, 41*, 774–785.

Wiener, R. L., Gervais, S. J., Allen, J., & Marquez, A. (2013). Eye of the beholder: Effects of perspective and sexual objectification on harassment judgments. *Psychology, Public Policy, and Law, 19*, 206–221.

Wilkinson, J. (2015, April 4). Sexually assaulted at UVA. *The New York Times*. Retrieved June 18, 2015, from *www.nytimes.com/2015/04/05/opinion/sunday/sexually-assaulted-at-uva.html?_r=0*.

Woodzicka, J. A., & LaFrance, M. (2001). Real versus imagined gender harassment. *Journal of Social Issues, 57*, 15–30.

Word, C. O., Zanna, M. P., & Cooper, J. (1974). The nonverbal mediation of self-fulfilling prophecies in interracial interactions. *Journal of Experimental Social Psychology, 10*, 109–120.

World Health Organization. (2014). Violence against women. Retrieved June 18, 2015, from *www.who.int/mediacentre/factsheets/fs239/en*.

Ziering, A. (Producer), & Dick, K. (Director). (2014). *The hunting ground* [Motion picture]. United States: RADiUS TWC.

PART III

THE SELF-CONCEPT IN RELATION TO GOOD AND EVIL ACTS

CHAPTER 12

False Moral Superiority

David Dunning

It is a Biblical story so iconic that some version of it appears in all four Christian Gospels. In the scene known as the Last Supper, Jesus tells his apostles that he will soon be arrested and that they will renounce and abandon him. Peter, one of his followers, protests vigorously, arguing that he would follow Jesus to prison and even to death. No, says Jesus, and tells Peter that he will deny knowing him three times before the cock crows the next morning.

The rest of the story is well known, as it is retold in countless churches every Easter. Judas Iscariot betrays Jesus, who is arrested and is led through Jerusalem to prison to await his trial. Peter closely follows behind, until spotted by a young girl, who accuses him twice of being Jesus' follower—an accusation that Peter forcefully denies. Finally, a crowd gathers and Peter again finds himself publicly disowning Jesus, cursing and swearing, shouting that he does not know the man. At that instant, a rooster crows, and Peter, recalling Jesus' prophecy, runs off to weep.

That one of the world's most prevalent religions places this story of human failing so prominently in its central story is telling. Even more telling is the specific failing Peter's story focuses on—on hubris, on the arrogance of thinking more generously of one's moral character than will actually be revealed in behavior.

But perhaps it is not surprising that a tale of human hubris would arise centrally in Christianity. All world religions exhort its adherents against hubris. In the Hindu *Bhagavad Gita,* Krishna counsels Arjuna to "be humble, be harmless, have no pretension" (13:7–8). In Islam, it is arrogance that provokes Allah to cast Satan from heaven and to drown the Pharoah's Egyptian army as they pursue Moses. As says the Koran, "So enter the gates of Hell, to dwell therein. Thus evil indeed is the abode of the arrogant" (16:29). Confucius notes that "the superior man has a dignified ease without pride; the mean man has pride without dignified ease." Even Greek mythology warns mightily against the sin of hubris. "The handsome hold the graves they won in Troy; the enemy earth rides over those who conquered," observes Aeschylus in *Agamemnon*.

This chapter focuses on whether people in their daily lives successfully adhere to these admonitions against hubris and toward humility. Do people see their character accurately? Do they correctly gauge the strength of their moral fiber—when it will succeed and when it will fail? Or do they suffer from the same false self-pride that ultimately shamed the Apostle Peter?

To foreshadow the central conclusion of this chapter somewhat, I discuss how recent social-psychological work suggests that people generally suffer from a false sense of moral superiority. They consider themselves more moral, ethical, generous, civic-minded, altruistic, and charitable than their peers. And in that perception, they are wrong. However, as I discuss in the chapter, the more revealing question is *how* and *why* they are wrong.

THE "HOLIER THAN THOU" PHENOMENON

World religions might emphasize humility so centrally because people show so little of it. Instead, people on average possess outsized and unrealistic views of their propensity to act in moral or self-sacrificing ways. Such self-impressions are easy to capture in studies on false moral superiority, in which people are asked to compare their moral character to that of their peers. People, on average, claim to perform more morally good behaviors than their peers do, while committing fewer sins (Allison, Messick, & Goethals, 1989). They also forecast that they will conduct themselves in the future in a more morally upstanding (and outstanding) way than their peers.

Being "Holier" than Others

For example, in one study of students at Williams College, 74% claimed that if a store clerk made a mistake and handed them back extra change they would give it back but that only 46% of their peers would do the same. Just over half said they would share their pizza with a hungry student but that only just over a third of other students would do likewise. A full 80% declared that they would refuse to copy from another students' exam but that only 56% of their peers would likewise remain honest (Goethals, 1986). Other studies find similar results: People place themselves on moral pedestals that they deny to their peers (Goethals, Messick, & Allison, 1991; Liebrand, Messick, & Wolters, 1986; Messick, Bloom, Boldizar, & Samuelson, 1985).

This research, however, leaves open an important question, one that has been the focus of research in my laboratory for the past 20 years. That question is which specific error people are making that allows them their false beliefs of moral superiority. There are two candidates. One is that people are roughly right about their own moral character if it were put to a test—they would actually refuse to copy from another student's test if given a chance to cheat—but that they are too cynical about the moral inclinations of their peers. This would be an error in social prediction; people would think themselves superior because they are wrong about their peers.

However, the other possible error is that people have their peers right—roughly half of their peers would, indeed, cheat—but respondents are too optimistic about their own personal moral character. They themselves would also cheat roughly half the time, just like their peers, but they fail to anticipate it. This would be an error in self-prediction; people would be mistakenly exaggerating the purity of their own personal better angels. Of course, people could also commit both errors—undue cynicism about their peers and unwarranted optimism about their own moral character.

Being "Holier" than Reality

Our work on the "holier than thou" effect gives a clear answer about which error people are making. First, replicating other work, we find that people forecast that they themselves will act in more socially desirable ways than their peers will. In our initial study, we asked each student in a large lecture psychology class whether they would buy a daffodil in a charity drive for the American Cancer Society taking place 4 weeks hence. We also asked them the percentage of students in the class who would also buy a daffodil. A full 83% of students predicted they would buy a daffodil but that only 56% of their peers sitting in the class would do likewise. The day after the charity drive ended, during a class exam, the entire class was surveyed about their behavior during the drive. The proportion of the class that had bought a daffodil: 43% (Epley & Dunning, 2000, Study 1).

In one of our follow-ups, we asked students in a similar class how many would vote in an upcoming presidential election. Of those eligible, 90% said they would. These students also predicted whether some other random eligible student would vote in the upcoming election. Here, the predictions were significantly less optimistic, with 75% of randomly selected peers forecast to vote. Actual voting rate, as assessed during a survey on a classroom exam the day after the election: 69% (Epley & Dunning, 2006, Study 1).

In short, we have found that people dramatically overpredict the likelihood that they will act in ethical, charitable, civic-minded, or socially desirable ways. The special moral pedestals they reserve for themselves are much too high to be supported by actual evidence. The rate they forecast for the same behaviors among their peers, however, is much closer to the actual rate we observe when we survey real behavior and constitutes in our view a remarkable achievement in social-cognitive accuracy that deserves more research scrutiny in of itself.

We have found this pattern of self-error but social accuracy under a wide variety of circumstances, in many different types of charity drives, across several political elections, in laboratory economic games such as the prisoner's dilemma, and in chances to volunteer one's services, such as to read for the blind or give blood. We have also seen it in motorists being willing to stop at crosswalks for pedestrians (Balcetis & Dunning, 2008, 2013, 2015; Balcetis, Dunning, & Miller, 2008; Epley & Dunning, 2000, 2006; Poon, Koehler, & Buehler, 2014). The same pattern of self-error but social accuracy extends to other behaviors that people care about, such whether their romances will survive (Epley & Dunning, 2006), they will excel in the academic classroom (Helzer & Dunning, 2012), or they can prudently handle their financial affairs (Koehler & Poon, 2006; Koehler, White, & John, 2011; Peetz & Buehler, 2009).

A BELIEF IN SELF-AGENCY

But why does the error fall toward the self? Accuracy in the prediction of others is somewhat easy to explain. People successfully navigate their social worlds only to the extent they largely anticipate how others will behave or react. A lifetime of observation should lead people to roughly accurate impressions of how humans behave in various situations, knowing that people will laugh at a party but hush in a church. Past work shows that people show a remarkable facility at counting the frequency of all sorts of events even when not asked to do so explicitly, such as how often the name of a flower has been mentioned during a laboratory session (Hasher & Chromiak, 1977; Hasher & Zacks, 1984; Hasher, Zacks, Rose, & Sanft, 1987) People also show remarkable accuracy when asked to gauge the frequency, prevalence, and range of social behaviors and attitudes among their peers. College students, for example, are quite good at describing the shape and range of opinions their peers attach to such social issues as abortion, international affairs, and drug use. They also accurately judge how often their peers attend religious services, have trouble getting to sleep, feel blue, and go to movies (Nisbett & Kunda, 1985).[1]

That said, one would expect that a similar accuracy aimed at the self would just be as beneficial, if not more so, to guide one's behavior through a complex life. So why does a rather rough but accurate wisdom about other people and human nature in general not transfer to oneself? Why do people hold themselves to be *exceptional*, that is, operating outside of the type of psychology that drives everybody else's behavior?

Work in my lab suggests some of the psychology of this exceptionalism, explaining why and when people consider themselves to be governed by different rules from those influencing other people. At the heart of this exceptionalism are people's beliefs about agency. People tend to believe they are *disjoint agents*, imposing their will upon the world regardless of external circumstances. In acting, they follow their intentions, preferences, desires, goals, and aspirations. As such, their actions are independent of other people's desires and the influence of external circumstances. In the language of causality, their behavior is *exogenous*—arrived at independent of any outside pressure. This is in distinction to *conjoint agency*, which is proactive behavior that takes other people and external circumstances into account as it is pursued. This type of agency is constrained by social obligations, the beliefs of others, and the limitations imposed by outside situational forces (Markus & Kitayama, 2003). In the language of causality, it is *endogenous*, nestled within a web of other causal influences.

I propose that people tend to think of themselves much more as disjoint agents than they do other people, who are construed as more conjoint (i.e., constrained and influenced) in their actions. This proposal fits several findings within our research and that of others. First, it fits people's beliefs that their actions and lives are more "open" and subject to the application of free will than that of their peers. People believe that their futures can take more plausible paths than those of their peers and that which path is taken is more unpredictable. Any future action they take is more a function of their desires and intentions than it is of personality constraints, situational forces, or the unfolding of inevitable fate (Pronin & Kugler, 2010). People also emphasize the active selves they are striving to be in the future (Williams & Gilovich, 2008), their potential and peak performance (Williams & Gilovich, 2012; Williams, Gilovich, & Dunning, 2012), relative to what they emphasize about others. When making predictions about the self, relative to others, they give more weight to their intentions (Koehler & Poon, 2006; Koehler et al., 2011; Kruger & Gilovich, 2004; Poon et al., 2014), aspirations (Helzer & Dunning, 2012; Peetz & Buehler, 2009, 2013), and plans (Buehler, Griffin, & Ross, 1994; Newby-Clark, Ross, Buehler, Koehler, & Griffin, 2000). In short, the self is a striver, exerting its will to overcome external obstacles. Others merely react to the conditions they fall into.

Direct comparisons between the self and other people affirm this belief that one's own future is more a function of one's striving than it is for other people. What matters is what one intends to do rather than the constraints that a person might make. People rate the time they get out of bed in the morning, the times they check their email, what to have for dinner, whether they skip or attend their college classes, and how long to work on homework to be more of a choice for themselves than they are for other people. They also construe decisions to conform to the choices of others to be more a matter of free choice for themselves than for other people. For example, if no one else complains about a person's cutting into a line and they go along with it, they are more likely to view their acquiescence as an active decision "not to make a scene" rather than just as staying quiet like everyone else (Helzer, 2012).

In perhaps the most telling example of how much more people emphasize their intentions and aspirations in self-prediction than in social prediction is a study by Helzer and Dunning (2012) in which people were paid for social predictions. Each person was involved in two predictions. In one, participants were asked to predict the upcoming exam performance of another student, with a chance to win up to $5 for accurate predictions. They were asked which of several pieces of information they wanted about the person whose performance they were assigned to predict, such as the person's score on the last exam in the course, the score he or she aspired to obtain on the upcoming exam, and how much the student planned to study. Participants tended to choose information about the student's past score on an exam over data about the score the student aspired to. Presumably, a person's past behavior contained a good deal of information about the constraints the student faced in getting a good score, and that is what participants wanted to know.

However, in a second prediction, we switched whose behavior was being predicted. The other student would now predict the participant's upcoming exam score, with the participant receiving up to $5 if that person predicted accurately. Participants were then asked which information they wished to share with the student making the prediction. Here, participants reversed their preferences—being more eager to give information about the score they aspired to in the next exam over data about how well they had performed in a previous exam in the same course. In short, when it came to self-prediction, what mattered were the intentions and goals of the participant—more in line with the agentic self—rather than evidence of past actual achievement (Helzer & Dunning, 2012).

THE ERROR IN SELF-AGENCY BELIEFS

But in this perception of self-agency, people appear to be wrong. Their behaviors are much more influenced by outside forces than their rather agentic views allow for.

Self-Agency Confronts Experience

How do we know? Evidence comes from two sources, including participants' own testimony once they experience a chance to be altruistic. Once people experience an event, they appear to renounce the importance of individual agency in moral or altruistic behavior.

Specifically, 4 weeks before another flower-driven charity drive for the

American Cancer Society on the Cornell University campus, Emily Balcetis and I (Balcetis & Dunning, 2008) asked college students to rate the personal character of those who would buy daffodils (e.g., whether they would stop to help a person fixing a flat tire) versus those who would not, as well the likely politics of buyers and nonbuyers. Participants were quite willing to make inferences about the traits and politics of buyers and nonbuyers. They were willing to rate buyers as more likely to engage in generous acts than nonbuyers and to be much more liberal in their politics.

In this, participants were clearly endorsing a *dispositional* point of view, one quite consistent with the idea of disjoint agency. Whether or not a person bought a flower depended greatly on their personality, preferences, and character. The choice to participate in the charity drive was driven by factors internal to the individual—the decision they actively wished to pursue—rather than produced by outside situational forces. Participants also predicted whether they would buy a daffodil and the percentage of their peers in a large lecture psychology class who would do likewise. Of this group, 83% predicted that they would buy a daffodil but that only 29% of their peers would.

Just after the charity drive concluded, a comparable group of students were asked whether they had bought a daffodil, and 44% had. They also filled out the same generous-behavior and political-leaning questionnaire that forecasters had faced, describing both a buyer and a nonbuyer. After experiencing the charity drive, participants appeared to swerve toward situationism in their thinking, refusing to make any personality inferences about buyers versus nonbuyers. That is, compared with those surveyed before the drive, experiencers refused to make any character or political inferences about buyers versus nonbuyers—often circling the exact noninformative midpoint of the scale (e.g., neither liberal nor conservative) in their descriptions. This refusal was evident not only among nonbuyers, whom one might expect to refuse to make any inferences in order to protect their own self-image, but was equally manifest among buyers (Balcetis & Dunning, 2008, Study 3).

Another study affirmed that the experience of the situation turned people into ardent situationists, claiming that decisions to help others depended more on outside influences than it did any factor residing within the individual. Participants were asked to rate the reasons why people would take part in a "relay for life" charity drive, in which college students pledged money to support a team walking or running around an athletic track for 24 hours. First-year students, who had never experienced the rather high-profile event before, tended to highlight internal reasons why a person might support the event, such as that the person was civic-minded, generous, or unselfish. However, older students, who had experienced the event at least once, tended to cite more external or situational factors in why a person might support the event, such as whether the person had any other time commitments or extra money, was in town for the event, or just happened to see the advertising for the drive (Balcetis & Dunning, 2008). Importantly, these attributions better matched the attributions made by people actually choosing to participate in the drive. Past supporters and nonsupporters both, at least to a marginally significant degree, were more likely to endorse situational rather than internal reasons for their past choices to support or not support the fund drive.

Self-Agency Confronts Reality

We have also tested the accuracy of people's beliefs about their own self-agency by asking them how they would be influenced by situational forces in a hypothetical experiment, as well as how much others would be influenced. We then compared their estimates to the actual influence these situational variations have when we run the experiment for real. In this research, our central question was whether people's beliefs in their agency would be reflected in their behavior. Would their actions be a function of their preferences more than the situational pressures we applied?

For example, it is well known, at least among social psychologists, that people are less likely to help others when they are surrounded by groups of people than when alone—the so-called bystander effect (Darley & Latané, 1968; Latané & Darley, 1968, 1970). What if we asked participants how they and others would behave in a bystander effect study and compare their impressions with behavior in an actual experiment? Would people show accurate intuitions about how much they or other people would be influenced by the crucial change of placing them in a group rather than keeping them alone? The belief of self as agent would likely cause people to deny that their behavior would be influenced by external circumstances. Whether they acted in a socially desirable way would depend on their own intentions and desires. However, this belief in agency would not be conferred to other people, and so others would be seen as being more likely to be influenced by outside circumstances.

Thus we decided to test whether people knew about the bystander effect and could anticipate how it would influence their own behavior versus that of other people. Participants were exposed to a role play in which an experimenter accidentally dropped a box of jigsaw puzzle pieces on the floor to assess whether others would help in picking up the pieces. Some participants were alone in the demonstration; others took part along with two other people. Those who took part in the group, relative to those experiencing the role play alone, thought that there was an 88% chance that they would help (relative to 92% for those in the alone condition) but that there was only a 50% chance that others would help (relative to 72% in the alone condition). Essentially, participants were estimating that placing them in the crowd would reduce the helping behavior of others by 22% but their own by only 4% (Balcetis & Dunning, 2013).

We then ran a comparable group of participants through an actual bystander experiment, essentially by not informing participants that the drop of the jigsaw puzzle box was staged. In the alone condition, 50% of participants helped pick up the pieces; in the group condition, the percentage fell to 23%. Overall, the percentage of helpers was much lower than the estimates provided for self and other, but the key finding was that the impact of the group condition, a drop of 27% from the alone condition, was virtually equal to the impact forecast for other people's behavior—and much larger than the drop anticipated for the self (Balcetis & Dunning, 2013).

Thus people tended to make self-predictions that rely heavily on a sense of self-agency, whereas their peer predictions recognize the potentially important role played by external forces. In these peer predictions, our participants turn out to be roughly accurate. It was in their self-perceptions that their belief in agency turns out to be misguided.

To be sure, at times people will concede that their behavior is influenced by external circumstances, but the cases in which people make such a concession are telling. Put simply, people concede that they can be influenced when the outside world pushes them to act in ways that match their already formed preferences and desires. We tested this idea in one of our earliest investigations into the holier-than-thou phenomenon. Participants were asked to estimate the likelihood that they or their college peers would be self-sacrificing. They were asked to consider an experiment in which they could volunteer to complete a long and dull experiment so that some other participant could be assigned to a shorter one.

Importantly, we told participants that we could vary this request along two dimensions. One was the degree of sacrifice. Would participants volunteer for a longer experiment if it were 25 minutes longer than the alternative versus only 5 minutes? The second dimension was whom participants might make the sacrifice for, a regular college student or a 10-year-old little girl. We predicted that participants would believe themselves to be unaffected by the size of the sacrifice but would think that the person they were sacrificing for would matter a great deal. But in these intuitions would they be right (Epley & Dunning, 2000, Study 4)?

Participants certainly had different opinions about how influential the size versus the beneficiary of the sacrifice would be. In terms of sacrifice, participants thought that the size of the sacrifice would have only a 5% impact on their choice to do it (reducing their volunteering for the longer experiment from 60% to 55%). Others would be more influenced, with a 16% impact (from 48% to 32%). However, when a version of the study was run in which participants had to make a real choice, the impact of the sacrifice's size was much more dramatic, from 50% to 13%—an impact of 37%. This estimate was clearly closer to the estimate made for others than for the self.

In terms of the beneficiary of the sacrifice, participants were much more likely to cite an influence for themselves, thinking that they were 36%

more likely to sacrifice their time for a little girl than for a nondescript college student (i.e., a rise in volunteering from 40 to 76%). They forecast that others would not be so influenced—with an impact of only 16% expected. The real impact when a version of the experiment involving real choices was run was −1% (i.e., the volunteer rate fell from 32 to 31% from the college student to little girl condition). Once again, forecasts made for other people showed more rough accuracy than those made for the self.

Self-Agency Confronts Culture

Cross-cultural work on the holier-than-thou phenomenon also implicates misguided beliefs about self-agency. If undue confidence in self-agency underlies the mistaken self-predictions that people make in the moral sphere, then members of some cultures should commit the error more than those from other cultures.

Specifically, individualist cultures, such as those in North America and Western Europe, celebrate the individual and emphasize that individual's autonomy, self-reliance, and personal achievement. These cultures are the ones most likely to construe the self as a disjoint agent, imposing his or her will against the environment, choosing freely, and acting mostly on intention and desire. This is in contrast to collectivist cultures, such as in Japan or India, which emphasize instead group goals and harmony over the individual's aspirations and in which people work interdependently to fulfill their complementary social roles. Agency in the collectivist sense involves more conjoint agency, in which a person's actions and influence occur under the constraints of social and external forces (Markus & Kitayama, 2003; Savani, Markus, & Conner, 2008; Savani, Markus, Naidu, Kumar, & Berlia, 2010; Stephens, Hamedani, Markus, Bersieker, & Eloul, 2009).

Work in our lab reveals that the holier-than-thou pattern of misprediction holds much more for members of individualist cultures than for those of collectivist ones. In one exploration, 9-year-old children attending an international summer school on the Mediterranean island of Mallorca were asked to predict how many of 10 candies they would keep and how many they would donate to the rest of the class if given the chance. Children from individualist countries (e.g., England, Germany) stated on average that they would donate 5.6 pieces of candy but that their peers would donate only 3.4 pieces—a small, sweet statement of moral superiority. When the time came to donate, they donated only 2.4 pieces, making their small declaration of superiority a false one. Children from collectivist countries (e.g., Spain, Mallorca) predicted they would donate 4.6 pieces against a figure of 3.4 for peers. At first blush, this looks like a similar but muted statement of false superiority, but collectivist children actually donated 4.5 pieces on average—closely matching their self-predictions. Both individualist and collectivist children, it turns out, were accurate in their social predictions, in that children on average donated 3.2 pieces, a figure again closely matching students' overall predictions.

Within a culture, people can differ in the individualism versus collectivism they display (e.g., Stephens et al., 2009). And we have found that this dimension at the level of the individual person also predicts the degree to which a person will express holier-than-thou self-perceptions. In a university in Nebraska, students were tested on their personal level of individualism versus collectivism. Three weeks later, they were asked whether they would participate in a charitable food drive conducted by a local chapter of the Boy Scouts. Individualists predicted that they would donate on average nearly 5 items, whereas collectivists stated they would donate less, about 3.7 items. Both groups predicted that peers would donate roughly 3 items. When the time came for the actual food drive, both groups turned out to be overly optimistic, but the individualist group even more so. Although they had predicted donating nearly 5 items, they in reality donated less than half an item each (meaning many donated nothing at all). Collectivists, more pessimistic in self-predictions (e.g., an average of 3.7 items), were more generous in the food drive, donating an average of 2.3 items.

RELATION TO ACTOR–OBSERVER DIFFERENCES IN ATTRIBUTION

A reader who is knowledgeable about the history of social cognition research by now would have developed a growing and bedeviling question. Herein, I suggest that people believe that their own behavior is driven by the force of their personalities, whereas the actions of others are shaped by external situational forces. This assertion, however, stands as a complete contradiction to one of social psychology's most classic hypotheses: the actor–observer difference in attribution, in which people explain their own behavior in terms of situational forces and other people's behavior in terms of their personalities (Jones & Nisbett, 1971), a hypothesis that was firmly supported by data (Nisbett, Caputo, Legant, & Marecek, 1973; Storms, 1973). How can the data from the holier-than-thou tradition be reconciled with this classic work?

A few moment's reflection reveals that the contradictions between the two research traditions are more superficial than real. Consider, first, attributions about the behavior of other people. Respondents in holier-than-thou studies clearly demonstrate a belief that the actions of others are sensitive to situational forces. But sensitivity to the situation need not imply a situational attribution. Such sensitivities can reveal an underlying personality trait. A person who always chooses the option with the most money can be called greedy. A person whose opinion always goes with the crowd can be called a conformist. Thus, citing a responsiveness to outside forces need not constrain a person to a situational attribution.

Now consider self-attributions. Classic work on the actor–observer difference in attribution, in a sense, highlighted the purely deterministic factors that produced people's behaviors. People's actions were determined by either their personalities (internal determinism) or by the situations (external determinism). Note that people in this classic work were being portrayed as organisms that reflexively responded to either set of causal determinants. There was no allusion to autonomy, free will, or personal intention (Malle & Knobe, 1997; Vazire & Doris, 2009).

Herein, I make that allusion and suggest that self and other beliefs differ exactly along this dimension: People believe their own behavior to be more freely chosen than they do the behavior of others. That is, the difference being highlighted in holier-than-thou work lies along a dimension, freedom of choice, that is completely outside the original analysis presented in actor–observer work (Jones & Nisbett, 1971), although other researchers later began to suggest and elaborate upon this dimension as research went on (Malle, 1999; Malle & Knobe, 1997).

FALSE MORAL SUPERIORITY AND BEHAVIORAL REGULATION

Does false moral superiority matter? Do outsized views of one's own moral character produce benefits or make people vulnerable to folly? This is a potentially important question worthy of future research, for the extant work already published suggests that false moral superiority might be both the very source of real morality and also the gateway to moral transgression.

Implications for Self-Regulation

The positive case begins with the observation that people often live up to (or down to) the labels they apply to themselves (Rotenberg, 1974; Thoits, 1985) or that are imposed by society (Kraut, 1973; Miller, Brickman, & Bolen, 1975; Rosenthal & Jacobson, 1992). Thus people's eagerness to assign moral traits to themselves—even unrealistically—could constrain them to act in a moral manner. That is, haughty self-views might create high standards that people feel compelled to live by.

Much research similar to the holier-than-thou work has shown that having people overpredict the quality of their future behavior has a measurable impact on that behavior. In 1980, Sherman phoned college students mentioning that the American Cancer Society (ACS) was calling people asking for their help and that he was conducting an independent survey looking to see how people would react to such phone solicitations. As such, he asked hypothetically if they would spend 3 hours helping to collect donations to the American Cancer Society if asked to do so. Nearly half said they would, although only 4% receiving a real request from the ACS out of the blue actually did so. However, when the prediction group itself was called 3 days later and given an actual request from the ACS to help, a full 31% agreed to donate their 3 hours. Self-predicting an altruistic act had conjured that act into reality.

Such effects have been observed in voting behavior, health habits, diet, and consumer purchases (Van Kerckhove, Geuens, & Vermeir, 2012). They appear to be strong to the extent that the individual holds such predictions closer to his or her self-identity; that is, people are more likely to vote if they state they will be "voters" rather than just "vote" (Bryan, Walton, Rogers, & Dweck, 2011), and will avoid unethical behavior more if they predict they will not be "cheaters" rather than that they will avoid "cheating" (Bryan, Adams, & Monin, 2013).

But this happy ending for self-labeling is not guaranteed. In my work, I have never observed such an effect as described above, perhaps because we interject a long period of time between people's predictions and tests of their actual behavior. In addition, people who overbelieve their ability to avoid temptation may place themselves in situations in which temptation wins. For example, an overbelief in one's ability to control a smoking habit may lead people to expose themselves to situations (e.g., other smokers) that make lighting up a cigarette too tempting an impulse to control (Nordgren, van Harreveld, & van der Pligt, 2009), or heavy drinkers may be led to sip that drink a little bit closer to excess (Jones, Cole, Goudie, & Field, 2012).

One can also imagine that an overbelief in one's moral sense might license people to engage in immoral behavior. That is, people tend to treat their moral behavior like a bank account they must keep in balance. An immoral behavior means a person must act in a moral way to balance the account (Jordan, Mullen, & Murnighan, 2011; Sachdeva, Iliev, & Medin, 2009)—and moral behavior today allows a person to indulge in a little self-interested, unethical, or undesirable behavior tomorrow (Kahn & Dhar, 2006; Monin & Miller, 2001). As such, an unshakeable belief in one's moral superiority might permit people to commit a few transgressions "now and then" with little harm to their self-views. And one way to license current misbehavior is to make optimistic forecasts of disciplined righteousness in the future (Khan & Dhar, 2007).

Of course, it might be the case that strong self-beliefs in one's moral nature could inspire *both* ethical and unethical behavior. What matters is the type of situation a person confronts. If given a chance to donate to a good cause, a firm self-belief in one's character may prompt one to donate. If given a chance to steal from the household's common fund, that same firm self-belief may justify a little theft. As such, future research will have to closely survey the exact pattern that false moral superiority prompts in subsequent moral behavior.

Implications for Social Regulation

False moral superiority also carries implications for the regulation of other people, and even of societies as a whole. As already described, people are quite willing to judge others based on the behavior those others exhibit in situations with moral overtones—at least before they experience those same situations themselves (Balcetis & Dunning, 2008). They expect such behavior to be a function of a person's personality and are quite willing to judge the other person's character and moral conscience once the other person's behavior is known (Epley & Dunning, 2000; Critcher & Dunning, 2013). They are disposed, for example, to extol those who give to charity as generous and altruistic and to assume that those who do not are stingy and greedy (Balcetis & Dunning, 2008). As applied to specific individuals, these judgments may be unfair, in that people refuse to apply those judgments to themselves, or to anyone else for that matter, once they have experienced the situation in question.

However, judgments of moral behavior that emphasize a person's character may go a long way toward promoting moral actions on the part of others and limiting immoral ones by ensuring that good behavior is rewarded, as least symbolically, and antisocial behavior is stigmatized. Recent work in psychology and anthropology has shown that stable cultures often arise when people will go out of their way to regulate the behavior of others—being willing to punish or reward others according to their behavior, even at a cost to the person doing the punishing or rewarding (Fehr & Fischbacher, 2004; Fehr & Gächter, 2002; Henrich et al., 2010). And one way to best regulate another person's actions is via his or her reputation (Fehr & Fischbacher, 2004; Milinski, Semmann, & Krambeck, 2002; Hardy & Van Vugt, 2006). A good reputation, one in which the person is seen as being concerned about others, draws cooperation and goodwill from others; a self-centered reputation draws social isolation.

As such, a false sense of superiority, even one people might abandon upon a little experience, might prove detrimental to other specific individuals yet beneficial to society as a whole. To the extent that people and their moral character are judged harshly for immoral actions and lauded for moral ones, people will be at times inappropriately judged for behavior attributable more to external circumstances than to their internal character. However, the ever-present threat of these judgments will give people incentives to act in prosocial ways.

Indeed, one sees this incentive at work in the most formal and codified norms that a society produces—namely, its law. In the Anglo-American legal tradition, at least, one finds that people are not punished for criminal actions so much as for their criminal intent (Hart, 2008; Jones, 2013). If a criminal action (an *actus reus*) occurs, it may not necessarily be a crime if no criminal intent (*mens rea*) exists. For example, if I put a teaspoon of sugar in a colleague's coffee but the sugar later turns out, without my knowledge, to have been ricin, a deadly poison, I have committed no crime, despite a "bad act" having occurred by my hand. I did not have any intent to harm my colleague, and so my actions do not qualify as a crime.[2] However, if I knowingly give my colleague the poison out of my own free will and intention, I am criminally liable. Further, it is intent, rather than the act itself, that often determines how serious a crime a person has committed. If I steal a colleague's car with the intention of selling off its parts, I have committed the serious crime of grand larceny. If I steal a car with only the more minor intention of just driving it around for an hour, I have committed the relatively less serious crime of joyriding (Morse, 1992).

Thus the presumption that moral behavior is a product of agents choosing freely lies at the heart of the formal social institution, the law, fully aimed at regulating social behavior (Jones, 2013). If people fail to use their presumed facility for free choice wisely, they will be punished. Note here that bad intentions themselves are not punished. One is not punished, for example, for wanting to murder another person. That wish must lead to an action that is illegal. It is the *acting* on such evil intentions that qualifies an individual for punishment (Dworkin & Blumenfeld, 1996).

The reliance of the law on this presumption of free will works for it in two ways. First, punishing people according to the malevolence of their intentions gives them an incentive to control the outcomes of those intentions. They are allowed to be human and to have malevolent wishes, but they not allowed to act on those wishes. This condition fulfills a major goal of the legal system, namely, the deterrence of crime (Geerken & Gove, 1975). Second, laypeople informally believe that others should be punished only to the extent that those others have evil intent. Thus, formally punishing people according to intent allows the law to be perceived as fair and just by the community at large. In terms of meting out retribution for criminal wrongs, another major function of the legal system, punishment again works to the benefit of the legal system by enhancing its stature and the stability of the society it supports (Carlsmith, Darley, & Robinson, 2002).

This leads to an important irony. Herein, we have shown that people believe their own actions to be the product of their own autonomous agency, even though their actual behavior fails to validate this belief in self-sovereignty. However, playing into this belief by exhorting people to use their autonomous free choice morally—or else!—may be just the right external push that impels people generally to act in kind and ethical ways. That is, society might successfully constrain people's behavior to be lawful only by prodding people to misjudge just how much their own behavior is constrained by outside forces. The law imposes a powerful constraint on people via convincing them that only they, via their own free will and willpower, have sway over their own behavior. Empirical evidence supports this assertion. Persuading people that their behavior is not subject to free will prompts them to cheat more on a laboratory task (Vohs & Schooler, 2008), and to help others less while aggressing against others more (Baumeister, Masicampo, & DeWall, 2009).

CONCLUDING REMARKS

I began this chapter by describing the Biblical story of Peter's denial, mostly to show just how far back and central the issue has been, at least in Western civilization, of people overclaiming a virtuous character that fails to emerge in their behavior. In work in my lab, my collaborators and I have found that people act much like Peter—overestimating the likelihood that they will engage in altruistic, ethical, or moral acts. They overestimate this likelihood relative to other people and also relative to the reality found in their own actions. That I end this chapter talking about the relevance of false moral superiority to the law in our modern times shows potentially just how entrenched and pervasive this illusion toward superiority might be.

However, the research described in this chapter does suggest a silver lining that might help people to achieve the humility their religions exhort them to adopt and to stay the ethical person the law requires them to be. In our work, we repeatedly find that people are remarkably accurate in their forecasts about others. They seem to possess a roughly accurate impression of peers in contemporary social life, and in that knowledge people might find ways to guide their own behavior more wisely. Their intuitions about other people may be clues as to when they will be tempted toward selfishness, antisocial behavior, or evil themselves.

Thus what people will have to recognize is the continuity between human nature and self-nature, and not to consider the latter to be different from the former. After all, in Biblical lore, Peter's denial set the stage for his subsequent redemption and a respected life as a principled and honorable man of faith. In using the wisdom they have about others in understanding themselves, people might similarly shape themselves toward becoming in reality the moral and giving individuals that they often mistakenly think they already are.

ACKNOWLEDGMENTS

The writing of this chapter was supported financially by a Fuller Seminary Thrive Center grant titled "Cognitive Habits of Intellectual Humility," funded by the Templeton Foundation.

END NOTES

1. Of course, there are times at which people grossly mispredict others (Gilovich, 1991; Nisbett & Ross, 1980; Ross, 1977), although that is not the focus of

the present examination of moral behavior. In our own work, we have found two general exceptions to accuracy in social prediction. The first involves how people react to situations involving emotion. In these circumstances, people experience "empathy gaps" in predicting how the self and other people will react to emotion-laden situations if they are not currently feeling the emotion itself (Van Boven, Loewenstein, Dunning, & Nordgren, 2013). The second circumstance involves anticipating the trustworthiness of others (Fetchenhauer & Dunning, 2010). People seem to underestimate other people's trustworthiness due to biased "experience sampling." At times, people trust others and get hurt, thus becoming more cynical about human nature in general. At other times, they decide a person is not trustworthy and thus do not trust him or her. However, this action deprives them from discovering that their pessimistic decision was unwarranted, that they were too cynical. This asymmetry in experience and feedback causes cynicism to grow, but not to be corrected.
2. Of course, in the law, there are always exceptions. Instead of having evil intent, I might be careless, thus causing a crime to occur. These crimes without intent fall into the category of negligence, in which people's behavior deviates from normal, thus creating a risk for a crime that a "reasonable person" would anticipate. The key is that negligence crimes are not considered as culpable, or worthy of punishment, as crimes with clear malevolent intent. Another category of crime, strict liability, also produces legal exposure to criminal prosecution even when it is conceded that it is impossible for the culprit, or any reasonable person, to have foreseen the crime that would occur (Morse, 1992).

REFERENCES

Allison, S. T., Messick, D. M., & Goethals, G. R. (1989). On being better but not smarter than others: The Muhammad Ali effect. *Social Cognition, 7*, 275–295.

Balcetis, E., & Dunning, D. (2008). A mile in moccasins: How situational experience reduces dispositionism in social judgment. *Personality and Social Psychology Bulletin, 34*, 102–114.

Balcetis, E., & Dunning, D. (2013). Considering the situation: Why people are better social psychologists than self-psychologists. *Self and Identity, 12*, 1–15.

Balcetis, E., & Dunning, D. (2015). *On the generality of the "holier than thou" phenomenon: Are people better social psychologists than self-psychologists?* Unpublished manuscript, New York University, NY.

Balcetis, E., Dunning, D., & Miller, R. L. (2008). Do collectivists "know themselves" better than individualists?: Cross-cultural investigations of the "holier than thou" phenomenon. *Journal of Personality and Social Psychology, 95*, 1252–1267.

Baumeister, R. F., Masicampo, E. J., & DeWall, C. N. (2009). Prosocial benefits of feeling free: Disbelief in free will increases aggression and reduces helpfulness. *Personality and Social Psychology Bulletin, 36*, 260–268.

Bryan, C. J., Adams, G. S., & Monin, B. (2013). "Cheating" vs. "being a cheater": Implicating the self prevents unethical behavior. *Journal of Experimental Psychology: General, 142*, 1001–1005.

Bryan, C. J., Walton, G. M., Rogers, T., & Dweck, C. S. (2011). Motivating voter turnout by invoking the self. *Proceedings of the National Academy of Sciences of the USA, 108,* 12653–12656.

Buehler, R., Griffin, D., & Ross, M. (1994). Exploring the "planning fallacy": Why people underestimate their task completion times. *Journal of Personality and Social Psychology, 67,* 366–381.

Carlsmith, K. M., Darley, J. M., & Robinson, P. H. (2002). Why do we punish?: Deterrence and just deserts as motives for punishment. *Journal of Personality and Social Psychology, 83,* 284–299.

Critcher, C. R., & Dunning, D. (2013). Predicting persons' goodness versus a person's goodness: Forecasts diverge for populations versus individuals. *Journal of Personality and Social Psychology, 104,* 28–44.

Darley, J. M., & Latané, B. (1968). Bystander intervention in emergencies: Diffusion of responsibility. *Journal of Personality and Social Psychology, 8,* 377–383.

Dworkin, G., & Blumenfeld, D. (1996). VI. Punishment for intentions. *Mind, 75,* 396–404.

Epley, N., & Dunning, D. (2000). Feeling "holier than thou": Are self-serving assessments produced by errors in self or social prediction? *Journal of Personality and Social Psychology, 79,* 861–875.

Epley, N., & Dunning, D. (2006). The mixed blessings of self-knowledge in behavioral prediction: Enhanced discrimination but exacerbated bias. *Personality and Social Psychology Bulletin, 32,* 641–655.

Fehr, E., & Fischbacher, U. (2004). Third-party punishment and social norms. *Evolution and Human Behavior, 25,* 63–87.

Fehr, E., & Gächter, S. (2002). Altruistic punishment in humans. *Nature, 415,* 137–140.

Fetchenhauer, D., & Dunning, D. (2010). Why so cynical?: Asymmetric feedback underlies misguided skepticism in the trustworthiness of others. *Psychological Science, 21,* 189–193.

Geerken, M. R., & Gove, W. R. (1975). Deterrence: Some theoretical considerations. *Law and Society Review, 9,* 497–513.

Gilovich, T. (1991). *How we know what isn't so: The fallibility of human reason in everyday life.* New York: Free Press.

Goethals, G. R. (1986). Fabricating and ignoring social reality: Self-serving estimates of consensus. In J. Olson, C. P. Herman, & M. P. Zanna (Eds.), *Relative deprivation and social comparison: The Ontario symposium on social cognition* (Vol. 4, pp. 135–157). Hillsdale, NJ: Erlbaum.

Goethals, G. R., Messick, D., & Allison, S. (1991). The uniqueness bias: Studies of constructive social comparison. In J. Suls & T. A. Wills (Eds.), *Social comparison: Contemporary theory and research* (pp. 149–176). Hillsdale, NJ: Erlbaum.

Hardy, C. L., & Van Vugt, M. (2006). Nice guys finish first: The competitive altruism hypothesis. *Personality and Social Psychology Bulletin, 32,* 1402–1413.

Hart, H. L. A. (2008). *Punishment and responsibility.* Oxford, UK: Oxford University Press.

Hasher, L., & Chromiak, W. (1977). The processing of frequency information: An automatic mechanism? *Journal of Verbal Learning and Verbal Behavior, 16,* 173–184.

Hasher, L., & Zacks, R. T. (1984). Automatic processing of fundamental information: The case of frequency of occurrence. *American Psychologist, 39*, 1372–1388.

Hasher, L., Zacks, R. T., Rose, K. C., & Sanft, H. (1987). Truly incidental encoding of frequency information. *American Journal of Psychology, 100*, 69–91.

Helzer, E. G. (2012). *The distinct understanding of agency in self and other: A metacognitive perspective on why we see ourselves as freer than the rest.* Unpublished doctoral dissertation, Cornell University, NY.

Helzer, E. G., & Dunning, D. (2012). Why and when peer prediction is superior to self-prediction: The weight given to future aspiration versus past achievement. *Journal of Personality and Social Psychology, 103*, 38–53.

Henrich, J., Ensimger, J., McElreath, R., Barr, A., Barrett, C., Bolyanatz, A., et al. (2010). Markets, religion, community size, and the evolution of fairness and punishment. *Science, 327*, 1480–1484.

Jones, A., Cole, J., Goudie, A., & Field, M. (2012). The effect of restraint beliefs on alcohol-seeking behavior. *Psychology of Addictive Behaviors, 26*, 325–329.

Jones, E. E., & Nisbett, R. E. (1971). The actor and the observer: Divergent perceptions of the causes of behavior. In E. E. Jones, D. E. Kanouse, H. H. Kelly, R. E. Nisbett, S. Valins, & B. Weiner (Eds.), *Attribution: Perceiving the causes of behavior* (pp. 79–94). New York: General Learning Press.

Jones, M. (2013). Overcoming the myth of free will in criminal law: The true impact of the genetic revolution. *Duke Law School, 52*, 1031–1052.

Jordan, J., Mullen, E., & Murnighan, J. K. (2011). Striving for the moral self: The effects of recalling past moral actions on future moral behavior. *Personality and Social Psychology Bulletin, 37*, 701–713.

Khan, U., & Dhar, R. (2006). Licensing effect in consumer choice. *Journal of Marketing Research, 43*, 259–266.

Khan, U., & Dhar, R. (2007). Where there is a way, is there a will?: The effect of future choices on current preferences. *Journal of Experimental Psychology: General, 136*, 277–288.

Koehler, D., & Poon, C. S. K. (2006). Self-predictions overweight strength of current intentions. *Journal of Experimental Social Psychology, 42*, 517–524.

Koehler, D. J., White, R. J., & John, L. K. (2011). Good intentions, optimistic self-predictions, and missed opportunities. *Social Psychological and Personality Science, 2*, 90–96.

Kraut, R. E. (1973). The effects of social labeling on giving to charity. *Journal of Experimental Social Psychology, 9*, 551–562.

Kruger, J., & Gilovich, T. (2004). Actions and intentions in self-assessments: The road to self-enhancement is paved with good intentions. *Personality and Social Psychology Bulletin, 30*, 328–339.

Latané, B., & Darley, J. (1968). Group inhibition of bystander intervention in emergencies. *Journal of Personality and Social Psychology, 10*, 215–221.

Latané, B., & Darley, J. (1970). *The unresponsive bystander: Why doesn't he help?* New York: Appleton-Century-Crofts.

Liebrand, W. B. G., Messick, D. M., & Wolters, F. J. M. (1986). Why we are fairer than others: A cross-cultural replication and extension. *Journal of Experimental Social Psychology, 22*, 590–604.

Malle, B. F. (1999). How people explain behavior: A new theoretical framework. *Personality and Social Psychology Review, 3,* 23–48.

Malle, B. F., & Knobe, J. (1997). Which behaviors do people explain?: A basic actor–observer asymmetry. *Journal of Personality and Social Psychology, 72,* 288–304.

Markus, H. R., & Kitayama, S. (2003). Models of agency: Sociocultural diversity in the construction of action. In V. Murphy-Berman & J. Berman (Eds.), *Nebraska Symposium on Motivation: Vol. 49. Cross-cultural differences in perspectives on self* (pp. 1–57). Lincoln: University of Nebraska Press.

Messick, D. M., Bloom, S., Boldizar, J. P., & Samuelson, C. D. (1985). Why we are fairer than others. *Journal of Experimental Social Psychology, 21,* 480–500.

Milinski, M., Semmann, D., & Krambeck, H.-J. (2002). Reputation helps solve the "tragedy of the commons." *Nature, 415,* 424–426.

Miller, R. L., Brickman, P., & Bolen, D. (1975). Attribution versus persuasion as a means for modifying behavior. *Journal of Personality and Social Psychology, 31,* 430–441.

Monin, B., & Miller, D. T. (2001). Moral credentials and the expression of prejudice. *Journal of Personality and Social Psychology, 81,* 33–43.

Morse, S. J. (1992). The "guilty mind": *Mens rea.* In D. K. Kagehiro & W. W. Laufer (Eds.), *Handbook of psychology and law* (pp. 207–229). New York: Springer Science+Business Media.

Newby-Clark, I. R., Ross, M., Buehler, R., Koehler, D. J., & Griffin, D. (2000). People focus on optimistic and disregard pessimistic scenarios while predicting their task completion times. *Journal of Experimental Psychology: Applied, 6,* 171–182.

Nisbett, R. E., Caputo, C., Legant, P., & Marecek, J. (1973). Behavior as seen by the actor and as seen by the observer. *Journal of Personality and Social Psychology, 27,* 154–164.

Nisbett, R. E., & Kunda, Z. (1985). Perceptions of social distributions. *Journal of Personality and Social Psychology, 48,* 297–311.

Nisbett, R. E., & Ross, L. (1980). *Human inference: Strategies and shortcomings of social judgment.* Englewood Cliffs, NJ: Prentice-Hall.

Nordgren, L. F., van Harreveld, F., & van der Pligt, J. (2009). The restraint bias: How the illusion of self-restraint promotes impulsive behavior. *Psychological Science, 20,* 1523–1528.

Peetz, J., & Buehler, R. (2009). Is there a budget fallacy?: The role of savings goals in the prediction of personal spending. *Personality and Social Psychology Bulletin, 35,* 230–242.

Peetz, J., & Buehler, R. (2013). Different goals, different predictions: Accuracy and bias in financial planning for events and time periods. *Journal of Applied Social Psychology, 43,* 1079–1088.

Poon, C. S. K., Koehler, D. K., & Buehler, R. (2014). On the psychology of self-prediction: Consideration of situational barriers to intended actions. *Judgment and Decision Making, 9,* 207–225.

Pronin, E., & Kugler, M. B. (2010). People believe they have more free will than others. *Proceedings of the National Academy of Sciences of the USA, 107,* 22469–22474.

Rosenthal, R., & Jacobson, L. (1992). *Pygmalion in the classroom: Expanded edition*. New York: Irvington.

Ross, L. (1977). The intuitive psychologist and his shortcomings: Distortions in the attribution process. In L. Berkowitz (Ed.), *Advances in experimental social psychology* (Vol. 10, pp. 173–220). Orlando, FL: Academic Press.

Rotenberg, M. (1974). Self-labelling: A missing link in the "societal reaction" theory of deviance. *Sociological Review, 22*, 335–354.

Sachdeva, S., Iliev, R., & Medin, D. L. (2009). Sinning saints and saintly sinners: The paradox of moral self-regulation. *Psychological Science, 20*, 523–528.

Savani, K., Markus, H. R., & Conner, A. L. (2008). Let your preference be your guide?: Preferences and choices are more tightly linked for North Americans and for Indians. *Journal of Personality and Social Psychology, 95*, 861–876.

Savani, K., Markus, H. R., Naidu, N. V. R., Kumar, S., & Berlia, V. (2010). What counts as a choice? U.S. Americans are more likely than Indians to construe actions as choices. *Psychological Science, 21*, 391–398.

Sherman, S. J. (1980). On the self-erasing nature of errors of prediction. *Journal of Personality and Social Psychology, 39*, 211–221.

Stephens, N. M., Hamedani, M. G., Markus, H. R., Bersieker, H. B., & Eloul, L. (2009). Why did they "choose" to stay? Perspectives of Hurricane Katrina observers and survivors. *Psychological Science, 20*, 878–886.

Storms, M. D. (1973). Videotape and the attribution process: Reversing actors' and observers' points of view. *Journal of Personality and Social Psychology, 27*, 165–175.

Thoits, P. A. (1985). Self-labeling processes in mental illness: The role of emotional deviance. *American Journal of Sociology, 91*, 221–249.

Van Boven, L., Loewenstein, G., Dunning, D., & Nordgren, L. (2013). Changing places: Empathy gaps in emotional perspective taking. In J. Olson & M. P. Zanna (Eds.), *Advances in experimental social psychology* (Vol. 48, pp. 117–171). New York: Elsevier.

Van Kerckhove, A., Geuens, M., & Vermeir, I. (2012). A motivational account of the question-behavior effect. *Journal of Consumer Research, 39*, 111–127.

Vazire, S., & Doris, J. M. (2009). Personality and personal control. *Journal of Research in Personality, 43*, 274–275.

Vohs, K. D., & Schooler, J. W. (2008). The value of believing in free will: Encouraging a belief in determinism increases cheating. *Psychological Science, 19*, 49–54.

West, S. G., & Brown, J. T. (1975). Physical attractiveness, the severity of the emergency and helping: A field experiment and interpersonal simulation. *Journal of Experimental Social Psychology, 11*, 531–538.

Williams, E. F., & Gilovich, T. (2008). Conceptions of self and other across time. *Personality and Social Psychology Bulletin, 34*, 1037–1046.

Williams, E. F., & Gilovich, T. (2012). The better-than-my-average effect: The relative impact of peak and average performance in assessments of the self and others. *Journal of Experimental Social Psychology, 48*, 556–561.

Williams, E. F., Gilovich, T., & Dunning, D. (2012). Being all that you can be: The weighting of potential in assessments of self and others. *Personality and Social Psychology Bulletin, 38*, 143–154.

CHAPTER 13

Making Relationship Partners Good
A Model of the Interpersonal Consequences of Compassionate Goals

Jennifer Crocker and Amy Canevello

Social scientists generally agree about what makes people good relationship partners. Relationship partners who provide support, respond to needs, and give trust make better partners than people who do not act in these ways (Reis, Clark, & Holmes, 2004; Rempel, Holmes, & Zanna, 1985). And most people would agree, we think, that people who are supportive, responsive, and trusting are not only good relationship partners—they are good people, period.

The question for most people is not "What qualities make a good relationship partner?" but, rather, "How can I find a relationship partner with these qualities?" Many people have "destiny" beliefs about relationship partners, assuming that the "right person" exists somewhere and that if they can simply find that person, they will have a good relationship partner (Knee, Patrick, & Lonsbary, 2003). Americans spend enormous sums of money and inordinate amounts of time in the search for good relationship partners—not only romantic partners, but also friends, roommates, employees, employers, and mentors. We network, advertise, recruit, post, screen, and entice, in hopes of finding good partners for our endeavors.

Often, however, this search yields disappointing results. The promising date, the initially likeable friend, the talented job prospect, the boss who dazzles—all can turn sour, as competing demands, conflicts of interests, and disagreements inevitably arise and relationship partners fail to deliver the anticipated supportiveness, responsiveness, and trust.

In this chapter, we argue that good relationship partners are made, not found; people *become* good (or bad) relationship partners in the context of interpersonal interactions. And the key to creating good relationship partners, we suggest, is intentions. In interactions between two people, one person's intentions affect whether the other person becomes a good or bad relationship partner.

In this chapter, we propose that people make others bad when they are driven by a motivational orientation we call the *egosystem* and have the intention to manage the impressions others have of them. Conversely, people make others good when they are driven by a motivational orientation we call the *ecosystem* and have the intention to be constructive and supportive and not harm others. We first explain what we mean by egosystem and ecosystem motivational orientations and the interpersonal goals that characterize these orientations. We describe how compassionate goals relate to other prosocial orientations and their unique associations with well-being and relational outcomes. We then present a model of how people make their relationship partners good and describe a program of research testing the model for different types of behaviors. Our research suggests that making others good starts with making oneself good—specifically, clarifying an intention to be constructive and supportive and not harm others. These intentions shape both intrapersonal and interpersonal processes that make relationship partners—and ourselves—good.

EGOSYSTEM AND ECOSYSTEM MOTIVATIONAL ORIENTATIONS

Our program of research begins with the idea that all human relationships are shaped by two fundamentally important motivational systems, which we call the egosystem and the ecosystem. Whereas the egosystem is primarily self-interested, in the ecosystem people care about others' needs in addition to their own. These two motivational systems build upon evolved motivational systems found in many animals: the self-preservation and species-preservation systems (Henry & Wang, 1998), also called the fight-or-flight and tend-and-befriend motivational systems (Taylor et al., 2000).

The self-preservation system is evolutionarily very old and found in species from reptiles to humans (Henry & Wang, 1998). It evolved to enable organisms to survive immediate threats to survival by activating the fight-or-flight response (Dickerson & Kemeny, 2004; Sapolsky, 1998).

The species-preservation motivational system evolved more recently and is found in all mammals, for whom reproduction requires not only giving birth but also caring for young. These two motivational systems interact. At relatively low levels of threat, the species-preservation system, when activated, down-regulates the self-preservation system, enabling the organism to attend to the needs of others even at some cost or danger to the self (Henry & Wang, 1998). However, at high levels of stress or threat the self-preservation system typically overwhelms the species-preservation system (Henry & Wang, 1998). Because parents must survive to care for their young, the self-preservation system and species-preservation system apparently function most of the time to protect young without sacrificing parents. Thus the species-preservation motivational system functions in a non-zero-sum framework—good for others and oneself—except under extreme threat, when self-preservation typically has priority. Note that neither of these systems is morally good or bad; both are necessary for humans and other mammals to survive and reproduce.

The self-preservation and species-preservation systems provide the biological structures onto which egosystem and ecosystem motivations in social relationships are scaffolded.

Egosystem Motivation

Like the self-preservation motivational system, the egosystem promotes self-interest. In the egosystem, people care about their own needs and desires more than others' (Crocker & Canevello, 2015). Egosystem motivation is characterized by distinct goals, beliefs about interdependence with others, and affective states. First, in the egosystem, people try to manage the impressions others have of them to get what they want; that is, they have *self-image goals* to display their desirable qualities and conceal their undesirable qualities from others (Crocker & Canevello, 2008). Second, when people have self-image goals, they tend to view interpersonal relationships as zero-sum in nature; when one person wins, the other loses. For example, people higher in self-image goals tend to agree with such statements as "One person's success depends on another person's failure," and "In order to succeed in this world, it is sometimes necessary to step on others along the way" (Crocker & Canevello, 2008). They also have zero-sum views of close relationships. For example, people with self-image goals toward their roommates and romantic partners tend to agree with such statements as "What is good for one person is often bad for the other," and "I will ultimately be better off if I focus on my own needs and don't think about my roommate's [partner's] needs" (Crocker, Canevello, & Lewis, 2015). Third, when people have self-image goals, they tend to feel afraid, confused, and conflicted because they feel competitive with others (Canevello & Crocker, 2015a).

Because egosystem motivation is scaffolded onto the self-preservation system, threats to desired images of the self activate the same physiological systems as, and therefore feel like, threats to survival. For example, threats to the social self elicit elevated cortisol levels (Blackhart, Eckel, & Tice, 2007; Dickerson & Kemeny, 2004).

Egosystem motivation need not lead people to behave in antisocial ways; people may act in prosocial ways when motivated by the ego system. Apparent selflessness and self-sacrifice can be motivated by self-image goals, as happens when people give so that relationship partners see them as kind or helpful (Crocker & Canevello, 2012). Unmitigated communion seems to be a form of prosocial orientation driven by the egosystem. People high in unmitigated communion sacrifice for others and feel that they cannot say "no" to others (Fritz & Helgeson, 1998; Helgeson, 1994). By being intrusive, overly nurturant, and overly protective, they try to establish or strengthen relationships by making others need them, thus gaining a sense of control in the relationship (Helgeson & Fritz, 2000).

Ecosystem Motivation

Like the species-preservation motivational system, the ecosystem is primarily focused on promoting the well-being of others. Ecosystem motivation is characterized by distinct goals, beliefs about interdependence with others, and affective states. First, in the ecosystem, people try to be constructive and supportive and not harm others; that is, they have *compassionate goals* to promote the well-being of others (Crocker & Canevello, 2008). Second, when people have compassionate goals, they tend to view interpersonal relationships as non-zero-sum in nature; when one person wins, the other needn't lose. For example, people higher in compassionate goals tend to disagree with such statements as "To give to others usually requires a sacrifice on the part of the giver" (Crocker & Canevello, 2008). They also have non-zero-sum views of close relationships. For example, people with compassionate goals toward their roommates and romantic partners tend to agree with such statements as "It is usually possible to resolve disagreements in mutually beneficial ways" and "It is usually possible for both individuals to get what they need" (Crocker et al., 2015). Third, when people have compassionate goals, they tend to feel clear, peaceful, and connected, because they feel cooperative with others (Canevello & Crocker, 2015a).

Just as the species-preservation motivational system does not function in a zero-sum framework, pitting the survival of the parent against the survival of the offspring, the ecosystem does not promote self-sacrifice but rather promotes behaviors that benefit both self and others in a non-zero-sum way. Thus the ecosystem is not designed to promote altruism in the narrow sense—behavior that benefits others with no benefit to the self in return (Batson, Ahmad, Lishner, & Tsang, 2002). It is this non-zero-sum quality that makes the ecosystem a sustainable motivational system.

Threats to the well-being of people one cares about activate the same physiological systems as, and therefore feel like, threats to the survival of one's offspring, and they elicit protective or caring responses. Just as the species-preservation system down-regulates the cortisol-based fight-or-flight response to stress (Henry & Wang, 1998), activation of the ecosystem down-regulates the cortisol response to psychological threats, thereby promoting prosocial responses to others (Abelson et al., 2014).

TRAITS OR STATES?

We find stable differences between people in egosystem and ecosystem motivation (Crocker & Canevello, 2008; Crocker, Canevello, Breines, & Flynn, 2010). At the same time, egosystem and ecosystem motivation ebb and flow within the same person over time (Canevello & Crocker, 2010; Crocker et al., 2015). In studies that measure characteristics of egosystem and ecosystem motivation repeatedly over time (goals, non-zero-sum beliefs, and affective states), we can estimate how much of the variability in egosystem motivation occurs between people consistent with personality traits, and how much occurs within people consistent with psychological states (see Crocker & Canevello, 2012, for a discussion). Using multilevel modeling, we can "carve up" the variability in goals into that portion that occurs between people (i.e., reflects dispositions or traits) and that portion that occurs within people (i.e., reflects temporary states). In one study, about 40% of the variability in compassionate and self-image goals occurred between people, and the remaining 60% of the variability occurred within people, suggesting that egosystem and ecosystem motivation are *both* personality traits and psychological states (Crocker et al., 2015).

HOW ECOSYSTEM MOTIVATION MAKES RELATIONSHIP PARTNERS GOOD: A GENERAL MODEL

How might compassionate goals make relationship partners good? A general model of the interpersonal consequences of compassionate goals is presented in Figure 13.1. We first describe the model in its general form and then illustrate how it works across a range of studies, including different samples, relationship types, relationship behaviors, and relationship outcomes. In describing the model, we refer to the two people in a dyadic relationship as the Actor and the Partner, following conventions in relationship science (Kenny, Kashy, & Cook, 2006). The model begins with

The Interpersonal Consequences of Compassionate Goals 275

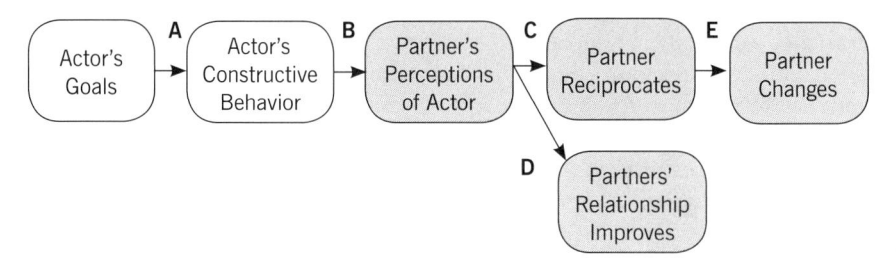

FIGURE 13.1. A general model of how actors' goals influence partners.

Actor's Goals → **A** → Actor's Constructive Behavior → **B** → Partner's Perceptions of Actor → **C** → Partner Reciprocates → **E** → Partner Changes; and **D** → Partners' Relationship Improves.

compassionate goals; we defer a discussion of what prompts people to have compassionate goals to a later section.

Path A: Actors' Goals Predict Actors' Constructive Relationship Behaviors

We propose that in close relationships, compassionate goals—intentions to be supportive and constructive and not harm relationship partners—predict a range of constructive behaviors toward partners. By "constructive relationship behaviors" we mean behaviors that promote the well-being of one or both of the relationship partners, or the relationship itself, in sustainable ways. Constructive relationship behaviors should not be confused with altruism (which can be costly to the self and therefore unsustainable over time), being positive, being nice, making the partner feel good, or doing what the partner wants. Although constructive relationship behaviors sometimes have these qualities, they need not. Sometimes being constructive requires having difficult conversations or saying "no" to relationship partners. For example, a manager with a compassionate goal might turn down an employee's request for a promotion if the manager believes the employee lacks the needed skills. A "no" response in this case would be good for the manager, the employee, and the organization. A romantically involved person might initiate a conversation about a partner's undermining behavior. Although having such a conversation might be uncomfortable and make the partner feel bad, it could be good for both people and for the relationship. Compassionate goals should predict *how* and *why* people deliver difficult messages, not whether they deliver them.

Studies show that compassionate goals are correlated with a range of constructive behaviors, including giving support (Crocker & Canevello, 2008), being responsive to partners (Canevello & Crocker, 2010), self-disclosing to partners (Jiang, Crocker, Canevello, Lewis, & Black, 2015), approaching conflicts with more understanding and less defensiveness (Canevello, Crocker, Lewis, & Hartsell, 2014), and approaching problems and difficulties in a relationship constructively (Canevello et al., 2014). Of course, correlation does not imply causality. To test the plausibility of causal effects, we examined associations over time between compassionate goals and constructive behaviors in a series of longitudinal studies. Results show that compassionate goals not only correlate with constructive behaviors; they also predict increases in constructive behaviors over time (e.g., Canevello & Crocker, 2010; Canevello et al., 2014; Crocker & Canevello, 2008; Jiang et al., 2015), consistent with the possibility that compassionate goals cause constructive relationship behaviors.

We have ruled out several alternative explanations for these associations. For example, associations between compassionate goals and constructive behaviors are not explained by the tendency to respond in socially desirable ways, by attachment anxiety or avoidance, or by self-esteem (see Crocker & Canevello, 2012, for a discussion). Males and females typically show similar effects; we have not found consistent gender differences in the effects of compassionate goals.

Self-image goals undermine these constructive relationship behaviors, either by attenuating the beneficial effects of compassionate goals (Crocker & Canevello, 2008) or by predicting decreases in constructive behaviors over time (Canevello & Crocker, 2010). In general, however, the negative or undermining effects of self-image goals are smaller and less consistent than the strong positive effects of compassionate goals on constructive behaviors.

In sum, when people have compassionate goals, they act in ways that are more constructive—good for their relationship partners and themselves, or good for the relationship itself.

One caveat regarding research on compassionate goals and constructive relationship behaviors concerns the self-report nature of the evidence. To date, studies have examined what people with compassionate goals report about their behavior, rather than observing the behavior itself. These self-reports do not allow us to distinguish between the possibility that actors' behavior has really changed and the possibility that actors are simply telling a nice story about themselves. This limitation is addressed by evidence regarding the next path in the model.

Path B: Partners Perceive Actors' Behavior

Path B hypothesizes that partners notice actors' constructive relationship behaviors. If partners do not notice actors' constructive behaviors, then actors' behavior will have little effect on partners.

In several studies of dyadic relationships, including college roommates, friends, and romantic partners, we have asked both people in the relationship to report their own constructive relationship behaviors and their partners' behaviors. These studies show that partners' perceptions of actors' behaviors are associated with actors' reports of actors' behaviors. Furthermore, partners notice *changes* in actors' constructive behaviors. For example, when actors' reports indicate increased support given by actors to partners over 3 weeks, partners corroborate this; that is, partners' reports indicate that actors have been more supportive over the same time period (Crocker & Canevello, 2008). Likewise, partners' reports confirm increases in actors' reports of increased responsiveness from day to day (Canevello & Crocker, 2010), increases in actors' constructive approaches to relationship problems (Canevello et al., 2014), and increases in actors' self-disclosure from week to week (Jiang et al., 2015).

These findings make two important points. First, they suggest that associations between actors' compassionate goals and actors' constructive relationship behaviors are not merely nice stories that actors tell about themselves. Rather, the changes in actors' behaviors are confirmed by their relationship partners. Second, they provide evidence for a key link between people's goals and their relationship partners; relationship partners notice the behaviors that those goals prompt.

Partners' perceptions of actors' behaviors are not perfectly associated with actors' reports; other processes can lead to dissociations between actors' reports and partners' perceptions. Our research has identified two sources of disconnection between actors' reports of their constructive behaviors and partners' perceptions. First, research suggests that the link between actors' reports of increased constructive behaviors and partners' perceptions of actors' behaviors may be attenuated or even completely eliminated when actors have both compassionate and self-image goals. Specifically, when we asked college roommates to report on their own and their roommates' supportive behaviors at two times during the first semester of college, actors' compassionate goals predicted increases in the support actors reported giving to partners, but partners corroborated this increase in support only when actors had low levels of self-image goals (Crocker & Canevello, 2008, Study 2). We cannot be certain precisely why this disconnection happened. It is possible that actors with high self-image goals were not truthful about the increases in their supportive behavior. Alternatively, actors' supportiveness might have increased, but their motivation to create a desired impression in partners might have somehow undermined how supportive their behavior appeared to partners.

A second source of disconnection between actors' constructive behaviors and partners' perceptions is projection. That is, partners' reports about actors' behavior may be based on partners' own behaviors rather than actors' behaviors. Research has shown, for example, that partners project their own responsiveness onto their relationship partners—highly responsive partners assume that actors are responsive, whereas less responsive partners assume that actors are less responsive (Lemay, Clark, & Feeney, 2007). In our research, we typically find evidence that partners' perceptions of actors' constructive behaviors reflect both projection and reality. For our purpose—understanding how actors' compassionate goals can make relationship partners good—the important point is that partners must notice actors' constructive behaviors in order for actors' goals to make their partners good.

Path C: Partners Reciprocate

People tend to reciprocate when they perceive changes in others' constructive behaviors, particularly when they perceive the other person's intentions to be benign rather than manipulative (Falk & Fischbacher, 2006; Gouldner, 1960). That is, partners who notice actors' constructive relationship behaviors respond by engaging in those same behaviors toward actors. For example, when partners perceive that actors have increased in supportiveness, partners become more supportive toward actors (Crocker & Canevello, 2008, Study 2). When partners perceive that actors have increased in responsiveness, partners become more responsive toward actors (Canevello & Crocker, 2010). And when partners perceive that actors have self-disclosed, partners tend to disclose in return (Jiang et al., 2015). In close relationships, these effects can be very strong. For example, in a weekly report study of college roommates, the partial correlation between week-to-week increases in partners' perceptions of actors' responsiveness and subsequent increases in partners' responsiveness to actors was $pr = .60$ (Canevello & Crocker, 2010, Study 1).

We did not expect that people reciprocate constructive behaviors because they feel obligated or pressured to do so. Instead, we expected that when others give freely, out of a genuine sense of caring, people want to respond in kind, freely and without feeling obligated to do so. For example, when a stranger ahead in line paid for people's coffee at a Connecticut Starbucks, the recipients "paid it forward," paying for the coffee of a stranger in line behind them. On Christmas Eve 2013, more than 1,000 people paid it forward in an unbroken string (Chen, 2013). It seems unlikely that people bought coffee for a complete stranger out of a sense of obligation or a feeling of pressure; indeed, people reported feeling happy about doing so. Many people paid forward more than they received in free coffee; one person contributed $100 to future coffee buyers.

Are there people who do not reciprocate changes in their relationship partners' constructive behaviors? Perhaps, although we have not uncovered any consistent moderators of this effect in our own research. Presumably, people with a strong tendency to be exploitative would be less likely to reciprocate constructive behaviors of relationship partners. The issue of who fails to reciprocate constructive behaviors of relationship partners provides an interesting question for future research.

To this point, we have shown that one person's compassionate goals can make his or her relationship partners good, prompting constructive behaviors in relationship partners. People with compassionate goals act more constructively (Path A in Figure 13.1), their relationship partners notice (Path B), and their relationship partners reciprocate (Path C). If you want your relationship partner to be more supportive, responsive, or disclosing, then set a compassionate goal and become more supportive, responsive, or disclosing yourself.

Path D: Perceiving Actors' Constructive Behavior Improves Partners' Relationship Experience

Partners who perceive actors' constructive behaviors may be more satisfied and committed and feel closer to actors, and their esteem for actors may increase. Indeed, a great deal of research suggests that perceptions of partners are crucially important to close relationships. For example, perceiving partners as responsive builds intimacy and closeness (Reis et al., 2004), and perceiving partners as having high regard for oneself fosters happy relationships (e.g., Murray, Holmes, & Griffin, 1996). Accordingly, we expect that when partners notice that actors with compassionate goals are engaging in more constructive behaviors, partners' relationship-specific experiences will improve.

Path E: Partners' Constructive Behavior Prompts Further Changes in Partners

Giving to others can be a profoundly transformative experience. Partners' reciprocation of actors' increased constructive relationship behaviors—partners becoming more supportive and responsive to actors and disclosing more to actors—may prompt deeper and more lasting changes in partners. Giving—whether one gives money, material things, time, or social and emotional support—has a wide range of beneficial effects on the giver. One well-documented effect of giving is improvements in the mood and well-being of the giver. For example, people who spend money on others are happier than people who spend money on themselves (Dunn, Aknin, & Norton, 2008). Giving is also good for the health of the giver; people with chronic illnesses who give to others show improvements in physical health (Post, 2005). Giving also promotes cooperation and social connection, decreasing feelings of loneliness (Cacioppo & Patrick, 2008). Other research suggests that when people give, their beliefs about themselves, others, and the world can change as a result. For example, when helpers are thanked for their efforts, their feelings of self-efficacy and social worth increase (Grant & Gino, 2010). Thus giving may prompt a variety of changes in the giver beyond improvements to health and well-being.

Because people tend to reciprocate constructive relationship behaviors, the direct cause of changes in the giver can be difficult to determine. People who give support or responsiveness and who disclose to others also tend to receive support, responsiveness, and disclosures from others, so giving and receiving are often confounded. Does giving or receiving lead to changes in the giver?

Research suggests that giving has benefits that may actually outweigh the benefits of receiving. In one study, people who provided autonomy support to close friends (i.e., acknowledging the other's perspective, providing choice, encouraging self-initiation, or being responsive) received more autonomy support in return, consistent with evidence that people tend to reciprocate constructive relationship behaviors (Deci, La Guardia, Moller, Scheiner, & Ryan, 2006). Both giving and receiving autonomy support correlated with the giver's well-being, but when entered together in analyses, giving, rather than receiving, autonomy support more strongly related to the giver's well-being. Longitudinal research also suggests that giving has benefits for well-being independent of receiving. Providing emotional support to a spouse uniquely predicted reduced risk of mortality for the helper over 5 years, independent of support received (Brown, Nesse, Vinokur, & Smith, 2003). Among bereaved people who experienced high loss-related grief, helping behavior predicted an accelerated decline in depressive symptoms for the helper 6–18 months following the loss, independent of support received (Brown, Brown, House, & Smith, 2008).

These findings suggest that when relationship partners reciprocate actors' constructive relationship behaviors, giving back to actors what they have received, partners' health and well-being may improve. These changes in partners due to what partners give to actors may occur above and beyond changes in what partners receive from actors. Based on these considerations, we hypothesize that compassionate goals predict increases in giving and receiving support, whereas self-image goals predict decreased giving and receiving support. Increases in giving support, in turn, may predict decreased distress, even controlling for support actually received or perceptions of support received.

We do not fully understand how partners' giving leads to deeper changes in partners. Self-perception processes might account for some changes in partners who give. For example, when people give and recipients express gratitude, givers might perceive that they have made a difference in recipients' lives, which might account for givers' increased self-efficacy and social worth (Grant & Gino, 2010). Alternatively, giving in response to receiving from someone with compassionate goals might prompt a shift in the giver's motivational orientation from egosystem to ecosystem (Canevello & Crocker, 2010).

Summary

In sum, our model suggests that people with compassionate goals make their partners good because, when people have compassionate goals, their intention to be supportive and constructive and not harm others promotes constructive relationship behaviors. Their relationship partners notice these constructive behaviors and reciprocate them. Partners' reciprocation of constructive behaviors prompts further changes in partners, ranging from improved mood and psychological well-being to physical health, self-efficacy, and so on. Thus partners not only act "good" (i.e., are responsive, supportive, and disclosing), but also they actually become happier, healthier, and "better" people. These changes in partners are separate from the benefits of receiving support, responsiveness, and disclosures.

TESTS OF THE MODEL

Our research has tested this general model in a range of participant samples with different constructive relationship behaviors and partner outcomes. Here we describe a few examples of findings from our studies to illustrate how people with compassionate goals make their relationship partners good and how people with self-image goals undermine these effects.

Social Support Given and Received and Change in Partners' Psychological Distress

The Roommate Goals Study

Our initial studies of compassionate goals tested only some paths of the model depicted in Figure 13.1. We were specifically interested in whether actors' compassionate goals predict change in the support their partners (in this case, college roommates) perceive from actors, whether partners reciprocate the change in support, and whether partners confirm that actors have given them increased support. In this study, 65 same-sex college roommate pairs (130 participants) completed pretest and posttest surveys including brief measures of social support received from and given to their roommates. Participants also completed 21 daily diary reports of their goals for the roommate relationship. Roommates were instructed to complete the surveys separately and not to discuss their responses with each other. We measured compassionate goals by asking students how much they wanted or tried to be supportive of their roommates, avoided doing anything that would harm their roommates, were constructive in their comments to their roommates, and similar items. We measured self-image goals by asking students how much they wanted or tried to get their roommates to see their positive qualities, avoided revealing their weaknesses, demonstrated their intelligence, and similar items.

We tested whether actors' chronic compassionate and self-image goals (averaged across 21 daily reports) predicted change in the support that actors reported giving to partners and whether actors' chronic goals predicted change in partners' reports of social support received from and given to actors, controlling for actors' goals (Crocker & Canevello, 2008, Study 2). Support given to roommates was measured by having students report how often they did things like "listen to your roommate talk about his or her private feelings," "give your roommate some information to help him or her understand a situation he or she was in," "pitch in to help your roommate do something that needed to be done," "joked or kidded to try to cheer your roommate up," and so on. Support received from roommates was measured with the same behaviors, but this time items asked how often roommates performed these behaviors.

As expected, actors' compassionate goals predicted increases in the support students (actors) said they gave to their roommates (partners). Actors' compassionate goals also predicted increases in partners' reports of the support partners received from actors and the support partners gave to actors. However, actors' compassionate goals predicted increases in partners' reports of support given and received only when actors were low in self-image goals. When actors were high in self-image goals, it didn't matter how much actors had compassionate goals; partners still didn't feel more supported or give more support back to actors. As discussed previously, actors' self-image goals apparently undermined partners' perceptions of actors' supportiveness and the support partners gave actors in return.

The path model depicted in Figure 13.2 shows how, though their goals, actors create the support they receive from their partners. In testing all path models, we controlled for variables preceding each path in the model (i.e., to the left in the figure). Actors with high compassionate and low self-image goals perceive that they receive increased support from roommates because their roommates feel more supported, and give increased support in return. With more compassionate goals and fewer self-image goals, people can create not just the perception that support is available to them but

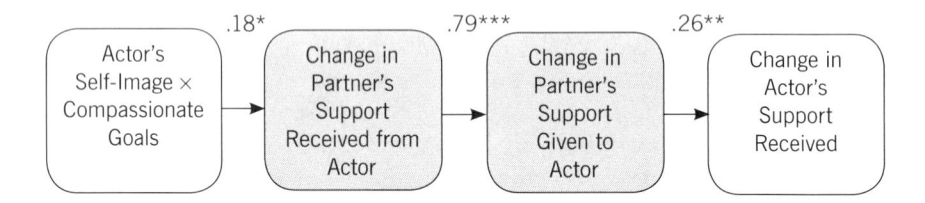

FIGURE 13.2. Actors' compassionate and self-image goals interact to predict change in support partners perceive, which predicts change in support partners give to actors, which predicts change in support actors receive. Different backgrounds mean that data were obtained from different people. All path coefficients are partial correlations. * = $p < .05$, ** = $p < .01$, *** = $p < .001$. Adapted from Crocker and Canevello (2008, Study 2). Copyright 2008 by the American Psychological Association. Adapted by permission.

also relationship partners who are actually more supportive. Notably, partners did not seem to reciprocate out of a sense of duty or obligation; when people had compassionate goals, they reported feeling more peaceful, clear, and connected and did not feel more pressured or obligated.

The Roommate Mental Health Study

Next, we examined implications of actors' compassionate goals and support given and received for symptoms of anxiety and depression in both actors and partners. In the Roommate Mental Health Study, 130 previously unacquainted college freshman roommate pairs (260 people) participated. Both members of the roommate pairs reported their compassionate and self-image goals and their symptoms of anxiety and depression (which we combined into a composite index of distress) and the support they gave to and received from their roommates at the beginning and end of the study and once a week in an online survey. Again, roommates were instructed to complete the surveys separately and not to discuss their responses with each other.

We first tested whether actors' compassionate and self-image goals predict change in the support actors receive from and give to their partners, which in turn predicts change in actors' symptoms of distress from pretest to posttest. Change in the support actors gave was strongly related to change in the support they received, so when examining the role of support actors gave to partners, we controlled for the support actors received from partners. Compassionate goals predicted giving increased support, controlling for self-image goals and support actors received. When actors gave more support to partners, actors' symptoms of anxiety and depression decreased from pretest to posttest, controlling for actors' compassionate and self-image goals and for support actors received. Thus actors' compassionate goals led to less distress in actors because of the support actors gave to partners, independent of the support they received from partners.

The finding that giving support predicts decreased distress, combined with evidence that roommates tend to freely reciprocate the support they receive, suggests that actors' goals may have an influence on roommates' distress through the social support that roommates give back to participants in social support transactions. When participants' goals lead them to provide increased support to roommates, roommates should perceive that support and reciprocate, which should then decrease roommates' distress. We tested this model, which is a specific version of the general model depicted in Figure 13.1.

Results are shown in Figure 13.3. When actors had chronically high compassionate goals (averaged across the 10 weekly reports), the support they gave to partners increased from pretest to posttest; when actors had chronically high self-image goals, the support they gave to partners decreased, consistent with Path A in Figure 13.1. Increases in the support

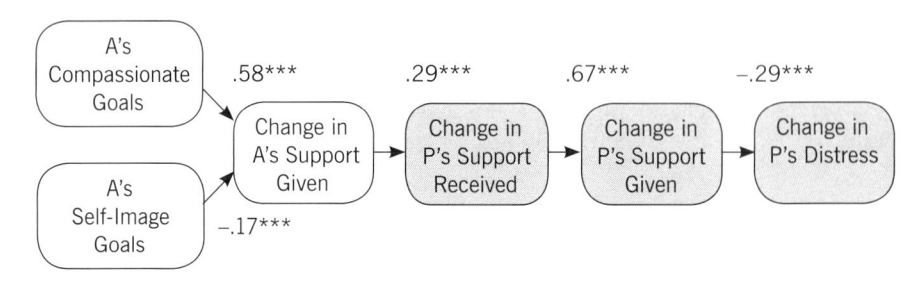

FIGURE 13.3. Path model of how actors' compassionate and self-image goals predict change in partners' distress through support actors give to partners, partners' perceived support received, and partners' reciprocation of support received. Different backgrounds mean that data were obtained from different people. All path coefficients are partial correlations. *** = $p < .001$. Adapted from Crocker and Canevello (2012). Copyright 2012 by Elsevier, Inc. Adapted by permission.

actors gave to partners predicted increases in the support partners reported receiving from actors, consistent with Path B in Figure 13.1. The more support partners perceived that actors gave them, the more support they reported giving actors in return. And the more support partners gave to actors, the less distress (i.e., anxiety and depression) partners reported. Thus, as our general model predicts, actors' goals indirectly influence partners' distress, because when actors have higher compassionate goals and lower self-image goals, actors give more support to partners, partners notice and reciprocate, and partners' giving support back to actors leads to decreases in partners' distress. As hypothesized, change in the support partners received did not predict change in partners' distress; only change in the support partners gave to actors predicted change in partners' distress. The changes in distress we observed were not momentary or short-term changes in mood; they were relatively long-lasting changes in mood that emerged over 10–12 weeks between pretest and posttest.

These results demonstrate one important way that people can make their relationship partners good. When people have compassionate goals, their relationship partners become less anxious and depressed, because actors give support to partners and partners reciprocate by giving support in return.

Responsiveness and Change in Partners' Relationship Quality, Compassionate Goals, Self-Esteem, and Interdependent Self-Construals

Good relationship partners are responsive—understanding, validating, and caring (Gable & Reis, 2006). They make others feel comfortable, valued, listened to, and understood. Responsiveness is not the same as social support; social support can either be responsive or unresponsive to recipients' needs (Collins, Guichard, Ford, & Feeney, 2006). The relationship literature emphasizes the importance of perceived partner responsiveness in close relationships. Indeed, Reis and his colleagues suggest that perceived partner responsiveness is a key to creating intimacy and closeness in relationships (Reis et al., 2004).

Changing Partners' Relationship Quality

We proposed that people with compassionate goals improve their partners' relationship quality by being responsive to their partners (Path A in Figure 13.1), which partners notice (Path B in Figure 13.1), resulting in improved relationship quality for partners (Path D in Figure 13.1).

We examined these associations in the roommate goals study, which included measures of both roommates' responsiveness and perceptions of the other's responsiveness, as well as relationship quality, in each of the 21 daily surveys. Responsive people are understanding, caring, and validating of their relationship partners; responsiveness was measured with items such as "I behave warmly toward my roommate." Perceived partner responsiveness was measured with a similar set of items (e.g., "My roommate behaves warmly toward me").

Results are depicted in Figure 13.4. As predicted, actors' compassionate goals one day predicted increases in their responsiveness to partners the next day; actors' self-image goals predicted decreases in their

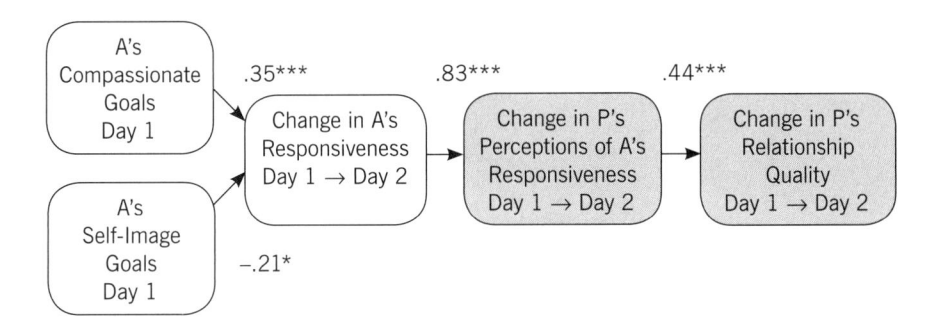

FIGURE 13.4. Path model of how actors' compassionate and self-image goals predict change in partners' relationship quality across 3 days through change in actors' responsiveness to partners and partners' perceptions of actors' responsiveness. Different backgrounds mean that data were obtained from different people. All path coefficients are partial correlations. * = $p < .05$, *** = $p < .001$. Adapted from Canevello and Crocker (2010, Study 1). Copyright 2010 by the American Psychological Association. Adapted by permission.

responsiveness to partners. Partners noticed the change in actors' responsiveness, and increases in partners' perceptions of actors' responsiveness predicted increases in partners' relationship quality.

Changing Partners' Goals

If actors' compassionate goals lead to increases in partners' perceptions of actors' responsiveness through the process depicted in Figure 13.4, might this lead, over time, to changes in other aspects of partners' relationships? That is, might actors with compassionate goals ultimately foster compassionate goals in their partners?

We tested whether actors' compassionate goals predict long-term change in partners' goals in the roommate goals study, examining whether actors' chronic goals (averaged across the 21 daily reports) predict change from pretest to posttest in actors' responsiveness, which partners notice, which leads to change in partners' goals from pretest to posttest (Canevello & Crocker 2010, Study 1). Results are depicted in Figure 13.5. As predicted, actors' chronic compassionate goals predicted increases in their responsiveness to partners 3 weeks later; actors' chronic self-image goals predicted decreases in their responsiveness to partners. Partners noticed the change in actors' responsiveness from pretest to posttest, and increases in partners' perceptions of actors' responsiveness predicted increases in partners' compassionate goals but did not predict change in partners' self-image goals.

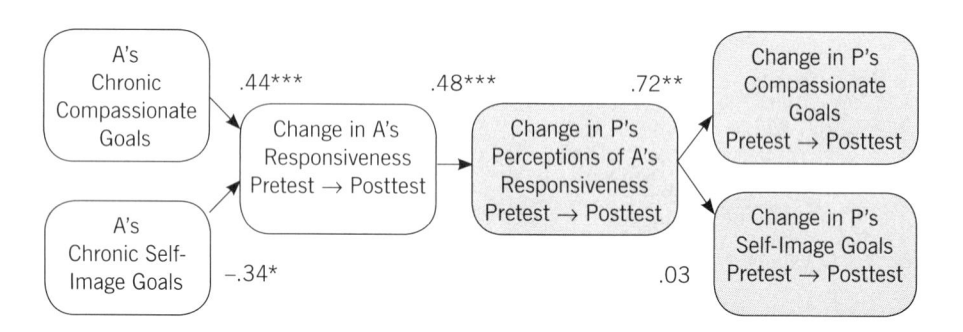

FIGURE 13.5. Path model of how actors' compassionate and self-image goals predict change in partners' compassionate and self-image goals through change in actors' responsiveness to partners and partners' perceptions of actors' responsiveness across 21 days. Different backgrounds mean that data were obtained from different people. All path coefficients are partial correlations. * = $p < .05$, ** = $p < .01$, *** = $p < .001$. Adapted from Canevello and Crocker (2010, Study 1). Copyright 2010 by the American Psychological Association. Adapted by permission.

Changing Partners' Responsiveness

Thus actors can increase their partners' relationship quality and compassionate goals; can they also increase how responsive their partners are to them? Although a great deal of research supports the view that perceived partner responsiveness is important in close relationships, less is known about how to create responsive partners. The model depicted in Figure 13.1 suggests that actors with compassionate goals are more responsive to partners, which partners notice and reciprocate. Thus actors with compassionate goals create more responsive relationship partners.

We examined these associations in the roommate mental health study, testing whether actors' chronic compassionate and self-image goals predict change in partners' responsiveness from pretest to posttest, which predicts change in partners' self-concepts from pretest to posttest (Crocker & Canevello, 2012).

We tested the path model depicted in Figure 13.6. Actors' chronic goals predicted change in their responsiveness to partners from pretest to posttest (Path A in Figure 13.1): actors' compassionate goals predicted increased responsiveness, whereas self-image goals predicted decreased responsiveness. Change in actors' responsiveness to partners predicted change in partners' perceptions of actors' responsiveness from pretest to posttest (Path B in Figure 13.1); in other words, partners noticed changes in actors' responsiveness. Change in partners' perceptions of actors' responsiveness in turn predicted increases in partners' responsiveness to actors from pretest to

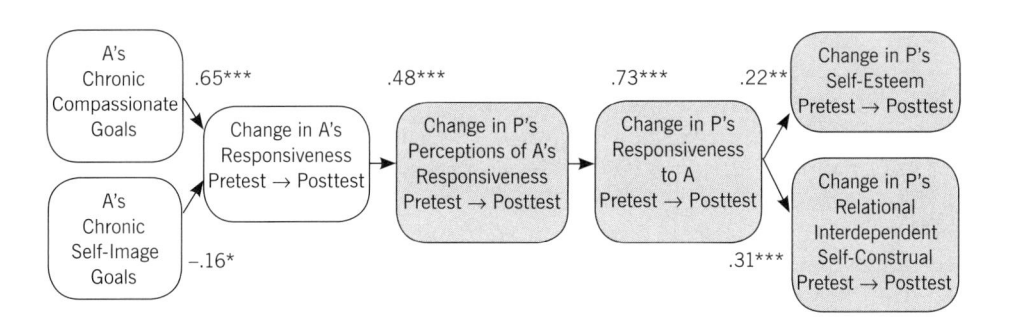

FIGURE 13.6. Path model of how actors' chronic compassionate and self-image goals predict change in partners' self-esteem and relational-interdependent self-concept through change in actors' responsiveness to partners, partners' perceptions of actors' responsiveness, and partners' responsiveness to actors across 10–12 weeks. Different backgrounds mean that data were obtained from different people. All path coefficients are partial correlations. * = $p < .05$, ** = $p < .01$, *** = $p < .001$. Adapted from Canevello and Crocker (2011). Copyright 2011 by John Wiley & Sons, Ltd. Adapted by permission.

posttest. Thus actors with compassionate goals created more responsive partners.

Changing Partners' Self-Esteem and Self-Construal

In the same study, we also tested whether partners' increased responsiveness predicted change in partners' self-esteem or relational interdependent self-construals (Path E in Figure 13.1). Both paths were significant, indicating that actors' goals ultimately predict change in their partners' self-esteem and relational self-construals, through partners' reciprocation of actors' responsiveness.

Self-Disclosure and Change in Partners' Trust

Good relationship partners trust each other. Trust allows people to reveal personal information about themselves that builds close relationships (Murray, Holmes, & Collins, 2006; Rempel et al., 1985). Rempel and colleagues suggested that "Trust is certainly one of the most desired qualities in any close relationship" (Rempel et al., 1985, p. 95).

Creating trust is a relationship process that typically evolves over time (Rempel et al., 1985). At first, people trust relationship partners who behave in trustworthy ways. Early in a relationship, people typically withhold trust until their partners have proven that they are trustworthy instead of giving trust until partners prove that they are untrustworthy. This approach can hinder the development of closeness. When people hold back from taking risks in a relationship, such as refraining from disclosing personal information, relationship partners may likewise decide not to take risks and also refrain from disclosing information (e.g., Murray et al., 2006).

We proposed that people with compassionate goals create more trusting relationship partners by taking a leap of faith and disclosing personal information to their partners. We hypothesized that actors with compassionate goals disclose personal information to relationship partners, regardless of their initial level of trust, because they want to be constructive and supportive (Path A in Figure 13.1). Partners notice the increased disclosure (Path B) and disclose more in return (Path C). Partners' increased disclosure, in turn, predicts increases in partners' trust in actors (Path E).

We tested this model in three separate data sets, including the roommate mental health study, a cross-sectional study of romantic couples, and a longitudinal study of romantic couples (Jiang et al., 2015). Figure 13.7 presents the results from the path model in the roommate mental health study, testing change from week to week. Actors' compassionate goals one week predicted increased disclosure to partners the following week, controlling for actors' initial levels of trust. That is, regardless of how much

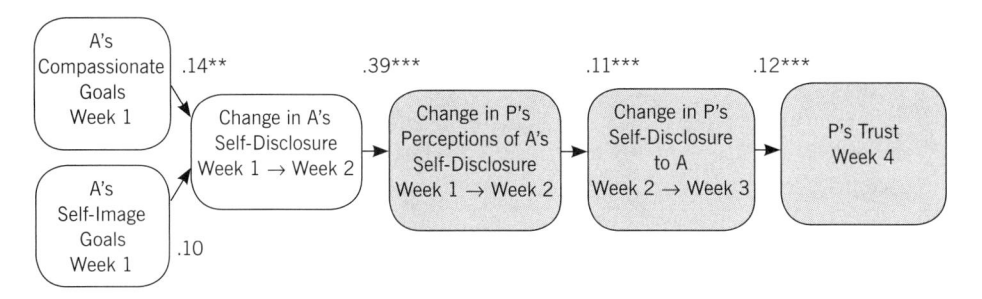

FIGURE 13.7. Path model of how actors' compassionate and self-image goals on Week 1 predict partners' trust on week 4 through change in actors' self-disclosure to partners from weeks 1 to 2, partners' perceptions of actors' disclosure weeks 1–2, and partners' disclosure to actors weeks 2–3. Different backgrounds mean that data were obtained from different people. All path coefficients are partial correlations. ** = $p < .01$, *** = $p < .001$. Adapted from Jiang, Crocker, Canevello, Lewis, and Black (2015). Adapted with permission from the authors.

actors trusted their roommates, if actors had compassionate goals, they disclosed more about themselves. Partners noticed the increased disclosure, and the more they perceived that actors had disclosed, the more partners disclosed in return. Thus, when actors had compassionate goals, their partners shared more personal information. Furthermore, partners' increased disclosure predicted increased trust in partners. Importantly, these processes were independent of how responsive actors were to partners, and they did not depend on actors' level of self-esteem.

These findings have important implications for creating trusting relationship partners. First, actors need not wait for partners to prove their trustworthiness before taking risks by self-disclosing. Regardless of their initial level of trust, actors with compassionate goals disclosed more, presumably because they wanted to be supportive and constructive. Second, when actors disclose to partners, partners notice and reciprocate. Thus the relationship becomes more open. Third, actors' disclosure leads to increased trust in partners. Finally, partner's trust increases in relation to partners' own disclosure to actors, not actors' disclosure to partners. This finding contradicts the intuitive view that people's trust increases when their relationship partners take risks by disclosing personal information. Instead, trust increases in people who take risks. We think of this finding as analogous to team-building exercises in which people fall into the arms of their teammates. No matter how many times people catch their teammates, they may not trust their teammates to catch them. It is only by falling into one's teammates arms that one learns to trust.

Summary

Taken together, these results support the general model of how people make their relationship partners good depicted in Figure 13.1. The results suggest that three processes (at least) can make relationship partners good. All of the processes start with actors' compassionate goals and the constructive relationship behaviors they foster. And all involve partners noticing actors' constructive behaviors.

First, when partners perceive actors' constructive behaviors, partners' relationship quality increases, partners develop more compassionate goals toward actors, and, in other findings, partners' regard for actors increases. Second, when partners perceive actors' constructive behaviors, partners reciprocate. Third, when partners reciprocate actors' constructive behaviors, deeper changes take place in partners, such as decreases in partners' symptoms of anxiety and depression, increases in partners' self-esteem, and increases in partners' relational interdependent self-construals. These changes in partners may have even further consequences for partners.

REMAINING ISSUES

Overall, our research suggests that people's compassionate goals can have powerful consequences for their relationship partners, influencing partners' constructive behaviors, relationship quality, interpersonal goals, mental health, and self-conceptions. People with compassionate goals make their relationship partners good.

Can People Make *Any* Relationship Partner Good with Compassionate Goals?

Are some relationship partners destined to be "bad," no matter how much people have compassionate goals toward them? Our model of how people can make their relationship partners good suggests limits on the ability for one person to make another good. First, as noted, when people have compassionate goals but also have self-image goals, their relationship partners tend not to notice increased supportive behaviors, and therefore partners do not reciprocate with increased supportive behaviors. Thus, in some circumstances, it seems that compassionate goals must be untainted by concerns with self-image or other egoistic motivations to make partners good. Second, although we discussed it only briefly, our research and others' indicates that partners can project their own behaviors onto actors. The process depicted in Figure 13.1 depends on partners noticing actors' increased behaviors. When partners are very low in responsiveness (or other constructive tendencies) and project their lack of responsiveness onto actors, partners might not notice or reciprocate actors' responsiveness. Partners may be "bad" or unresponsive regardless of actors' intentions. Likewise, when partners are high in responsiveness and project their own responsiveness onto actors, partners may be "good" responsive partners even when actors are "bad" and unresponsive. Third, some partners may simply lack the social awareness or sensitivity to detect actors' good intentions and reciprocate appropriately.

In general, however, our data suggest that people usually can make relationship partners good regardless of who the partner is. For example, in our studies of roommate relationships, we sometimes have roommate pairs from different racial or ethnic groups. On average, these cross-race roommate pairs tend to have lower quality relationships. But compassionate goals lead to improved relationship quality in these relationships, just as in same-race roommate relationships.

Compassionate Goals and Other Prosocial Orientations

Compassionate goals may strike the reader as similar to several other constructs related to prosocial motivation, such as empathic concern, communal orientation, and so on. Are compassionate goals distinct from other measures and constructs, or have we simply reinvented existing constructs? Researchers who have developed measures of prosocial orientations have differing theoretical perspectives and developed their measures for specific programs of research. However, the similarities and differences among these measures have rarely been systematically examined. Accordingly, we examined whether compassionate goals are a distinct aspect of prosocial orientations or simply a new name for existing measures and constructs.

Canevello and Crocker (2015b) conducted three studies examining associations among six different measures of prosocial orientations—compassionate goals (Crocker & Canevello, 2008), compassionate love for strangers (Sprecher & Fehr, 2005), communal orientation (i.e., endorsement of norms that people should respond to each others' needs; Clark, Oullette, Powell, & Milberg, 1987), communion (i.e., interpersonal warmth and kindness; Bakan, 1966; Spence, Helmreich, & Holahan, 1979), unmitigated communion (i.e., the tendency to sacrifice one's own needs for the sake of others; Fritz & Helgeson, 1998), and empathic concern for others in distress (Davis, 1983). Correlations among the measures indicated that they were all related, but not so strongly that they were redundant or interchangeable with each other; most correlations were approximately .50–.60. When we conducted factor analyses on the individual items in the six scales, 9 factors emerged, reflecting the original scales, except that communion items loaded on 2 factors (gentle/softhearted and aware/understanding) and communal orientation items loaded on 3 factors (not helpful, not avoiding others in need, and hurt when own feelings are ignored).

Importantly for our research, the items on the compassionate-goals scale loaded on a distinct factor, suggesting that they capture variability in the "space" of prosocial motivations that is distinct from the variability captured by other measures. Furthermore, compassionate goals explained unique variance in several outcomes related to relationship functioning (e.g., giving and receiving support, sense of belonging) and psychological well-being (e.g., self-esteem and depression) when we controlled for the other measures, indicating that compassionate goals capture an aspect of prosocial orientation not assessed by existing measures and constructs.

These results indicate that compassionate goals bear a family resemblance to other measures of prosocial orientations but that they are not identical. Compassionate goals capture a distinct aspect of prosocial orientations—intentions to be constructive and supportive—and explain things that other measures do not.

What Types of Relationships Benefit from Compassionate Goals?

The research we have described here has focused on new relationships, specifically relationships between college roommates who did not know each other prior to college. Are the processes described here limited to these new relationships?

Our recent studies have included friendship dyads, romantic couples, and married couples and suggest that compassionate goals have similar effects in many types of relationships. Indeed, effects of compassionate goals are remarkably similar across relationship types, suggesting that compassionate goals provide a powerful and general tool to make relationship partners good.

Where Do Compassionate Goals Come From?

Our model of how people with compassionate goals make their relationship partners good starts with compassionate goals. We have devoted little attention to where those compassionate goals come from, except to note that they are not completely fixed personality traits. Here we mention two findings from our research that provide clues to the origin of compassionate goals.

Compassionate Goals Depend on People's Affective States

Several findings suggest that compassionate goals decrease and self-image goals increase when people experience negative affect. For example, in the roommate mental health study, we found that symptoms of anxiety and depression predict change in people's goals from one week to the next. People higher in distress one week (a composite of anxiety and depressive symptoms) have less compassionate goals and more self-image goals the following week (Crocker et al., 2010). Likewise, people higher in chronic (trait) self-esteem have increased compassionate goals and decreased self-image goals 10–12 weeks later (Crocker & Canevello, 2012).

Compassionate Goals Are Contagious

People can "catch" compassionate goals from their relationship partners. We discussed this finding in the context of Figure 13.5, which shows that as partners perceive actors to be more responsive, partners develop more compassionate goals over time. Thus relationship partners' goals may be an important source of compassionate goals.

Compassionate Goals as a Choice

Finally, under certain circumstances people may choose either compassionate goals or self-image goals. Specifically, when people understand the benefits associated with compassionate goals for themselves, people they care about, and their relationships, and have the cognitive resources to think through the consequences of their actions, they may choose to act with the intention to be supportive and constructive.

Is There a Downside to Compassionate Goals for Actors?

The research we have described here suggests that actors' compassionate goals have a range of benefits for partners' behavior, experiences, and well-being. Are there costs of having compassionate goals that we have not considered here? In general, we think that compassionate goals are neither costly nor risky for actors. The types of constructive relationship behaviors that compassionate goals prompt, such as giving support, being responsive, and self-disclosing, rarely endanger the health or well-being of actors, and they do not cost money or even much time. Furthermore, our studies provide strong evidence that constructive relationship behaviors that follow from having compassionate goals are reciprocated by partners. In a very real sense, "what goes around comes around," and people with compassionate goals receive commensurate with what they give to their partners. Of course, compassionate goals might have costs in some circumstances. For example, psychopaths may be incapable of the emotional caring required to appreciate and reciprocate compassionate goals. Thus, when relationship partners are psychopaths, it may be risky to have compassionate goals. But it is probably risky to have relationships with psychopaths in any case, so we do not think compassionate goals noticeably increase the risk.

One potential danger of compassionate goals is the risk of exploitation. Caring people might be vulnerable to fraud, particularly scams that appeal for money on behalf of those in need. On the other hand, people who truly care about others' well-being may be judicious in helping others, whereas people with the self-image goal to appear caring might be more susceptible to appeals to help the needy and other forms of exploitation. Research that investigates the susceptibility of people with self-image and compassionate goals to exploitation could provide useful information about the limits of their costs and benefits.

Who Is the Actor and Who Is the Partner?

It is important to note that in all of the analyses described here, actors are also partners. In our analyses, as in life, each person is both an actor and a partner. Thus we caution the reader against assuming that their own experiences will improve only when their partners have more compassionate goals. Although we have focused on how one person's goals shape the other person's experience, people's goals even more profoundly shape their own experiences (see Canevello & Crocker, 2015b). For example, when actors self-disclose, actors' trust in partners increases. When actors are responsive to partners, actors' self-esteem increases. Thus, rather than viewing oneself as the endpoint of the process—the partner waiting for an actor to have compassionate goals—we think it is more helpful to view oneself as the starting point—the actor who can choose to have compassionate goals, and thus alter both actors' own and partners' experiences. While it is true that if our partners have more compassionate goals, our experiences will change, it is also true that if we have more compassionate goals, our experiences will change and our partners will, in all likelihood, become more of the people we want them to be.

CONCLUSIONS

Our research suggests that intentions toward relationship partners—specifically, *compassionate goals* to be constructive and supportive—make their relationship partners good. By carefully setting their intentions toward relationship partners, people can create the relationship partners they want.

REFERENCES

Abelson, J. L., Erickson, T. M., Mayer, S. E., Crocker, J., Briggs, H., Lopez-Duran, N. L., et al. (2014). Brief cognitive intervention can modulate neuroendocrine stress responses to the Trier Social Stress Test: Buffering effects of a compassionate goal orientation. *Psychoneuroendocrinology, 44*, 60–70.
Bakan, D. (1966). *The duality of human existence.* Chicago: Rand McNally.
Batson, C. D., Ahmad, N., Lishner, D. A., & Tsang, J. A. (2002). Empathy and

altruism. In C. R. Snyder & S. J. Lopez (Eds.), *Handbook of positive psychology* (pp. 485–498). Oxford, UK: Oxford University Press.

Blackhart, G. C., Eckel, L. A., & Tice, D. M. (2007). Salivary cortisol in response to acute social rejection and acceptance by peers. *Biological Psychology, 75*(3), 267–276.

Brown, S. L., Brown, R. M., House, J. S., & Smith, D. M. (2008). Coping with spousal loss: Potential buffering effects of self-reported helping behavior. *Personality and Social Psychology Bulletin, 34*(6), 849–861.

Brown, S. L., Nesse, R. M., Vinokur, A. D., & Smith, D. M. (2003). Providing social support may be better than receiving it: Results from a prospective study. *Psychological Science, 14,* 320–327.

Cacioppo, J. T., & Patrick, W. (2008). *Loneliness: Human nature and the need for social connection.* New York: Norton.

Canevello, A., & Crocker, J. (2010). Creating good relationships: Responsiveness, relationship quality, and interpersonal goals. *Journal of Personality and Social Psychology, 99*(1), 78–106.

Canevello, A., & Crocker, J. (2011). Interpersonal goals, others' regard for the self, and self-esteem: The paradoxical consequences of self-image and compassionate goals. *European Journal of Social Psychology, 41,* 422–434.

Canevello, A., & Crocker, J. (2015a). How interpersonal goals shape intrapsychic experiences: Self-image and compassionate goals and feeling uneasy or at ease with others. *Social and Personality Psychology Compass: Intrapersonal Processes, 9,* 620–629.

Canevello, A., & Crocker, J. (2015b). *Measures of prosocial orientations: Family resemblances and unique associations.* Unpublished manuscript, University of North Carolina at Charlotte, NC.

Canevello, A., Crocker, J., Lewis, K., & Hartsell, J. (2014). *Compassionate goals, constructive approaches to interpersonal problems, and upset feelings in relationships.* Manuscript in preparation.

Chen, T. (2013). Starbucks customers break 1,000 in pay-it-forward record. Retrieved from *http://abcnews.go.com/blogs/headlines/2013/12/starbucks-customers-break-1000-in-pay-it-forward-record*.

Clark, M. S., Oullette, R., Powell, M. C., & Milberg, S. (1987). Recipient's mood, relationship type, and helping. *Journal of Personality and Social Psychology, 53*(1), 94–103.

Collins, N. L., Guichard, A. C., Ford, M. B., & Feeney, B. C. (2006). Responding to need in intimate relationships: Normative processes and individual differences. In M. Mikulincer & G. S. Goodman (Eds.), *Dynamics of romantic love: Attachment, caregiving, and sex* (pp. 149–189). New York: Guilford Press.

Crocker, J., & Canevello, A. (2008). Creating and undermining social support in communal relationships: The role of compassionate and self-image goals. *Journal of Personality and Social Psychology, 95*(3), 555–575.

Crocker, J., & Canevello, A. (2012). Consequences of self-image and compassionate goals. In P. Devine & A. Plant (Eds.), *Advances in experimental social psychology* (Vol. 45, pp. 229–277). San Diego, CA: Academic Press.

Crocker, J., & Canevello, A. (2015). Relationships and the self: Egosystem and ecosystem. In M. Mikulincer, P. R. Shaver, J. A. Simpson, & J. F. Dovidio (Eds.), *APA handbook of personality and social psychology: Vol. 3. Interpersonal relations* (pp. 93–116). Washington, DC: American Psychological Association.

Crocker, J., Canevello, A., Breines, J. G., & Flynn, H. (2010). Interpersonal goals and change in anxiety and dysphoria in first-semester college students. *Journal of Personality and Social Psychology, 98*(6), 1009–1024.

Crocker, J., Canevello, A., Lewis, K., & Hartsell, J. (2015). *Nonzero-sum beliefs about romantic relationships: Predictors and implications for relationship stress and satisfaction*. Manuscript under revision.

Davis, M. H. (1983). Measuring individual differences in empathy: Evidence for a multidimensional approach. *Journal of Personality and Social Psychology, 44*(1), 113–126.

Deci, E. L., La Guardia, J. G., Moller, A. C., Scheiner, M. J., & Ryan, R. M. (2006). On the benefits of giving as well as receiving autonomy support: Mutuality in close friendships. *Personality and Social Psychology Bulletin, 32*(3), 313–327.

Dickerson, S. S., & Kemeny, M. E. (2004). Acute stressors and cortisol responses: A theoretical integration and synthesis of laboratory research. *Psychological Bulletin, 130*(3), 355–391.

Dunn, E. W., Aknin, L. B., & Norton, M. I. (2008). Spending money on others promotes happiness. *Science, 319*, 1687–1688.

Falk, A., & Fischbacher, U. (2006). A theory of reciprocity. *Games and Economic Behavior, 54*(2), 293–315.

Fritz, H. L., & Helgeson, V. S. (1998). Distinctions of unmitigated communion from communion: Self-neglect and overinvolvement with others. *Journal of Personality and Social Psychology, 75*, 121–140.

Gable, S. L., & Reis, H. T. (2006). Intimacy and the self: An iterative model of the self and close relationships. In P. Noller & J. A. Feeney (Eds.), *Close relationships: Functions, forms and processes* (pp. 211–225). Hove, UK: Psychology Press/Taylor & Francis.

Gouldner, A. W. (1960). The norm of reciprocity: A preliminary statement. *American Sociological Review, 25*(2), 161–178.

Grant, A. M., & Gino, F. (2010). A little thanks goes a long way: Explaining why gratitude expressions motivate prosocial behavior. *Journal of Personality and Social Psychology, 98*(6), 946–955.

Helgeson, V. S. (1994). Relation of agency and communion to well-being: Evidence and potential explanations. *Psychological Bulletin, 116*, 412–428.

Helgeson, V. S., & Fritz, H. L. (2000). The implications of unmitigated agency and unmitigated communion for domains of problem behavior. *Journal of Personality, 68*, 1031–1057.

Henry, J. P., & Wang, S. (1998). Effects of early stress on adult affiliative behavior. *Psychoneuroendocrinology, 23*, 863–875.

Jiang, T., Crocker, J., Canevello, A., Lewis, K., & Black, A. (2015). *Creating trust through self-disclosure: Compassionate goals predict increased trust in oneself and in relationship partners*. Manuscript in preparation.

Kenny, D. A., Kashy, D. A., & Cook, W. L. (2006). *Dyadic data analysis*. New York: Guilford Press.

Knee, C. R., Patrick, H., & Lonsbary, C. (2003). Implicit theories of relationships: Orientations toward evaluation and cultivation. *Personality and Social Psychology Review, 7*, 41–55.

Lemay, E. P., Jr., Clark, M. S., & Feeney, B. C. (2007). Projection of responsiveness to needs and the construction of satisfying communal relationships. *Journal of Personality and Social Psychology, 92*(5), 834–853.

Murray, S. L., Holmes, J. G., & Collins, N. L. (2006). Optimizing assurance: The risk regulation system in relationships. *Psychological Bulletin, 132*(5), 641–666.

Murray, S. L., Holmes, J. G., & Griffin, D. W. (1996). The self-fulfilling nature of positive illusions in romantic relationships: Love is not blind, but prescient. *Journal of Personality and Social Psychology, 71*(6), 1155–1180.

Post, S. G. (2005). Altruism, happiness, and health: It's good to be good. *International Journal of Behavioral Medicine, 12*(2), 66–77.

Reis, H. T., Clark, M. S., & Holmes, J. G. (2004). Perceived partner responsiveness as an organizing construct in the study of intimacy and closeness. In D. Mashek & A. P. Aron (Eds.), *Handbook of closeness and intimacy* (pp. 201–225). Mahwah, NJ: Erlbaum.

Rempel, J. K., Holmes, J. G., & Zanna, M. P. (1985). Trust in close relationships. *Journal of Personality and Social Psychology, 49*(1), 95–112.

Sapolsky, R. M. (1998). *Why zebras don't get ulcers: An updated guide to stress, stress-related diseases, and coping.* New York: Freeman.

Spence, J. T., Helmreich, R. L., & Holahan, C. K. (1979). Negative and positive components of psychological masculinity and femininity and their relationships to self-reports of neurotic and acting out behaviors. *Journal of Personality and Social Psychology, 37*(10), 1673–1682.

Sprecher, S., & Fehr, B. (2005). Compassionate love for close others and humanity. *Journal of Social and Personal Relationships, 22*(5), 629–651.

Taylor, S. E., Klein, L. C., Lewis, B. P., Gruenewald, T. L., Gurung, R. A. R., & Updegraff, J. A. (2000). Biobehavioral responses to stress in females: Tend-and-befriend, not fight-or-flight. *Psychological Review, 197*, 411–429.

CHAPTER 14

Evil Persons or Evil Deeds?
What We've Learned about Incarcerated Offenders

June P. Tangney, Dan V. Blalock,
Johanna B. Folk, and Jeffrey Stuewig

Where would you look to find the highest density of "evil" in the world today? Many might answer: in jails and prisons. Inmates are highly stigmatized (Moore, Stuewig, & Tangney, 2013), believed by some to be "evil people." And the United States has many of them. Currently, the United States has the highest incarceration rate of any country in the world. Each year nearly 12 million individuals become incarcerated in U.S. jails (Bureau of Justice Statistics, 2014), many on their way to lengthy sentences in state and federal prisons. How many of these millions of inmates are truly evil?

In this chapter, we introduce the construct of psychopathy, underscoring research showing that the large majority of incarcerated offenders are not evil psychopaths beyond the reach of treatment. We then describe what we have learned from 10 years of research with inmates about three key morally relevant characteristics—moral emotions of shame and guilt, criminogenic cognitions, and the capacity for self-control. Interventions are needed that target malleable individual differences predictive of postrelease success—an enhanced capacity for adaptive moral emotions, low criminogenic cognitions, and well-developed self-regulation skills.

EVIL DEEDS VERSUS EVIL PERSONS

Are there evil *people* in the world? In studying evil, social psychologists have long emphasized "the power of the situation." Classics such as Zimbardo's prison study (Haney, Banks, & Zimbardo, 1973) and Milgram's obedience studies (1963, 1974) serve to remind us that given certain circumstances, the "situation" can induce ordinary, even good, people to commit destructive deeds. It seems there *are*, however, some people whom many would describe as "evil"—psychopaths, as determined by Hare's (1991) Psychopathy Checklist—Revised (PCL-R). Psychopathy, as defined by the PCL-R, consists of two factors. Factor 1 assesses the "selfish, callous and remorseless use of others." It taps a personality style defined by people who are glib and superficial, egocentric and grandiose, lack feelings of remorse or guilt, lack the capacity to empathize with others, are deceitful and manipulative, and display shallow emotions. Factor 2 assesses a "chronically unstable and antisocial lifestyle," focusing more directly on criminal and other problematic behaviors. People who score high on Factor 2 are impulsive, have poor behavior control, need excitement, lack responsibility, display behavior problems early in life, and persist in antisocial behavior as adults. Although there is much debate, research suggests at least some biological basis for this individual difference (e.g., Blair, 2003, 2005; Debowska, Boduszek, Hyland, & Goodson, 2014; Kiehl et al., 2001; Kiehl, 2006). Fortunately, even in jails and prisons, such people are a clear minority (about 15–20%). For this minority of offenders, recidivism rates are exceptionally high, and evidence regarding the effectiveness of treatment is mixed and widely debated in the fields of psychology and criminology (Polaschek, 2014).

The vast majority of jail inmates, however, are not evil. Most people who cycle through the criminal justice system have the capacity for moral emotions. They may engage in bad (even evil) deeds, but they are not bad people. The potential for intervention is there.

SHAME AND GUILT: TWO KEY MORAL EMOTIONS

Shame and guilt are often mentioned in the same breath, as moral emotions that serve to encourage socially appropriate, prosocial behavior and to inhibit socially inappropriate, harmful behavior. Research over the past 25 years, however, underscores that these are distinct emotions with quite different implications for motivation and behavior (Tangney, Stuewig, & Mashek, 2007). A consistent theme emerging from much research over the past two decades is that shame and guilt are not equally "moral" emotions. On balance, guilt appears to be the more adaptive emotion, benefiting individuals and their relationships in a variety of ways (Baumeister, Stillwell

& Heatherton, 1994, 1995a, 1995b; Tangney, 1991; Tangney, Stuewig & Mashek, 2007). Coming largely from social and personality psychology, these studies have focused primarily on community (i.e., noncorrectional, nonclinical) samples. Here, we summarize initial findings underscoring the relative benefits of guilt compared with shame in four domains: (1) empathy, (2) anger and aggression, (3) psychological symptoms, and (4) moral behavior. We then describe what we have learned about shame and guilt from our study of inmates. We conclude this section by revisiting potential positive functions of shame in light of recent findings from the inmate study and from other laboratories studying shame-induced motivations in community samples.

What's the Difference between Shame and Guilt?

In brief, shame involves a negative evaluation of the global self; guilt involves a negative evaluation of a specific behavior (Lewis, 1971). Shame—about the self—is an acutely painful emotion typically accompanied by a sense of shrinking or of "being small" and by a sense of worthlessness and powerlessness. Although shame does not necessarily involve an actual audience present to witness one's shortcomings, there is often the imagery of how one's defective self would appear to others. Shame often leads to a desire to escape or to hide—to sink into the floor and disappear—and this powerful emotion often prompts defensive responses: denying or blaming the behavior on external circumstances or others involved in the situation.

In contrast, guilt is typically a less painful, devastating experience than shame because the focus is on the specific behavior, not the entire self. One's core identity or self-concept is not under attack. Instead of feeling defensive, people experiencing guilt focus on the act and its consequences. They feel tension, remorse, and regret over the "bad thing done." People feeling guilt often ruminate over their transgression, wishing they had behaved differently or could somehow undo the harm that was done. Rather than motivating avoidance and defense, guilt motivates reparative behavior—confession, apology, and attempts to fix the situation.

Guilt Is Good, Shame Is Bad?
Other-Oriented Empathy

First, there appears to be a special link between guilt and empathy observed at both the state and dispositional levels. For example, researchers have consistently demonstrated that shame-proneness and guilt-proneness are differentially related to the ability to empathize (Howell, Turowski, & Buro, 2012; Joireman, 2004; Leith & Baumeister, 1998; Martinez, Stuewig, & Tangney, 2014; Robinson, Roberts, Strayer & Koopman, 2007; Stuewig, Tangney, Heigel, Harty, & McCloskey, 2010; Tangney, 1991), a finding that is consistent across various ages and demographic groups (for a review, see Tangney, Stuewig, & Mashek, 2007). In general, guilt-prone individuals show high levels of empathy. Proneness to guilt consistently correlates with measures of perspective taking and empathic concern. In contrast, shame-proneness has been associated with an impaired capacity for other-oriented empathy and a propensity for problematic, "self-oriented" personal distress responses.

Anger and Aggression

Second, research has shown there is a link between shame and anger, again observed at both the dispositional and state levels. Helen Block Lewis (1971) first speculated on the dynamics between shame and anger (or humiliated fury) based on her clinical case studies, noting that clients' feelings of shame often precede expressions of anger and hostility in the therapy room. More recent empirical research has supported her claim. Studies of children, adolescents, college students, and adults have consistently shown that proneness to shame is positively correlated with feelings of anger and hostility and an inclination to externalize blame (Lutwak, Panish, Ferrari, & Razzino, 2001; Robinson et al., 2007; Stuewig et al., 2010; Tangney, Wagner, Fletcher, & Gramzow, 1992; Tangney, Stuewig, & Martinez, 2014). Not only are shame-prone individuals more likely to externalize blame and react with anger than their non-shame-prone peers, but, once angered, they are also more likely to manage and express their anger in a destructive fashion (Tangney, Wagner, Barlow, Marschall, & Gramzow, 1996). More shame-prone individuals handle their anger in more destructive fashions and situations that lead to more shame, which results in more negative consequences.

Psychological Symptoms

Regarding psychological adjustment, researchers consistently find that proneness to shame is related to a wide array of psychological symptoms, including depression, anxiety, eating disorder symptoms, subclinical psychopathy, and low self-esteem (Allan, Gilbert, & Goss, 1994; Fergus, Valentiner, McGrath, & Jencius, 2010; Harder, 1995; Hoblitzelle, 1987; Muris, Meesters, Bouwman, & Notermans, 2015; Sanftner, Barlow, Marschall, & Tangney, 1995). This relationship is robust across a range of measurement methods and across diverse age groups and populations. In concurrence with the clinical literature, empirical research finds overall that people who frequently experience feelings of shame are correspondingly more vulnerable to a range of psychological problems.

The findings for guilt and psychopathology are less clear-cut. The traditional view is that guilt plays a significant role in psychological symptoms. At least as early as Freud (1909/1955, 1917/1957, 1923/1961b), clinical theory and case studies make frequent reference to a maladaptive guilt characterized by chronic self-blame and obsessive rumination over one's transgressions (Blatt, 1974; Ellis, 1962; Freud, 1924/1961a; Hartmann & Loewenstein, 1962; Weiss, 1993). More recent theory and research, in contrast, has emphasized the adaptive functions of guilt, particularly for interpersonal behavior (Baumeister, Stillwell, & Heatherton, 1994; Tangney, 1991; Tangney, Wagner, Fletcher, & Gramzow, 1992; Tangney & Dearing, 2002).

Attempting to reconcile these perspectives, Tangney (1996) argued that once one makes the critical distinction between shame and guilt, there is no compelling reason to expect guilt over specific behaviors to be associated with poor psychological adjustment. Rather, guilt is most likely to be maladaptive when it becomes fused with shame. When a person begins with a guilt experience ("Oh, look at what a horrible *thing* I have *done*") but then magnifies and generalizes the event to him- or herself (" . . . and aren't I a horrible *person*"), many of the advantages of guilt are lost. Not only is a person faced with tension and remorse over a specific behavior that needs to be fixed, but he or she is also saddled with feelings of contempt and disgust for a bad, defective self. Ultimately, it is the shame component of this sequence—not the guilt component—that poses the problem.

In the case of guilt, there are typically a multitude of paths to redemption. Having transgressed, a person feeling guilt (1) often has the option of changing the objectionable behavior; (2) or even better yet, has an opportunity to repair the negative consequences; (3) or at the very least can extend a heartfelt apology. Even in cases in which direct reparation or apology is not possible, one can resolve to do better in the future. In contrast, a self that is defective at its core is much more difficult to transform or amend. Shame—and, in turn, shame-fused guilt—offers little opportunity for redemption. Thus it is guilt *with an overlay of shame* that most likely leads to the interminable painful rumination and self-castigation so often described in the clinical literature.

The empirical results are quite consistent with this view. Studies employing adjective-checklist-type (and other globally worded) measures of shame and guilt find that both shame-prone and guilt-prone styles are associated with psychological symptoms (Harder et al., 1992; Jones & Kugler, 1993; Meehan et al., 1996). On the other hand, when measures are used that are sensitive to Lewis's (1971) distinction between shame about the self versus guilt about a specific behavior (e.g., scenario-based methods such as the Test of Self-Conscious Affect [TOSCA], assessing shame-proneness and guilt-proneness with respect to specific situations), the tendency to experience "shame-free" guilt is essentially unrelated to psychological symptoms. Numerous independent studies converge: guilt-prone children, adolescents, and adults are not at increased risk for depression, anxiety, low self-esteem, and so forth (Fergus et al., 2010; Kim, Thibodeau, & Jorgensen, 2011; McLaughlin, 2002; Muris et al., 2015; Tangney & Dearing, 2002;

Tangney, Wagner, & Gramzow, 1992; Tilghman-Osborne, Cole, Felton, & Ciesla, 2008). In short, once one makes the critical distinction between shame and guilt, there does not appear to be a substantial personal cost for the interpersonally beneficial effects of guilt described thus far.

Risky, Illegal, and Otherwise Inadvisable Behavior

Finally, what are the implications of shame and guilt for actual moral *behavior*—various transgressions, risky behaviors, and other ill-advised deeds? There is the widely held assumption that because shame is so painful, it motivates people to avoid "doing wrong," decreasing the likelihood of transgression and impropriety (Barrett, 1995; Kahan, 1997). Initial research in this area provided surprisingly little evidence supporting this presumed adaptive function of shame.

In a study of college undergraduates, self-reported moral behaviors (assessed by the Conventional Morality Scale; Tooke & Ickes, 1988) were positively correlated with proneness to guilt but unrelated to proneness to shame (Tangney, 1994). For example, compared with their less guilt-prone peers, guilt-prone individuals were more likely to endorse such items as "I would not steal something I needed, even if I were sure I could get away with it"; "I will not take advantage of other people, even when it's clear that they are trying to take advantage of me"; and "Morality and ethics don't really concern me" (reverse-scored). In other words, results from this study suggest that guilt, *but not shame,* motivates people to choose the "moral paths" in life.

The notion that shame and guilt differentially relate to "moral behavior" is further supported by research on drug and alcohol abuse, aggression, and delinquency. In samples of children, adolescents, college students, and adults, shame-proneness has been positively related to aggression and delinquency (Ferguson, Stegge, Miller, & Olsen, 1999; Tangney et al., 1996; Tibbetts, 1997). Similarly, shame-proneness has been linked to substance use and abuse (Dearing, Stuewig, & Tangney, 2005; Meehan et al., 1996; Treeby & Bruno, 2012).

Proneness to "shame-free" guilt, on the other hand, does not show the same positive link to aggression, delinquency, and substance abuse. In fact, guilt-proneness is negatively related to alcohol and drug problems (Dearing, Stuewig & Tangney, 2005; Treeby & Bruno, 2012) and negatively related (Stuewig & McCloskey, 2005; Tangney et al., 1996) or inconsistently related (Ferguson et al., 1999) to aggression and delinquency.

The most direct evidence linking moral emotions with moral behavior comes from our longitudinal family study of moral emotions (Stuewig et al., 2015). In this study, 380 children, their parents, and their grandparents were initially studied when children were in the fifth grade. Children were recruited from public schools in an ethnically and socioeconomically diverse suburb of Washington, D.C. (60% of the sample is white, 31%

black, and 9% other; most children came from low- to moderate-income families; the typical parents had attained a high school education). The sample was followed up when the index children were 18–19 years old. At that time they participated in an in-depth social and clinical history interview, assessing their emotional and behavioral adjustment across all major life domains. Analyses of these extensive interviews show that moral emotional style in the fifth grade predicts critical "bottom-line" behaviors in young adulthood, including substance use, risky sexual behavior, and involvement with the criminal justice system.

More specifically, children who were more shame-prone in the fifth grade tended to start drinking at a younger age and to use a greater variety of drugs, were more likely to use heroin and other drugs, drove under the influence more often, and were more likely to engage in unprotected sex than their less shame-prone peers. In contrast, guilt-prone fifth-graders were less likely to have used alcohol by young adulthood, started drinking at a later age, were lower on polydrug use, were less likely to use heroin, marijuana, or other drugs, and drove under the influence less often than their less guilt-prone peers. Compared with peers who experienced guilt infrequently in fifth grade, these guilt-prone children were, in adolescence, less likely to be arrested or convicted or to have spent time in jail or juvenile detention. The majority of these links between early moral emotional style and subsequent behavioral adjustment held when controlling for family income and mothers' education. Thus this is not simply a socioeconomic status (SES) effect. Equally important, the effects largely remained even when controlling for children's anger in fifth grade. Thus these findings do not simply reflect that badly behaved children are inclined to become badly behaved adults.

In sum, among diverse samples drawn from the community, guilt appears to be the moral emotion of choice. Guilt-proneness is related to a variety of adaptive outcomes, including empathy, engagement in moral behaviors (e.g., not taking advantage of others), fewer alcohol and drug problems, and a lower likelihood of being involved in the criminal justice system. In contrast, shame-proneness is related to maladaptive outcomes, such as anger and hostility, externalization of blame, psychological symptoms, delinquency, substance use and abuse, and risky sexual behavior. But is this the case among people cycling through the criminal justice system? Among jail inmates charged with felonies?

Shame and Guilt among Jail Inmates

We began the George Mason University inmate study (Tangney, Mashek, & Stuewig, 2007) with some very basic questions. First, can we reliably measure shame- and guilt-proneness in an inmate population? For example, will inmates tell the truth? Will they be able to understand and respond to our scenario-based measures? Second, if so, are there individual differences in proneness to shame and guilt among serious offenders of a magnitude worth consideration? Or, as some might suggest, do most inmates essentially lack the capacity for moral emotions and thus become involved in illegal, harmful behavior? Third, if inmates vary in the propensity to experience shame and guilt, do shame and guilt appear to serve similar functions as in noncorrectional community samples? Fourth, and most socially relevant, does the propensity to experience guilt inhibit reoffense after release? Does shame-proneness promote desistence from crime in the future? If so, a long-term goal would be to develop interventions targeting inmates' capacity for these moral emotions.

Thus far, we have learned that we can reliably and validly assess individual differences in inmates' proneness to shame and guilt (Tangney, Stuewig, Mashek, & Hastings, 2011) using the Test of Self Conscious Affect—Socially Deviant Version (TOSCA-SD; Hanson & Tangney, 1995).[1] Moreover, there is considerable variance in inmates' proneness to shame and proneness to guilt. Inmates charged with felonies, on the whole, appear to have the capacity for moral emotions—some more than others. Importantly, individual differences in proneness to shame and guilt were differentially related to personality, adjustment, and past behavior in ways that closely parallel findings from noncorrectional community samples. For example, guilt-proneness was positively related to empathic concern and negatively related to psychological symptoms (e.g., anxiety, depression) and to preincarceration substance use and dependence. In contrast, shame-proneness was positively related to externalization of blame, aggressive attitudes, psychological symptoms (e.g., anxiety, traumatic stress, depression), and alcohol and drug problems (Tangney et al., 2011).

A key question is whether individual differences in proneness to shame and guilt, assessed during incarceration, can predict postrelease recidivism. In our longitudinal analysis of 476 jail inmates, guilt-proneness inhibited recidivism during the first year postrelease; shame-proneness did not (Tangney et al., 2014). Relative to those low on guilt, individuals who were higher on guilt-proneness at the outset of incarceration were significantly less likely to recidivate during the first year postrelease. The findings regarding shame were more complex. Mediational modeling revealed that shame-proneness positively predicted recidivism via its link to externalization of blame. That is, shame-proneness positively predicted externalization of blame (e.g., blaming others), which in turn positively predicted recidivism. Nonetheless, there remained a direct negative effect of shame on recidivism. That is, there was also evidence for a direct inhibitory effect of shame when unimpeded by externalization of blame. It therefore seems that shame can prompt multiple processes—some defensive and maladaptive in nature, others inhibitory and adaptive in nature.

In sum, the capacity for guilt may foster a lifelong pattern of generally following a moral path, motivating individuals to accept responsibility and take reparative action in the wake of failures or transgressions. The story for shame, however, may not be that simple.

Can Shame Be Useful and Adaptive? How and When?

For several decades, social-personality psychologists (Tangney, 1991; Tangney & Dearing, 2002; Tangney, Stuewig, & Mashek, 2007), clinicians (Gilbert & Irons, 2005; Lewis, 1971; Potter-Efron, 2002; Teyber, McClure, & Weathers, 2011), and authors of self-help books on addiction (e.g., Bradshaw, 1988) have emphasized the dark, destructive side of shame. In recent years, however, shame's image has been undergoing some significant rehabilitation. For example, Gausel, Leach, Vignoles, and Brown (2012) astutely observed that although few researchers have discussed shame's positive potential, a surprising amount of evidence already in print (including some portions of Tangney's early work) shows that there can be links between shame and motivations to repair, apologize, and reform (e.g., at the individual level, see De Hooge, Breugelmans, & Zeelenberg, 2008; De Hooge, Zeelenberg, & Breugelmans, 2010; at the group or collective level, see Gausel et al., 2012).

Given our current findings of two distinct paths *opposite in valence* from shame to recidivism (i.e., "inconsistent mediation"; MacKinnon, Fairchild, & Fritz, 2007; MacKinnon, Krull, & Lockwood, 2000), we think the question is not whether shame prompts prosocial motives (and perhaps behaviors) *or* self-defensive motives and responses. The key question facing the next generation of shame research is: For whom and under what conditions does shame serve moral, prosocial functions, and for whom and under what conditions are individuals vulnerable to a sense of threat leading to defensiveness, distance, and denial? Gausel and Leach (2011) suggest that shame may be especially useful in circumstances in which the failure or transgression is more as opposed to less reparable. This is an intriguing direction for future research because, although the causes and consequences of specific behaviors (eliciting guilt) are generally more reparable than more global traits and characteristics of the self (eliciting shame), the reparability of shame-eliciting events is certainly apt to vary. This suggests that an avenue for intervention with individuals plagued by unresolved feelings of shame (as well as unresolved feelings of guilt) may lie in helping individuals creatively construct reparative plans—future-oriented behavior-specific paths toward repair, redemption, and reintegration.

CRIMINOGENIC COGNITIONS: TOO LONG NEGLECTED BY PSYCHOLOGISTS

Thus far, we have focused on moral emotions, but morally relevant cognitions represent another key domain for understanding and intervening to reduce immoral, risky, or otherwise ill-advised behavior. For many years, psychology focused on moral reasoning, as conceptualized and measured by Kohlberg (1976), who was much influenced by Piaget. Unfortunately, moral reasoning à la Kohlberg has not lived up to its promise in predicting moral behavior, as highlighted in Blasi's (1980) comprehensive review. Research in the decades since that review has not shown otherwise.

A much more fruitful domain of morally relevant cognitions comes from the field of criminology. Andrews and Bonta (2010) have identified criminogenic cognitions (also referred to as criminal thinking) as one of the "big four" criminogenic needs (i.e., personal characteristics related to recidivism) and one of the more robust predictors of recidivism. As a result there have been increasing efforts in recent years to measure and alter criminal thinking among inmates. The earliest conceptualization of criminal thinking comes from Sykes and Matza (1957), who studied the thought patterns of juvenile delinquents and theorized that offenders use criminal thinking to reduce the cognitive dissonance produced when they act contrary to their moral standards. Walters (2012) defines criminal thinking as the "attitudes, beliefs, and rationalizations that offenders use to justify and support their criminal behavior" (p. 272). Criminal thoughts involve cognitive distortions theorized to propagate future criminal acts.

Criminal thinking is a moderately robust predictor of recidivism in some studies utilizing offender populations (see Andrews & Bonta, 2010; Walters, 2012, for meta-analytic support), but not in other, similar samples (Mills & Kroner, 1997; Simourd & Van De Ven, 1999; Taxman, Rhodes, & Dumenci, 2011). These disparate findings have promoted some investigation of moderators of the relationship between criminal thinking and recidivism. A recent study by Walters (2014) found that education level and, to a lesser extent, race and ethnicity moderate the relationship between criminal thinking and recidivism. For those who had completed 12 or more years of school, criminal thinking was effective in predicting recidivism, whereas it was not for those with fewer than 12 years of education. In addition, substance dependence symptoms have been found to moderate the relationship among "general population" jail inmates, but not among probationers with a history of substance misuse (Caudy et al., 2015). For individuals with higher levels of symptoms, the relation between criminal thinking and recidivism was attenuated, suggesting that criminal thinking may not be the primary driver of reoffense among individuals with a primary substance use disorder. Criminogenic cognitions are substantially more predictive of reoffense among inmates with a history of little or no substance misuse.

Treatment development and program evaluation have lagged behind measurement and prediction. Several correctional interventions have been developed that include efforts to reduce criminogenic thinking (e.g., Thinking for a Change, Bush et al., 1997; Impact of Crime, Folk et al., 2015; Cognitive Interventions Program, National Institute of Corrections, 1996; Reasoning and Rehabilitation, Ross & Fabiano, 1985), but typically criminal thinking is one of many targets of treatment. The field has yet to develop a theoretically informed, empirically supported cognitive-behavioral intervention aimed specifically at challenging and reducing criminal thinking.

This is precisely where clinical psychologists may be especially well placed to make a substantial contribution, owing to their special expertise in cognitive-behavioral theory (CBT) and associated techniques. Most dimensions of criminal thinking assessed by available measures are, at heart, cognitive distortions. Clinical psychologists are experts at using CBT techniques to reduce cognitive distortions—often in the context of internalizing disorders (e.g., depression, anxiety), but also in the context of externalizing behavior (e.g., aggression). To date, clinical psychologists have been largely absent from the treatment development in this area. (For a few notable exceptions, see Andrews & Bonta, 2010; Marques, Wiederanders, Day, Nelson, & van Ommeren, 2005; Morgan & Flora, 2002; Wormith et al., 2007; Zlotnick, Johnson, & Najavits, 2009).

Closer collaboration between criminologists and CBT-oriented clinical psychologists in the domain of criminal thinking is especially promising given Lipsey, Landenberger, and Wilson's (2007) systematic review of the efficacy of CBT, in general, for offenders. Results clearly support the utility of CBT as an effective recidivism reduction strategy, with the mean odds ratio of the CBT intervention effect being 1.53 ($p < .001$); this signifies that the odds of reincarceration were more than one and a half times as great for individuals in the treatment compared with the control group. Of note, use of cognitive restructuring (64% of studies reported the intervention utilized this) to recognize and modify criminogenic thinking in the intervention was positively related to effect size.

SELF-CONTROL: PUTTING GOOD INTENTIONS (MORAL AFFECT AND COGNITION?) INTO ACTION

Even when people's moral emotions and cognitions direct them to what they should or should not do, the question still remains whether people have the capacity to act accordingly. Many "evil deeds" can be reconceptualized as failures of self-control. In fact, Freud proposed that our ability to inhibit antisocial tendencies (i.e., self-control) is the basis for what makes us civilized (Freud, 1930/1961c). More recently, some scholars proposed that the majority of interpersonal and intrapersonal problems derive from a failure to maintain self-control (e.g., Baumeister, Heatherton, & Tice, 1994). When broadly discussing self-control, it is useful to think both of (1) individual differences in self-control (i.e., person variance: some people have a well-developed capacity for self-control; others are notably lacking in the ability or desire to exert self control) and (2) situational factors that influence how much self-control is required (e.g., a tempting dessert or forbidden love).

Recently, Hofmann and Kotabe (2012) put forth a taxonomy of required steps for successful execution of self-control. The first step in this taxonomy involves preventative self-control (i.e., the ability to make decisions early on that remove the need for in-the-moment self-control). For example, an individual intent on maintaining sobriety may remove all alcohol from his or her home. Once a conflict arises, however, individuals must recognize this conflict and make the decision to execute self-control behaviors. Thus to understand how self-control influences "evil deeds," we must examine both how individuals differ in their capacity for self-control (e.g., Tangney, Baumeister, & Boone, 2004) and how everyday contexts warrant the need to perform self-control behaviors (e.g., Hofmann, Baumeister, Förster, & Vohs, 2012).

Capacity for Self-Control and Self-Control Behaviors

The capacity for self-control is one of the most widely acclaimed predictors of whether a person is likely to engage in future undesirable actions (see de Ridder, Lensvelt-Mulders, Finkenauer, Stok, & Baumeister, 2012, for a meta-analysis). Although many of these undesirable actions may be as benign as eating too many potato chips (Friese & Hofmann, 2009), others are more severe, such as engaging in aggressive actions (Denson, DeWall, & Finkel, 2012), infidelity (Gailliot & Baumeister, 2007), and recidivism (Malouf et al., 2014). Most notably, trait self-control consistently predicts self-reported recidivism in offenders better than any other single measure (Malouf et al., 2014). Yet although we assume that high trait self-control implies a better ability to resist temptation, some research indicates that people higher in trait self-control might actually *use* self-control less often (e.g., Hofmann et al., 2012). That is, individuals higher in trait self-control may encounter fewer opportunities for "evil deeds" in their daily lives. Recent research also suggests that more beneficial habits may be the reason that those higher in trait self-control show more positive life outcomes and fewer negative ones (Galla & Duckworth, 2015).

IMPLICATIONS FOR TREATMENT AND POLICY

Although many incarcerated offenders have engaged in "evil deeds," the vast majority of inmates are not "evil persons." About four in five jail and prison inmates do not score in the psychopathic range on the PCL-R, which is perhaps today's most reliable indicator of "evil."

The theory and research reviewed here regarding moral emotions, moral cognitions, and the capacity for self-control have a number of direct treatment and policy implications. Findings underscore that inmates vary considerably in their capacity for moral emotions, in the degree to which they engage in criminal thinking, and in their capacity for self-control.

These characteristics have been directly linked to the likelihood of recidivism, and each is theoretically amenable to intervention.

Treatment Implications

We have come a long way since the grim conclusions of criminologists in 1970s that "nothing works," based on several highly cited reviews of the treatment literature (Martinson, 1974; Sechrest, White, & Brown, 1979). Since then, due to the development of more clearly articulated theories of change and more sophisticated research methods (e.g., meta-analysis, tighter control over program implementation), research clearly shows that (1) punishment is not effective (Petersilia, 2004; Pratt & Cullen, 2005) unless partnered with effective treatment and incentivized conformity (Cullen & Jonson, 2012), and (2) most treatment—especially CBT-based treatment—works (Cecil, Drapkin, MacKenzie, & Hickman, 2000; Cullen & Gendreau, 2000; Wilson, Gallagher, & MacKenzie, 2000). As Cullen and Gendreau (2001) observed, we need to now move from "nothing works" to "what works." Focusing on malleable predictors (i.e., factors that can be targeted and altered through intervention) of recidivism (e.g., moral emotions, criminogenic cognitions, capacity for self-control) seems a good bet. And here, social and clinical psychologists have an opportunity to make a substantial contribution.

Moral Emotions

From our perspective, restorative justice–inspired programs may be especially well suited for enhancing an adaptive "moral emotional style" among offenders. Restorative justice is a philosophical framework that calls for active participation by the victim, the offender, and the community with the aim of repairing the fabric of the community (Braithwaite, 1989, 2000). But these restorative justice–based interventions can be targeted toward offenders without the participation of their specific victims or communities. For example, the "Impact of Crime" workshop implemented in the adult detention center in Fairfax County, Virginia (Malouf, Youman, Harty, Schaefer, & Tangney, 2013; Folk et al., 2015) emphasizes principles of community, personal responsibility, and reparation. Utilizing cognitive restructuring techniques, caseworkers and group facilitators challenge common distorted ways of thinking about crime, victims, and locus of responsibility. As inmates grapple with issues of responsibility, the question of blame inevitably arises. And so, too, do the emotions of self-blame. Upon reexamining the causes of their legal difficulties and revisiting the circumstances surrounding their offenses and their consequences, many inmates experience new feelings of shame or guilt or both. At the heart of the restorative justice approach is a "guilt inducing, shame reducing" philosophy. Restorative justice approaches (e.g., Maruna, 2001) encourage offenders to take responsibility for their behavior, acknowledge negative consequences, feel guilt for having *done* the wrong thing, empathize with their victims, and act to make amends. But they are ultimately discouraged from feeling shame about *themselves*.

More generally, in the context of more traditional jail-based programs and services (e.g., parenting groups, anger management groups, substance abuse treatment), therapists and group facilitators can help inmates develop a more adaptive moral emotional style by (1) educating inmate clients about the distinction between feelings of guilt about specific behaviors and feelings of shame about the self, (2) encouraging appropriate experiences of guilt and emphasizing associated constructive motivations to repair or make amends, and (3) helping inmate clients recognize and adaptively respond to shame experiences (e.g., Dearing & Tangney, 2011).

Finally, an exciting direction for future research is to examine whether interventions aimed at decreasing defensive responses (e.g., motivational interviewing, acceptance-based therapies) are effective in helping people make constructive use of the pain of shame. The capacity to tolerate distress, to sit with and make use of feelings of shame, may also be a powerful moderator of the degree to which shame results in positive change versus denial and defense, and here mindfulness-based interventions may be especially promising.

Criminogenic Cognitions

As noted above, the development and evaluation of theoretically informed cognitive-behavioral interventions aimed specifically at challenging and reducing criminal thinking are in their infancy. We believe clinical psychologists are especially well placed to develop relatively brief CBT interventions specifically targeting distorted criminogenic thinking.

Self-Control

Despite the evidence that some individuals have higher self-control and that some individuals are better at preventing the need for self-control in the moment, we all inevitably face temptations from our environment. Along these lines, much work has focused on increasing self-control in the moment to overcome these short-term temptations (see Hagger, Wood, Stiff, & Chatzisarantis, 2010, for a meta-analysis). However, one particular individual difference—*beliefs* about self-control—has yielded both short-term and potentially long-term effects on undesirable behaviors. This research indicates that limited-resource beliefs (believing self-control "runs out" after a time) lead to more self-control failures (Job, Dweck, & Walton, 2010), as well as increased daily procrastination and lower achievement even weeks later (Job, Walton, Bernecker, & Dweck, 2015). Finally, although these self-control beliefs appear to be an individual-difference factor, this research also demonstrates that manipulation of these beliefs is a viable and potentially effective intervention.

Recent work on implementation intentions represents another promising line of research relevant to the enhancement of self-control and the curbing of "evil deeds." This research indicates that the specific process of mental contrasting (comparing one's current state with where one wants to be with regard to a specific goal), along with declaring specific implementation intentions (planning very specific "if–then" statements to move toward a certain goal), leads to desirable changes in a wide range of behaviors (Oettingen & Gollwitzer, 2010). Moreover, such implementation intentions have larger effects on changing undesirable behaviors when they are (1) specific (e.g., "*if* I feel my anger rise, *then* I will tell myself to stay calm and not aggress back"), (2) utilized by individuals who have behavioral control problems (e.g., heroin addicts), and (3) utilized in situations that overextend people's capacity to regulate their behavior (e.g., environmental temptations; see Gollwitzer & Sheeran, 2006, for a meta-analysis). This skill can be applied to a wide variety of behaviors and situations and, as such, is relevant to diverse populations, such as offenders who may struggle with self-control in a multitude of arenas.

Implications for Jail and Prison Policies

Research on moral emotions and criminal thinking has implications for more general jail/prison policies and procedures. Aspects of the incarceration experience itself may provoke feelings of shame and humiliation (Dunnegan, 1997; Gilligan, 1996; Smith, 1992), and it has been suggested that, particularly when punishment is perceived as unjust, such feelings of shame can lead to defiance and, paradoxically, an *increase* in criminal behavior (Sherman, 1993). This is especially troubling in light of Indermaur's (1994) finding that fully 90% of offenders view their sentences as unfair! Moreover, one domain of criminal thinking is negative attitudes toward authority (Tangney et al., 2012). Correctional officials can make policy decisions about specific practices (e.g., the manner in which strip searches are conducted, how inmates are addressed) or more general aspects of the jail/prison environment (e.g., "direct supervision" models of incarceration that place deputies in common living areas, as opposed to monitoring inmates down long corridors of peepholes) to minimize the potential for shame and humiliation and to enhance expressions of mutual respect between inmates and correctional staff.

Implications for Judicial Policy

Another area in which basic research on moral emotions has immediate applied implications involves judicial sentencing practices. As it becomes clear that imprisonment is both extremely costly and ineffective at reducing crime (Andrews et al., 1990; Bonta, 1996), judges understandably have begun to search for creative alternatives to traditional sentences. The trend toward "shaming" sentences has gained a good deal of momentum in recent years. Judges across the country are sentencing offenders to parade around in public carrying signs broadcasting their crimes, to post signs on their front lawns warning neighbors of their vices, and to display "drunk driver" bumper stickers on their cars. Other judges have focused on sentencing alternatives based on a restorative justice model (e.g., community service and other forms of reparation), which seem to be designed—at least implicitly—to elicit feelings of guilt for the offense and its consequences, rather than feelings of shame and humiliation about oneself. In seeking less costly and potentially more effective alternatives, judges have pretty much been operating in an empirical vacuum. Regarding shaming sentences in particular, there exist no systematic data on the effectiveness or nonmonetary costs of such efforts to publicly humiliate offenders, but our findings and those of others (see Jones, 2014, for a review) strongly suggest that this is a misguided approach to alternative sentencing. Rather than encouraging people to accept responsibility and make reparations, shame often provokes anger, aggression, denial, and externalization of blame.

CONCLUSIONS

In this chapter, we have distinguished between evil persons and evil deeds, citing data showing that the large majority of incarcerated offenders are not "evil" psychopaths beyond the reach of treatment. Rehabilitation efforts are best directed toward malleable (vs. static) characteristics that predict recidivism versus postrelease success. We have focused on three key morally relevant characteristics: moral emotions of shame and guilt, criminogenic cognitions, and the capacity for self-control. There are, no doubt, many more opportunities for synergy at the interface of psychology and criminology to enhance treatment of the high-risk, multineed, underserved individuals who cycle through our criminal justice system, with the ultimate benefits of reclaiming lives and improving public safety.

NOTE

1. Although our initial impression was that a population-specific version of the TOSCA would be necessary for jail inmates, our experience has been that inmates respond reliably to most psychological self-report measures when presented verbally by an interviewer or when presented via computer with both audio and visual supports. Reading comprehension, not ability to understand and respond to the content, can be a limiting factor for some.

REFERENCES

Allan, S., Gilbert, P., & Goss, K. (1994). An exploration of shame measures: II. Psychopathology. *Personality and Individual Differences, 17,* 719–722.

Andrews, D. A., & Bonta, J. (2010). *The psychology of criminal conduct* (5th ed.). Cincinnati, OH: Anderson.

Andrews, D. A., Zinger, I., Hoge, R. D., Bonta, J., Gendreau, P., & Cullen, F. T. (1990). Does correctional treatment work? A clinically relevant and psychologically informed meta-analysis. *Criminology, 28,* 369–403.

Barrett, K. C. (1995). A functionalist approach to shame and guilt. In J. P. Tangney & K. W. Fischer (Eds.), *Self-conscious emotions: The psychology of shame, guilt, embarrassment, and pride* (pp. 25–63). New York: Guilford Press.

Baumeister, R. F., Heatherton, T. F., & Tice, D. M. (1994). *Losing control: How and why people fail at self-regulation.* San Diego, CA: Academic Press.

Baumeister, R. F., Stillwell, A. M., & Heatherton, T. F. (1994). Guilt: An interpersonal approach. *Psychological Bulletin, 115,* 243–267.

Baumeister, R. F., Stillwell, A. M., & Heatherton, T. F. (1995a). Interpersonal aspects of guilt: Evidence from narrative studies. In J. P. Tangney & K. W. Fischer (Eds.), *Self-conscious emotions: The psychology of shame, guilt, embarrassment, and pride* (pp. 255–273). New York: Guilford Press.

Baumeister, R. F., Stillwell, A. M., & Heatherton, T. F. (1995b). Personal narratives about guilt: Role in action control and interpersonal relationships. *Basic and Applied Social Psychology, 17,* 173–198.

Blair, R. J. R. (2003). Neurobiological basis of psychopathy. *British Journal of Psychiatry, 182,* 5–7.

Blair, R. J. R. (2005). Applying a cognitive neuroscience perspective to the disorder of psychopathy. *Development and Psychopathology, 17,* 865–891.

Blasi, A. (1980). Bridging moral cognition and moral action: A critical review of the literature. *Psychological Bulletin, 88,* 1–45.

Blatt, S. (1974). Levels of object representation in anaclitic and introjective depression. *Psychoanalytic Study of the Child, 29,* 107–157.

Bonta, J. (1996). Risk-needs assessment and treatment. In A. T. Harland (Ed.), *Choosing correctional options that work: Defining the demand and evaluating the supply* (pp. 18–32). Thousand Oaks, CA: Sage.

Bradshaw, J. (1988). *Healing the shame that binds you.* Deerfield Beach, FL: Health Communications.

Braithwaite, J. (1989). *Crime, shame and reintegration.* Melbourne, Australia: Cambridge University Press.

Braithwaite, J. (2000). Shame and criminal justice. *Canadian Journal of Criminology, 42,* 281–298.

Bureau of Justice Statistics. (2014). *Jail inmates at midyear 2013—Statistical tables* (Publication No. NCJ 245350). Washington, DC: U.S. Government Printing Office.

Bush, J., Glick, B., & Taymans, J. (1997). *Thinking for a Change: Integrated cognitive behavior change program.* Washington, DC: U.S. Department of Justice, National Institute of Corrections.

Caudy, M. S., Folk, J. B., Stuewig, J. B., Wooditch, A., Martinez, A., Maass, S., et al. (2015). Does substance misuse moderate the relationship between criminal thinking and recidivism? *Journal of Criminal Justice, 43,* 12–19.

Cecil, D. K., Drapkin, D. A., MacKenzie, D. L., & Hickman, L. J. (2000). The effectiveness of adult basic education and life-skills programs in reducing recidivism: A review and assessment of the research. *Journal of Correctional Education, 51*, 207–226.

Cullen, F., & Gendreau, P. (2000). Assessing correctional rehabilitation: Policy, practice and prospects. In J. Horney, J. Martin, D. L. MacKenzie, R. Peterson, & D. Rosenbaum (Eds.), *Policies, processes and decisions of the criminal justice system* (pp. 109–175). Washington, DC: U.S. Department of Justice, National Institute of Justice.

Cullen, F., & Gendreau, P. (2001). From nothing works to what works: Changing professional ideology in the 21st century. *Prison Journal, 81*, 312–337.

Cullen, F. T., & Jonson, C. L. (2012). *Correctional theory: Context and consequences*. Thousand Oaks, CA: Sage.

Dearing, R. L., Stuewig, J., & Tangney, J. P. (2005). On the importance of distinguishing shame from guilt: Relations to problematic alcohol and drug use. *Addictive Behaviors, 30*, 1392–1404.

Dearing, R. L., & Tangney, J. P. (2011). Shame: An inevitable challenge in the therapy hour. In R. L. Dearing & J. P. Tangney (Eds.), *Shame in the therapy hour* (pp. 3–19). Washington DC: American Psychological Association.

Debowska, A., Boduszek, D., Hyland, P., & Goodson, S. (2014). Biological correlates of psychopathy: A brief review. *Mental Health Review Journal, 19*, 110–123.

De Hooge, I. E., Breugelmans, S. M., & Zeelenberg, M. (2008). Not so ugly after all: When shame acts as a commitment device. *Journal of Personality and Social Psychology, 95*, 933–943.

De Hooge, I. E., Zeelenberg, M., & Breugelmans, S. M. (2010). Restore and protect motivations following shame. *Cognition and Emotion, 24*, 111–127.

Denson, T. F., DeWall, C. N., & Finkel, E. J. (2012). Self-control and aggression. *Current Directions in Psychological Science, 21*, 20–25.

de Ridder, D. T. D., Lensvelt-Mulders, G., Finkenauer, C., Stok, F. M., & Baumeister, R. F. (2012). Taking stock of self-control: A meta-analysis of how trait self-control relates to a wide range of behaviors. *Personality and Social Psychology Review, 16*, 76–99.

Dunnegan, S. W. (1997). Violence, trauma and substance abuse. *Journal of Psychoactive Drugs, 29*, 345–351.

Ellis, A. (1962). *Reason and emotion in psychotherapy*. New York: Lyle Stuart.

Fergus, T. A., Valentiner, D. P., McGrath, P. B., & Jencius, S. (2010). Shame- and guilt-proneness: Relationships with anxiety disorder symptoms in a clinical sample. *Journal of Anxiety Disorders, 24*, 811–815.

Ferguson, T. J., Stegge, H., Miller, E. R., & Olsen, M. E. (1999). Guilt, shame, and symptoms in children. *Developmental Psychology, 35*, 347–357.

Folk, J. B., Blasko, B. L., Warden, R., Schaefer, K., Ferssizidis, P., Stuewig, J., et al. (2015). Feasibility and acceptability of an impact of crime group intervention with jail inmates. *Victims and Offenders*, 1–19. Available at *www.tandfonline.com/doi/abs/10.1080/15564886.2014.982777#preview.*

Freud, S. (1955). Notes upon a case of obsessional neurosis. In J. Strachey (Ed. & Trans.), *The standard edition of the complete psychological works of Sigmund Freud* (Vol. 10, pp. 155–318). London: Hogarth Press. (Original work published 1909)

Freud, S. (1957). Mourning and melancholia. In J. Strachey (Ed. & Trans.), *The standard edition of the complete psychological works of Sigmund Freud* (Vol. 14, pp. 243–258). London: Hogarth Press. (Original work published 1917)

Freud, S. (1961a). The dissolution of the Oedipus complex. In J. Strachey (Ed. & Trans.), *The standard edition of the complete psychological works of Sigmund Freud* (Vol. 19, pp. 173–182). London: Hogarth Press. (Original work published 1924)

Freud, S. (1961b). The id and the ego. In J. Strachey (Ed. & Trans.), *The standard edition of the complete psychological works of Sigmund Freud* (Vol. 19, pp. 12–66). London: Hogarth Press. (Original work published 1923)

Freud, S. (1961c). Civilization and its discontents. In J. Strachey (Ed. & Trans.), *The standard edition of the complete psychological works of Sigmund Freud* (Vol. 21, pp. 59–145). London: Hogarth Press. (Original work published 1930)

Friese, M., & Hofmann, W. (2009). Control me or I will control you: Impulses, trait self-control, and the guidance of behavior. *Journal of Research in Personality, 43*, 795–805.

Gailliot, M. T., & Baumeister, R. F. (2007). Self-regulation and sexual restraint: Dispositionally and temporarily poor self-regulatory abilities contribute to failures at restraining sexual behavior. *Personality and Social Psychology Bulletin, 33*, 173–186.

Galla, B. M., & Duckworth, A. L. (2015). More than resisting temptation: Beneficial habits mediate the relationship between self-control and positive life outcomes. *Journal of Personality and Social Psychology, 109*(3), 508–525.

Gausel, N., & Leach, C. W. (2011). Concern for self-image and social image in the management of moral failure: Rethinking shame. *European Journal of Social Psychology, 41*, 468–478.

Gausel, N., Leach, C. W., Vignoles, V. L., & Brown, R. (2012). Defend or repair?: Explaining responses to an in-group moral failure by disentangling feelings of shame, rejection, and inferiority. *Journal of Personality and Social Psychology, 102*, 941–960.

Gilbert, P., & Irons, C. (2005). Focused therapies and compassionate mind training for shame and self-attacking. In P. Gilbert (Ed.), *Compassion: Conceptualisations, research and use in psychotherapy* (pp. 263–325). New York: Routledge.

Gilligan, J. (1996). Exploring shame in special settings: A psychotherapeutic study. In C. Cordess & M. Cox (Eds.), *Forensic psychotherapy: Crime, psychodynamics and the offender patient: Vol. 2. Mainly practice* (pp. 475–489). London, UK: Jessica Kingsley.

Gollwitzer, P. M., & Sheeran, P. (2006). Implementation intentions and goal achievement: A meta-analysis of effects and processes. *Advances in Experimental Social Psychology, 38*, 69–119.

Hagger, M. S., Wood, C., Stiff, C., & Chatzisarantis, N. L. D. (2010). Ego depletion and the strength model of self-control: A meta-analysis. *Psychological Bulletin, 136*, 495–525.

Haney, C., Banks, C., & Zimbardo, P. (1973). Interpersonal dynamics in a simulated prison. *International Journal of Criminology and Penology, 1*, 69–97.

Hanson, R. K., & Tangney, J. P. (1995). The Test of Self-Conscious Affect—Socially

Deviant Populations (TOSCA-SD). Ottawa, Ontario, Canada: Department of the Solicitor General of Canada.

Harder, D. W. (1995). Shame and guilt assessment, and relationships of shame- and guilt-proneness to psychopathology. In J. P. Tangney & K. W. Fischer (Eds.), *Self-conscious emotions: The psychology of shame, guilt, embarrassment, and pride* (pp. 368–392). New York: Guilford Press.

Harder, D. W., Cutler, L., & Rockart, L. (1992). Assessment of shame and guilt and their relationship to psychopathology. *Journal of Personality Assessment, 59*, 584–604.

Hare, R. D. (1991). *The Hare Psychopathy Checklist—Revised*. Toronto, Ontario, Canada: MultiHealth Systems.

Hartmann, E., & Loewenstein, R. (1962). Notes on the superego. *Psychoanalytic Study of the Child, 17*, 42–81.

Hoblitzelle, W. (1987). Attempts to measure and differentiate shame and guilt: The relation between shame and depression. In H. B. Lewis (Ed.), *The role of shame in symptom formation* (pp. 207–235). Hillsdale, NJ: Erlbaum.

Hofmann, W., Baumeister, R. F., Förster, G., & Vohs, K. D. (2012). Everyday temptations: An experience sampling study of desire, conflict, and self-control. *Journal of Personality and Social Psychology, 102*, 1318–1335.

Hofmann, W., & Kotabe, H. (2012). A general model of preventive and interventive self-control. *Social and Personality Psychology Compass, 6*, 707–722.

Howell, A. J., Turowski, J. B., & Buro, K. (2012). Guilt, empathy, and apology. *Personality and Individual Differences, 53*, 917–922.

Indermaur, D. (1994). Offenders' perceptions of sentencing. *Australian Psychologist, 29*, 140–144.

Job, V., Dweck, C. S., & Walton, G. M. (2010). Ego depletion—Is it all in your head?: Implicit theories about willpower affect self-regulation. *Psychological Science, 21*, 1686–1693.

Job, V., Walton, G. M., Bernecker, K., & Dweck, C. S. (2015). Implicit theories about willpower predict self-regulation and grades in everyday life. *Journal of Personality and Social Psychology, 108*, 637–647.

Joireman, J. (2004). Empathy and the self-absorption paradox: II. Self-rumination and self-reflection as mediators between shame, guilt, and empathy. *Self and Identity, 3*, 225–238.

Jones, C. M. (2014). Why persistent offenders cannot be shamed into behaving. *Journal of Offender Rehabilitation, 53*, 153–170.

Jones, W. H., & Kugler, K. (1993). Interpersonal correlates of the Guilt Inventory. *Journal of Personality Assessment, 61*, 246–258.

Kahan, D. M. (1997). Ignorance of law *is* an excuse—But only for the virtuous. *Michigan Law Review, 96*, 127–154.

Kiehl, K. A. (2006). A cognitive neuroscience perspective on psychopathy: Evidence for paralimbic system dysfunction. *Psychiatry Research, 142*, 107–128.

Kiehl, K. A., Smith, A. M., Hare, R. D., Mendrek, A., Forster, B. B., Brink, J., et al. (2001). Limbic abnormalities in affective processing by criminal psychopaths as revealed by functional magnetic resonance imaging. *Biological Psychiatry, 50*, 677–684.

Kim, S., Thibodeau, R., & Jorgensen, R. S. (2011). Shame, guilt, and depressive symptoms: A meta-analytic review. *Psychological Bulletin, 137*, 68–96.

Kohlberg, L. (1976). Moral stages and moralization: The cognitive-developmental approach. In T. Lichona (Ed.), *Moral development and behavior: Theory, research, and social issues* (pp. 31–53). New York: Holt, Rinehart, & Winston.

Leith, K. P., & Baumeister, R. F. (1998). Empathy, shame, guilt, and narratives of interpersonal conflicts: Guilt-prone people are better at perspective taking. *Journal of Personality, 66*, 1–37.

Lewis, H. B. (1971). *Shame and guilt in neurosis.* New York: International Universities Press.

Lipsey, M., Landenberger, N. A., & Wilson, S. J. (2007). Effects of cognitive-behavioral programs for criminal offenders: A systematic review. *Campbell Systematic Reviews, 3*(6), 1–30.

Lutwak, N., Panish, J. B., Ferrari, J. R., & Razzino, B. E. (2001). Shame and guilt and their relationship to positive expectations and anger expressiveness. *Adolescence, 36*, 641–653.

MacKinnon, D. P., Fairchild, A. J., & Fritz, M. S. (2007). Mediation analysis. *Annual Review of Psychology, 58*, 593–614.

MacKinnon, D. P., Krull, J. L., & Lockwood, C. M. (2000). Equivalence of the mediation, confounding and suppression effect. *Prevention Science, 1*, 173–181.

Malouf, E. T., Schaefer, K. E., Witt, E. A., Moore, K. E., Stuewig, J., & Tangney, J. P. (2014). The brief self-control scale predicts jail inmates' recidivism, substance dependence, and post-release adjustment. *Personality and Social Psychology Bulletin, 40*, 334–347.

Malouf, E., Youman, K., Harty, L., Schaefer, K., & Tangney, J. P. (2013). Accepting guilt and abandoning shame: A positive approach to addressing moral emotions among high-risk, multineed individuals. In T. Kashdan & J. Ciarrochi (Eds.), *Mindfulness, acceptance, and positive psychology: The seven foundations of well-being* (pp. 215–239). Oakland, CA: Context Press.

Marques, J. K., Wiederanders, M., Day, D. M., Nelson, C., & Van Ommeren, A. (2005). Effects of a relapse prevention program on sexual recidivism: Final results from California's Sex Offender Treatment and Evaluation Project (SOTEP). *Sexual Abuse: A Journal of Research and Treatment, 17*, 79–107.

Martinez, A. G., Stuewig, J., & Tangney, J. P. (2014). Can perspective-taking reduce crime?: Examining a pathway through empathic concern and guilt proneness. *Personality and Social Psychology Bulletin, 40*, 1659–1667.

Martinson, R. (1974). What works?: Questions and answers about prison reform. *Public Interest, 35*, 22–54

Maruna, S. (2001). *Making good: How ex-convicts reform and rebuild their lives.* Washington, DC: American Psychological Association.

McLaughlin, D. E. (2002). Posttraumatic stress disorder symptoms and self-conscious affect among battered women. *Dissertation Abstracts International, Section B: The Sciences and Engineering, 62*, 4470.

Meehan, M. A., O'Connor, L. E., Berry, J. W., Weiss, J., Morrison, A., & Acampora, A. (1996). Guilt, shame, and depression in clients in recovery from addiction. *Journal of Psychoactive Drugs, 28*, 125–134.

Milgram, S. (1963). Behavioral study of obedience. *Journal of Abnormal and Social Psychology, 67*, 371–378.

Milgram, S. (1974). *Obedience to authority: An experimental view.* New York: Harper & Row.

Mills, J. F., & Kroner, D. G. (1997). The Criminal Sentiments Scale: Predictive validity in a sample of violent and sex offenders. *Journal of Clinical Psychology, 53,* 399–404.

Moore, K., Stuewig, J., & Tangney, J. (2013). Jail inmates' perceived and anticipated stigma: Implications for post-release functioning. *Self and Identity, 12,* 527–547.

Morgan, R. D., & Flora, D. B. (2002). Group psychotherapy with incarcerated offenders: A research synthesis. *Group Dynamics: Theory, Research, and Practice, 6,* 203–218.

Muris, P., Meesters, C., Bouwman, L., & Notermans, S. (2015). Relations among behavioral inhibition, shame and guilt proneness, and anxiety disorders symptoms in non-clinical children. *Child Psychiatry and Human Development, 46,* 209–216.

National Institute of Corrections. (1996). *Cognitive Interventions Program: Think.* Washington, DC: U.S. Department of Justice, National Institute of Corrections Information Center.

Oettingen, G., & Gollwitzer, P. M. (2010). Strategies of setting and implementing goals: Mental contrasting and implementation intentions. In J. E. Maddux & J. P. Tangney (Eds.), *Social psychological foundations of clinical psychology* (pp. 114–135). New York: Guilford Press.

Petersilia, J. (2004). What works in prisoner reentry?: Reviewing and questioning the evidence. *Federal Probation, 68,* 4–8.

Polaschek, D. L. (2014). Adult criminals with psychopathy: Common beliefs about treatability and change have little empirical support. *Current Directions in Psychological Science, 23,* 296–301.

Potter-Efron, R. (2002). *Shame, guilt, and alcoholism: Treatment issues in clinical practice* (2nd ed.). New York: Haworth Press.

Pratt, T. C., & Cullen, F. T. (2005). Assessing macro-level predictors and theories of crime: A meta-analysis. In M. Tonry (Ed.), *Crime and justice: A review of research* (Vol. 32, pp. 373–450). Chicago: University of Chicago Press.

Robinson, R., Roberts, W. L., Strayer, J., & Koopman, R. (2007). Empathy and emotional responsiveness in delinquent and non-delinquent adolescents. *Social Development, 16,* 555–579.

Ross, R. R., & Fabiano, E. A. (1985). *Time to Think: A cognitive model of delinquency prevention and offender rehabilitation.* Johnson City, TN: Institute of Social Sciences and Arts.

Sanftner, J. L., Barlow, D. H., Marschall, D. E., & Tangney, J. P. (1995). The relation of shame and guilt to eating disorders symptomotology. *Journal of Social and Clinical Psychology, 14,* 315–324.

Sechrest, L., White, S. O., & Brown, E. D. (Eds.). (1979). *The rehabilitation of criminal offenders: Problems and prospects.* Washington, DC: National Academy of Sciences.

Sherman, L. W. (1993). Defiance, deterrence, and irrelevance: A theory of the criminal sanction. *Journal of Research in Crime and Delinquency, 30,* 445–473.

Simourd, D. J., & Van De Ven, J. (1999). Assessment of criminal attitudes:

Criterion-related validity of the Criminal Sentiments Scale—Modified and Pride in Delinquency Scale. *Criminal Justice and Behavior, 26*, 90–106.

Smith, J. S. (1992). Humiliation, degradation and the criminal justice system. *Journal of Primary Prevention, 12*, 209–222.

Stuewig, J., & McCloskey, L. (2005). The impact of maltreatment on adolescent shame and guilt: Psychological routes to depression and delinquency. *Child Maltreatment, 10*, 324–336.

Stuewig, J., Tangney, J. P., Heigel, C., Harty, L., & McCloskey, L. (2010). Shaming, blaming, and maiming: Functional links among the moral emotions, externalization of blame, and aggression. *Journal of Research in Personality, 44*, 91–102.

Stuewig, J., Tangney, J. P., Kendall, S., Folk, J. B., Meyer, C. R., & Dearing, R. L. (2015). Children's proneness to shame and guilt predict risky and illegal behaviors in young adulthood. *Child Psychiatry and Human Development, 46*, 217–227.

Sykes, G. M., & Matza, D. (1957). Techniques of neutralization: A theory of delinquency. *American Sociological Review, 22*, 664–670.

Tangney, J. P. (1991). Moral affect: The good, the bad, and the ugly. *Journal of Personality and Social Psychology, 61*, 598–607.

Tangney, J. P. (1994). The mixed legacy of the super-ego: Adaptive and maladaptive aspects of shame and guilt. In J. M. Masling & R. F. Bornstein (Eds.), *Empirical perspectives on object relations theory* (pp. 1–28). Washington, DC: American Psychological Association.

Tangney, J. P. (1996). Conceptual and methodological issues in the assessment of shame and guilt. *Behaviour Research and Therapy, 34*, 741–754.

Tangney, J. P., Baumeister, R. F., & Boone, A. L. (2004). High self-control predicts good adjustment, less pathology, better grades, and interpersonal success. *Journal of Personality, 72*, 271–324.

Tangney, J. P., & Dearing, R. (2002). *Shame and guilt*. New York: Guilford Press.

Tangney, J. P., Mashek, D., & Stuewig, J. (2007). Working at the social–clinical–community–criminology interface: The George Mason University inmate study. *Journal of Social and Clinical Psychology, 26*, 1–21.

Tangney, J. P., Stuewig, J., Furukawa, E., Kopelovich, S., Meyer, P. J., & Cosby, B. (2012). Reliability, validity, and predictive utility of the 25-item Criminogenic Cognitions Scale (CCS). *Criminal Justice and Behavior, 39*, 1340–1360.

Tangney, J. P., Stuewig, J., & Martinez, A. G. (2014). Two faces of shame: Understanding shame and guilt in the prediction of jail inmates' recidivism. *Psychological Science, 25*, 799–805.

Tangney, J. P., Stuewig, J., & Mashek, D. J. (2007). Moral emotions and moral behavior. *Annual Review of Psychology, 58*, 345–372.

Tangney, J. P., Stuewig, J., Mashek, D., & Hastings, M. (2011). Assessing jail inmates' proneness to shame and guilt: Feeling bad about the behavior or the self? *Criminal Justice and Behavior, 38*, 710–734.

Tangney, J. P., Wagner, P. E., Barlow, D. H., Marschall, D. E., & Gramzow, R. (1996). The relation of shame and guilt to constructive vs. destructive responses to anger across the lifespan. *Journal of Personality and Social Psychology, 70*, 797–809.

Tangney, J. P., Wagner, P. E., Fletcher, C., & Gramzow, R. (1992). Shamed into anger?: The relation of shame and guilt to anger and self-reported aggression. *Journal of Personality and Social Psychology, 62,* 669–675.

Tangney, J. P., Wagner, P. E., & Gramzow, R. (1992). Proneness to shame, proneness to guilt, and psychopathology. *Journal of Abnormal Psychology, 103,* 469–478.

Taxman, F. S., Rhodes, A. G., & Dumenci, L. (2011). Construct and predictive validity of criminal thinking scales. *Criminal Justice and Behavior, 38,* 174–187.

Teyber, E., McClure, F. H., & Weathers, R. (2011). Shame in families: Transmission across generations. In R. L. Dearing & J. P. Tangney (Eds.), *Shame in the therapy hour* (pp. 137–166). Washington, DC: American Psychological Association.

Tibbetts, S. G. (1997). Shame and rational choice in offending decisions. *Criminal Justice and Behavior, 24,* 234–255.

Tilghman-Osborne, C., Cole, D. A., Felton, J. W., & Ciesla, J. A. (2008). Relation of guilt, shame, behavioral and characterological self-blame to depressive symptoms in adolescents over time. *Journal of Social and Clinical Psychology, 27,* 809–842.

Tooke, W. S., & Ickes, W. (1988). A measure of adherence to conventional morality. *Journal of Social and Clinical Psychology, 6,* 310–334.

Treeby, M., & Bruno, R. (2012). Shame- and guilt-proneness: Divergent implications for problematic alcohol use and drinking to cope with anxiety and depression symptomatology. *Personality and Individual Differences, 53,* 613–617.

Walters, G. D. (2012). Criminal thinking and recidivism: Meta-analytic evidence on the predictive and incremental validity of the Psychological Inventory of Criminal Thinking Styles (PICTS). *Aggression and Violent Behavior, 17,* 272–278.

Walters, G. D. (2014). Relationships among race, education, criminal thinking, and recidivism: Moderator and mediator effects. *Assessment, 21,* 82–91.

Weiss, J. (1993). *How psychotherapy works.* New York: Guilford Press.

Wilson, D. B., Gallagher, C., & Mackenzie, D. L. (2000). A meta-analysis of corrections-based education, vocation, and work programs for adult offenders. *Journal of Research in Crime and Delinquency, 37,* 347–368.

Wormith, J. S., Althouse, R., Simpson, M., Reitzel, L. R., Fagan, T. J., & Morgan, R. D. (2007). The rehabilitation and reintegration of offenders: The current landscape and some future directions for correctional psychology. *Criminal Justice and Behavior, 34,* 879–892.

Zlotnick, C., Johnson, J., & Najavits, L. M. (2009). Randomized controlled pilot study of cognitive-behavioral therapy in a sample of incarcerated women with substance use disorder and PTSD. *Behavior Therapy, 40,* 325–336.

CHAPTER 15

Dishonesty Explained
What Leads Moral People to Act Immorally

Francesca Gino and Dan Ariely

> There is no well-defined boundary between honesty and dishonesty. The frontiers of one blend with the outside limits of the other, and he who attempts to tread this dangerous ground may be sometimes in one domain and sometimes in the other.
> —O. HENRY, *Rolling Stones* (1912)

The accounting scandals and the collapse of billion-dollar companies at the beginning of the 21st century have forever changed the business landscape. These cases of corporate corruption add to a long list of instances of unethical behavior in organizations and society more broadly across a variety of settings (e.g., Frank et al., 2003): Employees violate company rules, workers sabotage their peers, consumers shoplift, students cheat on exams, citizens evade taxes, and managers overstate firm performance to shareholders. Such unethical behaviors are costly to organizations and economic systems more broadly (Graham, Litan, & Sukhtankar, 2002; Weber Kurke, & Pentico, 2003). For instance, organizations typically lose 5% of their revenues to fraud each year (Association of Certified

Fraud Examiners, 2012), a projected global fraud loss of more than $3.5 trillion. Between 40 and 50% of organizations do not recover any of their losses caused by fraud.

Dishonesty is not limited to prominent examples of one person or organization causing harm to many. Although less well publicized, the small transgressions of large numbers of people have at least as significant an impact on our daily lives. For instance, average workers commit occupational fraud that adds up to an estimated $994 billion in annual losses (Association of Certified Fraud Examiners, 2008). An estimated $16 billion in losses to the U.S. retail industry are due to the purchase, use, and then return of worn clothing (Speights & Hilinski, 2005). These losses are not caused by just a few people who regularly revolve their entire wardrobes, but by many individuals who return a single shirt or sweater after wearing it.

In fact, an increasing amount of empirical evidence in the social psychology and management literatures demonstrates that dishonesty often results not from the actions of a few people who cheat a lot but from the actions of a lot of people who cheat a little (Mazar, Amir, & Ariely, 2008; Gino, Ayal, & Ariely, 2009). When given the opportunity to act dishonestly, many individuals do cross ethical boundaries, if only by a small amount rather than to the maximum extent possible (Ayal & Gino, 2011; Gino et al., 2009; Mazar et al., 2008). For example, Mazar et al. (2008) conducted a series of experiments in which participants could cheat on tests by overreporting their performance with low odds of being caught: Participants only cheated in 6–20% of the possible instances in which they could cheat.

Given the economic and social importance of such dishonesty, scholars from various fields have begun to examine the motives behind it. In this chapter, we discuss what recent findings from the social-psychological and management literatures have to teach us about why unethical behavior is so prevalent in society and how they can help us understand the subtle ways in which we fail to follow our moral compass.

In reviewing various streams of research, we discuss different perspectives in the literature regarding the main causes of individuals' unethical behavior and provide a framework that centers on the number of times people face an opportunity to behave dishonestly. A first stream of research has focused on one single choice: whether to cheat or not for self-interested reasons when one faces this decision only once. A second stream of research has examined people's choices and behavior over two points in time when they could behave dishonestly. Finally, a third stream of research has focused on a longer term, examining people's actions over multiple opportunities to act dishonestly. We end by discussing an old but still existent debate on whether unethical behavior is the result of one's personality, the situation, or both.

ONE OPPORTUNITY TO ACT DISHONESTLY: SELF-CONCEPT MAINTENANCE AND THE "FUDGE FACTOR"

Research suggests that people lie and cheat on a daily basis, much more often than they care to admit (DePaulo et al., 1996; Fischbacher & Follmi-Heusi, 2013; Gino et al., 2009; Mazar et al., 2008; Schweitzer, Ordóñez, & Douma, 2004). For example, in one study, participants were paid according to the number of simple arithmetic problems they solved. When payment was based entirely on participants' reports of their performances and fudging of the numbers could not be linked to any individual, participants inflated their performances by 15% on average (Mazar et al., 2008). Employing a different paradigm, Fischbacher and Follmi-Heusi (2013) examined the extent of lying in a private dice game. In the study, participants were paid according to their reports of a roll of a die, with a higher payoff for higher rolled numbers. Because participants were able to cheat by reporting higher numbers and to receive larger payments without apparent risk of exposure, 40% of them lied on this task. Although participants were able to act dishonestly for monetary rewards without being caught, only 22% behaved unethically to the full extent. Shalvi, Dana, Handgraaf, and De Dreu (2011) found similar results: Only 20% of participants lied to the full extent in a similar dice game. Taken together, these studies suggest that when given the opportunity to behave dishonestly, many individuals do cross ethical boundaries, if only by "a little bit" rather than to the maximum extent possible.

But why do people cheat just a little? Research in social psychology has consistently demonstrated that people strive to maintain a positive self-concept both privately and publicly (Adler, 1930; Allport, 1955; Jones, 1973; Kruger & Dunning, 1999; Rogers, 1959; Rosenberg, 1979). Social identity theorists such as Schlenker (1982) and Tajfel (1982) have argued that people want to feel good about themselves and strive to maintain a positive self-image, even when doing so requires a degree of self-deception, pretense, or guile. Examples of the biases that allow us to hold on to a positive self-image include our ability to embrace successes as our own and reject failures as circumstantial (Hastorf, Schneider, & Polefka, 1970; Miller & Ross, 1975; Moore, 2007; Moore, Swift, Sharek, & Gino, 2010; Swift, Moore, Sharek, & Gino, 2013), as well as the illusion of control (Langer, 1975; Langer & Roth, 1975; see also Gino, Sharek, & Moore, 2011), which leads us to believe that we can influence chance events and attain better outcomes as compared with others (Alicke, 1985; Brown, 1986; Messick, Bloom, Boldizar, & Samuelson, 1985). Moreover, most of us are quite confident we can perform better than average across various tests and tasks (Alicke, Klotz, Breitenbecher, Yurak, & Vredenburg, 1995, Klar, 2002; Klar & Gilady, 1997; Moore, 2007). Related research has examined the need to maintain a positive self-concept with regard to one's moral self-image, showing that people typically attach high value to honesty and strongly believe in their own morality (Greenwald 1980; Sanitioso, Kunda, & Fong, 1990).

So, how can people maintain their positive self-concept while also benefit from cheating in situations in which they face only one opportunity to act dishonestly? In addressing this very question, Mazar et al. (2008) suggest that people act dishonestly to benefit in self-interested ways, but only up to a point at which they would not need to alter their image of themselves as honest individuals. More specifically, Mazar et al. (2008) identify self-concept maintenance as an important internal explanation for inhibiting dishonesty. People value honesty as an important part of their self-concept and devote effort to maintaining it (Greenwald, 1980). Self-concept can be defined as "a mental representation capturing our views and beliefs about ourselves" (Kenrick, Neuberg, & Cialdini, 2010). In six laboratory experiments, Mazar and colleagues (2008) provide evidence that self-concept maintenance is associated with honest behavior, even in situations in which dishonesty would have been undetected. For example, making moral standards salient to participants by either having them recall the Ten Commandments or sign an honor code inhibited dishonesty. Mazar and colleagues (2008) propose that a small amount of cheating "flies under the radar" (p. 639). In other words, people do not update their self-concept when engaging in minor acts of dishonesty. The authors assume there is a threshold beneath which being dishonest does not affect the self-concept, what they call the "fudge factor."

Internal processes and values that can determine the level of people's fudge factor are often grounded in socialization processes. Internalized values (e.g., being honest or generous toward others) and societal norms (e.g., behaving in appropriate ways such as being polite toward others) function as a benchmark against which people compare their behavior (Henrich et al., 2001). Compliance with these values and norms results in internal "rewards" (e.g., feeling good about yourself), whereas noncompliance results in internal "punishment" (e.g., feeling bad about yourself). Evidence for this internal punishment and reward system is provided by brain-imaging studies (De Quervain et al., 2004; Rilling et al., 2002). By looking at brain regions with functional magnetic resonance imaging (fMRI) that are activated in punishment-and-reward situations, the authors concluded that these regions were also activated by norm compliance (i.e., situations in which people behaved in ways consistent with accepted social norms, such as cooperating) and noncompliance (i.e., situations in which people behaved in ways inconsistent with accepted social norms). The internal punishment-and-reward system seems to be involved in norm-related behavior (e.g., acting in a fair or cooperative way in situations in which doing so is expected).

The threshold level of each person's fudge factor is influenced by other factors that can lead a person to view dishonest behavior as legitimate. One such factor is observing desired counterfactuals, namely, possible alternatives to events that have already occurred (Shalvi, Dana, et al., 2011; Shalvi, Handgraaf, & De Dreu, 2011). Counterfactual statements convey both the actual behavior and the hypothetical action; for instance, with the statement "If Dan had stopped by the grocery store, he would have arrived home later," one could highlight the outcome of an action that a person could have taken in the past (but did not). Thinking about and observing desired counterfactuals affects behavior (Kahneman & Varey, 1990; Morris & Moore, 2000).

In a cleverly designed experiment, Shalvi, Dana, et al. (2011) created a situation in which a participant could behave dishonestly without being caught. Participants had to throw a die underneath a cup. The experimenters made a small hole in the bottom of the cup through which only the participant could see the throw. Individual participants in one group had to throw the die three times and were instructed to remember and report the first throw. The participants were told that the other throws were intended to show that the experimenters did not manipulate the die (i.e., that the die was fair); in reality, this design offered the opportunity to present desired counterfactuals (e.g., obtaining a higher number on the second or third throw and thus earning more money by reporting it as if it were the outcome of the first throw). Participants in a second group could only throw the die once. Participants in both groups were told they would be paid the number of the first throw in Swiss francs at the end of the experiment. To eliminate external pressure to be honest, both the die throw and the claimed reward were completely anonymous.

Due to this design, it was not possible to investigate individual differences in behavior, but it was possible to draw inferences on the overall behavior of the sample. If all participants were to report their first throw honestly, no significant differences in die results would be expected between the two groups, and the expected distribution of the reported outcomes would be uniform. In reality, participants in the group that observed two more throws to verify the die reported significantly higher die results than participants who only threw the die once, a finding that seems to confirm the hypothesis that observing desired counterfactuals attenuates the degree to which people perceive dishonest behavior as unethical, which enhances dishonesty.

This finding is in line with the concept of "ethical maneuvering" (Shalvi, Dana, et al., 2011), or the tendency for people to run an internal cost–benefit analysis that leads them to view some lies as more legitimate than others. When faced with an opportunity to cheat, people employ internal mechanisms that assess contextual factors and determine how certain actions would affect their self-concepts. Ethical maneuvering refers to this process of making trade-offs between material self-interest and self-concept maintenance (Shalvi, Dana, et al., 2011). If it is true that people seek compromises when making ethical decisions, then they should avoid lies to a large extent because such lies would not be compatible with an "honest person" self-view. Consistent with these arguments, when Shalvi, Handgraaf, and De Dreu (2011) asked participants how unethical lying, with or without observing desired counterfactuals, is, participants perceived lying as less unethical when observing counterfactuals.

Observing desired counterfactuals is one of many types of justifications people make for their dishonest behavior. Another is contagious dishonesty, or the tendency for people to be more likely to engage in dishonest behavior when they see others similar to them do the same (Innes & Mitra, 2012; Gino et al., 2009; Gino & Galinsky, 2012). For instance, Gino and colleagues (2009) found that observing others engaging in unethical behaviors, such as cheating on a task by inflating their performance for greater pay, increases one's own unethical behaviors if these others are similar or are people one associates with (e.g., students from the same university). In one study, college students were asked to solve simple math problems in the presence of others, and they could earn money depending on their performance on this task. In some conditions, participants were given the opportunity to cheat by misreporting their performance and earning undeserved money. More importantly, in some conditions, participants were exposed to a confederate who cheated ostentatiously by finishing a task impossibly quickly and leaving the room with the maximum reward. The results showed that the level of unethical behavior among participants increased when the confederate was an ingroup member (indicated by wearing a plain T-shirt) but decreased when the confederate was an outgroup member (wearing a T-shirt from a rival university). Thus unethical behaviors are contagious: Just seeing another person act unethically influences us and leads us to behave unethically as well. Another type of justification occurs when an authoritative figure is asking the person to behave unethically, and thus one can rationalize the behavior by blaming the person in power (Milgram, 1974).

Generating justification for one's own unethical behavior is made easier by creativity (Gino & Ariely, 2012). People with creative personalities, our research shows, were more likely to cheat on performance tasks so as to earn more money than less creative people by lying more about how well they performed on the task. This tendency was especially true when there was ambiguity that could be interpreted in favor of the more creative person. In our studies, we also found that when creativity is encouraged, and thus people engage in tasks with a creative mind set, people are more likely to cheat on those tasks, as compared with situations in which creativity is not encouraged. Creativity, we suggested, fuels a person's ability to justify cheating and thus increases the extent to which people behave unethically, indicating that creativity can motivate dishonesty. That is, creativity allows people to convince themselves they are not actually acting without integrity as long as they do not overstep a self-designated boundary.

Importantly, people fail to anticipate that their desire to maintain a positive self-image as honest individuals influences their behavior when they face the opportunity to act unethically. In an experiment Mazar et al. (2008) used to test whether minor dishonesty flies under the radar, people who cheated a little bit did not update their beliefs about being honest. However, people judging others in the same situation expected them to view themselves as less honest.

BOUNDED ETHICALITY

The body of research that we've discussed, examining how people approach the choice of whether or not to behave unethically, has assumed that dishonest behavior is intentional—people are well aware of the choice they are facing and of the fact that their behavior is unethical when they do decide to cross ethical boundaries. However, another body of work has studied unintentional dishonesty. This research has suggested that people are subject to "bounded ethicality"; that is, their morality is constrained in systematic ways that favor self-serving perceptions, which in turn can result in behaviors that are inconsistent with their intended ethical standards (Banaji, Bazerman, & Chugh, 2003). Examples of such behaviors are overclaiming credit for group projects, ingroup favoritism, discrimination, and conflicts of interest. One of the main tenets of bounded ethicality is that people often engage in unethical behavior beyond their own awareness (i.e., unethical actions may occur implicitly or automatically), as their desire to be moral and deserving biases their perceptions of their decisions. That is, people (even those who care about being honest) often engage in unethical behavior simply because they do not recognize the moral implications of their actions (Bazerman & Banaji, 2004; Bazerman & Moore, 2008; Jones, 1991; Murnighan, Cantelon, & Elyashiv, 2001; Shu & Gino, 2012). For instance, experts such as doctors or financial advisors who are affected by conflicts of interest often decide not to disclose them because they do not realize that such conflicts of interest bias their advice to their benefit and create costs to the recipients (Schwartz, Gino, & Ariely, 2015).

Situational factors related to multiple demands from one's job and time pressure may make bounded ethicality more likely to occur. Chugh (2004) described the "messy, pressured, and distracting" conditions of managerial work as conducive to implicit or automatic mental processes. Time pressure and stress are two situational influences likely to accelerate mental processes and reduce the amount of information people feel is needed to make ethically sound decisions. Multiple task demands that require people's attention may produce similar effects. Situational factors such as these may also be exhausting, depleting self-regulatory resources to control unethical behavior. Thus, under the conditions most likely to be present in many people's lives in today's society, people are at the highest levels of risk for ethical failures.

TWO OPPORTUNITIES TO ACT DISHONESTLY: THE DYNAMIC AND MALLEABLE NATURE OF MORALITY

Research on the self-concept maintenance model has focused on situations in which people face one opportunity to act dishonestly. But what if there are two such opportunities? In their exploration of this question over the last decade, Monin and his colleagues (among other scholars) have argued that a person's morality is dynamic and malleable. Monin and Jordan (2009) suggest that, at any given moment, individuals may answer the question of how moral they are differently. That is, people perceive their own morality differently at different times:

> [A]s with the self-concept more generally (see Markus & Nurius, 1987), people's thoughts and behavior are often guided by a "working" level of moral self-regard that fluctuates from moment to moment according to situational influences. . . . We contend that situations actually can affect aspects of the self-concept. (Monin & Jordan, 2009, p. 10)

Three lines of research by Monin and colleagues are consistent with this view of one's own ethicality as malleable and dynamic: research on moral credentials, research on moral resentment, and research on moral compensation. We discuss each in turn.

Moral Credentials

The first line of research supporting the notion that morality is dynamic and malleable stresses the importance of considering the sequence in which moral choices and actions occur. That is, people commonly examine their decisions within the context of their recent behavioral history (Zhong, Liljenquist, & Cain, 2009). When individuals decide whether or not to engage in unethical behavior, they consider their previous moral and immoral actions, tracking their moral balance between moral credits (past good deeds) and moral debits (past bad deeds; Nisan, 1991). More specifically, Nisan's (1991) moral balance model suggests that people compute a personal moral balance based on their actions that are morally relevant within a given time frame and do not behave less ethically than their minimum standards. At any point in time, good deeds raise the balance, and bad ones lower it.

Consistent with Nisan's moral balance model (1991), Monin and Miller

(2001) conducted experiments in which they found that a prior moral act (even a token one) can license later morally questionable behavior. In one study, participants were presented with job-selection tasks. In their first such task, half of the participants were given the opportunity to select a stellar African American applicant, thus establishing nonracist credentials. The other half of the participants were in a control condition and were asked to pick from an all-white applicant pool. Compared with participants in the control condition, participants in the African American–candidate condition were more likely to say that a second, unrelated job in a police force identified as racist would be "better suited" for a white person than an African American person. This second task was designed to make it attractive for participants to favor a white person. However, this choice entails behaving in a way that feels unethical in a prejudice-conscious society; as a result, participants do not express this preference unless they have established their nonracist self-image with their first choice—what Monin and Miller (2001) labeled a *moral credential*.

Across various studies, Monin and Miller (2001) demonstrated that bolstering people's moral self-regard can liberate them to act less ethically in the future. Similarly, Mazar and Zhong (2010) found that people were more likely to cheat and steal after purchasing environmentally friendly products as opposed to conventional products. These studies demonstrate that socially conscious, ethical acts can secure a moral self that licenses socially undesirable behaviors even in unrelated domains. Interestingly, people do not seem aware of their tendency to keep their moral credits and debits in balance.

Moral Resentment

In a second stream of research, Monin and colleagues have found that learning about the behavior of heroes or saints can threaten people's moral self-regard in cases in which our behavior often falls short in comparison to theirs. As a result, they express resentment of these superior others, despite their clearly stellar and exemplary behavior (Monin, 2007). In one experiment, Monin and colleagues examined reactions to a target individual who refused to express opinions that contradicted his or her private beliefs. Although neutral judges appreciated this person and rated him or her positively on various dimensions, participants who had earlier expressed ideas that contradicted their beliefs without complaint expressed high levels of disliking for the target (Monin, Sawyer, & Marquez, 2008). Those who had willingly gone along with the problematic behavior perceived the target's exemplary behavior as a threat to their moral self-image and, consequently, derogated him or her (Monin & Jordan, 2009).

This research has direct implications for whistle-blowers, who are often lauded by the general public but scapegoated as the embodiment of treachery in their organizations. Monin et al. (2008) point out that it is common for heroes to be attacked by those closest to them. Hugh Thompson, Jr., the U.S. soldier who worked to stop the My Lai massacre during the Vietnam War, was shunned by his fellow soldiers and received numerous death threats (My Lai massacre, 2006). Frank Serpico, the New York police officer who exposed rampant corruption in the force, was shot in the face by fellow officers (Maas, 1973). The person who turned in a CD of photos showing the abuse of Iraqi detainees at the Abu Ghraib prison by U.S. soldiers during the Iraq War was taken into protective custody after receiving various threats from former colleagues (Rosin, 2004). Would-be whistle-blowers face incredible pressure to not report wrongdoing because it threatens both the material well-being and the psychological well-being of others' moral selves.

Moral Compensation

Finally, in the third stream of research, Monin and colleagues have demonstrated that a threat to individuals' self-concepts in a nonmoral domain may lead to moral derogation: Individuals may boost their own moral self-regard and put down others' morality as a result of such a threat. In one study demonstrating this phenomenon (Jordan & Monin, 2008), participants were asked to complete a boring task for the experimenter (a repetitive number-writing task). After completing the task, participants saw a confederate quit the same task without facing any negative consequence. As a result, participants elevated their ratings of their own morality and castigated the morality of the confederate, as compared both with participants who simply completed the boring task without seeing the confederate quit it and participants who simply observed the confederate quit the task without first having completed it themselves. Thus having completed an exceedingly boring and tedious task, together with witnessing another person avoid it, represented a threat to participants' general self-worth as rational, efficacious agents (Monin & Jordan, 2009). As a direct consequence of feeling threatened, participants compensated by boosting their moral self-regard and dimming their view of the other's morality.

Studies on moral credentials, moral resentment, and moral compensation provide robust and consistent evidence that our morality is malleable and dynamic. Monin's research examines influences on a person's moral self-regard by focusing on the person's past actions and others' current behavior—two moments in time that provide opportunities to act dishonestly. Yet one can also take a longer term view of morality. How do people behave, from a moral standpoint, when they encounter multiple opportunities to act dishonestly? We turn to the research stream that has addressed this question next.

MULTIPLE OPPORTUNITIES TO ACT DISHONESTLY: SELF-REGULATION IN THE MORAL DOMAIN

Unethical behaviors are often tempting because they offer short-term benefits, such as monetary rewards. For instance, a manager may gain a financial reward by inflating her expense report or her billable hours. The short-term benefits of unethical behavior, however, often risk inflicting long-term harm on one's reputation, established relationships, and long-term profitability. Thus many unethical behaviors are tempting in the moment but harmful over time. To resist the short-term temptation to act unethically, people need to exert self-control (Mead, Baumeister, Gino, Schweitzer, & Ariely, 2009). Self-control has been defined as "the ability to override or change one's inner responses, as well as to interrupt undesired behavioral tendencies (such as impulses) and refrain from acting on them" (Tangney, Baumeister, & Boone, 2004, p. 274). Self-control enables individuals to resist short-term temptations (e.g., the pleasure of eating cheesecake) to achieve long-term aims (e.g., losing weight; Loewenstein, 1996; Mischel, 1974; Myrseth & Fishbach, 2009).

In the near term, self-control, or self-regulation, is a finite resource (Baumeister & Heatherton, 1996; Heatherton & Baumeister, 1996; Muraven, Tice, & Baumeister, 1998). When exercised, self-regulatory resources become depleted, and subsequent self-control becomes much more difficult. Indeed, when people self-regulate their behavior (e.g., by not buying a tempting product they do not need), they consume self-regulatory resources and have few such resources available for a subsequent task. Compared with people who have not recently had to self-regulate their behavior, people who have done so are more likely to overeat, procrastinate, or shop impulsively (e.g., Baumeister, Bratslavsky, Muraven, & Tice, 1998; Vohs, 2006; Vohs, Baumeister, & Ciarocco, 2005; Vohs & Faber, 2007; Vohs & Heatherton, 2000; Kivetz & Simonson, 2002; Mischel, Shoda, & Rodriguez, 1989).

Just as people use self-control when dieting, they also use it to refrain from engaging in tempting, unethical behavior (e.g., submitting an inflated expense report or taking office supplies home). In a laboratory study, Muraven, Pogarsky, and Shmueli (2006) found that depletion of one's own self-regulatory resources predicted cheating on a problem-solving task. Mead and colleagues (2009) also found that individuals were more likely to misrepresent their performance when their self-control was depleted than when it was not. This research suggests that depletion of one's self-regulatory resources promotes cheating. Building on this work, Gino, Schweitzer, Mead, and Ariely (2011) demonstrate that resisting unethical behavior requires and depletes self-control resources. Gino, Schweitzer, et al. (2011) found that individuals with depleted self-control resources do not become less likely to recognize unethical behavior but do lack the willpower needed to resist tempting unethical acts.

Fortunately, people can replenish their self-regulatory resources over time. Specifically, Baumeister and Exline (1999) argue that people's willpower becomes stronger as it is exercised. The more often people engage in virtuous behaviors, the stronger the moral muscle grows, until behaving in virtuous ways becomes automatic—thus requiring little energy to enact. Although their model falls outside the moral domain, their findings add an important element to our understanding of how people regulate their morality over time. If individuals can struggle with but overcome their temptations and adhere to their moral beliefs, they might be able to have higher resolve in the future.

CROSSING ETHICAL BOUNDARIES: THE PERSON OR THE SITUATION?

The streams of research we've reviewed so far explain when and why people act dishonestly in the face of one, two, or multiple opportunities to cheat. Though different, these streams of research share the same assumption: that even people who care about morality cross ethical boundaries in predictable ways. In so doing, these research streams stress the role of social and situational forces on one's moral compass. Yet not every scholar sees the situation as being as powerful as this body of work implies when it comes to explaining unethical behavior. In fact, scholars interested in ethics have long discussed whether dishonesty is mainly the result of character flaws (the "bad apples" view), situational influences (the "bad barrel" view), or both (see, e.g., Treviño's [1986] person–situation interactionist model, or Jones's (1991) issue-contingent model). These different approaches focus on different sets of factors to explain the determinants of ethical decision making and unethical behavior.

Scholars who emphasize the impact of individual traits or characteristics in explaining unethical behavior suggest that morality is a relatively stable personality trait that people develop as they pass through different phases, or "stages," of moral development. For instance, expanding upon Piaget's three-stage framework of cognitive development, Kohlberg (1981) suggested that ethical behavior is determined by the sophistication (or stage) of a person's moral reasoning. Kohlberg proposed that moral judgment develops through a sequence of three levels comprising two stages each, for a total of six stages. Although individuals who have reached advanced stages may occasionally reason at a lower level, the central tenet of Kohlberg's model is that people at more developed stages make superior moral decisions to those at earlier stages (Gibbs, Basinger, & Fuller, 1992; Rest & Navarez, 1994). Kohlberg (1981) argued that "the nature of our sequence is not significantly affected by widely varying social, cultural, or religious conditions. The only thing that is affected is the rate at which individuals progress through this sequence" (p. 25).

Other views add situational variations to this model of the impact of individual traits on ethical reasoning and decision making. Rest (1986), for example, proposes a four-step process of ethical decision making: awareness, judgment, intention, and behavior. In this model, success at one stage does not imply success at subsequent stages. Thus a decision maker may possess moral judgment but, failing to establish moral intent in one context, may nonetheless engage in unethical behavior. Using Rest's words, "a person may have very sophisticated ways of making moral judgments, yet may prize other goals more, may fail to follow through, or may not behave morally" (Rest, 1986, p. 455).

Other fingers point at the situation, not the person. Scholars supporting this second perspective base their theories and empirical work on the assumption that, in most cases, situational forces overwhelm individual differences. Several well-known experiments are commonly discussed in support of this "situationist" account. For instance, in Milgram's famous experiment, an experimental assistant (an accomplice) asked each study participant to play the role of a teacher and administer "electric shocks" to another participant, the "learner" (who was actually a confederate or experimental assistant), each time the learner made a mistake on a word-learning exercise. After each mistake, the participant was asked to administer a shock of increasingly higher voltage, which began to result in apparent audibly increasing signs of distress from the learner. Over 60% of the study participants administered "shocks" through to the highest voltage, which was marked clearly as being potentially dangerous (Milgram, 1974). These results suggest that it is not individual character that causes one to inflict great pain on an innocent person but rather the situation in which an authority demands obedience. Similarly, in the famous Stanford prison experiment (Zimbardo, 1969), Stanford undergraduates were randomly assigned to be either guards or prisoners in a mock prison setting for a 2-week experiment. After less than a week, the experiment was abruptly stopped because the guards were engaging in sadism and brutality and the prisoners were suffering from extreme stress.

Both of these studies demonstrate two important dimensions that underlie many forms of unethical behavior: incremental steps and hierarchy. Incremental steps, or incrementalism, refers to the idea that terrible acts do not happen suddenly but rather result from a series of small, seemingly inconsequential steps. For example, in the Milgram experiments, the teacher appeared to start the "shocks" at a mere 15 volts and to increase the voltages in 15-volt increments. When people take initially incremental steps in a particular direction, they arrive at a new setpoint of behavior, from which they take a further step. Over time, a series of incremental steps can produce behavior that, at a distance, seems abhorrent. But to the individual taking the steps, the last act is simply one small step from the previous one (Gino & Bazerman, 2009; Tenbrunsel & Messick, 2004). The idea of incrementalism can provide insight into large-scale atrocities. For example, the Nazis in Germany did not start exterminating Jews immediately after taking power. Rather, their "final solution" resulted from a series of incremental steps made over an extended period of time. Notably, incrementalism is an effective technique for leading people down a new path, regardless of whether that path leads toward the production of good or evil.

In the unethical behavior uncovered in both the Milgram and the Stanford prison experiments, hierarchy also plays an essential role. Hierarchy is the predominant form of social organization in the world because it solves so many problems posed by the need to organize a collection of individuals (Magee & Galinsky, 2008). Halevy, Chou, and Galinsky (2011) note that hierarchy establishes a division of labor and reduces conflict by creating patterns of deference while motivating performance through the alluring rewards offered to the powerful. As a result, the human mind has evolved to be incredibly sensitive to one's own place in a social hierarchy and the behavior expected in that role. Research has shown that although people self-enhance on almost any dimension—from intelligence to attractiveness to morality and charity—individuals are remarkably accurate in their assessments of their own status, as well as that of others (Anderson, Srivastava, Beer, Spataro, & Chatman, 2006). For a hierarchy to function effectively and smoothly, those who are lower in the hierarchy must defer to those higher in the hierarchy. As a result, when an authority figure asks a lower-ranked individual to take some action, the person will often do it, even if that action would be considered unethical.

In addition to incrementalism and hierarchy, studies have identified other situational factors influencing individual dishonesty, such as incentive structures, organizational culture, job context (Ferrell, Gresham, & Fraedrich, 1989; Treviño, 1986), and even more subtle influences, such as ambient lighting (Zhong, Bohns, & Gino, 2010), the use of fake products (Gino, Norton, & Ariely, 2010), social bonds (Gino & Galinsky, 2012), and environmental wealth (Gino & Pierce, 2009). For example, Gino and colleagues (2010) found that participants who wore counterfeit sunglasses were more likely to cheat on various performance tasks by overreporting their performance, compared with participants who wore branded sunglasses.

Some of this research, such as studies focusing on the effects of ethics codes or ethical climate and culture in organizations, use a survey-based approach, which has the benefit of external validity but often involves correlational analyses. Other research, such as studies on the influence of subtle environmental factors, uses laboratory experiments. Although such studies may be criticized for a lack of external validity, they allow scholars to explore causal relationships in controlled environments. More recently, scholars have started using mixed approaches to the study of ethics. So, for instance, Gino and Pierce (2010) used data from emission testing markets to study illicit helping and hurting and paired their field data with laboratory studies to examine psychological mechanisms that cannot be explored in field settings.

Overall, this "situational ethics" approach provides relevant qualifications to the correspondence between moral traits and moral behavior by recognizing the moderating role of the situation in determining behavior. At least in its more liberal form, it suggests that morality is *malleable* and *dynamic* and that individuals with certain moral traits, even when they strongly value morality, may not behave consistently across different situations (Monin & Jordan, 2009).

CONCLUSIONS

Topical stories in the media exposing unethical practices in business and broader society have highlighted the gap between the decisions people actually make versus those they believe they should make. In recent decades, a large body of work across many disciplines—from social psychology and philosophy to management and neuroscience—has tried to tease out the reasons that people behave in ways inconsistent with their own ethical standards or moral principles. Antecedents of ethical decision making and dishonest behavior range from individual differences to situational forces that are so strong that they make individual choice all but irrelevant. In this chapter, we reviewed recent findings from the social psychology and management literatures and discussed how they can help us better understand why ethics is so hard to maintain in today's society.

We presented an organizing framework that focuses on the number of opportunities people face to behave dishonestly (one, two, or multiple opportunities). Though very insightful, this research has not examined how dishonesty occurs over the long run (e.g., years or even a lifetime). By taking a long-term perspective, future research could further our understanding of the antecedents and consequences of dishonesty. However, independent of the time frame considered (short vs. long term), the study of individuals' psychology and the influences of environment may prove particularly valuable as we try to understand corruption in organizations and society more broadly.

REFERENCES

Adler, A. (1930). *Individual psychology*. Oxford, UK: Clark University Press.

Alicke, M. D. (1985). Global self-evaluation as determined by the desirability and controllability of trait adjectives. *Journal of Personality and Social Psychology, 49*, 1621–1630.

Alicke, M. D., Klotz, M. L., Breitenbecher, D. L., Yurak, T. J., & Vredenburg, D. S. (1995). Personal contact, individuation and the better than average effect. *Journal of Personality and Social Psychology, 68*, 804–825.

Allport, G. W. (1955). *Becoming: Basic considerations for a psychology of personality.* New Haven, CT: Yale University Press.

Anderson, C., Srivastava, S., Beer, J. S., Spataro, S. E., & Chatman, J. E. (2006). Knowing your place: Self-perceptions of status in social groups. *Journal of Personality and Social Psychology, 91*, 1094–1110.

Association of Certified Fraud Examiners. (2008). 2008 Report to the Nations on Occupational Fraud and Abuse. Retrieved from *www.acfe.com/documents/2008-rttn.pdf.*

Association of Certified Fraud Examiners. (2012). 2012 ACFE Report to the Nations on Occupational Fraud and Abuse. Retrieved October 28, 2013, from *www.acfe.com/uploadedFiles/ACFE_Website/Content/rttn/2012-report-to-nations.pdf.*

Ayal, S., & Gino, F. (2011). Honest rationales for dishonest behavior. In M. Mikulincer & P. R. Shaver (Eds.), *The social psychology of morality: Exploring the causes of good and evil* (pp. 149–166). Washington, DC: American Psychological Association.

Banaji, M. R., Bazerman, M. H., & Chugh, D. (2003). How (un)ethical are you? *Harvard Business Review, 81*(12), 56–64.

Baumeister, R. F., Bratslavsky, E., Muraven, M., & Tice, D. M. (1998). Ego-depletion: Is the active self a limited resource? *Journal of Personality and Social Psychology, 74*, 1252–1265.

Baumeister, R. F., & Exline, J. J. (1999). Virtue, personality, and social relations: Self-control as the moral muscle. *Journal of Personality, 67*, 1165–1194.

Baumeister, R. F., & Heatherton, T. F. (1996). Self-regulation failure: An overview. *Psychological Inquiry, 7*(3), 1–15.

Bazerman, M. H., & Banaji, M. R. (2004). The social psychology of ordinary ethical failures. *Social Justice Research, 17*, 111–115.

Bazerman, M., & Moore, D. A. (2008). *Judgment in managerial decision making* (7th ed.). Hoboken, NJ: Wiley.

Brown, J. D. (1986). Evaluations of self and others: Self-enhancement biases in social judgments. *Social Cognition, 4*(4), 353–376.

Chugh, D. (2004). Societal and managerial implications of implicit social cognition: Why milliseconds matter. *Social Justice Research, 17*(2), 203–222.

DePaulo, B. M., Kashy, D. A., Kirkendol, S. E., Wyer, M. M., & Epstein, J. A. (1996). Lying in everyday life. *Journal of Personality and Social Psychology, 70*(5), 979–995.

De Quervain, D. J.-F., Fischbacher, U., Treyer, V., Schelthammer, M., Schnyder, U., Buck, A., et al. (2004). The neural basis of altruistic punishment. *Science, 305*, 1254–1258.

Ferrell, O. C., Gresham, L. G., & Fraedrich, J. (1989). A synthesis of ethical decision models for marketing. *Journal of Macromarketing, 9*, 55–64.

Fischbacher, U., & Follmi-Heusi, F. (2013). Lies in disguise: An experimental study on cheating. *Journal of European Economic Association, 11*, 525–547.

Frank, R., Bryan-Low, C., Pacelle, M., Smith, R., Berman, D., Mollenkamp, C., et al. (2003, October 3). Scandal scorecard. *Wall Street Journal*, p. B4.

Gibbs, J. C., Basinger, K. S., & Fuller, D. (1992). *Moral maturity: Measuring the development of sociomoral reflection*. Hillsdale, NJ: Erlbaum.

Gino, F., & Ariely, D. (2012). The dark side of creativity: Original thinkers can be more dishonest. *Journal of Personality and Social Psychology, 102*(3), 445–459.

Gino, F., Ayal, S., & Ariely, D. (2009). Contagion and differentiation in unethical behavior: The effect of one bad apple on the barrel. *Psychological Science, 20*(3), 393–398.

Gino, F., & Bazerman, M. H. (2009). When misconduct goes unnoticed: The acceptability of gradual erosion in others' unethical behavior. *Journal of Experimental Social Psychology, 45*(4), 708–719.

Gino, F., & Galinsky, A. (2012). Vicarious dishonesty: When psychological closeness creates distance from one's moral compass. *Organizational Behavior and Human Decision Processes, 119*(1), 15–26.

Gino, F., Norton, M., & Ariely, D. (2010). The counterfeit self: The deceptive costs of faking it. *Psychological Science, 21*(5), 712–720.

Gino, F., & Pierce, L. (2009). The abundance effect: Unethical behavior in the presence of wealth. *Organizational Behavior and Human Decision Processes, 109*(2), 142–155.

Gino, F., & Pierce, L. (2010). Robin Hood under the hood: Wealth-based discrimination in illicit customer help. *Organization Science, 21*(6), 1176–1194.

Gino, F., Schweitzer, M., Mead, N., & Ariely, D. (2011). Unable to resist temptation: How self-control depletion promotes unethical behavior. *Organizational Behavior and Human Decision Processes, 115*(2), 191–203.

Gino, F., Sharek, Z., & Moore, D. A. (2011). Keeping the illusion of control under control: Ceilings, floors, and imperfect calibration. *Organizational Behavior and Human Decision Processes, 114*(2), 104–114.

Graham, C., Litan, R. E., & Sukhtankar, S. (2002). *The bigger they are, the harder they fall: An estimate of the costs of the crisis in corporate governance*. Washington, DC: Brookings Institution.

Greenwald, A. G. (1980). The totalitarian ego: Fabrication and revision of personal history. *American Psychologist, 35*, 603–618.

Halevy, N., Chou, E., & Galinsky, A. D. (2011). A functional model of hierarchy: Why, how and when hierarchical differentiation enhances group performance. *Organizational Psychology Review, 1*, 32–52.

Hastorf, A., Schneider, D., & Polefka, J. (1970). *Person perception*. Reading, MA: Addison-Wesley.

Heatherton, T. F., & Baumeister, R. F. (1996). Self-regulation failure: Past, present, and future. *Psychological Inquiry, 7*, 90–98.

Henrich, J., Boyd, R., Bowles, S., Camerer, C., Fehr, E., Gintis, H., et al. (2001). In search of *Homo economicus*: Behavioral experiments in 15 small-scale societies. *American Economic Review, 91*, 73–78.

Innes, R., & Mitra, A. (2012). Is dishonesty contagious? *Economic Inquiry, 51*(1), 722–734.

Jones, S. C. (1973). Self- and interpersonal evaluations: Esteem theories versus consistency theories. *Psychological Bulletin, 79*, 185–199.

Jones, T. M. (1991). Ethical decision making by individuals in organizations: An issue-contingent model. *Academy of Management Review, 16*, 366–395.

Jordan, A. H., & Monin, B. (2008). From sucker to saint: Moralization in response to self-threat. *Psychological Science, 19*(8), 683–689.

Kahneman, D., & Varey, C. A. (1990). Propensities and counterfactuals: The loser that almost won, *Journal of Personality and Social Psychology, 59,* 1101–1110.

Kenrick, D. T., Neuberg, S. L., & Cialdini, R. B. (2010). *Social psychology: Goals in interaction.* Boston: Pearson Education.

Kivetz, R., & Simonson, I. (2002). Self-control for the righteous: Towards a theory of precommitment to indulgence. *Journal of Consumer Research, 29,* 199–217.

Klar, Y. (2002). Way beyond compare: Nonselective superiority and inferiority biases in judging randomly assigned group members relative to their peers. *Journal of Experimental Social Psychology, 38*(4), 331–351.

Klar, Y., & Giladi, E. E. (1997). No one in my group can be below the group's average: A robust positivity bias in favor of anonymous peers. *Journal of Personality and Social Psychology, 73*(5), 885–901.

Kohlberg, L. (1981). *Essays on moral development: Vol. I. The philosophy of moral development.* New York: Harper & Row.

Kruger, J., & Dunning, D. (1999). Unskilled and unaware of it: How difficulties in recognizing one's own incompetence lead to inflated self-assessments. *Journal of Personality and Social Psychology, 77*(6), 1121–1134.

Langer, E. (1975). The illusion of control. *Journal of Personality and Social Psychology, 32,* 311–328.

Langer, E. J., & Roth, J. (1975). Heads I win, tails it's chance: The illusion of control as a function of the sequence of outcomes in a purely chance task. *Journal of Personality and Social Psychology, 34,* 191–198.

Loewenstein, G. (1996). Out of control: Visceral influences on behavior. *Organizational Behavior and Human Decision Processes, 65*(3), 272–292.

Maas, P. (1973). *Serpico: The cop who defied the system.* New York: Viking Press.

Magee, J. C., & Galinsky, A. D. (2008). Social hierarchy: The self-reinforcing nature of power and status. *Academy of Management Annals, 2,* 351–398.

Markus, H., & Nurius, P. (1987). Possible selves: The interface between motivation and the self-concept. In K. M. Yardley & T. M. Honess (Eds.), *Self and identity: Psychosocial perspectives* (pp. 157–172). Sussex, UK: Wiley.

Mazar, N., Amir, O., & Ariely, D. (2008). The dishonesty of honest people: A theory of self-concept maintenance. *Journal of Marketing Research, 45,* 633–644.

Mazar, N., & Zhong, C. (2010). Do green products make us better people? *Psychological Science, 21*(4), 494–498.

Mead, N., Baumeister, R. F., Gino, F., Schweitzer, M., & Ariely, D. (2009). Too tired to tell the truth: Self-control resource depletion and dishonesty. *Journal of Experimental Social Psychology, 45*(3), 594–597.

Messick, D. M., Bloom, S., Boldizar, J. P., & Samuelson, C. D. (1985). Why we are fairer than others. *Journal of Experimental Social Psychology, 21,* 480–500.

Milgram, S. (1974). *Obedience to authority: An experimental view.* New York: Harper & Row.

Miller, D. T., & Ross, M. (1975). Self-serving biases in the attribution of causality: Fact or fiction? *Psychological Bulletin, 82,* 213–225.

Mischel, W. (1974). Processes in delay of gratification. In L. Berkowitz (Ed.), *Advances in experimental and social psychology* (Vol. 7, pp. 249–292). New York: Academic Press.

Mischel, W., Shoda, Y., & Rodriguez, M. L. (1989). Delay of gratification in children. *Science, 244*, 933–938.

Monin, B. (2007). Holier than me?: Threatening social comparison in the moral domain. *International Review of Social Psychology, 20*(1), 53–68.

Monin, B., & Jordan, A. H. (2009). Dynamic moral identity: A social psychological perspective. In D. Narvaez & D. Lapsley (Eds.), *Personality, identity, and character: Explorations in moral psychology* (pp. 341–354). Cambridge, UK: Cambridge University Press.

Monin, B., & Miller, D. T. (2001). Moral credentials and the expression of prejudice. *Journal of Personality and Social Psychology, 81*(1), 33–43.

Monin, B., Sawyer, P. J., & Marquez, M. J. (2008). The rejection of moral rebels: Resenting those who do the right thing. *Journal of Personality and Social Psychology, 95*(1), 76–93.

Moore, D. (2007). Not so above average after all: When people believe they are worse than average and its implications for theories of bias in social comparison. *Organizational Behavior and Human Decision Processes, 102*(1), 42–58.

Moore, D. A., Swift, S. A., Sharek, Z., & Gino, F. (2010). Correspondence bias in performance evaluation: Why grade inflation works. *Personality and Social Psychology Bulletin, 36*(6), 843–852.

Morris, M. W., & Moore, P. C. (2000). The lessons we (don't) learn: Counterfactual thinking and organizational accountability after a close call. *Administrative Science Quarterly, 45*, 737–765.

Muraven, M., Pogarsky, G., & Shmueli, D. (2006). Self-control depletion and the general theory of crime. *Journal of Quantitative Criminology, 22*, 263–277.

Muraven, M., Tice, D. M., & Baumeister, R. F. (1998). Self–control as a limited resource: Regulatory depletion patterns. *Journal of Personality and Social Psychology, 74*, 774–789.

Murnighan, J. K., Cantelon, D. A., & Elyashiv, T. (2001). Bounded personal ethics and the tap dance of real estate agency. In J. A. Wagner III, J. M. Bartunek, & K. D. Elsbach (Eds.), *Advances in qualitative organizational research* (Vol. 3, pp. 1–40). New York: Elsevier/JAI.

My Lai massacre hero dies at 62. (2006, January 6). *BBC News*, http://news.bbc.co.uk/2/hi/4589486.stm.

Myrseth, K. O. R., & Fishbach, A. (2009). Self-control: A function of knowing when and how to exercise restraint. *Current Directions in Psychological Science, 18*, 247–252.

Nisan, M. (1991). The moral balance model: Theory and research extending our understanding of moral choice and deviation. In W. M. Kurtines & J. L. Gewirtz (Eds.), *Handbook of moral behavior and development* (pp. 213–249). Hillsdale, NJ: Erlbaum.

Rest, J. R. (1986). *Moral development: Advances in research and theory.* New York: Praeger.

Rest, J. R., & Navarez, D. (1994). *Moral development in the professions: Psychology and applied ethics.* Hillsdale, NJ: Erlbaum.

Rilling, J. K., Gutman, D. A., Zeh, T. R., Pagnoni, G., Berns, G. S., & Kilts, C. D. (2002). A neural basis for social cooperation, *Neuron, 7,* 395–405.

Rogers, C. (1959). A theory of therapy, personality and interpersonal relationships as developed in the client-centered framework. In S. Koch (Ed.), *Psychology: A study of a science: Vol. 3. Formulations of the person and the social context* (pp. 184–256). New York: McGraw Hill.

Rosenberg, M. (1979). *Conceiving the self.* New York: Basic Books.

Rosin, H. (2004, May 17). When Joseph comes marching home: In a Western Maryland town, ambivalence about the son who blew the whistle at Abu Ghraib. *Washington Post,* p. C01.

Sanitioso, R., Kunda, Z., & Fong, J. T. (1990). Motivated recruitment of autobiographical memories. *Journal of Personality and Social Psychology, 59,* 229–241.

Schlenker, B. R. (1982). Translating actions into attitudes: An identity-analytic approach to the explanation of social conduct. In L. Berkowitz (Ed.), *Advances in experimental social psychology* (Vol. 15, pp. 194–248). New York: Academic Press.

Schwartz, J., Gino, F., & Ariely, D. (2015). *Experts know best, but for whom?: Understanding conflicts of interest in the marketplace* (Working paper). Manuscript in preparation.

Schweitzer, M., Ordóñez, L., & Douma, B. (2004). The role of goal setting in motivating unethical behavior. *Academy of Management Journal, 47,* 422–432.

Shalvi, S., Dana, J., Handgraaf, M. J. J., & De Dreu, C. K. W. (2011). Justified ethicality: Observing desired counterfactuals modifies ethical perceptions and behavior. *Organizational Behavior and Human Decision Processes, 115,* 181–190.

Shalvi, S., Handgraaf, M. J. J., & De Dreu, C. K. W. (2011). Ethical maneuvering: Why people avoid both major and minor lies. *British Journal of Management, 22,* s16–s27.

Shu, L., & Gino, F. (2012). Sweeping dishonesty under the rug: How unethical actions lead to forgetting of moral rules. *Journal of Personality and Social Psychology, 102*(6), 1164–1177.

Speights, D., & Hilinski, M. (2005). Return fraud and abuse: How to protect profits. *Retailing Issues Letter, 17*(1), 1–6.

Swift, S. A., Moore, D. A., Sharek, Z., & Gino, F. (2013). Inflated applicants: Attribution errors in performance evaluation by professionals. *PLoS ONE, 8*(7), e69258.

Tajfel, H. (1982) *Social identity and intergroup relations.* Cambridge, UK: Cambridge University Press.

Tangney, J. P., Baumeister, R. F., & Boone, A. (2004). High self-control predicts good adjustment, less pathology, better grades, and interpersonal success. *Journal of Personality, 72,* 271–324.

Tenbrunsel, A. E., & Messick, D. M. (2004). Ethical fading: The role of self-deception in unethical behavior. *Social Justice Research, 17,* 223–236.

Treviño, L. K. (1986). Ethical decision making in organizations: A person–situation interactionist model. *Academy of Management Review, 11,* 601–617.

Vohs, K. D. (2006). Self-regulatory resources power the reflective system: Evidence from five domains. *Journal of Consumer Psychology, 16*(3), 217–223.

Vohs, K. D., Baumeister, R. F., & Ciarocco, N. (2005). Self-regulation and self-presentation: Regulatory resource depletion impairs management and effortful self-presentation depletes regulatory resources. *Journal of Personality and Social Psychology, 8*, 632–657.

Vohs, K. D., & Faber, R. J. (2007). Spent resources: Self-regulatory resource availability affects impulse buying. *Journal of Consumer Research, 33*, 537–547.

Vohs, K. D., & Heatherton, T. F. (2000). Self-regulatory failure: A resource-depletion approach. *Psychological Science, 11*(3), 249–254.

Weber, J., Kurke, L., & Pentico, D. (2003). Why do employees steal? *Business Society, 42*(3), 359–374.

Zhong, C., Bohns, V. K., & Gino, F. (2010). A good lamp is the best police: Darkness increases self-interested behavior and dishonesty. *Psychological Science, 21*(3), 311–314.

Zhong, C. B., Liljenquist, K., & Cain, D. M. (2009). Moral self-regulation: Licensing and compensation. In D. De Cremer (Ed.), *Psychological perspectives on ethical behavior and decision making* (pp. 75–89). Charlotte, NC: Information Age.

Zimbardo, P. (1969). The psychology of evil: A situationist perspective on recruiting good people to engage in anti-social acts. *Research in Social Psychology, 11*, 125–133.

PART IV

GROUP PERSPECTIVES ON GOOD AND EVIL

CHAPTER 16

Bystanders and Emergencies
Why Understanding Group Processes Is Key to Promoting Prosocial Behavior

Mark Levine and Neil Wilson

When it comes to explanations for the psychology of good and evil, groups tend to get a bad press. Terms such as "mob violence," "mass hysteria," or even "peer group pressure" all convey the idea that groups somehow produce negative or atavistic behavior in otherwise rational and sensible individuals. Moreover, in explanations of the reasons people sometimes fail to help others in distress, group influence appears malign rather than benign. Concepts such as "pluralistic ignorance," "diffusion of responsibility," or "audience inhibition" all suggest that the presence of others undermines our natural propensity to help. The clear implication is that, in the absence of others, we are able to recognize and do the right thing; however, groups or group processes somehow contrive to make us lose our way.

In this chapter we argue that, despite its perseverance in popular media (and in more traditional social psychology textbooks; see Manning, Levine, & Collins, 2007), this view of the impact of groups on behavior is outmoded and unhelpful. We explore contemporary research that shows that, although groups can be implicated in negative and antisocial behavior, they can also be the foundation of prosociality and resistance to evil. We focus on behavior in emergency situations, showing how social-psychological explanations have begun to embrace a more nuanced and sophisticated view of the impact of the group on the individual. In particular, we explore an approach to understanding helping in emergencies that draws on insights from the social identity tradition. Social identity theory (Tajfel & Turner, 1979; Tajfel, 1981) and self-categorization theory (Turner, Hogg, Oakes, Reicher, & Wetherell, 1987) propose a way of thinking about the psychological relationship between the individual and the group that challenges the default notion that groups have a negative impact on decision making and behavior. At its heart, the social identity approach argues that people do not lose identity, and therefore behavioral control, in the presence of others. Rather, they can shift to a social identity and then act in terms of the norms and the values of that identity. Sometimes the norms of the social identity result in antisocial behavior. At other times, the values of the social identity favor prosocial action. By understanding the nature of social identity relations in emergency situations, we come to understand how the presence of others can sometimes inhibit and sometimes facilitate bystander intervention in emergencies.

A BRIEF HISTORY OF RESEARCH ON HELPING IN EMERGENCIES (OR WHY WE CAME TO THINK THAT GROUPS WERE BAD FOR HELPING)

Research on the psychology of bystander behavior is bound up with the story of the brutal rape and murder of Kitty Genovese. In the 50 years since Winston Moseley killed Kitty Genovese in the early morning of March 13, 1964, in the Kew Gardens district of New York, the idea of the 38 witnesses who failed to intervene has become enshrined in popular consciousness. A report in the *New York Times*, published 2 weeks after the murder, became the catalyst for an entirely new research paradigm in social psychology. The front-page article claimed that "for more than half an hour 38 respectable, law-abiding citizens in Queens watched a killer stalk and stab a woman in three separate attacks. . . . Not one person telephoned the police during the assault; one witness called after the woman was dead" (Gansberg, 1964).

Two young social psychologists, John Darley and Bibb Latané, read the article, were unconvinced by the public hand-wringing that this was an example of the malaise engendered by modern urban living conditions, and set out to demonstrate the psychological impact of the presence of others on emergency helping behavior. Their early, iconic experiments manipulating the number of bystanders to an emergency led to the discovery of the "bystander effect"—the finding that individuals are more likely to help when they witness an emergency on their own than in the presence of others (Latané & Darley, 1970).

It matters little that the facts in that original *New York Times* article were mistaken. In reality, there was no evidence that 38 witnesses had watched the murder (only three or four had seen Genovese and Moseley together for a short time, and not during the fatal stabbing) and some evidence of attempts to intervene (including phone calls to the police, as well as shouts of alarm that caused Moseley to withdraw). However, the original idea had taken root. The power of the story of the 38 transfixed and inactive bystanders came to dominate the psychological imagination (Manning et al., 2007). Hundreds of studies manipulating group size and helping behavior were carried out (Latané & Nida, 1981; Fischer et al., 2011). At the heart of this research was the idea that the presence of others is the key problem to be overcome in promoting social solidarity. Protecting future Kitty Genoveses meant overcoming the problem of group influence—and not (for example) tackling male proclivity for violence toward women or challenging the culturally embedded thinking of the prefeminist era (Cherry, 1995) that allowed gendered violence to remain invisible to bystanders.

THE BYSTANDER EFFECT DOESN'T HOLD IN VIOLENT OR DANGEROUS EMERGENCIES

It is important to acknowledge that two meta-analyses (Latané & Nida, 1981; Fischer et al., 2011) testify to the strength of the bystander effect. The point here is not that bystander effect research is somehow invalid, but rather that the focus on seeing group size as the problem has prevented us from exploring ways in which the group could be part of the solution. Some indication that groups can be key to promoting intervention can be found in Fischer et al.'s meta-analysis itself. Although they demonstrated a solid and sustained effect size for the bystander effect in more everyday emergencies (e.g., helping someone with a flat tire), they also show that the bystander effect does not hold for violent or dangerous emergencies (e.g., in which a victim is in immediate physical danger). In violent or dangerous emergencies, the presence of others, at the very least, does not inhibit helping and can often facilitate intervention. Fischer et al. (2011) suggest that this might have to do with the greater physiological arousal that attends violent and dangerous events. Drawing on the arousal cost–reward model of helping (Piliavin, Dovidio, Gaertner, & Clark, 1981; Dovidio, Piliavin, Gaertner, Schroeder, & Clark, 1991), they suggest that violent or dangerous events are more easily recognized as emergencies, which leads to greater aversive arousal and thus higher levels of intervention that function to reduce that arousal.

However, researchers using the social identity tradition have offered an alternative account. Rather than focusing on the arousal that attends emergencies, Levine and colleagues (Levine, Cassidy, Brazier, & Reicher,

2002; Levine, Prosser, Evans, & Reicher, 2005; Levine & Crowther, 2008) explore the social identity relationships between all those present at an emergency event. This includes the relationship between bystanders and victims, between bystanders and fellow bystanders, and, in the case of violence, between bystanders and perpetrators. They argue that, when bystanders and victims share a social identity, then bystanders are more likely to intervene. When bystanders and fellow bystanders share a social identity (and the norms of that identity favor intervention), then bystanders are more likely to intervene. When bystanders and perpetrators share a social identity (and the actions of the perpetrator threaten group reputation or interests), then bystanders are more likely to intervene.

To be clear, it is not that the social identity approach denies the importance of arousal in emergency decision making (see Scheepers [2009] for work on social identity and arousal), but rather it argues that the sense-making process associated with arousal is shaped by identity concerns. These include the salience of social identities (What kinds of social identities are important at the moment of the emergency?); the boundaries of social identity (Who is included and who is excluded from the relevant social identities?); the content of social identities (Do the norms and values of the relevant identity favor prosocial or antisocial action?); and the strategic interests of the identity (How will action or inaction reflect on the reputation of the group?).

THE SOCIAL IDENTITY MODEL OF EMERGENCY HELPING

This social identity approach to emergency intervention has been supported by a growing literature of empirical studies. For example, Levine and colleagues (Levine et al., 2002, 2005; Levine & Crowther, 2008), have conducted a number of experiments designed to explore different aspects of the bystander–victim–perpetrator relationships in emergency settings. They show that, in experiments in which participants read about or watch closed-circuit television footage of street violence, bystanders are more likely to say they will intervene when victims are ingroup members. For example, participants drawn from a university sample are more likely to say they will intervene when they read about a student being attacked in the street rather than when the victim is described as an ordinary member of the public. They are also more likely to intervene when fellow bystanders are ingroup members (and the norms of the group favor intervention). For example, in studies using confederates, in which the confederates present as either ingroup or outgroup members, the confederates influence likelihood of intervention only when they belong to the same group as the naive bystander. Taken together, Levine et al. (2002) argue that the identity

TABLE 16.1. Frequencies of Bystanders Helping (and % Help) by Shirt Condition for Study 1 and Study 2 in Levine et al. (2005)

	Study 1: Manchester United identity			Study 2: Football fan identity		
	Help	No help	% help	Help	No help	% help
Manchester United	12	1	92%	8	2	80%
Liverpool	3	7	30%	7	3	70%
Plain	4	8	33%	2	7	22%

Reflecting this narrative, the early social psychology literature on Holocaust rescue began with an attempt to identify the characteristics of individuals who were prepared to stand out from the crowd. This search for the "altruistic personality" (Oliner & Oliner, 1992) tapped into the idea that there must have been something about the personal qualities of those who rescued that distinguished them from the mass of ordinary people. In other words, it began with the idea that there might be something uniquely good about the personalities of those who were prepared to risk themselves to save others. This is an interesting contrast to the way research on the evils of the Holocaust developed. For example, Milgram's (1974) seminal work on obedience to authority makes the strong case that, under certain conditions, ordinary people will readily take part in murderous activity. More specifically, he rules out the idea that there needs to be anything deficient in the psychological makeup of individuals who are prepared to commit terrible acts. If people don't need to have pathological personalities to do bad, it seems logical to assume that they won't need to have altruistic personalities to do good. This might go some way toward explaining why reviews of the research on the idea of an altruistic personality (e.g., Piliavin & Charng, 1990) show that it is only weakly related to intervention behavior.

More recently, however, the Holocaust rescue literature has begun to move away from a focus on individuals to explore "collective" rescue. For example, scholars have examined why it was that there were differences in the survival rates of Jewish communities in different countries that fell under the shadow of the Nazis. For example, in Poland around 90% of the Jewish population perished, with 75% of Dutch Jews also being exterminated (Dawidowicz, 1986). However, in some countries, including Denmark and Bulgaria, almost the entire Jewish population was protected and survived. Some of this research focuses on the structural and political conditions that pertained in different countries. Clearly, the degree of control exercised by the Nazis, the political context of different occupied countries, or the period of the war when deportation of the Jews was proposed, all affected the opportunity and costs for those prepared to take part in rescue (Geras, 1995; Hilberg, 1993).

However, there is also a sizeable literature on the psychological components of this resistance. The literature clearly shows that resistance was possible and seeks to explore commonalities in the stories of collective resistance. Although there is no clear consensus on the relationship of social class, gender, political affiliation, or religion to rescue, there is general agreement that rescuers tend to share a worldview that Oliner and Oliner (1992) call *extensivity*. This is the idea that rescuers included victims as part of a common moral community with themselves, and thus they had an obligation to help those in need. Monroe (2004) extends this idea, drawing explicitly on ideas from the social identity approach, to argue that this notion of extensivity was not fixed but was dependent on the salience of social identities in context. Monroe points out that individuals with virtuous pedigrees before the war did not engage in rescue behavior, whereas some notable reprobates (Oskar Schindler, for example) showed conspicuous virtue during the Holocaust. Monroe thus points to the importance of understanding the impact of social context on identity and thus on the likelihood of rescue behavior.

A close examination of the two countries in which rescue was most successful (Denmark and Bulgaria) is informative in this respect. For example, Lidegaard (2013) writes about the rescue of Jews in Denmark, where less than 1% of Jews perished. He argues that, in a political context in which the Danish political class and the Danish king were able to retain a degree of autonomy, the very fabric of Danish national identity was constructed in inclusive terms. Lidegaard suggests that this process was begun in the prewar years, when social democratic governments attempted to inoculate the Danish population against the racist ideology of their German neighbor by stressing the shared identity of all Danes as "democratic citizens" rather than ethnic or religious compatriots. In this way they were able to deny the idea of a "Jewish problem" in Denmark. The nation was imagined in civic rather than ethnic terms: To be Jewish did not exclude one from the national polity.

When in October 1943 the Gestapo came to round up 7,500 Jews, the conditions for resistance were clearly established. The Danish king and the government made it clear that harming the Jews would lead to the end of any cooperation with the German regime, and the Danish population played an active role in helping Jews to flee across the water to neutral Sweden. Of course, the relatively small numbers and the close proximity of sanctuary in Sweden made the comprehensiveness of the rescue both feasible and possible. However, the very idea of the rescue was predicated on a way of thinking about the relationships between bystanders, victims, and perpetrators that paved the way for helping. This can clearly be seen in a statement issued by leading Danish politicians from different parties declaring that "The Danish Jews are an integral part of the people, and therefore all the people are deeply affected by the measures taken, which are seen as a violation of the Danish sense of justice" (Lidegaard, 2013).

It is important to note that this inclusive construction of Danishness did not protect everybody. The fact that it was a commitment to democracy and law that was central to Danishness, and not common race or religion, meant that those who didn't share these democratic values were not protected—even if they were ethnically Danish. Several hundred Danish communists (who had denounced the monarchy and supported the Hitler–Stalin pact) were first interned and then deported to the death camps. In other words, in this particular civic form of Danish national identity, Danes were prepared to defend the Jews, but not Danish communists who appeared not to endorse core democratic values. Inclusive category boundaries brought the Jews inside the national tent, but denial of the core values of the identity meant that communists were not afforded the protection of the group.

Similar themes can be seen in the story of the rescue of the Bulgarian Jews. The scale of the rescue was similarly impressive, though not quite so comprehensive as in Denmark. This has in part to do with the greater number of Bulgarian Jews and the more constrained circumstances of rescue. Jews could not simply be spirited away to a neutral country. The historical relationship between Bulgaria and Germany was also different. Bulgaria had been an ally of Germany in the First World War and had been punished in defeat by loss of territory and punitive reparations. One of the key aims of Bulgarian politicians was thus to regain territory and rid itself of reparations. This meant that in 1939, when war was declared, Bulgaria declared neutrality but entered into a pact with Germany in order to regain the territory it had lost in the First World War settlement. Part of the price of this agreement with the Germans was Hitler's insistence on the introduction of anti-Semitic legislation in Bulgaria. As the war progressed, Bulgaria agreed to further treaties with the Germans. In 1941, when Germany went to aid its Italian allies in Greece (by sending troops through Bulgaria), the Bulgarians agreed to a further treaty supporting the axis powers—and received the territories of Thrace, Macedonia, and Eastern Serbia by way of exchange.

By 1943, the pressure on Bulgaria to deal with their "Jewish problem" became intense. Adolf Eichmann's special envoy, the SS officer Theodor Dannecker, was pressing for the expulsion of Jews from Bulgaria and their dispatch to the concentration camps. This led to demonstrations by several thousand Jewish and non-Jewish Bulgarians who marched to the royal palace in protest. It has been described as second only to the Warsaw ghetto uprising as an act of resistance to the Holocaust (Genov & Baeva, 2003) and culminated in the king's categorically refusing any deportations from Bulgaria. The campaign was bolstered by a series of petitions, individual letters of protest by politicians, clergy, journalists, writers, and intellectuals, and assorted public demonstrations. Such was the success of the campaign that Bulgaria was the only case in which Jews largely survived within a country that was in the pro-German camp and where there were more Jews living at the end of the war than at the beginning (Ben-Yakov, 1990).

Using documents assembled by the historian Todorov (2001), Reicher, Cassidy, Wolpert, Hopkins, and Levine (2006) analyzed the way arguments to protect Jews were made by members of the Bulgarian establishment. They show that, in a similar vein as the Danish rescue, there was a strong and persistent construction of the Jews as part of the Bulgarian national category. They show how the Bulgarian identity of the Jewish people was repeatedly underscored using the conventional criteria of nationhood (common territory, language, culture loyalty). They also show how opinion formers worked hard to claim that even the inner psychic world of the Jews (their thoughts, feelings, private selves) was thoroughly Bulgarian. In doing so, they established the Jews as common category members with all Bulgarians, rather than as a group who are different by virtue of ethnic origin or religious persuasion. If Jews are Bulgarian, then an attack on the Jews is an attack on all Bulgarians, and thus must be resisted.

Reicher et al. (2006) also show how the norms associated with Bulgarian identity are used to oppose the deportation of the Jews. To be Bulgarian was to have "traditions of religious tolerance and humanity," "to protect humanity and freedom," "to be tolerant and honorable," and to have "humanity, justice and compassion for all those who suffer" (Reicher et al., p. 63). These noble and more universal values were used to argue for the importance of intervention on behalf of the Jews. Failure to act to resist deportation was presented as a failure of national character itself. Finally, Reicher et al. (2006) show how what they call category interests were also used to argue for the protection of the Jews. Political leaders argued that it would be against Bulgarian national interests in the long run to be seen to have cooperated with the anti-Semitic annihilationist plans of the Nazis. Bulgaria would "lose moral capital accumulated over many long years," and Bulgaria would be "morally at odds with public opinion" (Reicher et al., p. 65) in these other countries. At the same time, if the deportation of the Jews was in the German interest, it could not, by definition, be in the Bulgarian interest, and thus should be opposed by all Bulgarians.

Reicher et al. (2006) show how, taken together, category inclusiveness (the Jews are Bulgarians), category contents (Bulgarian values require protection of the Jews), and category interests (deportation of the Jews damages the reputation of Bulgarians) all served to mobilize ordinary Bulgarians in the rescue of Jews. However, as with the case of the Danish rescue, the availability of such inclusive categorization does not mean that everyone will be rescued. Todorov (2001) shows that this mobilization on behalf of the Jews was restricted to the Jews of "old Bulgaria." In the territories of Thrace and Macedonia, given to Bulgaria as part of the agreement with Germany in 1941, there was no attempt to make a case for the protection of Jews. The Bulgarians cooperated with deportation of Jews from these occupied territories. In total, 11,343 people were taken to Auschwitz and Treblinka. Twelve survived. There can be no clearer demonstration of the ultimate life-or-death implications that the construction and mobilization of social identities can have.

SOCIAL IDENTITY AND HELPING IN DISASTERS AND EMERGENCIES

A second way in which the importance of a group-level perspective on helping in emergencies is revealed can be found in the recent literature on behavior during life-threatening emergency events. The early orthodoxy on behavior in these kinds of emergencies took for granted that people would behave irrationally, selfishly, and potentially violently. Disaster response management was predicated on beliefs about the dangers of group-based psychological dysfunction in emergency settings. For example, Drury, Novelli, and Stott (2013) identify three psychological disaster myths that have plagued emergency planning. The first is the idea that there will be *mass panic*—that irrational or exaggerated fear will spread through people in the emergency, leading to behaviors that are unthinking, instinctual, and unconstrained by social rules. The second is that *civil disorder* will ensue— that people will take advantage of the emergency to engage in widespread criminality and wrongdoing. The third is that people will become *helpless* or suffer from "disaster syndrome" (Auf der Heide, 2004)—the idea that survivors will be too stunned or too passive to be able to help themselves.

There is general agreement between disaster sociologists, social psychologists, and those involved in disaster relief that these myths have led to poor and sometimes counterproductive responses to emergencies. For example, Solnit (2009) argues that the overmilitarized (as opposed to humanitarian) response by state and government officials to the Hurricane Katrina disaster in New Orleans in 2005 can in part be explained by the impact of these myths. Combined with a history of racial discrimination and deep racial distrust, these myths meant that black victims of the disaster were treated as dangerous and threatening (often being turned back toward danger at gunpoint when they tried to cross to safe areas), accused of looting when attempting to secure provisions that would help them survive the emergency (Henkel, Dovidio, & Gaertner, 2006), or starved of support that did not fit with the Federal Emergency Management Agency's (FEMA) agenda (Sobel & Leeson, 2006).

By way of contrast, researchers who have studied the actual behavior of people in life-threatening emergencies show that humans tend to cooperate and to help each other during times of crisis. Consider, for example, Proulx and Fahy's (2003) review of the emergency evacuation of the Twin Towers of the World Trade Center after they were struck by two hijacked planes on September 11, 2001. Even though the towers were more than 110 floors tall and the impact zones were on the upper floors of each tower, thousands of people escaped to safety from the floors beneath. Proulx and Fahy report that the overwhelming majority of people did not panic or act selfishly in a blind attempt to save themselves. Even though they knew they were in danger, they behaved in a calm and cooperative manner. People moved down the densely packed stairwells in a measured and orderly fashion. They paused to let firefighters ascend—or to help others who were dazed or injured. Where there was panic or distress, individuals were calmed by the behavior of the group. They took turns to help those who were in most need. Some office workers even stayed in the building to hold open doors and direct traffic.

This more positive view of behavior in emergencies is echoed in the work of John Drury and colleagues (Drury, Cocking, & Reicher, 2009; Drury & Reicher, 2010) in research on the survivors of the July 7, 2005, bombings in London. This attack involved four coordinated explosions (on three underground trains and a bus) during morning rush hour. The explosions killed 56 people and injured more than 700. Most of the survivors of the bombs were trapped in the dark, smoke-filled carriages among the dead and the dying. They had no way of knowing whether there would be more bombs or hazards from fire or electricity. There was also no means of communication with the survivors to reassure them about a rescue. They had every reason to believe they were still in mortal danger and every reason to try to save themselves if they were so inclined. Drury and colleagues collected data from more than 140 people who were present for the bombings, including 90 who had been on the trains. These data were made up of contemporaneous newspaper accounts (from 18 newspapers), which reported a range of statements from eyewitnesses and survivors, a corpus of 127 personal accounts which were given to official reviews, British Broadcasting Company websites, blogs, message boards, books, a radio documentary, and 27 interviews from primary respondents who had been in the bombings and were prepared to be interviewed directly. The data were coded and subjected to a thematic analysis. Drury and colleagues showed that the term *panic* was used by a few witnesses and survivors but mostly by commentators who did not witness events directly. Descriptions from the survivors tell the opposite story. Rather than selfishness and competition, mutual helping and concern predominated. People shared water, helped to stanch the flow of blood from those who were badly wounded, and generally provided emotional care and support. Interviewees described a sense of togetherness among survivors, using such terms as *unity, similarity, affinity, warmth,* and *empathy.* They contrasted this sense of togetherness to the sense of isolation, unpleasantness, and anomie they usually experienced as commuters on the busy underground system. Drury and colleagues argue that this helpfulness can be explained by the emergence of a shared social identity among victims of the event. They have found similar patterns in research on a variety of disaster scenarios, including soccer stadium crushes, music festival emergencies, building evacuations, ship sinkings, and other terrorist attacks. Survivors of these disasters who report feeling a common fate with others were more likely to report a feeling of shared identity. They also reported more instances of helping others or being helped by others during the emergency.

The role of shared identity in promoting helping behavior extends beyond emergency situations. Just as there are myths about irrational behavior during emergencies, so there are anxieties about behavior during mass gatherings of humanity more generally. As we have seen, traditional crowd psychology assumes that the crowd is inherently problematic. Crowd density is associated with danger, negative affect, and reduced cognitive performance. However, recent research on pilgrims to mass gatherings at Muslim and Hindu pilgrimage sites show that shared social identification can have positive benefits—particularly with respect to shared social support and helpfulness. For example, Alnabulsi and Drury (2014) studied pilgrims at the annual Hajj, or pilgrimage to Mecca. In 2012 the official number of pilgrims who gathered at specified spiritual locations at particular times—and who moved between locations in high-density flows—was more than 3 million. Given a recent history of crushing incidents and stampedes, Alnabusi and Drury (2014) were interested in whether shared identity might moderate both the behavior and the experience of pilgrims. They surveyed 1,194 pilgrims at the Holy Mosque—the site of Kaaba, a small black cube-shaped building that is the holiest site on earth for Muslims. At the height of the festival, the Holy Mosque is very crowded, with an average density of four people per square meter. However, nearer the Kaaba, the density levels can rise to six to eight people per square meter. The researchers measured density of the crowd, shared social identity with the crowd, and perceived safety. They found that, although increasing levels of crowd density reduced feelings of safety overall, this effect was moderated by identification with the crowd. More specifically, as density increased, those who had a higher level of identification with the crowd actually felt more safe. Their mediation analysis showed that this feeling of greater safety among high identifiers could be attributed to the fact that people felt that others in the crowd would be supportive and helpful toward them. Taken together, these findings suggest that identity, in the same way in which it leads to helping in emergencies, is also instrumental in the smaller and more mundane interactions in crowd settings—such as waiting in line, making space for others, or responding favorably to requests for help. Alnabusi and Drury (2014) argue that the role of collective identification is equally important to developing crowd safety solutions as the more usual engineering, mathematical, or architectural approaches.

Similar themes emerge in research by Nick Hopkins and colleagues (Tewari, Khan, Hopkins, Srinivasan, & Reicher, 2012; Pandey, Stevenson, Shankar, Hopkins, & Reicher, 2013) at the site of one of the largest gatherings of humanity on the planet—near Allahabad in northern India. Hopkins led a team that conducted a longitudinal study of Hindu pilgrims at a month-long religious festival in north India. This is an annual gathering at the confluence of the Ganges and Yamuna rivers, where pilgrims gather to perform sacred rituals and bathe in the waters of the Ganges. The event is on a 12-year cycle, and every 12 years (Maha Kumbh Mela) it is estimated that around 50 million people attend; 10 million can be on the site on a major bathing day. Every 6 years (Ardh Kumbh Mela) about 20 million people participate. In an ordinary year (Magh Mela), millions still attend, and hundreds of thousands of pilgrims (known as Kalpwasi) remain for the entire month. The conditions experienced by the Kalpwasis are very challenging. It is extremely cold, dusty, noisy, and crowded and with rudimentary sanitary facilities. These factors all combine to produce an environment that contains numerous potential stressors and threats to health and well-being. Tewari et al. (2012) showed that participation in the Mela, despite all these potential threats to health, had significant benefit to self-reported health status compared with those who remained in the villages. Pandey et al. (2013) further demonstrated that this greater resilience and positive sense of well-being resulted from a greater sense of connectedness to others and to both the feeling and the expectation that other pilgrims would be helpful and respectful toward them.

SOCIAL IDENTITY AND PERPETRATORS: TACKLING DEVIANTS WITHIN THE GROUP

So far we have seen how social identity dynamics among bystanders and between bystanders and victims can be central to the establishment of prosocial rather than antisocial behavior. We now move to consider the potential impact of social identity on the final key relationship in violent emergencies: the relationship between the group and the perpetrator. When situations involving violence arise, bystanders are forced to consider not only their relationship to the victim and other bystanders but also to those who perpetrate violence itself. Bystanders might therefore find themselves in the position of having to confront or resist a perpetrator in order to prevent or interrupt violence, putting themselves in a potentially dangerous situation.

According to Staub (2003, 2010), sharing some sense of collectivity with a violent perpetrator can confer upon one a potentially critical and powerful position—that of an "internal bystander" (a member of the perpetrator group who is not a perpetrator him- or herself). In discussing the conditions that foster the development of mass violence (e.g., genocide), Staub argued that internal bystanders can act as a social fulcrum, helping to shape collective norms regarding deviant acts in a positive or negative manner. Hence, whereas internal bystander passivity can tacitly enable and even encourage perpetration of violence by fellow group members, *intervening* against a violent perpetrator can convey a potent message concerning what is deemed acceptable behavior in terms of the group. Indeed, Staub (2010) noted that Nazi leaders in Germany consciously assessed the reactions of their own populace when anti-Jewish measures were first introduced. A general absence of resistance or protest against the measures was read as tacit acceptance, emboldening the Nazis and reinforcing the subjective legitimacy of their acts, thus allowing the intolerance of the Jews and ensuing violence to escalate to a massive scale. The *intra*group dynamics of a collective can thus play an important role in the emergence, and the cessation of violence.

One way in which group processes and social identity might function to actively promote prosocial action is through a social-psychological phenomenon known as the *black sheep effect* (Marques & Paez, 1994; Marques, Paez, & Abrams, 1998). This occurs when group members are seen to undermine or transgress some valued attitudinal or behavioral group norm and are thus perceived to threaten the reputation and image of the group and the associated social identity of group members. Consequently, in order to preserve the group's overall positivity and to uphold the legitimacy of its norms and standards, group members sometimes subject such deviants to greater negative judgment and derogation than they would if the deviant had belonged to an outgroup (Abrams, Marques, Bown, & Henson, 2000; Frings, Abrams, Randsley de Moura, & Marques, 2010).

Witnessing a member of a salient ingroup committing violence might thus be viewed as worse than witnessing an outgroup member behaving in the same manner, thus creating a greater willingness to intervene against an ingroup perpetrator. Of course, such a phenomenon depends on how strongly one identifies with the group in question, as well as the importance of the norm being transgressed (in this case, nonviolence; Frings et al., 2010). Hence, some group members might find it easier to psychologically distance themselves from a group image under threat or to disidentify with it and thus remain unperturbed by one of their own behaving badly (Eidelman & Biernat, 2003). There may also be some groups for whom recourse to violence is deemed more acceptable or even normative, and thus violent behavior would not be viewed as threatening to the group. Indeed, Frings et al. (2010) noted that the conditions under which group members might excuse or downplay the bad behavior of a rogue group member rather than acknowledging the threat posed by that person to the group, is still an open question.

Many studies have demonstrated the black sheep effect, usually through evidencing an exacerbated negative evaluation of ingroup relative to outgroup deviants. However, few studies have actually measured the willingness to confront or sanction such deviants, especially in the context of violence. Recent laboratory experiments have shown that group processes can have an impact upon bystander intentions to intervene and condemn nonviolent antisocial behavior, a process known as "informal social control." For example, Nugier, Chekroun, Pierre, and Niendenthal (2009) found that university students who read about a woman littering a public flowerbed indicated they would be more likely to actively condemn her when she was identified as a fellow student (ingroup) as opposed to a nonstudent (outgroup). Chekroun and Nugier (2011) found a similar result, as well as demonstrating that the effect was apparently underpinned by reactions of shame and embarrassment brought about because the antisocial behavior of an ingroup member threatened group image and social identity.

Although such examples pertain to the social control of relatively mundane and minor incivilities (e.g., littering), there exists some evidence to suggest that intragroup processes can also shape responses to violence. Wilson and Levine (2012) found that when participants read about or watched footage of street violence, they were more inclined to intervene in scenarios in which an outgroup perpetrator attacked an ingroup victim or an ingroup perpetrator attacked an outgroup member (reflecting a black sheep effect), compared with a situation in which the perpetrator and victim were both depicted as either ingroup or outgroup members. Outside the laboratory, Stott, Hutchinson, and Drury (2001) investigated collective disorder at the 1998 World Cup finals. Their ethnographic work revealed instances of the regulation of violence among Scottish soccer fans. The majority of these fans seemingly prided themselves on avoiding violent confrontation. When violence did arise from rogue members within the Scottish ranks, it was quashed by Scottish fans, who were concerned to uphold norms of nonviolence. Any violent fans were thus routinely condemned and restrained by their fellow group members.

According to Stott et al. (2001), this self-policing resulted from a desire among Scottish fans to maintain a positive impression of Scotland on the global stage. This was especially so because of the inevitable comparison of the Scots with stereotypically confrontational English fans (with whom there is a long history of rivalry); the World Cup finals provided the perfect stage for this to occur. In other words, the Scottish fans were particularly keen to appear well behaved, as doing so elevated the positivity of their group image above that of the English fans. Hence, the Scottish–English intergroup context shaped prosocial norms among the Scottish, which manifested in the intragroup regulation of ingroup violence.

Recently, programs in the United States aimed at ending the epidemic of sexual assaults against women in college campus communities (see Potter, Moynihan, & Stapleton, 2011) have increasingly targeted the role of bystanders (see Banyard, Moynihan, & Plante, 2007; Banyard, Plante, & Moynihan, 2004; Berkowitz, 2002). Moreover, some of these programs have begun to promote bystander action within specific social groups by focusing on men and groups in which norms of masculinity and appropriate male behavior can be addressed at a collective level (e.g., sports teams, fraternities). By emphasizing their efficacy and responsibility in preventing or halting sexual assault and by emphasizing prosocial male norms of intervention, such programs seek to enroll men as "social justice allies" for women (Fabiano, Perkins, Berkowitz, Linkenbach, & Stark, 2003), explicitly and collectively recruiting men in the regulation of male gendered violence.

Burn (2009) found that men reported being more willing to intervene in a sexual assault scenario when they knew the perpetrator and went on to argue that, by emphasizing group-level reputational threat (in other words, by taking advantage of black sheep effect processes), and by fostering a sense of collective responsibility, intervention might be facilitated when group deviants do arise (see also Banyard et al., 2004). Potter et al. (2011) also found that posters displayed on a college campus that depicted prosocial responses to potential sexual assault scenarios increased willingness to intervene when students positively identified with the people and situations in the posters (i.e., they found them familiar and relatable as part of a collective student experience), compared with when they did not.

Other programs have focused on debunking normative myths regarding how group peers view sexual assault. A social norms approach (e.g., Berkowitz, 2002) seeks to inform men that, in reality, other men strongly object to violence against women and also support intervention to prevent and stop it. In doing so, the approach addresses male misperceptions of gender-role expectations and of the norms held by peers regarding appropriate masculine behavior that might inhibit intervention (e.g., not appearing weak, or wishing to appear masculine; see Carlson, 2008). By revealing that, in fact, most men are uncomfortable with sexist and hypermasculine behavior, the approach encourages men to openly challenge attitudes that normalize violence or support rape myths (Berkowitz, 2002), empowered by the knowledge that they are upholding realistic male norms shared by their peers. They can thus begin to recalibrate positive collective norms of masculinity that enable and support intervention (see Katz, 1995).

In promoting the norm that most men *do* object to violence against women and would intervene to stop it, such approaches attempt to generate awareness of a kind of group-based normative support that sanctions attitudes and behaviors that are prosocial in their support of female victims of male violence. Research has shown that if people believe other members of their group have confronted a deviant, they are also encouraged to behave similarly (Frings et al., 2010). Likewise, believing that one's group holds collective norms that support or oblige intervention can encourage individuals to help victims of intimate partner violence (Baldry & Pagliaro, 2014) and also to intervene to prevent sexual assault (Fabiano et al., 2003). Moreover, social identity research in general has shown how public discourse can shape helping and intervention through promoting inclusivity and responsibility for victims (Reicher, Hopkins, Levine, & Rath, 2005; Reicher et al., 2006). It may be that such discourse can also, in some instances, target bystanders explicitly as members of a perpetrator group in order to effectively create social justice allies.

CONCLUSION

This chapter has argued that, although we know much about the potential for groups to produce antisocial behavior, we know comparatively little about how the power of groups can be harnessed to promote prosocial behavior. By reviewing recent evidence from laboratory and field experiments and exploring literatures in Holocaust rescue, emergency evacuation, and interpersonal violence, we have shown the importance of group processes to prosocial outcomes. Whether it is mobilizing communities to rescue Jews in the face of genocidal persecution, increasing the safety and resilience of those involved in mass (emergency) events, or developing programs to tackle perpetrators of (gendered) violence, a group-level approach promises important new insights.

The chapter describes the principles of a social identity approach to promoting prosocial behavior. It argues that a clear understanding of the social identity relationships among all those present in an emergency setting (bystanders, victims, and perpetrators) is central to the interpretation of behavior, and ultimately to the development of programs to promote prosociality. Knowing which social identities are salient, what the contents (the norms and values) of the social identities are, and where the boundaries of the social identities lie (who is included and excluded from the group) are the key to understanding (and thus harnessing) the impact of group processes in emergencies.

Since the early work in social psychology on the behavior of bystanders, group processes were always assumed to be the problem to be overcome rather than a potential resource to be harnessed. Groups were seen as part of the problem, not part of the solution. That is not to say, of course, that groups cannot turn bystanders into perpetrators or lead people to ignore the plight of others. The mistake is to assume that the impact of the group is *sui generis* a negative force on individual decision making and behavior. As we have seen in a variety of real-world examples, with life or death implications, group processes can empower individuals and societies to do the most heroic things. The challenge now is to learn how to harness group processes to promote all that is good—and tackle all that is evil.

REFERENCES

Abrams, D., Marques, J. M., Bown, N., & Henson, M. (2000). Pro-norm and anti-norm deviance within and between groups. *Journal of Personality and Social Psychology, 78*(5), 906–912.

Alnabulsi, H., & Drury, J. (2014). Social identification moderates the effect of crowd density on safety at the Hajj. *Proceedings of the National Academy of Sciences of the USA, 111*(25), 9091–9096.

Auf der Heide, E. (2004). Common misconceptions about disasters: Panic, the "disaster syndrome," and looting. In M. O' Leary (Ed.), *The first 72 hours: A community approach to disaster preparedness* (pp. 340–380). Lincoln, NE: iUniverse.

Baldry, A. C., & Pagliaro, S. (2014). Helping victims of intimate partner violence: The influence of group norms among lay people and the police. *Psychology of Violence, 4*(3), 334–347.

Banyard, V. L., Moynihan, M. M., & Plante, E. G., (2007). Sexual violence prevention through bystander education: An experimental evaluation. *Journal of Community Psychology, 35,* 463–481.

Banyard, V. L., Plante, E. G., & Moynihan, M. M (2004). Bystander education: Bringing a broader community perspective to sexual violence prevention. *Journal of Community Psychology, 32*(1), 61–79.

Ben-Yakov, A. (1990). Bulgaria. In I. Gutman (Ed.), *Encyclopedia of the Holocaust* (pp. 263–272). New York: Macmillan.

Berkowitz, A. D. (2002). Fostering men's responsibility for preventing sexual assault. In P. A. Schewe (Ed.), *Preventing violence in relationships* (pp. 163–196). Washington, DC: American Psychological Association.

Burn, S. (2009). A situational model of sexual assault prevention through bystander intervention. *Sex Roles, 60,* 779–792.

Carlson, M. (2008). I'd rather go along and be considered a man: Masculinity and bystander intervention. *Journal of Men's Studies, 16*(1), 3–17.

Chekroun, P., & Nugier, A. (2011). "I'm ashamed because of you, so please, don't do that!": Reactions to deviance as a protection against a threat to social image. *European Journal of Social Psychology, 41,* 479–488.

Cherry, F. (1995). *The stubborn particulars of social psychology.* London: Routledge.

Darley, J. M., & Batson, C. D. (1973). "From Jerusalem to Jericho": The study of situational and dispositional variables in helping behavior. *Journal of Personality and Social Psychology, 27*(1), 100–108.

Dawidowicz, L. S. (1986). *The war against the Jews, 1933–1945.* New York: Bantam.

Dovidio, J. F., Piliavin, J. A., Gaertner, S., Schroeder, D. A., & Clark, R. D., III. (1991). The arousal: Cost–reward model and the process of intervention: A review of the evidence. In M. Clark (Ed.), *Prosocial behavior* (pp. 86–116). Newbury Park, CA: Sage.

Drury, J., Cocking, C., & Reicher, S. (2009). Everyone for themselves?: A comparative study of crowd solidarity among emergency survivors. *British Journal of Social Psychology, 48,* 487–506.

Drury, J., Novelli, D., & Stott, C. (2013). Psychological disaster myths in the perception and management of mass emergencies. *Journal of Applied Social Psychology, 43,* 2259–2270.

Drury. J., & Reicher, S. (2010, November/December). "Crowd control": How we avoid mass panic. *Scientific American Mind,* pp. 58–65.

Eidelman, S., & Biernat, M. (2003). Derogating black sheep: Individual or group protection? *Journal of Experimental Social Psychology, 39*(6), 602–609.

Fabiano, P. M., Perkins, H. W., Berkowitz, A., Linkenbach, J., & Stark, C. (2003). Engaging men as social justice allies in ending violence against women: Evidence for a social norms approach. *Journal of American College Health, 52*(3), 105–112.

Fischer, P., Greitemeyer, T., Kastenmuller, A., Krueger, J. I., Vogrincic, C., Frey, D., et al. (2011). The bystander effect: A meta-analytic review on bystander intervention in dangerous and non-dangerous emergencies. *Psychological Bulletin, 137*(4), 517–537.

Frings, D., Abrams, D., Randsley de Moura, G., & Marques, J. (2010). The effects of cost, normative support, and issue importance on motivation to persuade in-group deviants. *Group Dynamics: Theory, Research, and Practice, 14*(1), 80–91.

Gansberg, M. (1964, March 27). 37 who saw murder didn't call the police. *The New York Times*, p. 1.

Genov, R., & Baeva, I. (2003). "Incomprehension of the nature of the race question": Saving the Bulgarian Jews from the Holocaust. In G. Halfdanarson (Ed.), *Racial discrimination and ethnicity in European history* (pp. 153–176). Pisa, Italy: Edizioni Plus, Pisa University Press.

Geras, N. (1995). *Solidarity in the conversation of humankind*. London: Verso.

Henkel, K. E., Dovodio, J. F., & Gaertner, S. L. (2006). Institutional discrimination, individual racism and Hurricane Katrina. *Analyses of Social Issues and Public Policy, 6*(1), 99–124.

Hilberg, R. (1993). *Perpetrators, victims, bystanders: The Jewish catastrophe 1933–1945*. New York: Harper Perennial.

Katz, J. (1995). Reconstructing masculinity in the locker room: The Mentors in Violence Prevention Program. *Harvard Educational Review, 65*(2), 163–175.

Latané, B., & Darley, J. M. (1970). *The unresponsive bystander: Why doesn't he help?* New York: Appleton-Century-Crofts.

Latané, B., & Nida, S. (1981). Ten years of research on group size and helping. *Psychological Bulletin, 89*(2), 308–324.

Levine, M., Cassidy, C., Brazier, G., & Reicher, S. (2002). Self-categorization and bystander nonintervention: Two experimental studies. *Journal of Applied Social Psychology, 7*, 1452–1463.

Levine, M., & Crowther, S. (2008). The responsive bystander: How social group membership and group size can encourage as well as inhibit bystander intervention. *Journal of Personality and Social Psychology, 95*(6), 1429–1439.

Levine, M., Prosser, A., Evans, D., & Reicher, S. (2005). Identity and emergency intervention: How social group membership and inclusiveness of group boundaries shapes helping behaviour. *Personality and Social Psychology Bulletin, 31*, 443–453.

Lidegaard, B. (2013). *Countrymen*. New York: Knopf

Manning, R., Levine, M., & Collins, A. (2007). The Kitty Genovese murder and the social psychology of helping: The parable of the 38 witnesses. *American Psychologist, 62*(6), 555–562.

Marques, J. M., & Paez, D. (1994). The "black sheep" effect: Social categorization, rejection of in-group deviants, and perception of group variability. In W. Stroebe & M. Hewstone (Eds.), *European review of social psychology* (Vol. 5, pp. 37–68). Chichester, UK: Wiley.

Marques, J. M., Paez, D., & Abrams, D. (1998). Social identity and intra-group differentiation as subjective social control. In S. Worchel, J. F. Morales, D. Paez, & J. C. Deschamps (Eds.), *Social identity: International perspectives* (pp. 124–141). New York: Sage.

Milgram, S. (1974). *Obedience to authority: An experimental view.* New York: Harper & Row.
Monroe, K. (2004). *The hand of compassion: Portraits of moral choice during the Holocaust.* Princeton, NJ: Princeton University Press.
Nugier, A., Chekroun, P., Pierre, K., & Niendenthal, P. M. (2009). Group membership influences social control of perpetrators of uncivil behaviours. *European Journal of Social Psychology, 39*(6), 1126–1134.
Oliner, S. P., & Oliner, P. M. (1992). *The altruistic personality: Rescuers of Jews in Nazi Europe.* New York: Free Press.
Pandey, K., Stevenson, C., Shankar, S., Hopkins, N. P., & Reicher, S. D. (2013). Cold comfort at the Magh Mela: Social identity processes and physical hardship. *British Journal of Social Psychology, 53*(4), 675–690.
Piliavin, J. A., & Charng, H. W. (1990). Altruism: A review of recent theory and research. *Annual Review of Sociology, 16,* 27–65.
Piliavin, J. A., Dovidio, J. F., Gaertner, S. L., & Clark, R. D. (1981). *Emergency intervention.* New York: Academic Press.
Potter, S. J., Moynihan, M. M., & Stapleton, G. J. (2011). Using social self-identification in social marketing materials aimed at reducing violence against women on campus. *Journal of Interpersonal Violence, 26*(5), 971–990.
Proulx, G., & Fahy, R. F. (2003). Evacuation of the World Trade Center: What went right? *Proceedings of the CIB-CTBUH International Conference on Tall Buildings October 20–23, Malaysia* (CIB Publication No. 290).
Reicher, S., Cassidy, C., Wolpert, I., Hopkins, N., & Levine, M. (2006). Saving Bulgaria's Jews: An analysis of social identity and the mobilisation of social solidarity. *European Journal of Social Psychology, 36*(1), 49–72.
Reicher, S., Hopkins, N., Levine, M., & Rath, R. (2005). Entrepreneurs of hate and entrepreneurs of solidarity: Social identity as a basis for mass communications. *International Review of the Red Cross, 87*(860), 621–637.
Scheepers, D. T. (2009). Turning social identity threat into challenge: Status stability and cardiovascular reactivity during inter-group competition, *Journal of Experimental Social Psychology, 45*(1), 228–233.
Sobel, R. S., & Leeson, P. T. (2006). Government's response to Hurricane Katrina: A public choice analysis. *Public Choice, 127,* 55–73.
Solnit, R. (2009). *A paradise built in hell: The extraordinary communities that arise in disaster.* New York: Viking.
Staub, E. (2003). *The psychology of good and evil: Why children, adults, and groups help and harm others.* New York: Cambridge University Press.
Staub, E. (2010). *Overcoming evil: Genocide, violent conflict, and terrorism.* New York: Oxford University Press.
Stott, C., Hutchinson, P., & Drury, J. (2001). Intergroup dynamics, social identity and the presence and absence of collective "disorder" at the 1998 Football World Cup Finals in France. *British Journal of Social Psychology, 40,* 359–384.
Tajfel, H. (1981). *Human groups and social categories.* Cambridge, UK: Cambridge University Press.
Tajfel, H., & Turner, J. C. (1979). An integrative theory of intergroup conflict. In W. G. Austin & S. Worchel (Eds.), *The social psychology of intergroup relations* (pp. 33–48). Monterey, CA: Brooks/Cole.

Tewari, S., Khan, S., Hopkins, N., Srinivasan, N., & Reicher, S. (2012). Participation in mass gatherings can benefit well-being: Longitudinal and control data from a North Indian Hindu pilgrimage event. *PLoS ONE*, 7(10), e47291.

Todorov, T. (2001). *The fragility of goodness*. London: Weidenfeld & Nicholson.

Turner, J. C., Hogg, M. A., Oakes, P. J., Reicher, S. D., & Wetherell, M. C. (1987). *Rediscovering the social group: A self-categorization theory*. New York: Blackwell.

Wilson, N. A., & Levine, M. (2012). *Social identity, violence and emotions: Bystander–perpetrator relationships in emergency intervention*. Unpublished manuscript.

CHAPTER 17

Remembering Historical Victimization
Potential for Intergroup Conflict Escalation and Conflict Reduction

Nyla R. Branscombe, Michael J. A. Wohl, and Ruth H. Warner

Past harms suffered by one's own group at the hands of another group are not simply chronicles found in a dusty history book. They are typically woven into the fabric of the group's identity, thus having consequences for intergroup attitudes and behavior (Rouhana & Bar-Tal, 1998). In this chapter, we address how both "good" (i.e., prosocial) and "evil" (i.e., antisocial) outcomes can flow from remembrance of historical victimization. We first consider the processes through which people can engage in harm doing toward members of other social groups—with little guilt or remorse—following reminders of their own group's historical victimization. Importantly, we discuss how negative attitudes and behaviors that stem from historical victimization are not merely directed toward members of the perpetrator group but also toward new groups not connected with the ingroup's victimization. We then examine the mechanisms that can lead to more benevolent outcomes when group members are reminded of their own historical victimization. Specifically, we discuss the necessary conditions for intergroup forgiveness and reconciliation, emphasizing when collective apology will be effective and why all too often it is not. We also address how memories of ingroup victimization can lead victim group members to help other victimized groups who are suffering. The central role of the meaning derived from historical victimization—in terms of the rights or obligations for current conduct that it implies—and how outgroups are differentially categorized depending on the meaning derived are emphasized.

At this juncture it is important to note that we focus on the consequences of remembering historical victimization for members of the victimized group. In doing so, we are not suggesting that historical victimization reminders have no relevance for the attitudes and behavior of perpetrator group members (see Sullivan, Landau, Branscombe, & Rothschild, 2012) or uninvolved third parties (see Warner & Branscombe, 2012). Instead, our objective is to examine how identifying as a member of a victimized group—and the ways in which outgroups are categorized and perceived—has implications for both prosocial and antisocial intergroup relations. Historical suffering is not neutral ground; suffering that stems from treatment that is perceived as unjust has implications for the social identity, morality, and emotions experienced by contemporary group members.

THE FUNCTION AND NATURE OF COLLECTIVE MEMORY

Members of a social group share a lineage. This is often expressed in terms of the group's "bloodline." The ancestral bridge, however, is not simply based on genetics. There is a bond that results from sharing a common history. Members of social groups have ancestors that have lived together, celebrated together, and—importantly—suffered together. Sharing these memories and formulating common beliefs about the sociopolitical context of those memories is a basic element of social identity formation.

According to Staub and Bar-Tal (2003), collective memories lurk below the surface, waiting to be brought to the fore. Particularly important, and having great impact, is the memory of ingroup suffering, even if all members (or oneself) did not experienced the suffering directly. For example, people who categorize themselves as members of a group experience vicarious empathy when informed of the suffering of a fellow group member (Avenanti, Sirigu, & Aglioti, 2010; Davis, 1994). Memories of such events help formulate shared beliefs about the ingroup and its relationship to other social groups (Bar-Tal, 2000). Group members tend to internalize the victimization experienced in the past, transforming it into a cultural narrative that becomes a prism through which their current sociopolitical realities are filtered. For example, memories of the Holocaust among Jewish people tend to elevate the perceived threat of Palestinians to the ingroup's continued existence, despite Israel's definitive military superiority (Wohl & Branscombe, 2008). In this way, collective memories are functional; attitudes and behaviors as they relate to intergroup conflict in the present reflect memories of past experiences (see Connerton, 1989). Put another way, group members experience the present in the context of their shared lineage and perceived connection (or self-categorization) with that lineage.

Volkan (1997) argued that groups that are unable to shed the memories of their historical victimization are likely to perpetuate feelings of powerlessness among their members. Eventually, the group's identity can become focused on their historical victimization. The consequence might be sensitivity to revictimization and a willingness to act in antisocial or aggressive ways in the name of group defense (see Staub, 2006). Indeed, victimization (or even the threat of it) has been used as justification for engaging in behavior that inflicts harm on enemies. For example, the victimization that Americans experienced during the September 11, 2001, attacks on the World Trade Center and the Pentagon was used as justification for the invasion of Afghanistan, and the threat of Saddam Hussein possessing weapons of mass destruction was used as justification for the invasion of Iraq. Thus prior ingroup victimization can legitimize or provide a reason for harming other groups who were not perpetrators of the actual suffering sustained by the ingroup. With that said, history is replete with examples of intergroup forgiveness of past wrongdoing and reconciliation with the former perpetrators of ingroup harm. Indeed, as Tutu (1999) suggested, humanity could not survive without forgiveness—through which victimized group members use their victimization experiences as a platform to advance intergroup good. Having suffered victimization might even make some group members believe they are morally obligated to help members of other groups that are currently suffering. In this chapter, we first address the evil that can stem from remembering past victimization and then turn our attention to factors that help promote positive intergroup relations in the face of historical ingroup victimization.

PAST VICTIMIZATION AS A LICENSE FOR HARM DOING

Memories of past victimization serve a number of functions. First and foremost, memories of past victimization help situate one's group within an intergroup dynamic—a dynamic in which one's own group is cast as victim and the other group is cast as perpetrator. By this process, one's group is placed on the side of the good, whereas the perpetrator group is placed on the side of evil.

Perceiving one's own group as good and the perpetrator group as evil has important implications for group members' social identity. According to Tajfel and Turner (1986), people are motivated to maintain a positive conception of the groups with which they identify. Morality is perhaps the most important dimension on which people evaluate their group (Leach, Ellemers, & Barreto, 2007). The victim role is attractive especially because victimhood enables a sense of moral superiority (see Moscovici & Perez, 2009). Specifically, following victimization, differences in the morality of one's own group and the perpetrator group become sharpened. The perpetrator group's goals and actions to achieve them are delegitimized. They are subsequently labeled cruel and uncaring—descriptors that paint the perpetrator group as less than human (see Baumeister, Stillwell, & Wotman, 1990; Leyens et al., 2000). Importantly, use of such descriptors increases the perceived likelihood that the perpetrator group is likely to revictimize if they have a chance.

The threat of revictimization heightens the perceived need for ingroup security, which can be addressed, in part, by acting against those who may pose a threat to the ingroup. Consequently, perceptions that a group has acted immorally toward one's own group can be used to justify behaving in an immoral fashion in response. Importantly, past victimization can also lead people to believe that other groups have ill intent toward one's own group (see Bar-Tal & Antebi, 1992). Such a siege mentality justifies aggressive, harmful behavior as a preemptive, defensive strike. Thus, although moral principles are typically framed as yielding prosocial (i.e., "good") behavior (e.g., Aquino, Freeman, Reed, Lim, & Felps, 2009), they can also be used as a tool to aggress against another group perceived to be evil.

Never Again: Immoral Behavior as a Defense against Future Victimization

Although it might be expected that people who themselves have a long history of suffering would "know better" than to harm others, the irony is that immoral behaviors can emerge from reminders of one's own historical victimization. The reason, according to Kelman (1992), is that groups that have recently experienced gross injustice are sensitive to the possibility that they might, once again, face a similar sort of threat that will require them to act to prevent new victimization. Bar-Tal and Antebi (1992) suggest that such sentiments are the central component of the siege mentality—a mental state in which members of a group hold the belief that the rest of the world has highly negative behavioral intentions toward them. Similarly, some people perceive the ingroup to be a perpetual victim—victimized by an array of enemies throughout its history (see Klar, Shori-Eyal, & Klar, 2013). Such appraisals of impending threat can arise from a history of group victimization and result in a desire to protect the group and its members. As Klar and colleagues (2013) make clear, among Israelis, the most frequently drawn lesson of the Holocaust is "never be a victim again," followed by "never let members of your group be victims." Importantly, such lessons can be drawn without personal experience with the ingroup's historical victimization; mere self-categorization as a member of a historically victimized group is all that is required.

Coupled with the notion that the ingroup must be on guard against those who might seek to victimize its members once again, there is often a perceived moral right to preemptive attack in the name of self-defense. Put another way, what would otherwise be considered immoral behavior becomes justified when it is framed as a means to protect the ingroup from potential new victimization. Indeed, the necessity of "doing evil to do good" has been used as a prelude to war and intergroup conflict by tacticians from Machiavelli to Robert McNamara, the "architect" of the Vietnam War.

Wohl, Branscombe, and Reysen (2010) suggested that collective angst—a group-based emotion focused on the future vitality of the ingroup—is an emotional mechanism linking historical ingroup victimization to intergroup harm doing. Collective memories of victimization typically carry an aversive existential tone (e.g., "they tried to destroy us"). Such existential threat elicits collective angst (e.g., "I'm anxious others will want to destroy us as well"), which in turn motivates group members to engage in ingroup protective action (e.g., "we must act to protect our group's future"). Thus, although an antecedent of collective angst might be memories of past victimization, this aversive group-based emotion has implications for responses to contemporary adversaries (i.e., the expected source of future harm) and ingroup protective actions.

In support of this contention, Wohl and colleagues (2010) found that regardless of the nature of the extinction threat experienced—whether from physical, cultural, or symbolic threats to the group—collective angst led historically victimized group members to favor policies aimed at solidifying the boundaries between the ingroup and the outgroup. For example, collective angst was elicited when Jews were reminded of the Holocaust. Among other consequences, collective angst heightened their desire to pass along Jewish traditions and to marry only fellow Jews. Although the Holocaust did not occur within the lifetime of participants, due to social categorization as a Jew, Holocaust reminders heightened concern for the group's future vitality. Moreover, extinction threat and the collective angst it evokes lead to behavior aimed at creating greater ingroup cohesion, as well as a desire for separation from those categorized as outgroups.

More recently, Mols and Jetten (2014) claimed that collective angst helps frame harm doing toward an outgroup as a necessary means of preserving the vitality of the ingroup. By examining the discourse of populist right-wing party leaders in Europe, they found that these leaders purposefully feed collective angst by expressing concerns about losing collective roots. In doing so, they provide (potential) followers with a historical justification for harsher treatment of migrants and minorities. Specifically, these leaders argue that group history shows that national survival depends on the group's ability to be strong in the face of threats. Providing further empirical support for this notion, Lucas, Rudolph, Zhdanova, Barkho, and Weidner (2014) found that heightened levels of collective angst predict support for exclusionary policies against immigrants. Thus, although direct experience with historical victimization may be absent, existential threat and memory of the victimization experienced by their ancestors can lead descendants to experience any new adversarial threat as reminiscent of that faced by their ancestors, and as a result they feel morally entitled to take action deemed necessary to reduce the threat (Bar-Tal & Antebi, 1992; Eidelson, & Eidelson, 2003).

Never Again: Laying Justification for Committing Evils

Reminders of past harms experienced by the ingroup can provide a license to engage in actions that harm others. Importantly, this license to harm others is not restricted to those who committed the historical harm. When the ingroup's historical victimization is salient, actions taken toward an entirely new enemy can be perceived as justifiable. We contend that historical victimization reminders undermine responsibility for harmful actions toward new enemies. In other words, historical victimization not only justifies the prospect of taking action against other social groups but also helps group members avoid feeling collective guilt that would otherwise be experienced when confronted by the harms they have committed against others.

Indeed, Wohl and Branscombe (2008) found that when Jewish North Americans were reminded of the Holocaust they felt less collective guilt for harm done to Palestinians, and this reaction was mediated by the increased illegitimacy of Palestinian actions and reductions in perceived Israeli responsibility for the conflict. However, when Jewish participants were reminded of another group's historical suffering (the Cambodian genocide) rather than their own group's Holocaust victimization, greater collective guilt for harm to Palestinians was experienced.

Because the existence of Israel today is rooted in the Holocaust experience (Teveth, 1996), perhaps the undermining of collective guilt depends on there being a link between the past victimization and current harmful actions toward Palestinians. To test whether this linkage between past victimization and present harm doing is necessary for collective guilt reduction, Wohl and Branscombe (2008) examined an instance in which such linkage was absent. The compelling case of American victimization by Japan's attack on Pearl Harbor in Hawaii in 1941 was utilized. There is little doubt that the Japanese bombing shattered Americans' sense of homeland security and served to bring the United States into the Second World War as a full combatant. Yet, because there is no connection between this instance of historical ingroup victimization and the war in Iraq, it was possible to assess whether a perceived link between the past and present is necessary for such historical reminders to undermine feelings of collective guilt for current ingroup harm doing. When reminded of such ingroup past victimization (vs. another group's past suffering—the Nazi invasion of Poland), Americans reported less collective guilt for harm sustained by Iraqis, and this lessened guilt was mediated by a sense of lowered American responsibility for the harm and increased legitimization of American actions due to al Qaeda terrorism. These effects of historical victimization reminders were specific to ingroup members (Americans); Canadians who were reminded of American past victimization (vs. another group's) did not show reductions in perceived American responsibility or increased legitimization of American harm to Iraqis. Indeed, under these conditions, Canadians expected Americans to feel considerably higher levels of collective guilt for their harm to Iraqis than they did. Thus reminders of the ingroup's historical victimization can lessen collective guilt felt for harm committed against a new adversary group—even when the historical and current intergroup conflicts are entirely unrelated. Furthermore, it is not simply a cognitive or mere contrast effect producing these results. Not only was the effect specific to ingroup members and absent in outgroup allies, but reminders of grave historical suffering on the part of any other group failed to lessen the perceived severity of subsequent ingroup harmful actions. Rather, reminders of past victimization experienced by one's own group alone evokes a sense of entitlement to harm others who are currently perceived as a threat to the ingroup and lessens feelings of collective guilt for harm doing by reducing perceived ingroup responsibility and encouraging legitimization of ingroup actions.

Threat and Competition between Victimized Groups

The negative consequences of historical victimization reminders are not restricted to former, current, or possible future enemies. Reminders of the ingroup's historical victimization not only increase sensitivity to outgroup threats but also increase motivation to define the victimization experienced by one's own group as incomparable to any other and thus of great significance. The consequence is that reminders of past victimization can yield negative responses to another victimized group, even if they are not directly threatening one's own group (i.e., there is no risk of harm doing from the other victimized group).

The desire to label the victimization experienced by one's own group as being greater than the other group's is strongest when both groups are in conflict. In such contexts, both sides claim to have experienced the greater harm (Noor, Shnabel, Halabi, & Nadler, 2012). The result is a reduced desire to find a solution to the conflict, which serves to continue the victimization of both sides (Noor et al., 2012; Sullivan et al., 2012). For example, willingness to forgive and seek reconciliation for the Troubles in Northern Ireland decreased alongside an increase in competitive victimhood (Noor, Brown, Gonzalez, Manzi, & Lewis, 2008; Noor, Brown, & Prentice, 2008). Importantly, the link between competitive victimhood and willingness to forgive was mediated by ingroup identification and outgroup trust such that higher identification and lower outgroup trust resulted in less willingness to forgive. Competitive victimhood also increases the perception that harm doing committed by the ingroup against an adversary was only in self-defense, and thus justified (Noor, Brown, Gonzalez, et al., 2008). Such justifications can be applied even when the suffering of the adversary group is made clear. For example, Jewish Canadians expressed entitlement to use any means necessary to defend the ingroup when reminded of Palestinian suffering—a desire that did not exist when Jewish Canadians were reminded of the suffering of neutral outgroups (Warner, Wohl, & Branscombe, 2014, Study 2).

Competition over victim status is not restricted to current adversaries; it can also exist among victimized groups that are not embroiled in conflict with each other (Noor et al., 2012; Sullivan et al., 2012). Although it would be reasonable to assume that victimized groups would recognize each other as compatriots in suffering, the existence of other victimized groups can pose a threat to the ingroup's victim role. As a result, one historically victimized group might respond negatively toward another historically victimized group. Indeed, Craig, DeHart, Richeson, and Fiedorowicz (2012) found that reminding white women of sexism (compared with a control condition) led to decreased pro-black responses. Additionally, to the extent that black Americans perceived their group to be victims of discrimination, more negative attitudes toward gay men and lesbians were expressed (Craig & Richeson, 2014, Study 1) and support for gay and lesbian civil rights was lowered (Craig & Richeson, 2014, Study 2). Craig and Richeson argued that reminders of ingroup victimization in these cases result in more negative intergroup attitudes because victimized group members are categorizing the other group as a competing identity outgroup. That is, when people self-categorize in terms of their racial group membership, sexual minorities are categorized as an outgroup. Instead of arousing empathy and increased common ground with the other victimized group, reminders of the ingroup's suffering serves as a social identity threat, resulting in increased ingroup bias and/or outgroup derogation. Presumably, it is difficult to see the commonalities in the suffering of the ingroup and the suffering of an outgroup when group membership is based on a different dimension or categorization. This can prevent a more inclusive victim recategorization and, potentially, increased reluctance to help another victim group in need.

Among victims, by construing all enemies (past and current) inclusively, reminders of past suffering can fuel current conflicts and lessen any guilt for ingroup harm doing. Reminders of past suffering can also lead to the denial of suffering of enemies and even reduce sympathy for other victimized groups. However, "never be a victim again" is not the only possible meaning that past victimization can evoke. Members of victimized groups can, at times, draw the lesson of preventing the suffering of others from remembrance of their own group's victimization (Klar et al., 2013). As is illustrated in the following, when past suffering is drawn on as a motivation to prevent intergroup conflict and the ingroup is seen as not uniquely victimized, more prosocial responses toward others can be evoked.

HOW GOOD CAN EMERGE FROM REMINDERS OF PAST VICTIMIZATION

Evil abounds in intergroup conflict, and, as outlined in the previous section, the collective memory of evil done against one's group can be used to justify harming other groups (Rouhana & Bar-Tal, 1998). In other words, evil can be perpetrated in response to remembrances of prior ingroup suffering. Importantly, however, over the course of human history some historically victimized group members have exhibited a capacity to see good in their (former) foes and have taken on the duty of assisting other victims. Indeed, Americans fought a bloody war for independence from their colonial British rulers. Now America and Britain are the closest of allies on the world stage. France and Germany have fought many wars against each other over the centuries. They now stand as brothers-in-arms within the European Union. And Israel, the Jewish State, calls Germany one of its strongest supporters and trading partners only decades removed from the Holocaust (Müller, 2011). Likewise, many Jewish Americans were supportive of the black civil rights movement in the United States in the early 1960s (Greenberg, 2010). More recently, remembering their own group's internment in camps during the Second World War, Japanese Americans protested against negative portrayals of Muslims, who, as a group, were deemed untrustworthy following the September 11th terrorist attacks (Murray, 2008). The point is that there is the potential for positive intergroup relations toward both former enemies and other groups with a history of victimization.

When considering the victimized group's perspective, forgiveness is a crucial step in promoting positive intergroup relations between former enemies. Forgiveness involves abandoning retribution against one's enemies and sets the stage for reconciliation and future positive intergroup relations (Bar-Tal, 2011). Shared experiences of victimization may lead one victimized group to have more positive attitudes toward another victimized group through recategorization and meaning-making processes (Craig & Richeson, 2012; Galanis & Jones, 1986; Warner et al., 2014).

How Intergroup Forgiveness Can Undermine Conflict

Intergroup forgiveness is at the heart of the psychology of good in the face of intergroup evil. Yet intergroup forgiveness is not an easy outcome for victimized group members to achieve. Thus it is important to ask what allows victimized group members to abandon their right to resentment, indifferent behavior toward members of the perpetrator group, or retribution seeking. Failure to ask risks glossing over the ambivalence, if not outright disdain, that many victimized group members feel toward the perpetrator group in the aftermath of harm that even the most heartfelt gestures of reconciliation on the part of the perpetrator group may not penetrate. Furthermore, our discussion is grounded in the belief that intuitions about intergroup forgiveness, likely stemming from experience with interpersonal forgiveness, are insufficient in understanding the rocky road to intergroup reconciliation. Thus the antecedents and consequences of intergroup forgiveness require empirical scrutiny. Next, we review theory and research on how and why intergroup forgiveness is (or is not) granted.

What Is Intergroup Forgiveness and Why Is It So Hard to Grant?

Since the late 1990s, psychological research has made remarkable strides in delineating the antecedents and consequences of interpersonal forgiveness (see Riek & Mania, 2012, for a review)—a prosocial response by a victim to a transgression perpetrator (McCullough, Pargament, & Thoresen, 2000). When people are victimized there is typically an associated increased desire to avoid, or even seek revenge against, their transgressors. When forgiveness is granted, memories of the transgressor, as well as the transgression, no longer motivate the victim toward these behaviors. Additionally, the victim who forgives tends to reap rewards in terms of psychological and physiological well-being (see Larsen et al., 2012; Toussaint, Owen, & Cheadle, 2012). Thus it would appear that in forgiveness there is great potential for good.

Akin to interpersonal forgiveness, intergroup forgiveness has been commonly conceived of as a prosocial act that yields positive outcomes (e.g., Noor, Brown, & Prentice, 2008; Wohl & Branscombe, 2005). Indeed, similar to its interpersonal sister, Wohl and Branscombe (2005), as well as Cehajic, Brown, and Castano (2008), found that intergroup forgiveness of historical victimization reduces the desire for psychological, as well as physical, distance from members of the perpetrator group. Intergroup forgiveness has been shown to be a positive predictor of harmony-oriented attitudes and behaviors (e.g., the seeking of means to resolve intergroup differences in order to enable peaceful coexistence; Noor, Brown, & Prentice, 2008). Given these outcomes, effort in uncovering avenues to facilitate intergroup forgiveness should be a good investment.

Wohl and Branscombe (2005) demonstrated that willingness to forgive a former perpetrator group is facilitated through a process of inclusive human categorization. Specifically, Jews were more forgiving of contemporary Germans for the Holocaust when they were induced to categorize members of both groups in terms of their common humanity. Likewise, Staub, Pearlman, Gubin, and Hagengimana (2005) demonstrated that Tutsi survivors who categorized the Hutu perpetrators of the genocide in Rwanda as humans like themselves and who perceived such harm doing as pervasive across human groups expressed greater forgiveness and exhibited reduced trauma symptoms. Of course, it could be argued that perceiving the humanity in the direct perpetrators, or even the descendents of those who harmed fellow group members, is not an easy feat. After all, when common humanity is highlighted, the boundaries between groups weakens, which has been shown to be threatening (Jetten, Spears, Hogg, & Manstead, 2000). According to social identity theory (Tajfel & Turner, 1986), group members are motivated to achieve and maintain a positive and distinct social identity. When intergroup distinctiveness is low, group members take action to reassert their uniqueness—action that can take on an antisocial or "evil" flavor (Jetten, Spears, & Postmes, 2006). Moreover, by placing perpetrators of intergroup harm into an inclusive, human category alongside one's own group, the value of that "human" category might be devalued. Such identity concerns may therefore undermine attempts at highlighting common humanity with the perpetrator group. Lastly, as Greenaway, Quinn, and Louis (2011) found, although common humanity increases forgiveness, it also reduces collective action to obtain restitution for the past harm experienced among historically victimized groups. Yet, once the common humanity wheels are set in motion, the resulting intergroup good appears to self-perpetuate. As shown by Noor, Shnabel, Halabi, and Doosje (2015), intergroup forgiveness results in perceiving an adversary group as trustworthy, like members of one's own group, which facilitates reconciliation.

Interestingly, perpetrator groups often seek to elicit intergroup forgiveness on the part of victim groups through the offer of a collective apology. Indeed, collective apologies have occurred with such frequency over the last few decades that Brooks (1999) has argued that humanity has entered an "age of apology." It is unknown precisely why there has been a recent upswing in the offer of collective apology, but the strong apology–forgiveness link that exists at the interpersonal level may well be part of the rationale (see Fehr, Gelfand, & Nag, 2010, for a meta-analytic review of the apology–forgiveness link). Despite the apologizer's presumably good intentions and desire to reconcile with the victimized group, the link between offering a collective apology and intergroup forgiveness on the part of victims is often absent (see Hornsey & Wohl, 2013 for a review).

In one of the first studies to assess the apology–forgiveness link at the intergroup level, Philpot and Hornsey (2008) exposed Australians to historical transgressions (incidents from the Second World War) against their ingroup and manipulated whether or not the perpetrator group was said to have offered an apology. The hypothesized boost in intergroup forgiveness was not observed; this may have occurred because an apology induces forgiveness in victims only if it is perceived to be costly for the perpetrator and therefore sincere, or if the official representative delivering the apology is believed to have the support of his or her population. More recently, Shnabel, Halabi, and Siman Tov-Nachlieli (2015) showed that collective apologies are frequently perceived to be insincere—a result in line with the findings of Blatz, Schumann, and Ross (2009), who showed that Chinese Canadians tended to believe that an official apology provided by the Canadian government for historical harms committed against their community did not reflect sincere remorse and instead was seen as an attempt to win votes in the next election. Similarly, qualitative work suggests that victimized group members are often ambivalent about apologies. For example, Chapman (2007) analyzed 6 years' worth of transcripts from the South African Truth and Reconciliation Commission (TRC) and noted the rarity with which victims mentioned forgiveness. This seemed to be consistent with the rareness of sincere apologies offered by these direct perpetrators and with victims' awareness of the exchange made by the perpetrators of their truth-telling for avoidance of prosecution for their actions. In a different intergroup context, Philpot, Balvin, Mellor, and Bretherton (2013) found that although some indigenous Australians reported forgiving white Australians for the forced removal and relocation of their children to white Australians' homes (i.e., the Stolen Generation), no participant indicated that the collective apology issued by the Australian government a half-century later helped them through the forgiveness process.

One reason that efforts to facilitate prosocial intergroup relations in the aftermath of historical victimization tend to fall flat concerns the psychology of trust (Hornsey & Wohl, 2013). A lack of intergroup trust is a defining characteristic of groups in conflict, especially among highly identified group members (see Dovidio, Gaertner, Kawakami, & Hodson, 2002; Tanis & Postmes, 2005). Without trust, efforts by the perpetrator group are likely to be perceived as hollow at best and duplicitous at worst by members of the victimized group. Providing empirical support for this supposition, Nadler and Liviatan (2006) showed that trust moderated the effect of conciliatory statements by the Palestinian leadership on Israelis' willingness to forgive. Specifically, a conciliatory statement by the Palestinian leadership (compared with the no-conciliatory-statement control) promoted forgiveness among Israelis who reported high preexisting levels of trust in Palestinians. When preexisting trust was low (the typical state of affairs during intergroup conflict), a conciliatory statement appeared to undermine forgiveness (compared with the no-conciliatory-statement control).

Unfortunately, trust (in the service of intergroup forgiveness) is not easy to induce. Among other reasons, ingroup members tend to be skeptical about the motives, intentions, and character of outgroup members (see Tanis & Postmes, 2005). Thus, when the perpetrator group makes reparative moves, victimized group members are apt to concern themselves with possible ulterior motives (see Philpot & Hornsey, 2008). Complicating matters further, any attempt at repairing the wrongs of the past is typically offered by a representative of the perpetrator group. The consequence is that victimized group members question whether the offer was merely a political decision to pacify, whether all (or even most) of the perpetrator group agrees with the offer of repair, or whether most members of the perpetrator group even understand the suffering sustained by the victim group. In practice, formal intergroup apologies often do have a strong political and thus strategic component. Moreover, due to social identity protective processes, many members of the perpetrator group are reluctant to accept collective guilt for historical harms the ingroup committed (see Wohl, Branscombe, & Klar, 2006). The outcome is, all too often, a lack of intergroup forgiveness on the part of historically victimized group members.

Creating the Psychological Infrastructure for Intergroup Forgiveness

According to the needs-based model of reconciliation (Shnabel & Nadler, 2008; Shnabel, Nadler, Ullrich, Dovidio, & Carmi, 2009), victimization robs the group of its power and agency. Accordingly, perpetrators who restore the victimized group's power can facilitate the forgiveness process (see Wenzel & Okimoto, 2010). A collective apology is often presumed to rectify the power imbalance created by victimization, particularly if accompanied by an admission of guilt by the perpetrator (Tutu, 1999). Although a collective apology may not be an ideal vehicle for victimized-group empowerment, the act of granting forgiveness might have intrinsic power restoration qualities. In forgiving the perpetrator group, the victimized group demonstrates its moral fortitude—that it is strong enough to look beyond the harms inflicted. Advocating that victimized groups forgive the perpetrator group as a means of achieving reconciliation can place an undue burden on them. Nonetheless, actually granting intergroup forgiveness does encourage the belief that enduring peace between groups in conflict is possible and desirable (Noor et al., 2015). Likewise, intergroup forgiveness can increase willingness to have contact with former perpetrator group members (Wohl & Branscombe, 2005).

To help ensure that the victimized group feels empowered, it is important for both sides to come to a common understanding of the past. To this end, discussions between representatives of the victimized and perpetrator groups are often fruitful. At the foundation of any discussion should be validation of the suffering experienced by the victims, which perpetrator groups are often tempted to downplay (Branscombe & Cronin, 2010; Wohl et al., 2006). Although it is challenging to their social identity and its moral image, perpetrator group members need to be empathetic witnesses to the suffering incurred by the victims. To the extent that perpetrator group members are able to do this, victim forgiveness is increased. Among victims who participated in the South African TRC and were given an opportunity to talk about the nature of the human rights violations they suffered, greater forgiveness of the perpetrators emerged (Kaminer, 2006). The use of these methods of reconciliation—through which victims convey their suffering at the hands of the perpetrator group—can be effective in unilateral intergroup conflicts, those in which the perpetrator and victim roles are clearly defined and recognized by the groups involved in the conflict (Klar & Schori-Eyal, 2015).

Acknowledging the harm done on both sides in bilateral conflicts, or conflicts in which both sides may be both victim and perpetrator, can also promote forgiveness. As discussed in the previous section, denying the suffering of the outgroup impedes reconciliation (Noor, Brown, & Prentice, 2008). Making salient the suffering of both sides in an intergroup conflict, and thereby inducing a common victim identity, decreases defensiveness and increases intergroup forgiveness (Shnabel, Halabi, & Noor, 2013). Key to such conflicts with simultaneous claims on victimhood is the idea of mutual forgiveness—rather than one group apologizing and the other forgiving—as clear-cut perpetrator and victim roles are not accepted by group members. Klar and Schori-Eyal (2015) examined mutual forgiveness and willingness to apologize in Israeli residents living in a town bordering the Gaza Strip. They found that Israeli residents exhibited little support for Israel's apologizing for military actions in the Gaza Strip, and they accepted little moral responsibility for such actions in this bilateral ongoing conflict situation because they do not accept the sole-perpetrator role. However, Klar and Schori-Eyal (2015) found considerable support among Israeli Jews for mutual forgiveness—the idea that Israelis and Palestinians need to forgive each other in order to move toward reconciliation.

A secondary benefit of intergroup discussions about historical victimization is that it provides an opportunity for intergroup contact. Indeed, Hewstone and colleagues (2004) reported that contact between Protestants and Catholics in Northern Ireland was positively associated with higher trust in the outgroup and with greater willingness to forgive its past misdeeds. Similarly, Cehajic et al. (2008) found that the contact between Bosnians and Serbs in Bosnia-Herzegovina predicted Bosnians' willingness to forgive Serbs through enhanced perspective taking, trust, and perception of outgroup heterogeneity. Thus bringing together members of conflicting groups in a context that promotes both frequent and good quality contact may be central to achieving forgiveness (Pettigrew & Tropp, 2006).

Intergroup contact can facilitate forgiveness in part because it provides opportunity to acquire new information about the perpetrator group. It is easy for victimized group members to cognitively freeze on preexisting negative beliefs about a perpetrator group (Halperin & Bar-Tal, 2011) and be unwilling to incorporate new positive information about the adversary group (see Porat, Halperin, & Bar-Tal, 2015). Needed to change this pattern are ways to help the victimized group see that the perpetrator group is able to change (see Halperin, Russell, Trzesniewski, Gross, & Dweck, 2011). Providing evidence of the importance of perceived change in the perpetrator group, Licata, Klein, Saade, Azzi, and Branscombe (2012) showed that victimized group members who are able to differentiate those who committed the historical harm from contemporary outgroup members report increased levels of intergroup forgiveness. Broadly speaking, then, when victimized group members, such as Christians in Lebanon, can be focused on ways the perpetrator group (Muslims in Lebanon) has changed from how it was (or was perceived to be) during the past civil war, intergroup trust may be built, and this can result in greater forgiveness and conflict resolution.

How Past Victimization Can Increase Prosocial Responses to Other Victimized Groups

Reminders of past victimization do not only influence intergroup relations among victim and perpetrator groups. Such reminders can also affect the ways in which victimized group members react to the suffering of other groups. At times, belonging to a group with a victimization history can lead to more positive attitudes and prosocial intentions toward members of other stigmatized groups. Victims who recategorize other victimized groups at a more superordinate level (e.g., "we are all victims") exhibit more positive intergroup attitudes (Gaertner & Dovidio, 2000). Reminders of victimization encourage this recategorization to the extent that they draw attention to similarities that members of different victimized groups share. Victimized group members may share a common experience of facing discrimination, disadvantage, stigma, or being subjected to violence (e.g., women and ethnic minorities). They may also share a common enemy or oppressor (e.g., African Americans, Mexican Americans, and Native Americans have all experienced harm at the hands of white Americans). When a common oppressor is perceived, different victimized groups may come to share similar goals—to reduce the disadvantages that their own and other stigmatized groups face.

To the extent that reminders of victimization increase perceived commonality between victimized groups, they can lead to more positive attitudes held by one victimized group toward another. For example, in one of the earliest social psychology experiments to examine the effects of reminders of victimization on judgments of members of a different victimized group, black undergraduates either read or did not read about a black individual who faced difficulties in life due to poverty and whose lawyer said he "was a victim of society." They were then asked to evaluate a mentally ill individual. Black participants who were reminded of blacks' status as victims were more tolerant of the mentally ill person than black participants who were not reminded of blacks as victims (Galanis & Jones, 1986). Although Galanis and Jones did not measure any mediating processes, they speculated that reminders of one's own group's victimization promote the drawing of connections between one's own victimization history and the experience of other victimized groups. Such shared experiences were believed to create sympathy for members of a different victimized group and to lead to a more positive view of them.

More recent research has offered additional evidence that belonging to a victimized group can sometimes produce positive attitudes toward different victimized groups by increasing perceptions of similarity. For example, members of minority groups in the Netherlands desire less social distance from minority outgroups they see as more similar compared with those they see as less similar (Hindriks, Verkuyten, & Coenders, 2014). Among Latino Americans, perceiving discrimination as due to race is associated with being more likely to believe that Latinos share a common fate with black Americans (Craig & Richeson, 2012, Study 1b). When the salience of discrimination against Latino Americans was manipulated, Craig and Richeson (2012, Study 5) found that Latino Americans who were reminded of discrimination against their group had more positive attitudes toward black Americans compared with Latino Americans who had not been reminded of discrimination. This effect was mediated by perceived similarity between the two disadvantaged groups.

Remembering victimization can result in not only more positive attitudes toward other victimized groups but, in addition, a greater obligation or duty to help other, unrelated groups who have also been victimized. This is especially likely when members of victimized groups consider the meaning or lesson of that victimization for their own group. One meaning taken from historical victimization and oppression may be to try to prevent such atrocities from happening again or to provide assistance to victims if they do (Klar et al., 2013; Murray, 2008). This meaning may be most likely when parallels are drawn between the victimization that one group experienced and that of another. For example, some Jewish leaders have stated that Jewish people have a moral obligation to help the Sudanese refugees fleeing the genocide in Darfur due to their group's own Holocaust history (Messinger, 2005; Peraino, 2006; Wiesel, 2004). The perceived similarity between the victimization history of one's own group and the victimization of another group can enhance the sense of obligation to act prosocially toward the other group.

We examined these processes in a number of studies involving Jewish or female participants (Warner et al., 2014). First, we asked Jewish participants to consider the lessons of the Holocaust for either the victimized group (Jews) or the perpetrator group (Germans). Thus their ingroup's victimization was always salient, but the meaning constructed was focused on one group or the other. We found that the Jewish participants perceived Jews as more obligated to provide assistance to other victimized groups and to do no harm to other victimized groups when they focused on the lessons of their group's victimization, for Jews compared with Germans (Warner et al., 2014, Study 1). Focusing on the meaning of victimization for one's own victimized group brought to mind a particular lesson—not letting others suffer as one's group has—and so highlights the experience of suffering that different victimized groups share. We replicated the lesson of the victimization focus effect with women by asking women to either consider the lessons of women's history of oppression for women or the lessons of it for men (Warner et al., 2014, Study 3). We then assessed how obligated women were to help blacks and to refrain from harming blacks, as well as how similar the oppression of women was to the oppression of other stigmatized groups. We found that perceived similarity of the groups mediated the effect of the lesson focus on moral obligation to help others and not do harm. Focusing on the lesson of women's oppression for women compared with men resulted in female participants perceiving their group's history of victimization as more similar to other oppressed groups' victimization, which in turn resulted in female participants perceiving women as incurring moral obligations to act prosocially toward blacks.

Experiencing collective victimization has long-lasting implications for members of victimized groups in how they think about and relate to members of other groups. The focus of experiencing collective victimization can shift from one of defensiveness and protection of the ingroup to one of avoiding continued intergroup conflict and suffering (Klar et al., 2013). Such a change in mind set can encourage intergroup forgiveness and assisting other victimized groups that are currently in need.

CONCLUSIONS

Reminders of one's own group's victimization can encourage "evil" and fuel harm doing toward not just the former perpetrator group (i.e., retribution) but, more critically, toward other, entirely new adversaries who were unconnected with the ingroup's original victimization. It is in this sense that reminders of past victimization can act as a license, or sense of entitlement, for current harm doing to others. The reason is that memories of one's own victimization can evoke a sense of perpetual ingroup threat (siege mentality) and elicit feelings of collective angst. Such angst leads victim groups to maintain separation from those categorized as outgroups. Threat and this "never again" understanding of intergroup relations lessens feelings of collective guilt for ingroup harm doing toward groups defined as "new enemies." Reminders of ingroup suffering, too, can have negative implications for responses to other victimized groups. When people self-categorize as members of a uniquely victimized group, they show less sympathy toward other victim groups that are categorized as competing outgroups. However, when they recategorize those outgroups as sharing a common inclusive ingroup with their own (e.g., "fellow victims"), a moral obligation to help those others can emerge.

Intergroup forgiveness is another form of good that can emerge from historical victimization. This can entail forgiving the direct perpetrators of the harm done to the ingroup (e.g., Rwandan survivors of the genocide or black South Africans following the dismantling of apartheid), forgiving the descendants of the historical perpetrators (e.g., Jewish people forgiving contemporary Germans), or mutual forgiving of those one's group has both been harmed by and done harm to (e.g., Jewish Israelis and Palestinians in the current conflict). One of the most critical factors encouraging intergroup forgiveness in each of these forms is recategorization—perceiving the harm-perpetrating group as human like one's own. Intergroup apology by a representative of the historical or current perpetrator group is not so frequently effective at instigating intergroup forgiveness in members of the victimized group. The reason is that such apologies are rarely perceived as sincere or effective at restoring power to the victims, although they can be effective when seen as genuine. Apology can be effective when the outgroup representative is perceived to be trustworthy and is not seen as merely serving his or her own interests. Likewise, when the suffering of the outgroup is acknowledged, it can be taken as a sign of genuine desire for forgiveness and reconciliation.

Which process will operate in the face of reminders of historical victimization—licensing of harm doing toward others or empathy and mutual forgiveness—fundamentally depends on the interpretation given to the past. Is its meaning "never forget and always be on guard to protect ourselves," or is its meaning "we have to be on guard never to be perpetrators and not do what was done to us"? How others are categorized is also central to how outgroups are likely to be treated. If they are categorized as "human" like us, or victimized like us, then good may be more likely to emerge than evil when our own past suffering is recalled.

REFERENCES

Aquino, K., Freeman, D., Reed, A., II, Lim, V. K. G., & Felps, W. (2009). Testing a social-cognitive model of moral behavior: The interactive influence of situations and moral identity centrality. *Journal of Personality and Social Psychology, 97,* 123–141.

Avenanti, A., Sirigu, A., & Aglioti, S. M. (2010). Racial bias reduces empathic sensorimotor resonance with other-race pain. *Current Biology, 20,* 1018–1022.

Bar-Tal, D. (2000). *Shared beliefs in a society: Social-psychological analysis.* Thousand Oaks, CA: Sage.

Bar-Tal, D. (2011). *Intergroup conflicts and their resolution: Social psychological perspective.* New York: Psychology Press.

Bar-Tal, D., & Antebi, D. (1992). Beliefs about negative intentions of the world: A study of the Israeli siege mentality. *Political Psychology, 13,* 633–645.

Baumeister, R. F., Stillwell, A., & Wotman, S. R. (1990). Victim and perpetrator accounts of interpersonal conflict: Autobiographical narratives about anger. *Journal of Personality and Social Psychology, 59,* 994–1005.

Blatz, C. W., Schumann, K., & Ross, M. (2009) Government apologies for historical injustices. *Political Psychology, 30,* 219–241.

Branscombe, N. R., & Cronin, T. (2010). Confronting the past to create a better future: The antecedents and benefits of intergroup forgiveness. In A. Azzi, X. Chryssochoou, B. Klandermans, & B. Simon (Eds.), *Identity and participation in culturally diverse societies* (pp. 338–358). New York: Wiley-Blackwell.

Brooks, R. L. (Ed.). (1999). *When sorry isn't enough: The controversy over apologies and reparations for human injustice.* New York: New York University Press.

Cehajic, S., Brown, R. J., & Castano, E. (2008). Forgive and forget: Antecedents and consequences of intergroup forgiveness in Bosnia and Herzegovina. *Political Psychology, 29,* 351–367.

Chapman, A. R. (2007). Truth commissions and intergroup forgiveness: The case of the South African Truth and Reconciliation Commission. *Peace and Conflict: Journal of Peace Psychology, 13,* 51–69.

Connerton, P. (1989). *How societies remember.* New York: Cambridge University Press.

Craig, M. A., DeHart, T., Richeson, J. A., & Fiedorowicz, L. (2012). Do unto others as others have done unto you?: Perceiving sexism influences women's evaluations of stigmatized racial groups. *Personality and Social Psychology Bulletin, 38,* 1107–1119.

Craig, M. A., & Richeson, J. A. (2012). Coalition or derogation?: How perceived discrimination influences intraminority intergroup relations. *Journal of Personality and Social Psychology, 102,* 759–777.

Craig, M. A., & Richeson, J. A. (2014). Discrimination divides across identity dimensions: Perceived racism reduces support for gay rights and increases anti-gay bias. *Journal of Experimental Social Psychology, 55,* 169–174.

Davis, M. H. (1994). *Empathy: A social-psychological approach.* New York: Hawthorne.

Dovidio, J. F., Gaertner, S. L., Kawakami, K., & Hodson, G. (2002). Why can't we just get along? Interpersonal biases and interracial distrust. *Cultural Diversity and Ethnic Minority Psychology, 8,* 88–102.

Eidelson, R. J., & Eidelson, J. I. (2003). Dangerous ideas: Five beliefs that propel groups toward conflict. *American Psychologist, 58,* 182–192.

Fehr, R., Gelfand, M. J., & Nag, M. (2010). The road to forgiveness: A meta-analytic synthesis of its situational and dispositional correlates. *Psychological Bulletin, 136,* 894–914.

Gaertner, S. L., & Dovidio, J. F. (2000) *Reducing intergroup bias: The common ingroup identity model.* Philadelphia: Psychology Press.

Galanis, C. M. B., & Jones, E. E. (1986). When stigma confronts stigma: Some conditions enhancing a victim's tolerance of other victims. *Personality and Social Psychology Bulletin, 12,* 169–177.

Greenaway, K. H., Quinn, E. A., & Louis, W. R. (2011). Appealing to common humanity increases forgiveness but reduces collective action among victims of historical atrocities. *European Journal of Social Psychology, 41,* 569–573.

Greenberg, C. L. (2010). *Troubling the waters: Black–Jewish relations in the American century.* Princeton, NJ: Princeton University Press.

Halperin, E., & Bar-Tal, D. (2011). Socio-psychological barriers to peace making: An empirical examination within the Israeli Jewish Society. *Journal of Peace Research, 48,* 637–651.

Halperin, E., Russell, G. A., Trzesniewski, H. K., Gross, J. J., & Dweck, C. S. (2011). Promoting the peace process by changing beliefs about group malleability. *Science, 333,* 1767–1769.

Hewstone, M., Cairns, E., Voci, A., McLernon, F., Niens, U., & Noor, M. (2004). Intergroup forgiveness and guilt in Northern Ireland: Social psychological dimensions of "The Troubles." In N. R. Branscombe & B. Doosje (Eds.), *Collective guilt: International perspectives* (pp. 193–215). New York: Cambridge University Press.

Hindriks, P., Verkuyten, M., & Coenders, M. (2014). Interminority attitudes: The roles of ethnic and national identification, contact, and multiculturalism. *Social Psychology Quarterly, 77,* 54–74.

Hornsey, M. J., & Wohl, M. J. A. (2013). We are sorry: Intergroup apologies and their tenuous link with intergroup forgiveness. *European Review of Social Psychology, 24,* 1–31.

Jetten, J., Spears, R., Hogg, M. A., & Manstead, A. S. (2000). Discrimination constrained and justified: Variable effects of group variability and in-group identification. *Journal of Experimental Social Psychology, 36,* 329–356.

Jetten, J., Spears, R., & Postmes, T. (2004). Intergroup distinctiveness and differentiation: A meta-analytic integration. *Journal Personality and Social Psychology, 86,* 862–879.

Kaminer, D. (2006). Forgiveness attitudes of Truth Commission deponents: Relation to commission response during testimony. *Journal of Peace Psychology, 12,* 175–187.

Kelman, H. C. (1992). Acknowledging the other's nationhood: How to create a momentum for the Israeli–Palestinian negotiations. *Journal of Palestinian Studies, 22,* 18–38.

Klar, Y., & Schori-Eyal, N. (2015). Gazing at suffering Gaza from suffering Sderot: Seeds of forgiveness and reconciliation amidst the turmoil? *Group Processes and Intergroup Relations, 18,* 624–643.

Klar, Y., Schori-Eyal, N., & Klar, Y. (2013). The "never again" State of Israel: The emergence of the Holocaust as a core feature of Israeli identity and its four incongruent voices. *Journal of Social Issues, 69,* 125–143.

Larsen, B. A., Darby, R. S., Harris, C. R., Nelkin, D. K., Milam, P. E., & Christenfeld, N. J. (2012). The immediate and delayed cardiovascular benefits of forgiving. *Psychosomatic Medicine, 74,* 745–750.

Leach, C. W., Ellemers, N., & Barreto, M. (2007). Group virtue: The importance of morality (vs. competence and sociability) in the positive evaluation of in-groups. *Journal of Personality and Social Psychology, 93,* 234–249.

Leyens, J. P., Paladino, P. M., Rodriguez-Torres, R., Vaes, J., Demoulin, S., Rodriguez-Perez, A., et al. (2000). The emotional side of prejudice: The attribution

of secondary emotions to ingroups and outgroups. *Personality and Social Psychology Review, 4*, 186–197.
Licata, L., Klein, O., Saade, W., Azzi, A., & Branscombe, N. R. (2012). Perceived outgroup (dis)continuity and attribution of responsibility for the Lebanese civil war mediate effects of national and religious subgroup identification on intergroup attitudes. *Group Processes and Intergroup Relations, 15*, 179–192.
Lucas, T., Rudolph, C., Zhdanova, L., Barkho, E., & Weidner, N. (2014). Distributive justice for others, collective angst, and support for exclusion of immigrants. *Political Psychology, 35*, 775–793.
McCullough, M. E., Pargament, K. I., & Thoresen, C. E. (Eds.). (2000). *Forgiveness: Theory, research, and practice*. New York: Guilford Press.
Messinger, R. (2005). Grassroots support to stop the Sudan genocide grows while world action wanes. Retrieved from *http://css.static.reliefweb.int/report/sudan/grassroots-support-stop-sudan-genocide-grows-while-world-action-wanes*.
Mols, F., & Jetten, J. (2014). No guts, no glory: How framing the collective past paves the way for anti-immigrant sentiments. *International Journal of Intercultural Relations, 43*, 74–86.
Moscovici, S., & Perez, J. A. (2009). A new representation of minorities as victims. In F. Butera & J. M. Levine (Eds.), *Coping with minority status: Responses to exclusion and inclusion* (pp. 82–103). New York: Cambridge University Press.
Müller, P. (2011). The Europeanization of Germany's foreign policy toward the Israeli Palestinian conflict: Between adaptation to the EU and national projection. *Mediterranean Politics, 16*, 385–403.
Murray, A. Y. (2008). *Historical memories of the Japanese American internment and the struggle for redress*. Stanford, CA: Stanford University Press.
Nadler, A., & Liviatan, I. (2006). Intergroup reconciliation: Effects of adversary's expressions of empathy, responsibility, and recipients' trust. *Personality and Social Psychology Bulletin, 32*, 459–470.
Noor, M., Brown, R., Gonzalez, R., Manzi, J., & Lewis, C. A. (2008). On positive psychological outcomes: What helps groups with a history of conflict to forgive and reconcile with each other? *Personality and Social Psychology Bulletin, 34*, 819–832.
Noor, M., Brown, R., & Prentice, G. (2008). Prospects for intergroup reconciliation: Social-psychological predictors of intergroup forgiveness and reparation in Northern Ireland and Chile. In A. Nadler, T. E. Malloy, & J. D. Fisher (Eds.), *The social psychology of intergroup reconciliation* (pp. 97–116). New York: Oxford University Press.
Noor, M., Shnabel, N., Halabi, S., & Doosje, B. (2015). Peace vision and its socioemotional antecedents: The role of forgiveness, trust, and inclusive victim perceptions. *Group Processes and Intergroup Relations, 18*, 644–654.
Noor, M., Shnabel, N., Halabi, S., & Nadler, A. (2012). When suffering begets suffering: The psychology of competitive victimhood between adversarial groups in violent conflicts. *Personality and Social Psychology Review, 16*, 351–374.
Peraino, K. (2006, May 29). A flight from genocide: Israel debates its moral obligations to the victims of Darfur. *Newsweek*, p. 34.
Pettigrew, T. F., & Tropp, L. R. (2006). A meta-analytic test of intergroup contact theory. *Journal of Personality and Social Psychology, 90*, 751–783.

Philpot, C. R., Balvin, N., Mellor, D., & Bretherton, D. (2013). Making meaning from collective apologies: Australia's apology to its indigenous peoples. *Peace and Conflict: Journal of Peace Psychology, 19*, 34–50.

Philpot, C. R., & Hornsey, M. J. (2008). What happens when groups say sorry: The effect of intergroup apologies on their recipients. *Personality and Social Psychology Bulletin, 34*, 474–487.

Porat, R., Halperin, E., & Bar-Tal, D. (2015). The effect of sociopsychological barriers on the processing of new information about peace opportunities. *Journal of Conflict Resolution, 59*, 93–119.

Riek, B. M., & Mania, E. W. (2012). The antecedents and consequences of interpersonal forgiveness: A meta-analytic review. *Personal Relationships, 19*, 304–325.

Rouhana, N. N., & Bar-Tal, D. (1998). Psychological dynamics of intractable ethnonational conflicts: The Israeli–Palestinian case. *American Psychologist, 53*, 761–770.

Shnabel, N., Halabi, S., & Noor, M. (2013). Overcoming competitive victimhood and facilitating forgiveness through re-categorization into a common victim or perpetrator identity. *Journal of Experimental Social Psychology, 49*, 867–877.

Shnabel, N., Halabi, S., & Siman Tov-Nachlieli, I. (2015). Group apology under unstable status relations: Perceptions of insincerity hinder reconciliation and forgiveness. *Group Processes and Intergroup Relations, 18*, 716–725.

Shnabel, N., & Nadler, A. (2008). A needs-based model of reconciliation: Satisfying the differential emotional needs of victim and perpetrator as a key to promoting reconciliation. *Journal of Personality and Social Psychology, 94*, 116–132.

Shnabel, N., Nadler, A., Ullrich, J., Dovidio, J. F., & Carmi, D. (2009). Promoting reconciliation through the satisfaction of the emotional needs of victimized and perpetrating group members: The needs-based model of reconciliation. *Personality and Social Psychology Bulletin, 35*, 1021–1030.

Staub, E. (2006). Reconciliation after genocide, mass killing and intractable conflict: Understanding the roots of violence, psychological recovery, and steps toward a general theory. *Political Psychology, 27*, 867–894.

Staub, E., & Bar-Tal, D. (2003). Genocide, mass killing and intractable conflict: Roots, evolution, prevention and reconciliation. In D. Sears, L. Huddy, & R. Jarvis (Eds.), *Handbook of political psychology* (pp. 710–755). New York: Oxford University Press.

Staub, E., Pearlman, L. A., Gubin, A., & Hagengimana, A. (2005). Healing, reconciliation, forgiving, and prevention of violence after genocide or mass killing: An intervention and its experimental evaluation in Rwanda. *Journal of Social and Clinical Psychology, 24*, 297–334.

Sullivan, D., Landau, M. J., Branscombe, N. R., & Rothschild, Z. K. (2012). Competitive victimhood as a response to accusations of ingroup harmdoing. *Journal of Personality and Social Psychology, 102*, 778–795.

Tajfel, H., & Turner, J. C. (1986). The social identity theory of intergroup behavior. In S. Worchel & W. G. Austin (Eds.), *The psychology of intergroup relations* (pp. 7–24). Chicago, IL: Nelson-Hall.

Tanis, M., & Postmes, T. (2005). A social identity approach to trust: Interpersonal perception, group membership and trusting behaviour. *European Journal of Social Psychology, 35*, 413–424.

Teveth, S. (1996). *Ben-Gurion and the Holocaust.* New York: Harcourt Brace.

Toussaint, L. L., Owen, A. D., & Cheadle, A. (2012). Forgive to live: Forgiveness, health, and longevity. *Journal of Behavioral Medicine, 35*, 375–386.

Tutu, D. (1999). *No future without forgiveness.* London: Random House.

Volkan, V. (1997). *Blood lines: From ethnic pride to ethnic terrorism.* Boulder, CO: Westview Press.

Warner, R. H., & Branscombe, N. R. (2012). Observer perceptions of moral obligations in groups with a history of victimization. *Personality and Social Psychology Bulletin, 38*, 882–894.

Warner, R. H., Wohl, M. J. A., & Branscombe, N. R. (2014). When do victim group members feel a moral obligation to help suffering others? *European Journal of Social Psychology, 44*, 231–241.

Wenzel, M., & Okimoto, T. G. (2010). How acts of forgiveness restore a sense of justice: Addressing status/power and value concerns raised by transgressions. *European Journal of Social Psychology, 40*, 401–417.

Wiesel, E. (2004, July 14). *On the atrocities in Sudan.* Remarks delivered at the Darfur Emergency Summit convened by the American Jewish World Service and the United States Holocaust Memorial Museum, New York.

Wohl, M. J. A., & Branscombe, N. R. (2005). Forgiveness and collective guilt assignment to historical perpetrator groups depend on level of social category inclusiveness. *Journal of Personality and Social Psychology, 88*, 288–303.

Wohl, M. J. A., & Branscombe, N. R. (2008). Remembering historical victimization: Collective guilt for current ingroup transgressions. *Journal of Personality and Social Psychology, 94*, 988–1006.

Wohl, M. J. A., Branscombe, N. R., & Klar, Y. (2006). Collective guilt: Emotional reactions when one's group has done wrong or been wronged. *European Review of Social Psychology, 17*, 1–37.

Wohl, M. J. A., Branscombe, N. R., & Reysen, S. (2010). Perceiving your group's future to be in jeopardy: Extinction threat induces collective angst and the desire to strengthen the ingroup. *Personality and Social Psychology Bulletin, 36*, 898–910.

CHAPTER 18

Organizations Matter

Arthur P. Brief and Kristin Smith-Crowe

Organizations are collectivities with more or less identifiable boundaries, hierarchies, rules and procedures, and communication systems. They engage in activities related to a set of goals, and the results of those activities have consequences for the organizations themselves, their members, and the societies in which they are embedded (e.g., Etzioni, 1964; Hall, 1977; Scott & Davis, 2007; Simon, 1964). Organizations come in a variety of shapes, sizes, and types, including, for instance, governments, armies, religious denominations, charities, and businesses. Largely because of our familiarity with the subject, this chapter focuses on the latter.

The principal message we want to convey is that understanding organizations matters for the social psychology of good and evil. We make two cases for our claim. One is that organizations have the capacity to create widespread good, as well as to perpetrate horrific evil. Here the case we make is an intuitive one: We give examples of companies doing wrong and doing good. The second case we make is based on our knowledge as social scientists: We argue that organizations are distinct from individuals and small groups. That is, understanding individuals and groups does not equate to understanding organizations; indeed, the "atomistic fallacy" is to generalize from individual (or group) behavior to that of higher-level entities (Alker, 1969). To this end, we review features of organizations likely to promote the production of good and evil: hierarchy and power, "tone at the top" and socialization, and moral blindness and automaticity. Further, we discuss the concept of emergence, which serves to connect these features of organizations to organizations' capacity to do good and evil. The chapter closes with a discussion of where to go from here.

ORGANIZATIONS HAVE THE CAPACITY TO DO GOOD AND EVIL

We begin with what the news media makes difficult to ignore: the capacity for organizations to perpetrate evil. For instance, although it happened more than 30 years ago, the Union Carbide pesticide plant gas leak in Bhopal, India, remains headline news today ("Bhopal's deadly legacy," 2014). More than 5,000 people were killed in the aftermath, and the leak has continued to plague Bhopal for generations due to environmental contamination, causing cancer, birth defects, and developmental problems. The toll is now at 600,000 people affected. The site has still not been cleaned. Nor has everyone faced justice. Although eight Indian executives were convicted of negligence ("Bhopal's deadly legacy," 2014), India considered Warren Anderson, the then chief executive officer of Union Carbide, to be a fugitive (Martin, 2014). Having been released on bail in the days after the tragedy, he left India never to return. He died in 2014.

Walmart, the largest private employer in the United States (Hess, 2013), comprising 11,000 stores and 2.2 million employees worldwide (Walmart, n.d.), is a plentiful source of corporate wrongdoing examples. They are routinely embroiled in controversies, including bribery (Barstow, 2012), mishandling hazardous waste (Clifford, 2013), sex discrimination (Hines, 2012), and violating workers' rights (Greenhouse, 2014; Trottman & Banjo, 2015). Walmart's treatment of its workers in particular made it an obvious context for Ehrenreich's (2001) investigation into the plight of the working poor. Notably, she used words such as *dictatorship* and *authoritarian* to describe the working conditions she experienced.

Her choice of terms recalls the too recent past when companies including BMW and Siemens, with little apparent respect for human rights and dignity, utilized Jewish slave labor (Cohen, 1999). It also recalls a lesser known chapter of history: the continuance of black slavery in the American South after the Emancipation Proclamation and into the 1940s (Blackmon, 2008). Economically devastated by the Civil War, the South rebuilt itself through alternative means of coerced labor. Among other schemes, local governments created convict leasing programs. Black men especially were targeted for arrests for trivial "offenses" (e.g., vagrancy, meaning not having immediate proof of employment) and severe punishments. Once in the system they were "leased" to private enterprises, including mines, lumber camps, quarries, farms, factories, railroads, and foundries, creating a source of revenue for government and a source of cheap labor for business. To illustrate the cruelty of the system, Blackmon (2008) tells the story of Green Cottenham. Arrested in 1908 in Shelby County, Alabama, for vagrancy, the 22-year-old black man was found guilty and sentenced to 30 days of hard labor. Because he was unable to pay the numerous fees assessed for the processing of his case, his sentence was extended to almost 1 year of hard labor, which he served in a coal mine operated by a subsidiary of U.S. Steel. As dangerous as it was unjust, under this system many prisoners leased to businesses died during their servitude of injury, disease, and murder; many more were brutalized by practices such as whippings.

At the other end of this spectrum are companies that are engaged in doing widespread good. Patagonia is one such company. Despite being in the retail industry, one of their causes is responsible consumerism. The average American buys 64 pieces of new clothing a year (Cline, 2012); correspondingly, the U.S. Environmental Protection Agency (n.d.) estimates that in 2012 textiles alone generated over 14 million tons of municipal solid waste. In response, Patagonia began their "Don't Buy This Jacket" (unless you really need it) campaign (Nudd, 2011) and promoted their Common Thread Initiative (Patagonia, n.d.) aimed at reducing unnecessary purchases of their products and the repair and recycling of existing products. They have reportedly repaired more than 26,000 and reused more than 41,000 items and recycled more than 56 tons of worn-out Patagonia clothes (Landwehr, 2013).

Microsoft is another company engaged in doing good on a large scale by tackling a significant societal evil: They are combating child sex trafficking. The U.S. Department of Homeland Security (2014) estimates that human trafficking is a $32 billion per year industry, making it the second most profitable criminal industry. Microsoft, finding existing knowledge about the use of technology in child sex trafficking lacking, created a research grant program in 2011 to fund research into understanding how child victims are recruited, abducted, and sold via technology, ultimately addressing questions including "how do 'pimps' advertise victims for sale online," "how do 'johns' search for their victims," and "how do 'pimps' confirm that a 'john' is not a law enforcement officer" (Microsoft Research, 2011). Rane Johnson-Stempson, the Education and Scholarly Communication Principal Research Director for Microsoft Research, described the first steps of the initiative as follows: "We thought the best way we could help is to first define the problem. Then it's much easier to build a technology solution that may disrupt it" (Microsoft, 2012). To date, this sponsored research has led to progress toward defining the problem, including understanding that the use of technology is more varied than previously thought ("spreading across multiple online sites and digital platforms") and that, despite the increased access of mobile technology throughout the world, variation in access implies the need for approaches tailored to targeted groups (Latonero et al., 2012).

ORGANIZATIONS ARE NOT SIMPLY REDUCIBLE

The examples we provide are illustrative of the capacity for organizations to do good and evil, but they do not address the questions of why or how organizations might do good and evil. Turning now to making our second case for why understanding organizations matters for the social psychology of good and evil, we identify various features of organizations that can facilitate both outcomes. These features are not necessarily unique to organizations, but they are key features of organizations, and they support our claim that organizations are not simply reducible to individuals or even small groups. Rather, organizations, particularly in terms of the horrific evils they may perpetrate and the widespread good they can produce, are emergent phenomena, albeit phenomena grounded in the dynamics of individuals and groups.

Before proceeding, we must express our considerable gratitude to John Darley (1992, 2001, 2005). There is no doubt that most of what we have to say is borrowed, directly or indirectly, from Darley's (1992) review of several important works (e.g., Arendt, 1963; Kelman & Hamilton, 1989; Lifton, 1986; Milgram, 1974) and, more importantly, the creative insights he drew from this collection. For instance, regarding the atomistic fallacy, Darley (1992), in focusing on the social production of evil, asserted that people tend to see that "behind evil actions lay evil doers who can be identified as possessing an inherent inward evilness" (p. 203). He goes on to argue that doing so "preserves our belief in a just and ordered world" (p. 203), for the evil individual is viewed as an exception; an outlier that can be dismissed or contained as a threat to the principles of order and justice. Darley (1992) concluded that

> individual-level psychology is largely irrelevant to the occurrence of a much more common source of evil actions—produced by what I call "organizational pathology." We now need to create . . . a psychology and sociology of how human institutions can purposely move or accidently lurch toward causing these actions, somehow neutralizing, suspending, overriding, or replacing the moral scruples of their members. That psychology will inevitably be a social and organizational one, rather than one centered on the individual. . . . (p. 217)

As our argument unfolds, the rationale for his conclusions will become apparent.

Hierarchy and Power

Although some organizations may be flatter with fewer hierarchical levels and others taller with more, all organizations are hierarchical by definition (e.g., Blau, 1968). Hierarchies are central to understanding how organizations produce evil and, we contend, also good. This is so, in part, because hierarchical position tends to covary naturally, for example, with power, status,[1] and what economists and sociologists call "decision rights" (Zuckerman, 2010). Decision rights reside at the top of organizational hierarchies but may be loaned to (but not owned by) those lower in the hierarchy (Baker, Gibbons, & Murphy, 1999). These rights are very broad, including, for example, hiring, training, job design, sourcing, capital, operating procedures, pricing, advertising, and product design (Baker et al., 1999). Of course, some of these decisions entail those higher in the hierarchy issuing orders to those below.

When we examine the bases of power (French & Raven, 1959) embedded in superior hierarchical positions, the import of hierarchy becomes even more apparent. Superior hierarchical positions entail legitimate power by definition (Emerson, 1962). For some individuals, especially those with politically conservative views, complying with this authority represents a *moral* obligation (e.g., Haidt, 2007). And, as noted by Darley (1992), Milgram (1974) argued that because of the necessity for organized action, humans have evolved to be obedient to authority. While legitimate power does not always produce obedience, it obviously can be a potent force in the good and evil actions of organizations. Also potent are coercive power (influencing subordinates through punishments such as verbal abuse, reduction in paid hours worked, threats of firing, and even dismissal) and reward power (influencing subordinates through rewards such as praise, pay increases, and promotions). Those in superior positions can and do materially and otherwise reward and punish their subordinates.

In organizations what power produces is obedience among lower-level organizational members (e.g., Brief, Buttram, Elliott, Reizenstein, & McCline, 1995; Brief, Dietz, Cohen, Pugh, & Vaslow, 2000; Kelman & Hamilton, 1989), perhaps in proportion to the economic need of those below, those whose families depend on their employment, and those living on the margins (e.g., Brief & Aldag, 1989, 1994; Brief, Konovsky, George, Goodwin, & Link, 1995). According to Milgram (1974), this occurs because people have defined themselves in a manner that renders them open to regulation: "the individual no longer views himself as responsible for his own actions but defines himself as an instrument for carrying out the wishes of others" (p. 134). Simon (1976) was even more blunt: "personal considerations determine whether a person will participate [in organizations], but if he decides to participate, they will not determine the content of his organizational behavior" (p. 203). Consistently, the sociologists Hamilton and Sanders (1992, p. 49) observed that persons in subordinate organizational positions do not see their situation as one of choice "but of role requirements and obligations."

Referent and expert bases of power (French & Raven, 1959) also can be seen to bolster the potential influence of those in superior hierarchical positions. Lower organizational participants can identify with those higher up. Such identification, which leads to referent power, could be rooted in the higher material rewards and status possessed by those higher up the hierarchy. Finally, due to the knowledge that organizational superiors have about the coordination of complex tasks, they also may have power based on their expertise (Darley, 2001).

Relevant to this chapter, a seemingly common way of manipulating power in the social psychology laboratory is to have participants recall an incident in which they had power over another individual or individuals and to describe that situation and how they felt (e.g., Galinsky, Gruenfeld, & Magee, 2003). Although this manipulation and others like it clearly address how a person with power feels, it is unknown to what extent the power episodes recalled by individuals relate to power as it exists in organizations. Moreover and obviously, the exercise of real and lasting influence over others on a daily basis, as is entailed in a superior hierarchical position, may not equate to the conditions commonly created in the laboratory. Of course, this ultimately is an empirical question (also see Darley, 2001, on such concerns).

Often the exercise of reward and punishment power within organizations involves making rewards and punishments contingent on some measure of performance, commonly defined in terms of goal attainment (Locke & Latham, 1990). While this can be an effective motivational tool, it can also lead to wrongdoing (Schweitzer, Ordóñez, & Douma, 2004). Ordóñez, Schweitzer, Galinsky, and Bazerman (2009) give these examples:

> At Sears' automotive unit, employees charged customers for unnecessary repairs in order to meet specific, challenging goals. In the late 1980s, Miniscribe employees shipped actual bricks to customers instead of disk drives to meet shipping targets. And in 1993, Bausch and Lomb employees falsified financial statements to meet earnings goals. In each of these cases, specific, challenging goals motivated employees to engage in unethical behavior. (p. 10)

Further, the exercise of power can create accountability, "the implied or explicit expectation that one may be called upon to justify one's belief, feelings, and actions to others" (Lerner & Tetlock, 1999, p. 255). A considerable amount of data shows that when the views of those to whom one is accountable are known, accountable individuals tailor their message to be in line with these views (e.g., an auditor's opinion reflecting the wishes of the client; see Buchman, Tetlock, & Reed, 1996; Hackenbrack & Nelson, 1996). Anticipating such findings, Tetlock (1985) argued that the study of judgment and choice needs to be broadened to take into consideration the impact of social and organizational context. Later, Tetlock and Mitchell

(2010) similarly argued that understanding moral decision making requires a "macrosocial psychological perspective that stresses the efforts of social beings to preserve their claims to desired identities in the eyes of the constituencies to whom they feel accountable" (p. 207). As examples of research consistent with this perspective, they cite Aquino, Freeman, Reed, Lim, and Felps (2009) and Warren and Smith-Crowe (2008). The former project focuses on the interactive effects of individuals' moral identity and situational primes and incentives on moral judgment and behavior; the latter focuses on the effects of internal emotional processes and external sanctions on shifts in moral judgments. In contrast to these examples, they characterize the typical research paradigm as entailing merely the observation of "only one step of one partner" (p. 207) and thus as not accounting for the reality of social, situational, and reciprocal influences.[2]

Others have made more general points along the same lines. Anteby (2013), in his ethnographic study of Harvard Business School, puts it this way:

> By constructing moral dilemmas as solely individual decision-making problems, we often forget that individuals operate in collective settings. Yet moral conduct rarely occurs ex cathedra or in context-free behavioral laboratories, as some scholarship might lead us to believe. . . . If we wish to discuss individuals' moral conduct we need in particular to look into the organizational conditions that give rise to or hinder such conduct. (p. 125)

Palmer and Yenkey (2015) drew on Granovetter's (1985) concepts of undersocialized and oversocialized theories of behavior to make the point that disregarding context is not the only possible form of myopia. They argue that much research on wrongdoing in organizations falls into one of two categories: either undersocialized, roughly in which individuals are assumed to essentially follow their self-interest in a social vacuum, or oversocialized, roughly in which individuals are assumed to enact the assumptions, values, beliefs, and norms of the groups in which they are embedded. In an effort to study organizational wrongdoing from a more integrated perspective, they conducted a multilevel study of the use of illegal performance-enhancing drugs among 198 cyclists embedded in 22 teams in the 2010 Tour de France. They theorized and found support for the hypothesis that individuals occupying roles within their teams that are crucial to their individual and team success are more likely to engage in wrongdoing due to the very high performance expectations placed on them by subordinates, peers, and superiors, as well as their own drive to perform at a high level. We turn next to discuss further common sources of expectations in organizations and how individuals come to learn of these expectations.

Tone at the Top and Socialization

We borrow the term "tone at the top" from the accounting literature, in which it commonly refers to "the ethical atmosphere created in the workplace by the organization's leadership" (Association of Certified Fraud Examiners, n.d., p. 1). The term was introduced by the National Commission on Fraudulent Financial Reporting (called the Treadway Commission), which claimed that it is a prime causal factor leading to fraudulent behavior and financial statement fraud (but see Brief, Dukerich, Brown, & Brett, 1996, who found null results for the effects of codes of conduct on willingness to engage in financial fraud). Tone at the top encompasses the normative idea of "ethical leadership," referring to how leaders ought to behave both in terms of demonstrating appropriate conduct and promoting such conduct among followers (Brown & Treviño, 2006; Ciulla, 2004). The empirical evidence, however, is mixed. Kish-Gephart, Harrison, and Treviño (2010) found no significant independent effect of code of conduct existence on ethical choice in their meta-analysis. Yet more recently there is evidence that formal systems, including codes of conduct, are more likely to be effective when they are reacting against informal systems that promote unethical behavior (Smith-Crowe et al., 2014). Further, Treviño, Den Nieuwenboer, and Kish-Gephart (2014) speculated that codes of conduct could be rendered effective if employees were to sign pledges before acting. Their speculation is based on an extrapolation of Shu, Mazar, Gino, Ariely, and Bazerman's (2012) finding that pledging honesty before acting made ethics more salient and reduced dishonesty. Also several studies have demonstrated significant, positive correlations between measures of ethical leadership and such follower outcomes as job satisfaction, affective organizational commitment, and work engagement (Treviño et al., 2014). Importantly, however, it seems that very few such survey research studies have shown significant relationships between ethical leadership and the ethicality of follower behavior (Detert, Treviño, Burris, & Andiappan, 2007; for exceptions see Mayer, Aquino, Greenbaum, & Kuenzi, 2012; Mayer, Kuenzi, Greenbaum, Bardes, & Salvador, 2009).

Another way to consider tone at the top is through the lens of organizational climate: shared perceptions of the goals that management wants accomplished and the appropriate means for accomplishing them, and the organizational rewards employees can expect in return for pleasing management (e.g., Kopelman, Brief, & Guzzo, 1990; Reichers & Schneider, 1990).[3] Organizational climate necessarily has a referent, for instance a climate for ethics (Victor & Cullen, 1987, 1988). Mayer, Kuenzi, and Greenbaum (2010), for example, using a sample of employees and their supervisors drawn from 300 organization units, reported a statistically significant, negative relationship ($r = -.29$, $p < .001$) between organizational ethical climate (e.g., "department employees have a lot of skills in recognizing ethical climate") and employee misconduct (e.g., "said or did something to purposely hurt someone at work"; Robinson & O'Leary-Kelly, 1998, p. 663). More recently, Arnaud and Schminke (2012) studied 648 individuals in 117 organization units, gauging two dimensions of organizational ethical climate (self-focused and other-focused reasoning) and ethical behavior (e.g., "padding an expense account"; Treviño & Weaver, 2001, p. 659). They found that the self-focused climate dimension correlated positively with unethical behaviors and the other-focused dimension correlated negatively. Thus research on a climate for ethics indicates that tone at the top influences ethical outcomes in organizations.

Whereas research on organizational climate deals with perceptions of what is valued and expected by management, research on socialization deals with how organizational members come to have these perceptions (Chao, 2012). That is, socialization entails learning the value systems and norms of the organization (Darley, 1996; Palmer, 2012; Schein, 1995), which obviously could support the production of good or evil. Building, for instance, on the works of Brief, Buttram, and Dukerich (2001) and Darley (2001), Ashforth and Anand (2003) perhaps provide the most comprehensive conceptual treatment of organizational socialization resulting in corrupt behaviors.[4] They argue that groups within organizations often create a psychological, and even a physical, "social cocoon," a microculture in which the norms may be very different from those of the wider organization or even the society in which the organization is embedded (Greil & Rudy, 1984; also see Cressey, 1986; Sutherland, 1949). Consistent with this idea, Aven (2015) found that corruption at Enron relied on far smaller social networks than did legitimate projects, which involved six times as many organizational members. Those members of corrupt networks initially communicated sparingly, as each communication regarding corrupt activity entailed the risk of detection. Over time, however, they learned to trust each other and became more "cavalier in their communications" (Aven, 2015, p. 994)—less secretive and more communicative.

In addition to developing trust, organizational members can be corrupted via role modeling, ideology, framing, reinforcement, and punishment. For instance, Palmer and Yenkey (2015) found that proximity to Tour de France cyclists unpunished for illegal performance-enhancing drug use was positively related to drug use, whereas proximity to cyclists punished for use of illegal drugs was negatively related to drug use. Members can "surrender" to or be "seduced" by such socialization (Moore & Gino, 2013): They can resist objectionable practices until yielding to them as inevitable (i.e., surrendering), or they can submit to the powerful attraction of the benefits (material and psychological) associated with engaging in them (i.e., being seduced). Members may also participate in wrongdoing despite their strong misgivings because they relinquish their agency to an authority figure, such as their boss (Werhane, Hartman, Archer, Englehardt, & Pritchard, 2013). Smith-Crowe and Warren (2014) theorize another possibility: Well-meaning organizational members may be made guilty, shamed, or embarrassed into coming to think of corrupt practices as ethical. They argue that in organizations in which corrupt practices are normative, members who do not engage in these practices may be sanctioned for allegedly harming the organization because they are not doing things as they should be done in the organization. These nonparticipants may then come to feel that they have morally transgressed against the organization and that they should engage in these practices.

We are unaware of research on the socialization of doing good, but an example suggests that the process may be different (more formal and sequenced; Van Maanen & Schein, 1979) from the socialization of doing evil. An example of such a structured socialization program is seen in the efforts of Salesforce.com. Salesforce.com is a publicly traded corporation that provides cloud computing applications. It is headquartered in San Francisco and has 13,300 employees and $4 billion in sales ("The world's most innovative companies," 2014). Forbes named Salesforce.com the world's most innovative company 4 years in a row, beginning in 2011. The company also is known for its philanthropic efforts. In 1999, when Salesforce.com was incorporated, Salesforce.com Foundation was created as a public charity. The charity's resources reflected the company's 1–1–1 integrated corporate philanthropy model committing 1% equity (1% of founding stock) to offer grants and monetary assistance to the needy, 1% percent time (for each employee, 6 paid days off a year) to volunteer at a nonprofit, and 1% product donated to nonprofits (Beato, 2014). Their 5-day orientation includes 1 day at the Foundation, where new employees not only are exposed to the 1–1–1 model in a classroom setting but also actually volunteer at a nonprofit. The volunteering portion of the model is reinforced in a number of ways, including $1,000 Champion Grants for nonprofits given in an employee's name when that employee completes 6 full days of volunteering at the nonprofit (Beato, 2014).

It is important for us to note at this point that although tone at the top and socialization tell organizational members what they should be doing and hierarchy and power dynamics compel them to heed these messages, none of these factors is deterministic. Organizational members are to some degree autonomous beings who make choices. Their autonomy is arguably limited, however, not only by these previously discussed features of organizations but also to the extent to which individuals' cognitive capacity is compromised. Next, we turn to a discussion of processes of a more insidious kind that contribute particularly to organizations doing evil by limiting individuals' cognitive capacity.

Moral Blindness and Automaticity

Here we consider the influence of organizations on members' cognitive capacity via the notions of System 1 and System 2 thinking (Stanovich, 1999; also see Kahneman & Frederick, 2002; Evans, 2008). System 1 thinking is characterized as unconscious, rapid, and automatic; System 2 thinking is characterized as conscious, slow, and deliberate (e.g., Evans, 2008). The two systems can be active concurrently in competition for control of overt behavior (Kahneman & Frederick, 2002; also see Baumeister, Masicampo, & Vohs, 2011).

Assuming a directive from above is judged to have moral content (e.g., the directive pertains to donating time or money to a charity or it entails harming customers or clients) and System 2 is engaged, recipients of the directive can be thought of as consciously choosing between right and wrong. In such cases, a recipient's moral character, "an individual's characteristic patterns of thought, emotion, and behavior associated with moral/ethical and immoral/unethical behavior" (Cohen, Panter, Turan, Morse, & Kim, 2014, p. 944), would likely come into play. This is to say that individual differences matter. But, in organizations, the assumption that issues are readily identified as having moral content, even among those with a strong moral character, often is questionable (Brief et al., 2001; Darley, 2001; Gioia, 1992). Several reasons for this are evident.

First, for example, organizational superiors may intentionally obscure the moral content of their directives (e.g., Bandura, 1999; Kreps & Monin, 2011; Tenbrunsel & Messick, 2004). One way this might be done is by the use of "euphemistic labeling" (or hygienic language; Bandura, 1990a, 1990b). Examples in business abound, at least pertaining to harmful acts: Cotton dust in a textile factory becomes "airborne particulates" (Jackall, 1988), financial fraud becomes "creative accounting," and mass firings become "right-sizing" (Kreps & Monin, 2011). Another way is to provide implicit rather than explicit directives. As Yeager (1986) pointed out, in results-oriented environments, "The implicit message received from top management may be that much more weight is attached to job completion than to legal or ethical means of accomplishment" (p. 110). When a superior manager sets a profit, sales, or market-share target for a subordinate and adds "and I won't take any excuses for failure," an implicit message is being sent.

A final mechanism for obscuring the moral content of a directive may be less intentional, relying simply on division of labor. The division of a task into discrete subtasks understandably can limit the perspectives taken by those assigned the subtasks (e.g., Ashforth & Anand, 2003; Brief et al., 2001; Darley, 1992; Kelman, 1973). Thus participants lower in the organization simply may not be able to see the moral content of the subtasks they are performing. For instance, it is difficult to imagine that the mill workers focused on producing the punch cards sold by IBM to Nazi Germany for use on IBM census machines to identify, incarcerate, and murder millions of Jews and others (Black, 2001) really understood their personal role in these atrocities. In contrast, IBM President Thomas Watson knew well what the Nazis were doing with IBM's technology; not only did IBM customize their technology for the Nazis' purposes, but he even visited the Bergen-Belsen concentration camp, where one of IBM's machines was in use.

One would anticipate that System 1 thinking is especially common in organizations whose members are busy, rushed, and otherwise cognitively preoccupied (e.g., juggling multiple tasks at the same time; Bazerman & Moore, 2013; also see Chugh, 2004). Although both Systems 1 and 2 have their advantages and disadvantages (including when System 2 monitors System 1), System 1, in particular, is seen by some to be open to biases (Kahneman, 2003; Milkman, Chugh, & Bazerman, 2009; Soll, Milkman, & Payne, in press). One of the biases that likely leads organizational members to erroneous intuitive judgments regarding the morality of received directives is self-interest (Darley, 2005; but see Miller, 1999). According to Moore and Loewenstein (2004), "self-interest is automatic, viscerally compelling, and often unconscious" (p. 189). Arendt (1978), the moral philosopher, observed that an organizational member "for the sake of his pension, his life insurance, the security of his wife and children [is] prepared to do literally anything" (p. 232).

More generally speaking, a number of related phenomena associated with System 1 thinking have been labeled "bounded ethicality," referring to instances in which people act unethically without their own awareness and fail to notice the unethical behavior of those around them (e.g., Bazerman & Gino, 2012; Bazerman & Tenbrunsel, 2011; Chugh, Banaji, & Bazerman, 2005; Gino, Moore, & Bazerman, 2009). An example of such is people acting in racist and sexist ways based upon their implicit attitudes and associations without being aware of doing so (Banaji & Greenwald, 2013; Chugh et al., 2005). Relatedly, Brief (2012) discusses the relevance of Haidt's (2001) influential theorizing to the understanding of organizational behavior. Essentially, Haidt argues that moral judgments often take the form of emotionally laden intuitions (and, if need be, rationales for the judgments are constructed post hoc, rather than judgments being the product of rational thought processes). Taking the case of judging the morality of a directive from above, we would expect, according to Haidt's thinking, that intuitions laden with positive emotions (e.g., pride) would be judged the right thing to do and that those with negative emotions (e.g., shame) would be judged as wrong (see also Smith-Crowe & Warren, 2014; Warren & Smith-Crowe, 2008). Brief (2012) also notes that emotions may be experienced unconsciously (Barsade, Ramarajan, & Westen, 2009).

Thus organizational members' cognitive capacity can be compromised, leaving them vulnerable to engaging in unintended unethicality or unethical outcomes resulting from an amoral decision-making process, meaning that moral aspects of the situation are not considered (Tenbrunsel & Smith-Crowe, 2008). For instance, Gioia (1992) recounts his and others' lack of moral awareness concerning the Ford Pinto case involving the 1970s car with a deadly design flaw. He notes the euphemistic language (*condition*, never *problem*) dictated by Ford's legal department, as well as the "overwhelming complexity and pace" of his job as Ford's recall coordinator. He argues that these factors, plus a corporate context that promoted business decisions based on cost–benefit analyses in which human injury and death could be simply monetized, acted to obscure the moral implications of the dangers of the Pinto, which, outside of the organizational context, he argues, would have been visible to him:

> Before I went to Ford I would have argued strongly that Ford had an ethical obligation to recall. After I left Ford I now argue and teach that Ford had an ethical obligation to recall. But, *while I was there*, I perceived no strong obligation to recall and I remember no strong *ethical* overtones to the case whatsoever. (p. 388, emphasis in original)

That unethicality can be unintended and even unnoticed in the face of severe consequences makes these processes insidious in their influence—they can lead good people astray such that they can end up unknowingly doing things against their own conscience. Also insidious is the way that small decisions and actions at the individual level can render significant evil at the organizational level. Researchers of corruption have discussed this phenomenon in terms of a number of individuals each making small contributions to what adds up to organizational corruption (e.g., Ashforth & Anand, 2003; Brief et al., 2001). We suspect that organizations can achieve significant good through a similar process. Next, we turn to the concept of emergence, our final point in support of our contention that organizations are not simply reducible.

Emergence

Emergent phenomena are those that arise from lower-level phenomena. According to Kozlowski and Klein (2000, p. 15), "many phenomena in organizations have their theoretical foundation in the cognition, affect, behavior, and characteristics of individuals, which—through social interaction, exchange, and amplification—have emergent properties that manifest at higher levels" (cf. Kozlowski, Chao, Grand, Braun, & Kuljanin, 2013). They further contend that too often emergent phenomena in organizations are treated as isomorphic to the lower-level phenomena in which they are grounded, whereas isomorphism is more often the exception than the rule, suggesting that the atomistic fallacy is a pervasive problem.

Instead, emergent phenomena are conceptually different from the lower-level phenomena from which they emerged (see Eidelson, 1997, for an interdisciplinary review of emergent phenomena). This difference is in part due to the contextual influences and constraints on emergence (Kozlowski & Klein, 2000), including the organizational features discussed above: hierarchy and power, tone at the top and socialization, and moral blindness and automaticity. Emergence is process oriented, it unfolds over time, and it is dynamic (Kozlowski et al., 2013; Kozlowski & Chao, 2012).

Our thinking about emergence in the context of the social psychology of good and evil has been influenced strongly by Martell, Emrich, and Robison-Cox's (2012) emergent theory of vertical gender segregation in organizations, which they define as "the overrepresentation of one group (e.g., men) versus another (e.g., women) in higher status managerial positions" (p. 138). They argue that vertical gender segregation is an emergent property of only small individual preferences for men over women. Their argument is in response to the seemingly paradoxical findings that although gender segregation at higher organizational levels is striking in its magnitude (e.g., there are more chief executives named John than there are female chief executives; Wolfers, 2015), the magnitude of individual gender bias is only slight, meaning that underlying the gender disparity at the upper echelons of organizations are not rabid misogynists bent on the oppression of women; rather, it seems that individuals generally have a mild preference for men over women. These findings have led some to conclude that gender bias does not explain vertical gender segregation in organizations. Martell and colleagues (2012), considering the problem from the perspective of emergence, argue that even modest individual-level gender bias can produce significant aggregate discriminatory effects.

In part, they rely on Schelling's (1971) work on racial diversity in neighborhoods. Schelling ran simulations to test the effects of individuals' preferences for neighbors of the same or a different race on overall patterns of neighborhood segregation. He constructed a "checker board" of 13 rows and 16 columns. Except for those on the edges, individuals each have eight adjacent neighbors; each individual belongs in one of two racial categories, equally represented. Schelling began by placing individuals in a random pattern on the board with about 25–30% of the squares left empty to allow individuals to move in order to satisfy their preferences. Assuming an individual-level preference (e.g., that 50% of the adjacent neighbors be of the same race), he then identified the dissatisfied individuals and began moving them on the board to spaces that would accommodate their preference. Of course, the more "demanding" the individual preference (i.e., the higher the proportion of same-race neighbors preferred), the greater the resulting levels of overall neighborhood segregation; but even relatively undemanding preferences for same-race neighbors resulted in segregation. Applying Schelling's simulation, for instance, one can see that even an individual-level preference for 25% (or 2 out of 8) of one's neighbors to be of the same race creates racial segregation out of the initial random pattern. As Martell et al. (2012) point out, such segregation is produced in the absence of any individual desire to live in a racially segregated neighborhood. Schelling (1971) demonstrates further that to the extent that one racial group outnumbers another (as whites do relative to blacks), individuals' preferences to be adjacent to same-race neighbors exacerbates the resulting segregation.

Martell et al. (2012) further rely on signaling theory to explain how substantial vertical gender segregation could be based on only mild gender bias at the individual level. Signaling theory suggests that in situations of information asymmetry, in which not everyone has access to the same information, decision makers look to signals to fill in the gaps (Connelly, Certo, Ireland, & Reutzel, 2011). For instance, employers cannot know in a very direct or definitive sense how motivated or intelligent a job candidate is. Instead, they can rely on signals such as the prestige of a candidate's bachelor-degree-granting institution. Martell et al. (2012) argue that the context of managerial promotions is necessarily ambiguous because the content of and criteria for managerial work is ambiguous. As such, signals become important. For instance, less positive performance appraisals for women, even if differences are slight, indicate that they are less worthy of promotion. Failure to be promoted can be compounded over time with being in a particular position for too long or appearing to be a late bloomer or generally moving too slowly up the corporate ladder, all of which signal they are unworthy of promotion. Eventually, the lack of promotion may suggest that one should not even be considered for future promotions. Thus Martell et al. (2012) argue that in the aggregate such processes produce gender segregation at the top of the organization, despite the absence of any strong bias against women. Indeed, Martell et al. (2012) suggest that these processes can be unintended, even invisible (see also Ditomaso, 2012).

Likewise, we assume that, in many cases, organizations do not deliberately pursue the production of evil. In contrast, our examples of organizations doing good represent a conscious intention to produce good. Here, too, we assume that emergence is a useful way to think about collective action and outcomes, but whether the emergent processes that produce good would be the same as those that produce evil is not something current research addresses.

CONCLUSION

We sincerely hope you have been persuaded that organizations matter and that a social psychology of individuals or groups is inadequate to understanding when, why, or how organizations produce good or evil. Rather, what is required is an organizational psychology, resting on and influenced by social psychology. Historically, such social-organizational approaches to the study of organizations were plentiful and influential (e.g., Katz & Kahn, 1966; Porter, Lawler, & Hackman, 1975; Weick, 1979). Today this is considerably less the case, with social psychologists interested in organizational phenomena seeking to generalize an individual-based social psychology developed via experiments conducted in the laboratory to the complex world of organizations. We think this shift is notable not because we do not value laboratory experiments or decontextualized research. We value both greatly. Indeed, some of our own work falls into these categories, and these kinds of research certainly inform our thinking and research more generally. Rather, we think this shift is notable because laboratory experiments and decontextualized research are simply not sufficient for understanding organizations, as Darley (e.g., 1992) has so clearly argued.

Given the tremendous good and evil that organizations are capable of producing, we urge social psychology to once again turn its astute eye toward organizations. While there are obvious and great needs for the development of fundamental theory and methodological innovations, it is important to strive for more. That more is the formulation and evaluation of organizational interventions designed to promote doing good and to inhibit behaving badly. For instance, it is one thing to demonstrate in a series of laboratory experiments that perspective taking reduces prejudice (e.g., Galinsky & Moskowitz, 2000) and another to devise a perspective-taking intervention to be implemented in a large, complex organization and to empirically ascertain whether that intervention yielded a meaningful decrease in prejudice and related behaviors. In other words, one needs to know whether the intervention *caused* a reduction in prejudice. Therefore, we are calling for social psychologists to take a stronger turn toward field experimentation, like their counterparts in behavioral economics (e.g., Harrison & List, 2004; Levitt & List, 2009; List, 2011). In the end, good and evil, in their many forms, are issues too crucial for social psychologists to limit their study of them by choice of theoretical perspective (individuals, groups, and/or organizations) or research setting (laboratory or field).

ACKNOWLEDGMENT

We thank Art Miller and Alex Romney for their helpful comments on earlier versions of this chapter, and to Teng Zhang for his bibliographic assistance.

NOTES

1. For more on hierarchy, power, and status covarying "naturally" in organizations, see Magee and Galinsky (2008).

2. Likewise, the study of power in the social psychology lab may provide a limited, or even inaccurate, view of power as it exists in organizations (see also Darley, 2001).
3. Related to the concept of organizational climate is organizational culture. Yet the notion of culture is confused: "[f]or every definition of what culture is there is an important contrary view" (Schneider, Ehrhart, & Macey, 2013, p. 370). Moreover, much has been written about quantitatively measuring climate at the organizational level of analysis (Schneider et al., 2013). For these reasons, we focus on organizational climate.
4. Numerous case studies have appeared in the popular press describing how people are socialized into wrongdoing at work, including accounts of Salomon Brothers (Lewis, 1989), Enron (McLean & Elkind, 2003), and Arthur Andersen (Toffler, 2003).

REFERENCES

Alker, H. R. (1969). A typology of ecological fallacies. In M. Duggan & S. Rokkan (Eds.), *Quantitative ecological analysis in the social sciences* (pp. 69–86). Cambridge, MA: MIT Press.

Anteby, M. (2013). *Manufacturing morals: The values of silence in business school education*. Chicago: University of Chicago Press.

Aquino, K., Freeman, D., Reed, A., Lim, V. K. G., II, & Felps, W. (2009). Testing a social-cognitive model of moral behavior: The interactive influence of situations and moral identity concerns. *Journal of Personality and Social Psychology, 97*, 123–141.

Arendt, H. (1963). *Eichmann in Jerusalem: A report on the banality of evil*. New York: Penguin Books.

Arendt, H. E. (1978). *The life of the mind*. New York: Harcourt Brace Jovanovich.

Arnaud, A., & Schminke, M. (2012). The ethical climate and context of organizations: A comprehensive model. *Organization Science, 23*, 1767–1780.

Ashforth, B., & Anand, V. (2003). The normalization of corruption in organizations. *Research in Organizational Behavior, 25*, 1–52.

Association of Certified Fraud Examiners. (n.d.). Tone at the top. Retrieved from www.acfe.com/uploadedFiles/ACFE_Website/Content/documents/tone-at-the-top-research.pdf.

Aven, B. L. (2015). The paradox of corrupt networks: An analysis of organizational crime at Enron. *Organization Science, 26*, 980–996.

Baker, G., Gibbons, R., & Murphy, K. (1999). Informal authority in organizations. *Journal of Law, Economics, and Organization, 15*, 56–73.

Banaji, M., & Greenwald, A. (2013). *Blindspot: Hidden biases of good people*. New York: Random House.

Bandura, A. (1990a). Mechanisms of moral disengagement. In W. Reich (Ed.), *Origins of terrorism: Psychologies, ideologies, theologies, states of mind* (pp. 161–191). Cambridge, UK: Cambridge University Press.

Bandura, A. (1990b). Selective activation and disengagement of moral control. *Journal of Social Issues, 46*, 27–46.

Bandura, A. (1999). Moral disengagement in the perpetration of inhumanities. *Personality and Social Psychology Review, 3*, 193–209.

Barsade, S. G., Ramarajan, L., & Westen, D. (2009). Implicit affect in organizations. *Research in Organizational Behavior, 29*, 135–162.

Barstow, D. (2012, April 21). Vast Mexico bribery case hushed up by Wal-Mart after top-level struggle. *The New York Times*. Retrieved from www.nytimes.com/2012/04/22/business/at-wal-mart-in-mexico-a-bribe-inquiry-silenced.html?_r=0.

Baumeister, R., Masicampo, E., & Vohs, K. (2011). Do conscious thoughts cause behavior? *Annual Review of Psychology, 62*, 331–361.

Bazerman, M. H., & Gino, F. (2012). Behavioral ethics: Toward a deeper understanding of moral judgment and dishonesty. *Annual Review of Law and Social Science, 8*, 85–104.

Bazerman, M. H., & Moore, D. A. (2013). *Judgment in managerial decision making* (8th ed.). Hoboken, NJ: Wiley.

Bazerman, M. H., & Tenbrunsel, A. E. (2011). *Blind spots: Why we fail to do what's right and what to do about it.* Princeton, NJ: Princeton University Press.

Beato, G. (2014). Growth force. *Stanford Social Innovation Review.* Retrieved from www.ssireview.org/articles/entry/growth_force.

Bhopal's deadly legacy [Editorial]. (2014, December 4). *The New York Times*. Retrieved from www.nytimes.com/2014/12/05/opinion/bhopals-deadly-legacy.html.

Black, E. (2001). *IBM and the Holocaust: The strategic alliance between Nazi Germany and America's most powerful corporation.* New York: Crown.

Blackmon, D. A. (2008). *Slavery by another name: The re-enslavement of black Americans from the Civil War to World War II.* New York: Anchor Books.

Blau, P. M. (1968). The hierarchy of authority in organizations. *American Journal of Sociology, 73*, 453–467.

Brief, A. (2012). The good, the bad, and the ugly: What behavioral business ethics researchers ought to be studying. In D. DeCremer & A. Tenbrunsel (Eds.), *Behavioral business ethics and shaping an emerging field* (pp. 17–46). New York: Routledge.

Brief, A. P., & Aldag, R. J. (1989). The economic functions of work. In K. Rowland & G. R. Ferris (Eds.), *Research in personnel and human resources management* (pp. 1–23). Greenwich, CT: JAI Press.

Brief, A. P., & Aldag, R. J. (1994). The study of work values: A call for a more balanced perspective. In I. Borg & P. P. Mohler (Eds.), *Trends and perspectives in empirical social research* (pp. 99–124). Berlin: deGruyter.

Brief, A. P., Buttram, R., & Dukerich, J. (2001). Collective corruption in the corporate world: Toward a process model. In M. E. Turner (Ed.), *Groups at work: Advances in theory and research* (pp. 471–500). Hillsdale, NJ: Erlbaum.

Brief, A. P., Buttram, R. T., Elliot, J. D., Reizenstein, R. M., & McCline, R. L. (1995). Releasing the beast: A study of compliance with orders to use race as a selection criterion. *Journal of Social Issues, 51*, 177–193.

Brief, A. P., Dietz, J., Cohen, R., Pugh, D., & Vaslow, J. (2000). Just doing business: Modern racism and obedience to authority as explanations for employment discrimination. *Organizational Behavior and Human Decision Processes, 81,* 72–97.

Brief, A. P., Dukerich, J., Brown, P., & Brett, J. (1996). What's wrong with the Treadway commission report?: Experimental analyses of the effects of personal values and codes of conduct on fraudulent financial reporting. *Journal of Business Ethics, 15,* 183–198.

Brief, A. P., Konovsky, M. A., George, J., Goodwin, R., & Link, K. (1995). Inferring the meaning of work from the effects of unemployment. *Journal of Applied Social Psychology, 25,* 693–711.

Brown, M., & Treviño, L. (2006). Ethical leadership: A review and future directions. *Leadership Quarterly, 17,* 595–616.

Buchman, T., Tetlock, P. E., & Reed, R. O. (1996). Accountability and auditors' judgments about contingent events. *Journal of Business Finance and Accounting, 23,* 379–398.

Chao, G. (2012). Organizational socialization: Background, basics, and a blueprint for adjustment at work. In S. Kozlowski (Ed.), *The Oxford handbook of organizational psychology* (pp. 579–614). Oxford, UK: Oxford University Press.

Chugh, D. (2004). Societal and managerial implications of implicit social cognition: Why milliseconds matter. *Social Justice Research, 17,* 203–222.

Chugh, D., Banaji, M., & Bazerman, M. (2005). Bounded ethicality as a psychological barrier to recognizing conflicts of Interest. In D. Moore, D. Cain, G. Loewenstein, & M. Bazerman (Eds.), *Conflicts of interest: Challenges and solutions in business, law, medicine, and public policy* (pp. 74–95). New York: Cambridge University Press.

Ciulla, J. (2004). *Ethics, the heart of leadership.* Westport, CT: Praeger.

Clifford, S. (2013, May 28). Wal-Mart is fined $82 million over mishandling of hazardous wastes. *The New York Times.* Retrieved from *www.nytimes.com/2013/05/29/business/wal-mart-is-fined-82-million-over-mishandling-of-hazardous-wastes.html.*

Cline, E. L. (2012). *Overdressed: The shockingly high cost of cheap fashion.* New York: Portfolio/Penguin.

Cohen, R. (1999, November 16). Germany adds $555 million to offer in Nazi slave cases. *The New York Times.* Retrieved from *www.nytimes.com/1999/11/16/world/germany-adds-555-million-to-offer-in-nazi-slave-cases.html.*

Cohen, T., Panter, A., Turan, N., Morse, L., & Kim, Y. (2014). Moral character in the workplace. *Journal of Personality and Social Psychology, 107*(5), 943–963.

Connelly, B. L., Certo, S. T., Ireland, R. D., & Reutzel, C. R. (2011). Signaling theory: A review and assessment. *Journal of Management, 37,* 39–67.

Cressey, D. (1986). Why managers commit fraud. *Australian and New Zealand Journal of Criminology, 19,* 195–209.

Darley, J. (1992). Social organization for the production of evil. *Psychological Inquiry, 3,* 199–218.

Darley, J. (2001). The dynamics of authority influence in organizations and the unintended action consequences. In J. Darley, D. M. Messick, & T. R. Tyler (Eds.), *Social influences of ethical behavior in organizations* (pp. 37–52). Mahwah, NJ: Erlbaum.

Darley, J. (2005). The cognitive and social psychology of contagious organizational corruption. *Brooklyn Law Review, 70*, 1177–1194.
Detert, J. R., Treviño, L. K., Burris, E. R., & Andiappan, M. (2007). Managerial modes of influence and counter productivity in organizations: A longitudinal business-unit-level investigation. *Journal of Applied Psychology, 92*(4), 993–1005.
Ditomaso, N. (2012). *American non-dilemma: Racial inequality without racism* (13th ed.). Ithaca, NY: Cornell University Press.
Ehrenreich, B. (2001). *Nickel and dimed: On (not) getting by in America.* New York: Picador.
Eidelson, R. J. (1997). Complex adaptive systems in the behavioral and social sciences. *Review of General Psychology, 1*, 42–71.
Emerson, R. (1962). Power-dependence relations. *American Sociological Review, 27*(1) 31–41.
Etzioni, A. (1964). *Modern organizations.* Englewood Cliffs, NJ: Prentice Hall.
Evans, J. (2008). Dual processing accounts of reasoning, judgment, and social cognition. *Annual Review of Psychology, 59*, 255–278.
French, J. R. P., Jr., & Raven, B. H. (1959). The bases of social power. In D. Cartwright (Ed.), *Studies in social power* (pp. 150–167). Ann Arbor, MI: Institute for Social Research.
Galinsky, A. D., Gruenfeld, D. H., & Magee, J. C. (2003). From power to action. *Journal of Personality and Social Psychology, 85*, 453–466.
Galinsky, A. D., & Moskowitz, G. B. (2000). Perspective-taking: Decreasing stereotype expression, stereotype accessibility, and in-group favoritism. *Journal of Personality and Social Psychology, 78*, 708–724.
Gino, F., Moore, D. A., & Bazerman, M. H. (2009). See no evil: Why we fail to notice unethical behavior. In R. M. Kramer, A. E. Tenbrunsel, & M. H. Bazerman (Eds.), *Social decision making: Social dilemmas, social values, and ethical judgments* (pp. 241–263). New York: Psychology Press.
Gioia, D. (1992). Pinto fires and personal ethics: A script analysis of missed opportunities. *Journal of Business Ethics, 11*, 379–389.
Granovetter, M. S. (1985). Economic action and social structure: The problem of embeddedness. *American Journal of Sociology, 91*, 481–493.
Greenhouse, S. (2014, December 10). Walmart illegally punished workers, judge rules. *The New York Times.* Retrieved from *www.nytimes.com/2014/12/11/business/walmart-illegally-punished-workers-judge-rules.html.*
Greil, A. L., & Rudy, D. R. (1984). Social cocoons: Encapsulation and identity transformation organizations. *Sociological Inquiry, 54*, 260–278.
Hackenbrack, K., & Nelson, M. W. (1996). Auditors' incentives and their application of financial accounting standards. *Accounting Review, 71*(1), 43–59.
Haidt, J. (2001). The emotional dog and its rational tail: A social intuitionist approach to moral judgment. *Psychological Review, 108*, 814–834.
Haidt, J. (2007). The new synthesis in moral psychology. *Science, 316*, 998–1002.
Hall, R. (1977). *Organizations: Structure and process.* Englewood Cliffs, NJ: Prentice Hall.
Hamilton, V., & Sanders, J. (1992). Responsibility and risk in organizational crimes of obedience. *Research in Organizational Behavior, 14*, 49–90.

Harrison, G. W., & List, J. A. (2004). Field experiments. *Journal of Economic Literature, 42*, 1009–1055.

Hess, A. E. M. (2013, August 22). The 10 largest employers in America. *USA Today*. Retrieved from *www.usatoday.com/story/money/business/2013/08/22/ten-largest-employers/2680249*.

Hines, A. (2012, June 6). Walmart sex discrimination claims filed by 2,000 women. *Huffington Post*. Available at *www.huffingtonpost.com/2012/06/06/walmart-sex-discrimination-women-_n_1575859.html*.

Jackall, R. (1988). *Moral mazes: The world of corporate managers*. New York: Oxford University Press.

Kahneman, D. (2003). Maps of bounded rationality: Psychology for behavioral economics. *American Economic Review, 93*, 1449–1475.

Kahneman, D., & Frederick, S. (2002). Representativeness revisited: Attribute substitution in intuitive judgment. In T. Gilovich, D. Griffin, & D. Kahneman (Eds.), *Heuristics and biases: The psychology of intuitive judgment* (pp. 49–81). New York: Cambridge University Press.

Katz, D., & Kahn, R. L. (1966). Organizations and the system concept. *Social Psychology of Organizations, 1*, 14–29.

Kelman, H. (1973). Violence without moral restraint: Reflections on the dehumanization of victims and victimizers. *Journal of Social Issues, 29*, 25–61.

Kelman, H., & Hamilton, V. (1989). *Crimes of obedience*. New Haven, CT: Yale University Press.

Kish-Gephart, J. J., Harrison, D. A., & Treviño, L. K. (2010). Bad apples, bad cases, and bad barrels: Meta-analytic evidence about sources of unethical decisions at work. *Journal of Applied Psychology, 95*(1), 1–31.

Kopelman, R. E., Brief, A. P., & Guzzo, R. A. (1990). The role of climate and culture in productivity. In B. Schneider (Ed.), *Organizational climate and culture* (pp. 282–318). San Francisco: Jossey-Bass.

Kozlowski, S. W. J., & Chao, G. (2012). The dynamics of emergence: Cognition and cohesion in work teams. *Managerial and Decision Economics, 33*, 335–354.

Kozlowski, S. W. J., Chao, G., Grand, J., Braun, M., & Kuljanin, G. (2013). Advancing multilevel research design: Capturing the dynamics of emergence. *Organizational Research Methods, 16*, 581–615.

Kozlowski, S. W. J., & Klein, K. J. (2000). A multilevel approach to theory and research in organizations: Contextual, temporal, and emergent processes. In K. J. Klein & S. W. J. Kozlowski (Eds.), *Multilevel theory, research, and methods in organizations* (pp. 3–90). San Francisco: Jossey-Bass.

Kreps, T., & Monin, B. (2011). Doing well by doing good?: Ambivalent moral framing in organizations. *Research in Organizational Behavior, 31*, 99–123.

Landwehr, D. (2013, September 22). Don't buy this jacket [Web log post]. Retrieved from *http://dlandwehr.com/2013/09*.

Latonero, M., Musto, J., Boyd, Z., Boyle, E., Bissel, A., Gibson, K., et al. (2012). The rise of mobile and the diffusion of technology-facilitated trafficking. Retrieved from *https://technologyandtrafficking.usc.edu/files/2011/08/HumanTrafficking2012.pdf*.

Lerner, J. S., & Tetlock, P. E. (1999). Accounting for the effects of accountability. *Psychological Bulletin, 125*, 255–275.

Levitt, S. D., & List, J. A. (2009). Field experiments in economics: The past, the present, and the future. *European Economic Review, 53,* 1–18.

Lewis, M. (1989). *Liar's poker: Rising through the wreckage on Wall Street.* New York: Norton.

Lifton, R. J. (1986). *The Nazi doctors: Medical killing and the psychology of genocide.* New York: Basic Books.

List, J. A. (2011). Why economists should conduct field experiments and 14 tips for pulling one off. *Journal of Economic Perspectives, 25,* 3–15.

Locke, E. A., & Latham, G. P. (1990). *A theory of goal setting and task performance.* Englewood Cliffs, NJ: Prentice Hall.

Magee, J. C., & Galinsky, A. D. (2008). Social hierarchy: The self-reinforcing nature of power and status. *Academy of Management Annals, 2*(1), 351–398.

Martell, R. F., Emrich, C. G., & Robison-Cox, J. (2012). From bias to exclusion: A multilevel emergent theory of gender segregation in organizations. *Research in Organizational Behavior, 32,* 137–162.

Martin, D. (2014, October 30). Warren Anderson, 92, dies; faced India plant disaster. *The New York Times.* Retrieved from *www.nytimes.com/2014/10/31/business/w-m-anderson-92-dies-led-union-carbide-in-80s-.html.*

Mayer, D. M., Aquino, K., Greenbaum, R. L., & Kuenzi, M. (2012). Who displays ethical leadership, and why does it matter?: An examination of antecedents and consequences of ethical leadership. *Academy of Management Journal, 55*(1), 151–171.

Mayer, D. M., Kuenzi, M., & Greenbaum, R. L. (2010). Examining the link between ethical leadership and employee misconduct: The mediating role of ethical climate. *Journal of Business Ethics, 95,* 7–16.

Mayer, D. M., Kuenzi, M., Greenbaum, R., Bardes, M., & Salvador, R. (2009). How low does ethical leadership flow?: Test of a trickle-down model. *Organizational Behavior and Human Decision Processes, 108,* 1–13.

McLean, B., & Elkind, P. (2003). *The smartest guys in the room: The amazing rise and scandalous fall of Enron.* New York: Portfolio Trade.

Microsoft News Center. (2012). Shedding light on the role of technology in child sex trafficking. Retrieved from *http://news.microsoft.com/2012/07/18/shedding-light-on-the-role-of-technology-in-child-sex-trafficking.*

Microsoft Research. (2011). The role of technology in human trafficking—RFP. Retrieved from *http://research.microsoft.com/en-us/collaboration/focus/education/human-trafficking-rfp.aspx.*

Milgram, S. (1974). *Obedience to authority.* New York: Harper & Row.

Milkman, K., Chugh, D., & Bazerman, M. (2009). How can decision making be improved? *Perspectives of Psychological Science, 4,* 379–383.

Miller, D. (1999). *Principles of social justice.* Cambridge, MA: Harvard University Press.

Moore, C., & Gino, F. (2013). Ethically adrift: How others pull our moral compass from True North, and how we can fix it. *Research in Organizational Behavior, 33,* 53–77.

Moore, D. A., & Loewenstein, G. (2004). Self-interest, automaticity, and the psychology of conflict of interest. *Social Justice Research, 17*(2), 189–202.

Nudd, T. (2011, November 28). Ad of the day: Patagonia. *Adweek.* Retrieved from *www.adweek.com/news/advertising-branding/ad-day-patagonia-136745.*

Ordóñez, L. D., Schweitzer, M. E., Galinsky, A. D., & Bazerman, M. H. (2009). Goals gone wild: The systematic side effects of overprescribing goal setting. *Academy of Management Perspectives, 23*(1), 6–16.

Palmer, D. (2012) *Normal organizational wrongdoing: A critical analysis of theories of misconduct in and by organizations.* Oxford, UK: Oxford University Press.

Palmer, D., & Yenkey, C. (2015). Drugs, sweat, and gears: An organizational analysis of performance enhancing drug use in the 2010 Tour de France. *Social Forces.* Available at *http://sf.oxfordjournals.org/content/early/2015/03/05/sf.sov046.abstract.*

Patagonia. (n.d.). Introducing the common threads initiative: Reduce, repair, reuse, recycle, reimagine. Retrieved from *www.thecleanestline.com/2011/09/introducing-the-common-threads-initiative.html.*

Porter, L. W., Lawler, E. E., & Hackman, J. R. (1975). *Behavior in organizations.* New York: McGraw-Hill.

Reichers, A. E., & Schneider, B. (1990). Climate and culture: An evolution of constructs. *Organizational Climate and Culture, 1,* 5–39.

Robinson, S. L., & O'Leary-Kelly, A. M. (1998). Monkey see, monkey do: The influence of work groups on the antisocial behavior of employees. *Academy of Management Journal, 41*(6), 658–672.

Schein, E. H. (1995). The role of the founder in creating organizational culture. *Family Business Review, 8*(3), 221–238.

Schelling, T. C. (1971). Dynamic models of segregation. *Journal of Mathematical Sociology, 1,* 143–186.

Schneider, B., Ehrhart, M. G., & Macey, W. H. (2013). Organizational climate and culture. *Annual Review of Psychology, 64,* 361–388.

Schweitzer, M. E., Ordóñez, L., & Douma, B. (2004). Goal setting as a motivator of unethical behavior. *Academy of Management Journal, 47*(3), 422–432.

Scott, W. R., & Davis, G. F. (2007). *Organizations and organizing.* Upper Saddle River, NJ: Pearson Prentice-Hall.

Shu, L. L., Mazar, N., Gino, F., Ariely, D., & Bazerman, M. H. (2012). Signing at the beginning makes ethics salient and decreases dishonest self-reports in comparison to signing at the end. *Proceedings of the National Academy of Sciences of the USA, 109,* 197–200.

Simon, H. A. (1964). On the concept of organizational goal. *Administrative Science Quarterly, 9,* 1–22.

Simon, H. A. (1976). From substantive to procedural rationality. In T. J. Kastelein, S. K. Kuipers, W. A. Nijenhuis, & G. R. Wagenaar (Eds.), *25 years of economic theory* (pp. 65–86). Oxford, UK: Oxford University Press.

Smith-Crowe, K., Tenbrunsel, A. E., Chan-Serafin, S., Brief, A. P., Umphress, E. E., & Joseph, J. (2014). The ethics "fix": When formal systems make a difference. *Journal of Business Ethics.* Available at *http://link.springer.com/article/10.1007%2Fs10551-013-2022-6.*

Smith-Crowe, K., & Warren, D. E. (2014). The emotion-evoked collective corruption model: The role of emotion in the spread of corruption within organizations. *Organization Science, 25,* 1154–1171.

Soll, J. B., Milkman, K. L., & Payne, J. W. (in press). A user's guide to debiasing. In G. Keren & G. Wu (Eds.), *Wiley–Blackwell handbook of judgment and decision making.* Hoboken, NJ: Wiley.

Stanovich, K. E. (1999). *Who is rational?: Studies of individual differences in reasoning*. Mahwah, NJ: Erlbaum.

Sutherland, E. H. (1949). *White collar crime*. New York: Dryden Press.

Tenbrunsel, A. E., & Messick, D. M. (2004). Ethical fading: The role of self-deception in unethical behavior. *Social Justice Research, 17*(2), 223–236.

Tenbrunsel, A. E., & Smith-Crowe, K. (2008). Ethical decision making: Where we've been and where we're going. *Academy of Management Annals, 2*, 545–607.

Tetlock, P. E. (1985). Accountability: The neglected social context of judgment and choice. *Research in Organizational Behavior, 7*, 297–332.

Tetlock, P. E., & Mitchell, G. (2010). Situated social identities constrain morally defensible choices: Commentary on Bennis, Medin, & Bartel (2010). *Perspectives on Psychological Science, 5*, 206–208.

Toffler, B. L. (2003). *Final accounting: Ambition, greed, and the fall of Arthur Anderson*. New York: Random House.

Treviño, L., Den Nieuwenboer, N., & Kish-Gephart, J. (2014). (Un)ethical behavior in organizations. *Annual Review of Psychology, 65*, 635–660.

Treviño, L. K., & Weaver, G. R. (2001). Organizational justice and ethics program "follow-through": Influences on employees' harmful and helpful behavior. *Business Ethics Quarterly, 11*(4), 651–671.

Trottman, M., & Banjo, S. (2015, January 15). Wal-mart accused of violating workers' rights. *Wall Street Journal*. Retrieved from www.wsj.com/articles/SB10001424052702304419104579322990073258798.

U.S. Department of Homeland Security. (2014). *Definition of human trafficking*. Retrieved from www.dhs.gov/definition-human-trafficking.

U.S. Environmental Protection Agency. (n.d.). Municipal solid waste generation, recycling and disposal in the United States: Facts and figures for 2012. Retrieved from www.epa.gov/epawaste/nonhaz/municipal/pubs/2012_msw_fs.pdf.

Van Maanen, J., & Schein, E. H. (1979). Toward a theory of organizational socialization. *Research in Organizational Behavior, 1*, 209–264.

Victor, B., & Cullen, J. B. (1987). A theory and measure of ethical climate in organizations. In W. C. Fredrick & L. Preston (Ed.), *Research in corporate social performance and policy* (pp. 51–71). London: JAI Press.

Victor, B., & Cullen, J. B. (1988). The organizational bases of ethical work climates. *Administrative Science Quarterly, 33*, 101–125.

Walmart. (n.d.) Our story. Retrieved from *http://corporate.walmart.com/our-story*.

Warren, D. E., & Smith-Crowe, K. (2008). Deciding what's right: The role of external sanctions and embarrassment in shaping moral judgments in the workplace. *Research in Organizational Behavior, 28*, 81–105.

Weick, K. E. (1979). *The social psychology of organizing* (2nd ed.). New York: McGraw-Hill.

Werhane, P. H., Hartman, L. P., Archer, C., Englehardt, E. E., & Pritchard, M. S. (2013). *Obstacles to ethical decision-making: Mental models, Milgram, and the problem of obedience*. Cambridge, UK: Cambridge University Press.

Wolfers, J. (2015, March 2). Fewer women run big companies than men named

John. *The New York Times*. Retrieved from *www.nytimes.com/2015/03/03/upshot/fewer-women-run-big-companies-than-men-named-john.html*.

The world's most innovative companies. (2014). Retrieved from *www.forbes.com/companies/salesforce*.

Yeager, P. (1986) Analyzing corporate offenses: Progress and prospects. In J. Post (Ed.), *Research in corporate social performance and policy* (pp. 93–120). Greenwich, CT: JAI Press.

Zuckerman, E. (2010). Speaking with one voice: A Stanford School approach to organizational hierarchy. *Research in the Sociology of Organizations, 28*, 289–307.

CHAPTER 19

Globalization and Terrorism
The Primacy of Collective Processes

Fathali M. Moghaddam, Victoria Heckenlaible,
Madeleine Blackman, Sarah Fasano,
and Daniel J. Dufour

There is widespread agreement that terrorism is evil, but little agreement as to why it has increased in the 21st century. Why did the most devastating terrorist attacks against the United States take place on September 11, 2001, and not September 11, 1970, or 1950? Why did violent fundamentalist groups such as the Taliban, al Qaeda, and Islamic State (IS) gain strength in the 21st century and not decades or centuries earlier? In this chapter we answer these questions by demonstrating the pivotal role of globalization in terrorism and radicalization (Moghaddam, 2008). We argue that 21st-century globalization is, in important ways, new and central to the macro, collective processes shaping terrorism. We use the April 15, 2013, Boston Marathon bombings as an illustrative case study to argue that macro collective processes and not the personality of individuals are the major factor leading to the rise of terrorism.

After 9/11, information about terrorist individuals and networks rapidly increased. However, there has been a lack of effective models to integrate and interpret this information. The staircase model of terrorism (Moghaddam, 2005) has been widely used to fill this gap, including in applied deradicalization programs such as TerRa, which has produced a practical deradicalization toolkit ("TerRa: Terrorism and Radicalisation," n.d.). The staircase model provides a clear guide to policies. Counterterrorist actions can be adjusted to fit the level of the staircase the radicalized individual has reached. Rapid, short-term action is needed against individuals who have reached the highest levels of the staircase, whereas longer-term policies are needed for people on the lower levels of the staircase. Throughout the different levels, the context, which includes extremist narratives aggressively propagated across the globe, is the most powerful factor shaping behavior. In this sense, the model gives priority to collective processes over individual processes. Nevertheless, the characteristics of individuals do matter on the staircase, as we learn from the case of the Tsarnaev brothers, the perpetrators of the Boston bombings; some individuals are more likely than others to move up the staircase.

According to the staircase model of terrorism, each level on the staircase is characterized by particular psychological processes. Throughout the different levels, the fundamentally important feature of the situation is how people perceive the building and how they see spaces and doors on each floor. As individuals climb up the stairway, choices become fewer and fewer, obedience and conformity increase, until only the destruction of life is possible. The perception of fairness and identity aspirations are key psychological processes on the ground floor. Those who reach the first floor are seeking ways to get ahead and achieve social mobility. When mobility is blocked, some individuals climb to the second floor, where frustration is intensified and aggression is channeled toward particular targets. Some individuals keep climbing up, and on the third floor they experience a shift in moral thinking, adopting a morality according to which the ends justify the means. They come to see terrorist violence as justified. Categorical thinking is accentuated among those who reach the fourth floor, as is their own sense of legitimacy. Finally, some individuals such as the Tsarnaev brothers take action to sidestep inhibitory mechanisms that prevent killing in most humans, so that they can carry out acts of violence and destruction on the final floor. These processes need to be understood in the larger context of globalization.

GLOBALIZATION IN THE 21ST CENTURY

Globalization involves increasing and large-scale economic, technological, social, political, and cultural integration around the world, enabling ideas and narratives to spread with a velocity previously unseen. A major motor for these changes is technological innovations, which are unpredictable and not confined in their effects by national boundaries. During the Arab Spring, social media spread the idea of revolution to overturn oppressive governments and restore national dignity across the Middle East and

North Africa. In the same way political activists communicate with each other through social media, terrorists exploit social media to propagate their narratives. Al Qaeda produces the English-language online magazine *Inspire*, while al Shabab in Somalia, IS, and the Pakistani Taliban all use various social media outlets to promote their message (Pradhan, 2014). The result is that radical, and once isolated, religious beliefs now have a global audience (Cronin, 2002/2003).

Technology-Driven Change

Contemporary globalization is driven primarily by powerful technological and economic factors. Technological changes are unpredictable and influenced by individuals and private entities. The enormous impact of social platforms, portable devices, and other technological innovations has been unprecedented. These have increasingly connected the world: Approximately 3 billion people use the Internet and approximately 2.3 billion have mobile broadband subscriptions (International Telecommunication Union, 2014). Now nearly half of the Earth's population is just a mouse click away. Individuals may connect and interact with distant communities. Statistics from social networking sites reflect this aspect, as approximately 10–15% of people's Facebook friends live in another country (Ghemawat, 2012).

The unprecedented connectivity facilitates a terrorist organization's ability to develop a global community of like-minded, radicalized individuals. Online forums are frequently used to plan violent attacks and recruit members. Among the many examples of this strategy is Revolution Muslim, an organization that sought to end "enemies of Islam" (Federal Bureau of Investigation, U.S. Attorney's Office, 2012, para. 4). The New York-based leader of the group used forums to connect and build relationships with fellow members (Federal Bureau of Investigation, U.S. Attorney's Office, 2012). The effectiveness of their forums demonstrates how new social networking platforms enable terrorist organizations to readily recruit vulnerable individuals and nurture group ideology.

In addition, technology facilitates remote group administration and fundraising (Cronin, 2002/03). Electronic mailing lists allow organizations such as al Qaeda to streamline communication and disseminate information, while giving administrators the ability to organize their groups and activities. Meanwhile, websites such as Silk Road are used to sell illegal goods, and platforms similar to PayPal and Kickstarter are used to transfer illegal funds for their activities. Combine electronic money management platforms with the globalizing economy, and terrorist organizations are able to discreetly transfer money while gaining huge profits from business conducted outside their homeland. Hezbollah, a prime example, reaps huge financial rewards from narcotics trafficking in Latin America (Kraul & Rotella, 2008). Now that terrorist groups have a global financial support network, the initiative of only one country to defeat them is very unlikely to succeed.

Extremists have further utilized social media networks to spread propaganda and share videos of executions, including that of American journalist James Foley (Anderson, 2014). Furthermore, they now use an even more effective "swarmcast" approach that utilizes Twitter. Due to Twitter's multiparty "flock" organization, it is nearly impossible for authorities to shut down extremist propaganda spread in this way. Ultimately, eliminating the top perpetrators will not halt the messages' spread, as they will only be replaced by other willing and able extremists. Ali Fisher from the Center on Public Diplomacy (CPD) describes this behavior as swarming, explaining that it is "akin to the way a swarm of bees or flock of birds constantly reorganizes in flight" (Fisher, 2014, para. 2). This format "marks a shift from the hierarchical and broadcast models of communication during conflict to a new dispersed and resilient form, the user curated 'swarmcast'" (Fisher, 2014, para. 2). Through swarmcast, organizations accomplish two main objectives: The first is to eulogize martyrs and extremist leaders, and the second is to reach a wide audience and inspire action.

Twitter swarmcasting efforts by terrorists successfully capture the attention of mass audiences through combining propaganda with widely popular subjects, such as the soccer World Cup. Perpetrators use hashtags to interject themselves into conversations around trending topics and utilize both English and Arabic in their posts. English allows them to reach a global audience while Arabic resonates with a religious audience that is helpful for recruitment (Fisher, 2014). Arguably, it is such social platforms that encourage individuals to travel across the globe to join extremist causes. Aqsa Mahmoud, for example, was a 20-year-old Scottish woman who left her home in Glasgow to marry a Syrian IS fighter ("Privately Educated Woman," 2014). However, social media propagandizing is not as successful in recruiting as it strives to be. According to the CPD, 99.6% of users retweeting propaganda had previously engaged in one form or another (Fisher, 2014). Propaganda in and of itself is not enough to radicalize or mobilize.

Economy-Driven Change

Globalization has changed economics in at least four key ways: more global brands, increased disparity of wealth between countries and socioeconomic classes, greater flow of goods and people, and an accessible global financial system. Globalization gives many Western and non-Western companies the ability to establish a global brand and dominance. Walmart, for example, reaches across the globe, opening as many as 20 stores in developing markets such as India (Sarkar, 2014). Similarly Sina Weibo, a Chinese alternative to Twitter, has been integrated into iPhones, an iconic American product (Wee, 2012). However, the booming success of global companies often threatens local companies and proves to be economically damaging to local employers, communities, and trades. This type of economic damage has been seen to provide an opportunity for radical individuals to cast foreign companies as villains akin to invasive species in their narratives (Moghaddam, 2008).

Although globalization lifts billions out of poverty, it simultaneously increases wealth disparity (Piketty, 2014). As global demand raises the price of goods, the poor can no longer afford them. For example, Colombia's rural poor can no longer afford their traditional grain quinoa because of its demand explosion in developed countries (Blythman, 2013). The fluctuating prices and market shifts then create a chasm between those who benefit from globalization and those who do not.

As the chasm grows wider, it becomes more and more difficult for the lower class to breach the gap or live comfortable lives. Some scholars (Cronin, 2002/2003) call this chasm the root of terrorism as communities compare their lives with the popular narrative of the West's limitless wealth, increasing feelings of disparity. J. R. Nassar (as cited in Hazbun, 2005) says people adopt dreams of the West and of obtaining wealth, but when they do not succeed the dreams become nightmares. He refers to this process as the migration of nightmares: Frustrated radicalized individuals blame the West for their disappointments and can react by committing acts of terrorism (Hazbun, 2005). Thus the collective threat being perceived by traditionalists and fundamentalists opposed to the spreading of Western values (Moghaddam, 2008) seems to be a manifestation of tension between those who have and those who do not (Cronin, 2002/2003, p. 35).

Security

A globalized economy rewards countries that make the migration of people and goods easier, creating an incentive for countries to become more interconnected. However, interconnectivity creates opportunities for terrorist attacks and infiltration into new territories. The United States, for example, scans only 4% of the many crates that gain entrance into the country (Bliss, 2012). The U.S. Department of Homeland Security warns that terrorists could try to sneak a dirty bomb into the United States by hiding it in a shipping container. The monetary rewards of international business have increased air travel around the world, thereby increasing opportunities for bombings. In February 2012, a Nigerian man tried to ignite a bomb that he had hid in his pants while on a flight. Fortunately, the device failed, and passengers were able to restrain him (Ariosto & Feyerick, 2012). However, the reality is that as more goods and people move around the world, so will terrorists.

Today there exists a growing do-it-yourself community that shares tips through online forums and blogs. Unfortunately terrorists such as al Qaeda exploit this free information sharing to incite violence by publishing articles about bomb making and networking. In their magazine *Inspire*, al Qaeda published an article aptly titled "Make a Bomb in the Kitchen of Your Mom" (2010, p. 33). An American living in Harlem downloaded this article and was in the process of building a pipe bomb when the New York Police Department arrested him in 2011 (Parascandola, 2014). Ultimately, as access to information increases, the threat of homegrown terrorism, attacks from foreign terrorists, and cyberterrorism increase in tandem.

As globalization increases global connectivity, local connections are partially replaced by online connections through Facebook, chat rooms, and online video games. As a result, homegrown terrorists can establish significant and meaningful social relationships with radicals outside their home communities. The recruitment process is considered homegrown in the sense that the terrorists can radicalize without ever traveling. Therefore, as the local community is becoming less important and less of a barrier to radicalization, globalization is inadvertently contributing to the rise in homegrown terrorism (Moghaddam, 2008).

Finally, not only are people becoming more connected, but the technology that runs our lives is also becoming more connected. Anything that is connected to the Internet is vulnerable to hacking, and, as cars, watches, and other daily tools are connected to the Internet, cyberterrorists will have more targets (Goodin, 2014). As of now, it seems that technical incompetence is the greatest barrier for terrorists, such as in the case of the underwear bomber mentioned previously (Ariosto & Feyerick, 2012).

Culture

Globalization is seen by many in the non-Western world as Americanization. Traditionalists and conservatives are wary of the spread of secular "Hollywood" values and the magnetic pull of American culture for youth in their societies. This perceived threat has mobilized ultraconservatives who suddenly feel that their narratives are under attack (Moghaddam, 2008). When culturally offensive art exhibits, such as those that spell the name of God in insects, are allowed under new ideals such as freedom of expression, the conservative narrative strengthens, because ultraconservatives propagate this as proof that secular freedoms will result in a morally degenerate society (Amara & Noueihed, 2012; Nagaty, 2013). Many Egyptians saw the overthrow of Mohammed Morsi as a direct attack on the conservative culture that he represented. This caused a rallying effect in which Ansar Bayt Al Maqdis, an Egyptian terrorist group, grew in strength (Cronin, 2002/2003). As globalization threatens traditional cultures, ultraconservatives are emboldened to fight against perceived threats, with America seen as the main source.

Backlash from traditionalists and fundamentalists has resulted in symbolic or identity-based violence. While globalization may reduce instrumental violence, the change has increased identity-asserting violence (Cronin, 2002/2003). Islamic extremists used the September 11th attacks to reassert their identity. The World Trade Center symbolized American capitalism, which had wooed the young with promises of glitz and glamor, making it the ideal target. Therefore, its destruction symbolized the terrorists' attack on and rejection of the entire system.

New technologies also provide small groups with opportunities to share their ideas. These include extremists both within the United States and in the rest of the world, in conflict zones such as Syria and Northwestern Pakistan. Likewise, the Internet gives small underground cells the opportunity to recruit more broadly. Terrorist organizations such as the IS share numerous English-language videos around the world via YouTube and Twitter (Khan, 2014). With technology and information sharing at a global scale, all groups, including terrorists, can spread their culture around the world.

Terrorists have been described as the "arch-globalizers" (Marsden, 2004); they exploit the openness provided by globalization to spread their narratives and connect radicalized individuals previously unreachable. This process of extremist narratives becoming globalized is directly and indirectly supported by certain dictatorial regimes (Moghaddam, 2013). Globalization has a particularly dangerous effect on two groups of people: those who have already radicalized and those who are ripe for radicalization. The staircase to terrorism, discussed in the following section, illustrates how the effects of globalization can move individuals to instigate extreme violence.

A CASE STUDY IN RADICALIZATION: THE TSARNAEV BROTHERS

Radicalization is the process in which people become frustrated by the discrepancy between their actual life conditions and their aspirations. The frustration can lead to an adoption of increasingly extreme ideologies as a solution to bridging this gap. Such individuals perceive serious threats to their identities and adopt extreme political, social, or religious beliefs as part of their coping strategies (Seul, 1999). Although in recent decades radicalization has often been associated with Islamic extremists, the process can happen in any community regardless of political, social, or religious beliefs.

In the United States, Islamic terrorist attacks account for only a small number of politically inspired killings despite their disproportionate amount of media coverage. A study by the University of North Carolina found that 190,000 Americans have been murdered since September 11, 2001, and that only 37 of those murders have been linked to Muslim terrorists (as cited by Obeidallah, 2015). The National Consortium for the Study of Terrorism and Responses to Terrorism analyzed data collected by the Global Terrorism Database to identify the groups responsible for the most terrorist attacks in the United States between 1970 and 2011. They found that only 1% of terrorist acts committed by major groups were Islamic extremists (LaFree, Dugan, & Miller, 2014). Rather than fixating on radical Islam, it is more useful to survey a diverse set of radicalization cases actualizing into violence. The radicalization process of the Boston bombers, for example, was guided by radical Islam. However, in the case of Wade Page, white supremacist ideology drove him to kill six and wound three in Oak Creek, Wisconsin, on August 2012 (Iyer, 2014). In 2014, David Malcolm Strickland killed 19-year-old Mollie Olgin because of her sexual orientation (Wong, 2014). Bernhard Laufer threatened to kill members of the Council on American–Islamic Relations, a leading Muslim civil rights organization (Algar, 2014). Each of these incidents was driven by a different ideological belief, located in a different region, and perpetrated by persons of varying gender, age, and race—yet they all radicalized.

The Staircase to Terrorism

The staircase to terrorism is a metaphor that organizes psychological findings on radicalization to direct future policy and research. Imagine a staircase at the center of a building. Everyone begins on the ground floor, and most people never move up to higher floors. Some individuals do move up the staircase, committing differing degrees of illegal activity, and few reach the final floor, where they carry out terrorist acts. Particular psychological processes characterize action and thought on each floor. As individuals climb the staircase, they come to see fewer and fewer available opportunities, until there are no other options than to climb to the final floor. Although it is possible for individuals to descend the staircase, each ascending step makes reintegration into society more difficult. If an individual does deradicalize, the path does not necessarily involve retracing the same steps down the staircase (Moghaddam, 2009).

A consistent theme on all floors is that of identity and, particularly, perceived threats to identity. Social identity theory posits that individuals are driven by the need to attain a positive and distinct identity (Tajfel & Turner, 1979). Social identity is based on memberships in groups, such as religious or racial groups. Individuals' perceptions of how fairly they themselves and their groups are treated determines what actions they will take. If individuals believe, due to race or class, for example, that it is impossible for them to achieve adequate identities, they are more likely to resort to deviant behavior (Tyler & Huo, 2002)

The Ground Floor

On the ground floor individuals seek opportunities to improve their social status and achieve what they see to be fair treatment for themselves and their groups. As more and more opportunities become unacceptable or closed to individuals, the ground floor becomes unlivable. Driven by discontentment, the individual is faced with two options: exit the current ground floor in favor of a new ground floor through changing contexts, or climb the staircase. On this floor and all floors perception is key, although it may not closely correspond to reality.

Leaving one's current ground floor for another can lead to completely new spaces, in a new country or lifestyle where the opportunities may appear brighter. These new ground floors may disappear or become an unacceptable option according to the individual's perception. For example, if the individual has a family, an international move may not be an option, or if the individual disapproves of military action, a military career would appear to be objectionable. When individuals perceive no more opportunities on the ground floor, they will begin to climb the staircase to terrorism.

The opportunities perceived are closely associated with perceptions of fairness and just treatment. If individuals perceive that their treatment on the ground floor is unjust, they will recognize fewer opportunities. They will believe that, although those opportunities may be an option for others, due to their gender, race, or religion, the opportunity is not an option for them. When people believe their world to be just and fair, they will believe it is possible to improve themselves, reach their aspirations, and acquire a unique and good identity. As a consequence of perceived injustice, feelings of shame and frustration grow to a point that compels these persons to take their first step onto the staircase.

Perceptions of unfairness can be exacerbated by relative deprivation—the process by which an individual compares him- or herself to peers and perceives him- or herself to be unfairly deprived of equality (Runciman, 1966; Collins, 1996). This perceived deprivation can equally affect the educated and noneducated, the well off and the impoverished, as globalization has increased individuals' abilities to compare their situations (Atran, 2003).

Our case study on radicalization focuses on an immigrant family who moved from Chechnya to the United States in 2002 (Jacobs, Filipov, & Wen, 2013). The mother, father, two daughters, and two sons settled in Cambridge, Massachusetts. The husband worked as a mechanic and the wife as a beautician. The couple had high hopes for the future of their children, particularly their two sons. They dreamed of an Olympic career for their eldest son, the New England Golden Gloves heavyweight champion, and immense academic success for their younger son, called the boy with the heart of gold (Jacobs, Filipov, & Wen, 2013; Reitman, 2013).

However, on April 15, 2013, the United States witnessed a horrific act of terror that killed three people and injured more than 260 others. The attack, now known as the Boston Marathon bombing, was planned and executed by Tamerlan and Dzhokhar Tsarnaev, the two young sons in the immigrant family who moved from Chechnya seeking prosperity. The brothers spent the majority of their lives in the United States seemingly assimilating into the culture and trying to find success in America. As survivors and bystanders alike attempted to understand, President Obama asked the question that seemed to haunt everyone: "Why did young men who grew up and studied here, as part of our communities and our country, resort to such violence?" (White House, 2013, para. 6). We address this question by interpreting the case of the Tsarnaev brothers through the lens of the staircase model.

THE GROUND FLOOR: TSARNAEV

Like everyone else, the Tsarnaev family began on the ground floor. Anzor Tsarnaev, the brothers' father, came from a family of seven, fighting to overcome the crippling poverty of their professional scavenger father (Jacobs et al., 2013). Impoverished as they were, with very few options available to them, four of the seven went on to become lawyers. As Anzor's siblings became more successful, greater opportunities became available to him. And yet, just as his siblings provided him with opportunities, they also provided a means for Anzor to feel jealous or deprived relative to them. The new perception, or expectation of ascendancy, built through his siblings' successes effectively lessened the amount of acceptable opportunities. Anzor was no longer willing to live the life of his father or to work as a mechanic in Kyrgyzstan, making him dissatisfied with his lifestyle.

As Chechens in Kyrgyzstan, the family faced oppression. The stifled opportunities, especially those within the middle class, was part of the reason why Anzor moved his family out of Kyrgyzstan and back to Chechnya (Jacobs et al., 2013). With this move, the Tsarnaev family entered into a new ground floor where life went well, as Anzor described. Unfortunately, war drove the family back to Kyrgyzstan.

Back in Kyrgyzstan, a ground floor that Anzor had already left once due to the lack of opportunities, he became bolder. Anzor would later tell his psychologist that while he was working a gang kidnapped and tortured him (Jacobs et al., 2013). Friends and his wife, Zubeidat, however, would explain that Anzor had become involved in illegal activities and that it had been a rival smuggling group that had taken him (Jacobs et al., 2013). If Anzor's story is true, then he remained on the ground floor during this time, avoiding deviant activity. If, however, Zubeidat's story is true, then Anzor took his first step onto the staircase by looking for illegal opportunities not condoned by Kyrgyzstan society. Whatever the reason for Anzor's troubles, the prevalence of Chechen oppression made it no longer safe for the Tsarnaev family to stay in Kyrgyzstan, and they accomplished their long desired move to the United States by seeking asylum in 2002 (Jacobs et al., 2013).

When the Tsarnaev family arrived in America in April 2002, they approached their new life with enthusiasm. The children enrolled in public school, and the parents sought employment. The family found itself on a new ground floor, where most of the opportunities to develop an identity came through the couple's children, mainly the eldest son, Tamerlan. Both parents devoted their lives to their children. Zubeidat, who claimed to have training as a lawyer, began work as a home health care provider (Jacobs et al., 2013). Anzor capitalized upon his skills as a mechanic while spending hours of his free time training his oldest son as a boxer.

At first the family was dazzled by new opportunities and Anzor's increased income. Anzor's profession apparently provided Tamerlan with a sleek white Mercedes and the ability to appear well off (Jacobs et al., 2013). The family was still comparing their life in America to that in Kyrgyzstan, making them feel privileged. However, this did not last. They became surrounded by successful Chechen immigrants (Reitman, 2013).

Life in the adopted land creates tensions for immigrants; they are torn between the desire to advance in the adopted society and the need to maintain their heritage and cultural identities. The Tsarnaev family provides an example of the victims of this tension and its detrimental effects. The family attempted to adapt in the West while maintaining their Muslim identities and values. Their preservation of their Muslim identities demonstrates how "conversion is integral to the policy of assimilation and the melting-pot ideology that has historically dominated in the United States" (Moghaddam, 2008, p. 59). When individuals adopt the ways of the West or another outgroup, they are inevitably weakening their ingroup heritage.

Of all the Tsarnaevs, the youngest son, Dzhokhar, having moved to America at the early age of 8, had the smoothest transition. He spoke English without an accent, drifted easily between social groups, and enjoyed a heterogeneous group of friends that spurred him academically (Reitman, 2013). At this point in his life, Dzhokhar had three avenues through which he could acquire an adequate identity: as a successful student, as a member of the Tsarnaev family, and as a friend to his Cambridge peers (Reitman, 2013; Wen, 2013). Dzhokhar was loved by both teachers and peers alike. He was even voted captain of the school's wrestling team. His grades, membership in the National Honor Society, ability to speak three languages, and unique background brought him a possible opportunity to attend a solid American university. At the same time, his brother Tamerlan grew more successful as a boxer, with the possibility of the Olympics looming closer (Jacobs et al., 2013). The Tsarnaev family stood a real chance to achieve the financial and social prestige they desired. However, even though

Dzhokhar's life seemed filled with increasing opportunities, his family's opportunities ultimately started to disappear (Reitman, 2013; Wen, 2013).

The First Floor

Individuals who move to the first floor do not see themselves as terrorists. They climb up because they perceive no more opportunities to improve their situation on the ground floor (Moghaddam, 2005). They seek alternative opportunities to improve their social status, options unavailable on the ground floor. They become willing to try unauthorized ways of "getting ahead." This deviant behavior does not have to be immoral or dangerous, but only unacceptable to the local society. If they fail in their attempts at social mobility, individuals start becoming isolated from society and begin to shift their belief systems.

THE FIRST FLOOR: TSARNAEV

When the Tsarnaev family first arrived, their identity was as the new family and victims of violent oppression with great potential. Friends took them in, sheltered them, and helped the couple find new careers. As time progressed, that identity dissipated, and they were no longer special. Now, they were just like any other immigrant family, struggling to get by. Increasing feelings of deprivation brought on strong feelings of frustration. Neighbors reported incidents in which Anzor lashed out at them, grabbing at their shovels and shouting. Their family apartment, which was so small the whole family could not fit around the kitchen table, only grew smaller as the children grew older. Marijuana became a popular pastime for the Tsarnaev children, as they became more American and less Chechen (Wen, 2013). Anzor's salary no longer seemed so large. In other words, as they began to settle down and experience life in the United States, the promise of a "fresh start in America" seemed to sour.

The souring that the Tsarnaev family experienced was associated with their inability to get ahead and improve their living conditions as they expected in America. When expectations of prosperity are unmet, individuals often experience immense dissatisfaction as they compare their expectations with their reality (Moghaddam, 2005, 2008). They were ultimately unable to adjust to life in the United States, as each member experienced personal failures within the culture that they did not successfully adapt to.

Between 2002 and 2008, the Tsarnaev family grew increasingly disenchanted with their new life. Anzor and Zubeidat began embracing tradition more and more as their time in the United States went on. In 2007, the couple arranged a marriage for their youngest daughter, 17 at the time, to a Chechen man of 20. She gave birth a month after the marriage. The eldest sister was married off soon after. It is possible that the couple's renewed devotion to a tradition they had both fled from in their youth was an attempt to control their children and bring order to their life. Renewed devotion also allowed them to reorient their identity. Unfortunately, the arranged marriages failed within a year; Ailina's husband had tried to strangle her (Jacobs et al., 2013). The failed marriages reflected badly on their identity as a traditional Chechen family. Anzor's mercurial temper grew worse as his health deteriorated to the point that he could no longer work full time; Zubeidat, who was working at a beauty parlor at the time, became the major breadwinner.

The Tsarnaev family is a reminder of how failure to achieve social mobility in the United States can foster feelings of relative deprivation and resentment among immigrants. The resentment often motivates them to cling tighter to what is left of their former identities. In such cases, individuals feel left behind and alienated by globalization and the progressive West. They turn to their cultural roots for comfort. According to Jacobs et al. (2013, para. 2), "as the stress of life in [the Tsarnaevs'] adopted country began to take its toll, the family turned to religion with mounting fervor." Rather than continuing to adapt to life in America, they began to define themselves in terms of their Chechen roots and Muslim faith. In an interview after the bombing, Zubeidat recalls telling Tamerlan, "We are Muslim, and we are not practicing our religion, and how can we call ourselves Muslims?" (Bodden, 2014, p. 61). Similar to many members of traditional society who decide to define their identity in terms of ethnic or historical group memberships, the Tsarnaev family ultimately saw the West as an unwelcoming and corrupt force trying to destroy their cultural heritage and identity.

In the case of the eldest brother, Tamerlan's rise to terrorism seems to have begun with his personal failure in America and the consequent devastation of his American identity. Unable to make friends and learn English before plunging into public high school, Tamerlan always struggled to fit in. "I don't have a single American friend," he once admitted, "I don't understand them" (Bodden, 2014, p. 54). When he graduated from high school in 2006, he was denied admission into the University of Massachusetts and was forced to attend community college, from which he would later drop out. His failure in the academic world left Tamerlan with one option: boxing. On the bright side, the awards and respect he began winning as a boxer in 2004 continued to grow. As a result Tamerlan's sense of self in his new community came from his boxing career and his dreams of becoming a U.S. Olympian. Even his family believed that his athletic success would be "their passport to respectability and their ticket to success" (Jacobs et al., 2013).

Dzhokhar seemed to have been more of a follower. Unlike his brother, he did not have a strong sense of self. Arguably the most well-adapted member of the Tsarnaev family, Dzhokhar was initially hardworking. However, he did not manage to develop the discipline required to continue to build on his initial successes at school. Nor was he able to escape the tensions in his family. He read the Koran when told to but avoided home as often as possible and would confess his disapproval to friends. Dzhokhar's identity as a functioning and loved member of both his family and his social circle became separated; friends never visited his home, and his family never attended school events. Dzhokhar was forced to choose between lifestyles. Part of Dzhokhar's need to maintain his sense of membership within his own family at the expense of his success in America may have been a result of negligence and uninterest on the part of his parents.

Dzhokhar did have initial success at Cambridge Rindge and Latin High School. He was one of 45 students granted a $2,500 college scholarship; he was also in the National Honor Society and was the captain and Most Valuable Player of the wrestling team. However, he received little attention from his family. Peter Payack, Dzhokhar's wrestling coach, admitted that he never saw the parents and was not even aware that Dzhokhar had an older brother (Wen, 2013). Dzhokhar never had his family rooting for him on the sidelines. Instead, the wrestling team became Dzhokhar's support system, providing him with the structure to keep him on the right track. The only praise that Dzhokhar received from his family was in regard to his education: "His parents had deemed him the brains of the family, destined to be the first to earn a US college diploma and become a high-earning professional" (Wen, 2013). The scholarly Dzhokhar seemed to represent an assimilation success story: an immigrant on the path toward prosperity in America. However, as his grades started to slip from a B-plus to a C-minus average, he was rejected by his dream schools. When he got to college, his grades suffered dramatically, and he seemed to be on a downward trajectory (Wen, 2013). As his academic dreams were lost, he began looking for opportunities for a new identity, and, led by his older brother, he started climbing the staircase.

The Second Floor

The second floor is a heavily emotion-laden platform, attracting individuals who are dissatisfied with the solutions they had found on the first floor and who continue to experience frustration. These individuals are influenced to turn their dissatisfaction into aggression against particular outgroups. The second floor is influenced by conspiracy theorists, racists, and other individuals harboring extreme prejudices, all pointing to targets for displaced aggression. This floor is particularly important in how it shapes the individual's belief system. Individuals who already blame "the Americans" for problems will seek a strong narrative that confirms this explanation, opening themselves to radical propaganda. Through the adoption of ideologies that justify displaced aggression against particular targets such as America, individuals begin to construct a new identity.

THE SECOND FLOOR: TSARNAEV

The frustrations of the Tsarnaev family escalated around 2009. Tamerlan could not find a job, and his only hope for success was through boxing. He spent his time in the gym and in front of the computer. The daughters, Bella and Ailina, were both divorced. The atmosphere at home was difficult because of the father's hostility. Ultimately, after filing for divorce, both parents ended up moving back to Dagestan, Kyrgyzstan. "I've been here for 10 years in this country and I have nothing to show for it. Nothing," stated Anzor Tsarnaev. "I have less than when I came here" (Jacobs et al., 2013). Thus the American Dream had not worked for them. The Tsarnaevs experienced failure, disappointment, and resentment as they compared their experiences with the expectations they had brought with them from Chechnya. They became disillusioned with the United States as a shared sense of inadequacy and dissatisfaction permeated the family.

The frustrations experienced by the family manifested themselves in different ways. Tamerlan began talking about conspiracy theories and developed a proclivity for casting public aspersions against American foreign policy. Tamerlan, Zubeidat, and Dzhokhar all espoused, at separate times, the opinion that the 9/11 attacks had been an inside job meant to turn the world against Islam. And Tamerlan was arrested that year for slapping his girlfriend.

Tamerlan's frustrations were soon amplified by problems in his boxing career. In 2010, after achieving the title of New England Golden Gloves heavyweight champion of the year and capturing the Rocky Marciano Trophy, a new rule prohibiting noncitizens from participating in the regional Golden Gloves championship created a glass ceiling for Tamerlan's boxing career. This shattered his world. Boxing was the one aspect of his self-concept that linked him to his adopted country. He felt like a failure. According to Ronald Schouten, a psychiatrist specializing in terrorism, "People who fail sometimes latch onto a cause that makes their anger legitimate" (quoted in Bodden, 2014, p. 61). Without boxing, he was simply an unemployed college dropout with no sense of self or purpose. Consequently, Tamerlan latched onto his faith in search of purpose. He began poring over the Koran, Islamic texts, and extremist websites. By 2011, Tamerlan's chauvinism and anti-American political views had become so extreme that the FBI launched a 3-month investigation, which only served to exculpate him (Jacobs et al., 2013).[1]

Dzhokhar ascended to the second floor during his freshman year of college. According to self-categorization theory, individuals will often inhibit certain aspects of their personal identity in order to join a group and achieve an adequate social identity (Moghaddam, 2008). At the University of Massachusetts at Dartmouth, in his attempts to find his niche, Dzhokhar sacrificed his identity as the scholar because he was more interested in his drug-dealing business and his social life. By the end of his freshman year at college, he was known for selling the best weed and earned about $1,000 a week (Wen, 2013). He grew increasingly reckless. He was notorious for driving irresponsibly, picking fights, and talking himself out of trouble. He also seemed to be struggling in striking a balance between his Western identity and his heritage. Terrorism expert Brian Fishman identifies this struggle as an issue of "divided loyalties," as individuals attempt to determine whether they are American first or Muslim first (Bodden, 2014, p. 61). When Dzhokhar began failing in school and his identity as a scholar slipped further away, he began identifying more closely with his ancestry and viewing himself and his family as oppressed Chechen Muslims. Like his brother, Dzhokhar eventually seemed desperate to distinguish himself and establish a strong Muslim identity. A professor at the University of Massachusetts recalled that when Dzhohkar wished to do a research paper on Chechnya, the professor was struck by how little Dzhokhar actually knew about his glorified homeland (Reitman, 2013).

Dzhokhar's radicalization can be tracked through trends on his Twitter account, where he had a tendency to post very negative comments, mainly about women. There are dangers in assuming too much from a person's online media posts, especially those of a teenager (Preston & Roston, 2013). However, looking at Dzhokhar's Twitter account as a whole, the main underlying theme is identity and internal conflict about what direction to take. He tweeted on May 1, 2012, about the turmoil he felt (Jahar, 2012b): "its so loud inside my head, too many thoughts #longnight." He often tweeted one statement and then directly contradicted the tweet later. On March 14, 2012, he tweeted (Jahar, 2012a), "drugs are a crutch for people who cant handle reality." This tweet is a direct contradiction to his lifestyle and samples of his other tweets. He tweeted a prodrug opinion on November 17, 2012 (Jahar, 2012h): "This night deserves Hennessy a bad bitch and an o of weed the holy trinity."

His contradictions went beyond the topic of drug use; Dzhokhar was unsure how to treat women and people of other ethnicities. He described women in a demeaning way in a tweet full of machismo on May 8, 2012 (Jahar, 2012c): "the juice needs to be well worth the squeeze otherwise i rather not waste my time." However, he backtracked on this opinion later when he apologized for his treatment of women and his judgments. He tweeted on December 24, 2012 (Jahar, 2012i), "My last tweets felt too wrong, I don't like to objectify women or judge anyone for their actions."

On racism and ethnicity, he showed a similar struggle, not understanding his actions and words fully. He tweeted about his own racist actions on May 30, 2012 (Jahar, 2012d), "it's no coincidence that i almost crashed into an asian dude. . . . " Later, however, he described himself as completely removed from racist actions, making a point to declare his innocence to the world. He tweeted on October 22, 2012 (Jahar, 2012g), "Foreign to racism, never been a part of it."

These tweets reveal a young man with a confused identity and mismatching opinions. His confused identity is key, as it drove him up the staircase in search of a positive and distinct identity. The desperate search made him vulnerable to extremist recruitment. Furthermore, as the basis for his identity—family, social, academic—became more and more disconnected, he became isolated. Isolation again heightened his vulnerability. As Dzhokhar ascended the staircase, his idea of a positive identity became defined by action in support of Islamic extremism.

The Third Floor

The most important change that takes place on the third floor is a shift in moral values. Having come to see the world as unfair and having identified a source for this unfairness on lower floors, individuals transition to "ends justifies means" thinking. They come to believe that they stand for justice and truth, whereas those who oppose them are evil. In such a world, where evil forces are powerful, it is justified to use whatever means are available to fight for justice and truth. This shift in moral thinking is accompanied with a sense that the world has changed; the individual has entered a new situation.

THE THIRD FLOOR: TSARNAEV

Because his parents were divorced and everyone else was working, Tamerlan had ample time. The inflammatory language of the many blogs and articles he read expressed the types of anti-Western attitudes and beliefs that he needed to validate his bitterness and provide him with a new cause to work toward. Stout (2002) explains that terrorism "is not senseless violence but rather the fruit of resentment and lack of empowerment that leads to acts against the civilian population" (p. 10). Tamerlan spent hours surfing the Internet exploring extremist media outlets associated with Islamist militants in the Caucasus. Feelings of resentment and bitterness led to his pursuit of terrorism and membership in extremist groups. Tamerlan's faith and radicalization now provided him with a new distinct and positive identity. His new identity redirected his energies. He no longer dreamed of representing the United States in the Olympics; he dreamed of destroying it. He had found a new sense of self and sought the validation that would accompany his membership in an extremist group.

Likewise, the positive student-based identity Dzhokhar had started to develop in high school faded. Dzhokhar abandoned his ambitions to do well in school, and his identity changed (Wen, 2013, para. 1):

> Starting in the winter of 2013, Jahar almost certainly knew his hopes of ever getting a college degree—and bringing honor to his family—were bleak, if not impossible. He had so prized his independence from his fractious clan, but had proved entirely unable to manage on his own.

Dzhokhar had always been the most autonomous member of his family and was the academic destined for success. No unfair regulation had robbed him of his opportunity to flourish. Rather, Dzhokhar had simply failed—he was the agent of his own demise. Similar to his brother, Dzhokhar ultimately clung to the only part of his identity that seemed within reach: his faith. He began spending more time at home with his brother, downloading radical Muslim publications focused on *jihad* and the enemies of Islam. Eventually, like Tamerlan, Dzhokhar manufactured and assumed an identity of Muslim extremism. The identity would help him to cope with the disappointment accompanying his failure while allowing him to direct the blame toward the United States.

Dzhokhar's moralization can be tracked through his Twitter account. His tendency toward self-deprecation is particularly interesting and exemplifies tensions he experienced. He regularly called himself lazy. On August 7, 2012, he tweeted (Jahar, 2012e), "Missed my first day of work today #trap I am a terrible employee." And he would publicly reprimand himself for sexist comments. However, as time passed, he accepted and justified his failings. Whereas once he reproached drug users, he began to brag about his own usage; it was the same for sexism, religion, and his academic failures.

The Fourth Floor

The major cognitive shifts that take place on the fourth floor involve more rigid categorical thinking, differentiating further between ingroups and outgroups, condemning the outgroup as evil and deserving of destruction. The world is now seen in more simplistic terms, through a prism that explains everything categorically. This worldview leads to further isolation, as individuals seek to locate themselves with the ingroup and exclude the evil outgroup.

THE FOURTH FLOOR: TSARNAEV

In January of 2012, Tamerlan traveled to Dagestan, Kyrgyzstan. Upon arrival, he became involved with the Union of the Just, which campaigns against human rights violations that victimize Muslims. The Union of the Just is characterized by a fundamentalist interpretation of Islam, believing in the establishment of an Islamic caliphate governed by Sharia religious law spanning the Caucasus. Tamerlan also allegedly made contact with a recruiter for the Islamist underground named Makhmud Mansur Nidal and prayed with members of the Islamic insurgency. The visit reflected his desire to further solidify his new radical Muslim identity by joining an active radical group. Those who join such groups accept a highly polarized worldview and narrow set of rules in exchange for simple answers and a comprehensive framework of social and moral norms and values. Furthermore, the ideological framing of us-versus-them creates a strong bond among members while alienating the West. For Tamerlan, membership in one of these groups would validate both his senses of self and of purpose while further distancing himself from America.

Despite his efforts to fit into these extremist groups, Tamerlan was still viewed as an outsider. Mukhamad Magomedov, deputy leader of the Union of the Just, admitted, "What gave him away was his appearance" (Jacobs et al., 2013). According to Jacobs et al. (2013), "he wore a long shirt of the type favored by Pakistanis. . . . He combed his hair with olive oil and darkened his eyes with kohl shadow, practices followed by devout Sunnis in some cultures, but not in Dagestan." This description demonstrates his failure to fit into the group to which he so desperately wished to belong. Ironically, his foreign habits ultimately inhibited his ability to blend in among the Muslims in Dagestan. He spoke in English-inflected Russian, chatted animatedly with strangers, and gave money to beggars on the street, all of which were uncharacteristic of the local culture. His failure to be accepted among the Muslims "back home" in Dagestan may have damaged his sense of self further. His new radical Muslim identity seemed illegitimate in the eyes of local radical Muslims.

The rejection closed this new ground floor and may have catalyzed the radicalization process. Upon his return, Tamerlan had grown a full beard and abandoned his flashy American clothing for traditional, dark garb. He spoke out publicly at least twice at local mosques, reprimanding the speakers for not being religious or aggressive enough; he was asked to leave by the community elders. Finally, he began downloading information from jihadist websites, such as articles from al Qaeda in the Arabian Peninsula's magazine *Inspire* on how to construct explosives (Jacobs et al., 2013).

The transition to terrorism is accomplished by cognitively redefining the morality of killing. In the case of the Tsarnaev brothers, the moral shift that justified killing Americans was accompanied by increasing anti-American beliefs and allegations against Americans that they were spearheading a war against Muslims. The Tsarnaev brothers adopted an "us-versus-them" narrative that allowed them to hide their feelings of failure and inferiority beneath layers of misplaced anger, hate, and envy. This abandonment of nuance enabled the Tsarnaevs to dehumanize innocent Americans and transform them into merely "agents of cultural destruction" who deserved to suffer. In this way, they maintained a just worldview depicting their victims as evil.

Tamerlan's social media posts indicate that he now saw himself as having a special role in fighting the United States, which was waging an "all out war against Islam" (Jacobs et al., 2013). He called for Muslims to band together and fight against America. One of his YouTube posts features an armed figure, presumably a terrorist, speaking in Russian. The figure states, "There will always be a group of people who will stick to the truth, fight for that truth . . . and those who won't support them will not win" (Jacobs et al., 2013). For Tamerlan, he was one of the special people "fighting for the truth," and America represented corruption in its purest form.

As time passed, Dzhokhar's tweets also became increasingly aggressive; he appeared less and less confused about his identity, and he became increasingly interested in taking action. For example, on April 7, 2013, he tweeted (Jahar, 2013): "If you have the knowledge and the inspiration all that's left is to take action." His account trends demonstrate an emotional preparation that took him further and further from the boy who once posted, on August 8, 2012 (Jahar, 2012f), "i wish i could apologize to the kids i bullied at a young age #iwasonsomefuckery i'm talking like first/second grade though. I've changed!"

According to the graffiti left on the boat that the authorities finally found Dzhokhar hiding in on Friday, April 19, 2013, he was convinced that the United States government was killing innocent Muslim civilians. He wrote, "I can't stand to see such evil go unpunished. . . . Fuck America" (Reitman, 2013, para. 8). Dzhokhar also wrote a poem on the side of the boat that said, "We Muslims are one body, you hurt one you hurt us all" (Wen, 2013). Both brothers saw themselves as part of a global struggle against the persecution and oppression of Muslims in which the United States was the main perpetrator.

The Fifth Floor

Human beings are influenced by what Lorenz (1966) terms *inhibitory mechanism* to limit physical harm against other humans. Most people feel distress when they physically harm another human being. Soldiers go through extensive military training in order to prepare for killing the enemy (Grossman, 1999). Modern weapons enable humans to sidestep inhibitory mechanisms, because they kill from a distance and there is no human-to-human interaction. For example, drone operators will not see the human targets of a drone attack they have launched sometimes thousands of miles away. Terrorists sidestep inhibitory mechanisms by dehumanizing the targeted others and condemning them as evil.

THE FIFTH FLOOR: TSARNAEV

Ultimately, Tamerlan's decision to bomb the marathon may have been an attempt to prove his allegiance to Islam and his legitimacy as a radical Muslim dedicated to fighting for the truth. The United States simply functioned as the scapegoat to elevate and affirm his identity as a devoted extremist. Justified by his own personal vendetta against America and the anti-Western ideology characteristic of radical Islam, Tamerlan bombed the Boston Marathon and became immortalized as a terrorist.

For Dzhokhar, his radicalization ended with one last public statement in a note he left in the Watertown boat where he was in hiding after the bombings ("Text from Dzhokhar Tsarnaev's Note," 2013, para. 4):

> God has a plan for each person. Mine was to hide in this boat and shed some light on our actions. The US Government is killing our innocent civilians but most of you already know that. As a [UI] I can't stand to see such evil go unpunished. We Muslims are one body, you hurt one you hurt us all. Well at least that's how muhhammad (pbuh) wanted it to be [for]ever. The ummah is beginning to rise. [UI] has awoken the mujahideen. Know you are fighting men who look into the barrel of your gun and see heaven, now how can you compete with that. We are promised victory and we will surely get it. Now I don't like killing innocent people it is forbidden in Islam but due to said [UI] it is allowed. All credit goes [UI]. Stop killing our innocent people and we will stop.

The Tsarnaev brothers redefined their act of terror as a practice of selfless benevolence through self-sacrificing motivation. Terrorists are often motivated by a need to remedy political or social injustice or to retaliate against a world they view as irredeemably corrupt and salvageable only through total destruction. In this way, both brothers justified their actions by defining the actions in terms of a divine mission: There was a need to bring justice to a world plagued by the evil and corruption of the United States. In one of his Twitter posts Dzhokhar writes, "It's kind of like we're living in this time where good is evil and evil is good" (Wen, 2013, para. 9). Tamerlan and Dzhokhar both claimed to be motivated by a strong sense of duty to preserve the truth. In another one of his Twitter posts Dzhokhar wrote, "There are people that know the truth but stay silent . . . and there are people that speak the truth but we don't hear them cuz they're the minority" (Russell, Abelson, Wen, Rezendes, & Filipov, 2013). Echoing the same sentiments as many of his brother's posts, Dzhokhar's statement conveys the narrative of oppression and corruption that the brothers ultimately used to justify their retaliation.

CONCLUDING COMMENTS

> The act of the two great brothers, Tamerlan and Dzhokhar, is but the true image reflected by the bloody deeds of [American] hands, reflected by the oppressive policies of your downtrodding regimes.
> —Letter from the Editor (2013)

Globalization is associated with enormous macrolevel changes around the world, including large-scale movements of cultures, values, and people. These processes have resulted in secular Western values spreading around the world, creating threats in the eyes of traditionalists and fundamentalists

(Moghaddam, 2008). Muslim fundamentalists have reacted with particular energy and violence, using Internet jihad to launch their extremist ideologies around the world. Internet jihad touches dissatisfied youth in many regions of the world, including the United States. The Tsarnaev brothers were two examples of Muslims in the United States who became ensnared in the web of Internet jihad and subsequently climbed up the staircase to terrorism. Their experiences and actions can best be explained by giving primacy to collective processes rather than personality characteristics and other idiographic factors. Undoubtedly the personalities of the Tsarnaev family members did play a role, but the larger context was more important.

The Tsarnaev brothers are far from unique. The radicalization they experienced and the violence they perpetrated is repeated by others. On January 7, 2015, Said and Cherif Kouachi, two brothers motivated by radical Islam, attacked the offices of the French satirical magazine Charlie Hebdo in Paris, France, killing 11 people and seriously injuring many others. The Kouachi brothers were born in France to immigrants from Algeria. Their life story is similar to that of the Tsarnaev brothers in that it involved a lack of social mobility in an affluent Western society and identification with a larger Islamic community perceived to be under attack. The two sets of brothers climbed up the staircase to terrorism experiencing similar psychological processes on each floor.

In another era, the Tsarnaev and Kouachi brothers might have joined street gangs and become local thugs. But in the 21st century era of globalization and Internet jihad, their aggressive, destructive energies became channeled through radical Islamic ideology. In another era, they might have fought battles against rival street gangs. But in this era they directed their energies against innocent American and French civilians, justifying their actions by asserting that they were "defending Islam." This pattern of would-be or actual street gang member transforming into "Islamic terrorist" is often repeated, as in the case of the 22-year-old Danish-born attacker who gunned down a Danish film director and a Jewish night guard in Copenhagen on February 14, 2015. According to the staircase model, long-term policies are needed to prevent such individuals from starting up the staircase. However, fast and short-term policies must be in place to eliminate threats from those who reach the highest floors. We have need of more practical long-term deradicalization policies, although some progress is being made ("TerRa: Terrorism and Radicalisation," n.d.).

NOTES

1. At this point, it is also important to note Tamerlan's mental status. He mentioned hearing voices and feared he had been brainwashed by the government into acting in ways he objected to. Unfortunately, Tamerlan never sought psychiatric

care, so the claims are unsubstantiated. As the claims cannot be verified, and as the object of this chapter is to demonstrate the radicalization process rather than to answer the question of why the brothers radicalized, we ask the reader to put aside questions into Tamerlan's mental health (Jacobs et al., 2013).

REFERENCES

Algar, S. (2014, June 17). Anti-Muslim maniac busted for sending death threats. *New York Post*. Retrieved from *http://nypost.com/2014/06/17/anti-muslim-maniac-busted-for-sending-death-threats*.

Amara, T., & Noueihed, L. (2012, June 12). Tunisian Salafi Islamists riot over "insulting" art. Retrieved from *www.reuters.com/article/2012/06/12/us-tunisia-salafis-clashidUSBRE85B0XW20120612*.

Anderson, J. L. (2014, August 20). The men who killed James Foley. *The New Yorker*. Retrieved from *www.newyorker.com/news/news-desk/men-killed-james-foley*.

Ariosto, D., & Feyerick, D. (2012, February 17). Christmas day bomber sentenced to life in prison. Retrieved from *www.cnn.com/2012/02/16/justice/michigan-underwear-bomber-sentencing*.

Atran, S. (2003). Genesis of suicide terrorism. *Science, 299*, 1534–1539.

Bliss, J. (2012, August 13). U.S. backs off all-cargo scanning goal with inspections at 4%. Retrieved from *www.bloomberg.com/news/2012-08-13/u-s-backs-off-all-cargo-scanning-goal-with-inspections-at-4-.html*.

Blythman, J. (2013, January 16). Can vegans stomach the unpalatable truth about quinoa? Retrieved from *www.theguardian.com/commentisfree/2013/jan/16/vegans-stomach-unpalatable-truth-quinoa*.

Bodden, V. (2014). *The Boston Marathon bombing*. Minneapolis, MN: ABDO.

Collins, R. L. (1996). For better or worse: The impact of upward social comparison on self-evaluations. *Psychological Bulletin, 116*, 457–475.

Cronin, A. K. (2002/2003). Behind the curve: Globalization and international terrorism. *International Security, 27*(3), 30–58.

Federal Bureau of Investigation, U.S. Attorney's Office. (2012, February 9). Leader of Revolution Muslim pleads guilty to using Internet to solicit murder and encourage violent extremism [Press release]. Retrieved from *www.fbi.gov/washingtondc/press-releases/2012/leader-of-revolution-muslim-pleads-guilty-to-using-internet-to-solicit-murder-and-encourage-violent-extremism*.

Fisher, A. (2014, July 8). Eye of the swarm: The rise of ISIS and the media Mujahedeen [Web log post]. Retrieved from *http://uscpublicdiplomacy.org/blog/-swarm-rise-isis-and-media-mujahedeen*.

Ghemawat, P. (2012). Actually, the world isn't flat [Video file]. Retrieved from *www.ted.com/talks/pankaj_ghemawat_actually_the_world_isn_t_flat*.

Goodin, D. (2014, April 2). "Internet of things" is the new Windows XP—malware's favorite target. Retrieved from *http://arstechnica.com/security/2014/04/how-new-malware-is-making-the-internet-of-things-the-windows-xp-of-2014*.

Grossman, D. (1999). *Teaching kids to kill*. Mascoutah, IL: Killology Research Group.

Hazbun, W. (2005). Globalization and terrorism: The migration of dreams and

nightmares [Review of the book *Globalization and Terrorism: The Migration of Dreams and Nightmares*, by J. R. Nassar]. *Comparative Studies of South Asia, Africa and the Middle East, 25*(3), 696–697.
- International Telecommunication Union. (2014, May 5). ITU releases 2014 ICT figures [Press release]. Retrieved from *www.itu.int/net/pressoffice/press_releases/2014/23.aspx*.
- Iyer, D. (2014, August 5). Oak Creek community marks two years since Sikh temple shooting. Retrieved from *www.nbcnews.com/news/asian-america/oak-creek-community-marks-two-years-sikh-temple-shooting-n171981*.
- Jacobs, S., Filipov, D., & Wen, P. (2013, December 15). The fall of the house of Tsarnaev. Retrieved from *www.bostonglobe.com/Page/Boston/2011-2020/WebGraphics/Metro/BostonGlobe.com/2013/12/15tsarnaev/tsarnaev.html*.
- Jahar. (2012a, March 14). Drugs are a crutch for people who can't handle reality [Tweet]. Retrieved from *https://twitter.com/j_tsar/status/179856279865532416*.
- Jahar. (2012b, May 1). It's so loud inside my head, too many thoughts #longnight [Tweet]. Retrieved from *https://twitter.com/J_tsar/status/197280781587062784*.
- Jahar. (2012c, May 8). The juice needs to be well worth the squeeze otherwise i rather not waste my time [Tweet]. Retrieved from *https://twitter.com/j_tsar/status/200048114793590787*.
- Jahar. (2012d, May 30). It's no coincidence that i almost crashed into an asian dude . . . [Tweet]. Retrieved from *https://twitter.com/j_tsar/status/207917365684473857*.
- Jahar. (2012e, August 7). Missed my first day of work today #trap I am a terrible employee [Tweet]. Retrieved from *https://twitter.com/j_tsar/status/232847035106217984*.
- Jahar. (2012f, August 8). I wish i could apologize to the kids i bullied at a young age #iwasonsomefuckery. i'm talking like first/second grade though. I've changed! [Tweet]. Retrieved from *https://twitter.com/j_tsar/status/233414998339248128*.
- Jahar. (2012g, October 22). Foreign to racism, never been a part of it [Tweet]. Retrieved from *https://twitter.com/j_tsar/status/260408778892120064*.
- Jahar. (2012h, November 17). This night deserves Hennessy a bad bitch and an o of weed the holy trinity [Tweet]. Retrieved from *https://twitter.com/j_tsar/status/270018393137086465*.
- Jahar. (2012i, December 24). My last tweets felt too wrong, I don't like to objectify women or judge anyone for their actions [Tweet]. Retrieved from *https://twitter.com/j_tsar/status/283231268315987968*.
- Jahar. (2013, April 7). If you have the knowledge and the inspiration all that's left is to take action [Tweet]. Retrieved from *https://twitter.com/J_tsar/status/321113224802099201*.
- Khan, A. (2014, June 20). What ISIL's English-language propaganda tells us about its goals. Retrieved from *http://america.aljazeera.com/watch/shows/america-tonight/articles/2014/6/19/how-isil-is remakingitsbrandontheinternet.html*.
- Kraul, C., & Rotella, S. (2008, October 22). Drug probe finds Hezbollah link. Retrieved from *http://articles.latimes.com/2008/oct/22/world/fg-cocainering22*.
- LaFree, G., Dugan, L., & Miller, E. (2012). IUSSD: Data on the terrorist attacks in the United States homeland, 1970–2011. Retrieved from *www.start.umd.edu/sites/default/files/files/publications/START_IUSSDDataTerroristAttacksUS_1970-2011.pdf*.

Letter from the Editor. (2013, Spring). Retrieved from *https://azelin.files.wordpress.com/2013/05/inspire-magazine-issue-11.pdf*.

Lorenz, K. (1966). *On aggression* (M. Wilson, Trans.). New York: Harcourt, Brace & World.

Make a bomb in the kitchen of your mom. (2010, Summer). Retrieved from *http://azelin.files.wordpress.com/2010/06/aqap-inspire-magazine-volume-1.pdf*.

Marsden, C. T. (2004). Hyperglobalized individuals: The Internet, globalization, freedom and terrorism. *Foresight: The Journal of Future Studies, Strategic Thinking and Policy, 6*(3), 128–140.

Moghaddam, F. M. (2005). The staircase to terrorism: A psychological exploration. *American Psychologist, 60*(2), 161–169.

Moghaddam, F. M. (2008). *How globalization spurs terrorism: The lopsided benefits of one world and why that fuels violence*. Westport, CT: Praeger Security International.

Moghaddam, F. M. (2009). De-radicalization and the staircase from terrorism. In D. Canter (Ed.), *The faces of terrorism: Multidisciplinary perspectives* (pp. 277–292). Chichester, UK: Wiley-Blackwell.

Moghaddam, F. M. (2013). *The psychology of dictatorship*. Washington, DC: American Psychological Association Press.

Nagaty, Y. (2013, April 2). Nude feminism challenges Islamist discourse. Retrieved from *www.al-monitor.com/pulse/originals/2013/04/feminist-nude-protests-islamism.html*.

Obeidallah, D. (2015, February 14). Are all terrorists Muslims?: It's not even close. Retrieved from *www.thedailybeast.com/articles/2015/01/14/are-all-terrorists-muslims-it-s-not-even-close.html*.

Parascandola, R. (2014, July 16). Terror magazine encourages attack on U.S. Open: NYPD official. Retrieved from *www.nydailynews.com/new-york/nyc-crime/terror-magazine-encourages-attack-u-s-open-nypd-official-article-1.1869108*.

Piketty, T. (2014). *Capital in the twenty-first century* (A. Goldhammer, Trans.). Cambridge, MA: Belknap Press.

Pradhan, N. (2014, July 31). Terrorism, Facebook, and Twitter: A love story. Retrieved from *www.digit.in/internet/terrorism-facebook-twitter-a-love-story-23462.html*.

Preston, J., & Roston, M. (2013, April 20). A closer look at the bombing suspect's Twitter account [Web log post]. Retrieved from *http://thelede.blogs.nytimes.com/2013/04/20/dzhokhar-tsarnaevs-jahar-twitter-account-prompts-scrutiny/?_r=0*.

Privately educated woman, 20, who went to Syria to marry an ISIL fighter. (2014, September 3). Retrieved from *www.telegraph.co.uk/news/uknews/terrorism-in-the-uk/11073923/Privately-educated-woman-20-who-went-to-Syria-to-marry-an-Isil-fighter.html*.

Reitman, J. (2013, July 17). Jahar's world. Retrieved from *www.rollingstone.com/culture/news/jahars-world-20130717*.

Runciman, W. G. (1966). *Relative deprivation and social justice: A study of attitudes to social inequality in twentieth-century England*. Oxford, UK: Routledge & Kegan Paul.

Russell, J., Abelson, J., Wen, P., Rezendes, M., & Filipov, D. (2013, April 19).

Brothers veered violently off track. Retrieved from *www.bostonglobe.com/metro/2013/04/19/relatives-marathon-bombing-suspects-worried-that-older-brother-was-corrupting-sweet-younger-sibling/UCYHkiP9nfsjAtMjJ-PWJJL/story.html*.

Sarkar, J. (2014, July 5). Reliance Retail set to take on Walmart. Retrieved from *http://timesofindia.indiatimes.com/business/india-business/Reliance-Retail-set-to-take-on-Walmart/articleshow/37796878.cms*.

Seul, J. R. (1999). "Ours in the way of God": Religion, identity, and intergroup conflict. *Journal of Peace Research, 36*, 553–569.

Stout, C. E. (2002). *The psychology of terrorism*. Westport, CT: Praeger.

Tajfel, H., & Turner, J. C. (1979). An integrative theory of intergroup conflict. *Social Psychology of Intergroup Relations, 33*(47), 74.

TerRa: Terrorism and radicalisation: Prevention, de-radicalisation, and citizenship. (n.d.). Retrieved from *http://www.terra-net.eu*.

Text from Dzhokhar Tsarnaevtion, and citizenship.ent [Press release]. Ry 22. Retrieved from *www.bostonglobe.com/metro/2014/05/22/text-from-dzhokhar-tsarnaev-note-left-watertown-boat/KnRIeqqr95rJQbAbfnj5EP/story.html*.

Tyler, T. R., & Huo, Y. (2002). *Trust in the law: Encouraging public cooperation with the police and courts*. New York: Russell Sage Foundation.

Wee, W. (2012, September 12). Apple's iOS 6 comes with Sina Weibo integration, in and outside of China. Retrieved from *www.techinasia.com/apples-ios-6-sina-weibo-integration-china*.

Wen, P. (2013, December 15). The fall of the house of Tsarnaev. Retrieved from *www.bostonglobe.com/Page/Boston/2011-2020/WebGraphics/Metro/BostonGlobe.com/2013/12/15tsarnaev/tsarnaev.html*.

White House. (2013, April 19). Statement by the President [Press release]. Retrieved from *www.whitehouse.gov/the-press-office/2013/04/19/statement-president*.

Wong, C. M. (2014, June 23). David Malcolm Strickland, suspect in 2012 shooting of lesbian teen couple, arrested in Texas. Retrieved from *www.huffingtonpost.com/2014/06/23/david-malcom-strickland-arrest_n_5521878.html*.

PART V

THE POSSIBILITIES FOR KINDNESS

CHAPTER 20

Benefits and Liabilities of Empathy-Induced Altruism
A Contemporary Review

C. Daniel Batson, Nadia Y. Ahmad, and E. L. Stocks

To judge one thing good and another evil can be quite subjective. Uncomfortable with such judgments, we shall focus on benefits and liabilities. Empathy-induced altruism has both, as we illustrated in the first edition of this book (Batson, Ahmad, & Stocks, 2004). We are pleased to have an opportunity to update and extend that analysis. In order to make room for more recent examples and evidence, we have abbreviated what was said in the first edition. To get a more complete picture you may want to look at the earlier chapter along with this one. As there, we begin with what we mean by empathy-induced altruism.

EMPATHY-INDUCED ALTRUISM

For more than 30 years, our colleagues and we have explored the possibility that the repertoire of human motivation is not limited to self-interest. Specifically, we have tested the *empathy–altruism hypothesis*, which states that empathic concern produces altruistic motivation (Batson, 2011). In this hypothesis, *empathic concern* refers to *other-oriented emotion elicited by and congruent with the perceived welfare of someone in need.*

Five quick points to clarify this definition: First, it does not refer to catching another's emotion (emotional contagion) but to responding emotionally to *the perceived welfare* of the other. Thus we can feel empathic concern (sympathy, compassion) for someone who is depressed or upset—or for an unconscious accident victim who is not feeling anything at all. Second, empathic concern is *congruent* in valence; it is positive when the perceived welfare of the other is positive, negative when the perceived welfare is negative. Third, it is *other-oriented* in that it involves feeling for the other, not simply reacting with emotion to his or her plight or feeling as the other feels. Fourth, although the term *empathy* is broad enough to include feeling empathic joy at another's good fortune (Smith, Keating, & Stotland, 1989; Stotland, 1969), not all empathic emotion is hypothesized to produce altruistic motivation—only the empathic concern felt when the other is perceived to be *in need*. Without need, there is no impetus for change. Fifth, perception of the other as in need and intrinsically valuing the other's welfare are the conditions that evoke empathic concern.

Altruism in the empathy–altruism hypothesis refers to *a motivational state with the ultimate goal of increasing another's welfare*. It is juxtaposed to *egoism—a motivational state with the ultimate goal of increasing one's own welfare*. In each of these definitions, *ultimate goal* refers to something sought as an end in the situation, not to a metaphysical first or final cause and not to biological function. Increasing the welfare of a person in need by providing help can be either an ultimate goal (altruistically motivated) or an instrumental means to benefit oneself (egoistically motivated).

Over 35 experiments have now been conducted to test the empathy–altruism hypothesis against various egoistic hypotheses that claim that the motivation produced by empathic concern is directed toward the ultimate goal of obtaining some self-benefit (see Batson, 2011, for a comprehensive review). With remarkable consistency, results of these experiments have supported the empathy–altruism hypothesis, leading to the tentative conclusion that it is true. But to conclude that empathy-induced altruism is within the human motivational repertoire is not grounds for unrestrained rejoicing. To be sure, this altruistic motivation offers benefits. However, it also has liabilities.

BENEFITS

More, More Sensitive, and Less Fickle Help

Even before tests of the empathy–altruism hypothesis, there was much evidence that empathic concern can increase the likelihood of helping (e.g., Coke, Batson, & McDavis, 1978; Krebs, 1975). Now that we know empathic concern produces altruistic motivation, we have reason to believe it can improve the quality of help as well.

Because altruistic motivation is directed toward the ultimate goal of increasing another person's welfare, empathy-induced altruism is likely to motivate help that is more sensitive to that person's need. Egoistic goals, such as gaining rewards and avoiding punishments, can often be reached even if the help does not alleviate the needy individual's suffering. For these goals, it's the thought that counts. But for the altruistically motivated, it's the other's welfare that counts. Experimental evidence supports this reasoning. Unlike those feeling little empathy, individuals induced to feel empathic concern tend to feel good if and only if the other's need is relieved (Batson et al., 1988; Batson & Weeks, 1996). Highlighting sensitivity to future consequences, Sibicky, Schroeder, and Dovidio (1995) provided evidence that empathic concern actually reduced helping when that help—although meeting an immediate need—would be detrimental in the long term.

Penner et al. (2008) provided evidence of increased sensitivity in a field setting. They assessed the level of empathic concern felt by parents for their children who were about to undergo an invasive and stressful treatment for pediatric cancer. Penner et al. found a significant negative correlation between the parents' level of empathic concern and the level of pain and distress their child experienced during treatment (as assessed by the child, by nurses, and by trained observers). What produced this correlation? The parents faced a situation in which sensitive care did not involve freeing their child from pain. That was not possible. Instead, it involved being there with and for the child during the pain. Parents feeling high empathy differed from those feeling low empathy in the way they interacted with their child during the treatment. High-empathy parents were more likely to offer supportive and normalizing communication (e.g., comforting, reassuring, and engaging the child in everyday, nonmedical activities such as reading and play) rather than invalidating communication (e.g., denying or minimizing the child's pain).

In addition to producing more sensitivity, empathy-induced altruistic motivation produces less fickle help. Research indicates that individuals experiencing relatively low empathy—and hence a relative predominance of egoistic over altruistic motivation—are far less likely to help when they can easily escape exposure to another's need without helping, or when they can justify to themselves and others a failure to help. Easy escape and high justification for not helping are common characteristics of many helping situations. We can almost always find a way to direct attention elsewhere or to convince ourselves that inaction is justified. However, research also indicates that individuals experiencing high empathy are likely to help even when these outs are readily available (Batson, Duncan, Ackerman, Buckley, & Birch, 1981; Batson et al., 1988; Toi & Batson, 1982). Further, unlike those feeling low empathy, individuals induced to feel high empathy are as likely to help when convinced that they will not think about the other's need in the future as when they think they will (Stocks, Lishner, & Decker, 2009).

Less Aggression

A second benefit is inhibition of aggression. To the degree that feeling empathic concern for someone produces altruistic motivation to maintain or increase that person's welfare, it should inhibit any inclination to aggress against or harm that person. This inhibitory effect was demonstrated by Harmon-Jones, Vaughn-Scott, Mohr, Sigelman, and Harmon-Jones (2004). They assessed the effect of empathy on anger-related left-frontal cortical electroencephalographic (EEG) activity following an insult. As predicted based on the empathy–altruism hypothesis, relative left-frontal cortical EEG activity—which is typically increased by insult and promotes aggression, and which increased in a low-empathy condition—was inhibited in a high-empathy condition.

Empathic feelings should not inhibit all aggressive impulses, only those directed toward the target of empathy. Indeed, it is easy to imagine *altruistic aggression*, in which empathy for Person A leads to increased aggression toward Person B, if B is perceived to be a threat to A's welfare (Hoffman, 2000). To test for such aggression, Vitaglione and Barnett (2003) had participants listen to an audiotaped interview in which a woman hit by a drunk driver talked about the impact of the accident on her life. Consistent with the idea of empathy-induced altruistic aggression, empathic concern felt for her was associated with feelings of anger toward the driver, which in turn increased motivation to punish him.

Increased Cooperation and Care in Interpersonal Conflict Situations

There is also evidence that empathy-induced altruistic motivation can increase cooperation and care in conflict situations. Paradigmatic of such situations is a one-trial prisoner's dilemma. In this two-person dilemma, it is always in each person's interest to defect (i.e., compete) regardless of what the other person does. Game theory and the theory of rational choice both predict no cooperation in a one-trial prisoner's dilemma because each theory assumes that only one motive exists—self-interest (egoism).

The empathy–altruism hypothesis predicts that if one of the two people is led to feel empathy for the other, the person feeling empathy will experience two motives—self-interest and empathy-induced altruism. Although self-interest can be best satisfied by defecting, altruism is best satisfied by cooperating. So the person feeling empathy should be more likely to cooperate. Batson and Moran (1999) and Batson and Ahmad (2001) both reported prisoner's dilemma experiments with precisely these results.

Rumble, van Lange, and Parks (2010) further found that inducing empathic concern for the other in a variant of an iterated prisoner's dilemma counteracted the detrimental effects of "negative noise"—the other person's occasional, unexpected noncooperative response.

Might induction of empathy-induced altruism be worth pursuing in real-world conflict situations, such as business or political negotiations? Or is allowing oneself to feel for the other in these situations too big a risk? Think, for example, of negotiations between management and labor, between Palestinians and Israelis, between Pakistanis and Indians. Empathy-induced altruism might prompt one to give ground. But it might also produce a better outcome for all. It might even save lives.

Research by Galinsky, Maddux, Gilin, and White (2008) suggests that empathic concern may have both of these effects on negotiations. It may prompt one to give ground, but it may also create a more positive environment that can, in the long run, produce a better outcome for all.

In one experiment, Galinsky and colleagues (2008) had MBA students in a negotiations course pair up and engage in a 30-minute two-party negotiation exercise. One student played the role of a Job Candidate and the other, a Recruiter. Eight issues were negotiated, including salary, work location, bonus, and vacation time. Both students knew that some of these issues mattered more to the Candidate, others more to the Recruiter. Joint gain could be maximized by being sensitive to which issue mattered most to whom and using this information to negotiate trade-offs. As a manipulation of perspective taking, the student in the Recruiter role was randomly assigned to one of three sets of instructions: (1) consider your own role carefully, (2) try to understand what the Candidate is thinking, and (3) try to imagine what the Candidate is feeling. The imagine-feelings instructions were similar to instructions used in previous studies to induce empathic concern.

Dyads with Recruiters assigned to one of the latter two sets of instructions produced greater joint gain than dyads with Recruiters assigned to consider their own role. For Recruiters who focused on the Candidate's thoughts, the difference was highly significant. For those who focused on the Candidate's feelings, it was marginal. Of particular interest was how the joint gains were achieved. Recruiters who focused on the Candidate's thoughts got more of what they wanted than did Recruiters who focused on the Candidate's feelings. Candidates negotiating with a Recruiter focused on their feelings got more of what they wanted than did Candidates negotiating with a Recruiter focused either on the Recruiter's role or (nonsignificantly) on the Candidate's thoughts.

These results led the researchers to conclude that, when negotiating, it is more effective "to 'think for' than to 'feel for' one's adversaries" (Galinsky et al., 2008, p. 383). Recruiters who imagined the Candidate's feelings—which presumably induced empathic concern (we cannot be sure because no measures of emotion were taken)—gave ground, benefiting the Candidate at cost to themselves. Recruiters who were able to get inside the Candidate's thoughts, as a skilled chess player might, got more of what they wanted.

But these results were in the short term, in a single negotiation. What about long-term effects in situations in which negotiators interact over time? In such situations, it seems possible that the goodwill produced by giving ground might tip the scales in favor of negotiators who imagine feelings. In the long run, those who imagine feelings, not thoughts, might end up with the better overall outcome.

Consistent with this possibility, Galinsky et al. (2008) found in a different negotiation exercise that Sellers who negotiated with an empathic Buyer (one focused on the Seller's feelings) were significantly more satisfied with the way they were treated during the negotiation than were Sellers who negotiated with a Buyer focused on their thoughts. This was true even though agreement on a sale was (nonsignificantly) more likely to be achieved in the latter case than the former. Whether these feelings of satisfaction lead to more productive subsequent negotiations seems worth exploring in future research.

Reduced Intergroup Conflict

When one thinks of trying to use empathy-induced altruism to reduce intergroup conflict (e.g., conflict between religious, racial, or ethnic groups), two problems immediately loom. First, these conflicts often have a history of intergroup disdain and mistrust, if not outright hostility. To feel empathic concern requires that one be other-oriented, attending with sensitivity to the other's plight. In the face of suspicion and antipathy, is other-oriented sensitivity not too much to ask (Cikara, Bruneau, & Saxe, 2011)? Second, both empathic concern and altruistic motivation are interpersonal processes. One feels and cares for another individual or individuals. Is it possible to feel empathic concern for members of another group, especially an outgroup?

To address these two problems, a key element in strategies using empathy-induced altruism to reduce real-world intergroup conflict has been to work from the interpersonal to the intergroup level by providing *personalizing contact* with one or more outgroup members (Brown & Hewstone, 2005; Pettigrew, 1997). Through such contact, members of one group are led to deal with members of the other group on a personal basis, not simply as one of *them*.

How can personalizing contact among individuals on opposite sides of an intergroup conflict be achieved? Obviously, it is not easy. More is required than simply bringing the antagonists together. Mere contact is likely to invite further antipathy and hostility (Pettigrew, 1998). One structural technique that has proved especially effective in creating nonadversarial personalizing contact, and thereby reducing intergroup conflict, is to introduce a *superordinate goal* (Sherif, Harvey, White, Hood, & Sherif, 1961). A superordinate goal is something that both sides in the conflict want but can attain only if the two sides join forces and work together. Potential antagonists find themselves united in the effort to reach a common goal. Strange bedfellows perhaps, but bedfellows nonetheless.

Think of the psychological consequences. When working together toward a common goal, hostility and aggression are counterproductive. Instead, members of one group must understand and appreciate what members of the other group want. They must attend with sensitivity to the perspective of those in the other group, which should increase feelings of empathic concern for them. And, importantly, these effects on empathy do not require that group members give up their own group identity in order to pursue the superordinate goal, which can be a problem when trying to reduce conflict by appealing to a common ingroup identity—"we're all one" (Dovidio, Gaertner, & Saguy, 2009).

Conflict-Resolution Workshops, Peace Workshops and Camps

Stephan and Finlay (1999) pointed out that perspective taking and induction of empathy are often explicit components of techniques used in conflict-resolution workshops and in peace workshops and camps. Conflict-resolution workshops typically involve three to six leading figures on opposing sides of an international conflict, who are brought together in a nonthreatening, neutral location for a brief workshop (rarely lasting more than a week). The off-the-record interaction is designed to encourage (1) better understanding of each other's position and (2) finding a path toward a mutually beneficial negotiated settlement. The exchange is guided by trained facilitators who establish ground rules and agenda. Perhaps the best-known examples of such workshops are those organized by Herbert Kelman and his colleagues that brought together Israeli and Palestinian representatives (Kelman, 1990, 1997; Kelman & Cohen, 1986; Rouhana & Kelman, 1994; also see Burton, 1986, 1987; Fisher, 1994).

Immediate goals of these workshops are for each side to understand the perspective of those on the other side and to begin to trust them. The long-range goal is superordinate—to find a mutually acceptable peaceful solution to the conflict (Kelman, 2005). To these ends, participants are encouraged to express their hopes and fears and to listen to one another's concerns, actively adopting the perspective of those on the other side but not losing track of real differences. In Kelman's (1997) words, "Out of these interactions, participants develop increasing degrees of empathy, of sensitivity and responsiveness to the other's concerns, and of working trust, which are essential ingredients of the new relationship to which conflict resolution efforts aspire" (p. 219).

Peace workshops and camps are typically designed for young people (teenagers) of warring factions. The workshops often last only 3–4 days; camps may last a month or more. In these workshops and camps, participants from the two sides of the conflict live together, spend free time together, exchange views in dialogue sessions under the direction of trained leaders, take part in structured exercises, and share cultural experiences. These activities provide personalizing contact, superordinate goals, and awareness of outgroup needs. They encourage cross-group friendships, perspective taking, and empathic concern for outgroup members.

A well-known example is the workshop program for Jewish and Arab youth at Neve Shalom/Wahat al Salam—the Hebrew and Arabic names for the same community (Bargal & Bar, 1992; also see Bar-On & Kassem, 2004). Less well known, but quite interesting because of a 1-year follow-up assessment of attitudes and behavior toward the outgroup, is a 4-day peace workshop in Sri Lanka that brought together Sinhalese (majority) and Tamil (minority) youth (Malhotra & Liyanage, 2005). At the time of the follow-up assessment, participants in this workshop expressed more understanding of and concern for the well-being of members of the other group than did either of two comparison groups—(1) youth who were nominated for the workshop but did not take part due to budget cuts and (2) youth from demographically similar schools not involved in nominating students. Further, after completing the assessment, members of each group were given a chance to donate part of their payment money to a program designed to help poor children of the outgroup. On average, workshop participants donated more than did those in the nonparticipant groups.

Reducing Conflict in Educational Settings

Empathy-induced altruism may also help reduce intergroup conflict in educational settings. The jigsaw classroom is a learning technique originally developed in the 1970s by Elliot Aronson and his colleagues to try to overcome racial tension and animosity in desegregated schools in Austin, Texas (Aronson, 2004; Aronson, Blaney, Stephan, Sikes, & Snapp, 1978). In a jigsaw classroom, students spend part of their school day in racially/ethnically mixed groups (ideally, five to six students per group). Each group is given a learning task, and each member of the group has one, but only one, part of the information the group needs to complete the task. As a result, each person in the group must rely on the contribution of every other person to succeed. Again, we see personalizing contact and superordinate goals, conditions for increased empathy. After about 8 weeks the groups are dissolved, new groups are formed, and each student must learn to work effectively with four to five more students in a new racially/ethnically mixed group. After another 8 weeks, new groups are formed once more, and so on.

Aronson et al. (1978) reported that liking for fellow group members increased as a result of the jigsaw experience; so did helping. Unfortunately, they did not report effects specifically on interracial liking and helping. However, in an earlier study, Weigel, Wiser, and Cook (1975) did report such effects. Weigel et al. found that working together in ethnically mixed (European American, African American, and Mexican American) interdependent groups significantly increased both cross-ethnic liking and helping behavior; it also reduced cross-ethnic conflict (also see Johnson & Johnson, 1987). In general, research suggests that programs such as the jigsaw classroom, which involve learning cooperatively in racially or ethnically mixed groups, increase cross-group friendships, especially close friendships (see Paluck & Green, 2009, and Stephan & Stephan, 2001, for reviews).

An internationally popular empathy-based program for elementary school children, Roots of Empathy, uses monthly visits to the classroom by an infant and parent to stimulate children's perspective taking and empathy (Gordon, 2004). Research suggests the program can increase sensitivity to the needs of classmates and reduce aggression, specifically bullying (Schonert-Reichl, Smith, Zaidman-Zait, & Hertzman, 2012).

Improving Attitudes toward and Action on Behalf of Stigmatized Groups without Face-to-Face Contact

Is it possible that empathy-induced altruism might be used to improve attitudes toward, and action on behalf of, stigmatized groups even without face-to-face contact? There is reason to think so.

Consider the practical advantages of using empathy inductions based on written, audio, or video accounts of individual outgroup members' lives—at least initially (see Batson & Ahmad, 2009, for discussion of the importance of this qualifier). Induction of empathy by such means is likely to be easier than using face-to-face methods such as conflict-resolution and peace workshops. As novels, movies, and documentaries show, it is relatively easy to induce empathic concern for a member of a stigmatized group. And it can be done in low-cost, low-risk situations. Rather than the elaborate arrangements required to create face-to-face personalizing contact, our reading, listening, or watching can evoke empathic concern as we sit comfortably in our own home. Perhaps it could prepare the way for personalized contact.

Consistent with this possibility, empathy inductions in which individuals read or hear about the plight of a member of a stigmatized group have been used to improve racial attitudes, as well as to improve attitudes toward people with physical disabilities, homosexuals, people with AIDS, the homeless, even convicted murderers and drug dealers (e.g., Batson, Chang, Orr, & Rowland, 2002; Batson et al., 1997; Clore & Jeffrey, 1972; Dovidio et al., 2004, 2010; Finlay & Stephan, 2000; Vescio, Sechrist, & Paolucci, 2003; see Batson & Ahmad, 2009, for a review). Empathy induced by taking the perspective of a member of a stigmatized group can not only increase positivity toward the individual and the group in general but also toward other members of the group as individuals (Shih, Wang, Bucher, & Stotzer, 2009). And perspective taking can lead to more positive subsequent face-to-face interactions and to more positive attitudes without decreasing awareness of the unique characteristics of the stigmatized group or their position of disadvantage (Todd, Bodenhausen, Richeson, & Galinsky, 2011). Underscoring the broad applicability of such empathy-induced attitude change, Shelton and Rogers (1981) found that inducing empathy for whales led to more positive attitudes, expressed in intention to help save whales. Schultz (2000) found that empathy induced for animals being harmed by pollution improved attitudes toward protecting the natural environment—so did Berenguer (2007).

Such empathy-inducing experiences can be presented in the form of entertainment, as was done with a radio soap opera designed to improve Tutsi–Hutu relations in Rwanda (Staub & Pearlman, 2009). Along with didactic messages about the roots and prevention of prejudice, the soap opera presented characters wrestling with problems known to all Rwandans, such as cross-group friendships, overbearing leaders, poverty, and memories of violence. The program featured the struggles of a young cross-group couple as they pursue their love in the face of community disapproval and as they work to start a youth coalition for peace and cooperation. Listeners are drawn into the young couple's struggles, evoking empathic concern. Follow-up measures indicated that listening to this reconciliation soap opera increased perspective taking and feelings of concern for a range of people in Rwandan society. Compared with individuals who listened to a soap opera focused on health issues, those who listened to the reconciliation broadcast were afterward more accepting of cross-group marriage and more willing to trust and cooperate with others in their community, including outgroup members (Paluck, 2009).

Self-Benefits

Shifting focus, empathy-induced altruism may also benefit the person who is altruistically motivated. Long-term studies of volunteers and providers of social support have noted improved psychological and physical well-being among these help givers (Brown, Nesse, Vinokur, & Smith, 2003; Brown et al., 2009; Luks, 1991). And there is evidence that volunteers who provide personal care live longer than nonvolunteers, even after adjusting for such personal characteristics as physical health and activity level (Oman, 2007).

At this point, however, it is not clear that these health benefits are due to empathy-induced altruism. They might be due to the esteem enhancement or the feelings of accomplishment and competence that volunteering provides, rather than to experiencing other-oriented concern. And even if the benefits are due to empathy-induced altruism, a caution is in order: Intentional pursuit of these health benefits may be doomed to failure. To use empathy-induced altruism as yet another self-help cure—providing a means to the ultimately self-serving ends of gaining more meaning and better health—involves a logical and psychological contradiction. As soon as benefit to the other becomes an instrumental means to gain self-benefits, the motivation is no longer altruistic.

LIABILITIES

Along with the benefits described, empathy-induced altruism has important liabilities that need to be considered.

Empathy-Induced Altruism Can Cause Harm

Altruistic motivation is potentially dangerous. As evolutionary biologists have long pointed out (e.g., Dawkins, 1976), altruism may lead us to incur costs in time and money, even loss of life. When 28-year old Lenny Skutnik was asked why he dove into the ice-strewn Potomac River to rescue a drowning plane-crash victim, he said, "I just did what I had to do." When first responders to the World Trade Center on 9/11 pushed forward to help trapped civilians in spite of flames, toxic gases, and other obvious dangers, many died. We do not know to what extent these heroic acts were motivated by empathy-induced altruism, but we do know that whatever prompted them put the actors squarely in harm's way.

Not only can empathy-induced altruism be harmful to the altruistically motivated person, but, at times, it can hurt the target. Balzac, one of our most astute observers of the human condition, graphically portrayed this irony in his classic novel, *Pere Goriot* (1834/1962). Goriot's selfless love spoiled his daughters, drove them from him, and, ultimately, destroyed both them and him. Balzac's message: Altruism may be part of human nature, but it, like aggression, must be held carefully in check lest it prove destructive.

Graham Hancock made a similar point in his scathing indictment of international aid programs in *Lords of Poverty* (1989). He condemned the efforts of such esteemed agencies as the World Bank, UNICEF, UNESCO, the United Nations Development Organization, the United Nations Food and Agriculture Organization (FAO), the European Development Fund, and AID. Many people would agree that these organizations are less successful than one might wish. Hancock's attack was more fundamental. He claimed that international aid is a transaction between bureaucrats and autocrats that inevitably leads to corruption and self-defeating dependency. His analysis highlights the danger of acting when we do not fully understand the nature of the need situation. And can we ever fully understand?

Even when helping is clearly appropriate, empathy-induced altruism can at times make matters worse, particularly when effective help requires a delicate touch. Think of surgeons. It is no accident, argued neurophysiologist Paul MacLean (1967), that surgeons are prohibited from operating on close kin. When operating on one's sister rather than a stranger, deep feelings of concern and a desperate desire to relieve her suffering may cause a normally steady hand to shake. Empathy-induced altruism could cost the sister her life.

Empathy-Induced Altruism Can Lead to Paternalism

Perhaps the most plausible account of the evolutionary roots of empathy-induced altruistic motivation is that it reflects cognitive generalization of human parental nurturance (Batson, 2011). If true, this account reveals a potentially serious liability. It suggests that a person for whom empathic concern is felt is metaphorically seen as childlike—dependent, vulnerable, and in need of care—at least in terms of ability to address the need in question. Consistent with this view, research has found that we feel greater empathic concern for more baby-faced or vulnerable adults (Dijker, 2001; Lishner, Batson, & Huss, 2011; Lishner, Oceja, Stocks, & Zaspel, 2008).

Sometimes, to be perceived as dependent, vulnerable, and in need of care poses no problem. Most of us happily defer to the expertise of physicians, police, firefighters, and mechanics when we need their help. At other times, however, the consequences can be tragic. Teachers and tutors can, out of genuine concern, fail to enable students to develop the ability and confidence to solve problems themselves. The result can be unnecessary dependence, low self-esteem, and a reduced sense of efficacy (Nadler, Fisher, & DePaulo, 1983). Physical therapists, physicians, nurses, friends, and family members can do the same for patients with physical or mental disabilities, as can social welfare efforts to care for the poor and disadvantaged. To see someone in need as dependent and vulnerable may lead to a response that perpetuates, even exacerbates, the problem. It may produce paternalism.

Effective parenting requires sensitivity about when to intervene and when to stand back, as well as how—if possible—to structure the child's environment to foster coping, confidence, and independence. Effective help requires much the same (Fisher, Nadler, & DePaulo, 1983). Recall the adage about teaching the hungry to fish rather than giving them fish.

If empathy-induced altruism based on generalized parental nurturance is to be sensitive to what another person really needs, it is essential that the person feeling empathy recognize and appreciate how the other feels about his or her situation. Drawing on her own practice as a physician and psychiatrist, Jodi Halpern (2001) presented the case of "Mr. Smith," a successful executive and family patriarch. Mr. Smith had experienced sudden paralysis from the neck down and was ventilator dependent. Seeing his helpless condition, Halpern felt—and tried to provide comfort by communicating—her deep sympathy and sorrow for him. He reacted with anger and frustration. Only after Halpern made an active effort to imagine "what it would be like to be a powerful older man, suddenly enfeebled, handled by one young doctor after the next" (2001, p. 87) was she able to appreciate and address his anger and frustration—and to set the stage for working *with* him rather than working *on* him. Similar sensitivity is especially important in trying to address needs produced by intergroup conflict, in which there are often preexisting power and status differences. For those with little power, a major need is to be heard (Bruneau & Saxe, 2012; Nadler & Halabi, 2006; Shnabel & Nadler, 2008).

Empathy-Induced Altruism Can Be Overpowered by Self-Concern

In addition to producing misguided attempts to help, empathy-induced altruism can be overpowered by egoistic motives. Altruism is neither all powerful nor all enduring. Batson, O'Quin, Fultz, Vanderplas, and Isen (1983, Study 3) found that when the cost of helping was high—taking shocks that were "clearly painful but of course not harmful"—the motivation even of individuals who had previously reported high empathic concern for a stranger in need became egoistic rather than altruistic. This finding led to the suggestion that concern for others is "a fragile flower, easily crushed by self-concern" (Batson et al., 1983, p. 718; also see Bunzl, 2007).

The ease with which egoistic self-concern can crush empathy-induced altruism is a function of the relative strength of each motive. Imagine a case in which a father sees his young daughter suddenly run into the street in front of an oncoming car. His desire to save her may outweigh all self-concerns, even concern for his own life. But we do not care for everyone in need as for a daughter.

Not All Needs Evoke Empathy-Induced Altruism

Many of the pressing social problems we face today do not involve personalized needs of the sort likely to evoke empathic concern. Empathy is usually felt for individuals (including individualized members of other species). Problems such as environmental protection, population control, and nuclear disarmament are global. It is difficult, if not impossible, to feel empathy for an abstract concept like *the environment*, *world population*, or *the planet*, although personalizing metaphors like Mother Earth may move us in that direction.

Even when we recognize that these global issues directly affect individuals, the sheer number of potential victims may act as a barrier to empathy.

We may be less likely to feel empathic concern for an individual in need when he or she is but one of many with the same need (Kogut & Ritov, 2005; Small, Lowenstein, & Slovic, 2007). To paraphrase Stalin, a person in need is a tragedy; a million in need is a statistic. Many of the problems we face today come at us in the form of statistics rather than as individual persons in need. The consequence, claimed Slovic (2007), is "psychic numbing" and "the collapse of compassion" (also see Epstein, 2006). Seeing numbers, not people, we cease to feel for them.

Not only is it difficult to evoke empathy for global needs and for needs involving large numbers, but many of these needs cannot be effectively addressed with a personal helping response. Issues regarding the environment, population, and disarmament must be addressed, at least in part, in political arenas and through institutional and bureaucratic structures. The process is long and slow, not the conditions under which emotion-based motivation such as empathy-induced altruism is likely to be effective (Hardin, 1977). Emotions, including empathic concern, diminish over time. And if empathic concern diminishes, so does empathy-induced altruism.

At the local level, this diminution may limit the ability of empathy-induced altruism to motivate the sustained helping efforts often required of community-service volunteers (see Snyder, Omoto, & Lindsay, 2004). Empathy-induced altruism may be effective in initiating volunteer action, but other motives may need to take over if a volunteer is to continue for the long haul.

Empathy Avoidance

What if you do not want to be altruistically motivated? As already noted, altruistic motivation can be costly; it can lead you to spend time, money, and energy on behalf of others. Awareness that empathy produces altruism may arouse an egoistic motive to avoid empathy in order to avoid the resulting altruistic motivation. Supporting this possibility, Shaw, Batson, and Todd (1994) provided evidence that *empathy avoidance* is likely when you are aware, before exposure to a person in need, that (1) you will be asked to help this person and (2) helping will be costly. Empathy avoidance may be aroused, for example, when you see a homeless person on the street, or hear about the plight of refugees, or see news footage of the ravages of famine. The result? You turn your head, cross the street, switch channels. It may also be aroused when the number of people in need is high. As noted earlier, this can lead to a collapse of compassion because the need seems overwhelming (Cameron & Payne, 2011; Slovic, 2007).

Empathy avoidance may be a factor in the experience of *burnout* among those who work in the helping professions (Maslach, 1982). But the conditions for empathy avoidance among helping professionals do not seem to be the ones specified by Shaw et al. (1994). Among professionals, empathy avoidance is more likely to result from the perceived impossibility of providing effective help than from the perceived cost of helping. Aware that limited resources (e.g., too little time) or the intractability of the need (e.g., terminal illness) makes effective help impossible, some welfare case workers, therapists, counselors, and chronic-care nurses may try to avoid feeling empathy in order to avoid the frustration of thwarted altruistic motivation (López-Pérez, Ambrona, Gregory, Stocks, & Oceja, 2013; Stotland, Mathews, Sherman, Hansson, & Richardson, 1978). They may turn their clients or patients into objects rather than people and treat them as such. Other professional helpers may, over time, find that their ability to feel empathic concern is exhausted, leading to what has been called *compassion fatigue*. There are limits to how often one can draw from the emotional well (for some possible antidotes, see Halpern, 2001).

Empathy avoidance may also occur in response to the suffering of members of the opposition in intergroup conflicts. Whether the opposition is a rival sports team or a national, tribal, or ethnic outgroup, their suffering may be more apt to produce *schadenfreude*—pleasure at their suffering—than empathic concern (Cikara et al., 2011; Hein, Silani, Preuschoff, Batson, & Singer, 2010).

Empathy avoidance may even have played an important, chilling role in the Holocaust. Rudolf Hoess, the commandant of Auschwitz, reported that he "stifled all softer emotions" in order to carry out his assignment—the systematic extermination of 2.9 million people (Hoess, 1959).

Empathy-Induced Altruism Can Produce Immoral Action

A surprising implication of the empathy–altruism hypothesis is that empathy-induced altruism can lead to immoral action. This implication is surprising because many people equate altruism with morality. The empathy–altruism hypothesis does not.

As noted at the outset, the term *altruism* in the empathy–altruism hypothesis refers to a motivational state with the ultimate goal of increasing another's welfare. The dictionary defines *morality* as: (1) "Of or concerned with principles of right or wrong conduct"; (2) "Being in accordance with such principles." Given these definitions, altruism stands in the same relation to morality as does egoism. An egoistic desire to benefit myself may lead me to unfairly serve personal needs and interests in violation of my standards of fairness. Similarly, an altruistic desire to benefit another may lead me to unfairly serve that person's needs and interests, again in violation of my standards. Consistent with this latter possibility, Batson, Klein, Highberger, and Shaw (1995) presented evidence that empathy-induced altruistic motivation can, indeed, lead people to give preferential treatment to a person for whom they feel empathy in violation of their moral principles of fairness (also see Blader & Rothman, 2014). Egoism, altruism, and motivation to act morally are, it seems, three distinct forms of motivation, each of which may conflict with another.

More broadly, there is evidence that empathy-induced altruism can lead to partiality in our decisions as a nation about who among the many in need will get our assistance. Several decades ago, *Time* magazine essayist Walter Isaacson (1992) commented on the photogenics of disaster. He raised the possibility that the decision to intervene in Somalia but not the Sudan occurred because those suffering in Somalia proved more photogenic, evoking empathic concern and altruistic motivation in a way that those in the Sudan did not. Paul Bloom (2013) recently made a similar point about the power of empathy to skew our moral judgment and public policy.

Empathy-Induced Altruism Can Undermine the Common Good

The empathy–altruism hypothesis predicts that empathy-induced altruism not only can lead to immoral action but also that it can lead us to act against the common good in social dilemmas. A *social dilemma* arises when three conditions co-occur. First, a person has a choice about how to allocate scarce resources (time, money, energy). Second, regardless of what others do, to allocate the resources to the group is best for the group as a whole, but to allocate the resources to a single individual (oneself or another group member) is best for that individual. Third, if all allocations are to separate individuals, each individual is worse off than if all allocations are to the group. In modern society, social dilemmas abound. They include recycling, car pooling, reducing pollution, voting, paying taxes, and contributing to public TV or the local symphony, to name but a few.

Guided by the assumption of universal egoism that underlies game theory, it has generally been taken for granted that in a social dilemma the only individual to whom one would allocate scarce resources is oneself. But the empathy–altruism hypothesis predicts that if you feel empathic concern for another member of the group, you will be altruistically motivated to benefit that person. So, if you can allocate resources to him or her, then rather than the two motives traditionally assumed to conflict in a social dilemma—self-interest and the common good—three motives are in play. If, along with egoism (self-interest), the altruistic motive is stronger than the desire to promote the common good, the latter will suffer.

How often do empathy-induced altruistic motives arise in real-world social dilemmas? It is hard to think of one in which they do not. They arise every time we try to decide whether to spend our time or money to benefit ourselves, the community, or another individual about whom we especially care. I may decline to participate in a neighborhood clean-up project on Saturday, not because I want to play golf but because my son wants me to take him to a movie. Whalers may kill to extinction, and loggers clear cut, not out of personal greed but to provide for their families.

Consistent with this empathy–altruism prediction, Batson, Batson, et al. (1995) found that research participants in a social dilemma allocated some of their resources to a person for whom they felt empathy, reducing the overall collective good. And Oceja and colleagues (2014) found that if there is reason to believe other individuals in the group have needs similar to the need that induced empathy, resources may be allocated to them as well.

Highlighting a situation in which empathy-induced altruism poses a greater threat to the common good than does self-interested egoism, Batson et al. (1999) found that when allocation decisions were to be made public, empathy-induced altruism reduced the common good more than did self-interest. Why? There are clear social norms and sanctions against pursuit of self-interest at the expense of what is best for all (Kerr, 1995): *Selfish* and *greedy* are stinging epithets. Norms and sanctions against showing concern for another's interests, even if doing so diminishes the common good, are far less clear. How do whalers and loggers stand up to the public outcry over depletion of natural resources? It is easy. They are not using these resources for themselves, but to care for their families.

If altruism poses such a threat to the common good, why are there no societal sanctions against it, such as there are against egoism? We can only speculate, but it may be because society makes one or both of two assumptions: (1) Altruism is always good; (2) altruism is weak. There is now rather clear evidence that each of these assumptions is wrong.

SUMMARY AND CONCLUSION

Overall, the research we have reviewed suggests that empathy-induced altruism is a more pervasive and powerful force in our lives than has been recognized. The ideas and evidence presented in the first half of the chapter reveal that it can be an important positive force in human affairs. It offers benefits in the form of more and more sensitive help for those in need, less aggression, increased cooperation in competitive situations, reduction of intergroup conflict, and improved attitudes toward—and more action on behalf of—stigmatized groups. It may also provide health benefits to the altruistic helper.

However, empathy-induced altruism is not always a force for good. To use its power wisely, we need to be aware not only of the potential benefits but also the liabilities. Empathy-induced altruism can, at times, bring harm to the altruistically motivated individual or to those in need. It can lead to paternalism. Unless strong, it can be overridden by self-concern. It is more suited to addressing personal than global needs. People may try to avoid feeling empathic concern when they know that to act on the resulting altruistic motivation would be either costly or ineffective. Empathy-induced altruistic motivation can produce immoral action. It can, for example, lead us to show partiality toward those for whom we care, even when our standards of fairness dictate impartiality. And it can lead us to act against the common good in social dilemmas. Indeed, when our action is public, empathy-induced altruism may pose a more serious threat to the common good than does self-interested egoism.

Lest we do more harm than good, these liabilities need to be taken into account in any attempt to make use of empathy-induced altruism to promote human welfare. Empathy-induced altruism may be prevalent and powerful, but it is not a panacea.

REFERENCES

Aronson, E. (2004). Reducing hostility and building compassion: Lessons from the jigsaw classroom. In A. G. Miller (Ed.), *The social psychology of good and evil* (pp. 469–488). New York: Guilford Press.

Aronson, E., Blaney, N., Stephan, C., Sikes, J., & Snapp, M. (1978). *The jigsaw classroom*. Beverly Hills, CA: Sage.

Balzac, H. de (1962). *Pere Goriot* (H. Reed, Trans.). New York: New American Library. (Original work published 1834)

Bargal, D., & Bar, H. (1992). A Lewinian approach to intergroup workshops for Arab–Palestinian and Jewish youth. *Journal of Social Issues, 48*, 139–154.

Bar-On, D., & Kassem, F. (2004). Storytelling as a way to work through intractable conflicts: The German–Jewish experience and its relevance to the Palestinian–Israeli context. *Journal of Social Issues, 60*, 289–306.

Batson, C. D. (2011). *Altruism in humans*. New York: Oxford University Press.

Batson, C. D., & Ahmad, N. (2001). Empathy-induced altruism in a prisoner's dilemma: II. What if the target of empathy has defected? *European Journal of Social Psychology, 31*, 25–36.

Batson, C. D., & Ahmad, N. (2009). Using empathy to improve intergroup attitudes and relations. *Social Issues and Policy Review, 3*, 141–177.

Batson, C. D., Ahmad, N., & Stocks, E. L. (2004). Benefits and liabilities of empathy-induced altruism. In A. G. Miller (Ed.), *The social psychology of good and evil* (pp. 359–385). New York: Guilford Press.

Batson, C. D., Ahmad, N., Yin, J., Bedell, S. J., Johnson, J. W., Templin, C. M., et al. (1999). Two threats to the common good: Self-interested egoism and empathy-induced altruism. *Personality and Social Psychology Bulletin, 25*, 316.

Batson, C. D., Batson, J. G., Todd, R. M., Brummett, B. H., Shaw, L. L., &

Aldeguer, C. M. R. (1995). Empathy and the collective good: Caring for one of the others in a social dilemma. *Journal of Personality and Social Psychology, 68*, 619–631.

Batson, C. D., Chang, J., Orr, R., & Rowland, J. (2002). Empathy, attitudes, and action: Can feeling for a member of a stigmatized group motivate one to help the group? *Personality and Social Psychology Bulletin, 28*, 1656–1666.

Batson, C. D., Duncan, B., Ackerman, P., Buckley, T., & Birch, K. (1981). Is empathic emotion a source of altruistic motivation? *Journal of Personality and Social Psychology, 40*, 290–302.

Batson, C. D., Dyck, J. L., Brandt, J. R., Batson, J. G., Powell, A. L., McMaster, M. R., et al. (1988). Five studies testing two new egoistic alternatives to the empathy–altruism hypothesis. *Journal of Personality and Social Psychology, 55*, 52–77.

Batson, C. D., Klein, T. R., Highberger, L., & Shaw, L. L. (1995). Immorality from empathy-induced altruism: When compassion and justice conflict. *Journal of Personality and Social Psychology, 68*, 1042–1054.

Batson, C. D., & Moran, T. (1999). Empathy-induced altruism in a prisoner's dilemma. *European Journal of Social Psychology, 29*, 909–924.

Batson, C. D., O'Quin, K., Fultz, J., Vanderplas, M., & Isen, A. (1983). Self-reported distress and empathy and egoistic versus altruistic motivation for helping. *Journal of Personality and Social Psychology, 45*, 706–718.

Batson, C. D., Polycarpou, M. P., Harmon-Jones, E., Imhoff, H. J., Mitchener, E. C., Bednar, L. L., et al. (1997). Empathy and attitudes: Can feeling for a member of a stigmatized group improve feelings toward the group? *Journal of Personality and Social Psychology, 72*, 105–118.

Batson, C. D., & Weeks, J. L. (1996). Mood effects of unsuccessful helping: Another test of the empathy–altruism hypothesis. *Personality and Social Psychology Bulletin, 22*, 148–157.

Berenguer, J. (2007). The effect of empathy in proenvironmental attitudes and behaviors. *Environment and Behavior, 39*, 269–283.

Blader, S. L., & Rothman, N. B. (2014). Paving the road to preferential treatment with good intentions: Empathy, accountability, and fairness. *Journal of Experimental Social Psychology, 50*, 65–81.

Bloom, P. (2013, May 20). The baby in the well: The case against empathy. *New Yorker, 89*, 118-n/a.

Brown, R., & Hewstone, M. (2005). An integrative theory of intergroup contact. In M. Zanna (Ed.), *Advances in experimental social psychology* (Vol. 37, pp. 255–343). San Diego, CA: Academic Press.

Brown, S. L., Nesse, R., Vinokur, A. D., & Smith, D. M. (2003). Providing support may be more beneficial than receiving it: Results from a prospective study of mortality. *Psychological Science, 14*, 320–327.

Brown, S. L., Smith, D. M., Schultz, R., Kabeto, M. U., Ubel, P. A., Poulin, M., et al. (2009). Caregiving behavior is associated with decreased mortality risk. *Psychological Science, 20*, 488–494.

Bruneau, E. C., & Saxe, R. R. (2012). The power of being heard: The benefits of "perspective giving" in the context of intergroup conflict. *Journal of Experimental Social Psychology, 48*, 855–866.

Bunzl, M. (2007). The next best thing. In K. A. Appiah & M. Bunzl (Eds.), *Buying freedom: The ethics and economy of slave redemption* (pp. 235–248). Princeton, NJ: Princeton University Press.

Burton, J. W. (1986). The procedures of conflict resolution. In E. E. Azar & J. W. Burton (Eds.), *International conflict resolution: Theory and practice* (pp. 92–116). Boulder, CO: Lynne Reiner.

Burton, J. W. (1987). *Resolving deep-rooted conflict*. Lanham, MD: University Press of America.

Cameron, C. D., & Payne, B. K. (2011). Escaping affect: How motivated emotion regulation creates insensitivity to mass suffering. *Journal of Personality and Social Psychology, 100*, 1–15.

Cikara, M., Bruneau, E., & Saxe, R. R. (2011). Us and them: Intergroup failures of empathy. *Current Directions in Psychological Science, 20*, 149–153.

Clore, G. L., & Jeffrey, K. M. (1972). Emotional role playing, attitude change, and attraction toward a disabled person. *Journal of Personality and Social Psychology, 23*, 105–111.

Coke, J. S., Batson, C. D., & McDavis, K. (1978). Empathic mediation of helping: A two-stage model. *Journal of Personality and Social Psychology, 36*, 752–766.

Dawkins, R. (1976). *The selfish gene*. New York: Oxford University Press.

Dijker, A. J. (2001). The influence of perceived suffering and vulnerability on the experience of pity. *European Journal of Social Psychology, 31*, 659–676.

Dovidio, J. F., Gaertner, S. L., & Saguy, T. (2009). Commonality and the complexity of "we": Social attitudes and social change. *Personality and Social Psychology Review, 13*, 3–20.

Dovidio, J. F., Johnson, J. D., Gaertner, S. L., Pearson, A. R., Saguy, T., & Ashburn-Nardo, L. (2010). Empathy and intergroup relations. In M. Mikulincer & P. R. Shaver (Eds.), *Prosocial motives, emotions, and behavior: The better angels of our nature* (pp. 393–408). Washington, DC: American Psychological Association.

Dovidio, J. F., ten Vergert, M., Stewart, T. L., Gaertner, S. L., Johnson, J. D., Esses, V. M., et al. (2004). Perspective and prejudice: Antecedents and mediating mechanisms. *Personality and Social Psychology Bulletin, 30*, 1537–1549.

Epstein, K. (2006, Spring). Crisis mentality: Why sudden emergencies attract more funds than do chronic conditions, and how nonprofits can change that. *Stanford Social Innovation Review*, 48–57.

Finlay, K. A., & Stephan, W. G. (2000). Reducing prejudice: The effects of empathy on intergroup attitudes. *Journal of Applied Social Psychology, 30*, 1720–1737.

Fisher, J. D., Nadler, A., & DePaulo, B. M. (Eds.). (1983). *New directions in helping: Vol. 1. Recipient reactions to aid*. New York: Academic Press.

Fisher, R. (1994). General principles for resolving intergroup conflict. *Journal of Social Issues, 50*, 47–66.

Galinsky, A. D., Maddux, W. W., Gilin, D., & White, J. B. (2008). Why it pays to get inside the head of your opponent: The differential effects of perspective taking and empathy in negotiations. *Psychological Science, 19*, 378–384.

Gordon, M. (2005). *Roots of empathy: Changing the world child by child*. Markham, Ontario, Canada: Thomas Allen & Son.

Halpern, J. (2001). *From detached concern to empathy: Humanizing medical practice*. New York: Oxford University Press.

Hancock, G. (1989). *Lords of poverty: The power, prestige, and corruption of the international aid business*. New York: Atlantic Monthly Press.

Hardin, G. (1977). *The limits of altruism: An ecologist's view of survival*. Bloomington: Indiana University Press.

Harmon-Jones, E., Vaughn-Scott, K., Mohr, S., Sigelman, J., & Harmon-Jones, C. (2004). The effect of manipulated sympathy and anger on left and right frontal cortical activity. *Emotion, 4*, 95–101.

Hein, G., Silani, G., Preuschoff, K., Batson, C. D., & Singer, T. (2010). Neural responses to ingroup and outgroup members' suffering predict individual differences in costly helping. *Neuron, 68*, 149–160.

Hoess, R. (1959). *Commandant at Auschwitz: Autobiography*. London: Weidenfeld & Nicholson.

Hoffman, M. L. (2000). *Empathy and moral development: Implications for caring and justice*. New York: Cambridge University Press.

Isaacson, W. (1992, December 21). Sometimes, right makes might. *Time*, p. 82.

Johnson, D. W., & Johnson, R. T. (1987). *Learning together and alone: Cooperative, competitive, and individualistic learning*. Englewood Cliffs, NJ: Prentice-Hall.

Kelman, H. C. (1990). Interactive problem-solving: A social psychological approach to conflict resolution. In J. W. Burton & F. Dukes (Eds.), *Conflict: Readings in management and resolution* (pp. 199–215). New York: St. Martin's Press.

Kelman, H. C. (1997). Group processes in the resolution of international conflicts: Experiences from the Israeli–Palestinian case. *American Psychologist, 52*, 212–220.

Kelman, H. C. (2005). Building trust among enemies: The central challenge for international conflict resolution. *International Journal of Intercultural Relations, 29*, 639–650.

Kelman, H. C., & Cohen, S. P. (1986). Resolution of international conflict: An interactional approach. In S. Worchel & W. G. Austin (Eds.), *Psychology of intergroup relations* (pp. 323–432). Chicago: Nelson-Hall.

Kerr, N. L. (1995). Norms in social dilemmas. In D. A. Schroeder (Ed.), *Social dilemmas: Perspectives on individuals and groups* (pp. 31–47). Westport, CT: Praeger.

Kogut, T., & Ritov, I. (2005). The singularity effect of identified victims in separate and joint evaluations. *Organizational Behavior and Human Decision Processes, 97*, 106–116.

Krebs, D. L. (1975). Empathy and altruism. *Journal of Personality and Social Psychology, 32*, 1134–1146.

Lishner, D. A., Batson, C. D., & Huss, E. (2011). Tenderness and sympathy: Distinct empathic emotions elicited by different forms of need. *Personality and Social Psychology Bulletin, 37*, 614–625.

Lishner, D. A., Oceja, L. V., Stocks, E. L., & Zaspel, K. (2008). The effect of infant-like characteristics on empathic concern for adults in need. *Motivation and Emotion, 32*, 270–277.

López-Pérez, B., Ambrona, T., Gregory, J., Stocks, E., & Oceja, L. (2013). Feeling at hospitals: Perspective-taking, empathy, and personal distress among professional nurses and nursing students. *Nurse Education Today, 33*, 334–338.

Luks, A. (with Payne, P.). (1991). *The healing power of doing good: The health and spiritual benefits of helping others.* New York: Fawcett Columbine.

MacLean, P. D. (1967). The brain in relation to empathy and medical education. *Journal of Nervous and Mental Disease, 144*, 374–382.

Malhotra, D., & Liyanage, S. (2005). Long-term effects of peace workshops in protracted conflicts. *Journal of Conflict Resolution, 49*, 908–924.

Maslach, C. (1982). *Burnout: The cost of caring.* Englewood Cliffs, NJ: Prentice-Hall.

Nadler, A., Fisher, J. D., & DePaulo, B. M. (Eds.). (1983). *New directions in helping: Vol. 3. Applied perspectives on help-seeking and -receiving.* New York: Academic Press.

Nadler, A., & Halabi, S. (2006). Intergroup helping as status relations: Effects of status stability, identification, and type of help on receptivity to high-status group's help. *Journal of Personality and Social Psychology, 91*, 97–110.

Oceja, L. V., Heerdink, M. W., Stocks, E. L., Ambrona, T., López-Pérez, B., & Salgado, S. (2014). Empathy, awareness of others, and action: How feeling empathy for one-among-others motivates helping the others. *Basic and Applied Social Psychology, 36*, 111–124.

Oman, D. (2007). Does volunteering foster physical health and longevity? In S. G. Post (Ed.), *Altruism and health: Perspectives from empirical research* (pp. 15–32). New York: Oxford University Press.

Paluck, E. L. (2009). Reducing intergroup prejudice and conflict using the media: A field experiment in Rwanda. *Journal of Personality and Social Psychology, 96*, 574–587.

Paluck, E. L., & Green, D. P. (2009). Prejudice reduction: What works? A review and assessment of research and practice. *Annual Review of Psychology, 60*, 339–367.

Penner, L. A., Cline, R. J. W., Albrecht, T. L., Harper, F. W. K., Peterson, A. M., Taub, J. M., et al. (2008). Parents' empathic responses and pain and distress in pediatric patients. *Basic and Applied Social Psychology, 30*, 102–114.

Pettigrew, T. F. (1997). Generalized intergroup contact effects on prejudice. *Personality and Social Psychology Bulletin, 23*, 173–185.

Pettigrew, T. F. (1998). Intergroup contact theory. *Annual Review of Psychology, 49*, 65–85.

Rouhana, N. N., & Kelman, H. C. (1994). Promoting joint thinking in international conflicts: An Israeli–Palestinian continuing workshop. *Journal of Social Issues, 50*, 157–178.

Rumble, A. C., van Lange, P. A. M., & Parks, C. D. (2010). The benefits of empathy: When empathy may sustain cooperation in social dilemmas. *European Journal of Social Psychology, 40*, 856–866.

Schonert-Reichl, K. A., Smith, V., Zaidman-Zait, A., & Hertzman, C. (2012). Promoting children's prosocial behaviors in school: Impact of the "Roots of Empathy" program on the social and emotional competence of school-aged children. *School Mental Health, 4*, 1–21.

Schultz, P. W. (2000). Empathizing with nature: The effects of perspective taking on concern for environmental issues. *Journal of Social Issues, 56*, 391–406.

Shaw, L. L., Batson, C. D., & Todd, R. M. (1994). Empathy avoidance: Forestalling feeling for another in order to escape the motivational consequences. *Journal of Personality and Social Psychology, 67,* 879–887.

Shelton, M. L., & Rogers, R. W. (1981). Fear-arousing and empathy-arousing appeals to help: The pathos of persuasion. *Journal of Applied Social Psychology, 11,* 366–378.

Sherif, M., Harvey, O. J., White, B. J., Hood, W. E., & Sherif, C. W. (1961). *Intergroup conflict and cooperation: The robber's cave experiment.* Norman: University of Oklahoma Book Exchange.

Shih, M., Wang, E., Bucher, A. T., & Stotzer, R. (2009). Perspective taking: Reducing prejudice towards general outgroups and specific individuals. *Group Processes and Interpersonal Relations, 12,* 565–577.

Shnabel, N., & Nadler, A. (2008). A needs-based model of reconciliation: Satisfying the differential emotional needs of victim and perpetrator as a key to promoting reconciliation. *Journal of Personality and Social Psychology, 94,* 116–132.

Sibicky, M. E., Schroeder, D. A., & Dovidio, J. F. (1995). Empathy and helping: Considering the consequences of intervention. *Basic and Applied Social Psychology, 16,* 435–453.

Slovic, P. (2007). "If I look at the mass I will never act": Psychic numbing and genocide. *Judgment and Decision Making, 2,* 1–17.

Small, D. A., Lowenstein, G., & Slovic, P. (2007). Sympathy and callousness: The impact of deliberative thought on donations to identifiable and statistical victims. *Organizational Behavior and Human Decision Processes, 102,* 143–153.

Smith, K. D., Keating, J. P., & Stotland, E. (1989). Altruism reconsidered: The effect of denying feedback on a victim's status to empathic witnesses. *Journal of Personality and Social Psychology, 57,* 641–650.

Snyder, M., Omoto, A. M., & Lindsay, J. J. (2004). Sacrificing time and effort for the good of others: The benefits and costs of volunteerism. In A. G. Miller (Ed.), *The social psychology of good and evil* (pp. 444–468). New York: Guilford Press.

Staub, E., & Pearlman, L. A. (2009). Reducing intergroup prejudice and conflict: A commentary. *Journal of Personality and Social Psychology, 96,* 588–593.

Stephan, W. G., & Finlay, K. (1999). The role of empathy in improving intergroup relations. *Journal of Social Issues, 55,* 729–743.

Stephan, W. G., & Stephan, C. W. (2001). *Improving intergroup relations.* Thousand Oaks, CA: Sage.

Stocks, E. L., Lishner, D. A., & Decker, S. K. (2009). Altruism or psychological escape: Why does empathy promote prosocial behavior? *European Journal of Social Psychology, 39,* 649–665.

Stotland, E. (1969). Exploratory investigations of empathy. In L. Berkowitz (Ed.), *Advances in experimental social psychology* (Vol. 4, pp. 271–313). New York: Academic Press.

Stotland, E., Mathews, K. E., Sherman, S. E., Hansson, R. O., & Richardson, B. Z. (1978). *Empathy, fantasy, and helping.* Beverly Hills, CA: Sage.

Todd, A. R., Bodenhausen, G. V., Richeson, J. A., & Galinsky, A. D. (2011). Perspective taking combats automatic expression of racial bias. *Journal of Personality and Social Psychology, 100,* 1027–1042.

Toi, M., & Batson, C. D. (1982). More evidence that empathic emotion is a source of altruistic motivation. *Journal of Personality and Social Psychology, 43*, 281–292.

Vescio, T. K., Sechrist, G. B., & Paolucci, M. P. (2003). Perspective taking and prejudice reduction: The mediational role of empathy arousal and situational attributions. *European Journal of Social Psychology, 33*, 455–472.

Vitaglione, G. D., & Barnett, M. A. (2003). Assessing a new dimension of empathy: Empathic anger as a predictor of helping and punishing desires. *Motivation and Emotion, 27*, 301–325.

Weigel, R. H., Wiser, P. L., & Cook, S. W. (1975). The impact of cooperative learning experiences on cross-ethnic relations and attitudes. *Journal of Social Issues, 31*, 219–244.

CHAPTER 21

Volunteerism
Multiple Perspectives on Benefits and Costs

Mark Snyder, Allen M. Omoto, and Patrick C. Dwyer

The importance of helping others has been widely recognized throughout history. The themes of benevolence and self-sacrifice can be found within the sacred texts of most of the world's religions, in the writings of philosophers, and in the stories passed down in many cultures (Dovidio, Piliavin, Schroeder, & Penner, 2006). There is, of course, the well-known Christian parable of the Good Samaritan who stopped to help an injured stranger left for dead on the side of a road (Luke 10:29–37). The virtue of helping continues to be recognized today; acts of helpfulness, especially extraordinary ones, are regularly featured in the news. Recently, the *New York Times* reported the story of a modern-day Good Samaritan, Wesley Autrey, a 50-year-old construction worker who, while waiting for the subway, sprang into action to help a stranger who had fallen onto the tracks:

> Mr. Autrey was waiting for the downtown local at 137th Street and Broadway in Manhattan around 12:45 p.m.... Nearby, a man collapsed, his body convulsing.... The man, Cameron Hollopeter, 20, managed to get up, but then stumbled to the platform edge and fell to the tracks, between the two rails. The headlights of the No. 1 train appeared. "I had to make a split decision," Mr. Autrey said. So he made one, and leapt. (Buckley, 2007)

Miraculously, both men survived, and Autrey was hailed as a hero, becoming known as the "Subway Samaritan." Although Autrey felt he was just doing the right thing, his story was widely praised and even mentioned by President George W. Bush in his State of the Union address ("President Bush's 2007 State of the Union Address," 2007).

Early social psychological investigations of helping focused primarily on the kind of helping demonstrated by Wesley Autrey—instances of one person assisting another person during an emergency (Snyder & Dwyer, 2013). In such situations, helping is spontaneously enacted in response to an unforeseen, immediate, and acute need. Much of this early work was inspired by news reports in the mid-1960s of instances in which bystanders *failed* to intervene in emergencies, often with tragic consequences. Classic studies examined the impact of situational factors, such as the number of people present in an emergency (Darley & Latané, 1968) or whether people were in a hurry (Darley & Batson, 1974), on whether assistance was provided. In many emergencies, action provides an immediate solution to a problem, although it can involve risk to the bystander who helps. In the case of Wesley Autrey, he put his life on the line by jumping into the path of an oncoming subway train. It may not be surprising that these spontaneous acts of seemingly selfless heroism receive considerable media attention. Moreover, for better or worse, the factors affecting bystander intervention in emergencies have received considerable attention in social psychology textbooks for many years (see Manning, Levine, & Collins, 2007, for a critique of this focus).

Contrast the case of the "subway samaritan" with that of Liz McCartney, who in the wake of the destruction of Hurricane Katrina in 2005 decided to get involved to help people affected by the storm. Her story illustrates a form of helping—volunteerism—that has begun to receive increasing attention from the public, the media, and researchers.

> From her home 1,000 miles away in Washington, Liz McCartney was haunted by images of the storm's destruction.... In February 2006, she and her boyfriend, Zack Rosenburg, went to New Orleans to volunteer.... Within two months, McCartney and Rosenburg opened the nonprofit St. Bernard Project, which focuses on helping those they consider most in need—senior citizens and families with children. The formula is straightforward: With donations, volunteers and skilled supervisors, homes get rebuilt—and people move home. (CNN, 2008)

There are many "everyday heroes" who, like Liz McCartney, give much time and energy on an ongoing basis to address a cause, problem, or issue. They are the volunteers who work on behalf of other people and their communities, by engaging in activities such as preparing and serving food at a homeless shelter, helping to clean up and preserve local environments, or serving as mentors or sources of support for troubled teens. Their services may be delivered over an extended period of time and can involve prolonged commitments to helping, thereby distinguishing them from the relatively short-term and spontaneous assistance provided by bystanders in emergencies (e.g., Omoto & Snyder, 1995). The conditions that inspire these volunteers involve problems that cannot be fixed quickly with a single act. Rather, these helpers must stay the course and provide assistance over time to produce tangible results. To be sure, not all volunteers will go on to start their own nonprofit organization, as Liz McCartney and her partner did, but, collectively, they do invest considerable time and energy in addressing problems for which there is no "silver bullet" fix. As with rebuilding after a hurricane or other natural disaster, recovery is possible only through repeated and sustained action.

Volunteerism is widespread; in the United States, some 31% of adult Americans volunteer annually (Center on Philanthropy Panel Study [COPPS], 2005), and volunteerism is found around the world (Gronlund, 2011). The scientific literature on volunteerism has grown to such an extent in the social sciences that one recent review concluded that research and theory on volunteerism "has assumed its rightful place at the core of the social sciences" (Wilson, 2012, p. 176). We focus in this chapter on this growing body of work on volunteerism, the people who engage in it, and the settings within which it typically takes place.

Specifically, we offer an overview of the processes of volunteerism. We review research and theory on why people volunteer, focusing specifically on research examining the psychological factors that lead people to become volunteers and that sustain them over time. We feel that this focus on the dynamics of volunteerism, considered from a variety of perspectives, reveals the importance and complexity of volunteerism. Moreover, consideration of the multiple causes and consequences of volunteerism leads naturally to focusing attention on the benefits and costs associated with volunteerism. Consequently, we discuss benefits and costs from the perspectives of volunteers themselves, the recipients of their services, the organizations that rely on volunteers, and society at large.

WHAT IS VOLUNTEERISM?

Volunteerism is an active and intentional process. Unlike other forms of helping in which a person reacts to a situation requiring a specific form of assistance (e.g., as when a bystander intervenes in an emergency), volunteers attempt to chart their own course from the outset. Whereas the "Subway Samaritan," Wesley Autrey, provided assistance in response to a stranger's immediate needs, Liz McCartney and her partner made an active decision to move across the country to help people affected by Hurricane Katrina. In defining volunteerism, we find it heuristically useful to identify six characteristic features (drawing on Snyder & Omoto, 2008, and their discussion of defining and characteristic features of volunteerism). First, volunteer actions must be performed voluntarily, on the basis of free will and as a result of personal choices. They are enacted beyond bonds of social obligation, such as those that often motivate care, support, and assistance to friends and family members. In fact, these other forms of helping, which unfold within existing relationships, may not be perceived as truly voluntary because of the sense of obligation that can flow from existing social pressures and expectations. Rather than social obligation, then, volunteerism predominantly derives from the influences of personal values and motives.

Second, volunteerism typically reflects deliberation and decision making. Whereas helping in an emergency may happen reflexively and without forethought, the decision to volunteer often involves considerable advance planning, a weighing of potential costs and benefits, and considerations of when, where, and how to get involved. Because of these deliberative processes, the influences of inner motives, values, and dispositions are likely to be amplified for volunteerism relative to other forms of helping.

Third, volunteerism frequently involves substantial time and effort, often extending over long periods of time. Compared with volunteerism, other forms of helping typically occur in a narrower window of time. For example, a bystander who intervenes in an emergency may provide crucial help in only seconds or minutes, whereas the efforts of volunteers are often sustained over a substantially longer time period. In fact, a survey of approximately 60,000 U.S. households suggested that people who had volunteered during the previous year contributed a median of 50 hours of service over the year (U.S. Bureau of Labor Statistics, 2015).

Fourth, volunteer activities are carried out without the explicit expectation of reward or punishment. This feature distinguishes volunteerism from work in the "helping professions," in which people provide care, assistance, and support that appear similar to the activities of volunteers but that are done as a means to an end (i.e., a paycheck). Moreover, in between volunteerism and paid work is participation in national service, such as through the Peace Corps, AmeriCorps, or Teach for America. In these programs, individuals voluntarily and intentionally provide assistance to others in exchange for a modest stipend, health insurance, scholarships and loan payments, and postservice readjustment funds (Corporation for National and Community Service, 2015). Similar to other forms of community service (e.g., those mandated as graduation or incarceration requirements; Stukas, Snyder, & Clary, 1999), these programs do not meet the full definition of volunteerism, despite also being long-term and planned actions intended to benefit others.

Fifth, volunteers serve individuals, groups, and causes who desire help. Volunteers' services typically are not imposed on recipients; rather, these services are often willingly sought out. The volunteer's goal of providing help should match the recipient's desire to receive it. And, sixth, volunteers typically carry out their activities through agencies or organizations. This definitional feature distinguishes volunteerism from informal acts of helping, such as assisting a neighbor. However, it is important to note that restricting volunteerism to actions performed through organizations, what might be termed "formal helping," has implications for judging the relative prevalence of volunteerism; areas with less well-developed networks of organizations that utilize volunteers will, almost by definition, report lower rates of volunteerism (see Wilson, 2012). Helpful actions occur outside of formal settings, of course, so it is also possible for general helpfulness to be high even if rates of formal volunteerism are relatively low.

In sum, we define volunteerism as deliberate action intended to be helpful, performed for people and causes who desire help, delivered on a recurring basis through an agency or organization, and extending over time. Further, volunteerism is performed freely, beyond bonds of indebtedness or obligation, and without expectation of reward or punishment.

WHY DO PEOPLE VOLUNTEER?

The question of why people give their time and energy free of charge has been a persistent "problem" for those interested in understanding human nature (e.g., Olson, 1965; Wilson, 2012). As framed by Hustinx (2010), "while no one wonders why someone may assume gainful employment, many ask why one would volunteer" (p. 420). This sense of mystification that volunteerism exists stands in sharp contrast with the fact that volunteerism is ubiquitous. To be sure, there are many barriers to volunteerism, so the question "Why do people volunteer?" poses challenges to researchers.

In our view, this "why?" question boils down to a question of motivation, especially given our definition of volunteerism that focuses on actions that are deliberate and freely chosen. In fact, psychologists have examined the motives that lead people to volunteer and the psychological functions served by volunteering (for overviews of relevant theorizing, see Mannino, Snyder, & Omoto, 2011; Snyder, Clary, & Stukas, 2000). Motivationally oriented inquiries into why people volunteer and what sustains their service over time carry forward the tradition of *functional* theorizing in psychology (e.g., Katz, 1960; Kelman, 1958; Smith, Bruner, & White, 1956). The functional approach to understanding social behavior focuses on the motivational bases underlying plans that people devise for themselves and subsequently act out in purposeful pursuit of goals (see Snyder & Cantor, 1998).

Theorizing about Motives for Volunteerism

Perhaps the most familiar application of the functional approach appeared in psychology in the 1950s and 1960s, when it was proposed by theorists interested in people's attitudes (see Katz, 1960; Kelman, 1958; Smith et al., 1956). According to this perspective, attitudes serve different functions, and psychological and social benefits arise from holding and expressing attitudes. A central tenet of this approach is that different people can hold the same attitude for different reasons and can derive different benefits from holding the same attitude. Thus the same attitude may serve different purposes, or functions, for different people, or even different purposes for the same person at different points in time.

Just as different functions may underlie people's attitudes, diverse functions may underlie people's actions (Snyder & Cantor, 1998). With regard to volunteerism, there are a variety of motives for getting involved, and volunteer behaviors that appear similar on the surface may reflect different motives for different people (Omoto & Snyder, 1995). Whereas one person may volunteer to express humanitarian values, another may do so in order to boost his or her résumé or gain new social contacts, and yet another may do so to learn about him- or herself, other people, or different groups or cultural practices.

Additionally, the deliberate and planned nature of volunteerism lends itself well to analyses of the functions that motivate this helping behavior. Because volunteerism is typically planned, the influence of dispositional and motivational factors is likely to be relatively large compared with that of situational pressures that may guide spontaneous and emergency help (Clary & Snyder, 1991). The more planning and deliberation on the part of the volunteer, the more dispositional and motivational forces can be expected to influence his or her behavior.

Assessing Motives for Volunteerism

Guided by functional theorizing, researchers have developed inventories to identify and measure motives for volunteerism. Whereas some of these inventories have been constructed in order to assess motives of generic relevance to volunteerism (e.g., the Volunteer Functions Inventory; Clary et al., 1998), others have been created to assess motives in the context of specific causes (e.g., Omoto & Snyder, 1995; Ouellette, Cassel, Maslanka, & Wong, 1995; Reeder, Davison, Gipson, & Hesson-McInnis, 2001; Schondel, Shields, & Orel, 1992). Across these various investigations, using different methods of measurement and data collected from many samples of volunteers from different demographic groups (e.g., Okun, Barr, & Herzog, 1998; Omoto, Snyder, & Martino, 2000), similar sets of motives emerge.

Despite some variability in the precise numbers and character of motives for volunteerism, several motives demonstrate noteworthy regularity (Clary et al., 1998; Omoto & Snyder, 1993, 1995; Snyder & Omoto, 2008). One of the most commonly identified motives for volunteering is the expression of personal *values*, including humanitarian concern for other people, and other guiding convictions, including religious and spiritual values. A different motive, but one that is also relatively other-oriented, stems from *community concern*; it includes the desire to help members of a community of people, regardless of whether the volunteer is a member of that community. In addition, people may be motivated to volunteer out of general self-oriented *social* concerns, such as the desire to make new friends and expand social networks. There are several other specific self-oriented motives that have been identified. Some people volunteer to obtain *career* benefits, such as bolstering their résumés or making new business contacts. Meanwhile, other people volunteer out of a quest for learning or *understanding*; they see volunteerism as a way of practicing their skills or of learning about themselves, other people, and groups or cultures. Additional self-oriented motives include volunteering in order to *protect* oneself from negative feelings, such as guilt over being better off than other people, or volunteering to approach or *enhance* positive mood and self states, such as feelings of self-worth or self-esteem.

Research employing inventories of motives has revealed considerable variability between people in the functions served by their volunteerism, a finding that aligns with functional theorizing that diverse motives can underlie the same behaviors. That is, specific motives may be important for some people but not necessarily for other people. Moreover, some people may volunteer to satisfy more than one motive (Kiviniemi, Snyder, & Omoto, 2002). The important point here is that, although people may engage in the same volunteer activities, they may be doing so for very different reasons.

In addition, these functions not only vary in strength between people, but they also may vary in strength within the same person across time and life circumstances (Snyder & Omoto, 2008). For example, research by Omoto and colleagues (2000) suggests that, whereas younger people are drawn to pursue volunteerism to satisfy interpersonal goals (e.g., forming relationships), the motives of older volunteers are relatively more generative and societally focused (e.g., fulfilling societal duties or obligations; see also Okun & Schultz, 2003). This shift in the motivational agenda for volunteering over the life course has important implications for organizations seeking to recruit volunteers. Knowledge of the motivational foundations for volunteering that are relevant for certain groups, such as older and younger adults, allows for "market segmentation" in recruitment campaigns and more specific targeting of potential groups of volunteers through functionally based appeals tailored to the motives of those groups.

Further, this variability in the motives that lead people to volunteer can be meaningfully linked with critical downstream events (Snyder & Omoto, 2008). In light of its ongoing and sustained nature, volunteerism has been conceptualized as a process that unfolds over time, through three sequential stages focused on antecedents, experiences, and consequences (Omoto & Snyder, 1995). It has been speculated that the relative importance of different motives may change over the course of this process (Snyder, Omoto, & Smith, 2009). In addition, differences in the reasons that lead people to volunteer (i.e., motivational antecedents) may predict later volunteer experiences and consequences, such as who will remain involved, the quality of services they provide, their assessment of their experiences, and even the amount of service they ultimately provide. Accordingly, we next turn to research that tests hypotheses about the initiation of volunteerism, as well as about the maintenance of volunteerism over time.

Using Motive-Matched Appeals to Recruit Volunteers

According to functional theorizing regarding attitude and behavior change, persuasive appeals will be more effective at changing a person's attitudes or behaviors if they address, or "match," the specific functions underlying them, a prediction known as the functional matching hypothesis (Snyder & Cantor, 1998). Within the context of volunteerism, this hypothesis has clear practical implications for organizations that rely on the services of volunteers. Specifically, it suggests that recruitment appeals (e.g., fliers, brochures, advertisements in newspapers, on television, online) should be more effective at eliciting interest from potential volunteers to the extent that they address the motives important to those volunteers.

This hypothesis has been tested in several studies. Clary, Snyder, Ridge, Miene, and Haugen (1994) tested it by having research participants complete an inventory assessing the personal importance of several possible volunteer motives and then watch a videotaped advertisement that portrayed a woman discussing how her volunteer experience fulfills her goals. This advertisement was either functionally matched or not in that the motive rated as most important by the participant was either the focus of the advertisement or was not mentioned. Afterward, participants rated the persuasiveness of the advertisement and their likelihood of volunteering in the future. The results of this experiment were consistent with the functional matching hypothesis. People who viewed a recruitment message that matched their personally relevant motives judged the advertisement as more persuasive and were more likely to volunteer in the future than people exposed to functionally nonmatched messages. Clary et al. (1998) conducted a similar study, this time examining the effectiveness of print messages in brochures. Again, supporting the functional matching hypothesis, participants judged recruitment brochures containing functionally matched messages as more persuasive than brochures containing appeals that were not functionally matched.

The functional matching hypothesis was further tested in a field study focused on recruiting volunteers for AIDS service organizations (Snyder et al., 2009). Specifically, three advertisements were constructed: one with a self-focused appeal, one with an other-focused appeal, and a control appeal that did not target any specific motive. These ads were run sequentially for periods of 5 consecutive days in campus newspapers at two different universities, with 2-week breaks in between ads during which responses were collected. People who responded to an ad completed a questionnaire that measured their self-focused and other-focused motives for AIDS volunteerism. The results of this field study showed that more people responded to ads appealing to specific motives than to the control ad. Further, consistent with the matching hypothesis, the other-oriented ad generated responses from people with higher scores on other-oriented motives than either of the other ads, although this matching pattern was not as strongly demonstrated for the self-focused ad. Taken together, though, the results of these studies provide compelling evidence that the judged and actual persuasive impact of recruitment messages are enhanced when the focus of a recruitment appeal matches the specific motives of potential volunteers.

The Role of Motives in Sustaining Volunteerism

Researchers also have examined, in longitudinal studies, the extent to which the motives that lead people to start volunteering are similar to those that sustain them over time (Snyder et al., 2009). These investigations raise intriguing questions regarding distinctions between factors affecting behavioral initiation and behavioral maintenance and also highlight important issues for organizations that rely on volunteers. The longer volunteers remain active, the more help they presumably provide to their organizations, especially because high turnover rates among volunteers can burden organizational resources (Gidron, 1985).

In a study of AIDS volunteers tracked over several years of service, Omoto and Snyder (1995) examined the relations between volunteers' motives and their duration of service. An intriguing pattern of associations emerged. Compared to four other motives that were assessed at the beginning of the study, the *values* motive was endorsed most highly by volunteers. That is, this relatively other-oriented, or "altruistic," motive emerged as a primary self-reported reason for volunteering, a finding that is consistent with research that has assessed motives for volunteering in other settings (e.g., Dwyer, Bono, Snyder, Nov, & Berson, 2013). However, when it came to predicting actual length of volunteer service, it was the relatively self-oriented motives (specifically understanding and personal development) that demonstrated predictive utility. Volunteers who reported relatively more "selfish" or self-oriented motives at the beginning of the study were the most likely to stick with their volunteer work over time (Omoto & Snyder, 1995; but see also Davis, Hall, & Meyer, 2003; Penner & Finkelstein, 1998).

In much the same way that motive matching is important for effective volunteer recruitment, the match between motives for volunteering and experiences as a volunteer may play a critical role in a volunteer's future involvement (or lack thereof). One study of college student volunteers revealed that the more their motives for volunteering were fulfilled by their volunteer experiences, the more satisfied they were, and the greater their desire was to volunteer in the future (Clary et al., 1998). Moreover, when given a choice, people prefer volunteer activities with benefits they expect will satisfy their most important motives (Houle, Sagarin, & Kaplan, 2005). That is, volunteers prefer activities perceived as best matching their motives.

Moreover, in a study of long-term hospice volunteers, Finkelstein (2008) found that volunteers were more satisfied if their experiences fulfilled their motives, and, in turn, more satisfied volunteers spent more time volunteering than less satisfied ones. Satisfaction, however, did not predict overall length of service in this study, and only weak associations between motive fulfillment and volunteer behavior were observed. Because most of the volunteers in this sample had already been volunteering for many years, they may have already developed a strong volunteer role identity (see Piliavin & Callero, 1991) that rendered less important the satisfaction of specific motives in sustaining their service into the future (Finkelstein, 2008).

Finally, recent research suggests that the importance of motive matching may be greater in certain contexts, namely weakly structured organizational environments, and play less of a role in guiding volunteer behavior in highly structured organizational environments (Stukas, Worth, Clary, & Snyder, 2009). In this research, an aggregate "Total Match Index" better predicted outcomes (e.g., satisfaction) than either personal motives or environmental benefits alone. In fact, it was the degree of match between volunteer motives and perceived benefits offered by the volunteer setting that appeared important in keeping volunteers involved.

Taken together, the results of these studies suggest multiple and complex roles for different motives in initiating and sustaining volunteerism. In addition, they point to the need to attend to the extent to which key motives are matched in recruitment appeals and volunteer experiences in attempting to ensure success in recruiting and retaining volunteers, let alone in maximizing their feelings of satisfaction. As we now discuss, the complex role of motivation in volunteerism is also reflected in the variety of ways in which volunteerism has both costs and benefits.

BENEFITS AND COSTS OF VOLUNTEERISM

It can be argued that acts of volunteerism are inherently "good," especially to the extent that volunteers provide services to people in need—services that are often desperately lacking in communities due to insufficient funding or political will. Despite the obvious benefits of volunteerism, however, there often are *costs* associated with volunteerism. At the very least, there are costs of time and energy for people who volunteer, costs that are incurred as direct and indirect byproducts of the very motives that bring people to volunteer service. Volunteers frequently expend or lose financial resources, including gas money getting to and from their volunteer assignments, meal and entertainment expenses when working with clients or other volunteers, and even taking time off from paid work to attend to volunteer tasks or meetings. Volunteers also may face less obvious emotional costs, such as distress at seeing other people suffer, as well as social costs, such as stigma by association, as when the people they help are members of socially marginalized groups.

Accordingly, we now consider some of the costs and benefits of volunteerism. Moreover, we take multiple perspectives into account in seeking answers to questions such as "Who benefits from volunteerism?" and "What are the costs of volunteerism?" We address these questions from the perspectives of *volunteers* themselves, the *recipients* of volunteer services, the *organizations* that rely on volunteers' efforts, and *society* at large.

Benefits and Costs to Volunteers

Volunteers often claim that they themselves benefit from their service. Indeed, a common refrain among volunteers is that they "get more than they give" (e.g., see Claxton-Oldfield, 2015). Findings from the growing body of research on the impact of volunteerism on volunteers are generally consistent with this idea (Wilson, 2012). Whether it is stronger social connections to their communities, improved mental health and psychosocial adjustment, or even improvements in physical health, research documents that volunteers receive a variety of benefits from the work they perform on behalf of others.

To begin with, volunteers often feel more socially connected as a result of their service. For example, in a study of older adult volunteers, a large majority reported an increase in the size of their social networks as a result of their service (Morrow-Howell, Kinnevy, & Mann, 1999). Similarly, volunteers become increasingly connected to their communities through their service, by forming bonds with other volunteers, staff, or service recipients at their volunteer organizations and developing stronger feelings of connection to their communities (Snyder & Omoto, 2008). Using data from a longitudinal study of volunteers, Omoto and Snyder (2002) found that by the time volunteers had served 3 months, 81% claimed to have at least one friend at their organization. Moreover, over their first 6 months, the proportion of volunteers reporting at least one close friend (rather than simply a friend) at their service organization nearly doubled (from 11.7

to 21.1%). Over this same period, the proportion of each volunteer's total social network that was made up of other AIDS volunteers increased from 22.5 to 36%. As these findings suggest, volunteers become increasingly surrounded by a community of people associated with their service organizations. Furthermore, as connections to a community of shared concerns increase, volunteers' general participation in the community, including through forms of civic engagement other than volunteerism (e.g., donating to charities, attending fundraisers, and engaging in social activism), also increase (Omoto & Malsch, 2005).

In a recent review, Wilson (2012) noted that mental health benefits for volunteers are among the outcomes frequently studied by researchers. For instance, in one 2-year longitudinal study of older adults volunteering for Experience Corps (a program in which volunteers work in public elementary schools to help boost students' academic achievement), volunteers reported fewer symptoms of depression and fewer functional limitations than a matched comparison group of people who were not volunteering for this program (Hong & Morrow-Howell, 2010). Similarly, volunteering by older adults has been shown to speed recovery from depression associated with the death of a spouse (Li, 2007). Moreover, volunteers at AIDS service organizations tracked over the course of their service reported *decreases* in loneliness and helplessness, perceived personal risk of contracting HIV, and stress in other areas of their lives, as well as *increases* in their sense of control, self-esteem, and self-confidence (Omoto & Snyder, 1996).

Other research suggests psychological benefits of volunteerism, including increases in sense of purpose and self-efficacy (Fraser, Clayton, Sickler, & Taylor, 2009), and also in life satisfaction and positive affect (Pavlova & Silbereisen, 2012). In an experimental study of welfare recipients, Cohen (2009) found that those assigned to serve as volunteers experienced greater sense of empowerment compared with a control group of welfare recipients who were not assigned to volunteer. Furthermore, longitudinal evidence on the impact of volunteerism suggests that volunteering enhances many aspects of well-being, including happiness, life satisfaction, self-esteem, and sense of mastery (Thoits & Hewitt, 2001).

Volunteers also seem to garner physical health benefits as a result of their service (e.g., Brown, Nesse, Vinokur, & Smith, 2003; Post, 2007). Lower levels of hypertension have been observed in regular volunteers (Burr, Tavares, & Mutchler, 2011), and in one longitudinal study, volunteering was positively related to improvement in self-reported health (Piliavin & Siegl, 2007). Research on older adults suggests that volunteering is associated with delayed mortality and that more (and more frequent) volunteering may confer even greater protective benefits (e.g., Oman, Thoresen, & McMahon, 1999; Harris & Thoresen, 2005). In fact, a meta-analysis of 11 studies of volunteerism among older adults (age 55 and over) revealed that volunteerism was associated with a nearly 50% reduction in mortality risk (Okun, Yeung, & Brown, 2013). Even after controlling for variables that could influence this effect (e.g., age, gender, socioeconomic status, marital status), a nearly 25% reduction in mortality risk was observed. Finally, archival studies of newspaper obituaries corroborate these findings: The more volunteer activities people engaged in during their lives, the longer they lived (Wallace, Anthony, End, & Way, 2015).

Thus, volunteers appear to benefit at the same time that they help others. However, and echoing our earlier discussion, volunteers' motives may also play a role in these benefits. In one study, for example, reduced mortality risk was found among older volunteers, but only among volunteers who volunteered for *other-oriented*, rather than self-oriented, reasons (Konrath, Fuhrel-Forbis, Lou, & Brown, 2011). Overall, volunteering may provide social, well-being, and health benefits to people who engage in it, but *why* and *how much* a person volunteers appear to partially determine *who* benefits most from their volunteer service.

At the same time that there are clear benefits of volunteering, volunteers experience costs from their service activities. As noted earlier, perhaps most obvious are practical costs, such as expenditures of time, energy, and financial resources. Among Red Cross volunteers, quitting has been found to be associated with personal issues such as competing job and family responsibilities, which can crowd out resources needed for volunteering (Hustinx, 2010); for example, when describing their decisions to quit volunteering, "respondents referred to the promising sports career of their child, the care for a sick mother, the new house that needed to be built, or the weekend trip with the family that could not be missed" (p. 250).

In addition to practical, "everyday" costs, volunteering can impose emotional costs. Depression, for example, is a common consequence of HIV caregiving (Ironson, 2007). Burnout also can be experienced in volunteer settings, and it appears to be greater among volunteers who feel they are wasting their time or who feel unappreciated (Kulik, 2007). Greater burnout has been observed among volunteers motivated by extrinsic reasons (Moreno-Jimenez & Villodres, 2010), a finding that is consistent with research showing that college students who volunteered for intrinsic rather than extrinsic reasons experienced greater well-being (Weinstein & Ryan, 2010). At minimum, these findings provide further evidence that people's motives for volunteering can influence the benefits and costs that they experience from their service.

Additionally, volunteerism is associated with social and reputational costs for some volunteers in some contexts. For example, because the beneficiaries of volunteer services are often members of socially stigmatized groups (e.g., people who are homeless, physically disabled, or who have mental illness), volunteers may experience stigma by association, or "courtesy stigma" (Goffman, 1963), due to their service. That is, the stigma associated with the service recipients may "spill over" and likewise taint volunteers. Persons living with HIV disease and AIDS, for example, are stigmatized due to their association with marginalized groups (e.g., sexual minorities), illegal activities (e.g., intravenous drug use), and disease, disfigurement, and death (Herek, 2008), and this stigmatization can negatively affect the perceptions and experiences of AIDS volunteers (Snyder, Omoto, & Crain, 1999).

Interestingly, it appears that the burden of stigma by association may affect only some volunteers. In a longitudinal study of AIDS volunteers, in fact, higher anticipated stigma by association deterred people with lower, but not higher, self-esteem from initiating volunteer service (Dwyer, Snyder, & Omoto, 2013). Three months later, greater stigma by association was related to less contact with an HIV-positive client in public, but again only among volunteers lower in self-esteem. Moreover, greater public contact with an HIV-positive client predicted less satisfaction among volunteers, but only among those with relatively lower self-esteem. From a resilience perspective, higher self-esteem appears to have buffered some volunteers from the pernicious effects of stigma by association as they provided assistance to a person living with HIV. These findings highlight the importance of considering individual differences among volunteers, and specifically differences in self-esteem, when attempting to understand the connections between social costs and a person's engagement and satisfaction with volunteerism.

Benefits and Costs to Recipients of Volunteer Services

The positive impact that volunteers have on the recipients of their services is readily apparent in many instances of volunteerism. For example, volunteer teachers or tutors can point to gains in educational advancement (e.g., exam grades, classes completed, certificates and diplomas earned) among the students they help. Similarly, for volunteers working for organizations such as Habitat for Humanity International (2015), the benefits to recipients are displayed when families move into new, low-cost, and well-built homes. Despite these seemingly obvious examples of the benefits of volunteerism for recipients, there have been relatively few systematic studies of the impact of volunteers on the individuals they serve. However, research in this area has begun to grow.

Volunteers can improve the functioning of recipients of services by providing social and emotional support, as well as practical assistance. Research on the impact of volunteers on people living with HIV illustrates these benefits (e.g., Crain, Snyder, & Omoto, 2000; Lindsay, Snyder, & Omoto, 2003; Omoto & Snyder, 1999). Compared with HIV-positive clients who did not have a volunteer, clients who had one reported better psychological functioning, perceptions that their lives were more manageable and less stressful, and improvements in their outlook on life. Moreover, the links between avoidant coping (e.g., ignoring stress, wishing for improvement, or using alcohol or drugs to feel better) and indicators of negative psychological functioning (e.g., symptoms of depression, anxiety, and fatigue) appeared to have been short-circuited among clients who were paired with a volunteer. These clients also took better care of themselves, although the effects of volunteers on specific indicators of physical health (e.g., number of AIDS related symptoms) yielded inconsistent results.

Other research has shown that volunteers can have a positive impact on the physical health of recipients of services, including the survival time of terminally ill patients. For example, in a study of hospice patients, those who had received visits from volunteers lived, on average, 80 days longer than patients who had not received visits (Herbst-Damm & Kulik, 2005). Although patients were not randomly assigned to receive visits, the patient groups were comparable on many background variables (e.g., age, gender, diagnoses) and the degree of longevity predicted by health status measured at baseline. Thus the key to extending longevity among patients in this study seems to have been visits by volunteers.

Further evidence of the benefits of volunteers on recipients of services comes from studies of mentoring programs that utilize adult volunteers to work with youth (e.g., Big Brothers/Big Sisters). In one meta-analysis of 55 studies, a modest positive effect on youth outcomes (e.g., academic achievement, social competence, employment/career development) was observed (DuBois, Holloway, Valentine, & Cooper, 2002). Moreover, when effects of programs based on empirically or theoretically sound mentoring models were compared with those of programs without sound theoretical foundations, the impact was stronger and clearer. Mentoring programs based on sound theory or research produced strong positive effects, whereas the impact of other programs was much smaller. Similarly, in research based on a national sample of adolescents, youth mentoring programs have been shown to have broad academic, psychological, and health benefits, although the mechanisms responsible for these effects is not yet clear (DuBois & Silverthorn, 2005).

Although the idea that receiving help could come with a downside may seem counterintuitive, theory and research suggests that there are costs associated with receiving volunteer services. For example, people may feel threatened when seeking or receiving help, especially when doing so highlights the unequal status of helper and recipient (Nadler, 2002). In these cases, receiving help can lead a person to feel dependent or incompetent (Halabi, Nadler, & Dovidio, 2011), and he or she may experience lower self-esteem as a result (e.g., Nadler & Fisher, 1986). These dynamics can reduce the likelihood that people will seek out or accept help when they are in a position of need. People also may be quite careful and deliberate about who or which agencies they approach for help (van Leeuwen, Tauber, & Sassenberg, 2011). Interestingly, recent work suggests that despite the stress associated with receiving help, helping someone else can restore a recipient's sense of self-competence (Alvarez & van Leeuwen, 2015). That is, helping another, "third person" can alleviate negative feelings associated with being a help recipient.

Benefits and Costs to Organizations

Perhaps the most obvious way that organizations benefit from volunteers is through cost savings. In many organizations, volunteers do tasks that would otherwise be done by paid staff. Put simply, organizations save money by incorporating volunteers into their programs (e.g., see Karn, 1983), even if service organizations typically do not report cost savings resulting from volunteer efforts. Handy and Srinivasan (2004) examined the economic benefits of volunteers in hospitals. Volunteers in these settings provide assistance to patients and perform other needed functions (e.g., staffing gift shops, organizing fundraising events, performing nonmedical services). In this research, administrative and clinical staff members and volunteers were surveyed at 31 hospitals in the greater metropolitan area of Toronto, Ontario, Canada, and an impressive "payoff" for the hospitals was documented. Specifically, every dollar spent on volunteers (e.g., through recruitment, training, supervision, recognition, and other administrative costs) resulted in an estimated benefit of $6.84, or a return on investment of 684%. Other studies of hospital volunteers have shown significant cost savings, while also finding that volunteers in patient settings positively influence patient satisfaction (e.g., Hotchkiss, Fottler, & Unruh, 2008). Thus, at least with regard to hospitals, the benefits (monetary and otherwise) of utilizing volunteers are substantial.

Further, and in keeping with the findings that volunteers enhance patient satisfaction, there are nonmonetary ways in which organizations benefit from incorporating volunteers into their activities. Volunteers can enhance the range and quality of services offered by organizations and provide ways for the organization to give more specific attention to the populations it serves. Volunteers also can bring specialized services and skills to an organization and can increase public support for organizations (Hager & Brudney, 2004). Related to this latter point, companies and organizations may feel obligated to "give back" to the communities within which they operate, and one way of doing so is through sponsoring volunteer activities by their paid employees. Such instances of "corporate-sponsored volunteerism" or corporate responsibility are becoming increasingly common (Bussell & Forbes, 2008). Corporate-sponsored volunteer programs not only benefit the surrounding community, but they also can have positive consequences for the sponsoring organization in public goodwill and at the bottom line. In one study, for example, employee participation in corporate-sponsored volunteerism was found to boost commitment to the organization (Brockner, Senior, & Welch, 2014).

In addition to the benefits of volunteers to organizations, however, costs must be considered. For example, recruiting and coordinating volunteers requires resources. Volunteers must be trained to ensure that they have the necessary skills and knowledge to effectively deliver services. Volunteers typically work part time. A larger number of part-time volunteers, as compared with fewer full-time paid employees, presents supervisory and management challenges and costs (Brudney & Duncombe, 1992). Paid staff may be perceived as more consistent and reliable than volunteers. Compared with paid employees, therefore, volunteers may not feel the same degree of commitment from an organization, which can exacerbate attrition problems.

In an attempt to assess both the costs and benefits of volunteers to organizations, Hager and Brudney (2004) created a "net benefits" score that captures the advantages and challenges faced by organizations that utilize volunteers. In their research, they found that net benefits tend to be greater the more an organization invests in volunteer management practices, such as screening and matching of volunteers to appropriate assignments. Thus, organizations with an identifiable volunteer coordinator had higher net benefits scores than organizations without one (Hager & Brudney, 2004). In short, volunteers, and especially their training and management, can represent real costs to organizations.

Benefits and Costs to Society

In 2013, a total of approximately 63 million Americans volunteered nearly 8 billion hours of service (Corporation for National and Community Service, 2014). The benefits to U.S. society from all of these hours of volunteer work can be estimated, at least in part, by using the Independent Sector's (2014) metric for converting volunteer hours into dollar equivalents. If an hour of volunteer service is worth $22.55 (as it was in 2013), the value of volunteerism in America in 2013 can be estimated as nearly $180 billion. For comparison purposes, this amount is approximately three times the U.S. federal budget for the Department of Homeland Security for that same year (U.S. Department of Homeland Security, 2013). Simply put, the monetary value of volunteer service is substantial.

Looking beyond the monetary value of volunteerism, the benefits of volunteerism may include a healthy and well-functioning society. Volunteerism and other forms of civic engagement (e.g., voting) create bonds of social capital, which are features of a societal structure that facilitate trust, a sense of belonging, and cooperative action for mutual benefit (Stukas, Daly, & Cowling, 2005; Wilson & Musick, 1997). Moreover, social capital is positively related to per capita income growth (Rupasingha, Goetz, & Freshwater, 2000) and negatively associated with the number of families within a community who are living in poverty (Rupasingha & Goetz, 2007). Higher levels of civic participation, including volunteerism, also have been linked to greater economic well-being (Helliwell & Putnam, 1995) and can buffer communities against the negative effects of economic downturn (e.g., Casey & Christ, 2005). Recently, the National Conference on Citizenship (2012) summarized the messages of research on civic participation and societal outcomes by concluding that civic engagement fosters more economically resilient communities and societies.

Volunteerism, it appears, also promotes community connectedness. As we noted earlier, the enhanced sense of community derived from volunteering in turn may encourage other forms of civic engagement, thereby magnifying and diversifying benefits to society (Omoto & Snyder, 2002). Moreover, many social movements begin as volunteer efforts (Snyder & Omoto, 2008); for example, people concerned about deterring criminal activity where they live may join together to start a neighborhood watch program, which may then become part of the larger network of law enforcement activities and associations in the community and across the nation (e.g., see *USAonWatch,* National Sheriff's Association, 2015). There are, no doubt, many other examples of people with common concerns coming together, first in small community meetings to identify problems and potential solutions and later developing into larger organizations with connections to national and international networks. In short, grass-roots community organizing is one example of volunteerism with potentially profound societal implications. One need only look to changes in the realms of women's rights, civil rights, mental health and prison reform, protections for animals, and the preservation of the natural environment to see vivid examples of the powerful potential of volunteer efforts to transform communities and society at large.

Because of these benefits, societal leaders and policymakers routinely seek to promote community service. Many legislatures and school boards acknowledge the value of public service and civic participation by instituting service learning requirements for graduation (Stukas, Clary, & Snyder, 1999). Initiatives at the federal level further reflect the perceived importance of service. In the 1990s, the U.S. Congress passed the National and Community Service Act and National Service Trust Act, creating the Corporation for National and Community Service and realizing then-President Clinton's vision of a domestic corps of volunteers who would provide services in areas of need (e.g., AmeriCorps, Learn and Serve America, Senior Corps). The largest of these programs, AmeriCorps, provides a modest stipend, health insurance, and education awards to its members. Although service in AmeriCorps may not meet a strict definition of volunteerism, its members provide societally significant services (for little financial gain). In fact, evaluations of the AmeriCorps program suggest that its services and activities help to strengthen communities, improve coordination between service organizations, and enhance the life skills and civic responsibility of its members (Aguirre International, 1999).

Other researchers have attempted to use psychological theory to better understand the effects of AmeriCorps service. In a recent longitudinal study, constructs used to understand volunteerism (i.e., personality, identity, and motivation) predicted AmeriCorps service experiences and outcomes, such as member satisfaction and future volunteering intentions and behavior (Maki, Dwyer, & Snyder, 2015). Moreover, and consistent with research findings on volunteers in many different contexts, AmeriCorps members were most strongly motivated to serve for values-based reasons. AmeriCorps members also reported relatively strong career-based reasons for their service, such as developing their résumés or getting a foot in the door where they wanted to work. Speaking to the broader community impact of AmeriCorps members and the potentially central role that motives can play, enhancement motivation predicted member satisfaction with AmeriCorps, but values motivation predicted members going "above and beyond" in performing additional, nonrequired AmeriCorps service.

Beyond the specific programs and services offered, communities in which individuals actively volunteer and work to meet each other's needs send powerful messages to their members. These activities provide concrete evidence that services are available to individuals who are in need, and, because these activities are often performed in public, they may also instill a societal norm of reciprocal helping and caregiving. In these ways, widespread volunteerism can promote the creation of caring communities and societies in which citizens willingly assume responsibility for assisting those in need.

In contrast to societal benefits, there is little research systematically addressing the costs of volunteerism to society. Some research has suggested that service learning programs, when required (i.e., "mandatory volunteerism"), can backfire and make participants less likely to volunteer when given the choice, although this appears to be true for those who did not freely choose to volunteer on their own initially (Stukas, Snyder, & Clary, 1999). Other research suggests that compulsory community service has positive future benefits on students and society, even if the benefits are unevenly achieved (Metz & Youniss, 2005).

However, we can speculate on possible negative consequences of volunteerism, in its strictest form, on society at large. Although efforts to promote volunteerism may on the surface seem to be a "good" thing, to the extent that they are perceived as coercive or manipulative, they too may run the risk of turning off potential volunteers and engendering reactance to such "good deeds." Additionally, it has been suggested that volunteerism may actually contribute to societal problems because it takes governments "off the hook" for helping to identify and solve societal problems. That is, the existence of charitable organizations, and the volunteers who staff them, make it relatively easy for governments or other entities to neglect their responsibilities to provide services to citizens and also are used to justify cuts to governmental agencies and "safety net" programs that provide critical support services (Milbank, 1998; Poppendieck, 1999).

Furthermore, it is possible that costs to individual volunteers (of the kinds discussed earlier in this chapter) could aggregate into costs to society. For example, individuals who experience burnout in their volunteering roles and activities may cease to be engaged and productive employees, voters, and citizens, as well. It is possible that the burdens of their volunteer service could spill over to negatively affect their functioning in other life and societal domains. Of course, these are but hypothetical possibilities. Systematic and well-controlled research is needed to gain a more complete understanding of the societal consequences of volunteerism, in terms of both benefits and costs.

CONCLUDING COMMENTS

In this chapter, we have examined volunteerism as a form of sustained prosocial action and considered theoretical and empirical perspectives on the motivational foundations of people's decisions to volunteer and to continue their service activities over time. In addition, we have attempted to highlight the benefits and costs of volunteerism across a wide range of targets and levels. Volunteerism clearly produces tangible benefits for volunteers themselves, for individuals who receive services, for the organizations that utilize volunteers, and for society at large. From these multiple perspectives, we can argue that volunteerism reflects one of the good sides of human nature—an active, purposeful, agentic side, in which individuals seek out opportunities to perform good works for others and for society, while also satisfying personal motives and improving their own lives. As such, it is quite understandable that societies might seek to promote volunteerism. However, and as we have discussed, there are potential and sometimes unrecognized costs associated with volunteerism. These costs must be identified, appraised realistically, and counteracted by organizations dependent on the services of volunteers and by communities and societies seeking to instill cultures of caring through the promotion of volunteerism. A greater appreciation of the benefits and costs of volunteerism, considered from multiple perspectives, should go a long way toward increasing the number and quality of prosocial actions—and, ultimately, the level of goodness in society.

REFERENCES

Aguirre International. (1999). *Making a difference: Impact of AmeriCorps State/ National Direct on members and communities 1994–95 and 1995–96*. San Mateo, CA: Author.

Alvarez, K., & van Leeuwen, E. (2015). Paying it forward: How helping others can reduce the psychological threat of help. *Journal of Applied Social Psychology, 45*, 1–9.

Brockner, J., Senior, D., & Welch, W. (2014). Corporate volunteerism, the experience of self-integrity, and organizational commitment: Evidence from the field. *Social Justice Research, 27*, 1–23.

Brown, S. L., Nesse, R. M., Vinokur, A. D., & Smith, D. M. (2003). Providing social support may be more beneficial than receiving it: Results from a prospective study of mortality. *Psychological Science, 14*, 320–327.

Brudney, J. L., & Duncombe, W. D. (1992). An economic evaluation of paid, volunteer and mixed staffing options for public services. *Public Administration Review, 52*, 474–481.

Buckley, C. (2007, January 3). Man is rescued by stranger on subway tracks. *The New York Times*. Retrieved from http://www.nytimes.com/2007/01/03/nyregion/03life.html.

Burr, J., Tavares, J., & Mutchler, J. (2011). Volunteering and hypertension risk in later life. *Journal of Aging and Health, 23*, 24–51.

Bussell, H., & Forbes, D. (2008). How UK universities engage with their local communities: A study of employer-supported volunteering. *International Journal of Nonprofit and Voluntary Sector Marketing, 13*, 363–378.

Casey, T., & Christ, K. (2005). Social capital and economic performance in the American states. *Social Science Quarterly, 86*, 826–845.

Center on Philanthropy Panel Study. (2005). *Key findings: Center on Philanthropy panel study*. Indianapolis: Indiana University–Purdue University.

Clary, E. G., & Snyder, M. (1991). A functional analysis of altruism and prosocial behavior: The case of volunteerism. In M. Clark (Ed.), *Review of personality and social psychology* (Vol. 12, pp. 119–148). Newbury Park, CA: Sage.

Clary, E. G., Snyder, M., Ridge, R. D., Copeland, J. T., Stukas, A. A., Haugen, J. A., et al. (1998). Understanding and assessing the motivations of volunteers: A functional approach. *Journal of Personality and Social Psychology, 74*, 1516–1530.

Clary, E. G., Snyder, M., Ridge, R. D., Miene, P., & Haugen, J. (1994). Matching messages to motives in persuasion: A functional approach to promoting volunteerism. *Journal of Applied Social Psychology, 24*, 1129–1149.

Claxton-Oldfield, S. (2015). Hospice palliative care volunteers: The benefits for patients, family caregivers, and the volunteers. *Palliative and Supportive Care, 13*, 809–813.

CNN. (2008, May 9). Katrina survivor: "I was gonna blow myself away." Retrieved from www.cnn.com/2008/LIVING/05/08/heroes.mccartney/index.html?iref=allsarch.

Cohen, A. (2009). Welfare clients' volunteering as a means of empowerment. *Nonprofit and Voluntary Sector Quarterly, 38*, 522–534.

Corporation for National and Community Service. (2014). Volunteering and civic life in America, 2014. Retrieved from www.volunteeringinamerica.gov.

Corporation for National and Community Service. (2015). AmeriCorps fact sheet. Retrieved from *www.nationalservice.gov/programs/americorps*.

Crain, A. L., Snyder, M., & Omoto, A. M. (2000, May). *Volunteers make a difference: Relationship quality, active coping, and functioning among PWAs with volunteer buddies*. Paper presented at the meetings of the Midwestern Psychological Association, Chicago, IL.

Darley, J. M., & Batson, C. D. (1974). From Jerusalem to Jericho: A study of situational and dispositional variables in helping behavior. *Journal of Personality and Social Psychology, 27*, 100–108.

Darley, J. M., & Latané, B. (1968). Bystander intervention in emergencies: Diffusion of responsibility. *Journal of Personality and Social Psychology, 8*, 377–383.

Davis, M. H., Hall, J. A., & Meyer, M. (2003). The first year: Influences on the satisfaction, involvement, and persistence of new community volunteers. *Personality and Social Psychology Bulletin, 29*, 248–260.

Dovidio, J. F., Piliavin, J. A., Schroeder, D. A., & Penner, L. A. (2006). *The social psychology of prosocial behavior*. Mahwah, NJ: Erlbaum.

DuBois, D. L., Holloway, B. E., Valentine, J. C., & Cooper, H. (2002). Effectiveness of mentoring programs for youth: A meta-analytic review. *American Journal of Community Psychology, 30*, 157–197.

DuBois, D. L., & Silverthorn, N. (2005). Natural mentoring relationships and adolescent health: Evidence from a national study. *American Journal of Public Health, 95*, 518–524.

Dwyer, P. C., Bono, J. E., Snyder, M., Nov, O., & Berson, Y. (2013). Sources of volunteer motivation: Transformational leadership and personal motives influence volunteer outcomes. *Nonprofit Management and Leadership, 24*, 181–205.

Dwyer, P. C., Snyder, M., & Omoto, A. M. (2013). When stigma-by-association threatens, self-esteem helps: Self-esteem protects volunteers in stigmatizing contexts. *Basic and Applied Social Psychology, 35*, 88–97.

Finkelstein, M. (2008). Predictors of volunteer time: The changing contributions of motive fulfillment and role identity. *Social Behavior and Personality, 36*, 1353–1364.

Fraser, J., Clayton, S., Sickler, J., & Taylor, A. (2009). Belonging at the zoo: Retired volunteers, conservation activism and collective identity. *Ageing and Society, 29*, 351–368.

Gidron, B. (1985). Prediction of retention and turnover among service volunteer workers. *Journal of Social Service Research, 8*, 1–16.

Goffman, E. (1963). *Stigma: Notes on the management of spoiled identity*. Englewood Cliffs, NJ: Prentice-Hall.

Gronlund, H. (2011). Identity and volunteering intertwined: Reflections on the values of young adults. *Voluntas, 22*, 852–874.

Habitat for Humanity International. (2015). *Habitat for Humanity frequently asked questions*. Retrieved from *www.habitat.org/how/FAQ.aspx*.

Hager, M. A., & Brudney, J. L. (2004). *Balancing act: The challenges and benefits of volunteers*. Washington, DC: Urban Institute.

Halabi, S., Nadler, A., & Dovidio, J. F. (2011). Reactions to receiving assumptive

help: The moderating effects of group membership and perceived need for help. *Journal of Applied Social Psychology, 41,* 2793–2815.
Handy, F., & Srinivasan, N. (2004). Valuing volunteers: An economic evaluation of the net benefits of hospital volunteers. *Nonprofit and Voluntary Sector Quarterly, 33,* 28–54.
Harris, A. H., & Thoresen, C. E. (2005). Volunteerism is associated with delayed mortality in older people: Analysis of the longitudinal study of aging. *Journal of Health Psychology, 10,* 739–752.
Helliwell, J., & Putnam, R. D. (1995). Economic growth and social capital in Italy. *Eastern Economic Journal, 21,* 295–307.
Herbst-Damm, K. L., & Kulik, J. A. (2005). Volunteer support, marital status, and the survival times of terminally ill patients. *Health Psychology, 24,* 225–229.
Herek, G. M. (2008). AIDS and stigma. In P. Conrad (Ed.), *The sociology of health and illness: Critical perspectives* (8th ed., pp. 126–134). New York: Macmillan.
Hong, S., & Morrow-Howell, N. (2010). Health outcomes of Experience Corps: A high commitment volunteer program. *Social Science and Medicine, 71,* 414–420.
Hotchkiss, R. B., Fottler, M. D., & Unruh, L. (2008). Valuing volunteers: The impact of volunteerism on hospital performance. *Health Care Management Review, 34,* 119–128.
Houle, B. J., Sagarin, B. J., & Kaplan, M. F. (2005). A functional approach to volunteerism: Do volunteer motives predict task preference? *Basic and Applied Social Psychology, 27,* 337–344.
Hustinx, L. (2010). I quit, therefore I am?: Volunteer turnover and the politics of self-actualization. *Nonprofit and Voluntary Sector Quarterly, 39,* 236–255.
Independent Sector. (2014). Value of volunteer time. Retrieved from *www.independentsector.org/volunteer_time.*
Ironson, G. (2007). Altruism and health in HIV. In S. Post (Ed.), *Altruism and health* (pp. 70–81). New York: Oxford University Press.
Karn, G. N. (1983). The true dollar value of volunteers. *Journal of Volunteer Administration, 1,* 1–19.
Katz, D. (1960). The functional approach to the study of attitudes. *Public Opinion Quarterly, 24,* 163–204.
Kelman, H. C. (1958). Compliance, identification, and internalization: Three processes of attitude change. *Journal of Conflict Resolution, 2,* 51–60.
Kiviniemi, M. T., Snyder, M., & Omoto, A. M. (2002). Too many of a good thing?: The effects of multiple motivations on task fulfillment, satisfaction, and cost. *Personality and Social Psychology Bulletin, 28,* 732–743.
Konrath, S., Fuhrel-Forbis, A., Lou, A., & Brown, S. L. (2011). Motives for volunteering are associated with mortality risk in older adults. *Health Psychology, 31,* 87–96.
Kulik, L. (2007). Explaining responses to volunteering: An ecological model. *Nonprofit and Voluntary Sector Quarterly, 36,* 239–255.
Li, Y. (2007). Recovering from spousal bereavement in later life: Does volunteer participation play a role? *Journals of Gerontology, Series B: Psychological and Social Sciences, 62,* S257–S266.
Lindsay, J. J., Snyder, M., & Omoto, A. M. (May, 2003). *Volunteers' impact on*

psychological and physical functioning of persons living with HIV. Paper presented at the annual meeting of the American Psychological Society, Atlanta, GA.

Maki, A., Dwyer, P. C., & Snyder, M. (2015). Understanding AmeriCorps service: Perspectives from psychological theory and research on volunteerism. *Analyses of Social Issues and Public Policy, 15*, 253–281.

Manning, R., Levine, M., & Collins, A. (2007). The Kitty Genovese murder and the social psychology of helping: The parable of the 38 witnesses. *American Psychologist, 62*, 555–562.

Mannino, C., Snyder, M., & Omoto, A. (2011). Why do people get involved?: Motivations for volunteerism and other forms of action. In D. Dunning (Ed.), *Social motivation* (pp. 127–146). New York: Taylor & Francis.

Metz, E. C., & Youniss, J. (2005). Longitudinal gains in civic development through school-based required service. *Political Psychology, 26*, 413–437.

Milbank, D. (1998, October 18). Spare a dime? *The New York Times*. Retrieved from *www.nytimes.com/books/98/10/18/reviews/981018.18milbant.html*.

Moreno-Jimenez, M., & Villodres, M. (2010). Prediction of burnout in volunteers. *Journal of Applied Social Psychology, 40*, 1798–1818.

Morrow-Howell, N., Kinnevy, S., & Mann, M. (1999). The perceived benefits of participating in volunteer and educational activities. *Journal of Gerontological Social Work, 32*, 65–80.

Nadler, A. (2002). Inter-group helping relations as power relations: Maintaining or challenging social dominance between groups through helping. *Journal of Social Issues, 58*, 487–502.

Nadler, A., & Fisher, J. D. (1986). The role of threat to self-esteem and perceived control in recipient reactions to aid: Theory development and empirical validation. In L. Berkowitz (Ed.), *Advances in experimental social psychology* (Vol. 19, pp. 81–123). New York: Academic Press.

National Conference on Citizenship. (2012). *Civic health and unemployment: II. The case builds*. Washington, DC: Author.

National Sheriff's Association. (2015). Neighborhood watch program. Retrieved from *www.nnw.org*.

Okun, M. A., Barr, A., & Herzog, A. R. (1998). Motivation to volunteer by older adults: A test of competing measurement models. *Psychology and Aging, 13*, 608–621.

Okun, M. A., & Schultz, A. (2003). Age and motives for volunteering: Testing hypotheses derived from socioemotional selectivity theory. *Psychology and Aging, 13*, 231–239.

Okun, M. A., Yeung, E. W., & Brown, S. (2013). Volunteering by older adults and risk of mortality: A meta-analysis. *Psychology and Aging, 28*, 564–577.

Olson, M. (1965). *The logic of collective action*. Cambridge, MA: Harvard University Press.

Oman, D., Thoresen, C. E., & McMahon, K. (1999). Volunteerism and mortality among the community-dwelling elderly. *Journal of Health Psychology, 4*, 301–316.

Omoto, A. M., & Malsch, A. (2005). Psychological sense of community: Conceptual issues and connections to volunteerism-related activism. In A. M. Omoto

(Ed.), *Processes of community change and social action* (pp. 83–102). Mahwah, NJ: Erlbaum.

Omoto, A. M., & Snyder, M. (1993). AIDS volunteers and their motivations: Theoretical issues and practical concerns. *Nonprofit Management and Leadership, 4*, 157–176.

Omoto, A. M., & Snyder, M. (1995). Sustained helping without obligation: Motivation, longevity of service, and perceived attitude change among AIDS volunteers. *Journal of Personality and Social Psychology, 68*, 671–686.

Omoto, A. M., & Snyder, M. (1996). [A longitudinal study of AIDS volunteers]. Unpublished raw data.

Omoto, A. M., & Snyder, M. (1999). [A study of helping relationships between AIDS volunteers and their clients]. Unpublished raw data.

Omoto, A. M., & Snyder, M. (2002). Considerations of community: The context and process of volunteerism. *American Behavioral Scientist, 45*, 846–867.

Omoto, A. M., Snyder, M., & Martino, S. C. (2000). Volunteerism and the life course: Investigating age-related agendas for action. *Basic and Applied Social Psychology, 22*, 181–198.

Ouellette, S. C., Cassel, B., Maslanka, H., & Wong, L. M. (1995). GMHC volunteers and the challenges and hopes for the second decade of AIDS. *AIDS Education and Prevention, 7*, 64–79.

Pavlova, M. K., & Silbereisen, R. K. (2012). Participation in voluntary organizations and volunteer work as a compensation for the absence of work or partnership?: Evidence from two German samples of younger and older adults. *Journals of Gerontology, Series B: Psychological Sciences and Social Sciences, 67*, 514–524.

Penner, L. A., & Finkelstein, M. A. (1998). Dispositional and structural determinants of volunteerism. *Journal of Personality and Social Psychology, 74*, 525–537.

Piliavin, J. A., & Callero, P. L. (1991). *Giving blood: The development of an altruistic identity.* Baltimore, MD: Johns Hopkins University Press.

Piliavin, J. A., & Siegl, E. (2007). Health benefits of volunteering in the Wisconsin longitudinal study. *Journal of Health and Social Behavior, 48*, 450–464.

Poppendieck, J. (1999). *Sweet charity?: Emergency food and the end of entitlement.* New York: Viking.

Post, S. G. (2007). *Altruism and health: Perspectives from empirical research.* New York: Oxford University Press.

President Bush's 2007 State of the Union Address. (2007, January 23). Retrieved from *www.washingtonpost.com/wpdyn/content/article/2007/01/23/AR2007012301075.html*.

Reeder, G. D., Davison, D. M., Gipson, K. L., & Hesson-McInnis, M. S. (2001). Identifying the motivations of African American volunteers working to prevent HIV/AIDS. *AIDS Education and Prevention, 13*, 343–354.

Rupasingha, A., & Goetz, S. J. (2007). Social and political forces as determinants of poverty: A spatial analysis. *Journal of Socio-Economics, 36*, 650–671.

Rupasingha, A., Goetz, S. J., & Freshwater, D. (2000). Social capital and economic growth: A county-level analysis. *Journal of Agricultural and Applied Economics, 32*, 565–572.

Schondel, C., Shields, G., & Orel, N. (1992). Development of an instrument to measure volunteers' motivation in working with people with AIDS. *Social Work in Health Care, 17,* 53–71.

Smith, M., Bruner, J., & White, R. (1956). *Opinions and personality.* New York: Wiley.

Snyder, M., & Cantor, N. (1998). Understanding personality and social behavior: A functionalist strategy. In D. T. Gilbert, S. T. Fiske, & G. Lindzey (Eds.), *The handbook of social psychology* (Vol. 1, 4th ed., pp. 635–679). Boston: McGraw-Hill.

Snyder, M., Clary, E. G., & Stukas, A. A. (2000). The functional approach to volunteerism. In G. R. Maio & J. M. Olson (Eds.), *Why we evaluate: Functions of attitudes* (pp. 365–393). Hillsdale, NJ: Erlbaum.

Snyder, M., & Dwyer, P. C. (2013). Altruism and prosocial behavior. In I. Weiner, H. A. Tennen, & J. M. Suls (Eds.), *Handbook of psychology: Vol. 5. Personality and social psychology* (pp. 467–485). Hoboken, NJ: Wiley.

Snyder, M., & Omoto, A. M. (2008). Volunteerism: Social issues perspectives and social policy implications. *Social Issues and Policy Review, 2,* 1–36.

Snyder, M., Omoto, A. M., & Crain, A. L. (1999). Punished for their good deeds: Stigmatization of AIDS volunteers. *American Behavioral Scientist, 42,* 1175–1192.

Snyder, M., Omoto, A. M., & Smith, D. M. (2009). The role of persuasion strategies in motivating individual and collective action. In E. Borgida, C. Federico, & J. Sullivan (Eds.), *The political psychology of democratic citizenship* (pp. 125–150). New York: Oxford University Press.

Stukas, A. A., Clary, E. G., & Snyder, M. (1999). Service learning: Who benefits and why? *Social Policy Report: Society for Research in Child Development, 13,* 1–19.

Stukas, A. A., Daly, M., & Cowling, M. J. (2005). Volunteerism and the creation of social capital: A functional approach. *Australian Journal of Volunteering, 10,* 35–44.

Stukas, A. A., Snyder, M., & Clary, E. G. (1999). The effects of "mandatory volunteerism" on intentions to volunteer. *Psychological Science, 10,* 59–64.

Stukas, A. A., Worth, K. A., Clary, E. G., & Snyder, M. (2009). The matching of motivations to affordances in the volunteer environment: An index for assessing the impact of multiple matches on volunteer outcomes. *Nonprofit and Voluntary Sector Quarterly, 38,* 5–28.

Thoits, P. A., & Hewitt, L. N. (2001). Volunteer work and well-being. *Journal of Health and Social Behavior, 42,* 115–131.

U.S. Bureau of Labor Statistics. (2015). Volunteering in the United States, 2014. Retrieved from *www.bls.gov/news.release/volun.nr0.htm*.

U.S. Department of Homeland Security. (2013). FY 13 budget in brief. Retrieved from *www.dhs.gov/xlibrary/assets/mgmt/dhs-budget-in-brief-fy2013.pdf*.

van Leeuwen, E., Täuber, S., & Sassenberg, K. (2011). Knocking on the outgroup's door: Seeking outgroup help under conditions of task or relational conflict. *Basic and Applied Social Psychology, 33,* 266–278.

Wallace, L. E., Anthony, R., End, C. M., & Way, B. M. (2015, February). *Giving back is good for you: An analysis of volunteerism and longevity based on obituaries.* Paper presented at the annual meeting of the Society for Personality and Social Psychology, Long Beach, CA.

Weinstein, N., & Ryan, R. M. (2010). When helping helps: Autonomous motivation for prosocial behavior and its influence on well-being for the helper and recipient. *Journal of Personality and Social Psychology, 98,* 222–244.

Wilson, J. (2012). Volunteerism research: A review essay. *Nonprofit and Voluntary Sector Quarterly, 41,* 176–212.

Wilson, J., & Musick, M. (1997). Who cares?: Toward an integrated theory of volunteer work. *Social Forces, 76,* 251–272.

CHAPTER 22

The Psychology of Heroism
Extraordinary Champions of Humanity in an Unforgiving World

Zeno E. Franco and Philip G. Zimbardo

It is curious that one of the most compelling and vexing of all human behaviors—acting heroically—has been almost totally ignored by the entire field of psychology. The terms *hero* and *heroism* do not exist in the lexicon of any introductory texts of which we are aware. In fact, Pallone and Hennessy (1998) noted that "society values heroism, but rarely studies its dynamics or antecedents" (p. 206). Apart from the works of Joseph Campbell, relatively few hero-related articles have been published in past decades, but finally researchers and theorists in psychology, as well as others outside our discipline, are focusing more attention on the phenomenon of heroic action.

There are several reasons that heroism was not systematically explored sooner, including ethical preclusions to presenting human participants with the types of risk situations that are equivalent to those encountered by heroic actors; the continued (and, we argue, erroneous) argument that heroism is simply a more extreme form of altruism, and, perhaps more subtly, the personal challenge that heroism presents those who study it—the question, "If I were placed in a situation in which heroic action was needed, would I answer the call despite the risks?" (Baumeister, Bratslavsky, Finkenauer, & Vohs, 2001; Franco, Blau, & Zimbardo, 2011). To date much of the work specifically on heroism has been theoretical or anecdotal, or has addressed perceptions of heroism rather than the behavior itself. Various taxonomies of heroic action, types, and individuals have been offered (Allison & Goethals, 2011, 2013; Franco et al., 2011). A number of attempts to define heroism have also been offered in an attempt to improve systematic study of heroism as a specific social and psychological phenomenon. Some of these definitions include ideas such as the following:

> Hence, we suggest that heroism emerges from a mix that includes neurogenic impulsivity (but not self-aggrandizement), sensitization to prosocial interpersonal environments, and a (more or less chance) encounter with an opportunity to behave impulsively in prosocial ways. By *heroism*, we mean a prosocial act, perhaps implicating the self in danger, the purpose of which is to right a wrong which is being done (or which is threatened) to another person . . . or, on occasion, to an object of significance (e.g., an effort to deface a patriotic or religious symbol). (Pallone & Hennessy, 1998, p. 208)

> An act of heroism means that a person takes responsibility and acts in a manner that changes the situation. (Ginzburg, Solomon, Dekel, & Neria, 2003, p. 472 [discussion of heroism in the context of military battle])

> Our definition of heroism is as a social activity: (a) in service to others in need—be it a person, group, or community, or in defense of socially sanctioned ideals, or new social standard; (b) engaged in voluntarily (even in military contexts, heroism remains an act that goes beyond actions required by military duty); (c) with recognition of possible risks/costs, (i.e., not entered into blindly or blithely, recalling the 1913 Webster's definition that stated, "not from ignorance or inconsiderate levity"); (d) in which the actor is willing to accept anticipated sacrifice; and (e) without external gain anticipated at the time of the act. (Franco et al., 2011, p. 101)

There are many theoretical ways to approach heroism, ranging from the practical, evolutionary psychology view that heroic action may make male risk-takers more attractive as mates (Kelly & Dunbar, 2001) to the mytho-philosophical aspects of the Homeric ideal of *kalos thanatos* (beautiful death) and its relationship to the destructive or self-sacrificial aspects of heroic action in extreme situations, thus offering clear relationships between the notion of heroism and psychoanalytic and existential aspects of psychology (Peklar, 2011). While it is impossible to cover the entire range of ideas that inform the exploration of heroism and set the frame for further scholarship and research on the nuances of heroic action, we nonetheless attempt here to provide a comprehensive overview of the domain. We have organized this chapter into four major sections.

First, we explore the notion of "everyday heroism," or the idea that heroism is not so rare and exceptional but rather is a fundamental part of human existence and is something that can be engaged in by anyone, notably by ordinary people. Second, psychological theories related to heroism as an *internal* process are offered from two major perspectives: a prosocial view based on the idea of positive psychology of heroism as a virtuous activity; and a more negative alternative view of heroism as an activity that can equally emanate from inappropriate risk taking, deviance, and even psychopathology. Third, we examine heroism as an *external*, socially constructed label given to (and taken away from) individuals based in part on their overt actions but also at the whim of the social group or by a particular cultural, temporal construction. Fourth, we provide some thoughts on how heroism can inform our views of the most extremely virtuous aspects of human nature, advancing the idea of heroes as important intercessors of mercy and social justice in an often harsh, complex world.

EVERYDAY HEROISM

Perhaps the reason that heroism has escaped the attention of modern psychology is in part because societies pay attention to only a very few individuals who achieve widespread fame for their actions. Thus the phenomenon seems so rare that normative research that attempts to contextualize these actions as part of a broader understanding of human behavior might seem pointless. However, the increasing focus on heroism brought with it the deepening recognition that heroic action is much more commonplace than one would at first suspect. In fact, one in five Americans (20%) in a national random sampling study reported having acted heroically at some point in their lives, and those from minority backgrounds reported even more frequent heroic activity (Zimbardo, Breckenridge, & Moghaddam, 2013). The findings suggest that the idea of "altruism born of suffering" (Vollhardt, 2009) may extend to the realm of heroic acts as well. Minorities may also be placed in situations (e.g., violent urban settings) that "call for" heroism more often than their nonminority counterparts.

One contemporary example of this can be drawn from the story of Feidin Santana, who witnessed the police shooting of Mr. Walter Scott, an African American man in South Carolina. Mr. Santana used a cell phone camera to record a police officer shoot Walter Scott eight times, apparently while he was fleeing. The officer was later charged with murder. Mr. Santana's action, not to intervene directly but later to come forward with the video despite intense fears about reprisals, are one example of how bystanders can be transformed into heroic actors, even when their actions are constrained by the situation (Queally & Zucchino, 2015). It is also reasonable to conjecture that minorities using approaches that bear witness to injustice in ways that create personal risk are born out of their own experience and the ability to imagine themselves in the shoes of the victim.

In our own work, we have increasingly moved away from the idea that heroism is only within the purview of an elect, somehow superior group, as is often suggested in historical or mythological views of the ideal. This work has brought us closer to an understanding that heroic activity is actually within the grasp of everyone. In so doing, the realization that "everyday heroism" that involves prosocial risk taking is something that everyone is capable of also brings the phenomenon into the realm of activities that are more easily and directly observed and studied by the behavioral sciences. The idea of the "banality of heroism" (Franco & Zimbardo, 2007) as a counteracting force to Hannah Arendt's (1964) "banality of evil" has important, far-reaching implications for reducing social injustice, for conflict resolution, and for accountability within social systems (Johnson & Friedman, 2014).

Theories of "the everyday" can assist in contextualizing this new understanding of heroism as a tactic used by many people in situations that come up in daily life that require moderate or even substantial risk taking but rarely gain attention beyond a small circle of family members, local community, or colleagues (De Certeau, 1998). Everyday activities are mundane, routine, and rhythmic, yet express fundamental social, political, and historical conditions (Nayar, 2010). Often, power relationships that allow evil to be perpetrated are also embedded in these everyday aspects of life, making their eradication nearly impossible without a commensurate positive activity fundamentally embedded in these same everyday structures of life.

Increasingly, the idea of everyday heroism is being incorporated into so-called "social fitness" or character education programs (Wenos, Trick, & Williams, 2014). Although advocating for more everyday heroism is an easy, positive message with potentially great impact to send out to citizens and especially our youth, a number of important empirical, philosophical, and ethical questions remain. For example, are the real risks associated with heroic activity things that most individuals are prepared to encounter? Could training to think about engaging heroically reduce individuals' risk perception in potentially harmful ways that overly minimize or simplify the nature of risk in crisis situations? Does teaching the idea of everyday heroism, which appears to be a powerful way to reach children with a positive psychology message, encourage them to take on issues and problems best left to adults? Heroism seems to be more frequently considered the domain of men, but are women actually *more* likely than men to act heroically in situations that typically fall within the everyday activity domains of females? And are these acts hidden from view or uncelebrated (Polster, 2014)?

Just to delve into the question of everyday heroism and gender as an example, it is widely noted that males performing acts of heroism and acts that involve physical rather than social risk are more prototypically viewed as heroic and more likely to receive major awards for heroism (Franco et al., 2011; Rankin & Eagly, 2008). Rankin and Eagly (2008), focusing in part on a feminist social constructivist view of heroism, also point out that heroism has a dual and combinatorial emphasis on risk and social benefit. Rankin and Eagly (2008) point out that "heroism would seem to be culturally androgynous, and women as well as men might be well represented as heroes" (p. 414). In fact, actual acts of heroism, such as Holocaust rescue, are at least as frequently performed by women (Becker & Eagly, 2004). Women more typically create and maintain social networks; and these networks were key to saving the lives of thousands of Jewish children from certain death by helping them escape from the Warsaw ghetto. Irena Sendler was a social worker who organized such a network of 19 women and 1 man that not only enabled the children to escape but that also could then move them from home to home and finally out of the city entirely. This Holocaust hero was responsible for giving new life to 10,000 survivors and their descendants, as told in her powerful biography (Mayer, 2011).

Further, experimental evidence suggests that including female heroic protagonists in research paradigms can meaningfully change reported perceptions of women's ability to perform high-risk acts that are typically seen as male roles, but the researchers also point out that many of the risks faced by women in their everyday lives go largely unnoticed, such as the fortitude required to care for and protect children in a difficult marriage (Rankin & Eagly, 2008). Interestingly, the recent movie series *The Hunger Games*, with a strong, heroic female lead character who is capable of engaging in high-risk activities, has been associated with a marked increase in young girls seeking training in archery (Hood, 2013).

PSYCHOLOGICAL THEORIES RELATING TO HEROISM

It is critical at this time to develop a comprehensive understanding of the theories that can inform our analysis and that, more importantly, can be meaningfully applied to future multi-disciplinary research on heroic action once we accept the argument that heroism is actually within the grasp of all of us: men and women, young and old, the politically connected and the disenfranchised, the physically mighty and the underdog. We first tackle the prosocial, largely positive theoretical aspects of heroism, including leadership, fortitude and grit, high-velocity cognition and improvisation, altruism, and positive aspects of time perspective. Following this exploration of the positive aspects of heroic action, we take the counterpoint, looking at the possibility for heroism to be motivated by factors grounded in deviance, including risk-taking behavior, impulsivity, and the psychopathological aspects of heroism. Collectively, these views of the internal psychology of heroic action provide a more nuanced and complex view of a set of behavioral/situational interactions that can, and do, occur for a number of reasons and across a wide variety of contexts.

Prosocial Theories

Leadership

Although the discussion on heroism in the last few years has, appropriately, refocused attention to the actions of "average" citizens and the capability of anyone to act heroically given the right mix of situational and dispositional factors, it is important to maintain some focus on the psychology and role of exceptional leaders who act in heroic ways. What is meant here is leaders who take on extraordinary personal, corporate, or national risks. It is easy to conflate the ideas of heroism and heroic leadership with the simpler idea of charismatic leadership, and much of the leadership and management literature can be accused of making this mistake (Arnulf, Mathisen, & Hærem, 2012; Carney, 2007). As noted earlier, at its core, the term *hero* implies the acceptance of significant personal risk, engaged in voluntarily. A charismatic leader might face, for example, the minor risk that by using powerful persuasive techniques the leader might alienate some followers. This is not the level of risk that we mean. Instead, the term *heroic leader* should be reserved for larger-than-life figures who take larger-than-life gambles to advance socially just ideals, transform societies, lead soldiers into battle (Wansink, Payne, & Van Ittersum, 2008), place companies at financial or security risk to prove a moral point (e.g., the satirical newspaper Charlie Hebdo, which refused to give in to threats, ultimately resulting in the deaths of 12 of its journalists; Somaiya, 2015), or lead nations out of existential crisis (Allison & Goethals, 2015). Examples run from Franklin Delano Roosevelt, Winston Churchill, Vaclav Havel, Nelson Mandela, and Dr. Martin Luther King, Jr., to name but a few.

For example, Warren Bennis (2007, pp. 2–3) noted in a special issue on leadership in *American Psychologist* that "[a]lthough heroic leaders may have commanded a disproportionate amount of people's attention in the past, psychology still does not know enough about how they develop and how they recruit and maintain their avid followers. Heroic or charismatic leadership is still an essential, unsolved part of the puzzle."

Of course, one criticism of the "great man" idea is that "great dictators" who are profoundly corrosive, such as Adolf Hitler, are often viewed through a heroic lens within their own cultural context (Haslam, Reicher, & Platow, 2013). We must acknowledge the negative aspect of some powerful individuals, such as corrupt politicians and destructive bosses, who are toxic leaders with a powerful allure (Lipman-Blumen, 2006). However, the positive impacts of heroic leadership must not be overlooked because of these negative counterexamples. In his discussion of the role of heroic leadership, Bennis (2007) emphasized the need for more research in this arena, noting, "[t]o this day, psychologists have not sorted out which traits define leaders, or whether leadership exists outside of specific situations, and yet we know with absolute certainty that a handful of people have changed millions of lives and reshaped the world" (p. 3).

One area in which much greater understanding is needed concerns the specific behaviors heroic leaders exhibit on encountering social or military crises. It is clear that President Franklin Roosevelt, for example, had to martial U.S. civilian support for entering into a long and costly war, reducing a range of options to a single course of unified action. Similarly, duty-bound heroes in the military, police, fire, and other first-response roles must rapidly select a specific course of action, creatively bring available resources to bear, and rally support from subordinates to the front lines of high-risk situations through a combination of effective orders, persuasion, and role modeling. Leaders in heroic roles—again, in situations in which existential threat is encountered—must also be acutely aware of the human instinct in their subordinates to abandon their posts for safer ground (Ruderman et al., 2006; Taylor, Rutkow, & Barnett, 2014). In our personal communications with a variety of disaster management leaders, we have seen suggestions that in order to be successful, heroic leaders probably employ both positive and negative leadership strategies. These figures call their followers to be engaged with missions greater than any one individual, and they acknowledge overall risk; but, simultaneously, leaders may suppress specific risk information that might increase the possibility of post abandonment by their subordinates.

From this perspective, heroic leaders can be seen as providing several key functions for the groups they manage, including maintaining situational awareness (O'Brien & O'Hare, 2007); rapid option narrowing (Thompson, 1995); active information filtration to subordinates (Finkelstein, Hambrick, & Cannella, 2009) to ensure that the subordinates remain focused on the present and do not have to consider the future risks; persuasion (Stewart, Smith, & Denton, 2012); and meaning making that is powerful enough that it allows individual followers to accept catastrophic personal loss as part of a larger social mission aligned with group identity (Haslam et al., 2013). In this sense, the followers of such heroic figures literally place their lives in the hands of their leader in order to be unencumbered by fears that would otherwise paralyze the execution of mission-critical tasks.

Fortitude and Grit

In our early work on heroism, we noted the importance of the idea of *fortitude* as one of the original subdefinitions of heroism from older dictionaries (Franco et al., 2011; Zimbardo, 2007). Harkening back to this reference, the definition of fortitude emphasizes the idea of one's ability to passively resist attack.

That strength or firmness of mind which enables a person to encounter danger with coolness and courage, or to bear pain or adversity without murmuring, depression, or despondency; passive courage; resolute endurance; firmness in confronting or bearing up against danger or enduring trouble." (*Webster's revised unabridged dictionary*, 1913, p. 588)

More recently, the positive psychology movement focused on the idea of "grit" as a psychological construct that emphasizes diligence and single-mindedness of purpose (Von Culin, Tsukayama, & Duckworth, 2014). There is increasing recognition of the importance of grit in individual success in a variety of life outcome domains, and these findings emphasize that talent alone does not account for long-term success (Duckworth, Peterson, Matthews, & Kelly, 2007).

The relationship between grit and engagement in activities that are meaningful over the long term, rather than immediately hedonically satisfying, relates in important ways to the passive courageousness expressed in the idea of fortitude. Fortitudinous heroes are involved in what can be described as epic adversity—for warriors, not a single combat in which success is a shining victory, but the punishing day-after-day human diminishment of trench warfare (Roper, 2000); for social heroes, fortitude is not actively seeking confrontation within a corrupt organization but passively and repeatedly resisting when bribes are offered time after time. These heroes have grit; they keep struggling toward meaningful goals despite often incredible odds.

High-Velocity Cognition, Action, and Improvisation

In our earlier work on heroism we highlighted the difference in speed of slow action found in laboratory studies of altruistic behavior in complex social situations as compared with reports of nearly instantaneous heroic activity, noting:

[A]ltruism and bystander intervention are typically accompanied by a period of deliberative indecision lasting from several seconds in fairly straightforward situations to several minutes in comparatively ambiguous contexts (Latané & Nida, 1981). In contrast, anecdotal accounts of physical risk heroism suggest that individuals are impelled to engage in split-second decisions that propel action despite situational complexity (Howerth, 1935; Shepela et al., 1999). (Franco et al., 2011, p. 103).

Recent research, performed at Yale University, on published interviews with Carnegie Hero Medal recipients has borne out the idea that extreme altruists do not think much before taking action (Rand & Epstein, 2014). In this research, participants read interviews from news stories about the heroic actions taken by those recognized through the Carnegie Award. Even after controlling for situations in which the hero had time to think through the situation, both human raters and textual analysis suggests the heroes acted rapidly, without much deliberation (Rand & Epstein, 2014). This evidence suggests that heroes, at least in facing physical risk situations, may depend largely on automatic, intuitive cognition and recognition-primed decision making (Klein, 1993; Sorensen, Øvergård, & Martinsen, 2014).

However, an underexplored aspect of heroism is also the ability to think creatively under pressure. In situations that are novel, with a rapidly closing window of opportunity to act, heroes must also be able to cobble together available resources or to act in ways that might not be immediately obvious in order to mount a heroic response. For example, one of the subway rescuers noted for heroic action in recent years, Wesley Autrey, a 50-year old construction worker, took a series of complex actions in rapid order to be able to effectively respond to the plight of Cameron Hollopeter, a 20-year-old college student, who had a seizure on a subway platform in New York. Hollopeter stumbled off the platform onto the subway tracks in front of an oncoming train. Wesley asked a woman standing on the platform to take charge of his two young daughters before leaping down into the track bed. Initially, he had hoped to drag Hollopeter to safety, but realizing there was no time, Wesley forced Mr. Hollopeter's body in between the tracks and forcibly held him down by placing his own body over him. As the subway train passed over them, there was only a clearance of one-half inch between the bottom of the train and the top of Wesley's skull—and his decapitation (Post, 2014).

Many accolades have been given to Wesley for his heroism, but a largely unstated aspect of these heroic actions was his ability to think on his feet. The rapid succession of considered actions suggests deep situational awareness, an understanding of the constraints and resources available, and an ability to develop and modify an action plan as necessary in a rapidly changing environment. This cognitive and behavioral picture is almost the exact definition of *improvisation* (Mendonça, Beroggi, & Wallace, 2001; Mendonça & Franco, 2013; Mendonça & Wallace, 2007). The relationship between improvisation and heroic action remains an underexplored area and is one that importantly nuances the evidence of rapid, automatic cognition in these circumstances.

Altruism

Although altruism alone does not tell the whole story of heroism (Franco et al., 2011), it is an important component, with some conceptualizing heroism as extreme extension of altruism (Monin, Sawyer, & Marquez, 2008; Oliner & Oliner, 1988; Staub, 1991). Research on extreme or extraordinary altruism has been gaining an increasingly robust evidence base, often using organ donors or similar acts as the prerequisite for this status. Although perhaps conceptually somewhat distinct from our definition of heroes, extreme altruists may provide unique insights into heroism. For example, current research has found biological differences in extreme altruists who donated a kidney to a nonrelative, including significantly larger right amygdalas and heightened blood oxygen level–dependent responses to fearful facial expressions, as compared with normal controls (Marsh et al., 2014).

Moreover, recent work on systematizing the theories of altruism (Feigin, Owens, & Goodyear-Smith, 2014) may also assist in classifying heroic activity. Feigin and colleagues (2014) suggest that two major types of altruistic behavior exist: pseudo-altruism, which is substantially influenced by external social rewards and punishments, and autonomous altruism, which is purely engaged in without consideration of external contingencies. From this perspective, the heroism of bystander intervention is to some degree normative, that is to say, those who react in situations of immediate physical peril are also aware of and responding to some degree to social norms and scripts about appropriate civic behavior. The moral obligation to act is also tied to the actors' "internal rewards even when these rewards are not directly observable" (Feigin et al., 2014, p. 4). Several subtheories—including social learning, normative, stage theoretic, arousal-reduction, cost–reward model, and bystander decision making—may all govern this form of heroic behavior. In contrast, the autonomous altruism view suggests that rather than "doing good to feel good about oneself," heroes "do good to make another person feel good" (Feigin et al., 2014, p. 5), even if it causes the heroic actor to experience negative emotions or physical pain or results in significant personal sacrifice.

Positive Aspects of Time Perspective

There is no research on the issue of temporal orientation differences between two major categories of heroes: physical risk versus social risk heroes. As we've noted elsewhere in this chapter, it is reasonable and conceptually appropriate to argue that in many cases physical risk heroes act impulsively, making the decision to act on the spur of the moment, captivated by the emergency of the situation they face. They are reactive to situational demands and have their behavioral response systems set to "Play," or "Forward action," but not to "Pause."

Whereas the initial evidence suggests that heroes in physical risk situations may use automatic processes to respond, with little consideration for anything but the present moment in time, the operational picture and time perspective may be quite different for social risk heroes (Boyd & Zimbardo, 2005; Stolarski, Bitner, & Zimbardo, 2011). Generally, social risk heroes are engaged in activities (e.g., whistle-blowing) that unfold over a period of time, often through a set of escalations (Faqihi, 2014). There are many examples of whistle-blowers who, upon identifying a wrong, attempt to point it out to their supervisors using established, internal channels. When this fails, the whistle-blower may threaten to use other channels to expose wrongdoing, and this may result in pressure from the wrongdoers designed to get the whistle-blower to back down. This cycle gradually escalates until the whistleblower feels there is no choice but to expose the wrongdoing through outside channels that can not be co-opted.

In such situations as these, the social hero has time to think about the consequences to him or herself and the sacrifices that may result (e.g., loss of career). However, they also are able to consider the future consequences of their failure to act. Often in social risk heroism, we see what appears to be a dual-time perspective, that is, an ability to attend to and act in the moment as necessary, while simultaneously maintaining an acute sense of how these actions (or omissions) will affect much later outcomes. The ability to maintain a focus on future states as a way to maintain an unwavering position when faced with serious present-moment pressure has been proposed as one of the ways social heroes are able to complete heroic tasks where others fail to do so (Franco & Zimbardo, 2007). Some Christians who helped Jews during the Holocaust reported that they imagined the guilt that they would feel in the future when they recalled failing to help when they could have done so (Zimbardo & Boyd, 2008).

One example of a social risk hero is Pvt. Joe Darby, who exposed the prisoner abuses perpetrated by his military police (MP) buddies in Abu Ghraib prison in Iraq in 2004. He had time to review the CD given to him by one of his friends that contained hundreds of images of prisoner abuses and then to decide to turn it over to a senior investigating officer—fully aware that all those MPs would be punished and that they would consider him a traitor. In fact, he had to be put in protective custody for 3 years, along with his wife and mother, because of threats to their lives.

Another social risk hero is Michael Winston, who challenged Countrywide Mortgage Company's illegal loan practices and unhealthy work conditions (asbestos in the ceilings). When he refused to retract those accurate allegations, he was offered bribes to cease and desist and was then fired. After several years he did win a jury settlement of millions of dollars against his former employer—which, amazingly, was overturned by a single judge without any new evidence (Morgenson, 2011)!

Deviance-Based Theories of Heroism

Although the positive psychology view of heroism as a valiant act done for prosocial reasons is often advanced, we have argued that this perspective runs the risk of not examining heroic acts engaged in by criminals or done for nonaltruistic reasons (Franco et al., 2011). Evidence for this argument was recently coalesced in an examination of the relationship between psychopathy and heroism by Smith, Lilienfeld, Coffey, and Dabbs (2013) and also hinted at earlier by Pallone and Hennessy (1998), who stated that it was their view "that heroism and violent criminality may share remarkably similar biological roots . . ." (p. 198). Although the authors note they are speculating, Pallone and Hennessy argued that neuropsychological disposition of risk-taking heroes and criminals similarly result in impaired estimation of costs, risks, and benefits of actions.

Risk-Taking Behavior and Impulsivity

It is easy to consider heroism as invariably motivated by positive intentions and engaged in only by "good" people. However, there are many examples in which the impulsivity that plays into deviant behavior also prepares individuals with checkered pasts to act in heroic ways. The swift, seemingly automatic reactions of physical risk heroes fit the literal definition of impulsivity offered by Eysenck and Eysenck (1978), that is, "non-planning" or action without thought (p. 1248). Although we discussed the positive aspects of present-time perspective as it relates to heroism, a more negative view can also be taken. For example, an individual's sole focus on the present may suppress considerations of the long-term negative consequences of heroic activity (e.g., injury, death), effectively lowering the barrier to entry into complex crisis situations without adequate thought.

We have identified a number of individuals who have been involved in criminal activity prior to, as well as after, a single heroic act that benefited others. For example, Jabar Gibson, a young man from Louisiana with a criminal record, acted in a way that many considered heroic in the midst of the failure of the U.S. and local governments to field an effective response to the humanitarian crisis in New Orleans after Hurricane Katrina. Mr. Gibson commandeered a school bus filled with people who wanted to go to a relief shelter in Texas and drove it there; he was lauded by many as a hero in that context (Franco & Zimbardo, 2007).

While Jabar Gibson is an extreme case, there are more commonplace examples of risk-taking tendencies being associated with heroic roles as well. For instance, many jobs that involve maintenance of public safety, including first responders but also the cultures of railway and utility workers, have developed an ethos involving risk taking and impulsivity as part of their role. Prosocial deviance in first responders is a well-documented phenomenon. For example, a number of studies document higher levels of impulsive sensation-seeking behaviors in police, with results more similar to both negative and positive deviance (drug users, rock climbers) as compared with normal controls (Fischer & Smith, 2004; Levenson, 1990). The willingness to take risks may involve routine rule bending in order to ensure efficiency within complex systems but may also require "exceptional risk-taking" to save other teammates or to preserve lives or the safety of the general public (Sanne, 2008, p. 647). In these contexts, willingness to take daily risks that are not specifically called out as heroic is viewed as part of the social contract between these workers and the society as a whole; thus their roles and the work itself is often viewed as representing a heroic endeavor even in the absence of a specific heroic action that gains notoriety.

Although early research on the so-called rescue personality associated with those in the field did not show differences in risk orientation between firefighters and controls (Wagner, Martin, & McFee, 2009), more recent research found that this group is less risk averse than professionals from other domains. Interestingly, ethnographic work on those performing high-risk jobs suggests that these roles are often accorded a degree of freedom from societal oversight and managerial supervision as "part of the bargain." Arguably these roles provide a place in society for those who depart from normative behavior, for those who are impulsive and sensation seeking, and who enjoy taking risks (Klee & Renner, 2013)—so long as the deviance is channeled into positive activity.

Psychopathy

In their multistudy examination of the relationship between negative deviant behavior and heroism, Smith and her colleagues (2013) found that scores on the Psychopathic Personality Inventory (PPI-I) factor Fearless Dominance provided some insight. The PPI-I spans three subscales—Social Potency, Fearlessness, and Stress Immunity—all of which were significantly associated with heroism as measured by the Activity Frequency Inventory (AFI; Lilienfeld, 1998), the Self-Report Altruism (SRA) Scale (Rushton, Chrisjohn, & Fekken, 1981), and Simonton's presidential war heroism historical ratings (Smith et al., 2013). In this study, the authors found that PPI-I Social Potency (i.e., low social fearfulness) was positively associated with "everyday heroism." This result expands on the bystander effect, suggesting that one reason heroes intervene when others do not may simply be because they are less concerned about the social implications of their actions. This is interesting given our earlier suggestion that heroism, regardless of whether it is manifested as physical or social heroism, has an inherently controversial element. In both physical and social risk contexts, having low social fearfulness may reduce barriers to entering crisis situations for heroes, whereas those who fear the social judgment of others hesitate and ultimately fail to act (Latané, Nida, & Wilson, 1981).

Historically, a few individuals who "buck the system" or who remain slightly "outside the law" have been considered not just rebels, but heroes. Robin Hood is perhaps one of the best known fictional examples of this concept. These individuals include mavericks, vigilantes, and common criminals who act once or occasionally in prosocial ways; however, ratings of these figures, even when their actions entail personal risk for social benefit, are more mixed, suggesting that their intentions are much more closely questioned by observers (Franco et al., 2011). Anecdotally, case after case can be identified throughout history of criminals who perform heroic acts in specific situations (Franco & Zimbardo, 2007), vigilantes who are viewed as heroic by an outgroup but as criminals by the broader society (Papageorgiou, 2014), and also individuals who use heroism as a redemptive path to correct past transgressions (Barbour, 1999; Hymer, 1995).

But even acknowledging this research probably does not go far enough in exploring the "dark side" of heroism. Some have argued for the existence of other connections between heroism and pathological behavior, suggesting that the desire for the accolades associated with heroism can, in some instances, lead individuals to fantasize about attaining the mantle of heroism (Pallone & Hennessy, 1998). Although relatively harmless in most cases, these fantasies are occasionally acted on, resulting in individuals intentionally creating high-risk events in order to be able to "save" potential victims. Examples of this include the impersonation of police or fire personnel and arson committed by firefighters in order to have the opportunity to fulfill the heroic aspect of their professional role (Lewis & Yarnell, 1951).

At the farthest extreme, heroism can involve what may be viewed as a positive transcendence of death, that is to say, an acceptance of death as an outcome that the individual has come to terms with as one possible consequence of taking necessary heroic action (Greenberg, Koole, & Pyszczynski, 2013), and heroism has even been looked at as "beautiful death" in literary contexts (Peklar, 2011). More negatively, heroic rescue fantasies may cover an underlying death wish (Pallone & Hennessy, 1998; Štrobl, 2003). In this sense, heroism has a destructive, socially distancing quality to it that may in part account for society's uneasy relationship with heroic figures. Perhaps because heroes are willing, in some cases, to accept self-annihilation (either literally or in terms of death to career, e.g., "political suicide") to prove a point, they are inherently mistrusted by others.

THE SOCIAL CONSTRUCTION OF HEROISM

We noted in our own work that whereas the *actions* related to heroism are fundamentally personal and internal, the interpretation of these actions and the ascription of heroic status is fundamentally a social and cultural process (Franco et al., 2011). How is it possible for an individual who engages in an extreme premeditated act of bravery at the risk of life and limb for a higher moral cause simultaneously to be both a "hero" and "monster"? Suicide bombers are considered by some to be heroes who die for their national cause, yet they are villains or monsters to the nation of the innocent victims they kill (Al Ali, 2011; Carretero-González, 2010; Karajica, 2014). Earlier suicide bombers were mostly young men trained in small groups by elders to kill the "enemy" with strapped-on explosive devices, but recently young women have been recruited for this deadly task, in part because they are less likely to elicit suspicion.

In our research, as noted earlier, we compared heroic actors who engaged in what we described as justified versus unjustified risk taking in a large community study using the Heroic Perceptions Measure (Franco et al., 2011). This distinction between types of risk suggests the idea that some risks are readily agreed on as reasonable by the general public, whereas others go above and beyond moral obligation to act. For example, taking a minor risk to assist an elderly person at a busy intersection might be referred to as "small h" heroism (Farley, 2012), but risking one's own life to save someone who had fallen onto the tracks of an oncoming subway train is not something that any individual is morally obligated to do. This can be interpreted as going too far, and in at least some cases these extramoral acts are viewed as controversial when successful by bystanders, family members, and even the actor themselves, looking back at the event with a better understanding of the consequences, and considered downright stupid when the action does not result in the desired outcome (Desmond, 2008b).

Thus despite our arguments that the decision to act heroically is an interior process, the mantle of heroism is rarely something that heroic actors assume for themselves. In fact, the title *hero* is something that is bestowed in a social context, by eyewitnesses, colleagues, agencies, governments, and the like (Desmond, 2008b; Franco et al., 2011). The relative merits of an act, the intentions of the actor, and the outcomes of the event are all used by the social structures around the actor to make a determination as to whether the act met the criteria for heroism.

In large social structures such as nations, the narrative of a hero's actions may also be molded to fit into a broader social narrative or state-sponsored propaganda (Desmond, 2008b). For example, Rankin and Eagly (2008) noted that one of the purported heroes of the Iraq War, Pvt. Jessica Lynch, was presented in the U.S. media as a war hero for reportedly actively exchanging fire with Iraqi forces after her Humvee was ambushed. She was later held as a prisoner of war in an Iraqi hospital, and a video of her and one of her fellow soldiers was aired on Al Jazeera television. U.S. Special Forces ultimately retrieved her from the Iraqi hospital. Pvt. Lynch returned to a hero's welcome in the United States, but she later noted in Congressional testimony that the Pentagon had created a heroic narrative around her actions, when in fact she had never fired her weapon in the ambush (it had jammed at the outset of hostilities). Ultimately Pvt. Lynch sought to correct the record in Congressional testimony, noting that there had in fact been heroic action during the ambush, as others had fought valiantly and several members of her unit were killed in the firefight, but they were not lauded publicly in the way that she was. She stated:

At the same time, tales of great heroism were being told. My parent's home in Wirt County was under siege of the media all repeating the story of the little girl Rambo from the hills who went down fighting.

It was not true.

I have repeatedly said, when asked, that if the stories about me helped inspire our troops and rally a nation, then perhaps there was some good. However, I am still confused as to why they chose to lie and tried to make me a legend when the real heroics of my fellow soldiers that day were, in fact, legendary. People like Lori Piestewa and First Sergeant Dowdy who picked up fellow soldiers in harm's way. Or people like Patrick Miller and Sergeant Donald Walters who actually fought until the very end.

The bottom line is the American people are capable of determining their own ideals for heroes and they don't need to be told elaborate tales.... The truth of war is not always easy. The truth is always more heroic than the hype. ("Misleading Information from the Battlefield," 2007)

Another aspect of the social construction of heroism involves controversy and the ability of the public to strip the heroic mantle from formerly heroic figures. One of the points we have made is that *in their own time*, heroes are often very controversial figures (Franco et al., 2011). Our contemporary culture has accepted Dr. Martin Luther King, Jr., as a hero, and a monument in his honor was recently erected in Washington, D.C. But during the 1960s, Dr. King was an incredibly controversial figure at the forefront of a movement determined to upset the established social order. Examples of how controversial he was are illustrated by the Federal Bureau of Investigation's (FBI) wiretap effort, accusations of communist collusion, and efforts even after Dr. King's death to discredit him ("Boston U. Panel Finds Plagiarism by Dr. King," 1991; Theoharis, 1999).

To make the intensity of this type of social controversy more tangible, consider the recent leaks of classified government data by Julian Assange of Wikileaks and Edward Snowden, which resulted in many news stories specifically asking the question, "hero or villain?" (Franco et al., 2011; "NSA Whistle-Blower Hero or Villain?," 2013). Currently, the U.S. population appears to remain very divided about the motivations and ultimate outcomes of these leaks, and it will probably take years, if not decades, for some consensus to emerge. In our own research, we found that, unsurprisingly, the perception of physical risk was positively associated with a participant's ascription of heroic status. But beyond this, actions that were coded by the researchers as involving justified risk were negatively associated with heroism. This suggests that unjustified risk, that is, the observer's view that an individual took actions exceeding what is generally considered acceptable, holds important clues to how heroic status is ultimately determined (Franco et al., 2011). Controversy, or contested views of why an individual took seemingly unjustified risks, may be the very early makings of the heroic narrative.

In another era, Daniel Ellsberg (2003) helped to end the Vietnam War earlier than it might have without his national exposé of the Pentagon Papers, in which he mimeographed thousands of pages of these government secrets, which revealed that all high-level military believed the war could not be won but did not know how to end it effectively. The Secretary of State under President Richard Nixon called Ellsberg "the most dangerous man in America," and he was tried for treason. Ellsberg publicly reported being willing to go to jail if his actions helped end that endless war in Vietnam. He was acquitted.

Importantly, Dr. Martin Luther King, Jr., and other heroic figures are not without personal failings. In fact, perhaps in part because of the idea that virtue, nobility, or correct intentions underpin heroism, personal failings often result in the public's withdrawal of support for a hero. As researchers, we have been suspicious of calling sports figures "heroes"; however, many members of the general public regarded Lance Armstrong's feats as an athlete and his courageous, public fight to survive cancer as heroic. Yet, as it became clearer that Armstrong's accomplishments were built on doping, the public responded at first with shock and disbelief and later anger (Franco, 2012). Ultimately, Armstrong's image was damaged beyond repair, and now almost no one would use the term *hero* to describe him. But a subtler, and perhaps more important, point is that in placing heroes on a pedestal, we fail to see their human side, their weaknesses, and the fact that they are just like everyone else in many ways. In a brilliant essay called "The Lie of Heroism," Matthew Desmond (2008a) noted:

> [B]ut in referring to firefighters always and only as heroes, do we not look straight through them? Or, better said, heroizing firefighters flattens their humanity, and all that is left are mythic creatures—virtuous, courageous, modern-day messiahs who offer up their bodies as living sacrifices for us. There are not one, but two ways to dehumanize. The first is to strip people of all virtue, the second is to cleanse them of all sin. (p. 58)

SOME ADVANCES IN OUR THINKING: THE POSSIBILITIES OF KINDNESS

> For you who love heroic things
> In summers dream or winter tale,
> I tell of warriors, saints, and kings,
> In Scarlet, sackcloth, glittering mail,
> And helmets peaked with iron wings.

> They beat down Wrong; they strove for Right
> In ringing fields, on grappled ships,
> Singing they flung into the fight;
> They fell with triumph on their lips,
> And in their eyes a glorious light.
>
> That light still gleams. From far away
> Their brave song greets us like a cheer;
> We fight the same great fight as they,
> Right against Wrong; we now and here;
> They, in their fashion, yesterday.
> —WILLIAM CANTON (quoted in *Heroism*, 1914, p. 3)

The Champion: Heroes as the Intercessors of Mercy and Justice

Although it is important to have a clear-eyed view of heroism, examining it in both its positive and negative lights, let us return for a moment to the idea of heroism as an extreme morality, a stance that offers the potential to act in ways that are good to such a degree that these acts stand distinctly apart from the norm, even if they are encountered in everyday life and are accessible to everyday people. In this sense, one of the key components of heroism is that it is conducted in the services of a *noble cause* (Martens, 2005). Arguably, without this critical component, actions cannot rise to the level of heroics.

It is easy to dismiss this view of heroism as a Pollyanna view of the world, a child's naive view of a clear right and wrong, with no shades of gray and little understanding for the nuance of the pressures and complexities of the human experience. Yet, although we are often uncomfortable with this most noble, romantic view of heroism, it is in fact what draws the hearts of children to the term *hero*, and the greatest achievements of heroes are forged in seeking what is simply just and good in a world that allows, condones, or conspires with evil. In this sense, heroism is the most potent antidote to evil. Although the psychology of the 20th century sought to understand evil in all of its various forms in the aftermath of the Holocaust, it is, from our perspective, the task of psychologists in this century to begin to understand the contours of heroism and how lessons taken from heroic activity can be used to strengthen the moral and ethical fiber of individuals, social systems, corporations, and governments.

One of the things that this line of thinking implies is that at their most potent, heroes serve as *champions*—literally someone able to stand up to evil on behalf of others who cannot, because they are too physically weak or incapacitated by fear or because they lack the political standing to effect change. In this context, heroes shield the weak with their bodies, words, and actions or with their offices or stations, by risking themselves in another's place. When construed in this way it becomes clear why, at their best, heroes are viewed as those who ensure human dignity and enforce justice when individuals, organizations, or societies fail to do so. Recent research on lay perspectives of the functions heroes play in the lives of others underscores the importance of the view of heroism as a shield, finding that study participants viewed heroes as enhancing the lives of others, promoting morals, and protecting people from outside threats (Kinsella, Ritchie, & Igou, 2015).

One such example is Cesar Chavez, who fought for years to create the United Farm Workers union despite intense and sometimes violent opposition by big farmer organizations.

Although many of his followers considered Chavez as "saintly," he once told a group of volunteers: "Nice guys throughout the ages have done very little for humanity," again emphasizing the importance of the heroic figure to personally "take the heat" on behalf of others to effect social actions that are transformative. Miriam Pawel tells his moving story in the biography *The Crusades of Cesar Chavez* (2014).

In our other works, we have focused on African American and African leaders who were centrally, and heroically, involved in the end of slavery and segregation in the United States and the policy of apartheid in Africa. But before these leaders could take that mantle, generations of others from varied backgrounds had to prepare the ground for these major social advances that moved social and economic systems away from oppression and toward equity. The easiest of these to recall is Abraham Lincoln, who said in his last speech, "Let us have faith that *right makes might,* and in that faith let us, to the end, dare to do our duty as we understand it" (Lincoln, 1991). Lincoln's assassination perhaps crystallized sentiment toward him as a heroic president who championed a difficult cause (Allison & Goethals, 2015).

But by looking only to these major historical figures, we often forget the smaller champions, the impassioned voices that seek out justice, sometimes at great personal cost. One example from the decades just prior to the Civil War was William Lloyd Garrison, a white abolitionist who published extensively on the injustices and immorality of slavery. Garrison stated in one of his antislavery newspapers, *The Liberator:* "I am aware that many object to the severity of my language; but is there not cause for severity? I will be as harsh as truth, and as uncompromising as justice" (Garrison, 1885). Although he did not meet the same fate as Lincoln, the risks were no less real. Garrison was sued for libel and imprisoned, chased by a mob of slavery supporters, and faced lynching had he not been saved by law enforcement. In reflecting on his life and illustrating the role of the champion in doing for others what oppression prevented them from doing for themselves, Garrison was eulogized by one of his colleagues who said, "Not for thyself, but for the slave, thy words of thunder shook the world" (Whittier, 1880).

Although each generation faces its seemingly unique challenges, we have wondered whether the moral relativism and social distancing that seems prevalent today is resulting in an equally powerful call to reestablish and redefine what heroism is in our own era. Examples of this range from the recent "real-life superheroes" movement (Svoboda, 2013) to calls for greater corporate accountability and stewardship on issues of societal importance (Anderson, 2006). The discipline of psychology as a whole has a long-standing emphasis on social justice, and these ideas have been systematized by Isaac Prilleltensky, among others (e.g., Johnson & Friedman, 2014; Prilleltensky & Huygens, 2014).

Social justice may be conceptualized as multifaceted and involving distributive, procedural, intrapersonal, interpersonal, developmental, informational, cultural, and retributive justice. Prilleltensky also suggests that human health and well-being are fundamentally tied to just outcomes for individuals and communities (Prilleltensky & Huygens, 2014). In this sense, the champion role of the hero is tied to what we have elsewhere argued is an "excess of what is good," an ethical/aesthetic state something akin to the Aristotelian value of *eudemonia*—the ideal of human flourishing (Franco, Flower, Whittle, & Sandy, 2015). We have noted, for example, that "[h]eroism focuses us on what is right with human nature. We care about heroic stories because they serve as powerful reminders that people are capable of resisting evil, of not giving into temptations, of rising above mediocrity, and of heeding the call to action and to service when others fail to act" (Zimbardo, 2007, p. 461). In this way, the hero creates a path toward a more perfect state of the human condition, and that is one of the key reasons heroes are revered and why societies seek to codify their thoughts and teachings. It is in looking toward the path of the individual hero that we are able to collectively achieve progress, and in this sense it is our potential for heroism that makes us human.

Mercy

In terms of the arguments about distributive, economic, and retributive justice, heroes enforce what is physically just, shielding others by ensuring that mercy is shown to those who are weak. The folk heroes of old, often cloaked in the mystique of the vigilante, embodied these ideas. From Batman to Zorro, these figures fought to protect the less fortunate from the evil and the cruel injustices of the world (O'Neil, 2013). Displaying the most extreme level of activity, heroes are the avengers where injustice has occurred, enforcing retribution in ways that seek to right wrongs while carefully ensuring that the cyclic nature of violence or oppression is avoided (Arteaga, 2010).

Although it is easy to dismiss this view as again just the stuff of youthful fantasy, the reasons that the world as a whole revered Nelson

Mandela was not just the personal risks and injustices he suffered but his ability to create a more merciful and just society in South Africa in the aftermath of apartheid, ensuring orderly retributive justice in a deeply fractured society. In fact, part of the reason Mandela and F. W. de Klerk were awarded the Nobel Peace Prize was their ability to "work for the peaceful termination of the apartheid regime" (Mednic, Christakis, & Fowler, 2010). Although it was perhaps an imperfect solution, this was accomplished in part through the truth and reconciliation process, which at its core is a nonpunitive approach to achieving acceptable retribution (Swartz, 2006).

Human Dignity

In terms of the ideas of interpersonal, developmental, procedural, and cultural justice, heroes enforce the ideal of human dignity. In this sense, while some heroes use their abilities to physically or metaphorically shield the weak from those things that diminish embodied existence (hunger, imprisonment, etc.), other heroic figures offer a psychological shield. In effect, these heroes take on the brunt of a boss's vitriol at work so that others who are less able to handle these interpersonal injustices are not so deeply harmed (Frost & Robinson, 1998; Metz, Brown, Cregan, & Kulik, 2014). Equally, whistle-blowers attempt to shield others from procedural injustice when, for example, governmental rules are being used to suppress important information about health impacts of toxic exposure (Glazer & Glazer, 1989; Qusqas & Kleiner, 2001; Zimbardo, 2007).

Intrapsychic Justice

Perhaps the most challenging is the idea of intrapsychic justice (Prilleltensky & Huygens, 2014). Making massive personal change requires encountering the fear of giving up one identity for another. In a very real sense, for those who experience transformational personal change, parts of one's identity are replaced or *have to die* in order for new elements of identity to come to the fore. One good example of this is individuals who are in drug and alcohol recovery. The fears associated with living a sober life are substantial and involve taking on the significant social risk of acknowledging addiction in settings in which this can cause social harm and of making amends with those damaged by the addict's past behavior (White & Sanders, 2013). But among the most significant is abandoning the addicted self in favor of the nonaddicted self. This is often described as requiring a deep intrapersonal form of bravery, working to, in the words of many addicts, "slay the dragon" of addiction (White & Sanders, 2013) and the often comfortable, though highly destructive, patterns of behavior that accompany it in exchange for a much less comfortable sober lifestyle. In part, this fear stems from facing, perhaps for the first time, difficult emotions and memories rather than suppressing them with drug use (McCullough, 2003). This same view of intrapsychic heroism can be applied to a number of other therapeutic situations as well in which a maladaptive, but deeply entrenched, identity is exchanged for a more adaptive one only through the encountering of "demons."

DISCUSSION

In this chapter we had a number of objectives, or missions, that we hope our readers will feel that we have accomplished. After briefly outlining what we have tried to do, Phil Zimbardo adds a postscript about his new heroic imagination project, whose goal is to educate people, especially youth, on how to become "heroes-in-training" by doing daily deeds of social goodness. The theme is that heroism can be learned and practiced by anyone rather than being a unique inborn trait.

In the most general sense, we have tried to portray heroism as a fascinating, complex and richly tapestried human phenomenon. We have tried to rescue it from earlier simplistic notions of select individuals born with special qualities that propelled them toward a heroic life, as well as a similar departure from the superhero genre our youth have inherited from Marvel comics. Although each superhero is endowed with superhuman abilities such as flying, immunity to bullets and fire, and more, what they lack is what every one of our young people possess—a brain that can imaginatively create and appreciate such marvelous feats.

We applaud the recent attempts by researchers around the world to begin to investigate the dynamics of heroism, following decades lacking any serious academic interest in this most central aspect of human nature. And we encourage our colleagues to continue to ask the hard questions about heroic motivation and action and to answer with solid experimental, correlational, survey, interview, and historical investigations. If that goal is accomplished, then maybe heroism will earn a new place in the lexicon of psychology textbooks and also within the positive, humanistic, and existential views of psychology—where its absence has been notably conspicuous.

We organized our ideas around four basic themes or topics. First, we explored the notion of "everyday heroism," or the idea that heroism is not a rare and exceptional human virtue but rather is a fundamental part of human existence. In a sense, we have democratized heroism by making it clear that it is a social action that can be engaged in by anyone, notably by ordinary people.

Second, we laid out some psychological theories related to heroism as an internal process that can be appreciated from two major perspectives: a prosocial view based on the idea of a positive psychology of heroism as a virtuous activity and also from a more negative, alternative view of heroism as an activity that can equally emanate from inappropriate risk taking, deviance, and even psychopathology. In retrospect, decades of prior inquiry did not adequately appreciate the efforts of a few researchers to highlight moral courage as the core mechanism between personal ideals, beliefs, action readiness, and the outcome behavior of taking heroic action (e.g., Monin et al., 2008; Oliner & Oliner, 1988; Staub, 2011).

Third, we contrasted these dispositional views with those that focus on external determinants. The notion is that heroism is always a socially constructed label given to (or taken away from) individuals based in part on their overt actions, but also based on cultural, historical, and time-based constructions. Consider also that heroes are more likely to be found in literate societies that document their actions, as well as among winners of wars rather than in the ranks of the losers.

Fourth, and finally, we tried to provide speculations on how heroism can inform our views of the most extremely virtuous aspects of human nature. We strongly advance the idea of heroes as important progenitors of mercy, dignity, and social justice in a complex world. We need heroes to represent humanity's endless struggle against evil, injustice, corruption, poverty, and discrimination. Heroes represent the ideal in human nature to which each of us can aspire.

Following Philip Zimbardo's TED presentation in 2009 on his journey from investigating evil to inspiring heroism (which has gone viral on the Internet with millions of viewers), he was encouraged by many attendees to develop more fully the heroic dimension of his vision. To do so, he created a San Francisco–based nonprofit foundation, the Heroic Imagination Project, or HIP. It is a novel education- and research-centered operation that helps people make morally courageous decisions in challenging situations in their lives—family, school, community, business, and nation. It advances ideas about how any person, regardless of age or background, can make a difference in creating a better world. HIP, through its website and in-class training programs, encourages everyone to imagine a new world in which every schoolchild and every adult is a hero in training. That means learning how to wisely and effectively stand up, speak out, and take heroic action against injustice of all kinds—bullying, prejudice, unjust authority, and apathy of passive bystanders in emergencies.

That is HIP's mission, which is now being realized through in-class training sessions of teachers and students—and, eventually, through programs for parents. In part, the training involves a totally new way of teaching that is a psychological revolution in its content—focused on many basic social-psychological themes, such as bystander effects, mind set, group dynamics, and more. But equally special is its unique method of delivery in which each lesson is organized around the same set of eight activities, triggered by having students watch provocative videos and then engaging in discussions and role-playing exercises. Teachers no longer lecture but are provided detailed scripts in which they become more like coaches determined to bring out the best in each student-player, as well as to create team camaraderie. This program is called Understanding Human Nature. It is now designed for high school and college use but will be reformulated soon for middle school and grade school use.

This new educational program is now a central part of many high school programs in Flint, Michigan. This community has been one of America's most depressed towns—in which the unemployment rate is up to 50% and the high school dropout rate an alarming 70%. As an impetus to get the community, civic, and business leaders to support these new programs, the organizing committee has transformed its name into Flint Hero Town, U.S.A. In addition, this program is operational in many California community colleges organized by the Psi Beta Honor Society, with its students teaching the HIP lessons in local high schools. The California State University system is also working with HIP to create a new science, technology, engineering, and math (STEM) heroes program. Finally, HIP's educational programs are going global. Thousands of high school teachers in Budapest, Hungary, are using them, as well as throughout Poland, and also in Corleone, Sicily (the "Godfather" town). Naturally, these programs will all be systematically evaluated and assessed on many dimensions to determine their effective impact. Once that is determined, then there can be evidence-based recommendations for its use in school systems everywhere. Will it help create a new global generation of everyday heroes? Time and data will tell (visit *www.HeroicImagination.org*).

ACKNOWLEDGMENTS

This chapter, and our past decade of work and thought on the psychology of heroic action, stems in part from a mentoring relationship established between Zeno Franco and Larry Raine, DrPH, MPH, at the U.S. Department of Homeland Security (DHS). During and after the September 11, 2001, terror attacks on the World Trade Center and the Pentagon, many acts of heroism occurred. While he was on a DHS Graduate Fellowship in 2004, Dr. Franco requested permission to examine some of the heroes and mavericks who responded to the 9/11 catastrophe. Although it was not directly related to the goals of the fellowship, Dr. Raine provided the freedom to pursue these ideas fully. A manuscript developed during the DHS fellowship was shared with Philip Zimbardo, who had been working on similar ideas, and the ensuing discussion has spanned more than a decade. In part as a result of this freedom to explore novel areas, the ideal of heroism and its formal study are enjoying a renaissance in psychology. Dr. Raine's approach proves that intellectual pursuits have a place in government as much as in the academy, and that the walls of the university are boundless.

REFERENCES

Al Ali, G. (2011). Hero or terrorist?: A comparative analysis of Arabic and Western media depictions of the execution of Saddam. *Discourse and Communication, 5*(4), 301–335.

Allison, S. T., & Goethals, G. R. (2011). *Heroes: What they do and why we need them*. New York: Oxford University Press.

Allison, S. T., & Goethals, G. R. (2013). *True heroes: An influence taxonomy of 100 exceptional individuals*. New York: Routledge.

Allison, S. T., & Goethals, G. R. (2015). *"Now he belongs to the ages": The heroic leadership dynamic and deep narratives of greatness*. New York: Palgrave Macmillan.

Anderson, S. (2006). New century challenges and executive success. *Mid-American Journal of Business, 21*(1), 9–12.

Arendt, H. (1964). *Eichmann in Jerusalem: A report on the banality of evil*. New York: Viking Press.

Arnulf, J. K., Mathisen, J. E., & Hærem, T. (2012). Heroic leadership illusions in football teams: Rationality, decision making and noise–signal ratio in the firing of football managers. *Leadership, 8*(2), 169–185.

Arteaga, R. L. (2010). *"The rarer action": Revenge and pity in* Titus Andronicus *and* The Tempest. Unpublished doctoral dissertation, California State University at Chico, Chico, California.

Barbour, D. H. (1999). Heroism and redemption in the Mad Max trilogy. *Journal of Popular Film and Television, 27*(3), 28–34.

Baumeister, R. F., Bratslavsky, E., Finkenauer, C., & Vohs, K. D. (2001). Bad is stronger than good. *Review of General Psychology, 5*(4), 323–370.

Becker, S. W., & Eagly, A. H. (2004). The heroism of women and men. *American Psychologist, 59*(3), 163–178.

Bennis, W. (2007). The challenges of leadership in the modern world: Introduction to the special issue. *American Psychologist, 62*(1), 2–5.

Boston U. panel finds plagiarism by Dr. King. (1991). Retrieved from *www.nytimes.com/1991/10/11/us/boston-u-panel-finds-plagiarism-by-dr-king.html*.

Boyd, J. N., & Zimbardo, P. G. (2005). Time perspective, health, and risk taking. In A. Strathman & J. Joireman (Eds.), *Understanding behavior in the context of time: Theory, research, and application* (pp. 85–107). Mahwah, NJ: Erlbaum.

Carney, S. (2007). Reform of higher education and the return of "heroic" leadership: The case of Denmark. *Management Revue, 18*(2), 174–186.

Carretero-González, M. (2010). Sympathy for the devil: The hero is a terrorist in *V for Vendetta*. In N. Billias (Ed.), *Promoting and producing evil* (pp. 199–210). New York: Rodopi.

De Certeau, M. (1998). *The practice of everyday life: Living and cooking* (Vol. 2). Minneapolis: University of Minnesota Press.

Desmond, M. (2008a). The lie of heroism. *Contexts, 7*(1), 56–58.

Desmond, M. (2008b). *On the fireline: Living and dying with wildland firefighters*. Chicago: University of Chicago Press.

Duckworth, A. L., Peterson, C., Matthews, M. D., & Kelly, D. R. (2007). Grit:

Perseverance and passion for long-term goals. *Journal of Personality and Social Psychology, 92*(6), 1087–1101.

Ellsberg, D. (2003). *Secrets: A memoir of Vietnam and the Pentagon Papers.* New York: Penguin.

Eysenck, S. B., & Eysenck, H. J. (1978). Impulsiveness and venturesomeness: Their position in a dimensional system of personality description. *Psychological Reports, 43*(3, Pt. 2), 1247–1255.

Faqihi, N. (2014). Choosing which rule to break first: An in-house attorney whistleblower's choices after discovering a possible federal securities law violation. *Fordham Law Review, 82*(6), 3341–3393.

Farley, F. (2012, January 19). Can you train someone to be a hero? *Science and Religion Today.* Retrieved from *http://www.scienceandreligiontoday. com/2012/01/19/can-you-train-someone-to-be-a-hero.*

Feigin, S., Owens, G., & Goodyear-Smith, F. (2014). Theories of human altruism: A systematic review. *Annals of Neuroscience and Psychology, 1*(1), 1–9.

Finkelstein, S., Hambrick, D. C., & Cannella, A. A. (2009). *Strategic leadership: Theory and research on executives, top management teams, and boards.* New York: Oxford University Press.

Fischer, S., & Smith, G. T. (2004). Deliberation affects risk taking beyond sensation seeking. *Personality and Individual Differences, 36*(3), 527–537.

Franco, Z. (2012). Lance Armstrong and the tenuous nature of heroism. Retrieved November 19, 2014, from *www.cnn.com/2012/08/24/opinion/franco-lance-armstrong.*

Franco, Z., Blau, K., & Zimbardo, P. G. (2011). Heroism: A conceptual analysis and differentiation between heroic action and altruism. *Review of General Psychology, 15*(2), 99–113.

Franco, Z., Flower, M., Whittle, J., & Sandy, M. (2015). Professional ethics and virtue ethics in community-engaged healthcare training. In D. Mitchell & R. Ream (Eds.), *Professional responsibility: The fundamental issue in education and health care reform* (pp. 211–229). Cham, Switzerland: Springer.

Franco, Z., & Zimbardo, P. (2007, Fall/Winter). The banality of heroism. *Greater Good,* 30–35.

Frost, P., & Robinson, S. (1998). The toxic handler: Organizational hero—and casualty. *Harvard Business Review, 77*(4), 96–106, 185.

Garrison, W. P. (1885). *William Lloyd Garrison, 1805–1879: The story of his life, told by his children* (Vol. 1). New York: Century.

Ginzburg, K., Solomon, Z., Dekel, R., & Neria, Y. (2003). Battlefield functioning and chronic PTSD: Associations with perceived self-efficacy and causal attribution. *Personality and Individual Differences, 34*(3), 463–476.

Glazer, M., & Glazer, P. M. (1989). *The whistleblowers: Exposing corruption in government and industry.* New York: Basic Books.

Greenberg, J., Koole, S. L., & Pyszczynski, T. (2013). *Handbook of experimental existential psychology.* New York: Guilford Press.

Haslam, S. A., Reicher, S. D., & Platow, M. J. (2013). *The new psychology of leadership: Identity, influence and power.* New York: Psychology Press.

Heroism: A reading list for boys and girls. (1914). New York: New York Public Library.

Hood, G. (2013). More girls target archery, inspired by "The Hunger Games." Retrieved November 19, 2014, from *www.npr.org/2013/11/27/247379498/more-girls-target-archery-inspired-by-the-hunger-games*.

Howerth, I. (1935). Heroism as a factor in education. *Phi Delta Kappan, 18*(1), 18–24.

Hymer, S. (1995). Redemption as a covert theme in psychotherapy. *Psychoanalytic Review, 82*(1), 21–40.

Johnson, C. V., & Friedman, H. L. (2014). *The Praeger handbook of social justice and psychology.* Santa Barbara, CA: ABC-CLIO.

Karajica, T. (2014). A hero or a villain, a terrorist or a liberator? In K. K. Ritzenhoff & J. Kazecki (Eds.), *Heroism and gender in war films* (pp. 35–47). New York: Palgrave Macmillan.

Kelly, S., & Dunbar, R. I. (2001). Who dares, wins. *Human Nature, 12*(2), 89–105.

Kinsella, E. L., Ritchie, T. D., & Igou, E. R. (2015). Lay perspectives on the social and psychological functions of heroes. *Frontiers in Psychology.* Available at *http://journal.frontiersin.org/article/10.3389/fpsyg.2015.00130/full*.

Klee, S., & Renner, K.-H. (2013). In search of the "Rescue Personality": A questionnaire study with emergency medical services personnel. *Personality and Individual Differences, 54*(5), 669–672.

Klein, G. A. (1993). *A recognition-primed decision (RPD) model of rapid decision making.* New York: Ablex.

Latané, B., & Nida, S. (1981). Ten years of research on group size and helping. *Psychological Bulletin, 89*(2), 308–324.

Latané, B., Nida, S. A., & Wilson, D. W. (1981). The effects of group size on helping behavior. In P. J. Rushton & R. M. Sorrentino (Eds.), *Altruism and helping behavior* (pp. 287–317). Hillsdale, NJ: Erlbaum.

Levenson, M. R. (1990). Risk taking and personality. *Journal of Personality and Social Psychology, 58*(6), 1073–1080.

Lewis, N. D. C., & Yarnell, H. (1951). Pyromania: Pathological firesetting. *Nervous and Mental Disease Monographs: Vol. 82.* New York: Coolidge Foundation.

Lilienfeld, S. O. (1998). *Fearlessness, antisocial behavior, and heroism.* Unpublished manuscript.

Lincoln, A. (1991). Address at Cooper Institute. In *Abraham Lincoln: Great speeches.* New York: Dover.

Lipman-Blumen, J. (2006). *The allure of toxic leaders: Why we follow destructive bosses and corrupt politicians and how we can survive them.* New York: Oxford University Press.

Marsh, A. A., Stoycos, S. A., Brethel-Haurwitz, K. M., Robinson, P., VanMeter, J. W., & Cardinale, E. M. (2014). Neural and cognitive characteristics of extraordinary altruists. *Proceedings of the National Academy of Sciences of the USA, 111*(42), 15036–15041.

Martens, J. W. (2005). Definitions and omissions of heroism. *American Psychologist, 60*(4), 342–343.

Mayer, J. (2011). *Life in a jar: The Irena Sendler project.* Middlebury, VT: Long Trail Press.

McCullough, L. (2003). *Treating affect phobia: A manual for short-term dynamic psychotherapy.* New York: Guilford Press.

Mednic, S., Christakis, N., & Fowler, J. (2010). The spread of sleep behavior influences drug use in adolescent social networks. *PLoS ONE, 5*(3), e9775.

Mendonça, D., Beroggi, G. E., & Wallace, W. A. (2001). Decision support for improvisation during emergency response operations. *International Journal of Emergency Management, 1*(1), 30–38.

Mendonça, D., & Franco, Z. (2013). Improvising. In K. Penuel, M. Statler, & R. Hagen (Eds.), *Encyclopedia of crisis management* (pp. 496–499). Thousand Oaks, CA: Sage.

Mendonça, D., & Wallace, W. A. (2007). A cognitive model of improvisation in emergency management. *Systems, Man and Cybernetics: Part A. Systems and Humans, IEEE Transactions on, 37*(4), 547–561.

Metz, I., Brown, M., Cregan, C., & Kulik, C. T. (2014). "Toxin handling" and well-being: The case of the human resources manager. *European Journal of Work and Organizational Psychology, 23*(2), 248–262.

Misleading information from the battlefield: Hearing before the Committee on Oversight and Government Reform House of Representatives, 110th Cong. (2007). Washington, DC: U.S. Government Printing Office. Retrieved from *www.gpo.gov/fdsys/pkg/CHRG-110hhrg42898/html/CHRG-110hhrg42898.htm*.

Monin, B., Sawyer, P. J., & Marquez, M. J. (2008). Rejection of moral rebels: Resenting those who do the right thing. *Journal of Personality and Social Psychology, 95*, 76–93.

Morgenson, G. (2011, February 19). How a whistle-blower conquered Countrywide. *The New York Times*. Retrieved from *www.nytimes.com/2011/02/20/business/20gret.html*.

Nayar, P. K. (2010). *An introduction to new media and cybercultures*. Malden, MA: Wiley.

NSA whistle-blower hero or villain? Our view. (2013, June 10). Retrieved November 19, 2014, from *http://www.usatoday.com/story/opinion/2013/06/09/nsa-whistle-blower-edward-snowden-editorials-debates/2406409*.

O'Brien, K., & O'Hare, D. (2007). Situational awareness ability and cognitive skills training in a complex real-world task. *Ergonomics, 50*(7), 1064–1091.

O'Neil, D. (2013). *Batman unauthorized: Vigilantes, jokers, and heroes in Gotham City*. Dallas, TX: Benbella.

Oliner, S. P., & Oliner, P. M. (1988). *The altruistic personality: The rescuers of the Jews in Nazi Europe*. New York: Free Press.

Pallone, N. J., & Hennessy, J. J. (1998). Counterfeit courage: Toward a process psychology paradigm for the "heroic rescue fantasy." *Current Psychology, 17*(2–3), 197–209.

Papageorgiou, I. (2014). The mountain-bandits of the Hellenic shadow theatre of Karaghiozis: Criminals or heroes? *Popular Entertainment Studies, 5*(2), 79–102.

Pawel, M. (2014). *The crusades of Cesar Chavez: A biography*. New York: Bloomsbury Press.

Peklar, B. (2011). The heroic death beneath the walls of Troy: Before and after Christ. *IKON, 4*(1), 293–302.

Polster, M. F. (2014). Eve's daughters: The forbidden heroism of women. In J. K. Zeig (Ed.), *The evolution of psychotherapy, the second conference*. New York: Routledge.

Post, S. G. (2014). Six sources of altruism: Springs of morality and solidarity. In V. Jeffries (Ed.), *The Palgrave handbook of altruism, morality, and social solidarity: Formulating a field of study* (pp. 179–194). New York: Palgrave MacMillan.

Prilleltensky, I., & Huygens, I. (2014). Well-being, justice, and social change. In H. L. Friedman, C. V. Johnson, J. Diaz, Z. Franco, & B. Nastasi (Eds.), *The Praeger handbook of social justice and psychology: Vol. 2. Well-being and professional issues* (pp. 3–33). Santa Barbara, CA: Praeger.

Queally, J., & Zucchino, D. (2015, April 8). Man who recorded Walter Scott shooting says his life has changed forever. *The Los Angeles Times*. Retrieved from *www.latimes.com/nation/nationnow/la-na-nn-videographer-south-carolina-20150408-story.html*.

Qusqas, F., & Kleiner, B. H. (2001). The difficulties of whistleblowers finding employment. *Management Research News, 24*(3/4), 97–100.

Rand, D. G., & Epstein, Z. G. (2014). Risking your life without a second thought: Intuitive decision-making and extreme altruism. *PLoS ONE, 9*(10), e109687.

Rankin, L. E., & Eagly, A. H. (2008). Is his heroism hailed and hers hidden?: Women, men, and the social construction of heroism. *Psychology of Women Quarterly, 32*(4), 414–422.

Roper, M. (2000, Autumn). Re-remembering the soldier hero: The psychic and social construction of memory in personal narratives of the Great War. *History Workshop Journal, 50*, 181–204.

Ruderman, C., Tracy, C. S., Bensimon, C. M., Bernstein, M., Hawryluck, L., Shaul, R. Z., et al. (2006). On pandemics and the duty to care: Whose duty? who cares? *BMC Medical Ethics, 7*(1), 5–11.

Rushton, P. J., Chrisjohn, R. D., & Fekken, G. C. (1981). The altruistic personality and the self-report altruism scale. *Personality and Individual Differences, 2*(4), 293–302.

Sanne, J. M. (2008). Framing risks in a safety-critical and hazardous job: Risk-taking as responsibility in railway maintenance. *Journal of Risk Research, 11*(5), 645–658.

Shepela, S. T., Cook, J., Horlitz, E., Leal, R., Luciano, S., Lutfy, E., et al. (1999). Courageous resistance: A special case of altruism. *Theory and Psychology, 9*(6), 787–805.

Smith, S. F., Lilienfeld, S. O., Coffey, K., & Dabbs, J. M. (2013). Are psychopaths and heroes twigs off the same branch?: Evidence from college, community, and presidential samples. *Journal of Research in Personality, 47*(5), 634–646.

Somaiya, R. (2015, January 8). The men behind the cartoons at Charlie Hebdo. *The New York Times*. Retrieved from *www.nytimes.com/2015/01/08/world/europe/the-men-behind-the-cartoons-at-charlie-hebdo.html*.

Sorensen, L. J., Øvergård, K. I., & Martinsen, T. J. (2014, April 7–10). *Understanding human decision making during critical incidents in dynamic positioning*. Paper presented at the International Conference on Ergonomics and Human Factors 2014, Southampton, UK.

Staub, E. (1991). Psychological and cultural origins of extreme destructiveness and extreme altruism. In W. Kurtines, J. Gewirtz, & J. Lamb (Eds.), *Handbook of moral behavior and development* (pp. 425–446). New York: Erlbaum.

Staub, E. (2011). *Overcoming evil: Genocide, violent conflict, and terrorism*. New York: Oxford University Press.

Stewart, C. J., Smith, C. A., & Denton, R. E., Jr. (2012). *Persuasion and social movements*. Long Grove, IL: Waveland Press.

Stolarski, M., Bitner, J., & Zimbardo, P. G. (2011). Time perspective, emotional intelligence and discounting of delayed awards. *Time and Society, 20*(3), 346–363.

Štrobl, D. (2004). Psychologické pasti záchranářství [The psychological traps of rescuing]. *Psychologie Dnes* (1), 14–15.

Svoboda, E. (2013). *What makes a hero?: The surprising science of selflessness*. New York: Penguin.

Swartz, S. (2006). A long walk to citizenship: Morality, justice and faith in the aftermath of apartheid. *Journal of Moral Education, 35*(4), 551–570.

Taylor, H. A., Rutkow, L., & Barnett, D. J. (2014). Willingness of the local health department workforce to respond to infectious disease events: Empirical, ethical, and legal considerations. *Biosecurity and Bioterrorism: Biodefense Strategy, Practice, and Science, 12*(4), 178–185.

Theoharis, A. G. (1999). *The FBI: A comprehensive reference guide*. Phoenix, AZ: Greenwood.

Thompson, F. (1995). Business strategy and the Boyd cycle. *Journal of Contingencies and Crisis Management, 3*(2), 81–90.

Vollhardt, J. R. (2009). Altruism born of suffering and prosocial behavior following adverse life events: A review and conceptualization. *Social Justice Research, 22*(1), 53–97.

Von Culin, K. R., Tsukayama, E., & Duckworth, A. L. (2014). Unpacking grit: Motivational correlates of perseverance and passion for long-term goals. *Journal of Positive Psychology, 9*(4), 306–312.

Wagner, S. L., Martin, C. A., & McFee, J. A. (2009). Investigating the "Rescue Personality." *Traumatology, 15*(3), 5–12.

Wansink, B., Payne, C. R., & Van Ittersum, K. (2008). Profiling the heroic leader: Empirical lessons from combat-decorated veterans of World War II. *Leadership Quarterly, 19*(5), 547–555.

Webster's revised unabridged dictionary. (1913). Springfield, MA: G. & C. Merriam.

Wenos, J., Trick, T., & Williams, J. A. (2014). Creating socially fit heroes and reducing the incidence of bullying in elementary physical education. *Journal of Physical Education, Recreation and Dance, 85*(7), 36–41.

White, W., & Sanders, M. (2013). Heroism and addiction recovery revisited: An interview with William White. Retrieved from *www.williamwhitepapers.com/pr/2013%20Heroism%20and%20Addiction%20Recovery%20Revisited.pdf*.

Whittier, J. (1880). Garrison. *Friends Intelligencer, 36*, 383.

Zimbardo, P. (2007). *The Lucifer effect: Understanding how good people turn evil*. New York: Random House.

Zimbardo, P., & Boyd, J. (2008). *The time paradox: The new psychology of time that will change your life*. New York: Simon & Schuster.

Zimbardo, P. G., Breckenridge, J. N., & Moghaddam, F. M. (2013). "Exclusive" and "inclusive" visions of heroism and democracy. *Current Psychology, 32*(3), 221–233.

Index

Note: *f*, *n*, or *t* following a page number indicates a figure, note, or table.

Abstract concepts, 455–456
Acclimation, 103–104
Accountability, 395–396
Acculturation framework, 102–103
Action, heroism and, 501–502, 507–510
Activity Frequency Inventory (AFI), 506
Adaptation
  aversive racism and, 97
  competition and, 20–22
  fitness conflicts and, 28–29
  free will and, 42
  good and, 31–33
  implications of, 34–36
  killing and, 24–25, 26*f*
  overview, 4
  shame and guilt and, 306
Addiction, 306. *See also* Substance use/abuse
Adjustment, 301
Adolescents, 302–303
Adultery, 9
Affect
  compassionate goals and, 292–293
  media violence effects and, 131
  sexual violence and, 8, 232–233, 238–239
Affective traits, 123*f*
Aftermath of genocide, 163–164. *See also* Genocide
Agency, 46–47
Agentic state, 194

Aggression
  dehumanization and, 144
  demonization of unconscious processes and, 71
  empathy–altruism hypothesis and, 446
  evolutionary perspective and, 33–34
  media violence effects and, 119–120, 124–129, 128*f*, 129*f*, 130–134, 134*f*
  Milgram experiments and, 202
  overview, 123–124
  self-control and, 309
  sexual objectification and, 8, 232–233
  shame and guilt and, 301, 303–304
Alcohol, 231. *See also* Substance use/abuse
Altruism. *See also* Empathy-induced altruism
  bystanders and, 174
  ecosystem motivation and, 273–274
  evolutionary perspective of, 31–33
  heroism and, 501, 502–503
  "holier than thou" phenomenon and, 251–252
  Milgram experiments and, 202
  overview, 12, 444
Altruistic personality, 351
Ambivalence, 55–56, 55*f*
Anger
  empathy–altruism hypothesis and, 446
  evolutionary perspective and, 35
  media violence effects and, 131, 134*f*
  shame and guilt and, 301

525

Antagonistic coevolution, 23–25, 26f. *See also* Evolutionary perspective
Anti-homicide mechanisms, 24–25, 26f, 36
Antinaturalistic fallacy, 35
Antisocial behavior, 161–162
Anxiety
　bias and, 56
　compassionate goals and, 276
　evolutionary perspective and, 36
　sexual violence and, 225
　shame and guilt and, 301, 302–303
Apology
　historical victimization and, 368
　intergroup forgiveness and, 377–379, 384
Appraisals, 121f
Arousal, 121f, 347
Arrogance, 8, 250. *See also* Moral superiority to others
Assessment
　aversive racism and, 98
　heroism and, 506
　volunteerism and, 472–474
Assimilation, 103–104
Atomistic fallacy, 390–391, 393
Attentional functioning, 133–134, 134f
Attitudes
　aversive racism and, 98, 109
　general aggression model (GAM) and, 122f
　general learning model (GLM) and, 123f
　genocide and mass killing and, 165–168
　media violence effects and, 121
　research on obedience to authority and, 199
　volunteerism and, 472
Attributions
　actor–observer differences in, 259–260
　bias and, 53–55
　demonization of unconscious processes and, 80–81
Authoritarian personality, 96, 164. *See also* Personality
Authoritarianism, 202
Authority. *See also* Obedience; Power; Respect for authority
　genocide and mass killing and, 166
　Milgram experiments and, 190
　moral blindness and, 400–402
　organizational settings and, 393–396
　research on obedience to, 193–200
　tone at the top and, 397–399

Automatic processes. *See also* Unconscious processes
　bias and, 53, 62–63
　habits and, 83
　organizational settings and, 390–391, 400–402
　overview, 65n
Autonomy, 44–46, 48–49
Aversive racism. *See also* Racism
　consequences of, 99–101
　intention and, 109–113
　overview, 96–99, 112–113
　perpetuation of disadvantage and, 107–109
Avoidance
　bias and, 56–57
　compassionate goals and, 276
　empathy–altruism hypothesis and, 456–457
Awareness
　aversive racism and, 109–111, 112–113
　bias and, 107–113
　compassionate goals and, 291
　demonization of unconscious processes and, 78–79
　empathy–altruism hypothesis and, 456–457
　organizational settings and, 400–402
　racism and, 95–96
　unconscious processes and, 5

B

Bad, 81–87
Behavior
　actor–observer differences in attributions and, 259–260
　bystanders and, 174
　ecosystem motivation and, 274–281, 275f
　evolutionary perspective and, 34–36
　free will and, 43
　heroism and, 501–502
　"holier than thou" phenomenon and, 251–252
　research on obedience to authority and, 199
　self-agency beliefs and, 252–259
　self-control and, 309
　sexual violence and, 8, 233–237, 240
　shame and guilt and, 303–304
Behavior scripts, 122f
Behavioral confirmation, 56, 238
Behavioral control, 83–84
Behavioral regulation, 260–264
Behaviorism, 78–79

Beliefs
  collective memory and, 368–369
  demonization of unconscious processes and, 80–81
  general aggression model (GAM) and, 122f
  general learning model (GLM) and, 123f
  good versus evil and, 162
  moral resentment and, 330–331
  organizational settings and, 395–396
  in self-agency, 252–259
  self-control and, 311–312
Benefit-delivering mechanisms, 31–32
Benevolence, 467. *See also* Volunteerism
Bias. *See also* Group membership; Racism; Stereotyping
  ambivalence and, 55–56, 55f
  aversive racism and, 96–101, 112–113
  awareness and, 95–96
  color-blind inclusiveness and, 101–109
  dishonesty and, 324–325
  exclusion and, 56–57
  ingroup biases and, 53–55
  intention and, 109–112
  overview, 4–5, 52–57, 55f, 64–65
  perpetuation of disadvantage and, 107–109
  responsibility for, 57–64
  social categorization and, 5
Big Five personality traits, 199. *See also* Personality
Black sheep effect, 359–360, 361. *See also* Group processes
Blaming victims, 172. *See also* Victims
Body shame, 239
Boston Marathon bombing, 421–435. *See also* Radicalization; Terrorism
Bounded ethicality, 328–329, 401. *See also* Ethical behavior; Unethical behaviors
Burnout, 456–457
Bystanders. *See also* Group processes; Helping behaviors
  emergencies and, 347–348
  everyday heroism and, 496–498
  genocide and mass killing and, 160, 171–174
  helping in disasters and emergencies and, 355–358
  Holocaust and, 350–355
  overview, 345–346, 362
  perpetrators and, 358–361
  research on, 346–347
  self-agency beliefs and, 256–257

  social identity model and, 348–350, 351t
  violence and, 347–348

C

Capital punishment, 1–2
Caring behavior, 446–448
Categorical thinking. *See also* Bias; Social categorization
  automaticity and, 62–64
  aversive racism and, 96–99
  overview, 5, 64–65
Categorization, social. *See* Social categorization
Category activation, 62–64. *See also* Bias
Causality
  compassionate goals and, 275–276
  free will and, 43
  organizational settings and, 405
Character, 497
Cheater detection, 36
Cheating, 324–328. *See also* Dishonesty
Children, 302–303
Choice. *See also* Free will
  bias and, 60
  demonization of unconscious processes and, 72
  empathy–altruism hypothesis and, 446–448
  ethical boundaries and, 328–329
  free will and, 43
  habits and, 84
  obedience experiments and, 211
  organizational settings and, 395–396
  self-agency beliefs and, 253–254
  volunteerism and, 470
Christianity, 71–74. *See also* Demonization of unconscious processes; Free will; Soul, concept of
Civil disorder, 355
Closed-mindedness, 162
Cognitive control, 133–134, 134f
Cognitive mechanisms
  bias and, 28, 63–64
  criminal offenders and, 306–308
  evolutionary perspective and, 36
  general aggression model (GAM) and, 121f
  heroism and, 501–502
  media violence effects and, 130–131, 134f
  organizational settings and, 400–402
  self-control and, 308–309
  sexual violence and, 8, 232–233, 238–239

Cognitive-behavioral theory (CBT), 308, 310
Cognitive-evaluative mechanisms of "good" and "evil," 25–28
Cognitive psychology, 77–79
Cognitive revolution, 77–79
Cognitive tuning, 194
Collapse of compassion, 172. See also Compassion
Collective angst, 371–372
Collective memory, 368–375
Collective resistance, 175–177
Collectivism
 group processes and, 358–359
 intergroup forgiveness and, 383
 media violence effects and, 125–126
 self-agency beliefs and, 258–259
Color-blind inclusiveness. See also Racism
 harmony and, 104–107
 overview, 101–107, 112–113
 perpetuation of disadvantage and, 107–109
Common good, 458–459
Common identity, 111–112. See also Group membership
Commonality frames, 105–107. See also Color-blind inclusiveness
Communal orientation, 291–292
Community service, 470, 483–486. See also Volunteerism
Compassion, 172, 456
Compassion fatigue, 457
Compassionate goals. See also Goals
 constructive behaviors associated with, 275–276
 ecosystem motivation and, 274–281, 275f
 overview, 9, 273, 290–294
 research on, 281–290, 282f, 284f, 285f, 286f, 287f, 289f
 risks associated with, 293–294
Compassionate love, 291–292
Compensation, 331
Competition
 evolutionary perspective of, 20–21, 23
 fitness conflicts and, 29
 fitness costs and, 21–22
 helping behavior and, 356
 killing as evil and, 23
 past victimization and, 373–375
Computer-based simulations, 198
Conditioned emotions, 123f
Conflict, 376–381, 446–451
Conflict resolution, 449–451
Conflicts of interest, 328–329

Confluence model, 233
Conformity
 actor–observer differences in attributions and, 259–260
 genocide and mass killing and, 6–7, 178
Conjoint agency, 253, 258. See also Self-agency
Conscious processes. See also Intentionality
 aversive racism and, 98
 habits and, 82–84
 organizational settings and, 400–402
 overview, 69–71, 75f, 87–88
Conservative attitudes, 199. See also Attitudes; Political attitudes
Constraints, 43
Constructive relationship behaviors, 274–281, 275f. See also Behavior; Relationships
Contact hypothesis, 171
Contagion, 293, 327
Contempt, 35
Contextual factors. See Situational factors
Control, 5, 199
Cooperation
 ecosystem motivation and, 279–280
 empathy–altruism hypothesis and, 446–448, 451
 helping behavior and, 355–356
Corporate corruption, 9, 322–324, 391–392. See also Dishonesty; Organizational settings
Cost–reward model, 347
Counterfactual statements, 326–327
Creativity, 327–328
Criminal behavior, 262–263, 303–304
Criminal offenders. See also Evil people; Incarceration; Perpetrators
 cognitive mechanisms and, 306–308
 good versus evil and, 161–162
 group processes and, 358–361
 overview, 298, 313
 self-control and, 308–309
 shame and guilt and, 304–305
 treatment and policy and, 309–313
Criminogenic conditions, 306–308, 311
Criminology, 9, 298
Crisis, 355–358
Cross-cultural factors. See Cultural factors
Cultural factors. See also Cultural functioning; Cultural identity
 free will and, 41–42
 globalization in the 21st century and, 420–421

heroism and, 498
media violence effects and, 125–126
organizational settings and, 406n
racism and, 95–96
self-agency beliefs and, 258–259
Cultural frame intervention, 111–112. See also Interventions
Cultural functioning. See also Cultural factors; Cultural identity
bias and, 57
color-blind inclusiveness and, 102–104
free will and, 43–44, 46–47, 48
Cultural identity. See also Cultural factors; Cultural functioning; Social identity
color-blind inclusiveness and, 102–104
cultural frame intervention and, 111–112
staircase model of terrorism and, 422–435

D

Dangerous emergencies, 347–348. See also Emergencies; Violence
Dating violence, 126–127
Death penalty. See Capital punishment
Debriefing procedures, 241
Deceit, 9–10. See also Dishonesty; Truthfulness
Decision making
dehumanization and, 152–153
demonization of unconscious processes and, 80–81
general aggression model (GAM) and, 121f
moral judgment and, 334
organizational settings and, 402
research on obedience to authority and, 196
self-agency beliefs and, 255–256
volunteerism and, 470
Defenses
evolutionary perspective and, 36
immoral behavior as, 370–372
killing and, 24–25, 26f
"Deflategate" at the Super Bowl, 9
Dehumanization
benefits of, 152–153
future harm and, 145–147
genocide and mass killing and, 168–169
harm and, 141–145, 146t, 152
objectification and, 7–8
overview, 6, 140–141, 153–155
past harm and, 149–152
present harm and, 147–149
research on obedience to authority and, 194
sexual violence and, 233
Delegitimization, 168–169
Deliberation, 470
Delinquency, 126–127, 303–304
Demonic possession, 76
Demonization of unconscious processes. See also Unconscious processes
good versus evil and, 161–162
influences, 71–81
overview, 69–71, 75f, 87–88
Depression
sexual violence and, 225
shame and guilt and, 301, 302–303
volunteerism and, 478
Deradicalization programs, 415–416. See also Terrorism
Desensitization, 122f, 132
Desire. See also Intentionality
demonization of unconscious processes and, 80–81
evolutionary perspective and, 27
free will and, 43
Destiny beliefs, 270–271
Destruction, 168–170
Determinism, 4, 516
Developmental factors, 333–334
Deviance-based theories, 504–507
Deviant group members, 358–361. See also Group processes
Difficult life conditions, 164–166. See also Societal factors
Dignity, 514
Disasters, 355–358
Discomfort, 56
Disconnection, 148, 277
Discrimination. See also Bias; Racism
historical victimization and, 374
intergroup forgiveness and, 381
organizational settings and, 403–404, 405
responsibility for, 58–59
Disgust, 35, 148–149
Dishonesty. See also Corporate corruption; Deceit
ethical boundaries and, 328–329, 333–336
nature of morality and, 329–331
overview, 322–324, 336
self-concept maintenance and, 324–328
self-regulation and, 332–333
Disjoint agency, 253. See also Self-agency

Disobedience, 194, 196, 199. *See also* Obedience
Dispositional factors
  heroism and, 499
  obedience experiments and, 207
  self-agency beliefs and, 255
  volunteerism and, 472
Domestic violence, 121, 126–127
Dominative racism, 97. *See also* Racism
Dual identity, 111–112. *See also* Group membership

E

Eating disorder symptoms, 301
Ecological momentary assessment (EMA), 241
Economics, 418–419
Ecosystem motivational orientation. *See also* Compassionate goals; Motivation
  overview, 271–272, 273–274
  personality traits and, 274
  psychological states and, 274
  relationships and, 274–281, 275f
Educational settings, 450–451
Egalitarianism, 97–98
Egoism, 444, 455, 458–459
Egoistic hypothesis, 444, 445
Egosystem motivational orientation. *See also* Motivation
  overview, 271–273
  personality traits and, 274
  psychological states and, 274
Emergence, 402–404
Emergencies. *See also* Bystanders; Helping behaviors
  bystanders and, 347–348, 362
  helping behavior and, 355–358
  overview, 345–346
  research on, 346–347
  social identity model and, 348–350, 351t
Emotions, 151. *See also* Moral emotions
Empathy. *See also* Empathy-induced altruism
  benefits of, 444–453
  collective memory and, 368
  dehumanization and, 6, 142, 151
  good versus evil and, 162
  Milgram experiments and, 202
  overview, 12
  research on obedience to authority and, 199
  shame and guilt and, 300–301
  unconscious processes and, 81–82

Empathy avoidance, 456–457. *See also* Avoidance; Empathy
Empathy–altruism hypothesis, 12, 443–444, 453–459, 459–460
Empathy-induced altruism. *See also* Altruism; Empathy
  benefits of, 444–453
  liabilities of, 453–459
  overview, 12, 443–444, 459–460
Empowerment, 379–381
Engagement, 500–501
Environmental factors, 82–85, 455–456
Error management theory, 28
Ethical behavior. *See also* Unethical behaviors
  dishonesty and, 328–329, 333–336
  false moral superiority and, 261
  "holier than thou" phenomenon and, 251–252
  shame and guilt and, 303–304
Ethical factors
  bias and, 65
  dishonesty and, 324–325
  Milgram experiments and, 186, 188–189
  obedience experiments and, 210–211
  research on obedience to authority and, 196, 200
Ethical leadership, 397–399. *See also* Leadership
Ethical maneuvering, 326–327
Ethnicity. *See also* Group membership; Racism
  cultural identity and, 103–104
  dehumanization and, 142
  empathy–altruism hypothesis and, 451
  media violence effects and, 127–129, 128f, 129f
  organizational settings and, 403–404
  staircase model of terrorism and, 430
Euphemistic labeling, 400
Evil. *See also* Evil people
  bystanders and, 174
  cognitive-evaluative mechanisms of "good" and "evil," 25–28
  evolutionary perspective and, 19–20, 33–34
  exploitation of, 30–31
  fitness conflicts and, 28–29
  genocide and mass killing and, 159–160, 161–162
  heroism and, 516
  justification for, 372–373
  Milgram experiments and, 190–191
  organizational settings and, 391–392

Index

overview, 1–3
perspectives on, 4–5
Evil people. *See also* Criminal offenders; Evil; Psychopathology
    overview, 9, 299, 313
    shame and guilt, 299–306
Evolutionary perspective
    antagonistic coevolution, 23–25, 26*f*
    cognitive-evaluative mechanisms of "good" and "evil," 25–28
    comparing with other theoretical perspectives, 33–34
    demonization of unconscious processes and, 78–79
    empathy–altruism hypothesis and, 453
    exploitation of evil, 30–31
    fitness conflicts and, 28–29
    free will and, 42
    good, 31–33
    human psychology and, 20–21
    implications of, 34–36
    killing as evil and, 22–23
    overview, 4, 18–20, 36–37
    self-preservation system, 271–272
Exclusion
    bias and, 56–57
    dehumanization and, 142, 151
    discrimination and, 58–59
    genocide and mass killing and, 168–169
Executive functioning, 133–134, 134*f*
Executive processes, 85–86
Exogenous behavior, 253
Expectancy effects, 56
Expectations
    actor–observer differences in attributions and, 259–260
    bias and, 56–57
    general aggression model (GAM) and, 122*f*
    general learning model (GLM) and, 123*f*
    volunteerism and, 470
Experiential factors, 230
Exploitation of evil, 30–31
Exploitation of others, 83, 293–294
Exposure to violent media. *See* Media violence effects
Extremism. *See* Radicalization; Terrorism

F

Failure, 429
False moral superiority. *See* Moral superiority to others
Fear, 36
Feminist social constructivist view, 498
Fight-or-flight response, 273–274
Fitness conflicts, 28–29
Fitness costs
    competition and, 21–22
    evolutionary perspective and, 27–28
    overview, 19–20
Flexibility, 34–36
Forgiveness
    historical victimization and, 367–368, 375–383, 384
    Milgram experiments and, 206
    overview, 2, 10–11
Fortitude, 500–501
Free will. *See also* Choice
    autonomy and, 44–46
    consequences of the belief in, 44–45
    demonization of unconscious processes and, 72
    disbeliefs in, 45–46
    obedience experiments and, 214–215
    overview, 4, 41–44
    self-agency beliefs and, 253–254
    self-regulation and, 48–49
    volunteerism and, 469–470
Freudian theories, 74–77, 87
Friendships, 292. *See also* Peer relationships; Relationships
Functional approach, 471–472, 474–475

G

Gambling, 10
Game theory, 446–448
Gaming violence effects. *See also* Media violence effects
    dehumanization and, 143, 149
    general aggression model (GAM) and, 122*f*
    overview, 5–6
Gender
    bystanders and, 347
    compassionate goals and, 276
    dehumanization and, 142–143
    heroism and, 497–498
    historical victimization and, 374
    research on obedience to authority and, 196, 199
    sexual violence and, 232–233, 234, 238–239, 242*n*
    social identity model and, 349
General aggression model (GAM), 6, 120–122, 121*f*, 122*f*. *See also* Media violence effects
General learning model (GLM), 121–122, 123*f*. *See also* Media violence effects

Genetic factors, 21–22, 29
Genocide. *See also* Holocaust; Mass atrocities
  bystanders, 171–174
  defining, 163
  good versus evil and, 161–162
  group processes and, 358–359
  Milgram experiments and, 189–192, 202
  overview, 6–7, 159–164, 178
  perpetrators of, 164–171
  victims, 174–178
Giving behavior, 279–280
Global Terrorism Database, 422
Globalization, 12, 415–421, 435–436
Goal pursuit, 110–111
Goal-directed behavior, 83
Goals. *See also* Compassionate goals
  conscious processes as evil intentions, 85–86
  empathy–altruism hypothesis and, 449
  free will and, 43–44
  sexual violence and, 233, 239–240
  volunteerism and, 470–471
Good
  bystanders and, 174
  cognitive-evaluative mechanisms of "good" and "evil," 25–28
  evolutionary perspective of, 19–20, 31–33
  forgiveness and, 375–383
  genocide and mass killing and, 161–162
  historical victimization and, 375–383
  organizational settings and, 391–392
  overview, 2–3
  perspectives on, 4–5
  unconscious processes as, 81–87
Good intentions, 109–113. *See also* Intentionality
Good people, 200–204
"Good person–evil deeds" thesis, 201–204
Gratification delay, 44
Gratitude, 47
Grit, 500–501
Group conflict, 165–166
Group membership. *See also* Bias; Intergroup attitudes; Status; Stereotyping
  aversive racism and, 97
  color-blind inclusiveness and, 102–104
  cultural frame intervention and, 111–112
  dehumanization and, 145–147, 149–150

  deviant group members and, 358–361
  empathy–altruism hypothesis and, 448–452
  exclusion and, 56–57
  genocide and mass killing and, 165–168, 166–167
  good versus evil and, 162
  harm doing and, 369–370
  harmony and, 104–107
  historical victimization and, 367–368, 369–375
  ingroup biases and, 53–55
  intergroup forgiveness and, 375–383
  media violence effects and, 127–129, 128*f*, 129*f*
  overview, 10
  perpetuation of disadvantage and, 107–109
  rationalization and, 150
  reconciliation and, 150–151
  stereotype content model and, 55–56, 55*f*
Group norms, 6–7, 178. *See also* Norms
Group perspectives, 10–12
Group processes. *See also* Bystanders; Social identity
  deviants and, 358–361
  helping in disasters and emergencies and, 355–358
  historical victimization and, 367–375, 383–384
  intergroup forgiveness and, 375–383
  overview, 345–346, 362
  research on, 346–347
  social identity and helping and, 350–355
Guilt, 299–306. *See also* Moral emotions

H

Habits, 82–84, 123*f*
Harassment, 236–237
Hard choices, 60. *See also* Choice
Harm
  dehumanization and, 141–152, 146*t*, 153–155
  empathy–altruism hypothesis and, 453–454
  overview, 140–141, 152
  past victimization and, 369–375
Harming others
  evolutionary perspective of, 21–22
  Milgram experiments and, 191–192
  overview, 5–8
Health, 478–479

Index

Helping behaviors. *See also* Bystanders; Emergencies; Rescuer behavior; Selfless behavior; Volunteerism
  belief in free will and, 45–46
  bystanders and, 173–174
  in disasters and emergencies, 355–358
  empathy avoidance and, 456–457
  genocide and mass killing and, 170–171
  Holocaust and, 350–355
  motives for, 472
  overview, 362
  research on, 346–347
  social identity model of, 348–350, 351t
  violence or emergencies and, 347–348
Helplessness, 355, 478
Heroic Imagination Project (HIP), 516–517
Heroic Perceptions Measure, 508
Heroism. *See also* Helping behaviors; Selfless behavior; Volunteerism
  everyday heroism, 496–498
  kindness and, 510–515
  overview, 13–14, 467–471, 494–496, 515–517
  psychological theories and, 498–507
  social construction of, 507–510
Hierarchical views
  dehumanization and, 147
  moral judgment and, 335
  organizational settings and, 393–396
Historical victimization. *See also* Victimization
  collective memory and, 368–369
  forgiveness and, 375–383
  good from, 375–383
  as a justification for harm doing and, 369–375
  overview, 367–368, 383–384
Hitler, Adolf, 86–87
"Holier than thou" phenomenon. *See also* Moral superiority to others
  actor–observer differences in attributions and, 259–260
  behavioral regulation and, 260–264
  overview, 250–252
  self-agency beliefs and, 252–254, 258–259
Holocaust. *See also* Genocide
  bystanders and, 173–174
  collective memory and, 368–369
  conscious processes as evil intentions and, 86–87
  empathy avoidance and, 457
  genocide and mass killing and, 165–166

  group processes and, 358–359
  heroism and, 498
  immoral behavior as a defense against future victimization and, 370–371
  intergroup forgiveness and, 382–383
  Milgram experiments and, 187, 189–192, 201–204
  social identity and helping and, 350–355
  survivors, 177–178
  victims and, 176
Homicide. *See also* Killing; Murder; Premeditated murder
  evolutionary perspective and, 22–25, 26f, 33
  intent and, 60
  statistics regarding, 27
Hostility, 131, 134f
Human nature
  evolutionary perspective and, 34–36
  free will and, 41–42
  unconscious processes and, 81–82
Human psychology, 20–21
Humility, 250
Hygienic language, 400
Hypnotic therapies, 75–76
Hypocrisy, 109–111. *See also* Aversive racism

I

Identity. *See also* Cultural identity; Social identity
  cultural frame intervention and, 111–112
  staircase model of terrorism and, 422–435
  terrorism and, 422
  volunteerism and, 478
Ideologies
  dehumanization and, 145, 147–148
  genocide and mass killing and, 165–168, 178
  good versus evil and, 162
Illegal behavior, 303–304. *See also* Criminal behavior
Immediacy behaviors, 234–236. *See also* Nonverbal behavior
Immigration, 103–104, 142
Immoral behavior. *See also* Behavior; Morality
  empathy–altruism hypothesis and, 457–458
  justification for, 372–373
  past victimization and, 370–372
Implementation intentions, 83

Implicit Association Test (IAT), 98
Implicit attitudes, 98. *See also* Attitudes
Implicit biases, 101, 110–111. *See also* Bias
Improvisation, 501–502
Impulse control
  evolutionary perspective and, 33–34
  free will and, 48–49
  intent and, 60
  media violence effects and, 134, 134f
Impulsive action, 121f
Impulsive processes, 81–82, 505–506. *See also* Unconscious processes
Incarceration, 298, 309–313. *See also* Criminal offenders
Incrementalism, 335
Indigenous people, 142, 150
Individual differences
  bystanders and, 173–174
  dishonesty and, 326, 333–336
  genocide and mass killing and, 170–171
  motivational systems and, 274
  research on obedience to authority and, 199
  self-control and, 308, 311–312
  shame and guilt and, 305
  social interaction model of objectification and, 229–230
Individualism, 258–259
Individuation, 171
Infidelity, 309
Informal social control, 359–360
Information processing, 79
Informed consent, 196
Infrahumanization, 151. *See also* Dehumanization
Ingroup membership. *See also* Group membership; Intergroup attitudes
  aversive racism and, 97
  color-blind inclusiveness and, 102
  deviant group members and, 360
  empathy–altruism hypothesis and, 448–451
  genocide and mass killing and, 166–168
  harmony and, 104–107
  perpetuation of disadvantage and, 107–109
Inhibitory mechanism, 434
Institutional racism, 95–96, 107–109. *See also* Racism
Institutional review board (IRB), 196
Instrumental gain, 169

Insults, 198
Integration, 103–104
Intentionality. *See also* Conscious processes; Responsibility; Unconscious processes
  bias and, 53, 57–64, 65, 109–112
  compassionate goals and, 291
  conscious processes and, 85–87
  criminal actions and, 262–263, 265n
  dehumanization and, 147
  ecosystem motivation and, 278–279
  evolutionary perspective and, 27
  false moral superiority and, 262–263, 265n
  overview, 4
  self-agency beliefs and, 253–254
  self-control and, 308–309
  social categorization and, 5
Interactionism, 207, 215–216
Interconnectivity, 419–420
Intergroup attitudes. *See also* Attitudes; Group membership
  empathy–altruism hypothesis and, 448–451
  forgiveness and, 375–383, 384
  genocide and mass killing and, 165–168, 170–171
  historical victimization and, 367–375
Interpersonal conflicts, 446–448
Interpersonal dynamics, 8–9, 149–150
Interventions, 109–113
Intrapsychic justice, 514–515. *See also* Justice
Islamic State of Iraq and Syria (ISIS), 161, 162
Islamic State of Iraq and the Levant (ISIL), 161
Islamic terrorist attacks. *See* Radicalization; Terrorism

J

Jail inmates, 304–305, 312. *See also* Criminal offenders; Prisons
Jealousy, 24–25, 26f, 34
Judgment, 395–396. *See also* Moral judgment
Judicial policy. *See* Policy
Justice, 511–515
Justifications
  dehumanization and, 154
  dishonesty and, 327–328
  heroism and, 507–508
  organizational settings and, 395–396

Index

K

Killing. *See also* Homicide; Murder; Premeditated murder
  cognitive-evaluative mechanisms of "good" and "evil," 26–27
  evolutionary perspective of, 22–25
  justifying in the staircase model of terrorism, 433–434
Kin altruism, 31–32. *See also* Altruism
Kindness, 12–14, 510–515

L

Law, 262–264, 265*n*
Leadership
  genocide and mass killing and, 6–7, 176–177, 178
  heroism and, 499–500
  moral blindness and, 400–402
  organizational settings and, 397–399
Legal settings, 58–59, 61–62, 65
Liberal attitudes, 199. *See also* Attitudes; Political attitudes
Life conditions, 164–166. *See also* Societal factors
Loneliness, 279–280, 478
Low-income populations, 142
Lying. *See* Deceit; Dishonesty

M

Machiavellianism, 202
Marginalization, 103–104
Marriage, 292. *See also* Relationships
Mass atrocities. *See also* Genocide; Terrorism
  bystanders, 171–174
  defining, 163
  good versus evil and, 161–162
  Milgram experiments and, 201–204
  overview, 159–164, 178
  perpetrators of, 164–171
  victims, 174–178
Mass panic, 355
Mass violence, 11–12. *See also* Mass atrocities; Terrorism
Media violence effects. *See also* Violence
  dehumanization and, 143, 149
  mechanisms of, 130–134, 134*f*
  overview, 5–6, 119–120, 124–130, 128*f*, 129*f*, 135
  theoretical frameworks, 120–124, 121*f*, 122*f*, 123*f*
Memory, collective, 368–375
Memory tasks, 98
Mercy, 511–515

Milgram experiments. *See also* Obedience; Obedience experiments
  moral judgment and, 334–335
  moral responsibility and, 200–215
  overview, 7, 185–193, 215–216
  research on obedience to authority and, 193–200
Military action, 162
Mixed bias, 55–56, 55*f*. *See also* Bias
Modern racism, 97–98. *See also* Racism
Moral balance model, 329–330
Moral blindness, 390–391, 400–402
Moral character, 8
Moral compensation, 331
Moral conflicts, 211
Moral credentials, 329–330
Moral disengagement strategies, 147–148, 154, 194
Moral emotions. *See also* Morality
  criminal offenders and, 310–311
  self-control and, 308–309
  shame and guilt, 299–306
  treatment and policy and, 312–313
Moral exclusion, 168–169. *See also* Exclusion
Moral judgment, 333–336, 395–396. *See also* Judgment
Moral reasoning, 306–307
Moral resentment, 330–331
Moral responsibility, 5, 200–215. *See also* Responsibility
Moral superiority to others. *See also* Morality; Self-concept
  actor–observer differences in attributions and, 259–260
  behavioral regulation and, 260–264
  "holier than thou" phenomenon and, 250–252, 258–259
  overview, 8–10, 249–250, 264, 265*n*
  self-agency beliefs and, 252–259
Moralistic anger, 35. *See also* Anger
Moralistic fallacy, 35
Morality. *See also* Moral emotions; Moral superiority to others
  dehumanization and, 142–143, 144
  dishonesty and, 329–331, 333–336
  empathy–altruism hypothesis and, 457–458
  ethical behavior and, 336
  evolutionary perspective and, 34–36
  good versus evil and, 161
  heroism and, 503
  Milgram experiments and, 203
  past victimization and, 370–372

Morality (*continued*)
  research on obedience to authority and, 199
  self-control and, 308–309
  shame and guilt and, 303–304
Morality beliefs, 162
Mortality risk, 479
Motivation. *See also* Ecosystem motivational orientation; Egosystem motivational orientation
  bystanders and, 173–174
  color-blind inclusiveness and, 106
  conscious processes as evil intentions, 85–87
  demonization of unconscious processes and, 80–81
  empathy–altruism hypothesis and, 444, 445
  historical victimization and, 373–374
  Milgram experiments and, 201–207
  sexual violence and, 233, 239–240
  sexually objectifying behaviors and, 8
  volunteerism and, 471–476
Multicultural integration, 103–104. *See also* Assimilation
Murder, 60. *See also* Homicide; Killing; Premeditated murder

N

Narcissism, 202
National Consortium for the Study of Terrorism and Responses to Terrorism, 422
Natural selection, 18–19, 29, 33
Needs, 455–456
Negativity bias, 2–3
Negotiations, 447–448
Nonconscious processes. *See* Unconscious processes
Nonverbal behavior. *See also* Behavior
  aversive racism and, 101
  objectification and, 227–228
  sexual violence and, 234–236
Nonviolent strategies of dealing with conflict, 162
Normalization of violence
  genocide and mass killing and, 165–166
  Milgram experiments and, 204–205
  role of bystanders in, 171–174
Norms. *See also* Group processes
  genocide and mass killing and, 6–7, 178
  group norms, 6–7, 178

  group processes and, 358–359
  organizational settings and, 398
  overview, 346
Numbness, 172

O

Obedience. *See also* Authority; Milgram experiments; Obedience experiments; Respect for authority
  genocide and mass killing and, 166
  research on, 193–200
  social identity model and, 351
Obedience experiments. *See also* Milgram experiments; Obedience
  ethical considerations in, 188–189
  Holocaust and, 189–192
  moral responsibility and, 200–215
  overview, 7, 185–193, 215–216
  research on obedience to authority and, 193–200
Objectification. *See also* Sexual violence
  nonverbal behavior and, 235–236
  overview, 7–8, 241–242
  physical behaviors and, 236–237
  verbal behavior and, 236
Objectification theory, 238–239
Oppression, 381
Ordinary people, 200–204
Organizational settings. *See also* Corporate corruption
  automaticity and, 400–402
  bias and, 65
  discrimination and, 61–62
  emergence and, 402–404
  hierarchy and power and, 393–396, 406*n*
  moral blindness and, 400–402
  moral resentment and, 330–331
  overview, 11, 390–392, 404–405
  socialization and, 390–391, 406*n*
  tone at the top and, 397–399
  volunteerism and, 482–483
Ostracism, 36
Other-oriented empathy, 300–301, 473, 475. *See also* Empathy
Outgroup membership. *See also* Group membership; Intergroup attitudes
  aversive racism and, 97
  color-blind inclusiveness and, 102
  deviant group members and, 360
  empathy–altruism hypothesis and, 448–451
  genocide and mass killing and, 166–168

Index

harmony and, 104–107
perpetuation of disadvantage and, 107–109

P

Panic, 356
Parental involvement, 124
Parenting, 445–446, 454–455
Passivity of bystanders. *See* Bystanders
Passivity of victims, 174–175. *See also* Victims
Paternalism, 454–455
Path model, 285–289, 285f, 286f, 287f, 289f
Peace, 449–451
Peace workshops and camps, 449–450
Peer relationships, 124, 292. *See also* Relationships
Perceptions, 175–176
Perceptions of others
  actor–observer differences in attributions and, 259–260
  bias and, 64–65
  compassionate goals and, 276–278
  dehumanization and, 147–150
  empathy-induced altruism and, 444
  free will and, 47
  good versus evil and, 162
  harm doing and, 369–370
  "holier than thou" phenomenon and, 250–251
  self-agency beliefs and, 257–259
Perceptual processes, 77–78
Perceptual schemata, 122f, 123f
Performance-enhancing drugs, 9–10
Perpetrators. *See also* Criminal offenders
  dehumanization and, 151
  evolutionary perspective of, 23
  genocide and mass killing and, 160, 164–171
  group processes and, 358–361
  intergroup forgiveness and, 379–381
  Milgram experiments and, 189–190, 201–207
  sexual violence and, 226, 227–229, 228f, 240–241, 242n
  social identity and, 358–361
Personal factors, 229–230. *See also* Individual differences
Personality
  altruistic personality, 351
  aversive racism and, 96–99
  general aggression model (GAM) and, 122f
  general learning model (GLM) and, 123f
  heroism and, 505–506
  motivational systems and, 274
  research on obedience to authority and, 194, 199
  sexually objectifying behaviors and, 8
Personality disorders, 121
Personalization, 171
Perspective taking, 447–448, 449–451, 452
Persuasion, 474–475
Physical behaviors, 236–237. *See also* Behavior
Physical risk heroes, 503–504. *See also* Heroism
Physiological measures, 98
Plagiarism, 9
Pluralistic ignorance, 171
Pluralistic societies, 102–103
Policy, 309–313, 416
Political attitudes, 199. *See also* Attitudes
Political ideology, 162
Politicide, 165–166. *See also* Genocide
Post hoc rationalization, 150. *See also* Rationalizations
Poverty, 381–382
Power. *See also* Authority
  dehumanization and, 153
  genocide and mass killing and, 174–175
  habits and, 83
  intergroup forgiveness and, 379–381
  moral blindness and, 400–402
  organizational settings and, 393–396, 406n
  sexual violence and, 232, 233
Preconceptions, 4–5
Preexperimental screenings, 196
Prejudice. *See also* Bias; Racism; Stereotyping
  automaticity and, 63
  aversive racism and, 96–101, 112–113
  color-blind inclusiveness and, 101–109
  individual-level, 96
  organizational settings and, 405
  origins of, 57
Prejudice-reduction techniques, 109–113. *See also* Interventions
Premeditated murder, 22–23, 60. *See also* Homicide; Killing; Murder
Preparatory moral disengagement, 145
Prisons. *See also* Criminal offenders; Jail inmates
  overview, 9
  shame and guilt and, 304–305
  treatment and policy and, 312

Projection, 277–278
Promotion, 404
Prosocial action. *See also* Cultural functioning
  compassionate goals and, 291–292
  egosystem motivation and, 273
  forgiveness and, 376
  free will and, 47
  genocide and mass killing and, 170–171
  group processes and, 345–346, 362
  intergroup forgiveness and, 381–383
  media violence effects and, 129–130
Prosocial theories, 499–504
Protective factors, 124, 125–126
Psychic numbing, 168
Psychological factors
  free will and, 72
  genocide and mass killing and, 164–166, 168–170
  overview, 20–21
  personality traits and, 274
  psychological models, 59–61, 65, 108–109
  symptoms, 301–303
  terrorism and, 416
  well-being and, 225, 478
Psychopathic Personality Inventory (PPI-I), 506
Psychopathology. *See also* Evil people; Moral emotions
  aversive racism and, 96–99
  demonization of unconscious processes and, 76–77
  genocide and mass killing and, 169
  heroism and, 506–507, 516
  overview, 298, 299
  shame and guilt and, 299–306
Psychopathy Checklist—Revised (PCL-R), 299
Psychotherapies, 76
Punishment
  criminal offenders and, 310
  dishonesty and, 325–326
  obedience experiments and, 213–215
  organizational settings and, 395
  research on obedience to authority and, 195, 197
  volunteerism and, 470

R

Racial attitudes. *See also* Racism
  aversive racism, 96–99
  dehumanization and, 142
  genocide and mass killing and, 165–166
  media violence effects and, 127–129, 128f, 129f
  organizational settings and, 403–404
Racial segregation, 403–404
Racism. *See also* Bias; Stereotyping
  ambivalence and, 55–56, 55f
  aversive racism, 96–101
  awareness and, 95–96
  color-blind inclusiveness and, 101–109
  historical victimization and, 374
  intention and, 109–113
  moral credentials and, 330
  organizational settings and, 403–404
  origins of, 57
  overview, 5, 52, 64–65
  responsibility for, 57–64
  staircase model of terrorism and, 430
Radicalization. *See also* Terrorism
  case study in, 421–435
  globalization in the 21st century and, 416–421
  overview, 415–416, 436
Rape, 226. *See also* Sexual violence
Rational choice, 446–448. *See also* Choice
Rationalizations
  conscious processes as evil intentions, 86–87
  dehumanization and, 149–152
  demonization of unconscious processes and, 80–81
Rebound effects, 107–108
Recidivism
  criminogenic conditions, 307
  self-control and, 309
  shame and guilt and, 305
Reciprocal altruism, 31–32. *See also* Altruism
Reciprocal dehumanization, 150, 151. *See also* Dehumanization
Reciprocity, 278–280, 293–294
Reconciliation
  dehumanization and, 150–151
  historical victimization and, 367–368
  intergroup forgiveness and, 380
Reconciliation blocking, 150–151
Redemptive violence, 161, 162
Refugees, 142, 147, 382–383
Rehabilitation, 9
Relational factors, 231–232

Relationships
  compassionate goals and, 274–294, 275f, 282f, 284f, 285f, 286f, 287f, 289f
  ecosystem motivation and, 274–281, 275f
  empathy–altruism hypothesis and, 446–448
  evolutionary perspective of, 19–21
  fitness conflicts and, 29
  killing and, 24–25, 26f
  overview, 8–9, 270–271
  quality of, 285–286, 285f
Religious belief, 249–252
Religious fundamentalism, 162
Remorse, 161–162
Reproduction, 42
Rescuer behavior. *See also* Bystanders; Helping behaviors
  bystanders and, 173–174
  genocide and mass killing and, 170–171
  social identity model and, 350–355
Resentment
  dishonesty and, 330–331
  identity and, 427
  staircase model of terrorism and, 431
Resiliency, 124
Resistance, 174–177, 352–353
Resource allocation, 458–459
Respect for authority, 166, 199. *See also* Authority; Obedience
Response latency procedures, 98
Responsibility. *See also* Intentionality
  belief in free will and, 44–46
  bias and, 57–64, 60, 65
  evolutionary perspective and, 34–36
  heroism and, 495
  Milgram experiments and, 200–215
  research on obedience to authority and, 194
Responsible autonomy, 43
Responsiveness
  compassionate goals and, 284–289, 285f, 286f, 287f, 289f, 290–291
  ecosystem motivation and, 278–279
Restorative justice-inspired programs, 310–311
Revictimization, 370
Reward and punishment, 395, 470. *See also* Punishment
Right-thinking persons, 5
Right-wing authoritarianism, 162

Risk factors. *See also* Media violence effects
  aggression and, 123–124
  genocide and mass killing and, 165–166
  overview, 122–124
  sexual violence and, 237
Risk-taking behaviors, 505–506, 508
Romantic fallacy, 35
Romantic relationships, 291–292. *See also* Relationships
Roommate Goals Study, 281–283, 282f
Roommate Mental Health Study, 283–284, 284f, 287, 288–289, 289f
Roots of Empathy program, 451

S

Sacrifice, 257–258
Schadenfreude, 457
Screenings, 196
Security, 419–420
Self-agency, 252–259, 254–259
Self-attributions, 260. *See also* Attributions
Self-categorization theory, 346, 429–430. *See also* Group processes
Self-concept. *See also* Moral superiority to others
  behavioral regulation and, 260–261
  dishonesty and, 324–328, 329–331
  "holier than thou" phenomenon and, 250–252
  moral compensation and, 331
  overview, 8–10
  volunteerism and, 478
Self-concern, 455
Self-construal, 288
Self-control
  criminal offenders and, 308–309
  dishonesty and, 332–333
  treatment and policy and, 311–312
Self-dehumanization, 148, 149. *See also* Dehumanization
Self-disclosure, 288–289
Self-esteem
  aversive racism and, 96
  compassionate goals and, 276, 288
  conscious processes as evil intentions, 86
  shame and guilt and, 301, 302–303
  volunteerism and, 473, 478
Self-fulfilling prophecy, 56
Self-image
  color-blind inclusiveness and, 101–102, 108–109
  compassionate goals and, 281–283, 282f

Self-image (*continued*)
  ecosystem motivation and, 277
  goals and, 272
  overview, 8–10
Self-interest, 446–447
Selfishness
  automaticity and, 65*n*
  habits and, 83
  helping behavior and, 356
  volunteerism and, 475
Self-labeling, 260–261
Selfless behavior. *See also* Helping behaviors; Heroism; Volunteerism
  automaticity and, 65*n*
  helping behavior and, 356–357
  self-agency beliefs and, 252–259
Self-objectification, 238–239. *See also* Objectification
Self-policing, 360
Self-preservation system, 273–274
Self-protective processes, 172
Self-regulation
  dishonesty and, 332–333
  ethical boundaries and, 328–329
  false moral superiority and, 260–264
  free will and, 48–49
  psychopathy and, 298
Self-Report Altruism (SRA) Scale, 506
Self-report measures, 98
Self-sacrifice, 467. *See also* Volunteerism
Self-serving processes, 80–81
Self-worth, 473
Sensory processes, 77–78
Separatism, 103–104
Sexism, 374
Sexual assaults, 7–8
Sexual infidelity, 24–25, 26*f*
Sexual minorities, 374
Sexual objectification, 8, 226–227. *See also* Objectification; Sexual violence
Sexual violence
  bystanders and, 360–361
  deviant group members and, 360–361
  methodological obstacles and, 240–241
  overview, 225–226, 241–242
  social interaction model of objectification and, 226–240, 228*f*
Sexually aggressive behavior, 127, 142–143
Shame, 299–306. *See also* Moral emotions
Shared social identity, 357. *See also* Social identity
Shoplifting, 10
Signaling theory, 404

Situational ethics, 336. *See also* Ethical behavior
Situational factors
  dishonesty and, 333–336
  ethical boundaries and, 328–329
  general aggression model (GAM) and, 122*f*
  genocide and mass killing and, 165–166
  heroism and, 499
  Milgram experiments and, 201–204
  obedience experiments and, 207
  self-agency beliefs and, 255–256
  self-control and, 308
  sexually objectifying behaviors and, 8
  social interaction model of objectification and, 231–232
Social attitudes, 199
Social categorization. *See also* Categorical thinking
  automaticity and, 62–64
  aversive racism and, 96–99
  color-blind inclusiveness and, 101–109
  overview, 5, 64–65
  perpetuation of disadvantage and, 107–109
Social cognition, 96–97, 259–260
Social connection, 279–280
Social construction, 507–510
Social control, 359–360
Social dilemma, 458–459
Social dominance, 202
Social dominance orientation (SDO), 147, 162
Social engineering, 167
Social fitness, 497
Social-identification theory, 207–211
Social identity. *See also* Cultural identity; Identity
  bystanders and, 347–350, 351*t*
  genocide and mass killing and, 6–7, 176–177, 178
  helping in disasters and emergencies and, 355–358
  Holocaust and, 350–355
  intergroup forgiveness and, 380
  overview, 362
  social interaction model of objectification and, 237
  staircase model of terrorism and, 422–435
  terrorism and, 422
  violence or emergencies and, 347–350, 351*t*

Index

Social identity theory, 346. *See also* Group processes
Social interaction model of objectification (SIMO). *See also* Objectification
  antecedents phase of, 228f, 229–232
  interaction consequences phase of, 228f, 237–240
  interaction phase of, 228f, 234–237
  methodological obstacles and, 240–241
  overview, 7–8, 224–240, 228f, 340–341
  preinteraction mediators phase of, 228f, 232–234
Social justice, 511–515
Social media, 416–418
Social psychology
  color-blind inclusiveness and, 108–109
  conceptualizations of good and evil in, 2–3
  dehumanization and, 143
  genocide and mass killing and, 163–164, 178
  good versus evil and, 161–162
  Holocaust and, 351
  Milgram experiments and, 186–187, 189–192
  organizational settings and, 404–405
Social regulation, 262–264
Social risk heroes, 503–504. *See also* Heroism
Social support, 281–284, 282f, 284f, 285
Social withdrawal, 152
Socialization, 397–399
Socialization experiences, 96, 390–391, 406n
Societal factors, 164–166, 170, 483–486
Sociocultural processes, 97
Soul, concept of, 42–43, 71–74
Staircase model of terrorism, 415–416, 422–435. *See also* Terrorism
States, 274
Status. *See also* Group membership
  aversive racism and, 96
  color-blind inclusiveness and, 102–109
  dehumanization and, 147
  evolutionary perspective of, 21–22
  genocide and mass killing and, 169
  harmony and, 104–107
  killing and, 24–25, 26f
Stereotype content model, 55–56, 55f, 167
Stereotyping. *See also* Bias; Group membership; Racism
  automaticity and, 63
  aversive racism and, 98–99, 110

  dehumanization and, 145–148, 154–155
  evolutionary perspective and, 28, 36
  general learning model (GLM) and, 123f
  genocide and mass killing and, 167
  historical victimization and, 374
  intergroup forgiveness and, 381
  media violence effects and, 127–129, 128f, 129f
Stigma, 381, 451–452
Stimulus–response (S–R) chains, 77–78
Stranger anxiety, 36
Strong emotion, 148
Substance dualism, 42–43
Substance use/abuse, 231, 303–304, 306
Suffering of others, 457
Suicide terrorism, 30–31, 507–508. *See also* Terrorism
Superiority, sense of, 250. *See also* Moral superiority to others
Superordinate goal, 449. *See also* Goals
Survival
  ecosystem motivation and, 273–274
  free will and, 42
  genocide and mass killing and, 175–176
Survivors, 177–178. *See also* Victims
Symbolic racism, 97–98. *See also* Racism

T

Task demands, 328–329
Technological change, 417–418
Teen dating violence, 126–127
Temporal orientation, 503–504
TerRa program, 415–416, 436. *See also* Terrorism
Terrorism. *See also* Mass violence
  exploitation of evil and, 30–31
  globalization in the 21st century and, 416–421
  good versus evil and, 161, 162
  overview, 11–12, 415–416, 435–436
  radicalization and, 421–435
Terrorist threat, 148–149
Test of Self-Conscious Affect (TOSCA), 302–303, 313n
Thoughtful action, 121f, 501–502
Threat, 148–149, 373–375
Time perspective, 503–504
Tone at the top, 397–399. *See also* Organizational settings
Torture techniques, 162
Tractability, 34–36
Traits, 274

Treatment, 309–313
Trust, 288–289, 289f, 379
Truthfulness, 9–10. *See also* Deceit
Tsarnaev brothers, 421–435

U

Uncertainty, 27–28
Unconscious processes. *See also* Automatic processes; Demonization of unconscious processes; Intentionality
 aversive racism and, 98–99, 110–111
 bias and, 53
 color-blind inclusiveness and, 101–109
 demonization of, 71–81
 habits and, 82–84
 historical views of, 71–77
 organizational settings and, 400–402
 overview, 5, 69–71, 75f, 87–88
Understanding Human Nature program, 517
Unethical behaviors. *See also* Ethical behavior
 corporate corruption and, 322–323
 dishonesty and, 327
 ethical boundaries and, 328–329
 justification for, 327–328
 moral credentials and, 329–330
 moral judgment and, 333–336
 moral resentment and, 330–331
 overview, 336
 self-regulation and, 332–333
Unintentional processes, 53, 78. *See also* Automatic processes; Intentionality; Unconscious processes

V

Values, 97, 398, 435–436
Verbal behavior, 101, 236. *See also* Behavior
Victimization, 10–11. *See also* Historical victimization

Victims
 blaming of, 172
 dehumanization and, 151
 deviant group members and, 360
 evolutionary perspective of, 22–23, 24–25, 26f
 genocide and mass killing and, 160, 168–169, 174–178
 intergroup forgiveness and, 379–381
 Milgram experiments and, 190, 205
 sexual violence and, 226, 227–229, 228f, 240–241, 242n
Violence. *See also* Media violence effects; Sexual violence
 bystanders and, 347–348
 dehumanization and, 154–155
 domestic violence, 121, 126–127
 evolutionary perspective and, 33–34
 group processes and, 358–361
 objectification and, 7–8
 risk factors and, 123–124
Virtual reality simulations, 198
Visuospatial functioning, 134
Volunteerism. *See also* Helping behaviors; Heroism; Selfless behavior
 benefits and costs of, 476–486
 motives for, 471–476
 overview, 12–13, 467–471, 486
 recruiting volunteers, 474–475
 sustaining, 475–476

W

War, 144, 165–166
War on Terror, 161. *See also* Terrorism
Whistle-blowing, 198, 330–331
Willpower, 48–49

X

Xenophobia, 36

Z

Zimbardo's prison study, 186